SUEZ

SUEZ

KEITH KYLE

St. Martin's Press
New York

For Suzy, her book

First published in the United States of America in 1991

Printed in Great Britain

ISBN 0-312-06509-4
ISBN 0-312-08722-6 (pbk.)

Library of Congress Cataloging-in-Publication Data

Kyle, Keith.
Suez/Keith Kyle.
p. cm.
Includes bibliographical references and index.
ISBN 0-312-06509-4
1. Egypt—History—Intervention, 1956. I. Title.
DT107.83.K95 1991
962.05'3—dc20 91-11386
CIP

Contents

Maps and Illustrations

Maps

Illustrations

Between pages 336 and 337

Acknowledgements

The first person who deserves acknowledgement is Peter Hill of the BBC, the producer of the four-part television series on Suez which I wrote and presented in 1976 as part of the nightly *Tonight* programme and of my one-hour special, *Secrets of Suez*, transmitted on BBC 2 in 1986, who suggested that I wrote this book and worked hard to promote it. The next is Dr Wilfrid Knapp, Lecturer in Politics at St Catherine's College, Oxford, who by making his extensive collection of documents from the Eisenhower Library, Abilene, available to me set me off to a head-start with my own work in that excellent library.

My three main employers, *The Economist*, BBC Television and the Royal Institute of International Affairs, have, over a long period, given me opportunities and experiences which find reflection in these pages. Although this is not a Chatham House book, the fact that I was working there during the period when I was writing it meant that I had ready access to the Institute's admirable library and press library facilities. The Director, Admiral Sir James Eberle, and the two librarians, Nicole Gallimore and Susan Boyde and their staff have given me every support and encouragement. I am indebted also to the courtesy and efficiency of the staffs of the London Library, the Public Record Office at Kew, the Ministry of Defence Library at the Old War Office Building in Whitehall, the British Library and the Newspaper Library at Colindale, the British Library of Political and Economic Science, the Imperial War Museum, the Dwight D. Eisenhower Library at Abilene, Ka., the Seeley G. Mudd Manuscripts Library, Princeton University, N.J., the Diplomatic and Military Branches of the National Archives in Washington D.C., and the Dag Hammarskjöld Archive at the Royal Library, Stockholm.

I had the good fortune to attend two seminars on Suez at St Antony's College, Oxford, in 1986 and at the Woodrow Wilson Center for International Scholars at the Smithsonian castle in Washington D.C. in 1987, each organised jointly by these two bodies. For the thirtieth anniversary of the war I attended the Ben-Gurion Centennial symposium, *The Suez Crisis: A Retrospective 1956–1986* at Beersheva and Sde Boqer, and immediately afterwards in Cairo the symposium on *The Suez Canal Nationalisation*, organised by the Egyptian Committee of Afro-Asian Solidarity. From all four of these occasions I gained new insights into different aspects of the story.

In October 1987, I had the honour of being invited to take the chair for a seminar of the RAF Historical Society on 'The Air Aspects of the Suez Campaign, 1956'. The published *Proceedings* give an indication of the rich harvest of reminiscence that this reaped.

For material about Anthony Eden I was able to consult the Avon Papers, which are kept at the library of the University of Birmingham.

I am grateful for Lord Romsey's permission to have access to the beautifully arranged archives of the late Earl Mountbatten of Burma at Broadlands and to their curator, Mrs Molly Chalk, for guidance in using them. Dr Anthony Seldon, the editor of *Contemporary Record*, allowed me to make use of the transcripts of interviews that he conducted with Admiral Sir Guy Grantham and Admiral Sir Robin Durnford-Slater, which form part of an oral history archive at present in the keeping of Dr John Barnes.

Major sources for the British side of the story were two Oxfordshire neighbours and diarists, Sir Evelyn Shuckburgh and William Clark. Sir Evelyn has been generous with his time and material in supporting my work. William Clark, a friend of long standing whose conversation has illuminated my understanding of Suez from 1956 onwards, sadly did not, at the time when I was commissioned to write this book, have long to live. Thanks to the generosity of his relatives, Lady Goodhart and Lord Hemingford, I have enjoyed complete access to his unpublished papers and tape recordings.

Churchill College, Cambridge, is a great repository of unpublished autobiographic material, of which I have drawn particularly on the memoirs of Admiral Sir William Davis, General Sir John Cowley, Lord Hankey, Sir Alexander Cadogan and Admiral Sir Manley Power.

A man for whose crisp memory and whose perceptive and often witty comments at the age of eighty-eight I feel a particular admiration is the late Marshal of the RAF Sir William Dickson, who responded most warmly to my approach.

Similarly Air Marshal Sir Denis Barnett was very helpful. Group Captain (ret.) Gordon Key was of great assistance over interpreting the records of Bomber Wing, Cyprus. For coverage of the air campaign generally I have relied heavily on the documentary sources which Air Commodore Henry Probert, Head of the Air Historical Branch at Lacon House, placed at my disposal. He was also very responsive to my layman's questions on Service matters. On the various military plans Colonel John Sellers, of the Royal Military College, Camberley, helped me greatly to find my way.

On the diplomatic side I received help from Lord Sherfield (Sir Roger Makins), Sir Harold Beeley, Sir Patrick Dean, Sir Donald Logan, the late Lord Caccia, Sir Archibald Ross, Sir Michael Weir, Adam Watson, Nigel Clive, Ronald Higgins and Robert Belgrave. The late Sir Philip de Zulueta was kind enough to talk to me about 10 Downing Street in those days.

Sir Anthony Nutting on two occasions discussed with me the events of 1956. I had also interviewed him for BBC television in 1976. Other politicians who were kind enough to give me their time were Lord Home of the Hirsel, Lord Thorneycroft, Lord Carr of Hadley, Lord Hailsham, the Earl of Selkirk, Aubrey Jones and Julian Amery.

On the French political scene I had advice from Emile Noël who was Guy Mollet's *chef de cabinet*; in addition I was able to use the unedited transcripts of my interviews for television with Christian Pineau (1976) and Maurice Bourgès-Maunoury (1986).

In Cairo I received generous help from Mohamed Heikal, who, besides sharing his own information, supplied a research assistant to translate documents from his personal archive. Amin Hewedy, military writer and former Minister of Defence, was very helpful in answering my questions both in Cairo and, subsequently, in Washington. I should also like to thank Engineer Ezzat Adel, the Chairman and Managing Director of the Suez Canal Authority, Engineer Abu Baqr, his predecessor, and General Abdul Mun'im al-Nagar. In the course of several conversations HE Yusif Sharara, the Egyptian Ambassador in London, spoke of his experience in 1956 as a junior member of the Egyptian delegation to the UN in New York and of his impressions of Mahmoud Fawzi. I am indebted to Abdul Majid Farid, Chairman of the Arab Research Council, and Dr Yazid Sayigh for their assistance over material in Arabic.

Jordanians who have contributed to my understanding of the 1956 situation in Jordan included Professor Ali Mahafzah, Dr Jamal Sha'er, Samir Mutawi, Suleiman Musa, Dr Yacub Zayaddin, Mureywad Tell, and Major-General Ali Abu Nuwar.

In Israel I had the great advantage of the help and co-operation of Colonel (Res.) Mordechai Bar-On, then a Member of the Knesset and in 1956 the head of the bureau of Moshe Dayan. Other Israelis who assisted included Shimon Peres, General (Res.) Rahavam Ze'evi, Chief of Staff of the Southern Command in 1956, Professor Yehoshafat Harkabi, Dr Benny Morris and Yitzhak Noam, the editor of *Erev Erev* (Eilat). I was able to use the unedited transcript of my 1976 interview for television with Moshe Dayan. I would like to thank Professor Ilan Troën of the Ben-Gurion University of the Negev for making available to me sections of the translated version of David Ben-Gurion's Diary for 1956 and to thank his publishers, Frank Cass, for their generosity in letting me have pre-publication access to material intended for inclusion in their book *The Suez–Sinai Crisis 1956. Retrospective and Reappraisal*, edited by S. I. Troën and M. Shemesh (1990). Dr Lewis Glinert of the School of Oriental and African Studies, assisted me with Hebrew-language material.

For the American side of the story I have benefited from interviews with Ambassador Henry Byroade, Ambassador Raymond Hare, Ambassador

Herman Eilts, the late Miles Copeland, and Wilbur C. Eveland. I was able to refer to the 1976 transcript of an interview with Robert Amory of the CIA. I am especially indebted for access to American documents to Dr William J. Burns, the author of *Economic Aid and American Policy Toward Egypt*, and to Donald Neff, author of *Warriors at Suez*. I owe it to the personal courtesy of Dr William Z. Slany, the State Department Historian, and Dr John P. Glennon, Editor-in-Chief of the admirable *Foreign Relations of the United States 1955–57* series, that I obtained the earliest permissible access to the relevant volumes of the series, most of which only came off the press in 1990.

For his recollections of his experiences with the UN in 1956 I would like to thank George Ivan Smith. The late Evan Luard kindly gave me permission to print his letter of resignation from the Diplomatic Service as Appendix B and also made available to me a pre-publication version of Vol. 2 of his *History of the United Nations*.

The book has gained greatly from the comments and suggestions of the following who read various parts of it in MSS: Sir Evelyn Shuckburgh, Sir Harold Beeley, Sir Donald Logan, Colonel John Sellers, Air Commodore Henry Probert, Dr Avi Shlaim, Dr Roger Owen, Robert Belgrave and especially Piers Dixon. The responsibility for the text is mine alone.

I should like to express my warm appreciation for the personal enthusiasm and professional skills that Christopher Falkus and Hilary Laurie of Weidenfeld and Nicolson have brought to the task of turning a manuscript into a book.

My original typescript and many subsequent revisions were put on word processor by the dexterous hands of my sister-in-law Jane Sherriff, who with her husband Vernon and my three nieces Maria, Amy and Tiffany operated what amounted to a cottage industry in support of my work. My admiration is unstinted for the cheerfulness and skill with which Jane coped with what must have seemed an endless task. But I owe most of all to my wife Susan without whom this book could not have been undertaken.

Author's Note

For purposes of comparison, £1.00 in 1991 is worth the equivalent in purchasing power of 11.1p in 1956. In 1956 the US dollar was 2.75 to the pound sterling; the Egyptian pound (£E1.00) was worth £1.044.

In the main text I have not attempted to conform with any of the standard transliterations of Arabic names.

The moral for British Governments is clear.
Like most respectable people, they will make
poor criminals and had better stick to respectability.
They will not be much good at anything else.

A. J. P. Taylor

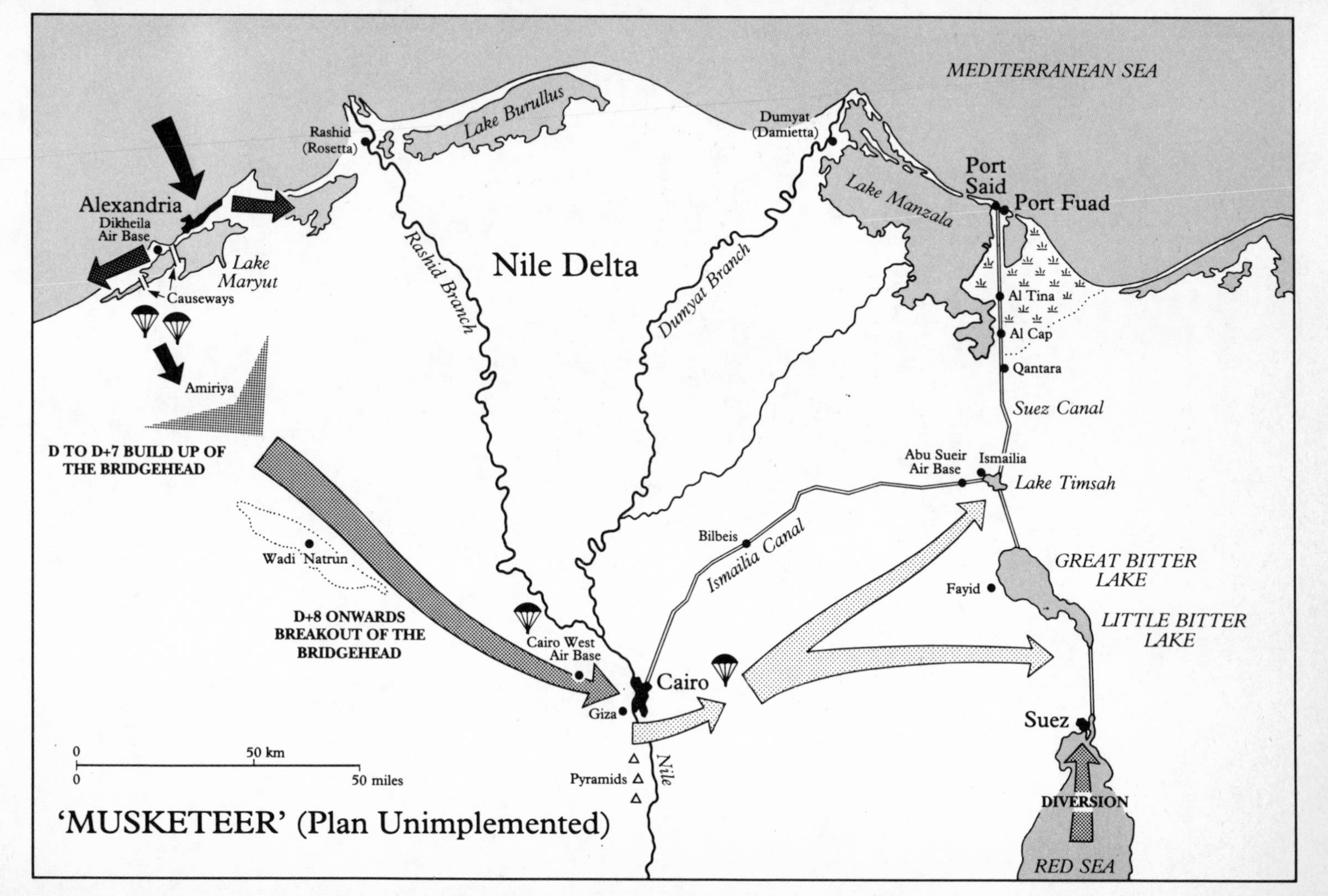
MEDITERRANEAN SEA
Lake Burullus
Rashid
(Rosetta)
Dumyat
(Damietta)
Port
Said
Port Fuad
Lake Manzala
Alexandria
Dikheila
Air Base
Lake
Maryut
Causeways
Rashid Branch
Nile Delta
Dumyat Branch
Al Tina
Al Cap
Qantara
Amiriya
Suez Canal
D TO D+7 BUILD UP OF
THE BRIDGEHEAD
Abu Sueir
Air Base
Ismailia
Lake Timsah
Bilbeis
Ismailia Canal
Wadi Natrun
GREAT BITTER
LAKE
Fayid
D+8 ONWARDS
BREAKOUT OF THE
BRIDGEHEAD
Cairo West
Air Base
LITTLE BITTER
LAKE
Cairo
Giza
Suez
0
50 km
0
50 miles
Pyramids
Nile
DIVERSION
RED SEA
'MUSKETEER' (Plan Unimplemented)

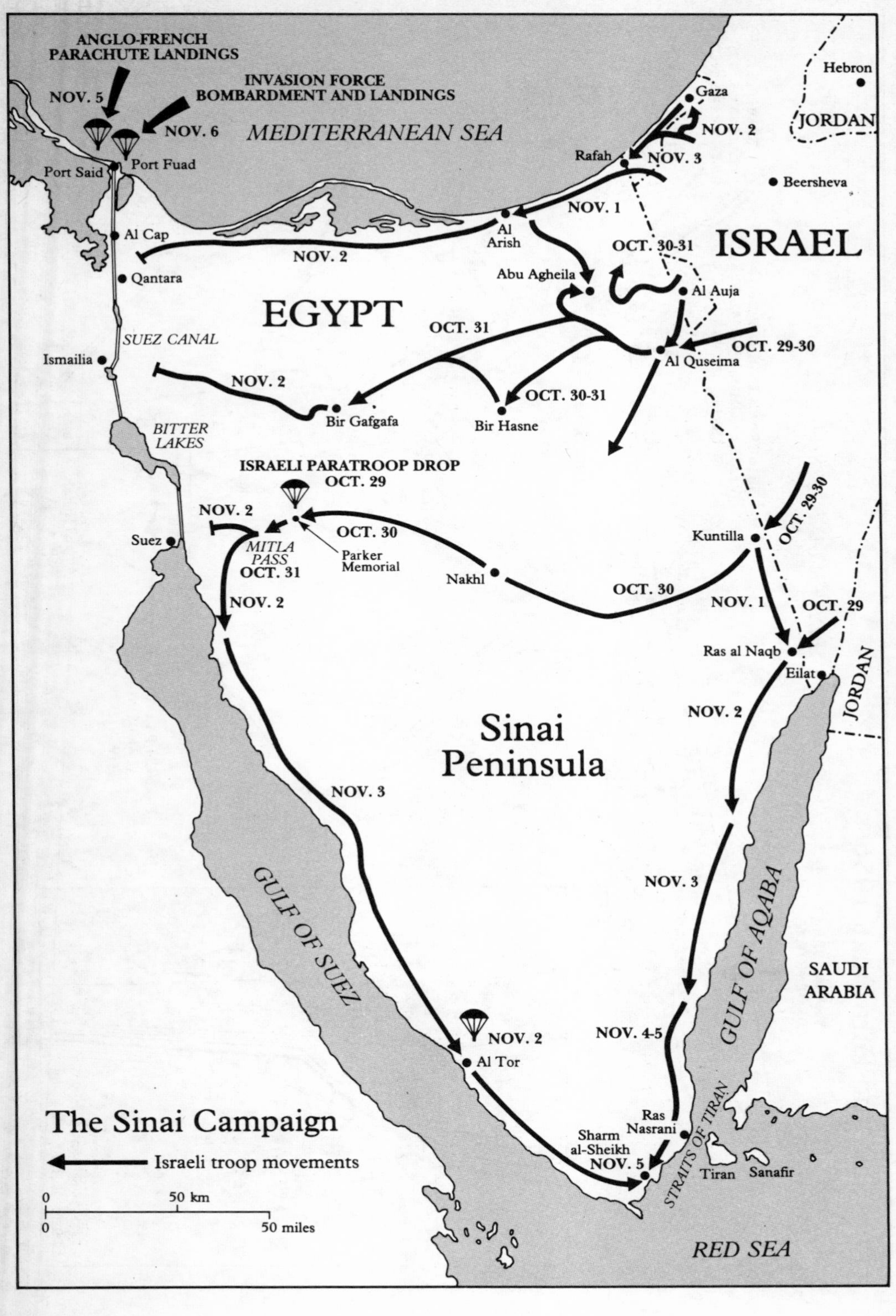
ANGLO-FRENCH PARACHUTE LANDINGS
NOV. 5
INVASION FORCE BOMBARDMENT AND LANDINGS
NOV. 6
MEDITERRANEAN SEA
Port Said
Port Fuad
Al Cap
Qantara
SUEZ CANAL
Ismailia
BITTER LAKES
Suez
Hebron
Gaza
JORDAN
NOV. 2
Rafah
NOV. 3
Beersheva
NOV. 1
Al Arish
NOV. 2
OCT. 30-31
ISRAEL
Abu Agheila
Al Auja
EGYPT
OCT. 31
Al Quseima
OCT. 29-30
NOV. 2
OCT. 30-31
Bir Gafgafa
Bir Hasne
ISRAELI PARATROOP DROP
OCT. 29
NOV. 2
MITLA PASS
OCT. 31
OCT. 30
Parker Memorial
Nakhl
Kuntilla
OCT. 29-30
OCT. 30
NOV. 2
NOV. 1
OCT. 29
Ras al Naqb
Eilat
JORDAN
NOV. 2
Sinai Peninsula
NOV. 3
NOV. 3
GULF OF SUEZ
GULF OF AQABA
SAUDI ARABIA
NOV. 4-5
NOV. 2
Al Tor
Ras Nasrani
Sharm al-Sheikh
NOV. 5
STRAITS OF TIRAN
Tiran
Sanafir
RED SEA
The Sinai Campaign
Israeli troop movements
0
50 km
0
50 miles

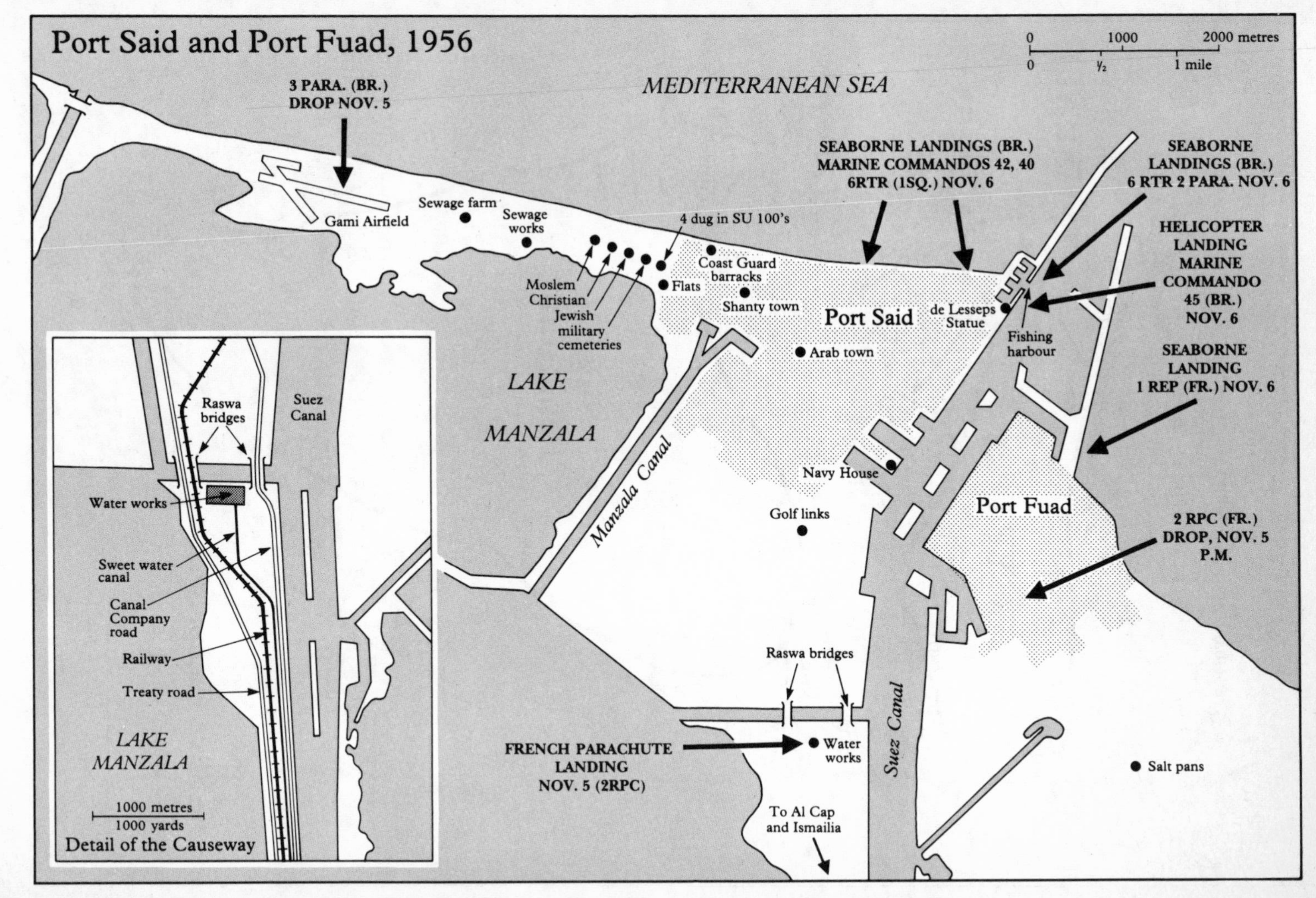
Port Said and Port Fuad, 1956
0 1000 2000 metres
0 ½ 1 mile
MEDITERRANEAN SEA
3 PARA. (BR.) DROP NOV. 5
Gami Airfield
Sewage farm
Sewage works
4 dug in SU 100's
Moslem
Christian
Jewish
military cemeteries
Coast Guard barracks
Flats
Shanty town
SEABORNE LANDINGS (BR.) MARINE COMMANDOS 42, 40 6RTR (1SQ.) NOV. 6
Port Said
Arab town
de Lesseps Statue
Fishing harbour
SEABORNE LANDINGS (BR.) 6 RTR 2 PARA. NOV. 6
HELICOPTER LANDING MARINE COMMANDO 45 (BR.) NOV. 6
SEABORNE LANDING 1 REP (FR.) NOV. 6
LAKE MANZALA
Manzala Canal
Navy House
Golf links
Port Fuad
2 RPC (FR.) DROP, NOV. 5 P.M.
Raswa bridges
FRENCH PARACHUTE LANDING NOV. 5 (2RPC)
Water works
Suez Canal
Salt pans
To Al Cap and Ismailia
Raswa bridges
Suez Canal
Water works
Sweet water canal
Canal Company road
Railway
Treaty road
LAKE MANZALA
1000 metres
1000 yards
Detail of the Causeway

Preface

Those who are old enough to remember Suez tend to remember very clearly where they were when it occurred. I do so myself. I was at the time the Washington Correspondent of the *Economist*, a paper which prides itself on the extent of its coverage of American domestic affairs. On Tuesday, 30 October 1956, I was standing in the National Press Club, which is on the top floor of the National Press Building in Washington, watching the news coming through on the agency ticker. I was looking out for the two items that were preoccupying most people in America at that time, the last stages of the American presidential election, and the epic story of the Hungarian revolution. The news that came through was the terms of an ultimatum delivered by the British and French to Egypt and, nominally but apparently not substantively, to Israel.

I was not alone in that city (or, indeed, elsewhere) in being taken by surprise. Again, like most people in Washington, I never for a moment supposed, given the wording and the context, that what I saw should be taken at its face value or could be anything other than some form of collusion between Britain, France and Israel (though how formal this was, I had yet to find out). There was, by chance, something which I could do instantly by way of personal comment. The next day I was to have a meeting to which I had been much looking forward. There had been, some time before, an item in the British press to the effect that the Conservative Party, worried at its weakness in the House of Commons in backbenchers interested in foreign affairs, was prepared to look abroad, if necessary among non-party members, to find potential party candidates.

I was both keen on politics (especially after close study of the American model) and without party affiliation (since being a Liberal while up at Oxford). I had long been an admirer of Sir Anthony Eden, a sentiment which had grown in enthusiasm as I had watched what I still consider to be his amazing series of diplomatic achievements in 1954–5. Viewed from a distance of 3,000 miles, the old Tory party seemed, under his leadership and with the prominence of such attractive personalities as Rab Butler and Iain Macleod, to have taken on the appearance of a reformed character. When it was announced that the Conservative vice-chairman in charge of candidates was coming to Washington to conduct interviews, I had made the necessary arrangements.

From the Club I went immediately to my office desk on which was poised a very primitive fax machine which whirred noisily around, shuddered and sent out smoke signals while transmitting a message. The messages I sent were to the Conservative vice-chairman at his Washington hotel and to the Party's Central Office in London cancelling an interview which, I said, 'served little purpose in view of the Anglo-French aggression against Egypt'.

In the next three weeks, I witnessed the beginning of the extraordinary ice age in the 'special relationship', when official Britain in Washington (though not the British press) was frozen out in a quite unprecedented way. I was invited (as were others) by the new British Ambassador to keep him informed of what I might learn of American official thinking, to which he had absolutely minimal access. After this, I went home to Britain for a few weeks and thus experienced at first hand the intensity of the feelings expressed on both sides of the Suez issue. Every member of the editorial staff of my paper except one had taken, I discovered, the same position as myself. Petrol rationing had been introduced and the West End of London was transformed for those of us using public transport into the pleasing dimensions of a village. It was, I remember, very cold.

One evening, I went to dine as a guest in the Oxford and Cambridge Club. There were very few people there and we afterwards sat down alongside a small group who were gathered round the only fire. They were talking. The subject was the one being discussed all over Britain. As we came up, each of the young men who were there was recounting in turn his horror story of some respected organ or institution which had let him down by falling below his expectations on the great issue of the hour.

'Of course, I have cancelled my subscription to the *Observer*', one said and there were murmurs of approval. 'It's such a shame about the list of Oxford dons protesting in *The Times*,' said another. 'I shan't ever be able to go to my tutor's sherry parties again.' There was an undercurrent of mutual sympathy. 'And then', said a third, bringing out, as it were, the crowning example of how the establishment had betrayed all decent folk, 'there's the *Economist*!' He paused at the horror of it; noticing us in earshot, listening, not part of the circle, he addressed us. 'Do you read the *Economist*?' 'No', I answered, 'I write it'. The group was for a moment silent, as if stunned, took one look at one another, and, then, sadly and without a word, departed.

Both in Washington and in London (where people were anxious to trade for gossip from Washington) I picked up all I could about what had gone wrong. I was often in the Press Gallery of the House to see the moving spectacle of a still desperately harried government. And I was in the Bagehot Room, known affectionately to the staff of the old *Economist* building as 'the honky tonk', where Permanent Secretaries and others were debriefed over a rather superior lunch, when Sir Frank Lee, an old friend of the paper who was then Permanent Secretary to the Board of Trade, declared that all constitutional textbooks must be rewritten and those passages excised which gave the impression that the government in Britain is run by civil servants who put words into the mouths of Ministers. Over Suez, Ministers had taken over the machine and by and large run it by themselves. I recall venturing to suggest that the textbooks might, on the contrary, use Suez as a footnote to support the proposition that this had been tried once and the outcome was such that it would never be attempted again.

After a few brief weeks, the subject of Suez, so intensively, so hectically debated, silently departed. The British people had been brought to the edge of an abyss and had drawn back. They had not liked what they had seen and had sensed. The bitter divisions separating husband and wife, friend and friend, dinner partners and workmates were more characteristic of other, less happy lands. By mutual consent Suez, as a topic of conversation, had become taboo.

I have now revisited as a historian the ground I partially trod as a journalist. As I read through the material, I can hear again the voices of Eisenhower and Dulles uttering their words, can sense the immense charm and authority of Anthony Eden, the stuttering doggedness under fire of Selwyn Lloyd in the House, the extraordinarily hypnotic quality of Hammarskjöld's accented English. But thirty years have passed. Much has changed, perspectives altered, the period distanced. Because of the Thirty Year Rule, documents on the British side for 1956 and 1957 are only now available in the 'history factory' at Kew Gardens with its crematorium chimney, where the Public Record Office is housed. It seemed the right time to look back on those days. I hope that I have been able to bring to the task something of what Oxford (and, most especially, A. J. P. Taylor) taught me about the writing of history. If there is one thing about which I have to confess a twinge of disappointment, it is that I have not found evidence that has shown that my reaction in 1956 was wholly misplaced.

Although this account has been written disproportionately from British and American documents because of their relative availability, as much use as practicable has been made of other primary sources. In no other country, including until the summer of 1990 the United States (where the amount of earlier, piecemeal declassification had nevertheless been substantial, and the work of the Eisenhower Library at Abilene, the place in Kansas where the cowboy trail used to end, has been exceptionally useful to scholars), had there been such a general release of material for this period as at the British Public Record Office in January 1987.

Some British material has been held back. The release of documents under the Thirty Year Rule can be considered fairly generous, provided that it is borne in mind that three levels of censorship have been at work. During the most crucial phases of the story, the key meetings were held either with no civil servants at all or on the basis that no written record should be kept. In respect of some things, therefore, there was never anything to erase in the first place. Secondly, there was, immediately after the events described in the later chapters, a systematic destruction of the most compromising records. The most notorious instance was the documentation about the secret meetings at Sèvres between Israel, France and Britain which are treated in Chapter 17. But there was a wider purge in Whitehall shortly after that, from which scraps like the Chief of the Air Staff's 'Points for PM' of 26 October and the First Sea Lord's speaking notes for 29 October have survived.

Different civil servants had different attitudes towards the problem of records. Some co-operated in the work of destruction. Others – W. R. Darracott, the secretary of the Egypt (Official) Committee which planned details of the occupation of Egypt, is the best example – made special provision for documents to be 'lost' if there was a change of government. (In Mr Darracott's case, the file with its endorsement to that effect is now to be found in the PRO at Kew.) Others began reconstructing later what had happened in the critical days when they had been excluded from receiving their normal intake of papers; and traces from their detective work can sometimes be found on the dockets.

The third level of censorship is the normal 'weeding' that occurs before each annual release of papers. There are quite a number of such omissions for 1956, including the minutes of one whole Cabinet meeting and all but two of the operational files concerning 'psychological warfare' against Nasser. The PRO does not have the practice, common in the United States, of declassifying portions of documents, leaving other portions 'sanitised' (blacked out). A single reference to a covert operation may therefore serve to keep an entire record off bounds. (Nor can one imagine a British equivalent to the records of telephone conversations that are available at the Eisenhower Library at Abilene, including, for example, one conversation between the Secretary of State and the Director of the CIA about a covert operation at the height of the Suez crisis against the Government of Syria.)

Nevertheless it is not the case, as I was told by seemingly everyone after entering on this work, that I should find nothing. Documents are not everything – Suez should teach that, if it teaches nothing else – but when added to evidence of other kinds, they help.

The main part of this book tells the story of a single year. But I have tried to place it in some historical perspective – in regard to the recent history of the Middle East, to Britain's position in the world, and to the thirty-five years that have passed since. Despite the curiously dated character of some of the material and of the particular controversy that it describes, there is a surprising amount about the international order and relations between states that has relevance to the student of international affairs today.

It is also, of course, at the human level a story about two men, each of whom came to think that the other was a bit mad. On the only occasion when I met him, at the British Embassy in Washington, I was impressed by Sir Anthony's superb good manners, by the care and complete concentration that he devoted to one young man asking him questions about the Geneva conference on Indo-China. I was a little shocked when an unknown civil servant, noticing the time that his master had spent with me and having elicited from me the above impression of him, volunteered that I would not think like that if I had to work for him and recommended that I read *Tribulations of a Baronet*, the memoir by Eden's brother of their scarcely sane father. But it is to Abdul Nasser that this book has constantly to refer, since, without him, there would have been no Suez crisis of this particular kind. It is difficult now to recapture the extent to which he had become an obsession in Britain, even before the seizure of the Canal Company. The single word 'Nasser', spoken or written in fear, derision or loathing became the curse-word of the times, only separated by a decade, it should be remembered, from the emotions of the Second World War. But to understand the spirit of Britain during Suez one needs to sense the polemical spin which British people in those strangely turbulent days imparted to the simple military rank of 'Colonel'.

Keith Kyle

1

Swing-Door of the British Empire

If the Suez Canal is our back door to the East, it is the front door to Europe of Australia, New Zealand and India. If you like to mix your metaphors it is, in fact, the swing-door of the British Empire, which has got to keep continually revolving if our communications are to be what they should.
Anthony Eden, House of Commons, 23 December 1929.

'If Persia is allowed to get away with it, Egypt and other Middle Eastern countries will be encouraged to think that they can try things on; the next thing may be an attempt to nationalise the Suez Canal.' Emanuel Shinwell, Minister of Defence in Clement Attlee's Labour Government, was addressing the Chiefs of Staff on 23 May 1951, after Persia, then the largest Middle Eastern oil producer, had had what so good a socialist as Shinwell considered the effrontery to apply to her principal source of wealth the policy of nationalisation that at home his government had made so peculiarly its own.[1]

The company which had created and, until nationalisation, owned the Persian oil industry was British, with fifty-one per cent of its shares owned by the British Government. The Anglo-Iranian Oil Company[2] managed and controlled the refining and the marketing of the liquid 'black gold' for which the war-smitten industries of Europe were acquiring an addictive thirst. The oil refinery on the island of Abadan, the largest in the world, was Britain's biggest single overseas asset. The oil was shipped to Europe through the Suez Canal[3] which, though popularly thought of in terms of passenger liners and general commerce, was in the course of becoming a virtual adjunct of the oil industry. Now all was endangered by what the weekly periodical *Time and Tide* termed 'frenetic and rackitic nationalists'. In fact the immediate danger was not from a 'new man' but from an old aristocrat of disinterested motives but populist style, Dr Mohamed Mossadeq, the Persian Prime Minister, whose personal extravagances of behaviour – his much publicised simplicity, his iron bed, his pyjamas, his ready tears – were accounted by many Westerners as the marks of a self-indulgent buffoon.[4] It seemed to be more than a symbolic gesture when, in November 1951, Dr Mossadeq, having nationalised his oil, stopped off in a Cairo already poised to defy Britain to immense popular applause.

After the Second World War, in which the Middle East had been for her a principal theatre of operations, Britain was at this time still, if only just, the principal power in the region, linked to Iraq, Egypt and Jordan by old-style military alliances and to the Gulf states and sheikhdoms by even older-style patron–client relationships of one sort or another. These were the 'special positions' on which Britain's status rested. Many of these now seemed unsafe and what had always been the central dynamic of Britain's world position, her industrial strength, was in very questionable order. But oil gave to the Middle East and the exercise of influence there a new importance. It was no longer only a place to go through on the way to somewhere else: now it was a destination in its own right. Above all, given the low state of Britain's currency reserves, her rulers could not but be aware that oil was far cheaper to get out of the ground in the Middle East than anywhere else and could be paid for in sterling.

A military reply to Dr Mossadeq's act of nationalisation could not be given in the heat of the moment because the forces were not ready. By the time they were, United States envoys were in place in Teheran as self-appointed mediators. This was the last capacity in which Britain wanted to encounter her wartime allies; it was an experience that made them thereafter highly alert to the dangers of being, as Winston Churchill put it, 'whittled on substance'.[5]

At the decisive Cabinet meeting on 27 September 1951, the Foreign Secretary, Herbert Morrison, backed by the Defence Minister, put a powerful case for the use of force at Abadan. Otherwise, Morrison said, 'Egypt might be emboldened ... to bring the Suez Canal under Egyptian control and British legal rights in many parts of the world would be placed in jeopardy'.

But this view did not prevail around the Cabinet table. The Prime Minister, Clement Attlee, in his clipped, laconic manner, gave three reasons against. The first and foremost was that, as both President Truman himself and his Secretary of State, Dean Acheson, had made abundantly clear, a policy of force would not have the support of the United States. 'We could not afford to break with the United States on an issue of this kind', the Prime Minister said. Secondly, it was not obvious that the course proposed, the occupation of Abadan, would have the desired result of overthrowing Mossadeq. It might, on the contrary, unite the country around him. And, thirdly, there was the United Nations.

Forty years ago, the UN had far more appeal in Britain to people of all political persuasions than it has had since, until the time of the Gulf War of 1991. At this early phase of its life the UN was dominated by the United

States, as it has become again in 1991, as a perhaps temporary consequence of the Gulf War. If Britain attempted to find a solution by the use of force, Attlee warned the Cabinet, she could not expect much support in the UN, where Latin American and Asian states would follow Washington's lead.[6] Use of force for the settlement of international disputes was explicitly outlawed by the Charter, except in the most immediate circumstances of self-defence or for the purpose of implementing decisions of the UN itself.

The 'Crown Prince'

Attlee's decision to withdraw from Abadan had to be implemented amidst the clash and turbulence of a British general election. On 26 September, just one week after the Prime Minister had announced that the country was to go to the polls, the Persians ordered the final expulsion of the British staff from Abadan. On 8 October, following on with uncanny rapidity, Nahas Pasha, Prime Minister of Egypt, proclaimed the abrogation of the Anglo-Egyptian Treaty of 1936, the only legal basis for the presence of British troops on Egyptian soil, and also the Convention of 1899 which validated the Anglo-Egyptian Condominium over Egypt's former colony in the Sudan. In the election-time atmosphere, the Tories and much of the popular press presented the Middle East news as cumulative evidence of Labour incompetence.

The election of 1951 was Winston Churchill's last chance of becoming Prime Minister. Almost 77 years old, he was not expected, if he won this time, to stay long at Number Ten. His successor had been known for a decade, since he had been recommended to the King during the Second World War as the man Churchill felt was equipped to take his place if a vacancy at the top should suddenly occur.[7] Since then Anthony Eden had been the Tory 'Crown Prince'. As his expertise lay in foreign affairs, it was fortunate for him that Labour clumsiness in this field should feature so highly in the Tory campaign.

'Abad*an*, Sud*an*, Bev*an*!' (the last being the left-wing bogeyman who had resigned from Attlee's Cabinet and threatened to overturn his leadership), screamed Lord Beaverbrook's *Daily Express*. Labour and its main supporter among the popular papers, the *Daily Mirror*, countered with the charge that, judging from the way they evidently wanted to behave in the Middle East, the Conservative leaders were not to be trusted to steer clear of World War III. 'Whose Finger On The Trigger?'[8] was the *Mirror*'s challenge.

'Scuttle' had been Churchill's reverberant word to describe what he felt about a Labour Government's withdrawals. It had been used as far back as 1925 by the young Anthony Eden when he told the House that the British ought not to 'scuttle like flying curs at the sight of our own shadow' from Iraq.[9] But Churchill set his stamp on it when excoriating post-war policy on Egypt and Persia. Not to scuttle was a course to which the new Tory Government, which came in after 25 October with a not-very-convincing majority of seventeen seats, was most evidently committed. How the Tories in power were to behave when Shinwell's prediction proved correct is the story of Suez.

Anthony Eden, who under such pressing conditions of Middle Eastern crisis became for the third time the British Foreign Secretary, was in the awkward position that, while his rapid succession to the premiership was universally expected, he lacked any experience of the domestic departments of state. To all outward appearance he was in October 1951 very much the same man, moving through well-preserved middle age, who had been the matinée idol of the 1930s. A gallant survivor of the trenches in the First World War – an ordeal of which he was to write most movingly in his last book, *Another World* – he had been in that decade the very model of the gifted and handsome young hero striving to prevent a recurrence of the horrors of war.

He was the younger son of a baronet, a landowner in County Durham whose uncontrollable rages and eccentric whims could only be tolerated within the dimensions of a great house, and of a mother who was a compulsive gambler, dissipating much of the family inheritance. Through her he was a Grey, which family had over generations contributed proconsuls and statesmen including a Prime Minister. After coming back from the war with an MC but also, as he put it, 'with my illusions intact, neither shattered nor cynical, to face a changed world',[10] Eden went up to Oxford to get his First in Oriental Languages – Persian and Arabic – with a view to a diplomatic career. But he allowed himself to be diverted into politics, entering Parliament for the safe seat of Warwick and Leamington in December 1923. Less than three years later, the young Eden (still under thirty) became Parliamentary Private Secretary to the Foreign Secretary and his destiny was fixed.

When in 1931 the National Government was formed, Eden became Foreign Under-Secretary and, in 1934, Lord Privy Seal with special responsibility for League of Nations Affairs within the Foreign Office. He became known to the public, at a time when flying was still thought of as something of an adventure, as a pioneer of airborne diplomacy. Always impeccably dressed, wearing the black homburg hat which he made fashionable, Eden was in 1934 the first British Minister to visit Hitler; in 1935 he was the first to visit Stalin. In December 1935, at the age of 38 he became Foreign Secretary, not so young as the first Foreign Secretary, Charles James Fox, who was 33, but the youngest since 1851. His had been an irresistible rise.

That rise was not universally applauded. A Tory peer and ex-Cabinet Minister described Eden in his diary at this time as 'fussing and fidgeting, very self-conscious and blushing with handsomeness – vain as a peacock with all the mannerisms of the *petit maître* – very studied costume, moustache curled inside out – that always galls me – altogether a most uncomfortable dinner companion'. Earlier, Lord Crawford and Balcarres had asked the Prime Minister (Baldwin), 'Can your Foreign Secretary frown?'[11] The cutting edge seemed to show when Eden broke with Neville Chamberlain in February 1938 over the policy of appeasing Mussolini. When the appeasement policy fell into rapid disrepute, Eden existed in the public eye second only to Churchill as the expression of an alternative Tory leadership.

Looking back on that period of office as he did again and again during the Suez crisis, Eden's main regret was the decision, in which he had fully participated, to make no stand against Hitler's reoccupation of the Rhineland in 1936. He had been only too well aware of the plausible arguments that had been used in London to undermine the initial, rather crumbly, French instinct for firmness: the country would not have been politically united behind such a stand, the Germans were only marching into their own backyard, the peace treaty that was being broken was outdated and vindictive. Retrospectively, Eden, like others, endorsed the 'lesson' that the right time to stop a predatory dictator was at the beginning, when he made his first move. But he was also ready to face up to the awkward fact that such early action, in seemingly blurred circumstances, would inevitably be controversial. Yet, given the right lead, he thought the country would be sure to respond and show that it had absorbed what it had been taught at such appalling cost.

In the period of opposition to Munich, Winston Churchill, though he must have been disappointed at Eden's limp style as a public speaker, hailed him as the 'one strong, young figure standing up' against the tides of drift and surrender. After the first year of war (when he was successively Dominions Secretary and War Minister), Eden returned to the Foreign Office for the duration. By the time that the Conservatives were swept out of power in 1945, it had become accepted that Eden would shortly take over the lead. 'I am most anxious to handle matters', Churchill wrote to him on 7 May 1946, 'so as to make the formal transference, when it occurs, smooth and effectual'.[12] The recipient of that note could hardly have understood this to mean 'in nine years' time'.

The role of *prince-héritier* is not a normal one in British politics and, for all of Eden's lasting popularity in the country at large, it was not one from which the party in opposition derived much satisfaction. 'Why do you not like my Anthony?' Churchill one day suddenly asked his Chief Whip, James Stuart. Stuart replied that, while Eden was no doubt first-class at the Foreign Office, he feared that it was only too apparent that he lacked knowledge of economics, housing, fuel, education and other matters on which he was having to speak. 'Well, you'll have to have him,' was Churchill's only reaction.[13] Eden had certain concepts for the post-war world. They had a centrist, cross-party sound: for industry, the development of co-partnership and profit-sharing; for Britain's world role, the notion of the 'three interlocking circles'. These circles – the Anglo-American alliance, the Commonwealth of Nations, and the union of Western Europe conveniently overlapped only at the point of Great Britain.[14] By adding them together in such a way as to make them seem cumulative rather than just confusing, Britain, despite her loss of momentum after two World Wars and the declining sickness that appeared to afflict her once remarkable economy, might still be dressed up to look the part of a World Power. It was striking that this same metaphor of three circles, at once exalted and vague, was shortly to be propounded as a vision for Egypt by Eden's historic opponent, Gamal Abdul Nasser.

French and British at Suez

The situation in Egypt with which immediately on returning to the Foreign Office Eden had to cope was the culminating effect of the long story of relations between that country and Britain. It was a story which so hung over the course of the Suez crisis that it must briefly be summarised here. Gamal Abdul Nasser, whose name and personality so dominate what was said and done in 1956, used to say that, instead of the Suez Canal being dug for Egypt as its ruler had been promised just a hundred years before, Egypt had become the property of the Canal.

The Universal Company of the Suez Maritime Canal, which was formally constituted on 20 December 1858, owed its existence and form to the exceptional personality of a former French diplomat of Basque origin, Ferdinand de Lesseps. He had the inspiration and drive, the guile, the charm and the cheek to capitalise on a previous friendship with Mohamed Said (after whom Port Said is named) when he became Viceroy of Egypt to gain the concession to dig a sea-level canal through the desert between the Mediterranean and the Red Sea and to operate it for ninety-nine years after it had opened. De Lesseps's scheme for piercing the one-hundred-mile isthmus of Suez which linked Asia to Africa was based on the correct perception – not shared by many – that the two seas were at the same level, and on the decision to exploit a succession of lakes, which would thereby shorten the length of the Canal. On one of them, Lake Timsah, the Canal Company eventually established its headquarters in a new European-style town intended for its employees and named Ismailia after Said's successor.

The Universal Company was, despite its name, a company with French shareholders and French management and its sole capital asset, the Canal, was constructed by French brains, Egyptian sweat and the money of both. Being French, its construction was ruthlessly and at times hysterically opposed by Britain. It is scarcely too much to say that the celebrated Lord Palmerston made of his ability to obstruct the Suez venture a measuring rod of his prestige and power. In 1858, by 290 votes to 62 the House of Commons, in obedience to his argument that as a hopelessly non-commercial venture the Canal could only be a cover for a French policy conceived in hostility to Britain, refused all British support.[15] Like some other great promoters of the period (King Leopold II of the Belgians was another), de Lesseps possessed an exceptional ability to combine articulation of great ideals – free and universal access to his artificial waterway and its neutrality in time of war – with marked commercial guile. It was difficult to tell where one began and the other broke off. He did make great efforts to broaden international participation in the investment; however, Britain was almost wholly successful in organising a boycott. As a result Said was obliged to take up on behalf of Egypt far more than her original allotment of shares in the enterprise.[16]

It was an important part of Egypt's historical contention in 1956 that the Canal was no gift from outside but was built largely at Egypt's expense. Certainly the *firman* (decree) which de Lesseps induced Said to sign was exceptionally favourable to his under-capitalised enterprise. Egypt supplied free, forced labour, lavish land grants and customs exemptions. When eight years later the Turkish Sultan, by virtue of his ultimate powers of sovereignty over Egypt, was able to force alterations in these unequal terms, the Viceroy Ismail agreed to pay the Company heavily in cash for concessions withdrawn. With the money thus obtained de Lesseps was able to finish the work with machinery. Cairo later reckoned, not unreasonably, that the Egyptian contribution towards the cost amounted to more than one and a half times the total of that made by others.[17] On the other hand it could be argued that, without de Lesseps, there would have been no Canal, though it would surely have been built at a later time.

Judgments on Ismail's performance as a ruler, once highly moralistic, tend, when looked at in comparison with Third World indebtedness today, to be a great deal more charitable. He is given the credit for wishing to modernise and develop his country. But having had the satisfaction of seeing the Suez Canal opened with great ceremony in November 1869, six years later the Khedive (as the Viceroy was now called) was in such financial straits that it became known in Whitehall that he was seeking a purchaser for the forty-four per cent of the Company's shares that he owned. Britain, having done all she possibly could to abort the Canal, jumped at this late chance of joining it. The Prime Minister, Benjamin Disraeli, overriding the opposition of both Foreign Secretary and Chancellor of the Exchequer, instantly acquired them for £4 million advanced by Rothschilds. The coup excited the popular imagination. 'To this country', said *The Times*'s leader of 27 November 1875, 'will belong the decision on every question, whether scientific, financial or political; administration and negotiation will be in our hands, and, as we have the power, so we shall have the responsibility before the world'.

The local press went wild: Birmingham knew that 'an Englishman feels proud now that he can "paddle his own canoe" on his own canal'; Cheltenham considered that 'Egypt is as necessary to England as Alsace and Lorraine to Germany', and Bristol felt that, holding the Canal, 'we hold Turkey and Egypt in the hollow of our hands, the Mediterranean is an English lake and the Suez Canal is only another name for the Thames and the Mersey'. Disraeli did not seem out of line when he wrote to the Queen: 'It is vital to your Majesty's authority and power at this critical moment that the Canal should belong to England.'[18]

These instant comments set the metaphors which lasted. As descriptions of what had happened, they were highly misleading. The Canal Company never owned the Canal, which remained Ottoman (and subsequently Egyptian) territory. It was a private joint-stock company which had a concession to operate the Canal until November 1968, when everything was to revert to the Egyptians. Still less did Britain's purchase of forty-four per cent of the shares involve a British takeover of the Company. The British Government was entitled to only three directors on a board of thirty-two. British ships were by far the largest users but not until 1883, after an immense row and a threat to build a rival British canal, were seven additional seats reserved for private British shipowners. The character and style of the Universal Suez Canal Company remained not only French but the French of the *ancien régime*. The Company's headquarters were not in Cairo or in Alexandria but in a Parisian building in the rue d'Astorg. Nevertheless, within seven years of Disraeli's purchase a fresh event had occurred which served to reinforce for the ensuing seventy years the excited impressions instilled in 1875.[19]

The 'Temporary' Occupation

This event, occurring not under the imperialist Disraeli but under the anti-imperialist Gladstone, was to provide detailed self-justification for Colonel Nasser and his Free Officers. By the end of the 1870s relations between Egypt and her international creditors had deteriorated to the point at which Ismail had been deposed, British and French Financial Controllers had been installed with sweeping powers and even for a short period, which was not forgotten by Nasser when he came to deliver his celebrated rodomontade at Alexandria on 26 July 1956, the portfolios of Finance and Public Works in the Egyptian Cabinet were given to an Englishman and a Frenchman. This coincided with the first great upsurge of Egyptian nationalism, which was in rebellion not only against external interference but also against the non-Arab cosmopolitanism of Alexandria and Cairo, with an Albanian ruling dynasty descended from a soldier of fortune, Turks and Circassians holding privileged positions in the court and army, and British, French,

Maltese, Cypriots, Greeks, Italians, Armenians, Lebanese as well as the religious minorities, Jews and Copts (Christians), prominent in business and the professions.[20]

The man who emerged as the hero of this uprising was a native Egyptian officer, Colonel Ahmad Arabi, who became briefly Minister of War and to whom Colonel Nasser looked as a precursor. Claiming that their nationals and their property were in danger, Britain and France intervened with a joint ultimatum, France taking the lead. The people exploded on to the streets of Alexandria on 11 June 1882, when Egyptians rioted against their foreign-seeming city and at least fifty Europeans were killed. This *émeute* laid the foundation of the myth, fortified by a very few widely separated instances in Cairo in 1919 and in 1952, that the Egyptian mob was a particularly volatile and incalculable beast.

French public opinion turned abruptly against a forward policy in Egypt so that, a month after the riot, the Royal Navy went in to bombard the fortifications of Alexandria alone, while the French Navy was sailing immaculately away. After the bombardment was over, a major fire destroyed much of the commercial area of the city. Since the Khedive took refuge with the British, all subsequent acts were performed in his name. A military expedition was despatched under Sir Garnet Wolseley, a soldier whose preparations were always so meticulous as to turn 'All is Sir Garnet!' into a military expression. De Lesseps, behaving as was his wont in the manner of a sovereign entity, telegraphed to Arabi: 'The English shall never enter the Canal, never. Make no attempt to intercept my Canal. I am there.' But Sir Garnet was there too and, going through the Canal, landed at Ismailia. A quick victory at Tel al-Kebir and Egypt was at Britain's mercy. To a national-minded Egyptian, the Canal was the invasion-route through which the latest foreign ruler had arrived.[21]

Gladstone learnt the hard way that it was much easier to march into Egypt than to disengage from it, once political and military responsibilities had been assumed. The 'temporary' occupation lasted seventy-four years. According to the historian A. J. P. Taylor, the British promise to withdraw, made originally in a circular to the Powers, was repeated sixty-six times between 1882 and 1922. 'But the condition', Taylor says, 'was the restoration of order; and this condition was never fulfilled to British satisfaction'.[22] Until 1904 Suez was the occasion for recurrent diplomatic tension between the British and their defaulting partner, the French. Since the French had made the mistake of sailing away, the British did not scruple to dismantle most of the machinery of the Dual Control over the country's economy. France became, therefore, the main promoter of international control over Egypt and the Canal; Britain's role was that of defender of Egypt's rights, since the Khedive's 'Egypt' was the creature (a rather sullen, petulant creature sometimes, but still the creature) of Britain.[23]

The principal international instrument governing the Suez Canal, an instrument much cited during the crisis of 1956, was the Convention of Constantinople of 1888 between Turkey (the nominal sovereign of the Canal) and the European Powers of the day. It substantially confirmed a compromise worked out by France and Britain – French principles and British exceptions. It started off with a fine flourish: 'The Suez Maritime Canal shall always be free and open in time of war as in time of peace to every vessel of commerce or of war, without distinction of flag.' In time of war the Canal was to be not so much 'neutralised' – de Lesseps's favourite expression does not in fact appear in the Convention – as made into a safe corridor for any and all belligerents. The signatories were not to keep any war vessels stationed in the Canal or raise any defence structures along its banks, but they were each entitled, if they so wished, to maintain two warships in or off the two ports of access, Port Said and Suez.

Under Article X, reflecting the interests of Britain, the Convention was not to interfere with the measures which the Khedive might find it necessary to take to secure the defence of Egypt and the maintenance of public order by his own forces (which forces were commanded by British officers). This was to give the British all they wanted in two World Wars, and afterwards it gave the Egyptians their text for denying passage to the commerce of Israel. Only one substantive article (XIV) and, by inference, the preamble referred to the Suez Canal Company. The Article said that the Convention was permanent and not bound by the limits of the concession. The preamble said that the Convention's purpose was to 'complete the system' established by the two *firmans* (decrees) issued by the Egyptian Viceroy in 1854 and 1856.

The phrase 'complete the system' resounded in the polemics of 1956. If 'the system' meant non-Egyptian management, the Company's concession had been given 'an international impress'. If, as the Egyptians plausibly contended, it meant that the principles of free and open navigation in peace and war extended by internal Ottoman decrees were now made international law, there was no connection between treaty and concession.

One other aspect of the 1888 Convention calls for some attention. On French insistence machinery was established for the international supervision of the Canal's operation. It was rudimentary but, even so, Britain took steps to ensure that it would be inoperative. Under Article VIII the Agents in Egypt (the chief diplomatic representatives) of the signatory Powers were to meet once a year – and more often if summoned by any three of their number – to take note of whether the Treaty was being observed. As Britain only agreed to sign the Convention provided it did not come into effect so long as 'the current emergency' compelled the 'temporary' British occupation, the Agents never met.[24]

Egypt was governed according to the 'advice' which was proffered to the Khedive and his Ministers by the British Agent and Consul-General, who was until 1908 the formidable Earl of Cromer. It was never part of the

Empire; it was always a 'veiled protectorate'. Although his personal ascendancy was unimpeded and his efficient supervision of the Egyptian administration served the interests of the foreign (mainly non-British) bondholders well, Cromer found his style cramped by the residual power of the French. His zeal for major reform ran into vetoes and delays which they were still able to interpose.[25] However in 1904, with the Entente Cordiale, French tiresomeness over Egypt ceased while Britain got out of France's way in Morocco. Britain then withdrew her reservations to the Constantinople Convention, which at last came into effect with the exception that France agreed that the Agents under Article VIII should even now never meet.

Despite all these arrangements Egypt, and hence the Suez Canal, remained juridically part of the Ottoman Empire. That ceased in 1914 when the Khedive Abbas Hilmi II, who had wearied of the British connection, sided with his sovereign, the Sultan of Turkey, in going to war on behalf of Germany. Abbas Hilmi was instantly deposed, Egypt was made a British Protectorate, and two of the ex-Khedive's uncles were in succession installed with the title of Sultan.

The Suez Canal was treated, at least from 1916, as a British territorial possession. According to Farnie's *East and West of Suez*, 'Britain infringed almost every article of the [Constantinople] Convention ... British lawyers provided the legal formulae which justified such an extension of belligerent rights.'[26]

With the war over and the principle of self-determination predominant, Egyptian nationalists, now organised as the Wafd Party, demanded a final end to 'temporary occupation'. On 28 February 1922, after riots in 1919 and years of disturbance, the British unilaterally proclaimed that Egypt was 'an independent, sovereign state', over which the Sultan Fuad was to reign as King. Four matters, however, were to be 'absolutely reserved to the discretion of HMG' until such time as it became possible to reach agreement on them. These were not small matters; indeed they went right to the root of the question of whether Egypt was or was not, in the modern European sense of the term, a sovereign state. The four matters were: the security of the communications of the British Empire (which meant British participation in guarding 'the swing-door of the Empire', as Anthony Eden called the Suez Canal in 1929); the defence of Egypt against all foreign aggression or interference (which meant that in time of war or the prospect of war Britain should be able to resume her military presence in the whole country); the protection of foreign interests and of minorities; and the future government of the Sudan. In the privately expressed opinion of Lord Lloyd of Dolobran, British High Commissioner in Cairo from 1925 to 1929, 'To tell a country she is independent while you keep an army of occupation is not only a contradiction in terms but a fraud'.[27]

Eden, Nahas and the War Experience

Egyptian politics now took on a recognisable rhythm. Elections were held, which the Wafd Party, led since 1927 by Mustafa Nahas Pasha, always won, at least to the extent of being the largest party. At intervals Nahas was called on by the Palace to become Prime Minister. Conflict between him and the Palace would follow. The King (Fuad until 1936, his son Farouk thereafter) would choose the moment when he considered Nahas was sufficiently undermined for it to be safe to dismiss him. In 1936 when Nahas was in power following the succession of the young Farouk, the Anglo-Egyptian Treaty was negotiated with Anthony Eden, the young Foreign Secretary of Britain.

Eden's Treaty with Nahas – which ensured Eden's appearance on Egyptian stamps – started off with a bold simplicity reminiscent of the Constantinople Convention: 'Article I. The military occupation of Egypt by the forces of His Majesty the King and Emperor is terminated.' But that did not mean that all British troops were to go away. 'In view', Article VIII said, taking a deep breath, 'of the fact that the Suez Canal, while being an integral part of Egypt, is a universal means of communication and also an essential means of communication between the different parts of the British Empire, HM the King of Egypt, until such time as the High Contracting Parties agree that the Egyptian Army is in a position to ensure by its own resources the liberty and entire security of the navigation of the Canal, authorises HM the King and Emperor to station forces in Egyptian territory in the vicinity of the Canal ... with a view to ensuring, in co-operation with the Egyptian forces, the defence of the Canal.' These forces however were to be strictly limited to a maximum of 10,000 soldiers, 400 airmen, and certain support staffs, and to areas narrowly defined next to the Canal and well away from the main centres of population. The Egyptian Government undertook to build suitable barracks, which it did not do. Article VIII was scrupulous to specify that, 'The presence of these forces shall not constitute, in any manner, an occupation and will in no way prejudice the sovereign rights of Egypt'.[28]

But there was also the Alliance (Articles IV to VIII): in the event of Britain being involved in war, imminent danger of war, or even 'apprehended international emergency', Egypt was to make her whole territory and facilities available and to enact such emergency measures as martial law and war censorship. In the Second World War Britain took full advantage of these facilities. Egypt was officially neutral until, for purposes of becoming a founder-member of the United Nations, she qualified as 'a peace-loving country' by declaring war. She was nevertheless a base and battlefield. Allied armies swarmed all over her territory, there was a vast military headquarters in her capital and a base of comparable proportions in the desert towards the Suez Canal, and the whole British people identified themselves with the campaigns in the Western Desert.

The wartime encounter did not, in general, serve to endear the two peoples to each other. Egypt's neutrality, though in time it came to suit the British Government, was not readily understandable to British troops. Also, Britain ran up heavy debts to Egypt in the course of 'defending' her. Egypt was in consequence not a popular country in Britain after the war; thousands of returned servicemen conveyed the impression of 'an ungrateful people'. In the middle of the Suez crisis in 1956 a reader's letter in the left-wing weekly *Tribune* was to ask: 'How many of [your correspondents] have had the "privilege" of defending this filthy race from the onslaught of German forces at El Alamein only to be spat upon, hissed at, booed at, and in many cases even murdered?'[29]

The nadir of Egypt's history as a sovereign state was reached in 1940 when the Government of Ali Maher Pasha, who was regarded as an Italianophile singularly ill-disposed towards the British presence, was removed on British 'advice' and in 1942 when, on 4 February, with their armoured carriers drawn up round the Palace, the British required King Farouk to appoint Nahas Pasha as Prime Minister or abdicate. Farouk, who was not a strong character, gave in to this ultimatum. Thus Nahas, the most popular of the politicians, was imposed by imperial will, while Ali Maher, who was in 1955–6 to become Britain's favoured candidate for the succession when Britain next dreamed of toppling Egyptians from the seat of power, was cast out.

By accepting public humiliation to retain his throne, the King had irrevocably alienated young nationalist officers like Gamal Abdul Nasser and Anwar Sadat.[30] Abdul Nasser was twenty-four at the time of the British coup and was stationed as a lieutenant in the Sudan. The son of a post-office clerk he had benefited from one of the indirect consequences of the Anglo-Egyptian Treaty. Following its signature, entrance to the Military Academy was opened for the first time to all social classes; almost all the Free Officers who changed the regime in 1952 would not otherwise have had commissions.

'What is to be done now that the die is cast and we have accepted what has happened on our knees in surrender?', Nasser later quoted himself as asking in 1942 in a letter to a friend. 'As a matter of fact, I believe that the Imperialist was playing with only one card in his hand for the purpose of threatening us. But, once the Imperialist realizes that some Egyptians are ready to shed their blood and meet force with force, he will beat a hasty retreat like any harlot rebuffed.'[31] Nasser was a tall, handsome, well-built man of austere tastes, great political ambition and the soul of a conspirator.

The Idea of Arab Unity

Nahas Pasha fulfilled British expectations by running for two and a half years a government that was firmly on the Allied side in the war. In September and October 1944 he presided at Alexandria over the meetings of the Preparatory Committee of Arab Prime Ministers which drew up the Protocol for the Arab League. This was the first positive step towards Arab unity, about which there had hitherto been much intellectual theorising and some inconclusive intrigue among the Asian Arab states.[32] Egypt's attitude to Pan-Arabism had hitherto been ambivalent. In many respects she seemed the natural metropolis of a Pan-Arab world, midway between the North African and the Asian Arabs, with much the highest population of any Arab state, having in Cairo and Alexandria the Arab world's largest city and its largest seaport, and in Al-Azhar University the ancient centre of Islamic learning. Yet the focus of Pan-Arabism had been in Asia; Egypt had often seemed detached, preoccupied by her own concerns.[33] Now Nahas took the lead, the Protocol was agreed, and the Pact to set up the League was signed in the following March. The Western patron of this move towards Arab union was considered to be Anthony Eden.

This reputation was only half-deserved. It arose mainly from two speeches – on 29 May 1941 and on 24 February 1943 – in which he expressed interest in advancing the idea. They were important because, in the days when Arab governments were in the practice of clearing their moves in advance with London, Eden's approval gave it the mark of legitimacy. Yet he did not encourage Nahas's decisive meetings at Alexandria and made it known that he would rather have had them postponed. The reason was clear: if in the autumn of 1944 the Arab states were to begin acting together, they were likely to act on issues which would be embarrassing to the West. They would want to organise opposition to the French in Syria and to the Jews in Palestine. Already the Palestine question was swelling in size until it would become the catalyst that determined alignments, unhinged emotions and tormented judgements throughout the Middle East.[34]

The day after the conclusion of the Alexandria meeting, Nahas was dismissed by King Farouk. The usual succession of royal nominees followed while, in opposition, Nahas sought to restore his credentials as the people's favourite. Once the war was over Egypt set herself to remove all British forces from Egyptian soil and to do so in a way that would no longer permit Britain to dictate her foreign policy. Although the 1936 Treaty ran for twenty years, either party was entitled to reopen talks on its provisions after ten. Egypt did so and it was Attlee's decision to respond, before any negotiations began, by an offer to withdraw all troops that aroused Churchill's first use of the rasping reproof of 'Scuttle'.

An agreement was reached for evacuation by September 1949 and on a

Joint Board of Defence to decide on action to be taken, including a British re-entry to the bases if there were an attack on Egypt or on one of her immediate neighbours, but it was never ratified by Egypt. Such an agreement presupposed a degree of underlying consensus about the nature of the threat which was simply not present, except in some particularly anglophile circles. The Wafd, being out of office, was able to articulate enough popular opposition to ensure that the agreement was withdrawn. The nominal breaking point came over the King's claim to rule over Sudan. The real reason, as Elizabeth Monroe, the *Economist*'s Middle East expert, put it in her little classic, *Britain's Moment in the Middle East*, 'was the endemic one: Egypt wanted evacuation without conditions; no Prime Minister could consent to a continuing British alliance and survive'.[35]

In the absence of a new agreement, the British left the Delta cities but sat tight on their vast estate in the Canal Zone, where a most elaborate accumulation of railways, roads, airfields, ports, barracks, stores and workshops were all under exclusively British control. The numbers of troops exceeded the Treaty limit by many times, so did the area that they filled.[36] But Nahas Pasha, when he came back to power for the last time, was no longer coming in under the guns of British tanks. In October 1951, he rejected out of hand the offer of membership of a Western military alliance headed by the United States and opted instead for confrontation with Britain. A few days later, the men he had to confront were once again those whom he had known in time of war: Winston Churchill and Anthony Eden.

But there was one other circumstance drastically affecting every relationship in the Middle East and profoundly conditioning the climax of the Suez affair which must now be considered: the upheavals consequent on the birth of the State of Israel.

2

A Jewish State

The most spectacular event in the contemporary history of Palestine – more spectacular in a sense than the creation of the Jewish State – is the wholesale evacuation of its Arab population . . . The reversion to the status quo ante *is unthinkable.*

Moshe Sharett, Foreign Minister of Israel, private letter, 15 June 1948.

The Jewish thrust into the Negev has for the first time in history split the Arab world: there is now no practicable land communication between Egypt and the other Arab States – a feat never achieved even by the Crusaders.

General Sir Gerald Templer, Vice-Chief of the Imperial General Staff, 29 October 1948.

One matter about which Churchill and Eden could not agree during the Second World War was whether at the end of it to proclaim a small Jewish state within Palestine, over which Britain had exercised since 1923 a League of Nations Mandate. A Cabinet committee had proposed it; Churchill, who called himself a Zionist, had backed it, the War Cabinet had endorsed it in principle. It would have been a very small state indeed (only a little more besides a coastal strip and even then needing to include several overwhelmingly Arab areas); it should be proclaimed at the moment of victory in Europe, when everyone was looking the other way and, to distract Arab attention, a large new Arab state ('Greater Syria') would be proclaimed at the same time. But Eden was against it from the outset. He listed 'no fewer than four major errors' in the Cabinet Committee's reasoning, warning that, 'The protracted and costly, maybe disastrous, resistance which I anticipate will be aroused . . . will be headed by leaders as yet unknown, the potential Titos of the Arab world'. Moreover, he saw another danger which counted heavily with him. If the Cabinet persisted with partition, the prospect was of 'losing to America our pre-eminence in a part of the world which is of great importance to us'.[1] Thus Britain's opportunity passed of playing one more time the role of victorious World Power in the Middle East. From then on it was to be downhill all the way.

The existence of the British partition plan was a state secret that was well kept. By the time the war ended it had fallen victim not only to Eden's resistance but to Churchill's dwindling enthusiasm. The assassination of Lord Moyne, the British Minister of State in the Middle East, by members of *Lehi,* a Jewish terrorist group of which Yitzhak Shamir was one of the three top leaders, profoundly moved him, so that he wondered if 'our dreams for Zionism' were to 'end in the smoke of assassins' pistols'. He was also irritated by the backseat driving of American opinion which, as Europe was being liberated, was demanding that Britain comply with Jewish objectives in Palestine without much regard for practical consequences. On 6 July 1945, at the very end of his first Premiership, Churchill wrote in a minute that Britain should show no desire to keep the Palestine Mandate 'while the Americans sit and criticise ... Somebody else should have their turn now'.[2]

While there were individuals in the Conservative Party including Churchill to whom the Zionists could look for sympathy, the influence of Jews in British politics forty years ago was exercised mainly through the Labour Party. There was a Zionist plank in the Labour platform in 1945 and Jewish expectation was high that a Labour Foreign Secretary would be much more amenable than an Eden whose name was popularly associated with the launching of the Arab League. Great was the disillusionment when it was found that Ernest Bevin was resolved to negotiate a bi-national settlement in an undivided Palestine, maintaining strict limits on further Jewish immigration.

Sovereignty and unlimited immigration being the Zionist requirements, their position and that of Britain and especially of Bevin personally were on a collision course. Massive civil disobedience, especially to the immigration laws, was organised by the mainstream Jewish organisations in Palestine headed by David Ben-Gurion, while terrorist action against British rule was the work of minority, 'dissident' groups, mainly the *Irgun* (IZL) led by Menachim Begin and Shamir's *Lehi* (known to the British as 'the Stern Gang'). Dramatic scenes involving European displaced persons, the pathetic survivors of the Holocaust, were acted out on the amplified screen of American media projection at the very moment when the securing of American support against the Russians was the pre-eminent British concern.

The 'de-Satanisation' of Bevin in Israeli scholarship has only begun in the last few years.[3] There was attributed to him at the time an implacable determination to do the Jews down, and even Churchill, who admired Bevin's sterling performance in office generally, referred in later minutes to his 'anti-Semitism', a characterisation for which there is little biographical support.[4] It was, therefore, in no mood of gratitude to Britain that Ben-Gurion proclaimed the sovereign independence of the State of Israel, while carefully avoiding mention of any boundaries, on 14 May 1948, just a few hours before the Mandatory Power silently disappeared with no handover, no firework display and no end-of-term speech by a member of the Royal Family. It had been the Zionist Churchill who had first made the proposition openly – in line with his end-of-the-war minute – that Britain should simply abdicate from the problem and throw it into the hands of the infant United Nations. When he made this view public on 1 August 1946 he revealed that, had he remained in power, he had planned to take this step earlier.

When Bevin, after struggling on for another six months, announced on 14 February 1947 what was in effect the adoption of Churchill's policy, the motive was no doubt the same. British troops were suffering losses at the hands of Jews, culminating in the huge civilian and military casualty list when British headquarters in the King David Hotel was blown up by Begin's terrorists. Britain's good name was in constant danger in the United States and elsewhere. Bevin said, when last-minute pressure was applied in April 1948 for British forces to stay behind to help the UN, that British public opinion would not tolerate the presence of the British army in Palestine one moment longer, so aggrieved was it at 'the irresponsible backseat driving of the United States'.[5]

British statesmanship over Palestine may have appeared broken-backed and unconstructive – giving the problem to the UN when London had found it insoluble, criticising the partition plan which the UN produced, and then sulkily harassing all efforts at its implementation. But there was a kind of shaky and obtuse consistency behind the British moves. Not even that could be said for what the United States produced. She supported the partition of Palestine; American propaganda contributed mightily to the air of unstoppable momentum behind this solution, and the arm-twisting by Americans with powerful connections went a long way to ensure the two-thirds vote of the General Assembly that, on 29 November 1947, endorsed the setting up of a Jewish state and an Arab state linked together by an Economic Union. But within the Administration there was not the steady commitment to the Jewish state to match that of the Soviet Union, which saw in the Zionist cause the surest available instrument for breaking up the British Empire in the Middle East. The State Department was notably unconvinced, avoiding a leadership role in the UN, acquiescing dubiously in pressures from elsewhere, and in so far as its own staff were concerned, pursuing a hands-off policy towards the vote on Resolution 181, the partition Resolution.

Resolution 181 was accepted immediately by the Jewish leadership in Palestine, although the boundaries created by the partition would be, in the absence of their universal acceptance in the region, strategically indefensible – with several cross-over points, a narrow coastal plain looking up at Arab hills, and a Jewish state with barely a majority (and probably, if the Bedouin nomad could be counted, not even that) of Jewish people, and containing areas heavily populated with Arabs.[6] Still for Jews it was at last the early prospect of a state, with sovereignty and control over immigration.

The majority population of Palestine, the Palestinian Arabs, did not accept the verdict (and did not acknowledge the General Assembly's juridical right to pronounce it) until 15 November 1988. It was also rejected by the states in the region. Since the Assembly had ordered various preliminary steps to be taken that could only by their nature be conducted voluntarily there was, as the Mandate ended, no Arab state constituted for part of the country, no Economic Union negotiated for the whole and no remaining authority capable of splitting up the assets. In the view of the regional states and of the Palestine Arab people there was, when the British left, literally nothing – *res nullius,* no legal authority.

The American State Department reproached the Jews for having told them that, once the Assembly had spoken, it would be grumpily but respectfully obeyed.[7] The British, who knew better, neither took part in the vote nor assisted the UN in any way. That would be to take sides in the Middle East, they said, and moreover to take the opposite side to that of their military allies, Egypt, Transjordan and Iraq.

The United States, confronted with the reality of Arab opposition, wavered. The Jews in the first instance expected to be defended by an international force upholding the authority of the United Nations. Since the British absolutely refused to allow their own troops to take part and the Soviet Union would not be welcome, this in practice meant a force largely supplied by the United States. Ralph Bunche, the American who was secretary of the UN Palestine Commission, called for one highly mechanised division to establish the Commission in Jerusalem, which, under the terms of the partition resolution, was to belong to neither successor state but to enjoy a special status as an International City. But a military assessment submitted to President Truman estimated that to enforce partition would require 80,000 to 100,000 men. Truman, realising that this requirement would involve partial mobilisation, decided with the unanimous support of his advisers, that American troops would not be involved.[8]

From that point on, the United States turned about and attempted frantically to find ways of averting the endgame of partition and the prospect of anarchy as the close of British rule remorselessly approached. All that the UN could manage in the time was to agree to send one man, a Swedish Mediator, with a modest staff.

Before midnight on 14/15 May, David Ben-Gurion had pre-empted the hiatus by his proclamation of the State of Israel and, just eleven minutes after the expiration of the Mandate at midnight, to the shock and shame of the unalerted American delegation to the UN, President Truman contrived the *de facto* recognition of the State.[9] The Soviet Union followed with *de jure* recognition just a few hours later. This sudden lurching of American policy was not the first, nor was it to be the last time that Truman, facing a presidential election which many assumed he could not win, abruptly grabbed the tiller of Middle East policy and swung it round in a Zionist direction. From the events of 1948 derived the assumption that every fourth year (and 1956 was a fourth year) American policy towards the region would either be paralysed or, if active, would do nothing that would disoblige Israel.

Ben-Gurion and the Arab Refugees

David Ben-Gurion, the man who on 14 May became the Prime Minister and Minister of Defence in the first Israeli Government and was to hold the same combination of posts in 1956, was a man of sixty-two in the year of independence and therefore seventy years old at the time of Suez. He was a short, stocky man with a large head, a conspicuous mane of white, protruding hair, a bit like Lloyd George, and a manner of moving that was both quick and jerky. He was often compared to a lion and certainly when displeased he roared and growled. In temperament he is described by his authorised biographer as 'a man of extremes, passionate in his feelings, fierce in his feuds, harsh in his battles'.[10] Short of small talk, he often appeared as lacking in consideration for his colleagues. Yet, to quote another Israeli writer, 'he was surrounded or surrounded himself with young and, in a way, awe-struck disciples'.[11]

Though not literally an audodidact (he was a law graduate from a Constantinople university), Ben-Gurion often behaved like one. He was a true bibliophile and his conversation and speeches were studied (sometimes to the point of overload) with a remarkable range of self-taught reference from ancient history, the sciences, comparative religion, military doctrine and classical Greek. He was a compulsive diarist, sometimes to be seen scribbling his account of conversations as they were taking place. These contemporaneous impressions were interspersed with his (sometimes incautious) aspirations and lengthy historical or philosophical digressions.

Ben-Gurion was a man who cared greatly about his place in history, often saying that battles had to be won twice, the first time on the field of action, the second time in the history books. There are, for example, grounds for thinking that he did not wish to be remembered as an expeller of Arabs but, to say the very least, he did not place obstacles in the way of the vast demographic movement that was now let loose and has loomed over each subsequent stage of the Arab–Israeli conflict.

The movement out of the country among upper- and professional-class Arabs, the natural leaders of their local communities, began as soon as the partition resolution was passed. Between November and the end of March there were spasmodic but increasing incidents of violence between the Arab and Jewish communities, starting with Arab attacks on isolated Jewish settlements and harassment of Jewish traffic and leading on to heavy Jewish reprisals; in the last six weeks of the Mandate there was civil war; after 15 May the new-born State of Israel was fighting against five attacking states. In the first period of five months an estimated 75,000 Arabs had deserted their homes; the figure had reached 400,000 by the end of British rule; it was approaching 800,000 by the end of the year. The existence of this enormous mass of refugees pressing on Israel's boundaries has ensured that in over forty years Israel has not been able to become a normal state; and it contributed the second powder trail (the Canal story being the first) that led directly to the Suez War.

Israel possessed such an obvious self-interest in the Arabs leaving and showed such subsequent determination that, once gone, they should not come back that there is a temptation to assume that there must have been a Jewish master-plan in operation to bring about the migration in the first place. But this was not the case, despite the fact that there were a number of Jews, like the Zionist official Yosef Weitz, who agitated in favour of what they called a policy of 'transfer' (which would have meant wholesale expulsion). Likewise, it was only a minority who 'officiously strove' to keep the Arabs from leaving, and many took steps which had the effect of encouraging their departure. Also, once they had left home, if only for a short time and if only for a short distance, they were not to be allowed to return.

Devices of psychological warfare used by Jewish commanders to throw Arab villagers onto the defensive and diminish their capacity for menace contributed to the climate in which Arabs left, according to a contemporary Jewish intelligence report of June 1948 unearthed by Benny Morris, the author of *The Birth of the Palestinian Refugee Problem*. The report places the main responsibility on Jewish military moves, real or rumoured; in only a small proportion of cases does it attribute evacuation to Arab orders. The shocking story of Deir Yassin, the Arab village near Jerusalem, which on 9 April was stormed by a mixed force from the *Irgun* and the Lehi under Menachem Begin's command, after which more than 200 villagers including old men, women and children were put to death was, according to the same report, 'a decisive accelerating factor'. Arab radios used it as the basis of a 'Jewish atrocity' campaign which had the unintended effect of multiplying the incentives for flight. Later, once the Arabs saw what a present was being made to the Jews, the same radios were desperately urging people to stay at home.[12]

The nearest to a general Israeli expulsion order that has emerged is an operational plan – Plan 'D' dated March 1948 – listing various ways of taking possession of the Jewish State in a climate of hostility. 'Enemy population centres located in or near our defensive system' were to be either physically destroyed or encircled and searched. 'In the event of resistance [to the search] the armed force must be wiped out and the population must be expelled outside the borders of the State.'[13] As Morris points out, during

April–June the Jewish commanders seldom faced the dilemma whether or not to carry out the plan in all its severity: the villagers had already fled.

The general impression to be drawn from the private reactions of the Jewish leadership, including Ben-Gurion, is one of astonishment and wonder at the vanishing of the Arabs. The Israeli scholar Shabtei Teveth is the latest to point out that there is still a lack of detailed work using Arab sources on what exactly made the first 75,000 go before the fighting became more generalised in April, the argument being that these early refugees generated the migration mood before most of the factors usually cited had been brought substantially to bear. Pending such research it can be said that, from what is known about refugees, it does not seem so very strange that, with the approaching end of civil order as they had known it and the likelihood of a period of anarchy to follow, large numbers of people should be overtaken by panic. It does not require the explanation that used to be given in Israel, that there was an Arab master-plan, conveyed by Arab radio, calling for a general evacuation so as to make easier a crushing Arab conquest. This assertion was used to support Israeli failure to let the Arabs return but evidence to support it, including any evidence whatever of the supposed radio transmissions, is manifestly lacking.

There is a parallel absence, despite the existence of Plan 'D' and of such individuals as Yosef Weitz, of evidence of a Jewish master-plan. Ben-Gurion was too much concerned not only with his own reputation but with that of the nascent Israeli Defence Forces, as the Jewish militias became after independence, to countenance that. Also there were elements in the Jewish community, for example in the civic leadership in Haifa, in certain settlements that were on good terms with their Arab neighbours, in the left wing of Ben-Gurion's first coalition Government, who were definitely opposed to the departure of the Arabs. But when Ben-Gurion and colleagues in the leadership perceived the 'miracle' of the disappearing Arabs, they were determined that it should be irreversible and were not above helping it on in those places where it failed automatically to occur.[14]

'The most spectacular event in the contemporary history of Palestine – more spectacular in a sense than the creation of the Jewish State,' wrote Moshe Sharett, the first Israeli Foreign Minister, in a private letter on 15 June 1948, 'is the wholesale evacuation of its Arab population ... The reversion to the *status quo ante* is unthinkable ... Even if a certain backwash is unavoidable, we must make the most of the momentous choice with which history has presented us so swiftly and so unexpectedly.' And the next year, in 1949, when he was defending before the first Knesset (Israeli Parliament) a highly unpopular diplomatic gesture of offering to receive back a maximum of 100,000 refugees, Sharett took credit to himself for having, as he said, educated the Israeli public to oppose a general right of return.[15]

When in mid-July the IDF captured Ramle and Lydda, two towns in the

'Arab State' but uncomfortably close to Tel Aviv, the Arab population did not spontaneously oblige. Some firing in the streets of Lydda produced a decision to clear both towns of their Palestinian inhabitants. The military leaders, Ygal Allon and Yitzhak Rabin, asked Ben-Gurion, who was at their headquarters, 'What shall we do with the Arabs?' He made a gesture which was interpreted as 'Drive them out'. Rabin immediately issued an order: 'The inhabitants of Lydda must be expelled quickly without attention to age.' A similar order was made for Ramle. Ben-Gurion wrote to a left-wing Minister, 'In Lydda and Ramle explicit orders were given not to drive the inhabitants away, and it transpired that they were driven away.'[16] Both patterns – spontaneous flight and the formula of that Ben-Gurion letter – marked Allon's and Rabin's capture of the south later in the year.

The First Arab–Israeli War

The Arab states showed sufficient regard for international law and the British Mandate to wait until the latter was over before committing their forces to the war that was already going on in Palestine. They did not recognise any government in Palestine – neither a government of 'the Arab State' (which would have involved acknowledgement of the validity of a 'Jewish State') nor, which was more surprising, a Government of All-Palestine, Arabs being in the majority in the country as a whole. This omission was a product both of the rivalries of the Arab states and of the confused state of Palestinian political leadership. They informed the UN that they were acting on the *res nullius* principle. Since all civil government had expired, they were responding to the appeal of the population 'for the sole purpose of restoring peace and security and establishing law and order'.[17]

The initiator of Pan-Arab action was Iraq, one of the two potential centres of leadership in the Arab world; the most doubtful starter was the other, Egypt. Since the end of the war her line had been that she could not take on both of her two opponents, Britain and the Zionists, at once; and getting rid of the British had priority. As late as 13 May 1948 Abdul Rahman Azzam, the Egyptian Secretary-General of the Arab League, felt that he had to tell the Syrian President that Egypt would not invade Palestine. This was also the opinion of Jewish Intelligence.

But yet when it came to the point, without consulting his Prime Minister or preparing the army, King Farouk gave the order to advance. He was affected, as all Arabs were, by the huge waves of refugees, but he was also driven by dynastic jealousy of King Abdullah of Jordan, who had been made the titular Commander-in-Chief of the Pan-Arab forces and was (rightly) suspected of planning to acquire the Arab fragment of partitioned Palestine for himself. If there was to be a victory parade Farouk wanted to be part of it.[18] Gamal Abdul Nasser, who was serving in the expedition as a major, afterwards wrote: 'This could not be a serious war. There was no concentration of forces, no accumulation of ammunition and equipment. There was no reconnaissance, no intelligence, no plans. Yet we were actually on the battlefield.'[19]

The first Arab–Israeli War was militarily disastrous for the Arabs, except for King Abdullah's Arab Legion. It nearly doubled the already large total of Arab refugees, it smashed what was left of the Egyptian King's reputation, it increased the size of Israel well beyond the boundaries recommended by the UN, it gave Abdullah, now known as King of Jordan, rule over those parts of Palestine still left to the Arabs except for Gaza, and it led, instead of the international regime that had been planned for Jerusalem, to the partitioning of the city between Israel and Jordan. The Arab Legion, commanded by General John Bagot Glubb, a British officer in King Abdullah's direct employ, known by all as Glubb Pasha, and in the upper ranks largely British-officered, was the only Arab force that emerged with any military glory, capturing East Jerusalem, including the whole of the Old City, even the Jewish Quarter, and denying to the Israelis the position of Latrun which is the key to the hills leading up to Jerusalem on the main road from Tel Aviv. The other Arab states, however, felt with good reason that Abdullah had intended from the outset to share Palestine with the Jewish State and many of his future Palestinian subjects resented Glubb's sound military tactic of keeping his small fighting force in being rather than sacrificing part of it in defence of the towns of Ramle and Lydda.

The Arab–Israeli war was fought as a series of short campaigns (15 May to 11 June, 9 to 18 July, 15 to 22 October, 22 December to 7 January 1949) alternating with truces and cease-fires. The military course of the war has been many times described and it is no part of the purpose of this book to do so again. But several features of the story deserve brief mention. The first is that, with the way the 'cold war' was developing in Europe, the overriding consideration for Britain and the United States was to ensure that, no matter how much their analysis of the Palestine situation might differ, they must not find themselves fighting a surrogate war against each other. To avoid this they both scrupulously adhered to the ban on weapons supply voted for in the UN Security Council. This meant that Israel was deprived of any American help, which would have been very serious for her if she had not just in time made the connection with a major supplier in Communist Czechoslovakia. The result was that, whereas the Israelis started by being outgunned and the first truce was rightly described by the Israeli military historian (and later President) Chaim Herzog as 'a welcome respite for the hard-pressed Israeli forces',[20] from then onwards they essentially held strategic superiority. For the Arab states the British arms embargo meant that their military ally, to whom their armed forces were linked, was not around when she was most needed.

Secondly, the attitude of Israel towards the United Nations evolved fast during the war. At first, after the passage of Resolution 181 and the Arab rejection, the Jews had looked to the international community for help. But rapidly they realised that they must stand on their own feet and rely on their own wits. The UN did not intervene to uphold its verdict by force but sent instead a Mediator, a member of the Swedish royal family, Count Folke Bernadotte of Wisburg, who had won much applause for his courageous wartime missions on behalf of (mainly Jewish) refugees. Bernadotte successfully arranged the first and second truces, which, though violated by both sides, were violated to decisively greater effect by the Israelis. Then, as was to be expected of a man with his background, he pressed hard for the return of the refugees, to be met with intransigence from Sharett. This was the beginning of a permanently tense relationship with the UN. A resolution, adopted by the UN General Assembly in December 1948 and confirmed every year, said that each refugee was entitled either to return or be compensated for his losses. The Israelis were never near to accepting – or even contemplating – such a formula. 'I don't accept', Ben-Gurion had written in his diary in the summer of 1948, 'the formula that "we should not encourage their return". Their return must be prevented ... at all costs.'[21]

Bernadotte had also assumed the task of proposing his own political settlement. His first draft was worked up in considerable isolation from the Powers, although he calculated that he would need Anglo-American support if the scheme was to be more than acadamic. He proposed to change the boundary lines of Resolution 181, so that Israel would be more compact, incorporating territories like Jaffa and western Galilee which she held by military conquest and in return yielding to the Arabs the Negev, a dry area of mountain and desert reaching down to the Red Sea in the shape of an inverted pyramid. In Jewish hands this would drive a wedge between Egypt and the Asian Arab world and, though awarded to Israel by the UN, was presently in Arab military occupation. But in addition to this Bernadotte proposed Jordanian sovereignty over Jerusalem and some international limitations on Israel's ability to admit immigrants, two proposals that in the circumstances were exceedingly ill-advised. He dropped both these latter proposals for the second draft, on which he had British and American advice.[22] But between the submission and the publication of this revised plan, the Mediator was murdered in the streets of Jerusalem by a hitherto unheard-of Jewish group, whose name was a flag of convenience for Yitzhak Shamir's Lehi.[23]

A third feature of 1948 was the lesson Israel supplied in the creation of 'new facts'. Britain and America joined in endorsing Bernadotte's second plan and thought to carry it through on the wave of emotion that followed his death. Israel had no intention of abandoning the Negev. People it might not have, water it might not have, but it had what the rest of Israel lacked, it had size. Ben-Gurion used to say that Carthage fell because it had no hinterland. He not only thought, from his reading about King Solomon's mines, that the Negev was full of minerals, but that only the Jews had the capacity and the will to turn the desert into a land of milk and honey. If a port could be built on the six-mile sea frontage on the Red Sea's Gulf of Aqaba, commerce could be opened with the Afro-Asian world. There was direct contradiction between this ambition and the Arabs' stress on their own territorial contiguity.

The third and fourth campaigns of 1948 were short, sharp onslaughts by which the Israelis commanded by Ygal Allon cleared the Egyptians out of southern Palestine, except for the 4,000 troops at Faluja, including Major Gamal Abdul Nasser, who held out after they had been surrounded, and except for the small coastal area next to Egyptian Sinai known as the Gaza Strip. These were battles in which Jordan's Arab Legion took no part. While the UN called for a return to the lines of the second truce, the IDF, in two strikes exquisitely timed to fit the electoral clock in the United States, rubbished Bernadotte by tearing up Egypt's bargaining card in the Negev.[24] The Israeli position was that there was going to be no swop: Negev was theirs by right of Resolution 181, Western Galilee by right of conquest. Any chance that the United States was going to stick firmly to the Bernadotte plan was abandoned when President Truman, only days away from the election, answered a taunt from his opponent by saying that Israel was entitled to every piece of territory offered her in the resolution unless she chose to give anything up.

Israel only overreached herself with a final offensive at the turn of the year when her troops crossed the Egyptian frontier at Al Auja and made across the desert for Al Arish, the administrative centre of Sinai on the Mediterranean coast. This aimed to wrap up the remainder of the Egyptian expeditionary force, and at the same time take the Gaza Strip. Not only did the UN Security Council order another cease-fire (that might have been evaded) but Britain, citing her obligations under the very alliance with Egypt which Egypt was so anxious to see abrogated, sent an ultimatum to Israel, delivered and orally reinforced by the Americans. Ben-Gurion, feeling he had gone too far, ordered a total, immediate withdrawal from Egyptian soil. Even this rebuff was accepted in cheeky fashion. Bevin arranged personally for five RAF reconnaissance planes to see if the Israelis had gone. The Israelis shot them all down and then dragged parts of the wreckage over to their side of the international border to show that they had been intruding.[25]

The final cease-fire between Egypt and Israel on 7 January 1949 was followed by a General Armistice Agreement between them negotiated by Ralph Bunche at the UN Headquarters on Rhodes. An Armistice Demarcation Line, which reflected the military status quo, was laid down which was 'not to be considered in any sense as a political or territorial boundary'.

A considerable zone on either side of Al Auja, the main invasion route into Sinai or into Palestine, was to be demilitarised. A United Nations Truce Supervision Organisation (UNTSO) was to have freedom to operate on both sides of the line. The Agreement was never intended to last for ever; its purpose was 'to facilitate the transition from the present truce to permanent peace in Palestine'.

The armistice with Egypt was followed by similar agreements with all Israel's other enemies except for Iraq, which remains to this day in a state of war with her. There being no common frontier between Iraq and Israel, the Iraqi troops abandoned their sector of the front and went home as the result of an arrangement between Israel and Jordan for which Moshe Dayan, the Israeli military negotiator, exacted a high price. Dayan, like all Israelis, was very aware of the narrowness – at one point only nine miles wide – of Israel's 'wasp-waist' and of the fact that, in general, the Jews were on the plain looking up at the Arabs in the hills. To get agreement, which he badly wanted, King Abdullah was forced to give up a strip of hill positions in an area known as 'the Little Triangle', where the separation of villagers from their orchards and fields was the cause of much future trouble during the build-up to Suez.[26]

No War, No Peace

1949–50 was the year of attempted peace, with 'proximity talks' (which often led to informal direct contacts) arranged by the UN's Palestine Conciliation Commission of the United States, France and Turkey. The Arab League had laid down a policy of non-recognition of the existence of Israel and this formally governed all Arab policies. But in private there were many indications from both Egypt and Jordan that peace was attainable on terms which included the right of return for the Palestinians and changes of border. Egypt wanted a common frontier with Jordan in the southern Negev, Jordan a corridor to the Mediterranean. Ben-Gurion was at one time prepared to offer such a corridor, but at a width only of metres while the King required one of a few kilometres. But, apart from toying with the Jordan option, Israel was losing interest in an early peace.[27] On 27 February 1950 two Israeli diplomats, Abba Eban and Gideon Rafael, told by their Egyptian interlocutor that Egypt was above all interested in the principle of the territorial continuity of the Arab world, replied firmly that, if that meant the southern Negev and Eilat, no Israeli Government would agree to any territorial concession there. 'If such a concession is indeed vital to the Egyptians, it would be best not to begin negotiations at all.'[28] It was simpler, too, to represent Israel's problem as an existential one: to be or not to be.

The real ulcer of Egyptian–Israeli relations was, however, to be Gaza.

Gaza was a place that had seen better times. It had been a prosperous trading centre before the First World War but had since dwindled. The town had a small, undeveloped harbour and a little local industry. The 'strip' of Palestine which remained in Egyptian occupation at the time of the cease-fire was only five miles wide and about twenty-eight miles long. This small and backward area had been turned by the circumstances of the 1948 combustion into the most vivid single symbol of the unsolved Palestine question. Onto the 86,000 original inhabitants had been decanted 203,000 more.[29] (By 1990, the total had grown to 600,000 making it the most densely populated area in the world.) Israel's first inclination was to say that Gaza should come to her and, since Egypt was thought to be willing to withdraw from Palestine altogether, this seemed for a while a possibility. Ben-Gurion displayed, both in 1949–50 and later in 1956–7, a perplexing uncertainty about what he wanted as regards Gaza, though he often sought to conceal this from his subordinates by statements that were both vigorous and cryptic. To have Gaza would bring Israel entirely up to the international frontier with Egypt in the south, but it would put the Israelis under a pressing obligation to do something about the refugees there. At a time when he apparently thought they numbered no more than 100,000, Ben-Gurion carried the proposal to offer to resettle them inside Israel by a majority vote in the Cabinet. But Egypt was in the end unprepared to withdraw, especially after the UN proved willing to come in and finance a minimum programme of relief.[30] In March 1950 Sharett, who had all along been opposed to absorbing the Strip and its human load, cabled his envoys Rafael and Eban, 'There is no place to settle those refugees who number 210,000 and they would increase [our] Arab minority to 450,000, thereby jeopardising the State of Israel'.[31]

The Arab population from that part of Palestine which was now Israel remained, therefore, on the rim, looking in, enduring primitive temporary accommodation, waiting to go home, sustained by annual resolutions of the UN General Assembly. On the West Bank, following requests from large meetings of notables in that traumatised community, the part of Palestine remaining to the Arabs was, with the exception of Gaza, formally annexed to Jordan in April 1950. The Jordanian Parliament was now reconstituted with twenty members each from the East and West Banks, with refugees given the right to vote. Despite Palestinian opposition to a separate deal with Israel, King Abdullah kept up secret negotiations until, on 20 July 1951, he was assassinated at the Al Aqsa Mosque in Jerusalem. Since the fact of his direct contacts with the Israelis in defiance of the Council of the Arab League's ban was by then widely known, the manner of the old man's death served to draw a line of blood across the pursuit of peace. After a year's interval, during which the brainstorms to which the King's son, Talal, was subject were found to be too disabling, Abdullah was succeeded by his sixteen-year-old grandson Hussein, who had been by him when he was killed.

The administration of a long, winding and unmarked border between Jordan and Israel, which Palestinians felt they had every right to cross as they were simply returning to their homes or fields, to contact their families or to harvest their crops, was an odious and delicate function for the Jordanian security authorities and their expatriate commander. To the Israelis such returning Arabs were illegal 'infiltrators'. Punishment must be severe and exemplary, not only of those who had crossed but of those in Jordan who could be presumed to have allowed them to cross. To erase the notion that their inhabitants' absence was temporary, very many Arab villages were obliterated by bulldozer.

Gaza differed in never being annexed by Egypt, which even halfheartedly allowed a phantom 'All-Palestine Government' to operate for a few months from the Strip. The refugees did not have Egyptian citizenship and were not allowed to get jobs in Egypt. The Strip was administered by the Egyptians who kept a military force there, but since Egypt was a poor country with her own severe social problems she did not feel able to extend much help. The one large exception to this was in the field of higher education, where, especially as the number of Egyptian universities increased in the 1950s, Palestinians were generously treated. For this reason the Palestine Students Union became the principal voice of the Palestinians in Cairo. From 1952, when he headed an all-party list of candidates on a platform of self-reliance, until 1956, the PSU's President was Yasser Arafat, who, like King Hussein, began in these years his career of Arab leadership.

Israel, scarcely able to believe her luck at having achieved what one member of the first Knesset described as 'a more or less homogeneous state', turned to a massive programme of Jewish immigration and absorption. Ben-Gurion, though saying often that he would go anywhere at any time for the sake of peace, no longer seemed to have it in the forefront of his mind. He reckoned he had got the measure of the UN. It had tiresome obsessions, such as the internationalisation of Jerusalem, but no force to see them fulfilled. He entered in his diary a remark by Abba Eban, whom he would have considered a natural peace negotiator, that, 'An armistice is sufficient for us. If we chase after peace, the Arabs will demand of us a price – borders or refugees or both.'[32]

The Tripartite Declaration and the Suez Blockade

The world had to accommodate itself to a prolonged period of 'No war, no peace' in the Middle East. The UN Security Council raised the absolute ban it had imposed on the supply of arms to the area, whereupon Israel expressed alarm at the speed and scale with which Britain responded by entering into arms contracts with the Arab states. (Many of these contracts, as far as Egypt was concerned, were later put into suspension when relations deteriorated in 1951 and were to provide a main element in the background of Britain's relations with Neguib and Nasser.) Israel still saw herself as the small underdog surrounded on all sides by hostile and potentially predatory neighbours. Remarks made by the Foreign Office News Department in Whitehall in April 1950 that the Israelis already had enough arms for internal and external security were sharply resented.[33]

On 25 May 1950 the United States, Britain and France issued a pronouncement about their intentions in the Middle East. This was always subsequently called the Tripartite Declaration and it was, on the face of it, an old-fashioned *diktat* by the Great Powers. They recognised that the Arab states and Israel needed to maintain 'a certain level' of armed forces for internal security, self-defence and what was described in the Cold War context as 'the defence of the area as a whole'. On the other hand they were determined not to create an arms race and declared their 'unalterable opposition to the use of force or the threat of force'. Consequently, should they find that any state was 'preparing to violate frontiers or armistice lines' (which for this purpose were elevated to the status of frontiers), they would 'immediately' take action 'both within and outside the United Nations' to prevent such violation.[34]

What the declaration only hinted at, but what was implemented by secret tripartite machinery, was the actual process used for arms control. A Near East Arms Co-ordinating Committee (NEACC) met in Washington and regularly examined requests from any of the three powers to supply armaments to the region. It was an interesting exercise in rationing and balance and, (though there were other factors involved,) it did limit the flow of war materials as long as these three were the only principal sources. The records of NEACC show the system under strain before September 1955: it was never absolutely clear whether Arab states as a whole or each individually were to be 'balanced' against Israel, for example. But it was to be the bursting on the scene of Soviet arms supplies to Egypt that finally wrecked this major attempt at collective self-restraint.[35]

Quite apart from the arms control feature, the Tripartite Declaration, with its prospect of intervention against whoever was deemed the aggressor, became a talisman of both British and American Middle Eastern policy in the next six years: and, for France, which had substantially lost her former footholds in the Levant, it served as proof that she was still, in a sense, present. For the Americans it formed an argument for use against the Israelis and the Zionist lobby whenever they agitated that her exposed position required that Israel have more weapons; it also gave them some control over the pace of British arming of the Arabs. For the British the great virtue of the Tripartite Declaration lay in its involving the United States in military action in the event of Israeli aggression. For example, Britain's whole footing in Jordan depended on the Anglo-Jordanian Alliance of 1946 which, as Professor Wm Roger Louis has put it, aimed 'in euphemistic language ... to reconcile a straightforward old-fashioned military treaty with the Charter of the United Nations'.[36] Now extended to the swollen Kingdom on both banks of the river, this promised to involve Britain in war with Israel, should that state ever take the military initiative on the West Bank. It became Britain's policy to ensure that, if ever she did have to intervene against Israel, it should be as America's ally under the Tripartite Declaration rather than alone under the bilateral Treaty.

'No war, no peace' for a prolonged period raised additional questions. The most important was whether, given the terms of the General Armistice Agreement, there was any way in which, for example, Egypt could still legitimately exercise belligerent rights against Israel. Or, putting it the other way, it was a question of whether, by treating a transitional armistice as an indefinite status quo, Israel was to be permitted to stall for ever on the fate of the refugees and the disposition of boundaries. Iraq, by cutting off the pipeline and Egypt by cutting off Israel-bound cargoes of oil through the Suez Canal, continued to prevent a revival of the major oil refinery at Haifa. In 1950, with Nahas Pasha back in power in Cairo, the naval blockade regulations, modelled on British practice in two world wars, were tightened. At the same time Egypt acquired from Saudi Arabia two uninhabited islands, Tiran and Senafir, which are located in the narrow Straits of Tiran, the entrance into the Gulf of Aqaba from the Red Sea. For much of its width these Straits are amazingly shallow; shipping can pass only through the narrow Enterprise Channel that flows swiftly between the Egyptian shore and the island of Tiran. If Israel were to carry out her declared intention of building a port at Eilat, on the Gulf of Aqaba, the islands could help in making such a port useless.[37]

The belligerent rights which Egypt continued to enforce were bitterly resented by both sides of the British House of Commons, since under them British oil could no longer be shipped to Haifa. The degree of Egypt's unpopularity in Britain was revealed in March 1951, when Hugh Gaitskell, the Chancellor of the Exchequer, had to defend the agreement by which Egypt could draw down annual amounts from the large debit balance Britain had run up 'defending Egypt' during the Second World War. Tories and Socialists were equally hostile to the agreement, and bitter about the loss of currency caused by the run down of the Haifa refinery. In the atmosphere of the House of Commons, to kick Egypt was made to appear a politically safe thing to do. Egypt's two quarrels – with Israel and with Britain – threatened to become entwined with each other.[38]

On 12 June 1951 the UN Truce Supervisors formally reported that the Egyptian embargo was a hostile and aggressive act in breach of the Armistice Agreement. On 16 August the Security Council adopted by eight votes to nil a resolution declaring that Egypt should end all restrictions on transit through the Suez Canal and explicitly refuting Egypt's theory of self-defence. The Soviet delegate, it was noticed, was not his usually vociferous self in support of Israel. He was instead one of the three abstainers, having taken virtually no part in the debate. Russia, the backer of Israel from the outset, was preparing to change sides.

The resolution having been passed, who was to implement it? Once more, as in Palestine, Britain was the one permanent member with troops on the spot and, unlike in Palestine, this was a resolution that Britain had sponsored. The maintenance of 'free passage' against all challengers was the most internationally respectable argument for the presence of so many Britons in arms on Egyptian soil. Two months after the Security Council vote, the problem was bequeathed to the new Conservative Government. It came up in the first meeting of the Churchill Cabinet and provoked the first clash between Churchill and Eden. Churchill propounded a principle – 'to keep the Suez Canal open to the world, using such force as might be necessary for the purpose' – and proposed to apply it in the case of oil tankers for Haifa. Eden supplied a damper: the principle was 'fully endorsed' but 'precipitate action' would not be expedient. Eden won. Nothing happened.[39] Eden advised the Cabinet as late as January 1954 that the Egyptians had quite a strong legal case on grounds of self-defence because their war with Israel had not been legally terminated. Although the issue was frequently raised by awkward questioners in the House of Commons, it was not until five years after its passage that the Security Council resolution of 1951 was to appear in Sir Anthony Eden's shop window as the much-needed certified proof of Egypt's international bad behaviour.

3

Eden and Nasser

We did not need an agreement nearly as much as Neguib. If HM Embassy did nothing for six months except avoid giving things away, he would be very content. At one point he said I should be a 'patient, sulky pig'.
Robin Hankey's briefing by Winston Churchill on going to Cairo, 22 May 1953.

I was impressed by Nasser, who seemed forthright and friendly although not open to conviction in this Turco–Iraqi business.
Eden to Churchill, 21 February 1955.

In October 1951 Anthony Eden started on three and a half years of remarkable diplomatic achievement which enhanced immensely his status on the world stage. In Europe, acceptance of West Germany's rearmament by other Western nations was achieved through the Western European Union. In the Far East, the punishing French military involvement in Indo-China was ended by diplomacy and the prospect of American military intervention for the time being averted. In the Middle East, there were Anglo-Egyptian agreements over the Sudan and over the Suez Canal Base and a resolution, both political and economic, of the unpromising relationship with Persia. Even East–West relations in Europe seemed to be thawing out, with a solution of the Trieste dispute between Italy and Jugoslavia, followed, just after Eden had moved into Number Ten, by the Austrian State Treaty which marked the first Russian retreat from a European country occupied in the war.

The extent of Eden's personal contribution to this brighter international scene, of course, varied; other nations, other personalities, including other British ones, were involved. But it would be perverse to deny that the British Foreign Secretary's sureness of touch had become a major national asset. His pre-Suez biographer, William Rees-Mogg, wrote of his command of the art of deferred timing: 'Like a jockey riding a winning race, when Eden moves he moves fast, but he is always concerned not to make his run prematurely.'[1] He had, however, to pay a political price for his run of successes, one of which, Indo-China, was at the expense of the United

States, and two of which, the Sudan and the Suez base, were at the expense of his reputation as an anti-appeaser with significant elements in his own party.

No less than Churchill, Eden was perfectly aware of the need to be closely allied to the United States. But, to an extent that sometimes commended him to left-wing sections of the Opposition benches, he was more alert than most to the dangers of such an alliance shading into subservience. 'The British should not allow themselves to be restricted overmuch by reluctance to act without full American concurrence and support', he told the Cabinet when he was Prime Minister in October 1955. 'We should frame our own policy in the light of our interests and get the Americans to support it to the extent we can induce them to do so.'[2] In a succession of Far Eastern issues (Vietnam in 1954, the Chinese offshore islands of Quemoy and Matsu in 1955) the American Secretary of State, John Foster Dulles, who was to be a principal in the Suez drama, played the part of the hawk, while Eden assumed the role of dove. The irony implicit in the intensive interplay between the two men at the time of Suez arises out of this past history of their relationship.

On the domestic scene what was worrying Eden as Britain's leader-in-waiting was the emergence of what eventually became known as the Suez Group – an organised faction (analogous, its members felt, to the group that formed round Churchill in the 1930s) of critics of Eden's policy towards Egypt. In the eyes of one who was at that time a leading member of the Suez group, Julian Amery, whose father had been one of Churchill's group at the time of Munich, the Suez story was a classic case of appeasement chicken coming home to roost.[3]

When the Conservatives took over in 1951, Egyptians, stirred up by the Muslim Brotherhood, had already launched a guerrilla war against the British in the Canal Zone. The Labour Government's orders to send in reinforcements were confirmed, until over 80,000 troops were tied down, doing no more than protect themselves. The Egyptian army stood aside, but the local civilian authorities, including the police, were hostile. Ninety per cent of the 60,000-strong Egyptian labour force employed by the British went on strike. Workers had to be imported from Cyprus and Mauritius. The Royal Navy had to help the Canal Company to keep the Canal traffic moving, giving rise to the Egyptian accusation that the Canal Company was departing from political neutrality.

On 25 January 1952, the British army ordered the surrender of the police barracks at Ismailia, where the hundred regular police had been reinforced by nearly seven times that number of armed auxiliaries. On the direct orders of the Minister of the Interior in Cairo, the Ismailia police put up hours of fierce and sustained resistance, surrendering only in the evening when forty-six of their number had been killed.

This in turn provoked an immediate reaction the next day in Cairo.

Large mobs burst in upon and set fire to British-owned and other foreign and foreign-seeming buildings in the centre of the city – Shepheard's Hotel, Thomas Cook, BOAC, Barclay's, the Swedish and Lebanese consulates, the French Chamber of Commerce, the ten largest cinemas, European-style bars and restaurants owned by Italians, Greeks and Jews, the British Council, where the Council representative was killed, and, most bloodily, the Turf Club, where nine guests, including the Canadian Trade Representative, perished. This *razzia* went on for twelve hours without police intervention until the Egyptian army cleared the streets. Primarily it was directed against property; otherwise, far more than twenty people (including eleven Britons) would have died.[4]

This series of episodes had important consequences. The Egyptians had displayed their ability, in some circumstances, to wage a guerrilla uprising capable of imposing on the British, for all their overwhelming conventional strength on the ground, what would prove to be unacceptable costs. In the quality of resistance at Ismailia they had shown unexpected spirit, which later was to impose caution on British military commanders, on General Keightley in 1956 in particular. British military assessments since 1948 tended to swing widely between exaggerated anticipation of Egyptian capacity for prolonged guerrilla war and contemptuous dismissal of Egyptian military prowess. The Cairo mob of 1952 massively reinforced the legend, born in Alexandria seventy years before, of the Egyptians' propensity to frenzy. 'The horrible behaviour of the mob puts them lower than the most degraded savages now known', wrote Churchill to Eden. '. . . They cannot be classed as a civilised power until they have purged themselves.' Anarchy in the streets gave King Farouk the perfect excuse to dismiss Nahas whose regime, Peter Mansfield wrote, 'gave off the smell of death'.[5] Six months later, during the night of 22–23 July (1952), when the King and his latest Ministers were at the summer capital of Alexandria, the Egyptian army took over Cairo.

In the morning of 23 July Colonel Anwar Sadat appeared on the radio and proclaimed the revolution.[6] Its declared leader was General Mohamed Neguib, a popular, avuncular figure of Sudanese origin, who was known to have been at odds with the Court. But it was clear from the outset that the long-run conspiracy had been in the hands of a younger group of colonels, majors and their equivalents in the air force known as the Free Officers. What was not at all clear at first was who among that group was pre-eminent. There were three days of uncertainty, days during which the British army in the Canal Zone, which had been often thought of as Farouk's ultimate guarantor, did not raise a finger to safeguard his throne.

Ahmed Mortada al-Maraghi, the Minister of the Interior who was to play a shadowy role later on during the Suez conflict, returned from Alexandria to Cairo to arrange an accommodation with the new rulers. On 26 July the King abdicated and left on his yacht after installing Ali Maher as Prime Minister. The monarchy was for a time preserved with a three-man Council of Regency that included Prince Abdul Monheim, the son and one-time heir apparent of the last Khedive deposed in 1914, to rule in the name of Farouk's baby son. At first the Free Officers exercised their new power only through the Revolutionary Command Council (RCC). Within six months Neguib himself had replaced Ali Maher as Prime Minister and, in March 1953, the monarchy was ended and Neguib became President.

'I am not opposed to a policy of giving Neguib a good chance provided he shows himself to be a friend', pronounced Churchill on 19 August. And a week later, 'The more I read the news from Egypt the more I like the Neguib programme. We ought to help Neguib and Co. all we can unless they turn spiteful. It is most important that we should not appear to be defending the landlords and Pashas against the long overdue reforms for the *fellaheen.*' Alongside a later message on plans for land reforms he wrote: 'Down with the Pashas and Up the *Fellaheen*!'[7]

Initial expectations in London about the new regime were conditionally favourable. It was felt that Egypt was well rid of the feckless corruption and petulance of Farouk. Because the new rulers were soldiers and airmen it was hoped that they would be more conscious of the strategic threat from Russian Communism and more responsive to the proposal of a military alliance with the West. In one respect relations immediately became easier. The officers agreed to simplify matters by negotiating with Eden a separate agreement on the future of the Sudan ahead of other issues, which was signed on 12 February 1953. Unfortunately from the political angle, this gave the appearance of leaning rather far towards meeting Egyptian claims for the 'Unity of the Nile', though, as events were to show, the terms left quite sufficient opportunity for the forces of Sudanese independence to assert themselves. But there was to be a three-year transition period before a vote should decide between complete independence and a link with Egypt; the background noises and charges of ill-faith arising from what was in effect an endlessly prolonged election campaign kept the issue from dying down.

From the outset this agreement was sharply criticised by Amery's group which was chaired by an ex-Minister, Captain Charles Waterhouse, and included two types of members – the elderly contemporaries of Churchill, like Lord Hankey, the arch-mandarin[8] who was now a director of the Suez Canal Company, the elder Amery and Lord Killearn, the ex-Ambassador in Cairo and author of the 1942 coup, and young Tory MPs such as Enoch Powell, Fitzroy Maclean and Julian Amery himself. The group was encouraged by various signs of behind-the-scenes Prime Ministerial approval.[9]

Churchill had been raging to his private secretaries against Eden, 'speaking of "appeasement" and saying he never knew before that Munich was situated on the Nile', adding that if Eden were to offer resignation he would accept it and take the Foreign Office himself.[10] He told the Cabinet that he doubted whether Eden's proposed settlement 'would command a sufficient measure of support inside the Conservative Party'. However Eden's nerve held. He was able to refute the Prime Minister by an unusually impressive performance to a meeting of Conservative MPs, though he left hostages to fortune by relying heavily on the argument that a quick Sudan deal would make for a much more satisfactory negotiation about the Canal.

This was of capital importance to the Suez Group. Its members believed strongly in sustaining the British Commonwealth as a military and political entity. Their view was that, now that India had gone, the British presence on the Suez Canal was the only possible way of making geopolitical sense of the Commonwealth. Without it Britain could not be a World Power.[11] Believing this, the group was alarmed by rumours that Eden, under American pressure, was beginning to consider a complete British withdrawal from the Canal Zone. In a report to Winston Churchill on his latest trip to Egypt, Lord Hankey in February 1953 declared his conviction that the British were 'heading straight for a disaster far more serious than the evacuation of Abadan'. All the civilian and service staffs in the Canal Zone lay under the shadow of 'Operation Scuttle'. 'Appetite', Hankey wrote, 'comes with the eating and the evacuation of the British forces is certain to be followed by a violent agitation for Egypt to declare the concession at an end and to take possession of the Suez Canal.' The letter ended with a sentence that was absolutely key to this whole type of thinking, for Englishmen, who, with the earth still moving under them from the end of Empire in India, were trying to find some solid ground. 'If we cannot hold the Suez Canal, the jugular vein of World and Empire shipping communications, what can we hold?'[12]

Churchill and Eden were in complete agreement that it made no sense to keep 80,000 troops in the Canal Zone when Britain was short of resources and there were in any case other pressing military claims. They wanted an agreement that would allow this number to be reduced drastically, while safeguarding the peacetime operation of the military workshops and stores and locking Egypt into a multilateral alliance. The strategy was to enlist the military and financial resources of the United States behind British diplomacy. The British ideal, as *The Economist* once put it, was that Britain should negotiate from American strength.

When, in June 1952, Churchill's Ministers were brought by the Treasury right up against the grim realities of Britain's economic position, Eden as Foreign Secretary produced a memorandum for the Cabinet on 'British Overseas Obligations'. It started out by briskly accepting the Treasury's position that maintenance of all existing policies was 'placing a burden on the country's economy which it is beyond the resources of the country to meet' and then proceeded to run through the various geographic areas in succession showing that none of the major obligations overseas, such as the defence of the Middle East, could be cut speedily without Britain's 'sink[ing] to the level of a second-class power'. In the rather longer run, relief would be contingent on the setting up of international defence organisations. 'Our aim', wrote Eden, 'should be to persuade the United States to assume the real burdens in such organisations while retaining for ourselves as much political control – and hence prestige and world influence – as we can.'[13]

'Ike' and John Foster Dulles

In January 1953, for the first time in twenty years, the party in power in the White House was about to change. Churchill and Eden went to Washington during the transition to renew old friendships with the new President, General Eisenhower, but also to tie down detailed plans for a joint Anglo–American approach to Egypt as tightly as possible with the dying administration. With any luck, these plans would then get in under the wire with the new men as part of their inheritance. American policy in the Middle East had not covered itself with glory in the years since the war; there was an inclination as late as the mid-nineteen-fifties to assume that Britain would take the lead. In two areas, Palestine and Saudi Arabia, the United States was for quite different reasons more deeply involved. The wavy, lurching quality of the American contribution to the Palestine problem has already been touched upon. The Saudi Kingdom was beginning to reflect that, whereas it had traditionally turned to Britain for guidance in international affairs, its new economic enrichment was owed exclusively to American enterprise and in particular to Aramco, the jointly owned subsidiary of four American majors which was making the desert give up its abundant oil wealth. At the end of 1950 an epoch-making agreement between Aramco and King Ibn Saud split the profits of the operation with him on a fifty-fifty basis. Though in form a commercial agreement, this was heavily backed by the agencies of the American Government.

In the opinion of Professor Wm Roger Louis, this arrangement 'signified as great a revolution at the time, as the political transfer of power in India'.[14] Not only did it mean that Ibn Saud, followed shortly by his son Saud, now looked to the United States rather than to Britain; not only did it mean that an unsophisticated monarch would in future have tens of millions of dollars to dispense out of his privy pocket, but it also meant that a new standard had been set for the terms of the proper economic relationship of the Arab world to the West.

The change in administration brought 'Ike' Eisenhower to the Presidency. His whole military career as a senior commander had been associated with America's commitment to Europe. He knew intimately Churchill, Eden and Harold Macmillan, who had been a particularly helpful and congenial

Resident Minister at his headquarters in North Africa during tense days that were critical for his reputation. Both American political parties had wanted Eisenhower as their presidential candidate after the war, not only because of his military fame, but because of the impression he made of a decent sunny personality, epitomised by his nickname and his face-splitting smile. He alone had enabled the Republican Party to win for the first time since 1928, dragging the congressional party in, like a heavy load, a long way behind him.

In assessing the personality of this President, there was a great divorce between the media and the message. Much of the press corps in Washington, domestic and foreign, together with other elements with whom they interacted in that highly political city, wrote Eisenhower off as merely a constitutional monarch, a role which he very successfully performed. When it came to the substantive tasks of a chief executive, the impression created was of a non-intellectual, rather too much given to the temptation to relax. His press conferences, which he held with conscientious regularity, produced replies which, though their oral punctuation was not impossible to follow, looked more than a bit strange when reproduced in cold print.

The great mass of the people were quite impervious to such criticisms of their President. His reputation was almost entirely independent of that of his party. It went down as his went up. During his first term he had a succession of serious illnesses, including a heart attack. All this and the pronounced personality of his Secretary of State, John Foster Dulles, led many people, including Anthony Eden, to suppose that the President was not the effective decision-maker in American foreign policy. In this they were mistaken as the release of documents from the Eisenhower presidency has shown.

The reaction that has resulted from the realisation of this has now probably gone too far, portraying Dulles as a messenger and technician. Eisenhower had a considerable grasp of international affairs and pronounced views; Dulles never forgot that he was the President's servant and reported to him with regularity. Except when he was ill, Eisenhower was an active participant, sometimes himself writing the first draft of important messages, eloquent rushes of meaning fighting to break free from a rather stilted form; at others, inserting key passages. However the President was not given to the sustained study of issues. He could not, and did not pretend, to match Dulles in matters of detail which were often critical and, in consequence, failed on some major occasions to persist with instincts that were sound. Eisenhower set a framework, but within it Dulles's assiduous application, his talent for draftsmanship, his penchant for conceptual formulation and, above all, the trust which the President came to rest in his judgement made him a very powerful force.

John Foster Dulles was, in the words of Samuel Flagg Bemis, 'the only religious leader, lay or clerical, ever to become Secretary of State'[15], and some of his pronouncements and the vocabulary he preferred reflected a lifetime of filling lay offices in the Presbyterian Church. A large, sombre figure with downward-curving lips and hands thrust deep into his pockets, he was given at his regular press conferences and occasional interviews in depth to formulating theoretical concepts of foreign policy in sometimes embarrassingly memorable phrases. During the 1952 presidential campaign he had written about the 'liberation of captive peoples' in a way that suggested a more activist policy against the Soviet Union; Europe was threatened in 1954 with an 'agonising reappraisal' of America's commitments there; and at the outset of 1956, summing up his experiences to date, he told *Life* magazine: 'The ability to get to the verge without getting into war is the necessary art ... [I]f you are scared to go to the brink, you are lost. We walked to the brink and we looked it in the face.'

Strong men blanched at the prospect of even one more such phrase. The word on Washington's Embassy Row, according to a British diplomat, was 'Three brinks and he's brunk'.[16] In his *New York Times* column, James Reston wrote of the Secretary, 'He doesn't stumble into booby traps; he digs them to size, studies them carefully, and then jumps.' But, for all his waywardness, Foster Dulles had formidable professional skills. As a leading international lawyer he was able to present a technically complex case with great address; his ideas, developed in longhand on yellow legal pads, were never negligible; and his knowledge of international relations was prodigious. He had a certain wintry charm, which had its appeal but totally escaped Winston Churchill. After he had met him for the first time in Washington in January 1953, the aged Premier went off to bed muttering that he wished to have no more to do with a man whose 'great slab of a face' he disliked and distrusted.[17] This was not a passing thought. Six months later Churchill was remarking to his doctor that Dulles was 'clever enough to be stupid on a rather large scale'.[18]

Dulles's relations with Eden – one prima donna with another, but of a very different type – were to be of critical importance at the time of Suez. Lord Sherfield, who as Sir Roger Makins was British Ambassador in Washington throughout Eisenhower's first term and knew both men well, says that the difference sprang from the fact that Dulles was a thinker who needed time to develop his thoughts whereas Eden was intuitive. He lost patience with Dulles's monologues and would himself make throw-away remarks which Dulles would seldom catch.[19] Evelyn Shuckburgh, who served Eden first as private secretary and then as Assistant Under-Secretary in charge of the Middle East, a man of musical tastes, thought that Eden and Dulles were 'like two lute strings whose vibrations never coincide. The tempo of their minds was not in harmony.'[20] But Eden had not got on well with Dean Acheson, Dulles's Democratic predecessor, either. Apart from quirks of personality, the situations of the two countries made for a friction that had, for compelling reasons, to be dressed up as harmony.

Dulles was not the only leading personality entrusted with America's international relations: it was his creative ingenuity and access to the President that in a short time gave him pre-eminence. But at the outset Eisenhower rather gave the impression of picketing Dulles around with influential counterweights. Apart from his wartime Chief of Staff who was made Dulles's first Under Secretary of State (to be replaced by ex-President Herbert Hoover's son, another Herbert and another engineer, by the time of Suez), there were the only two nationally well-known politicians (other than the Vice-President) in the Cabinet, Harold Stassen and Henry Cabot Lodge. They were both involved in foreign affairs and, as it happened, they were to take opposite stands towards Britain and France over Suez. Stassen, who had charge first of foreign aid and then of disarmament, had been proclaimed a 'boy wonder' on becoming the extremely eloquent Governor of his state (Minnesota) in his early thirties and ever since was brimming over with presidential ambitions. In the National Security Council he became the most persistent advocate of 'sticking by old friends', even, as he was forced to admit in November 1956, when they were in the wrong.

Henry Cabot Lodge bore two surnames each of which would have placed him socially at the apex of New England 'aristocracy'. The son and namesake of the man who more than any other was responsible for the Senate's rejection of the Versailles Peace Treaty and the League of Nations, he was himself, as a prominent member of the Senate, the principal promoter of General Eisenhower's elevation to the presidency. As a reward for this achievement he chose the job (which carried Cabinet rank) of US Permanent Representative at the United Nations, where his assiduity and devotion to international institutions could complete the national rejection of his father's isolationism. Facile and adept and a good manager, Lodge was not a great thinker. His political relationship to Eisenhower meant that he had direct access to the President but on any difficult problem he normally deferred to Dulles. However, though his instincts were quite the opposite to his father's on American membership of international organisations, they were not all that different when it came to weighing up with extreme scepticism the merits of being entangled in the 'colonial' policies of Britain and France.

Churchill's Last Stand

Eisenhower was placed on the alert, one month after his inauguration, by the 'urgency and somewhat frightening phraseology' of a letter from Churchill on the subject of Egypt. 'Our forces are in ample strength to resist any attacks,' the letter said, '... Nearly half the effective Egyptian army, about 15,000 men, stands on the eastern side of the Canal watching Israel. They could easily be forced to surrender, perhaps, indeed, merely by cutting off supplies.' The President told the National Security Council that Britain should not assume his Administration's agreement to something more than he had agreed with its predecessor.[21]

The Egyptians were not unaware of the belligerent mood in which their great opponent was approaching the negotiations on the Suez Zone. 'Negotiations with the British will never come to a satisfactory result unless we use force, concentrating on guerrilla warfare,' stated the Planning Section of the Egyptian General Staff. At a General Staff meeting, it was resolved that Britain, rather than Israel, should be treated as the most threatening enemy. Preparations for a new round of guerrilla warfare in the Canal Zone were put in train; the evacuation of Sinai was ordered and implemented in conspiratorial fashion. On a single night, after much preparation and many decoys, the main units were withdrawn across the Canal.[22] Faced with the same choice under much more harrowing conditions three years later, Nasser was to make the same decision.

To Churchill's great chagrin, his wish to bring the Americans from the outset into negotiations with Egypt was frustrated because the Egyptians did not want them – they said the British must leave first – and Eisenhower declined to force his way in as an uninvited guest. 'We cannot feel free and sovereign until they go,' Nasser said. 'We have a record of sixty-five promises that they were going to be withdrawn but they are still there.'

Although most Western visitors (even Lord Hankey) came away from Neguib liking him, there was an increasing view that he was what Hankey termed 'a military dictator in chains'. Handling the chains were the young lower middle class officers who had carried out the revolution. Their motives seemed all the more suspect in that they took military advice from ex-officers of the German army, who had been supplied, it emerged much later, courtesy of the CIA.[23] Their leader had at first been difficult to identify, but as the months went by it emerged that he was Gamal Abdul Nasser. 'I believe we are up against a determined anti-British movement,' wrote John de Courcy Hamilton, an old Cairo hand among British officials. 'The young officers think we are on the decline as a Great Power; they have a real hatred politically for us in their hearts. No amount of concession or evacuation on our part will evoke the slightest gratitude in return. Whoever Egypt may want in the future as an ally, it will not be us.'[24]

'As you will have noticed,' one Foreign Office official wrote to the head of chancery at the Cairo Embassy on 25 April, two days before the Anglo–Egyptian negotiations on the Suez base began, 'there has been a change of approach to the talks.'[25] There had indeed. Anthony Eden had gone into hospital for a mutilating gall bladder operation and Winston Churchill, as he had threatened earlier in the year, had assumed the additional functions of Foreign Secretary. He immediately issued instructions that 'our attitude should be that it is not we who are seeking talks'.

Unsurprisingly, with this approach, the first round of talks from 27 April to 6 May got precisely nowhere. Dr Mahmoud Fawzi, the Egyptian Foreign Minister, a professional diplomat inherited from the previous regime, conducted them on behalf of Egypt but in the presence of the leading soldiers, including both Neguib and Nasser. He ended this round by suggesting, pleasantly, that the British might like to seek new instructions from London.

Jefferson Caffery, the peppery Southern gentleman who represented the United States in Cairo under both Democrats and Republicans, epitomised what the British most dreaded – the Americans as neutral mediator. In his reports to the State Department he did not mix his words. 'It is apparent that the impasse in which the British now find themselves stems from the mistaken line of Middle Eastern policy which the British Foreign Office has been pursuing for some time (*vide* Iran, for instance) . . . With the deterioration of the British power position in the Middle East, the London Foreign Office has been tragically incapable of developing a new basis for satisfactory relationships with the peoples of the area.'[26]

On 11 May Churchill delivered one of his last great speeches in the House of Commons. It is generally remembered for his plea for a 'parley at the summit' following the death the previous March of Josef Stalin. But there was also a passage on Egypt which was deplored as much in Washington as it was in Cairo. In summarising the story of the negotiations so far, Churchill did precisely what Eisenhower had been afraid of: he publicised what the Americans regarded as the highly confidential talks with the 'lame duck' Truman Administration, he exaggerated the degree of identity of views that these had established and gave the impression that the new Administration was equally committed. This was not at all the image that the Americans wished to convey. Neither did they wish to see insulted Neguib and the Free Officers, in whom they reposed considerable hope once yesterday's business of the British occupation could be got swiftly out of the way.

But Churchill was enjoying himself in the House of Commons, drawing the last ounce of response from an audience which on a good day he could still totally command. 'One of the disadvantages of dictatorship is that the dictator is often dictated to by others', he declared to the obvious delight of the whole House. General Neguib, whose name Churchill rasped out in comically inaccurate fashion, had got altogether the wrong idea. 'We did not, let me repeat, seek these negotiations. We complied with the Egyptian desire for them. They asked for them and they have now – to quote the violent outpourings of General Neguib reported in today's newspapers – washed their hands of them.'

As he said this, the Prime Minister turned slowly round and, with each side of a House hanging on his every word and gesture, mimicked the handwashing act. 'We may await the development of events', he declared, 'with the composure which follows from the combination of patience with strength.'[27]

The speech was delivered (with the minimum of advance notice to Washington) just as Dulles, accompanied by Harold Stassen, was flying into Cairo, at the beginning of his first overseas tour as Secretary of State, to find out for himself if Egypt had the makings of a reliable ally. He was shaken by his reception. The paper *Al Misri,* for example, carried on its front page an open letter from its publisher bitterly attacking American policy. 'The fact which you must realise is that all the Arab peoples hate you and have no confidence in you.' *Al Ahram* said that Egypt watched the Anglo-American co-operation in evil with serenity. Because of the intensity of this anti-Western feeling, Dulles recommended to the National Security Council on 1 June that any kind of Middle East Defence Organisation founded on Egypt was out. Instead the West should concentrate on building a strong 'Northern Tier' made up of Turkey, Iraq, Syria and Pakistan (with the possible addition of Persia). In a radio broadcast he set a tone which Whitehall was to find particularly disobliging. Damage was being done to America's name by the belief that her alliance with France and Britain required that she preserve and restore 'old colonial interests'. The United States must, therefore, stop being 'ambiguous' about this. 'Western unity' must not be allowed to prevent the pursuit of 'our traditional dedication to political liberty'.[28]

Still convinced that time was on Britain's side and that a bloody clash with the Egyptian army, if the Egyptians brought it about, would teach them a very salutary lesson, Winston Churchill as Acting Foreign Secretary was now briefing Lord Hankey's son, Robin Hankey, who was setting out for Cairo, the Ambassador having fallen sick. 'If HM Embassy did nothing for six months except avoiding giving things away, he would be very content,' Hankey was told. His role in Egypt should be that of 'a patient, sulky pig'. Churchill felt pretty sure of the American President. 'Of Mr Foster Dulles he seemed to despair.' He sent his envoy off with the thought that, 'The Egyptians would come round all right when they found how determined we were.'[29]

Robin Hankey was soon reporting that Nasser was the man with whom to do business. He was 'intelligent and thinks with his head rather than his heart and he can be approached without publicity'.[30] No better government in Egypt was in sight. Americans and British were repeatedly assured by Nasser and others that once agreement over the Canal Zone was reached the Egyptians would be their friends and would join in arrangements for the defence of the Middle East. But Hankey added ominously, 'There may well be a tendency for the Egyptians to make difficulties for the Suez Canal Company once our fighting troops are withdrawn.'[31]

Churchill having been felled by a stroke while Eden was still on the sick list, Lord Salisbury was in charge of the Foreign Office during the second round of negotiations between the end of July and the third week of October. During these sessions the main features of what became the Anglo-

Egyptian Agreement of 1954 were thrashed out. British fighting troops were to evacuate the country completely in eighteen months. The stores and workshops of the base would be kept in full working order by British technicians. British troops were to have rights of re-entry if Egypt or certain neighbouring countries were attacked (though not by Israel). The new treaty was to last for seven years. Two points were still outstanding: whether the 4,000 British technicians still on Egyptian soil should wear uniform and whether Turkey (a Nato member) should be included among the regional states, an attack on whom should trigger a British return.

These might seem – and were certainly thought by Dulles – to be very secondary matters. But in October Churchill, battered but game, was once again on board and insisting that the wearing of British uniforms was 'a matter of cardinal importance to us'.[32] Nasser complained to Caffery, 'If we keep on retreating, we shall be hung in the streets one day when you depart for other shores.'[33] The talks were again adjourned: they had still one more year to go.

This postponement had a decisive effect on the West's relations with Egypt. Major economic assistance from the United States, which at the end of 1953 could have been forthcoming, and the resumption of arms supplies from Britain would both have been expected to follow an agreement. These could have kept Egypt substantially with the West. But Churchill could still exert influence in Washington. His urgent pleas, which prevailed with Eisenhower, that Egypt should get no economic rewards until the terms were agreed were couched in openly political terms. The danger was 'that the offended Conservatives might add their voices to that section of the Socialist party who criticize the United States'. At any time, he insisted, the 'increasingly angered section' of the Tory party might 'cancel our modest majority'.[34]

On 16 December (1953) Dulles found Eden, who was now back in charge at the Foreign Office, in a distinctly jumpy mood when he tackled him in his relentless way over a private lunch in Paris about further concessions to Egypt. Afterwards Sir Pierson ('Bob') Dixon, a senior Whitehall official shortly to go to New York as Permanent Representative to the UN, asked an American colleague to convey to Dulles the following message: 'Mr Eden's position is such that if the debate in the House goes badly at this particular time he might have to leave the Cabinet to please the rebels'.[35]

Gamal Abdul Nasser in Command

During the first four months of 1954 Egypt was in the grip of a power struggle which pitted the popular General Neguib, who wanted to be a real executive President and was willing to play the card of a return to pluralist democracy to bring it about, against the Free Officers. By April Nasser, assuming the office of Prime Minister, was the undisputed ruler of Egypt, with the backing of the army but with as yet no great popular appeal.[36] He had been the CIA's candidate from early on when the Agency's Director Allen Dulles, John Foster's brother, had arranged to short-circuit Neguib (with whom Caffery continued to conduct business) and to establish warm, informal relationships out of the public eye with Nasser and three other young officers. Since January 1953 this operation had been under the supervision of Allen Dulles's chief representative for the Middle East, Colonel Kermit ('Kim') Roosevelt, the quiet, preppy grandson of Theodore Roosevelt. Apart from full-time CIA agents, he had Miles Copeland, a 'CIA alumnus' now working in Cairo for an American consultancy firm, at the Ministry of the Interior, reorganising the police files and 'gaming out' how one would defeat an anti-Nasser coup. Part of the CIA team was even co-operating in the manufacture of anti-American propaganda, all in the interests of preventing Nasser, as the most desirable available Egyptian leader, from being toppled.[37]

On 9 March, (1954) before he had decisively won, Nasser sent a message to Kermit Roosevelt to say that he still wanted a settlement with Britain and that, if Britain would make concessions on uniforms, Egypt would accept the right of re-entry in the event of an attack on Turkey. Nasser claimed this was the last chance for agreement; otherwise Neguib would make a popular issue of his willingness to defy Britain.[38] Eden at this point persuaded the Cabinet to give up the whole idea of having Servicemen in or out of uniform, on Egyptian soil after the evacuation of the Canal Zone. Instead the base should be operated and maintained by civilian contractors. Happily Churchill also was in the process of changing his outlook as he absorbed the strategic consequences of the United States's test explosion of a hydrogen bomb. The difference between the atomic and hydrogen weapon struck him as being as great as those between the bow and arrow and the first atomic bomb. It removed, as far as he could see, the case for staying in the Canal Zone.[39] In a further approach to the British by way of Roosevelt, Nasser, by now Prime Minister, asked for fresh talks to be quick and carried out in secret so that the open negotiations could be extremely brief and decisive.[40]

Even so it took until the end of July before Heads of Agreement were published, and it was October before the detailed treaty was signed. Since the existing treaty was due to expire in 1956, a new seven-year agreement only extended the link for five more years. The removal of British troops, the end at last of the 'temporary occupation', was to take place by stages to be completed in June 1956. Detailed clauses defined the status of the Canal base until 1961. A rather pointed question had been asked the previous January in a British Cabinet Committee: 'If the base is held to be essential in war, what is the use of an agreement that will only last until 1961?' To which the reply by the Chief of the Imperial General Staff had been: 'During the succeeding seven years we shall do our best to induce in the Egyptians a sense of military responsibility.'[41]

By June 1956, when the last of the troops were to leave the Canal Zone, the atmosphere had utterly changed. The civilian contractors had been installed with extraordinarily little fuss. Persuaded that they were undertaking a vital national duty, some of the best-known firms in Britain – Vickers-Armstrong, George Wimpey, ICI, Balfour Beatty, John Laing, Austin and Rootes Motors – set up the Suez Contractors Organisation to try to make some sense of the immense, sprawling legacy of the Second World War. (One depot alone had a perimeter of seventeen miles).[42] The Egyptian military were helpful; organised thievery on a grand scale dramatically ceased. But the British Government which had fought so tenaciously over the precise details of the base now seemed to have lost interest in retaining it.

When General Sir Charles Keightley, the Commander-in-Chief, Middle East Land Forces, and the British Ambassador, Sir Humphrey Trevelyan, made a tour of the base in June, they noted a fundamental change in military assumptions since the treaty had been signed less than two years before. Then, strategic planning was based on 'the comparative probability of a major war'. Now, they said, it was based on 'the comparative improbability of a major war'. Then, too, the hope existed that the Egyptian Revolutionary Government was potentially an ally of the West with its armed forces dependent on British armaments and training. Now, this hope was not entertained.

In the face of this turnabout Sir Humphrey still recommended sticking to the base. But to judge from the handwritten minutes to his cable the logic of that policy no longer carried conviction in Whitehall. 'It is difficult to understand', ran one, 'why [the Ambassador] thinks it politically important for us to maintain our position in the base until the end of the Agreement since he acknowledges that there is no hope at all of the Egyptians agreeing to extend its validity.'[43] It had taken a long time for the Egyptian message to sink in but finally it had. At a meeting Eden held at Chequers on 9 June 1956 as part of the rigorous cut back of the Forces dictated by financial necessity, the Chiefs of Staff confirmed that their military planning now assumed that Britain would not retain the base after 1961. The War Office promptly set about plans to withdraw equipment and warn contractors about reducing their staff. Prestige still mattered. The new shut down must be seen as a move 'to previously prepared positions', not on any account as 'a simple abandonment of our Middle East positions'.[44] But in the strategic and economic context of 1956, 1954 already seemed a long time ago.

For the final stages of the negotiation and the signature of the Anglo-Egyptian Agreement in October 1954 Britain was represented in Cairo by Anthony Nutting, the Minister of State. Afterwards he had a long talk with

Colonel Nasser at the Nile Barrage about future bilateral relations in a context that was to become known as NECMU – the New Era of Co-operation and Mutual Understanding – and also about the settlement of the Palestine problem. As to the first, Nasser promised to tone down Egyptian propaganda broadcasting whose shrill endorsement of every anti-colonial or anti-traditionalist movement within transmission range of Cairo Radio was regarded by the British as a chronic threat to their 'special positions'. On the question of Palestine, Nasser indicated a readiness to negotiate that was to tantalise both Eden and Foster Dulles for the next twelve months and more.[45]

Nasser's immediate task was to show that, unlike his civilian predecessors, he had negotiated an agreement that he could sell to the Egyptian people. The Islamic fundamentalists of the Muslim Brotherhood, the *Ikhwan*, sharply attacked its terms: the 1936 treaty, which had only two more years to run, was to be extended by five years; the Turkey clause tied Egypt irrevocably to the West; the British civil contractors would be an occupation army in disguise. Nasser outfaced his critics, behaved calmly under fire when eight shots rang out as he addressed a public meeting on 26 October, and used the incident to smash the Brotherhood, six of whose leaders were sent to their execution.[46] As an exercise of power this worked in Egypt, though the immediate effect in parts of the Arab world was to cause him to be dismissed as a mere military dictator. The first large demonstration in Jordan at which the name of Nasser was heard was one denouncing him for his repression of the *Ikhwan*.[47]

Mission in Search of a Hero

But Gamal Abdul Nasser aimed to be a great deal more than a Zaim or a Shishakli (short-lived military dictators of Syria) or indeed than a Neguib. His reflections on the movement that he was leading were circulating in Cairo, having been put together from notes of his conversation and edited by his journalist friend Mohamed Heikal under the title *The Philosophy of the Revolution*. This was the thin volume that was subsequently to be spoken of by the French and British Prime Ministers as if it was the equivalent of Hitler's *Mein Kampf*, though how such a comparison could have survived any acquaintance with the two books is a puzzle.[48] 'Despite a certain awkwardness of style ... and a tendency to lose himself in anecdote', wrote the British Ambassador, Sir Ralph Stevenson, at the time of publication, 'the book throws a not unfavourable light upon its writer's own beliefs ... His book has a certain breadth of vision, humanity and idealism which one might be excused for not expecting from a man of his background. It is encouraging to be able to record that this idealism and moral conviction appear to be standing the test of time.'[49] When Eden met

Nasser the following February (1955) he made a graceful reference to *The Philosophy of the Revolution.*

The small book is loosely autobiographical, calling on the author's experiences in the army during the Palestine war and in the plotting and carrying out of the overthrow of the King. He refers quite frankly to his experiment with assassination, though he claims that, after one try, he rejected it as a method. He deplores the egotism of so-called experts to whom he and his fellow-officers had turned for advice once they had found themselves in power. 'The word "I" was on every tongue ... I had many times met eminent men – or so they were called by the press – of every political tendency and colour, – but when I would ask any of them about a problem in the hope he could supply a solution, I would never hear anything but "I".'

When later on it became fashionable to treat the book itself as evidence of egomania, the passage usually cited was one near the end when the author quoted the title of Pirandello's work *Six Characters in Search of an Author*. Nasser wrote: 'For some reason it seems to me that within the Arab circle there is a role wandering aimlessly in search of a hero. And I do not know why it seems to me that this role, exhausted by its wanderings, has at last settled down, tired and weary, near the borders of our country and is beckoning us to move, to take up its lines, to put on its costume since no one else is qualified to play it.' This could, of course, be taken to mean – as evidently it was by a surprising variety of people – that the ruler of Egypt saw himself as 'the Pharaoh of a vast Arab empire stretching from ocean to ocean', or it could more reasonably be taken as a poetic re-statement of a proposition often made, not least by Englishmen, namely that Egypt was the natural metropolis of the Arab world. Nasser himself says: 'Here let me hasten to say that this role is not one of leadership ... it is such a role as to spark this tremendous power latent in the area surrounding us.' The story of the political union with Syria in 1958 (which is outside the scope of this book) would suggest that Nasser had no plan worked out for the creation of an empire.

Nasser then goes on to refer, as if he were Anthony Eden, to three circles which most conveniently interlock only at the point of his own country. There is the continent of Africa, about which, writing like a nineteenth-century Khedive, he says: 'We will never in any circumstances be able to relinquish our responsibility to support, with all our might, the spread of enlightenment and civilisation to the remotest depths of the jungle.' There is also the Arab world and the world of Islam. Like Eden also, he calls attention to the importance for the modern world of oil, 'the sinew of material civilisation'. The Arab world should stop thinking of itself as weak. With oil far cheaper to produce in the Middle East than elsewhere, it should, in any proper ordering of contemporary values, be seen as strong. 'And now I go back to that wandering mission in search of a hero to play it. Here is the role. Here are the lines and here is the stage. We alone, by virtue of our place, can perform the role.'

Alpha and Baghdad

Towards the end of 1954, following the signature of the Suez Base Agreement, Sir Anthony Eden[50] took two major Middle Eastern initiatives – the one in public, the other hidden in deepest secrecy. The first was designed to pursue the idea first ventilated by Dulles of a Western defensive system that, accepting Egypt's self-exclusion, would be based on the Northern Tier of states. The second was to build on Nutting's conversation with Nasser so as to produce a permanent solution to the problem of Palestine. The first became the Baghdad Pact; the second was known to Eden, Dulles and the very few initiates among their officials as project Alpha. In practical terms each policy was the enemy of the other.

'The analogy of Trieste has been much in my mind', was the message that Eden instructed his Ambassador on 4 November (1954) to convey to Foster Dulles.[51] In the case of that apparently intractable Italo-Jugoslav dispute, British and American diplomats working as one team first spent much time labouring with one side to fine down its minimum requirements, then they switched to the other side and so on until success. Eden thought that the Palestine problem was too poisonous to leave as it was, too destabilising, too much of a temptation for 'the Bear' to create trouble. Dulles from the first reacted favourably. His own mind, he said, had been moving in the same direction. But where to start? With what country? And on what item? It was fairly soon agreed that the side with which to start should be the Arab one and the country should be Egypt. Nasser was the only Arab leader who, if agreement were reached, might make it stick.[52]

At a meeting in Paris Dulles gave a vivid description of the power and influence of the Zionist lobby in the United States. He had, he said, just about twelve months left in which to do something on Palestine before another election would make action impossible. He and Eden jointly appointed a small official team headed by Evelyn Shuckburgh, Assistant Under-Secretary of State at the Foreign Office for the Middle East, and Francis Russell, Counsellor at the American Embassy at Tel Aviv, to take charge of the enterprise. Shuckburgh had just come back from a tour of the Middle East, during which he had met Nasser. When over the dinner table another Free Officer, Major Salah Salem, had burst out that, even if Israel accepted the 1947 partition frontiers, the Arabs could not make peace with her, Nasser had quickly corrected him. There were things which a strong government like his could do which weak ones could not, he said. But he did not think the time ripe, because the Israelis were not yet ready to pay the price.

'Nasser has shown himself to be a man of courage,' Shuckburgh wrote, 'capable of leading rather than following public opinion.'[53] There was also the conversation at the Nile Barrage: what Egypt wanted, Nasser had told Nutting then, was full continuity with Jordan so as to end the physical separation of the Arab world. Unlike King Farouk, he would not mind if Jordan had all the connecting land, including the Gaza Strip.[54] What this meant, though, was that the Israelis would have to pay for peace by giving up the Negev. One thing was certain for Britain and the United States: if they were serious about Alpha they were committing themselves not only to working confidentially with Nasser but to helping him build up his standing in the Arab world.

But Eden's other initiative tended to work in precisely the opposite direction. Nasser made no bones about this over the dinner table to Shuckburgh. A military pact of the kind Eden had in mind – based as it would be on Iraq – would fracture Arab autonomy and solidarity, would split Iraq and ruin everything. There was, however, a certain sense of urgency about Britain's relations with Iraq. Just as Britain had attempted with manifest lack of success to transform her bilateral (and unequal) treaty with Egypt into a more respectable multilateral arrangement, she had been trying to do the same with Iraq. In this case the unpopular bilateral treaty, which placed the major air base at Habbaniya and the lesser one at Shaiba in the hands of the RAF and gave Britain the right to provide service instructors and technical advisers to the Iraqi armed forces, was due to expire in 1957.

The difficulty lay, as British officials saw it, in persuading Iraqi servicemen and politicians that an alliance with Britain in any form, given her straitened economy and the approaching loss of her principal *place d'armes* in the Suez Canal Zone, would still be worth it for them. 'It is difficult to give a satisfactory assurance on this point', noted one Whitehall official (Paul Falla), 'since we cannot disguise the discrepancy between the forces required to hold the Middle East and the forces we can make available in the region.' This provoked a sharp dissent from Eden (the asperity of whose marginalia was normally directed at foreigners rather than at his own officials): 'I don't agree with this. New plans for Turkey. These minutes are too negative. Turkey is capital in all this and a Turkish base that covers N.E. Iraq.'[55]

The opportunity to promote an alternative Middle East policy to one based on Egypt arose from a combination of two circumstances. Turkey, having first made a point of establishing the principle, which was of capital importance to her, that she was a European state by having herself accepted as a member of the Council of Europe and of Nato, was now ready to pursue a dynamic policy in the Middle East. More than Eden or the Iraqis, the Turks were the propulsive force behind the new initiative. And, secondly, the strongest and most Anglophile political leader of Iraq, General Nuri es-Said, had in August 1954 been recalled from a sickbed in London to become, for the twelfth time, Prime Minister and Minister of Defence.

Foremost Arab leader of the old school – that of men who had seen service under the Ottoman Empire – companion-in-arms of Lawrence of Arabia in the Arab Revolt, and arch-manipulator of Iraqi politics, Nuri possessed a personality and charm which succeeded in captivating many generations of British politicians and diplomats.

In 1941 Britain had by force of arms reinstated the Regent of Iraq, Crown Prince Abdul Ilah, son of the last Hashemite King of the Hedjaz, and General Nuri es-Said after they had been overthrown by a wartime revolution. Governments in Baghdad did not normally last more than a year or two, but ministerial jobs were rotated among a small class of élite landowners, manipulating what was in outward appearance a parliamentary system. Whether in or out of office Nuri played a masterful part within this system. He was, says the Egyptian historian and diplomat Ahmed Gomaa, 'known more as a born intriguer, a man who did not know a straight line'.[56] He had two priorities: the reorganisation of the Asian Arab world so as to create a Greater Syria, closely linked with Iraq (a scheme referred to as the 'Fertile Crescent') and the long term economic development of Iraq, to which purpose he conscientiously dedicated a high proportion of the country's income from oil.

The British Embassy in Baghdad was under no illusions about the threat of social revolution. 'I understand you can ride?' was the cheery manner in which Robert Belgrave, a new Third Secretary, was greeted on arrival at the Embassy in Baghdad by the Counsellor, Humphrey Trevelyan, in 1950. It was made plain that the query was not social. 'I am going to bequeath an agreeable duty, which is that on Fridays instead of coming to the office you will go out foxhunting with the Crown Prince's pack, because there you will meet the young officers, the young doctors and the young lawyers who sooner or later are going to carry out a revolution in this country.'[57] But it was to be another eight years before this happened, in the most bloody possible way: the young King Faisal, his uncle the Crown Prince, and Nuri were all killed. When it did most of Belgrave's riding companions took part, most especially the vet who, the least considered of the party, turned out to be a top Communist agent. Only Brigadier Qassim, the revolutionary chief, had been too austere a personality for such pursuits.

In 1954–5 the British felt that they must move fast if they were going to work with Nuri. He was by now very deaf – he 'kept touching his hand and his ear as though he was in pain', noticed Shuckburgh – but ideas poured out of him, another British official observed, so abundantly that it was never clear which one was a firm proposal.[58] Only Trevelyan seemed to view the Iraqi Premier with some detachment. A little later when he was Ambassador in Cairo he observed that he had never known anything Nuri had attempted to succeed except in internal Iraqi politics; and indeed, it was a fact that even in handling relations with Jordan, which ought to have been easy because of the dynastic link, Iraq's hand was often ineptly played.

Once back in power Nuri briskly fixed for himself a docile Parliament (which he did more outrageously than ever before) and started organising the new pact with the knowledge that he was acting with Eden's approval.

Eden, however, did not expect it to happen so fast. It was in keeping with Nuri's style that a great deal of manœuvring should precede any action. But this was to reckon without Adnam Menderes, the abrasive Turkish Prime Minister. On a visit to Baghdad in mid-January (1955), Menderes kept the Iraqi Parliament, waiting to hear him speak until Nuri could be induced to sign a communiqué announcing that Iraq and Turkey would conclude a treaty of mutual defence in the immediate future, the signature of which would be open to 'other interested countries'.[59]

Instantly Nasser summoned a meeting of the Arab states at prime ministerial level in Cairo. Nuri did not attend on a plea of ill-health, which was partly genuine. The occasion found the Egyptian Premier out of his usual calm and controlled humour since, if Egypt stuck to the Arab League policy of forming no outside alliances and the others, following Iraq's lead, did not, Egypt would soon find herself not as the Arab leader but as an outsider. Finding the proceedings bogging down in desultory exchanges of no great purpose, Nasser shouted: 'Egypt will not be intimidated. We shall carry on even if the Arab necklace is broken and all the beads scattered.'[60]

In early February the prime ministerial conference dwindled to a halt. 'After fifteen days of meetings totalling seventy-five hours', said Cairo Radio with disgust, 'Arabs came out not knowing whether they had decided anything or agreed on anything or whether they had in fact conferred at all.' But the British realised that the discordance of their two policies – Alpha and Baghdad Pact – was occurring far sooner than they had expected. The pact 'could, at least for the time being, seriously hamper the Anglo-American endeavour to promote an Arab-Israeli settlement'. The official advice was, however, quite clear. Nasser had hinted to the British that if Nuri would accept six months' delay differences could be worked out. But this, the Foreign Office decided, would 'lose what is possibly the last initiative of the ageing Nuri, discourage seriously the Turks, and still offer no real prospect ... through the Arab League'.[61]

On 24 February 1955, the Turco-Iraqi Pact was signed in Baghdad. Right up to the end it was the Turk, Menderes, who had to force the pace. Drafts and redrafts between the two capitals were exchanged by way of Whitehall, so the British Government was kept scrupulously informed. The effect of Nuri's redrafts was to eliminate most of the substance, since even now the old Ottoman officer did not really trust the Turk. Menderes asked Nuri whether the mountain of labour of the past weeks and months was really to produce such a ridiculous mouse of an agreement. Finally, the Turkish Prime Minister arrived abruptly on Nuri's doorstep and stayed till the treaty was signed.[62] The two agreed to co-operate over defence and invited additional members. Moreover any one member could conclude special agreements with any other member, a provision intended to accommodate Britain's special relations with Iraq. The policy of the Baghdad Pact had been launched.[63]

Eden Meets Nasser

The approaching signature of the Pact did not create an ideal atmosphere for the one and only meeting that brought face-to-face the two primary contestants of the Suez conflict: Eden and Nasser. This took place on 20 February at the British Embassy, when Nasser and his Foreign and Defence Ministers were invited to dinner to meet Eden and the Chief of the Imperial General Staff, who were on their way to the Far East. Eden greeted his chief guest in Arabic, which seems to have surprised Nasser and perhaps disconcerted him. Eden asked him whether this was the first time that Nasser had been in the Embassy. Nasser said it was; he was interested, he said, to see the place from which Egypt had been governed. 'Not governed', Eden demurred lightly, 'advised, perhaps'. There was a photo-opportunity and Nasser seized Eden's hand and clawed it rather awkwardly in a gesture of amiability.

They went in to dinner and the serious talk of the evening. There are two recently available accounts of this occasion, the Foreign Office record accessible since 1987[64] and the account published in 1986 (in *Cutting the Lion's Tail*) by Mohamed Heikal, who was not an eye-witness but who was in close touch with those on the Egyptian side who were. This differs in some respects from an earlier version by Heikal in *Nasser: The Cairo Documents*, published in 1972, which portrayed a much more dramatic confrontation between the two men.

Eden sought to flatter Nasser by offering him what he described as the same presentation about the nature of the military threat in the Middle East as had been made to the Commonwealth Prime Ministers who had recently met in London. Nuclear weapons would indeed be used against a Russian military threat to the south but this did not remove, as Nasser seemed to suppose, the need to be able to resist with conventional weapons. In reply Colonel Nasser expounded his own geopolitical doctrine, which stressed above all the primacy of the internal front. This, he said, in a world of ideological war, supplied the element of defence in depth. The Arab peoples, including himself, all had a complex about fear of foreign domination, especially domination disguised as area defence. For that reason, pacts with outside powers were abhorrent to them.

This led the Egyptian Prime Minister onto the subject of the impending pact between Iraq and Turkey. 'A mere handful of people in Baghdad' were behind it; it would do Britain no good at all. It was not Egyptian propaganda that had started the opposition to the agreement; the trouble had sprung out of the ground. When Eden asked what was wrong with Iraq having a link with Turkey when there was a Turkey clause in Egypt's own agreement with Britain, Nasser said that he had accepted that clause only to avoid a breakdown. It is unlikely that he believed Eden's perfectly true observation that the British Government had been as much surprised by the speed of the Turks and Iraqis as the Egyptians themselves.

In a climate set by the imminence of the signature in Baghdad, Eden decided not to introduce the substance of Alpha to the extent that Dulles had hoped and that had been anticipated in the Foreign Office brief.[65] He did however say that Egypt was the only Arab state in a position to move towards a settlement with Israel. Nasser replied mildly that it was a matter of timing. No solution was to be found in partial settlements. The frontier problems were on their own insoluble and could only be dealt with in the context of a comprehensive settlement, including the future of the Palestinian refugees. Eden agreed and expressed his desire to be of help.

Some years later, after the Suez conflict, Nasser in a television interview quoted himself as having said that Eden had behaved as if he had been 'a prince among beggars', and in his earlier book Heikal makes this the main theme of the encounter as if Eden had been condescending throughout.[66] *Cutting the Lion's Tail* treats Nasser's remark as a (sartorial) aside, made in 'amused astonishment' in response to the evening dress worn by the British party, which for part of the time included ladies.[67] This seems more likely, since Eden was naturally well-mannered and was genuinely impressed by Nasser's vigour and manly dynamism. Whatever became true later it seems doubtful if Nasser in 1955 'clearly regarded Eden as the personification of all he disliked in the British', as Eden's authorised biographer Robert Rhodes James suggests.[68] Heikal says that Nasser 'felt the occasion had been a useful one and that Eden was the sort of person with whom it might be possible to do business'. And the British official account concludes that: 'The spirit of the discussion was friendly and frank throughout and the Egyptian Prime Minister referred repeatedly to the great improvement in Anglo-Egyptian relations.' The prospects seemed set fair that NECMU had a long run ahead of it.

4

Arms and the Dam

Unpleasant things which we might instigate should have the appearance of happening naturally . . . Egypt as a neutralist would be more tolerable than as a Communist satellite.
John Foster Dulles to Harold Macmillan, 3 October 1955.

We are afraid that Nasser, whether innocently or deliberately, is dangerously committed to the Communists. Consequently we believe that it would be advantageous, in any event, to overthrow him if possible.
Harold Macmillan, telegram to Washington, 28 November 1955.

Eight days after Nasser had dined with Eden in Cairo, four days after the Turco-Iraqi Pact had been signed at Baghdad, an event occurred which started the real countdown to the Suez war. On the night of 28 February/1 March the armed forces of Israel and Egypt clashed in Gaza in circumstances that changed radically the priorities of the Nasser regime and brought to the forefront the almost forgotten cause of the Palestinian Arabs, clustered in their tents and huts like rabbit-hutches in the refugee camps.

The Israeli doctrine of inflicting a stunning military reprisal for a string of border incidents that were individually minor had been first applied against Jordan in October 1953, on the eve of David Ben-Gurion's dramatic decision to retire from office and live in the Negev desert. It took only eight days from his re-emergence as once more Minister of Defence (though not yet Prime Minister) on 20 February 1955 – the day of the Eden–Nasser encounter – for him to authorise the short, sharp shock which exposed the inability of Egypt's army, even under a military government, to give Palestinians adequate protection. Both instances – Qibya, 1953, and Gaza, 1955 – were the handiwork of a swashbuckling, overweight young officer (he was 25 years old in 1953) possessed of great courage and with what a military historian (who at the time of writing is the President of Israel) has called 'an uncanny feel for battle'. Chaim Herzog adds that Ariel ('Arik') Sharon was 'also a most difficult person to command'.[1]

A reserve officer, Sharon had been taken away from his history studies at the Hebrew University to recruit, train and lead a specialist counter-terrorist commando called Unit 101. It was hoped that it would combat a feeling of ineffectiveness and frustration in the Israeli Defence Forces that had followed the high points of the War of Independence. The problem to be dealt with was that of Arab 'infiltration' across the long, unmarked border offering no physical obstacle to illegal crossing. It began, according to Glubb Pasha in a report to the Foreign Office, as simply the movement of refugees back to their lands or to find lost relatives. The penalty for crossing the armistice lines was sometimes summary and meant to be exemplary. 'The Jews were ... not a little elevated by their successes and decided to shoot ... on sight. Any patrol meeting an Arab shot him dead and left his body rotting in the fields.' Finding themselves fired upon, the 'infiltrators' came armed and fired back. Unarmed Israeli civilians including women and children also came to be among their victims.

Glubb, commanding both the Arab Legion and the Jordanian police, claimed to have made headway with curbing the amount of illegal border-crossing. But, he reported in 1953, infiltration of a new type was now occurring by refugees who had gone to Damascus, been armed and paid with Saudi money, and 'who aimed only to kill'. The incident in October at the Israeli village of Yehud, when a hand-grenade was tossed through a window killing a woman and her two babies being one of this type, he offered Israeli security full co-operation in tracing the offenders.[2] The Israelis decided to use Sharon.

On 14/15 October 1953 the new scale of night-time reprisal raids which Unit 101 inaugurated against the Jordanian village of Qibya can be gauged by the fact that forty-five buildings, including the school and the reservoir, were blown up and sixty-six people, including many women and children, killed. Sharon claims to have been surprised and shocked when the casualty list appeared and explains it in his memoirs by saying that 'some Arab families must have stayed in their homes rather than running away', that the houses were large with cellars and back rooms and that his men had not been able to search them all before placing the explosives.[3]

Ben-Gurion had in the case of the Qibya raid been sufficiently apprehensive of world opinion that he emphatically denied over Israeli radio that any members of the Israeli forces had taken part. It had just been a spontaneous response by enraged frontier settlers to Arab atrocities. Since the end of the war no fewer than 421 Israelis, he added, had been killed individually in such incidents. Britain, the United States and the UN Security Council condemned the raid in harsh terms and made the fruitless demand that those responsible be brought to justice.

As his last act before surrendering office in December 1953, Ben-Gurion invested his favourite General, Moshe Dayan, as the Chief of Staff. Known everywhere by his black eye-patch (which, though it gave him a suitably piratical look, he detested wearing), Dayan was to play a decisive catalyst's role in the story of Suez. Much later, in 1979, as Foreign Minister, he was to negotiate the peace treaty between Israel and Egypt. A quarter of a century before he was already, according to a British diplomat, 'credited with political ambitions and said by some to covet the role of Foreign Minister'.[4] For all that, as a soldier he was very much the dashing man of action.

Although Moshe Dayan did not invent the doctrine of reprisal and was originally opposed to the creation of Unit 101, he made them a central part of Israeli defence policy, merging 101 with the paratroops and making Sharon the commander of the 202 Paratroop Battalion. In a lecture to commanders in 1955 he told them that Arab authorities would only take the highly invidious steps necessary to prevent their own people from violating the border if their failure to do so was made too obviously painful. Reprisals, therefore, should not be aimed at particular gangs of infiltrators; they would be aimed at whatever would give the authorities the biggest incentive to avoid a repetition.[5]

Reprisals did not lapse during 1954. Nine were carried out, seven against Jordan but none with the impact and casualties of Qibya. The Prime Minister, Moshe Sharett, was known to prefer the weapon of diplomacy to military battle; most authorised raids were small-scale. After one such episode, Anthony Eden asked the Israeli Ambassador, Eliahu Elath, why, when according to Israeli announcements all the recent frontier incidents had been caused by Egyptian inroads from Gaza, Israel's acts of physical retaliation should all be directed against Jordan, Britain's ally. Of course, the Foreign Secretary added, he was not suggesting that he would prefer Israel to retaliate upon Egypt.[6]

With Ben-Gurion back, Sharon was authorised to hit three Egyptian camps in Gaza and blow up the headquarters building and pump-house. Sharett had weakly sanctioned what he had been told would be a small operation which would only cause very few casualties. He was faced with one in which thirty-six Egyptian and Palestinian soldiers and two civilians had been killed, twenty-nine soldiers and another two civilians wounded and nine Israelis had been lost. Ben-Gurion indicated to Sharon his personal approval. For Nasser it changed everything.[7]

There had been for some time a small Palestinian reconnaissance unit which had been used for occasional patrols in Israeli territory. But the evidence produced by documents captured in the course of the Sinai campaign the following year supports the view that, in the weeks prior to the raid, Colonel Nasser had been attempting to bring the Palestinians in Gaza under tighter control to avoid further incidents.[8] Young Palestinians like Khalil Wazir (the future PLO leader Abu Jihad who was assassinated in Tunis in 1988) were, however, organising sabotage groups among the refugees and were eager to provoke war. Wazir and Yasser Arafat, the Cairo-based President of the Union of Palestinian Students, calculated that, taking account of the normal Israeli pattern of reprisal, it should be possible to provoke such a disproportionate display of Israeli violence as to force the Egyptian army into the fight. That this was far from Nasser's thoughts was clear from a visit he paid to Gaza just before Sharon's attack when he told the Egyptian garrison that he did not intend to allow the Armistice Demarcation Line to become a battleground and that he did not believe the Israelis would either.

Abu Jihad claimed later that it was his commando that precipitated the Gaza raid by sabotaging an Israeli water storage and pumping facility at Faluja. 'We used a lot of TNT and the explosion made a big flood', the Palestinian guerrilla leader told the British writer Alan Hart with satisfaction. '. . . I saw seeds and plants from Jewish settlements being swept along by the floodwaters. We were very happy.' Sharon says that it was the murder of an Israeli orange grove worker that was the actual trigger.[9]

The Gaza incident did not produce war because the Egyptian armed forces were no more ready for it now than they had been before the revolution. According to Major Salah Salem five years later, Egypt had at the time only six serviceable planes. Thirty others were grounded because Britain had stopped delivering spare parts during the long-drawn-out negotiations of the Base Agreement. Tank ammunition would last for a one-hour battle. Nearly sixty per cent of Egyptian tanks were in need of major repairs. Their artillery was no better.[10]

From this moment on Nasser's priorities were changed; he was still wedded to the economic development of Egypt but the overriding need was to ensure Egyptian rearmament from whatever sources it could be obtained. As Heikal puts it, the raid was treated 'as a message from Ben-Gurion to Nasser that building hospitals and schools and steel mills was not going to protect Egypt from a ruthless neighbour'.[11]

In the immediate aftermath there were large Palestinian demonstrations in Gaza. Egyptian and UN offices were smashed. Slogans read: 'If you want to save us, train us. If you want to save us, arm us.' Arafat led a student demonstration at the Arab League's headquarters in Cairo. Nasser in response allowed Arafat to go to Gaza to draw up a report, which called for the arming of the Palestinians. Two days after the raid the Egyptian military leadership had decided to reinforce Gaza with ten battalions of National Guards, for which Palestinians were recruited under Egyptian leadership.

In addition some Palestinians received special training as members of the 141 *Fedayeen* Battalion (*fedayeen* meaning self-sacrificers or commandos) as the Arab answer to Ariel Sharon. The gaol at Gaza was visited to recruit men who had been imprisoned for illegal infiltration across the Israeli borders. On 15 March the Egyptian War Minister, Maj-Gen. Abdul Hakim Amer, arrived in Gaza to set up the new force which was placed under the command of Colonel Mustafa Hafez of Egyptian Army Intelligence. The battalion started with fifty volunteers; by the year's end there were 700 trained for hit-and-run raids within Israel. At the same time the Egyptian army garrison was instructed to take up a much more active defence of the Gaza line.[12]

Diplomatically, Israel's action at Gaza left a deplorable impression. Relations between Israel and the Eisenhower Administration in the United States had in any case reached a low ebb. The United States in 1954 had gone so far as to suspend financial aid for a while to insist on Israel's not pressing forward unilaterally with a major water scheme in the demilitarised zone alongside Syria. Speeches from State Department officials caused offence, especially when Henry Byroade, the young ex-brigadier-general in charge of the Near East, suggested that Israel's Law of the Return, welcoming any Jew anywhere in the world to come to Israel as a citizen, created legitimate concern for her neighbours. So did his further admonition that if Israel wanted to be treated as a normal state she should take steps to become more Middle Eastern. Such opinions aimed an arrow at the very pupil of Israel's eye, said Moshe Sharett in the Knesset.[13] Eisenhower, although not anti-Semitic, was, according to his authorised biographer, Stephen E. Ambrose, 'uncomfortable with Jews' and not interested in hearing their point of view. At the same time the other superpower, the Soviet Union, had confirmed her complete change of side since 1947–8 by casting two pro-Arab vetoes during 1954.[14]

This feeling of isolation served not to make Israel more cautious but to make her more importunate. 'Give us reliable security undertakings, not the imprecise words of the Tripartite Declaration', Israel's envoys said to the West. Since the disharmony following Ben-Gurion's return between Ben-Gurion and Sharett was no secret, Sharett's men would convey heavily that only greater international understanding of Israel would suffice to safeguard Sharett's position and prevent raids worse than that of February. Nor was this just bluff. In April (1955) Ben-Gurion proposed that Israel end the Gaza nuisance once and for all by driving the Egyptians from the Strip. Sharett warned the Cabinet that if they followed Ben-Gurion's way the British could be expected to come in on Egypt's side (as they had threatened to do in December 1948) and the Americans would again cut off all economic aid. The chances of Israel getting a much-wanted security guarantee would vanish. Ben-Gurion's proposal was defeated by nine votes to four.[15]

On this occasion the Western deterrent had again worked. But its continued potency was precarious. Yet both John Foster Dulles and the British Foreign Office believed that time was on the Arabs' side, that the Israelis' military successes simply ensured them a short-term respite, which they should hasten to make use of to get the best deal they could. In the long run, however much the Israelis armed, they could not hope to compete with the vast manpower potential of the Arab world. Dulles's exasperation at the Israelis' failing to accept the logic of that assessment was enhanced by the belief that time was also not on the side of the West as a whole in the Middle East. Yet everything the allies wished to do was thwarted by the primacy of the Arab-Israeli dispute.

'The centre of infection in the region is Israel', wrote Sir John Nicholls, who became British Ambassador in Tel Aviv in the autumn of 1954, after he had been a few months in his post, 'and I believe that we must treat the Israelis as a sick people.' Almost every individual Israeli bore some psychological trace of 2,500 years of Jewish history which had left him with a legacy – 'unsureness, over-confidence, emotional instability, fierce intolerance, superiority complex, inferiority complex, guilt complex' and the deep conviction that the world was in his debt. 'It is not reasonable to expect', the Ambassador concluded, 'that a nation made up of individuals so psychologically unstable should be capable of a mature foreign policy'. It was much more likely that Israel would 'embark on an apparently suicidal policy in a state of national exaltation, based on a compound of mystical conviction that somehow Jehovah would intervene to save his people and shrewd calculation that US Jewry might turn out to be his chosen instrument'. Nicholls deduced from this a practical warning: Britain should not rely on the Israelis coolly reckoning the odds. They might risk war, even in the face of Britain's commitments to Jordan, before the balance of military power should turn decisively against them.[16]

Eden at Number Ten

On 6 April 1955 Anthony Eden at last replaced Winston Churchill in the Prime Minister's bed at Number Ten, a piece of furniture which both men favoured for the transaction of much official business.[17] In the end the old man, now eighty years old and showing it, tiptoed off the scene in the middle of a newspaper strike, and Sir Anthony, without the slightest political tremor, assumed the inheritance. He now had to prove that the misgivings about his lack of domestic experience and inability to entrust foreign policy to someone else were unjust. He immediately called an election (though he need not have done for another eighteen months), fought it impressively as, among other things, the first television election[18] and emerged with an increased majority (sixty instead of seventeen), the first time that had been achieved since 1900. This was a good beginning.

The astonishing thing is how rapidly that impression crumbled, how very short was the honeymoon period. The new Prime Minister's worst mistake was perhaps his first: after the longest conceivable notice, he seemed to be caught unprepared to form his new Cabinet. A patch-up of Churchill's team was accepted for the duration of the election, but Eden still seemed to be no nearer picking his own team when it was over nor was he ready until the end of December. This involved him in the clumsiness of first sending Harold Macmillan, a major political figure with wartime diplomatic experience, to the Foreign Office, thereby apparently fulfilling his own need to become almost entirely disengaged from foreign affairs, and then, eight months later, sending him away again. Indeed it appears from the diary kept while he was at Number Ten by Eden's Press Secretary, William Clark, that Eden was trying to shift Macmillan to the Treasury only five months after taking office.[19]

At the end of September, a basically pro-Conservative columnist, Henry Fairlie, was writing in the *Spectator* that 'there is no point in concealing the fact that [Eden's] first six months in office have not been encouraging'. More and more criticisms were being made 'by those who know' of the Prime Minister's refusal to take decisions. Why, for example, was there no new Government? 'The answer is that Sir Anthony Eden has been dithering. He has made up his mind, changed it, made it up again and changed it again.' This and other remarks in the press (and Eden was the most compulsive reader of political comment) did neither his reputation nor his self-confidence any good. He became obsessive about not appearing to dither.

To the public at large, although there was a certain dull inevitability about the succession, Eden nevertheless was an immensely reassuring and, to some, even an exciting figure. At fifty-eight he seemed a young Prime Minister, not only because his predecessor so clearly belonged to an older generation but because of his own retained good looks and his second marriage to the much younger Clarissa Churchill. His social and economic approach seemed broadly progressive and, in contrast to those inner circles who were so quick to denigrate, the general mood was to wish him well.

There was another contrast too: between the debonair good manners and unruffled charm for which Sir Anthony Eden was renowned and which epitomised his diplomatic fame and the intense rages into which he was liable to break out in the privacy of his immediate staff. People who were going to work close to him were advised to read the slim volume called *Tribulations of a Baronet* which his elder brother, Sir Timothy Eden, had written about life with their eccentric and volatile father. 'Do remember that he has quite extraordinary fits of temper,' William Clark was warned by a Foreign Office official. 'He will denounce you in a way that will make you want to slap his face. Don't do it. It is part of a physical defect. Don't resign. Wait until, which he will do eventually, he apologises.' 'That', interposed another colleague, 'is the nastier part of it.'[20]

Eden's principal Cabinet colleagues were, as the most senior of them, R. A. ('Rab') Butler, has put it, 'at the receiving end of those innumerable telephone calls, on every day of the week and at every hour of the day which characterised his conscientious but highly strung supervision of our affairs'.[21] Calls were particularly liable to come in the early hours as the Prime Minister made his way through the early editions of the newspapers;

and not all Ministers were able, as was Lord Home, the Commonwealth Relations Secretary, to control the rush of queries by cutting back on the supply of information to Number Ten.[22]

The other problem of an Eden premiership was his health. With an earlier medical record that did not suggest that he was very robust, he had had an attack of jaundice in 1952 and in April 1953 had been operated on twice for gallstones. The operations were not a success; serious damage was done to his bile duct, which left him liable to sudden fevers and jaundice. He had to be operated upon again in Boston, which did not solve the problem permanently but gave him a fresh chance, and he was not back on duty till October 1953. He was left, as he put it vividly in a memorandum prepared in January 1957, 'with a largely artificial inside. It was not thought that I would lead an active life again. However, with the aid of drugs and stimulants, I have been able to do so.'[23] Advised eventually by his doctor that he could take any job except that of Foreign Secretary, he allowed himself to be persuaded by Churchill that it was to that post that he should return. Having tested himself at its punishing routine he felt capable physically of Number Ten. But it had been noticed in his Private Office that he had everywhere to be accompanied by a great chest of pills and at times required injections.[24] It was a question whether his health would stand the strain of a crisis and whether the nature of his disability was not enhancing a pronounced tendency to fuss.

Eden gave his successor at the Foreign Office only a very short grace before bombarding him with the type (though not with the literary bite) of minutes that he himself had found so tiresome when coming from Winston Churchill. Moreover, even in the first months of his premiership he seemed to be distancing his views on the Middle East from those of his old department. Men like his former private secretary Evelyn Shuckburgh might still think primarily of Alpha. In the instructions dated 4 August issued to him as the new ambassador to Cairo, Sir Humphrey Trevelyan might be told that 'it is our policy to give [Egypt] such help as we are able', with a view to persuading Nasser 'to play a major part in achieving a settlement'.[25] But a reading of the Prime Minister's testy minutes over the summer would already have given quite a contrary impression.

What caused Eden aggravation was his minute scrutiny of Egyptian press reports about events in the Gulf. There the undefined political boundaries lost in the wastes of sand were under pressure from oil companies wanting to prospect. A group of eight villages, known collectively by the oasis name of Buraimi, whose 9,000 inhabitants had managed to live hitherto without visible allegiance to any state whatsoever, were claimed, six by the ruler of Abu Dhabi, two by the Sultan of Muscat, both places where Britain had a 'special position', including responsibility for their foreign policy. If any oil was to be found nearby, which was thought to be a distinct possibility, and these claims were upheld, the concession would go to the British-led Iraq

Petroleum Company. The King of Saudi Arabia precipitated the trouble by sending into the villages a posse of riders, their saddle bags bulging with gold, to aid the memories of the villagers about early traditions of Saudi overlordship. In the case of that claim becoming accepted, any oil concession would be a dollar one to the Aramco subsidiary.

Nasser's propagandists took the side of King Saud; their arguments against Britain's colonial-style relationship with the Gulf sheikhdoms rang a bell with Americans. Also, as the British did not fail to note, they coincided with American economic interests. Buraimi, as an irritant in Anglo-American relations throughout the whole of this period, running up to the Suez crisis and carrying on beyond it, gained a significance that was entirely disproportionate to its real importance – especially as oil, though found elsewhere in Abu Dhabi, was not in fact found there.

In mid-June (1955), only two months into the Eden premiership, the Prime Minister read in the press summary Egyptian accounts of British 'aggression' against Saudi Arabia. 'This is gross impertinence by those people who are likely to be attacked and destroyed by Israel before long,' he spluttered. 'I hope we give them no help.' At the foot of an outgoing telegram he queried, 'Anything in our power to hurt Egyptians without hurting ourselves'? The desk officers strove to reason with Number Ten and Macmillan commented, 'I think we have to bear in mind that Egypt must be an important factor in any Middle East defence system. We also need Nasser's co-operation for Alpha.'[26] Early in July Eden was at it again. On another Buraimi telegram he wrote: 'Foreign Secretary. This kind of thing is really intolerable. Egyptians get steadily worse. They should be told, "No more arms deliveries while this goes on".' But Macmillan was advised by Shuckburgh and others that, if Nasser went, they would only get someone worse. 'We have an interest therefore in giving him such support as is necessary to maintain him in power, which includes providing a certain amount of toys for his armed forces.'[27]

The Launching of Alpha

Henry Byroade, the young American Assistant Secretary of State, was switched from Washington to the Cairo Embassy at the beginning of 1955 as part of the Alpha policy in order to have as ambassador someone of the same age as Nasser – thirty-seven – who was also a former military officer. If Nasser was to play the role intended for him in making peace with Israel, it was thought desirable that a high-ranking American should be on terms of personal friendship with him. To the extent that this was possible, which was a limited one, Byroade succeeded in that aim; it did not take his Washington chiefs long to regret it. On 26 March and 3 April he saw Mahmoud Fawzi, the Foreign Minister, and on 5 April he saw Nasser.

Nasser said that he was keen to go ahead, Fawzi even using the expression that 'the iron was now hot'. But, said Nasser, there must be no misapprehension about Egypt's terms. The price for recognition of Israel's existence was the whole of the Negev. He warned that he was unwilling to bargain; when he said 'No corridor' he meant it. Israel's southern boundary should be to the north of Beersheva.[28] Colonel Nasser, the former intelligence officer at Falluja, required the results of the breach of the second truce of 1948 to be wiped out.

From this moment onwards Alpha was doomed, doomed not only because Nasser never endorsed in any way the British and American plans for him to propose the cession to Egypt and Jordan only of two triangular areas of desert touching at the apexes, possibly with a flyover bridge and an underpass, but also because, even if he had done so, there was not the slightest prospect of the Israelis accepting. Neither State Department nor Foreign Office had measured the intensity of Israel's refusal to give up territory for peace.[29] Not all Israelis had the same rhapsodic involvement with the Negev as did David Ben-Gurion, who wanted to see the whole weight of Israel shift from the Mediterranean plain towards the south. He was against big cities, which brought out the worst in men. 'This country', he said 'Isn't just a Jewish hotel'. He visualised many of the inhabitants of Tel Aviv and Jerusalem taking their industries with them and resettling in communities of no more than ten or fifteen thousand apiece scattered through the Negev's arid grandeur. But almost all Israelis did feel that the Negev lent some body and substance to a state which in other respects seemed so narrowly constricted. Moshe Sharett, the advocate of diplomatic methods and peaceful solutions, was every bit as much opposed to Negev concessions as Ben-Gurion. Hot and barren wastes the Negev might appear to be, but for Israel there was a sense of 'manifest destiny' about the future role of the Red Sea port of Eilat.[30]

Alpha did not only deal with the Negev. A document of fifty pages was assembled, containing reference to all aspects of a possible settlement. Territorial adjustments that might ease the co-existence of Israel and Jordan were listed in detail. The refugees were nominally to retain their choice between repatriation or compensation, but that choice was to be heavily weighted against repatriation. Britain and the United States would first find out from the Israelis what was the maximum number that they would be willing to receive back – it was optimistically thought that this might be some 75,000 – and then the numbers would be kept down to this order by stressing what a nasty time the returning refugees might be expected to have, compared with the certainty of financial grants (half of which would be underwritten by the United States and a sixth by Britain). Resettlement on the land would be assisted by a scheme that was being separately promoted by a special envoy, Eric Johnston, president of the Movie Picture Association of America, for developing the waters of the Jordan River system and making a fair division of them between Israel and her Arab neighbours. It was all in vain.[31]

One reason the intensity, though not the fact, of Israeli opposition was not sufficiently taken into account was that, until nearly the end of 1955, the approach had been made entirely to Egypt, in the hope that a really firm offer could then be put to Israel.[32] The Egyptians were skilful at keeping Alpha in play. Mahmoud Fawzi, a diplomat of the old order, subtle, allusive, (rather oriental, some Egyptian colleagues would say who knew that he had been stranded in Japan for the whole of the war) would give the impression that much progress was possible. Nasser would then often pull back, plead bad timing but still keep the door open. They were both, as in October–November 1955 and in July 1956, liable to reopen the subject themselves whenever a tilt towards the West seemed expedient.

Arms for Nasser

By the autumn of 1955 Byroade was seriously concerned about the failure to make progress with the Egyptians on any front. Despite his sustained attempts to raise American weapons for the Egyptian forces, not to mention the efforts of the CIA, whose clout in Washington when it came to delivery of carrots for their clients turned out to be exceedingly meagre,[33] Egypt was still largely dependent for arms supplies on the British and the French. Because Britain and France were secretly operating the arms control system through the Washington Committee, they were dribbling out in infuriatingly slow instalments such amounts as they had contracted to supply. Moreover the temptation to use the export licence procedure to attempt fine steering of pressures and penalties proved irresistible to British and French politicians.[34]

On 9 June Byroade was candidly warned by Nasser that on 23 May the Soviet Union had offered to supply Egypt with all she needed in the way of arms and that an Egyptian mission would leave for Moscow the following week.[35] This initiative represented a striking shift in Soviet policy. Stalin had never been interested in providing arms for nationalists who were not Communists, and Khrushchev says in his memoirs that at first Nasser was judged as a bourgeois Latin-American style dictator. Apparently it was Tito who advised that his Egyptian protégé's ideas had genuinely socialist content.

Byroade lectured the Egyptian Premier about the epidemic consequences of Communism once allowed in, while Nasser proclaimed himself confident of being able to handle his own domestic Communists so that they would gain no advantage from a Russian connection. It was true that Egyptian Communists were not united; of three factions, two (the Workers' Vanguard and *al-Riya*) were either currently led or had been founded by Egyptian Jews, while the third and much the largest group, the Democratic Movement for National Liberation, which had started out, unlike the others, supporting the Free Officers, had transformed itself into the United Egyptian Communist Party in complete opposition to Nasser just as he was thinking of turning to Moscow. During the first half of 1955 the colonel put 750 communist members behind bars.[36] 'The difficulty in dealing with this fellow', Byroade told Washington, 'is that he honestly agrees with our criticism [about the] dangers of Egypt's policies in the longer run, yet seems convinced he must move as he does in the short run.'

Having been told that the mission to Moscow had been deferred, the American Ambassador tried, in a series of increasingly frantic telegrams over the summer, to squeeze out of the Pentagon Nasser's (relatively) modest request for American arms. Eisenhower, casting a professional eye over the list, found that 'it did not represent a particularly potent military force'. On 2 July the President ruled that there should be a concerted effort to 'woo' Nasser. But while flattery of the Egyptian ruler went on apace – he had Dulles's 'full confidence', he was told, he had world stature as a man of peace, Egypt was entitled both by history and her present strength to be the leader of the Arab states – somehow this failed to translate itself into hardware. The Pentagon said it could supply most of the items on the list but appended a price-tag which was approximately the same as Egypt's entire, swiftly dwindling dollar reserve.[37]

On 15 August Byroade received an interesting visit from his opposite number in Washington, Ahmed Hussein, who, although an ex-Minister from royal times, was regularly consulted by Abdul Nasser during his lengthy and rather frequent trips home. Hussein now gave the American an extremely detailed impression of Nasser's conversation. Nasser had told him that he was 'in a real box'; he understood well enough the dangers of Soviet domination but, since Gaza, his fellow-officers on the Revolutionary Command Council and in the army as a whole had been desperate for arms, and word was getting out of the immense bounty that Dmitri Shepilov, the young editor of *Pravda* (who next year was to become Soviet Foreign Minister), had put on offer during his visit to Cairo the previous month. Shepilov had not only talked of 100 MiGs, 200 tanks and some Ilyushin jet bombers but had said that they could be paid for in cotton, Egypt's main export crop of which she possessed large unsold stocks. Once Egypt agreed, the weapons would start arriving in thirty days. Nor was this all. The Russians hinted too that the cotton could also be made to pay for them to build for Egypt a colossal multipurpose dam on the Nile at Aswan, in Upper Egypt near the Sudanese border, knowing that this monumental project was near the top of the Free Officers' civil programme. Egypt would not have to choose between economic and military expenditure. Thanks to Russia, she could have both arms and the dam.

Ahmed Hussein said he had urged Nasser to scrap the military regime at once and not wait until next January to install a regular and broader government. In the meantime he appealed to Byroade to think of some dramatic turn in American policy that would enable the Egyptian Prime Minister to marshal sufficient support to turn down the Soviet offers.[38]

In the early evening of 19 September, just as British and American Alpha-makers were preparing to sit down in Whitehall to plot the course of peace through Nasser, the State Department in Washington received a most urgent cable from Cairo. Egyptian acceptance of a Soviet arms offer was probable, perhaps even the following day. The Soviet offer was 'said to be almost embarrassing in size'. Under Secretary Hoover instantly suggested to Byroade that Egyptians be warned of the likely severity of American reactions, to which Byroade replied that they had been told that so often that further repetition would be useless. On 21 September he reported that, 'Late last night we were told by [a] highly reliable source that Egypt's arms deal with Russia was now definitely decided', at which point the conversation was interrupted by other persons breaking in. Tipped off by his American colleague, Trevelyan the same day informed London.[39]

The news caused the utmost alarm and consternation in both capitals. If true, it meant an end to the idea of arms control in the Middle East (or, alternatively and for some people even worse, the acceptance of Soviet Russia, which Eden seemed to favour but Macmillan and Dulles did not, into the charmed circle of arms-controllers). As F. E. Erasmus, the South African Minister of Defence, was to put it shortly afterwards, it also looked as if the plan to defend the African continent along the Northern Tier in Asia had already been leap-frogged by the potential foe. Harold Macmillan cabled Dulles to say: 'This cannot be allowed to go on.'[40] Dulles's first thought was to worry what the Israelis would do. He feared a pre-emptive strike in a mood of desperation before the arms were delivered.

The shock-effect in the Foreign Office, as the incoming reports made clear that Nasser had passed the point of no-return, produced a series of high-level official memoranda. In a note to Macmillan, Shuckburgh asked himself if it were possible to write off Egypt and build Britain's position on an alignment with Israel or, alternatively, with other Arab states. The answer was 'No'. If with Israel, Britain would lose the whole Arab world, which meant she would lose the oil. If with other Arabs, Egypt would pose as the most fanatical anti-Israeli, anti-imperialist state and would be 'irresistible to all Arabs'. Consequently, 'we must somehow keep Egypt on our side even to the extent of paying a very high price which may well include having to abandon Israel'. If Russia were to be active in the Middle East Britain must either outbid her or lose her main source of fuel. 'It has long been my firm belief', wrote Shuckburgh, 'that the continued support of Israel is incompatible with British interests.'

Shuckburgh's official superior, Sir Harold Caccia, who was Deputy Under-Secretary of State, added a minute agreeing with much of this desperate argumentation, but he was not sure that Britain need to go so far as the complete abandonment of Israel. 'Before we come to a final answer on price, we may have to get rid of Nasser, especially if he becomes publicly committed to the contract.'[41] That the contract was already sealed was made clear to Trevelyan by Abdul Hakim Amer, the War Minister and Commander-in-Chief. General Amer said that the Free Officers were strongly anti-communist but they had got nothing from the Americans and had made use of the Russians as the British had done in 1941.[42]

On the evening of 26 September Humphrey Trevelyan, on urgent instructions, sought an immediate audience with the Egyptian Prime Minister. When Colonel Nasser received a message to this effect in the Revolutionary Command Building he was in the company of two of his old CIA friends, including Colonel 'Kim' Roosevelt. They had been with him for three and a half hours, filling him with 'prognostications ("speaking strictly unofficially and as an old friend") of what is in store for him', and, in between Nasser's outbursts about Egypt's ability to 'fight Israelis indefinitely on [a] guerrilla basis, with knives, etc.', apparently getting him to agree to their drafting for him a public statement in which he would 'soften the blow' by committing himself to reducing tensions with Israel. Repeatedly he asserted his desire to avoid war, his faith in John Foster Dulles and the absolute necessity, if he was to survive in office, of his having acquired the arms. In his subsequent cable to Allen Dulles, the CIA director, Roosevelt expressed his remaining conviction, attributed also to Henry Byroade and Eric Johnston, that 'Nasser remains our best, if not our only, hope here'.

Miles Copeland, who was present in the room with Roosevelt, describes in *The Game of Nations* how the two Americans and Nasser together watched the lights of Sir Humphrey's Bentley as it pulled out of the Embassy on the opposite bank of the Nile and worked its way across the bridge. The Americans advised Nasser to stress the technical truth that the deal had been made with Czechoslovakia – Israel's old supplier – rather than with Russia. Nasser informed Trevelyan that ten or twelve days before Egypt had signed a purely commercial transaction to bring her strength up to the level of Israel's. Egypt had been dominated by Britain for seventy years; there was no intention now of substituting Russian domination. Following the CIA advice he mentioned that Egypt had gone to Prague for the weapons but managed to mispronounce the word as 'brag' so that it was not understood.[43]

The following day (27 September) the Foreign Office's News Department released the news of the arms contract without notifying Nasser or warning Trevelyan. Scooped by the British, Nasser turned up unexpectedly at the opening of an army photographic exhibition and, in place of the conciliatory speech drafted by the Americans, made a violent one documenting his case with an authentic passage from a British intelligence report which blamed the Israelis for belligerence at Gaza and an unofficial and inaccurate French account of the quantity and variety of British military sales to Israel.[44]

The West in Shock

The Foreign Secretary was now in the United States for the opening of the UN General Assembly. On 26 September, with the deal not yet publicly confirmed, he and Dulles engaged in rather wild speculation. 'Nasser cannot have thought out all the consequences of his move', said Macmillan. 'We could tell him frankly that we cannot tolerate it ... The world will not allow the USSR to become the guardian of the Suez Canal. We could make life impossible for Nasser and ultimately bring about his fall.' This struck a chord with Dulles. 'We did not all work so hard to get a Suez base agreement in order to turn the base over to the Soviets,' he said, to which Macmillan quickly responded, 'We have not yet completed our withdrawal from the Suez base. If we had your support, we might call the whole thing off.'

The officials, Russell and Shuckburgh, tried to get their masters to focus on the chances of exploiting the arms deal to advance Alpha. 'I believe Israel would be more disposed now to make a settlement,' mused Dulles. 'She might give up a bigger slice of the Negev.'[45] On 30 September Harold Caccia sent a consensus of Foreign Office views to Macmillan. 'We do not consider', he said, 'that our main object should be to oust Nasser.' Three answers to the arms contract were suggested, two of them to be supplied by America: American adherence to the Baghdad Pact; the immediate provision by America of eighty Centurion tanks to Iraq, and a British announcement advising Sudan to proclaim her immediate independence (and therefore separation from Egypt). These measures, if snappily carried out in obvious response to Nasser's behaviour, might discredit the Egyptian Prime Minister to the point where he was thrown out by the Egyptians themselves. Nasser's wisdom in having first got rid of the monarchy was clearly displayed in the absence in these memoranda of any neat explanation of the mechanism by which a recalcitrant Egyptian government was to be toppled.

Caccia, however, did go on to speculate as to whom they were likely to get should Egyptians be induced to remove Nasser, on the assumption that, if Britain knew what she wanted, she could still influence the choice. 'We would prefer', he said, 'not to be faced by one military dictator after another in Egypt.' Some form of democratic regime would be best and, Caccia added mysteriously, 'the man who looks to us the best candidate has been mentioned in my separate message'. The first draft of this letter, preserved in the Public Record Office, shows that the name was the familiar one of the seventy-three-year-old Ali Maher, who had presented himself at every juncture of recent Egyptian history, including the 23 July revolution, as the man to be sent for, and who had been in 1940 the Prime Minister whom the British had found so unacceptable.[46]

With the arms deal now public property the Americans and British each passed through two radically different stages in their reaction. The first was all pressure and menace, with George Allen, a high-ranking State Department professional, being sent to Cairo to read the riot act. The American press sounded off in advance about the ferocious message that he would bring, but once in Cairo his fangs were drawn in advance by the ubiquitous Kim Roosevelt who persuaded him of the counterproductive effect of mere threats. Responding to Allen's now subdued manner Nasser was reported to be 'relaxed and obviously making [a] special effort to be friendly'. But his message was clear: Gaza had changed everything; the Americans had not been forthcoming with arms at prices he could afford; the French had cancelled a contract for political reasons; Herut, the Israeli opposition under Begin with his policy of naked aggression, had just doubled its representation in the Knesset and he would double it again in another election within a year.[47] In his turn, Trevelyan tried to convince the Egyptians that the arms deal was incompatible with the new Anglo-Egyptian Agreement. Nasser earnestly represented that he was trying to avoid having Soviet technicians permanently on Egyptian soil. The deal was a once-for-all affair to cope with a particular problem. He was quite capable of taking care of domestic Communists.

The West switched quite quickly to a second stage. 'So we shall have to live with it,' Macmillan told Eden. 'Our interest is not to represent it as a great diplomatic defeat but rather to try to minimise it.'[48] A somewhat artificial distinction came to be made in Whitehall between doing nothing to help Nasser personally and, on the other hand, taking up energetically long-term schemes that would show Britain's interest in the welfare of the Egyptian people long after Nasser would have left the scene. The main example of this was suitably dramatic: the plan, much favoured by the Free Officers and apparently spoken of by Shepilov, to undertake the largest civil engineering project in the world at Aswan, near the Sudan border. This, with an immense lake reservoir, would regulate the flow of the Nile, on whose caprices Egypt had always depended for her very existence, and provide as well a major generator of electricity and a source of irrigation. On being told by Dulles that the High Dam was only feasible with the aid of the World Bank, Macmillan noted, 'I am in favour of this matter being pursued in Washington without delay.'[49]

John Foster Dulles, whose attitudes towards the non-aligned were capable of being more relaxed and philosophical than his Manichaean image might suggest, told Macmillan that he was opposed to taking any threatening or drastic steps. 'Unpleasant events which we might instigate should have the appearance of happening naturally'; otherwise the entire Arab world might be aligned against the West. True, Nasser was trying to emulate Tito; but 'Egypt as a neutralist would be more tolerable than as a communist satellite'. Dulles then deployed his favourite thesis about what had been going on in the Soviet Union since the death of Stalin. 'Up to the time of [the] Geneva [Summit in July 1955], Soviet policy was based on intolerance which was the keynote of Soviet doctrine. Soviet policy is now based on tolerance which includes good relations with everyone and basically alters many other things.'

Among the many things that were so altered, in Dulles's estimation, was that, with Westerners exchanging visits and developing good relations with Moscow, it was impossible to object to other countries such as Egypt doing the same. In any case, American aid had become so widespread and was so burdensome to the donor that it was impossible to pre-empt the Russians whenever they might choose to concentrate their efforts on a particular country. The Americans were in favour of waiting to see how the Russians got on with their programme of military aid to Egypt; American experience suggested that they might find it more of a liability than an asset.[50]

The reactions of the West, at first so visibly upset by what Dulles and Macmillan now agreed to refer to as 'the Czechoslovak arms deal', seemed to have gone full circle. In the region itself things looked more clear-cut. In making the deal Nasser had crossed a rubicon. He had shown to the Arab world that he was not, as uncharitable critics had alleged, an American stooge, nor was he a traditional military dictator like the Syrian Shishakli. He possessed the nerve to defy the West and to sup with the devil. He could measure up to the Israelis whatever the West might say. This was the foundation of Nasser's success as a hero of the Arab nation. He was still not a particularly popular figure with the Egyptian masses but the process of becoming so had begun. However much traditional rulers might look askance at the company Abdul Nasser was keeping, nationalists everywhere were turning towards Cairo.

Israel's Countdown to War

For many Israelis the countdown to war had begun. Dulles was told by Abba Eban, the immensely fluent and energetic Israeli Ambassador both to Washington and to the UN, that the general reaction was 'Let's not sit here like a rabbit waiting for the kill.'[51] According to Israeli intelligence, Nasser would have 300 medium and heavy tanks of the latest Soviet type, 200 MiG 15 jet fighters and 50 Ilyushin bombers which could bring destruction and death to cities like Tel Aviv and Haifa. There were also large quantities of anti-tank guns, anti-aircraft guns and supporting material. In Moshe Dayan's opinion it would take the Egyptians six to eight months to absorb these weapons, after which they would effectively wipe out the advantage Israel had hitherto enjoyed in quality.[52] The Chief of Army Intelligence,

Colonel Yehoshafat Harkabi, thought differently – that the Egyptians would take far longer to gain any competence with their new weapons.[53] But it was Dayan's time-frame that governed the policy recommendations of the Ministry of Defence. He, as Dulles had foreseen, wanted pre-emptive action at once.

As was frequently to happen in Israel, where the whole country votes as one constituency with many competing party lists and near-perfect proportional representation, a long pause occurred between the election of the Third Knesset at the end of July and the formation of a new coalition government on 2 November. In the meantime Moshe Sharett carried on, knowing that Ben-Gurion would shortly again take over the premiership. In a last bid to avoid another war Sharett made a circuit of the 'Big Four' Foreign Ministers who were assembling for the Foreign Ministers' conference at Geneva. From the three western Ministers he pleaded for arms to match those now possessed by Egypt as the only way of preserving peace. From Dulles and Macmillan he got little change. Dulles told him sharply that the United States would not stand for a preventive attack by Israel. Since it was his view that Israel was bound to be the loser in any unrestrained arms race, she should learn to rely on the Tripartite Declaration for her security. Macmillan said that the Israeli Government should be thinking about the concessions it could make to bring about a peace settlement. Only with Edgar Faure, the Prime Minister of France, whom Sharett saw in Paris in the last stages of tiredness after a punishing day at the Palais Bourbon, was the story different. The weary Faure cut short the long harangue on which Sharett was just beginning with the disarming remark that Israel's arms request would be granted.[54]

On 2 November Ben-Gurion was confirmed in office as Prime Minister and Minister of Defence. Already on 23 October he had ordered Dayan to start preparing a plan for a major operation in Sinai. The aims would be both to capture the Gaza Strip and also to uncork the bottle of the Red Sea by taking Sharm al-Sheikh, the southernmost point in Sinai, and the two islands controlling the entrance into the Gulf of Aqaba and thus access to the new port which the Israelis had now begun building at Eilat.[55]

Egypt had determined that the blockade of Israel was to be strictly enforced in the Egyptian waters of the Straits of Tiran. Foreign ships using these waters must notify their times and destination in advance. On the shore at Ras Nasrani, opposite the island of Tiran, Egyptian artillery was mounted, to be aimed at any non-complying vessel. To Israel's huge disappointment the maritime powers, after some talk of the rights of innocent passage, of using naval escorts and of taking a case to the International Court of Justice, decided to acquiesce. In a classic text of appeasement Harold Macmillan told the Commons: 'We are maintaining our legal position, but for practical purposes we have accepted [the] situation.'[56]

Israel had been served notice that, if she wanted to secure the use of Eilat, she was on her own.

Earlier in the year Dayan had sent six officers across the Egyptian border to undertake a ground reconnaissance of the very difficult terrain between Eilat and Sharm al-Sheikh. The white mountain landscape is of an astonishing, almost ethereal beauty, but the task of identifying faint and treacherous tracks that could with real determination be used by military vehicles was an arduous one. The party was landed by boat and later picked up by Piper Cub; they had managed to complete their work undetected.[57]

In mid-November (1955) British intelligence was reporting that the Israelis were intending to 'drive to Suez across Sinai in an endeavour to trap Egyptian forces, thereby causing Nasser's downfall'. These reports were in substance correct. On 10 November General Dayan recommended formally 'an early confrontation with the Egyptian regime, which is striving for the destruction of Israel, in order to bring about a change of regime or a change in its policy'. Although this was not like a reprisal raid, since the Gaza Strip and Straits of Tiran would be occupied and kept, the attack would be limited in that the whole of Sinai would not be occupied and there was no question of crossing the Suez Canal. It was Ben-Gurion who now hesitated. Being back at the top and having in any case a difficult coalition to handle, he was not ready to hold the whole world at defiance.

According to Colonel Mordechai Bar-On, who ran Dayan's office, Ben-Gurion 'very much apprehended the intervention of the powers, Great Britain in particular, should Israel take the initiative'. He abandoned the larger plan and on 5 December he submitted to the Cabinet a more limited scheme to seize the Straits of Tiran, but this was rejected by a majority of nine. He then addressed the entire High Command, giving three reasons against preventive war: a philosophical one – wars seldom end wars; a practical one – an Israeli aggression would bring about a total embargo on arms sales, and a fanciful one – the supposed British desire for military bases in the Negev, which had some basis in 1946–8 but none now, might prompt them to intervene on the side of the Arabs. The special unit that had been assembled for the operation was dispersed.[58] Ben-Gurion, anxious that the morale of his soldiers should not be affected, ordered a massive reprisal on the Syrians who had made minor attacks on Israeli fishing vessels on the Sea of Galilee, without causing casualties. The scale of the reprisal can be assessed by the fact that seventy-three Syrians were killed.[59]

Eden at the Guildhall

Anthony Eden was much exercised in his mind about Nasser, as well he might be considering the extent to which his personal reputation had become bound up with the policy of supporting him. In mid-October he called for an assessment from the British Ambassador of the Egyptian leader's personal position and of the potential opposition to him. Sir Humphrey Trevelyan's reply was categoric. 'There are at present no reliable signs of the regime losing its grip . . . or of its opponents gaining ground. On the contrary, the acceptance of Soviet arms has added to his prestige and given him, at least temporarily, what he had always lacked, a measure of personal popularity.' As for possible rivals, Neguib was a broken reed, Ali Maher never mentioned, Nahas lying low. Another military leader might turn out to be no different from Nasser.[60]

With this assessment in mind Eden decided to write a letter of reproach to be conveyed to Colonel Nasser. It went through many drafts. In one of these Nasser was to be reminded of the time when he 'took my hand in his and assured me that a new chapter had opened in our relations'. From that day forward, Nasser was to be told, Egypt had never ceased to attack Great Britain, the Egyptian press to call her 'the enemy' and to abuse her and her allies 'in and out of season with a vehemence worthy of the Kremlin'. 'If Nasser wishes to continue to denounce Britain and to oppose British policy on every occasion, let him say so,' the draft went on. 'If not, he should carry out his promises and he will not find us backward.' There was much anxious discussion about whether this letter should be sent until the decisive view was expressed by the Prime Minister's Private Secretary, Guy Millard. 'Would he listen? Should we not be making ourselves look rather silly? How would it look if it becomes public?' The message was not sent.[61] 'You should know', Macmillan was warned by his Permanent Under-Secretary, 'that the Prime Minister is much exercised about the Middle East and is in two minds, oscillating between fear of driving Nasser irrevocably into the Soviet camp and a desire to wring the necks of Egypt and Syria.'[62]

Once a year at the Guildhall the Prime Minister addresses the City of London, usually about some aspect of foreign affairs. On 9 November Eden used this occasion to lift the veil a little on Alpha. He made it public that he himself was available should his services as peacemaker between Arab states and Israel be required and he gave a broad hint of the basis on which peace might be made. 'The position today is that the Arabs take their stand on the 1947 and other UN resolutions,' he said. 'The Israelis, on the other hand, found themselves on the Armistice Agreement of 1949 and on the present territory they occupy. Between these two positions there is, of course, a wide gap, but is it so wide that no negotiation is possible to bridge it?'[63]

Interestingly enough, although the official Arab League position remained opposed to any recognition of partition, the speech was quite well received in Arab capitals. Nasser let it be known that, with the confidence of new strength, he was now willing to enter into serious confidential negotiations through intermediaries with Israel. Fawzi told Trevelyan that these must be indirect: the Egyptians would not have any proposed CIA-staged secret meeting between Nasser and Ben-Gurion or their representatives. But the wily Foreign Minister said again what he had said before: 'The iron is now red hot'. Macmillan told Eden not to rely too much on this. 'I only met Fawzi once and I thought him smooth and false. Perhaps he is a Liberal.'[64]

It was among the Israelis that the Guildhall speech created an explosion. The very idea of the 1947 boundaries retaining any legitimacy as part of an intended compromise was unthinkable. It reeked of the Bernadotte Plan. Ben-Gurion told the American Ambassador, 'it is an attempt to eliminate Israel'. If the British wanted to take Israel's territory away from her they would need to send troops to do it.[65] To the *New York Herald Tribune* he made it clear that this especially applied to the Negev. 'We are going to enter the period of solar power,' mused the old man. 'We have an endless supply in the Negev. We will desalt water and pump it over the Negev ...'

High Dam and 'Lucky Break'

In 1953 when Eugene Black, the American President of the World Bank, had first visited the Aswan site (where there already was, not far away, a small hydroelectric dam), his imagination had been fired by the scale and potential of the new scheme conceived by the Greek engineer Adrien Daninos. When eighteen months later the Bank was officially approached, the Free Officers had had a survey completed by a German combine, the Hochtief and Dortmund Union, a design picked, and a consortium, including British and French firms as well as the German combine, formed in the hope of taking on the immense task of completion. The Bank's experts reported that the scheme was technically sound and financially feasible.

It was for a dam 365 feet high and just over three miles long across the crest, with a reservoir able to store 45,890 billion cubic feet of water, which would be sufficient to regulate the flow of the Nile throughout the year. There would be a power house with an initial capacity of 720,000 kw which could later be doubled, a transmission line to Cairo, conversion of 700,000 acres to perennial irrigation and the reclamation and settlement of another 1.3 million acres. A large lake would be created (now known as Lake Nasser) and some 70,000 people, most of them on the Sudanese side of the border, would need to be resettled.

The Bank insisted that, for the country to benefit fully from the scheme, much more would have to be spent on ancillary works than the Germans had allowed for and a much larger fund would be needed to compensate the Sudanese. Whereas the Egyptians had reckoned the cost at £E241 million, the World Bank thought it would be necessary to make provision for £E470 million [$1.3 billion] of which £E333 million would be spent in the first ten years. Much of this, of course, would be spent in Egyptian currency, but Egypt would have a gap of $400 million in foreign exchange. The World Bank would be prepared to put up, on the basis of Egypt's creditworthiness, a loan of $200 million, which left no room for further large loans, so that the remaining $200 million would need to come as a gift from governments.[66]

On 20 October Sir Anthony Eden invited Winthrop Aldrich, the American Ambassador in London, to come to Number Ten on 'a matter of the greatest importance and urgency'. Less than a month after news of the arms deal, he told his visitor that the Russians had again offered to finance the dam. It was vital that the West prevent this from happening. There was no time to wait for the World Bank with its lengthy procedures. The European consortium was poised to go ahead at once, using suppliers' credits provided that Egypt's obligations were guaranteed by the western governments. But if Egypt defaulted in a big way, Britain might find herself at risk for far more than she could handle, well over a $100 million. Eden said he was turning urgently to the United States for help. The Americans were asked to square the World Bank so there would be no hard feelings if it were short-circuited, to promise to pump in enough aid to Egypt in future years so that she would not be liable to default, and to advise whether despite everything there was not some way that World Bank finance could be brought in later by the back door. The Prime Minister seemed to Aldrich to be quite obviously agitated and more than usually given to exaggeration.[67]

The idea of taking up the High Dam appealed to Dulles as a means of making it 'highly impractical for Egypt to switch to a Soviet and Satellite status', even though Nasser was beholden to the East for weapons. It never appealed in the same way to some of his powerful colleagues in Washington. George Humphrey, the Treasury Secretary, who was the only Cabinet member besides Dulles who had a warm personal relationship with the President, complained afterwards that Dulles 'used money as a tool of his trade. I just didn't like it at all.' In every meeting of the National Security Council at which Aswan was to come up he would growl that it was a complete betrayal of the free enterprise system. He was a consummate nay-sayer, any positive note from Dulles inviting from him contrapuntal gloom.

The British pushed hard and obtained negotiations in Washington with Humphrey and the Under Secretary of State, Herbert Hoover Jr, a man whose stiff bearing and very prominent hearing aid contributed to an impression of remoteness and lack of human warmth. 'It developed right away', said Humphrey, 'that this partnership affair with Britain – I asked them what basis it would be on and it was just what I thought: they'd take ten per cent and we'd take ninety per cent.'[68] The Eden proposals seemed to the Americans to show that Britain had not thought the matter through: the arithmetic did not add up; the existing consortium could on no account, without international competitive tendering, be backed by either the United States or the World Bank, nor would the British get away with treating a swifter release of Egypt's blocked sterling balances as their contribution.

The Americans would want real money or, as the British Ambassador, Sir Roger Makins, put it pithily, 'HMG cannot expect to get into the poker game unless they are willing to put up the ante.'[69]

Towards the end of November, Eden's enthusiasm for western sponsorship of the dam became ever more pressing. He had received intelligence reports of a most troubling nature. These represented the first of a stream of such reports attributed to a new and supposedly highly reliable source from within Prime Minister Nasser's immediate entourage, obtained by an agent code-named 'Lucky Break'. The information was supported by documents, including one entitled 'Popular Socialism'. The drift of the 'Lucky Break' material was that Nasser was far more under Soviet influence than had been supposed and that, in return for Soviet support for his ambitions, he was prepared to allow the Russians to play any role in the area that they chose.[70]

The impression that this made in Eden's circle can be gauged from the comments of the two Oxfordshire diarists, Evelyn Shuckburgh and William Clark. On 29 November Clark, a liberal internationalist with leanings towards the Third World, wrote, 'It is clear that Nasser has gone further than I had ever supposed towards a tie-up with the Communists. It is impossible to believe that we can go on supporting him in the long run.' 'He must go,' the Prime Minister's Press Secretary went on, as if writing of an impressive butler caught pinching the silver, 'though I feel sad about that as I liked him and would have thought him trustworthy. Can we find anyone as good, let alone better?'[71] Shuckburgh, perhaps because he had seen more MI6 reports than Clark, was more sceptical. On 28 November he wrote, 'It begins to look as if Nasser is even more unreliable than he seemed and may even be consciously handing over his country to Communism. But I do not quite believe it. I think he thinks himself supremely clever and is playing East off against West to the last moment.'[72]

The source of 'Lucky Break's' prolific information, which continued for at least another six months, remains uncertain. Nasser had surrounded himself with an eclectic group of advisers, whose views ranged from the political right to the political left. It seems likely that some right-wing person with that access found this way of expressing his alarm at the increasing influence of ideological rivals.

The immediate effect of this information was to strengthen Eden's eagerness to complete the arrangement for building the High Dam. In a dramatic cable to Eisenhower, who had hitherto been kept out of play because he was recovering from a heart attack, he declared, 'I hate to trouble you with this, but I am convinced that on our joint success in excluding the Russians from this contract may depend the future of Africa.' Eden referred to 'Lucky Break's' disturbing information which he was having passed over to the Americans and declared that, if the Egyptian delegation currently on its way to Washington returned empty-handed, 'I fear the Russians are certain to get the contract. Poland will act as stooge in this case, as Czechoslovakia did for the arms.'[73]

Herbert Hoover told the British Ambassador that he was indeed impressed by the 'Lucky Break' evidence of Nasser's slide to the left, but queried if it would not be better in that case to find an alternative to Nasser somewhere. If he was really lost to the West, the Dam should be a present for a successor.[74] This was a question to which Shuckburgh struggled to draft an answer. If it should be that Nasser is a communist puppet, Shuckburgh wrote, 'the right course would be to overthrow him rather than to offer him an immense and burdensome bribe'. In a passage which he deleted he went on: 'It looks very much as if the only possible ways of disrupting the present course of the Egyptian regime are: (i) the death of Nasser; (ii) a free hand to the Israelis.'[75]

Finally the answer was sent to Makins: 'We are afraid that Nasser, whether innocently or deliberately, is dangerously committed to the Communists. Consequently, we believe that it would be advantageous, in any event, to overthrow him if possible ... But we obviously cannot afford to hold everything up whilst we are considering this.'[76]

On 14 December the offer was made. The scheme was divided into two stages. For the first preparatory stage, the British and American Governments were to provide grants (the British share was £5.5 million) for foreign exchange costs, to be spent under World Bank supervision but not at World Bank cost since all its conditions, such as a final agreement between Egypt and Sudan, would not at that time have been met. The World Bank loan would be available in the subsequent phase, while Egypt was to undertake to 'allocate its [total] resources in a manner designed to assure high priority to the development, carrying on and completion of the High Dam'. The two Governments would, in addition, 'consider sympathetically' giving further support for the second stage 'in the light of conditions then existing and of progress and performance' during the first stage.[77] It was clear that there would have to be competitive tender and that the American money would have to come not, as Britain had hoped, from the Export–Import Bank, but from foreign aid funding which would require congressional support. While the early stages would be fully financed, subsequent ones would depend on British, American and World Bank judgements on the condition of the Egyptian economy. In Washington the Egyptian Finance Minister seemed very pleased with the offer, but the final decision on whether it should be accepted on these terms rested with Gamal Abdul Nasser alone.

5

Turning against Nasser

Egypt has stolen the public of Jordan and turned it against its own Government.
General John Bagot Glubb (Glubb Pasha), 28 November 1955.

He [Eden] was quite emphatic that Nasser must be got rid of. 'It is either him or us, don't forget that.'
Evelyn Shuckburgh, *Descent to Suez*, 12 March 1956.

When Sir Anthony Eden faced the new year, 1956, he had at last formed his own Cabinet. Harold Macmillan had finally been persuaded to move over to the Treasury after insisting that his rival, Rab Butler, who now became Lord Privy Seal and Leader of the House of Commons, should not be designated as Deputy Prime Minister. Although, as Macmillan told his biographer Alastair Horne, Eden had 'kept on sending me little notes, sometimes twenty a day, ringing me up all the time' while he was Foreign Secretary, he had enjoyed the job and did not relish the change.[1] To ensure that no high-ranking politician should split control of foreign policy with him again Eden promoted Selwyn Lloyd, who had devilled as his subordinate at the Foreign Office for three years and was a Cabinet Minister of only eight months' standing. He was to be the Foreign Secretary of Suez, though in relation to that crisis, Macmillan was to play a powerful and unsettling role.

Selwyn Lloyd was not and could not have been the complete lay figure he was sometimes made out to be. His rather pedestrian manner, his lack of verbal agility – it was once written of him that he was used to repeating prepositions like a stuck machine-gun – and a certain dogged gameness in face of adversity made it easy to dismiss him as no more than an average Tory member with a Service background (for a while, he used in politics his wartime rank of Brigadier). The son of a Welsh Liverpool dentist, brought up in a devoutly Methodist and strictly teetotal household, Selwyn Lloyd inherited some of his father's brusqueness of manner. 'He came', writes his biographer, D.R. Thorpe, 'from a background where people were honest and straight: therefore, when he was embroiled in a world where people told lies and put the knife in, he was completely out of his depth.'[2] He had a 'larky' sense of humour which did not go down well with the civil servants who worked for him.

The new Foreign Secretary was conscious of the rapidity of his promotion to head one of the most senior departments of state and, above all, of the fact that he owed everything to Eden. He was not likely to offer himself as a rival centre of power. He exasperated his officials by the incessant reference of daily decisions to the Prime Minister, prompting such remarks as 'It becomes daily more apparent that we have no Secretary of State.' Before the war, on the Northern circuit he had been a barrister of achievement rather than sparkle. Yet it should be remembered that he had shone as a first-class staff officer during the war and received repeated promotion. As a backbencher he had been the one member of a Royal Commission on Broadcasting stacked with members of the Establishment to come out with a well-argued minority report in favour of commercial television and had then pursued the matter to success within his party.

Unlike Eden himself or his own Minister of State, Anthony Nutting, Lloyd had not taken to foreign affairs from the start as if it were his predestined field. When Churchill offered him the post of Minister of State in 1951 he confessed that he did not really like 'abroad' or foreigners, that he had never been to a foreign country save in the army and had never listened to a foreign affairs debate in the House.[3] But three years at the Foreign Office and short tours at the Ministries of Supply and Defence had given him a certain familiarity with international issues and personalities. Eden thought he had a quick way with papers and a 'safe pair of hands'. His reputation had prospered most in New York, where he had attended the sessions of the General Assembly of the United Nations and had developed a good personal relationship with Dag Hammarskjöld, the Swedish Secretary-General, which showed to advantage during the severe strains which were to come.

Lloyd's political deputy at the Foreign Office, the lean and handsome Anthony Nutting, was the heir to a baronetcy. He was still only thirty-five years old, having enjoyed an irresistible rise through the ranks of organised Conservatism. Invalided out of the army, he had passed the rest of the war as a diplomat, acting for part of 1942 as Eden's Private Secretary and thus forming a link which was to be central to the rapid rise and eventual destruction of his political career. Entering the House in 1945 and following a spell as chairman of the Young Conservatives, he shot to the top as chairman of the National Union of Conservative and Unionist Associations in 1950 and of the Conservative National Executive Committee the following year. In 1951 Nutting had been made Foreign Under-Secretary and appeared, much more obviously than Selwyn Lloyd, to be the natural understudy to Anthony Eden. So much did his parliamentary performance seem to resemble that of the older man that *Punch* portrayed him as a glove puppet, labelled 'Eden's Eden'. Eden, moreover, stood by him when, in the autumn of 1955, personal gossip, fed by items in the New York gossip columns, caused him to be called back to London rather abruptly from the UN and created considerable political pressure for him to be moved from the Foreign Office.[4]

Lloyd and Nutting had, as their principal professional adviser, Sir Ivone Kirkpatrick, a small, immensely energetic and self-confident Irishman, who was, in the words of his biographer Sir Con O'Neill, 'probably the only man in the senior branch of his service with no university education or indeed any formal education after the age of seventeen'. He left school to join the army during World War I and, after being wounded, was sent to neutral Holland where he operated as a spymaster. He was lively company, quick-witted but intimidating. 'He was so sharp', says Sir Evelyn Shuckburgh, 'that he cut.' Sir Ivone took great pride in thinking, working and deciding very fast, 'perhaps too fast', adds O'Neill, himself no slouch. His minutes suggest that he took particular satisfaction from the spectacle of representatives of unsatisfactory smaller states departing from his presence with their tails between their legs.

An unusually large part of Kirkpatrick's official career had been spent in dealing with one country, Germany. He had been at the Berlin embassy during the whole of Hitler's peacetime rule, in charge of broadcasting to Germany during the Second World War, as High Commissioner there after it. He treated his latest Foreign Secretary with ill-concealed scorn. 'His only ambition is not to get into trouble,' he remarked dismissively of him in February 1956. He was to act in the Suez crisis as a personal adviser and draftsman for Eden. Unfortunately his background – his imperial pride, his fluent but high flown literary style, his absolute conviction that any apparent imitators of Hitler should be identified and stamped out shortly after birth – did not make him a cool counsellor for an edgy prime minister. Instead of counteracting Eden's temperament he served to feed his dubious historical analogies.[5]

Selwyn Lloyd's replacement at the Ministry of Defence was widely considered the most eccentric appointment of Eden's new team. A lawyer and a former courtier (to Edward VIII and the Nizam of Hyderabad), Sir Walter Monckton had been sent by Winston Churchill to the Ministry of Labour to keep industrial relations out of the headlines. He succeeded brilliantly, though at what economists subsequently reckoned was a heavy cost in inflationary settlements. By the end of 1955 Sir Walter was feeling very tired and demanded a less wearing occupation if he were to stay in politics. The Ministry of Defence was thought to qualify. Monckton subsequently lamented to the short, quick, witty but not very forceful airman who was now appointed to the new post of Chairman of the Chiefs of Staff Committee, Marshal of the RAF Sir William Dickson, that he should never have taken the job. 'I was told that Defence would be a piece of cake, a rest cure,' he was wont to lament.[6]

Opposing these men was a rejuvenated Labour leadership, the youngish Hugh Gaitskell, an economist and ex-public schoolboy, having taken over from a superannuated Clement Attlee. The new leader did not wait for the New Year recess to be over before moving in to challenge a maladroit Government right down the line including, to its surprise, on foreign policy. Since Gaitskell did not in the least share his own left-wing's distaste for the commitment to Nato, he directed his fire on policy towards the Middle East, against what he held to be the Government's appeasement of Nasser and against its persistent failure to arm Israel, especially with the Centurion tanks the Israelis particularly wanted. The Opposition Front Bench now not only presented the most pro-Israeli image of any British party in the eight years since the creation of that state, but in doing so it had the satisfaction of knowing that it was echoing unease at the Government's policy in many Conservative quarters.

The new Cabinet did nothing to enhance the position of its head, especially within his own party. Henry Fairlie, for instance, was writing at the end of December of 'the almost unbelievable series of mistakes which the Government has committed' and of the 'terrifying lack of authority at the top'. Much the most telling attack came in the *Daily Telegraph*, the favourite paper of many Conservatives, on 3 January 1956, in a signed article by its very reputable Deputy Editor, Donald McLachlan. He asked, 'Why are the men who triumphed at the polls last May now under a cloud of disfavour with their supporters?' By way of reply, McLachlan described 'a favourite gesture of the Prime Minister's which is sometimes recalled to illustrate this sense of disappointment. To emphasise a point he will clench one fist and smack the open palm of the other hand – but the smack is seldom heard.' The simile was to haunt Eden for the remainder of his term. The article went on to catalogue 'a whole series of changes of mind about Government policies, half-measures and postponement of decisions', mainly in the domestic sphere, but also touching briefly but woundingly on the Middle East, where observers had been dismayed by 'the clumsy courtship of unfriendly and fickle Arab statesmen'. The first international crisis this new reshuffled team had to face was Jordan.

Jordan Excretes the Pact

Following the Turkish state visit to Teheran in October (1955) with its high pressure salesmanship, the Shah of Persia had joined up as an additional member of the Baghdad Pact, in return for which Britain honoured his request to refer to his country in future as Iran. The next stop appeared to be Jordan, where the Turkish President, Celal Bayar, was booked to go in November. The Foreign Minister, Fatin Rüstü Zorlu, told the British Ambassador briskly that he was eager to 'play the hand together as we did in Teheran'[7] and sign up the young King Hussein, Abdullah's grandson, for what was in effect an anti-Nasser league. Eden and Macmillan, who were about to start promoting the Aswan High Dam, hesitated. These two ways at first seemed to them too crassly opposite, as long as Nasser had not definitely committed himself politically to the Soviet Union. 'I am somewhat apprehensive that the effect on Egypt of Jordan joining at this time might be unfortunate,' Eden wrote to Macmillan on 6 November. Dulles was also discouraging; if Jordan, a state bordering on Israel, joined, that would be a further obstacle to American membership of the Pact. As it was, Iran's accession seemed to be upsetting the Russians. 'It might be better to keep it a paper pact.'[8]

The Turks forged ahead. President Bayer and Zorlu visited Amman and came away with the news that they had brought Hussein to the edge of membership. It simply required a little extra push from the British to finish the job.[9] The successive messages which London was receiving, in terms of increasing urgency, from General Glubb contributed to the pressure. Glubb portrayed the rapid spread of Egyptian influence, immensely aided by Saudi gold which was corrupting everybody in sight, as an immediate challenge to Britain's position. 'The one ambition of the Egyptians', he said, 'is to dominate the Middle East and to this purpose it is essential for them to get rid of British and American influence.'[10] At the inaugural meeting of the Baghdad Pact's Council of Ministers on 21 and 22 November, Macmillan was thoroughly converted by the Turkish Premier, Menderes, and by Nuri to the view that Jordan must come in.[11]

Since the Jordanian King wanted a larger army (which would have to be paid for by the British Treasury), General Sir Gerald Templer, the Chief of the Imperial General Staff, was chosen to go to Amman to make an offer. He was a peppery general and very highly strung. 'A bundle of nerves, yet a strong character,' was Macmillan's judgement on first meeting him.[12] He did not readily sit still. A compulsive smoker, he had the habit of stubbing his cigarettes in a subordinate's sherry glass.

'Shouting and punching the table, making the tea cups and the coffee cups on it dance', according to a Jordanian eye-witness,[13] Sir Gerald Templer told the young monarch and his senior Ministers that, if Jordan did not decide now to take sides with her real friends, she would be risking her present regime and her very existence as an independent state. If she chose correctly there would be the extra battalions and tanks and the beginnings of a Jordanian air force. There would also be the renewal of the 'solemn undertaking to give immediate aid in the event of armed attack from any quarter'.[14]

The mission was a complete failure. The King wanted to sign a letter of intent to join, but his Ministers prevaricated. The three from the West Bank, whose tactics were orchestrated by Nasser's man Anwar Sadat who was installed in the Egyptian Embassy, demanded time to prepare public opinion and to consult Egypt. The Prime Minister, who was a Circassian, was not going to invite trouble for his own minority by imposing an unpopular policy. Templer kicked his heels for a number of days and then left, complaining that, 'The trouble is that none of them has got any bottom.'[15] He had probably been the wrong person to send; he certainly should not have been sent so hastily. Edward Fouracres, who was in charge of Information at the British Embassy, reported that his visit should have had months of preparation. As it was, public opinion on the West Bank was solidly against the Baghdad Pact while that on the East Bank, though less politically conscious, was preponderantly the same. The reason Fouracres gave was simple: pro-Pact arguments were all about the Russian menace whereas people wanted to hear about the Palestine problem and the refugees.[16]

General Templer did not leave unnoticed. Egyptian propaganda made great play of the rebuff of the celebrated victor of Malaya. Jordan slid rapidly towards chaos. Governments fell in quick succession, rioting and disorder filled the streets of the capital; the fragile state seemed in danger of collapse. Glubb eventually restored order but not as rapidly as had been confidently predicted. Over the turn of the year Major Ali Abu Nuwar, Hussein's chief aide-de-camp, was sent secretly by the King to see Abdul Nasser. Cairo Radio, alleging that Templer had used the threat of cutting off Jordan's British subsidy, had stated that Egypt, Saudi Arabia and Syria were prepared jointly to replace it. Now Nasser was told that the King wished to dismiss Glubb Pasha. If the British were to retaliate by ending the subsidy, would the three allies pay? Put on the spot, Nasser apparently replied, 'I disagree with the timing of your operation.' He proposed that the King postpone any such move until June at least, when the British evacuation of the Suez Canal Zone should be complete. As long as they had troops in the base, Ali Abu Nuwar remembers him saying, the British could rush them with great speed and effect into Jordan.[17]

Samir Rifai was appointed Prime Minister of Jordan on 9 January (1955), promising that his government would not 'participate or link up with any new alliances'. This had a notable calming effect. Eisenhower, the next day, noted in his diary: 'We tried to make the British see the danger of ... pressuring Jordan to join the Northern Tier Pact. They went blindly ahead and only recently have been suffering one of the most severe diplomatic defeats Britain has taken in many years.'[18]

The crisis over the Baghdad Pact served to emphasise what some Jordanians considered the supreme anomaly of their kingdom's excessive dependence on a foreign general who in many respects had gone native. Suleiman Nabulsi, an East Banker who had been Minister of Finance and Ambassador to London and who was now the most prominent of the nationalist admirers of Colonel Nasser, was offered a portfolio in Rifai's Cabinet. 'Glubb was in the Premier's office when I was invited to join the present Cabinet,' he said subsequently. 'Of course I refused. The trouble with Glubb is that he has been here too long . . . He knows the country better than we do. He has his personal policy which he will not give up.' 'The Emperor of Jordan', Nabulsi said on 15 January, 'must give up.'[19]

These sentiments were also those of the King, who, besides, had a number of specific complaints, the most important of which was his aversion to the tactical retreats from large sections of the West Bank which Glubb had recommended, on military grounds, in the event of Israeli attack. Probably because he was aware of how much his position was being undermined, in mid-January Glubb put forward to the British Government a remarkable new plan. Dated 'Amman, 18 January', it was the first of the fancy war scenarios of 1956, of which there were to be a number, and it supplied an answer to a problem that had just been ventilated in the conference of Middle East ambassadors that Selwyn Lloyd had convened on taking over the Foreign Office. On this occasion there was a consensus that, if Britain failed to take swift and effective steps to support an Arab country attacked by Israel, 'our credit in the Middle East would be irretrievably lost'. But the crucial additional question put (but not answered) was what should happen if 'following a preventive attack launched by Israel on Egypt, Jordan joined in on Egypt's behalf'.[20]

Glubb's answer was related to the terms of Eden's Guildhall speech. The British and Jordanians should work out a permanent borderline with Israel that would correspond to Eden's conception of a compromise. If the Israelis then struck at Egypt the Arab Legion would immediately advance into Israel, but only up to the prearranged line. British troops should be flown into Jordan in support of the Legion. On pain of British intervention Israel would then be called on to cease fire. The operation, its author confessed, 'is precarious but it is essential to discuss it fully'. Whitehall comment was that the Legion would be cut to pieces in an Israeli counter-attack; Eden's own reaction was that 'Glubb should be told this is quite unacceptable'.[21]

Glubb's scheme might be refused, but the problem remained. The British joint planners and the Chiefs of Staff Committee to which they reported devoted a surprising amount of time in 1954–56 to the prospect of war between Britain and Israel. On 26 January 1956 the Chiefs endorsed an elaborate operational plan for such a war called Operation *Cordage*, which provided for the 'neutralisation' of the Israeli air force, the imposition of a naval blockade, the 'punishment' of Israeli ground forces from the air, and commando raids at various points on the Israeli coast. Intensive attacks on military targets would be launched by carrier-based planes, while two Canberra bomber squadrons and five fighter/ground attack squadrons of the RAF, based on Cyprus, were to take out the airfields. Even so, the Arab Legion would be badly mauled and the Israelis would have occupied the line of the Jordan in two to three weeks. But six months' blockade was thought to be enough to convince them to 'withdraw and sue for peace'.[22]

A logical course, if an Israeli attack was really thought to be imminent, would have been to have staff talks between Egypt and Jordan. Humphrey Trevelyan did in fact suggest it, but as the Foreign Office replied to him, 'the Legion is still commanded by Glubb and has many British officers in it . . . But the Egyptians have declared Glubb to be "an enemy of the Arabs" . . . Glubb himself can hardly be expected to welcome such talks . . .'[23] The anomaly of Glubb's remaining where he was and indeed of Britain's bilateral obligation as a whole was becoming more apparent. The Pasha himself warned on 17 February that the young King had told him the day before that, if fighting began between Israel and either Egypt or Syria, he would immediately order the Arab Legion to attack Israel. Glubb's mortal enemy, Colonel Salaheddin Mustafa, the Egyptian Military Attaché, had been heard to boast how the British would be undone. Egypt, made the victim of Israeli attack, would invoke Jordanian aid. The British officers would refuse to act; 'Jordan, assisted by Egypt, will rise and destroy the British.' Glubb concluded: 'We are drifting towards disaster with no plan and no advice from HMG.'[24]

On 29 February King Hussein, who knew that his ADC, Major Ali Abu Nuwar had a coup against Glubb ready planned, asked him: 'Can you do it tomorrow?' Next morning the major reported that preparations had been completed. British officers' telephones had been cut; guard had been placed on their homes. The King went on cue to the Prime Minister's office: Samir Rifai (who was not in the plot) was ordered to dismiss Glubb immediately and have him out of the country in two hours.[25] The reason for this churlish procedure was the awe which the Pasha's personality and British backing created and the fear that, if he were to be given any longer, he would be able to rally substantial forces to his obedience.

By coincidence Selwyn Lloyd was dining on the evening of 1 March with Gamal Abdul Nasser in Cairo. He had returned to the Foreign Office to find the contradictions of British policy had become more strident: Alpha was still officially in play, the Aswan High Dam was to involve Britain in a £5.5 million gift to the Egyptian regime, yet Eden was speaking more and more as if Nasser were the enemy. There had been a significant exchange in the Cabinet on 22 February when Ministers had been startled to hear Selwyn Lloyd say in connection with Egyptian propaganda against British policies that it was not to be expected, if Egypt showed such hostility, that Britain should treat her as a friendly state and provide financial assistance towards the dam. On that occasion, Lloyd's colleagues had objected rather pointedly that they had thought that the aim of British policy over the dam was not to confer a favour on Nasser but to forestall the Russians.[26] Having failed to win Cabinet support for an invitation to Nasser to visit Britain, Lloyd arranged, as Eden had done the preceding year, to stop off at Cairo on the way to the Far East in the hope of clarifying his own mind about the Egyptian ruler.

The talks went quite well. Lloyd renewed Britain's support for the Aswan Dam. Nasser asked for the present membership of the Baghdad Pact to be frozen, in which case he would cease all attacks on it. Lloyd replied that he would have to consult other Pact members first.[27] Over dinner Nasser readily responded to Lloyd's invitation to tell the story of how he had overthrown the King and come to supreme power in Egypt. As he lovingly went into the details, he left the impression on his British listeners that he was first, last and always a professional conspirator. The news of Glubb's abrupt dismissal reached junior British officials of the party during dinner but they did not inform the Foreign Secretary till afterwards. During the night he was repeatedly on the phone to Eden, who attempted to persuade him to fly immediately to Amman to confront the King. Lloyd did not consider this a good idea but was convinced that Nasser had promoted the coup and during the dinner party had been aware of it. Apparently this was not so. Hussein's action had taken place some months before Nasser had expected it, and he only heard of it when Mohamed Heikal telephoned him in the morning. A resentful and weary Selwyn Lloyd presented himself for a farewell meeting to find himself being smoothly congratulated on a neat demonstration of British aplomb in arranging to have the inconvenient Pasha unseated.

Selwyn Lloyd's resentment and incoherence were unconcealed. Nasser, he reflected, had deteriorated since their first meeting three years before, when he had commented favourably on the personality of the colonel. 'He smiled a great deal more, for no apparent reason. He had lost the simplicity I had rather liked in 1953. He did not exactly condescend but he gave the impression that . . . he could do more harm to us than we could do to him.'[28]

With these unsettling thoughts Selwyn Lloyd moved on to Bahrein, where his motorcade was stoned by a football crowd just leaving the stadium. The slogans shouted were mainly directed at Sir Charles Belgrave, who, though a civilian had been, like Glubb, directly employed by the Ruler for a long time to make his government work. By the time Lloyd got to Karachi for a South-East Asia Treaty Foreign Ministers' meeting he was so visibly preoccupied with what was happening to Britain's traditional position in the Middle East that R. G. Casey of Australia offered to handle dossiers in which his colleague was showing little interest.[29]

Glubb Pasha, the Englishman on whom all Arabs doted, was a British newspaper reader's legend. His going, without warning, seemed like a notice to quit from the whole Middle East. The immediate reaction in Britain was even more anti-Eden than it was anti-Nasser. Bitter attacks on the Foreign Office appeared in the *Daily Mail* and the *News Chronicle*. Eden went around saying that he was 'utterly mystified by the whole event and wonders if the King of Jordan has brainstorms like his father'. It was a crisis, too, that coincided with the breakdown of the attempt to agree with Archbishop Makarios over a constitutional settlement for Cyprus, the one place in the Middle East where British troops could be firmly anchored in British soil. It also coincided with a serious misunderstanding with France over the Middle East. According to William Clark's diary, rumours of the Prime Minister's collapse were to be heard on all sides. Randolph Churchill (who had always begged his father not to hand the country over to Eden) wrote in Lord Beaverbrook's *Evening Standard*: 'I was told that the Prime Minister was doing his best. I do not doubt it. And that is why I am sure there has got to be, and quickly, a change at 10 Downing Street.'

Accounts of Eden's handling of this crisis leave an impression of a man overwrought and unsure of himself. His ex-secretary, Evelyn Shuckburgh, who had been present at the crucial Chequers meetings on 3 and 4 March, jotted down on 7 March, 'He seems to be completely disintegrated – petulant, irrelevant, provocative at the same time as being weak. Poor England, we are in total disarray.' The following day Shuckburgh noted, 'Today both we and the Americans really gave up hope of Nasser and began to look around for means of destroying him.'[30]

The Prime Minister was reaching for some decisive act – breakoff of the treaty with Jordan, reversal of the evacuation of the Suez Canal Zone which was not yet complete, landing of troops in Bahrein, entry of the United States into the Baghdad Pact – while addressing a stream of telegrams to the King of Jordan. None of these moves was made. Eisenhower declined the umpteenth invitation to join the Pact. Although Lord Salisbury, the Lord President of the Council, and Rab Butler among senior Ministers favoured a clean break with Amman, which would at least have the merit of relieving Britain of the bilateral obligation to fight Israel, Harold Macmillan took a firm and decisive stand against writing off traditional British influence in Jordan. Glubb, who was now back in London, advised, 'Do not pull out . . . Stop sending telegrams and let the dust settle down.'[31]

Exhausted physically and extremely tense, Anthony Eden on 7 March faced the House of Commons at the conclusion of a debate on the Middle East. Only too aware that he had little to say, he made the mistake of becoming engaged from the outset of his speech in petty debating points, in one case against a little-known Labour politician who was no longer even in the House. 'Somehow it was unreal, a nightmare,' wrote William Clark.[32] The Prime Minister suffered what was for a British politician the worst of disasters: he lost his temper and lost the House. Still, he refused to give up Jordan and he dug himself in even more emphatically than before behind the Tripartite Declaration. 'I do not consider that [the Declaration] is a light engagement that we have to carry . . .' he said. 'It is very serious indeed for the people of this country.'[33] A few days later he was able to make a decisive move: he had Archbishop Makarios III of Justinia Nova and All Cyprus arrested and deported to the Seychelles.

The strains of the terrible weekend that followed Glubb's dismissal immensely hardened Eden's attitude to Nasser. It is true that Glubb in

London took a broadminded view of his fate, considered his quarrel with the King to be purely personal and generational and urged that support continue to be given to Jordan.[34] Nevertheless, if one wished to make a case for Egyptian conspiracy against British interests, it could be constructed exclusively out of Glubb's own cables during the preceding six months. Shuckburgh describes Eden at this time as 'violently anti-Nasser, whom he compares to Mussolini'. In Lloyd's absence, Nutting was busy feeding the Prime Minister with anti-Nasser material to use in prodding the Foreign Secretary into more effective lobbying of Foster Dulles in Karachi. Nutting himself cabled his chief, 'This may be unwelcome to Americans but the fact remains that appeasement has not paid.'[35] On 12 March, when there was more news of trouble in Bahrein, Eden was quite emphatic that Nasser must be got rid of. 'It is either him or us, don't forget that,' he said.[36]

From Alpha to Omega

Having backed for a whole year the efforts to get Alpha off the ground, Eisenhower decided to see if it really had any future by sending an especially trusted envoy in great secrecy to the Middle East to sound out both sides on the prospects of peace. It was an affair of Allen Dulles as much as of his brother, Foster; all arrangements for Operation Gamma were in the hands of the CIA.[37] The envoy chosen was a Texan called Robert Anderson, who had been Secretary of the Navy and Deputy Secretary of Defense, but at the beginning of 1956 was in private life. 'My confidence in him is such', the President wrote in his diary when he had not quite decided that he was going to run for a second term, 'that at the moment I feel nothing could give me greater satisfaction than to believe that, next January 20, I could turn over this office to his hands. His capacity is unlimited and his dedication to this country is complete.'[38] In 1987 Robert Anderson was sent to prison for tax evasion and illegal banking in the Caribbean.[39]

In January and again in March Anderson went *sub rosa* to the Middle East armed with wide powers as a plenipotentiary, conferring several times each with Nasser and Ben-Gurion, imposing on their understanding the additional strain of his unfathomable Texan accent and operating a shuttle between them. When Eden and Lloyd came over to Washington to confer with Eisenhower and Dulles at the very end of January, Anderson had not yet reached any firm conclusions. The Americans were therefore very tentative. Eden, too, in these days before Glubb's dismissal, seemed very much in two minds, saying that Nasser had limitless ambitions and that he did not know how long they could go along with him. To this Dulles observed that they might soon know whether their whole attitude towards Nasser would have to change.[40]

It was the end of March before Anderson presented his final report.

Nasser had said he was ready to make peace, after which 'Israel would be treated like any other country', but there were two serious questions: refugees and 'territorial continuity'. Ben-Gurion knew how to trump this peace offer: he proposed direct talks between him and Nasser. But to this Nasser would never agree. 'Four times', said Anderson to Ben-Gurion, 'Nasser mentioned the murder of Abdullah and said: "I cannot stake myself and my government on this game." '[41] From the outset Anderson and Nasser never truly communicated, though Nasser told Byroade that he was 'much impressed' with the special envoy. The main trouble was that they were working to completely different timetables. Anderson's was propelled by awareness of Zionist pressure, whose intensity was related to the (inaccurate) estimate that the Egyptian armed forces would have absorbed their new weapons by June or shortly thereafter and to the American election calendar. 'It is quite unrealistic to believe that this situation can be maintained in status quo for a period of months, either three or six,' Allen Dulles wrote on 29 January. 'Before then Israel will either have moved to destroy Nas[se]r or pressures for resumption of arms shipments to Israel will have become so impelling as to be irresistible.'[42]

Assuming that Nasser wanted a settlement in the first place (an assumption that was challenged by Israelis at every turn, notwithstanding Ben-Gurion's statement to Anderson that, 'If only [Nasser and I] could meet, I know there would be peace in ten days'), the Egyptian Premier's main preoccupation was the difficulty of selling a 'reasonable' settlement to other Arab rulers. Nasser asked for plenty of time in which, first, there would be American probes to establish a basis for agreement, and then steps to change the atmosphere to one in which a favourable response might be expected from the Arab states. In the meantime the settlement could be worked out in detail. Only then would Nasser set to work on his job of 'Arab leadership'.

The Americans tried conscientiously to go along with this schedule. In February they produced an eight-step timetable, in which the UN was allotted a major instrumental role in purifying the atmosphere. The UN, they told Ali Sabri (the Director of Nasser's Political Office who was handling most of the details for him), 'would not be informed in any way of the existence of secret preparations for a settlement but would be "used" by the United States in concert with Nasser . . .' to ease tensions.[43] This was not likely to be, even at the best of times, a very rapid process, but the Americans were prepared to make a gallant effort to fit it into their own constricted timetable. It seemed to Nasser that the Americans simply failed to understand the magnitude of the task he would be undertaking. He was, he said on 18 February, 'deeply concerned' at the apparent belief that the whole thing could be settled quickly.[44]

On 24 February John Foster Dulles was given a sharp reminder of the domestic political dimensions of his problem when he appeared before a public hearing of the Senate Foreign Relations Committee and was subjected to several hours of questioning. Much of it, from such pro-Zionist Democrats as Wayne Morse of Oregon and Hubert Humphrey of Minnesota, was of a hostile or sardonic nature. The Secretary had to defend his policy of not selling planes and tanks to Israel and not entering into a security pact with her while at the same time shipping tanks to Egypt's ally Saudi Arabia, which, it had to be admitted under interrogation, was an absolute monarchy with an absolute detestation of Jews.[45] Dulles stuck doggedly to his argument that an arms race was a hopeless proposition for a small state like Israel; she should rely rather on the UN and the Tripartite Declaration. To the Democrats, some of whom were openly derisive, he pitched a memorable appeal. 'Our difficulty', he said, '... derives very largely from the fact that the Arabs believe that the United States, when it confronts problems which relate to Israel, is in the last analysis dominated by domestic political considerations.' He therefore expressed the fervent hope that 'in the pending political campaign the discussion will be on such a level as to dissipate the idea'.[46] Before he went abroad in early March, remembering what General Marshall had had to put up with in 1948, Dulles felt it necessary to tell Eisenhower, in the presence of the Chief of the White House Staff, that he hoped there would be no White House pressure in his absence to make arms available to Israel.[47]

When the American Ambassador in Tel Aviv, Edward Lawson, saw Ben-Gurion for the first time after Dulles's testimony he thought he had never found him 'so emphatic, forceful or so emotionally upset and, on several occasions, so near to tears'. 'None of us would be living', the Israeli Premier said, 'if Israel had relied on the UN in 1948.' Egyptian bombers were only ten minutes away from Tel Aviv and Haifa. The best way to ensure peace was to let Israel have arms. Deterrence was, after all, the principle of Nato. On 2 March, in a bitter dressing down of the Israeli Ambassador, Abba Eban, Dulles complained of 'the political campaign being waged by the Israelis against the Administration ... the paid advertisements, the mass meetings, the resolutions, the demands of Zionist organisations, the veiled threats of domestic political reprisals ...'[48]

However obliging Nasser might or might not be in general – and in February he did sign a secret letter to Eisenhower pledging himself to the peace process[49] – Anderson's mission was doomed, just as Alpha had always been, by the complete unpreparedness of Ben-Gurion or for that matter Sharett to consider for a moment Nasser's two sticking points – territorial continuity and the right of return for the Palestinian refugees. Nonetheless, for Anderson the main disillusionment occurred on 5 March in Cairo when he discovered that, even if a peace plan were to be agreed in secret, Nasser was not after all willing to propose it as his own idea. This was not at all what Americans had meant when they had talked continuously about Egypt assuming the position of leadership in the Arab world.[50] It was this thought that predominated when Anderson came to report to his President.

Eisenhower wrote in his diary after debriefing his envoy that, while Israeli officials were 'completely adamant in their attitude of making no concession whatsoever in order to obtain peace', it was Nasser who in his opinion had proved to be the 'complete stumbling block'. Because he wanted to be the most popular man in all the Arab world, he had to take into account public opinion in each of the Arab countries. 'The result is that he finally concludes he should take no action whatsoever – rather he should just make speeches, all of which must breathe defiance of Israel.'[51]

On paper it would seem that by the end of March London and Washington had made rather similar adjustments to their policies. At the January summit they had both been agnostic about Nasser and both frustrated by him. During March they had both moved to what in the Foreign Office was called 'the new doctrine' and in the State Department's memorandum to the White House of 28 March was labelled Omega. The memorandum containing the new doctrine drawn up by Nutting and officials has still not been released, although Nutting refers to it in his account of Suez called *No End of a Lesson*.[52] The Omega Memorandum has. The Nutting draft proposed to shift the main burden of peace-making onto the UN, thus releasing British policy from its captivity to Nasser's whims, and to concentrate rewards, in economic and military aid, on Britain's genuine Arab friends. There would no longer be any overriding instruction to give priority to Alpha, though any development helpful to peace would be encouraged on its own merits. One can infer, both from the fact that the document has not been made public and from later cross-references, that covert action against Nasser was discussed.

It was significant of the edgy nature of the mood in Downing Street that Eden blew up on the open telephone line to Nutting at the Savoy Hotel over Nutting's use in his memorandum of the phrase 'neutralising Nasser'. Eden did not want him neutralised. 'I want him ——ed'. In his book (published in 1967) Nutting said the word used was 'destroyed'. Later, in 1986, he would say that in fact it was 'murdered'.[53]

The Omega Memorandum contains nothing so dramatic. Yet in its way it is as decisive a document. The primary purpose, as Dulles wrote, was 'to let Colonel Nasser realize that he cannot co-operate as he is doing with the Soviet Union and at the same time enjoy most-favoured-nation treatment from the United States'. Any open break should be avoided and Nasser must be left a bridge back to good relations with the West should he so desire. There then followed an action list to be co-ordinated with Britain: current negotiations on the High Aswan Dam were to languish, arms shipments to Egypt were to be denied export licenses and action held up even on requests for food and other humanitarian aid. Iraq was to be given a powerful radio station to counter Nasser's propaganda, Britain to be encouraged to hang on to her bilateral relationship with Jordan, and

American support (but still not membership) of the Baghdad Pact to be upgraded. Though American arms were still not to be supplied directly to Israel, Canada and France were now to be encouraged to send some modern weapons. (Canada later grumbled about the way she was being used as a surrogate and in the end withdrew her offer; France vastly exceeded the amount that was agreed.)[54]

But the greatest emphasis in this important set of decisions (and the pebble in the shoe of Anglo-American co-ordination) was on the need to build up King Saud of Saudi Arabia as an opposite pole to Nasser in the Arab world. This raised again the vexed issue of the villages around the oasis of Buraimi, which ran in counterpoint to the Suez story and was afterwards regarded by the Americans as a paradigm of Eden's 'colonialist' behaviour. Buraimi had been described by Dulles at the Washington conference in January as the most difficult difference between the two countries. It led Eisenhower to burst out in exasperation that 'surely the British would not maintain that every mile in every borderline in the whole area would be a matter of British prestige'.[55]

What had happened over Buraimi the previous September had been that international arbitration over the fate of the eight villages, proceedings which the Americans had been happily congratulating themselves on bringing the Saudis at long last to accept, had been thrown over suddenly, completely and, in the end, violently by the British. When British officials learnt to their astonishment that their preliminary plea of wholesale Saudi bribery was about to fail, the British arbitrator abruptly resigned, prompting the Belgian president to do the same, thus throwing the whole process into confusion. Britain then declared the arbitration broken off and stubbornly refused to resume it.[56]

One month later, on 26 October (1955), by Eden's personal decision, military force was used. A scratch unit of Trucial Levies led by the British ejected the fifteen armed policemen with whom Saudi Arabia was currently occupying the disputed oasis. The Prime Minister had decided that the Americans were, for their own good, not to be warned in advance. 'We cannot', he told them afterwards, 'allow this primitive, irresponsible and expansionist power to seize control of sources from which we draw an essential part of our fuel.'[57]

One main result of the long Anglo-Saudi estrangement over Buraimi was that Saudi gold, in large quantities, was available for purposes broadly parallel to Nasser's in Jordan and elsewhere. Since the ample supplies of gold originated with Aramco, the British blamed American money for 'being spent on a vast scale to promote Communism in the Middle East', as Harold Macmillan put it.[58] The United States resolutely refused to act as though King Saud was a lost cause for the West. To the contrary, it was to be part of the new Omega programme that a new American air base agreement was to be promptly concluded with the King and that in return some of his military needs should be met at once. The British had to be told that a 'generous agreement' was expected of them on Buraimi.[59]

The White House meeting on 28 March did not confine itself to discussing diplomatic moves against Egypt. Dulles brought also a list of enforcement measures should they be needed. Planning for 'possibly more drastic action' was ordered, though the specifics were deleted when the Omega Memorandum was declassified. To implement the new policy the 'Omega Group', an inter-agency task force, was set up under Raymond Hare, who was presently to replace Henry Byroade as Ambassador to Cairo.

Leaving aside the special case of Buraimi, Anglo-American relations over the Middle East presented something of a paradox in the first part of 1956. Their policies had each described roughly the same parabola; yet in Washington there was a definable sense of unease and lack of harmony. Dulles expressed it best on 27 March when he spoke to Lester Pearson, the experienced External Affairs Minister of Canada, about 'the rather jittery attitude' shown by the British. They were doing a number of things rather hurriedly and without prior consultation such as the seizure of Buraimi, the bid to put Jordan into the Baghdad Pact and the exiling of Makarios. Pearson sympathised. He was particularly worried, he said, about Eden. He was not reacting very well to the strains and pressures of the present situation. Dulles noted that Pearson referred to the fact that Eden's father had been 'quite eccentric'.[60]

The same sense of lurching had hit the British Embassy in Cairo. In April the Ambassador, Humphrey Trevelyan, was alarmed at the flood of reports reaching him of a change of tone and direction of British policy resulting in American demurrers. An anti-Nasser drive was 'quite impossible unless we have not only full American support but active American co-operation in a joint policy'. He was much put out on hearing 'the loose talk in Whitehall' which the Treasury's representative, Frederic Milner, brought with him to Cairo. 'High officials in the Treasury particularly seem to have been very free with their proposals on what to do with Nasser, which included the most extreme solutions', he complained. 'Milner has been asked to keep his mouth shut tight here.'[61]

The question of a joint policy between Britain and the United States came up at a meeting Dulles held with Democratic and Republican leaders of Congress on 10 April. 'We believe that unless and until we can bring the UK around to our view', he told them bluntly, 'it would be a mistake to identify ourselves too closely with them in the Near East.' The British had made a number of mistakes in the area. 'They are in a state of undeclared war with Saudi Arabia. In Jordan the British went ahead against our advice ... Moreover in Egypt the British have very bad relations with Nasser.'[62] Quite evidently, despite Omega, Dulles did not wish American policy to be characterised in that fashion.

Agents of the British special intelligence service MI6 were taking up extreme positions on the subject of Nasser that had their CIA colleagues worried. On 1 April the CIA's Major Wilbur C. Eveland, who had been operating mainly from Beirut and Damascus and who with a colleague from Cairo had been taking part in London in several days of talks with MI6, cabled at length to Allen Dulles about the picture disclosed of the new British position. Conveyed by George Kennedy Young, the deputy MI6 director, and based mainly on six months of the 'Lucky Break' material, this reassessment portrayed Nasser as having accepted full-scale collaboration with the Soviet Union, and as being prepared to allow the Russians whatever role they wanted in order to ensure himself of support for his aims. These aims were defined as nothing less than the total destruction of Israel, complete domination of all Arab governments and the elimination of all western positions in the Arab world. Egypt must therefore from now on be regarded as an out-and-out Soviet instrument.[63]

There was a sweeping and absolute quality about this analysis that grated on the American agents and was not borne out by their own sources. MI6 was not modest in its approach. 'The cream of the take', they were represented as saying, had been passed to the CIA for months past. Some of it indeed had been attached to a 'most secret note of Egyptian intentions, of whose authenticity we are entirely satisfied' and which portrayed the Egyptians plotting the overthrow of every single Arab monarchy by means of intelligence agents disguised as educators with the ultimate aim of forming a United Arab States. This had been passed on direct from Eden to Eisenhower on 15 March.[64] The time had now come for the Americans to stop making belittling remarks and to say decisively whether they accepted these reports or found them 'phoney'. If the latter, what evidence did the CIA have for a different view of Nasser?

In his book *Ropes of Sand*, Eveland says that Young actually stood over him when he was drafting his cable to ensure that direct quotes attributed to MI6 appeared in the text. 'Britain is now prepared to fight its last battle', the British had said. 'No matter what the cost we will win.' MI6 had not been prepared at that stage to hand over details of the covert operations that it had in mind but its officials had mapped out a sequence. First, Syria's government must be overthrown. The primacy of Syria could be explained by the extremely fragile nature of her institutions and the fierce competition between Communists, Ba'thist, Nasserites and pro-Iraqi factions to take over. Young and his colleagues were confident of being able to bring this off alone, but if necessary they would bring in Iraq and Turkey. Next MI6 was interested, with Iraqi help, in exploiting splits in the royal family of Saudi Arabia to hasten the fall of King Saud.

Violent reaction of some sort was to be anticipated from Nasser to these initiatives. British response would be proportionate, ranging from sanctions intended to isolate him to the use of force to bring him down. Apparently from the CIA text it appears that the British visualised the use of both

British and Israeli forces for that purpose, although nothing is said about any possible co-ordination between the two. 'Special operations' by Israelis against newly acquired Egyptian planes, tanks and ammunition as well as an 'outright attack' on Gaza were contemplated as 'extreme possibilities'. The Israelis were also mentioned in connection with Syria, though so far, Young stipulated, only in terms of discussion with them, not yet with a view to enlisting their positive support.

Until it came to coping with Egyptian reaction the Americans, so it would appear, would only be asked to play a supporting role and the British, if necessary, would go ahead without them. But dealing with Nasser under these circumstances might be rather a different matter and British plans would depend on how far the Americans could be counted on. Specifically, Britain must face the possibility that Nasser might close the Suez Canal and she would like to know how the United States would react to that.[65]

Reflecting six months later, at the height of the Suez crisis, on the reasons for the parlous state of the alliance, Winthrop Aldrich, the American Ambassador in London, reminded Dulles that 'last spring' the British had proposed 'a number of immoderate and obviously impractical courses of Western counter-action'.[66] All the British advice was not, however, unwelcome. Allen Dulles, it seems clear, was considerably interested in the idea of a coup in Syria, though not at such a breakneck speed as MI6 had proposed. Work on that front went ahead throughout the summer and into the autumn of 1956. When co-ordination between Britain and the United States had reached vanishing point over Egypt, the CIA was in close touch with what MI6 and the Iraqis were plotting to do about Syria and was even supplying money to finance it. The deadline for Operation *Straggle* was several times postponed. It was finally fixed for, of all times, the night of 29 October 1956.[67]

Teeth for Tripartite Declaration

Joint American and British staff talks in Washington on what the two powers were to do under the Tripartite Declaration, should the *casus foederis* arise, were set in motion at Eden's talks with Eisenhower at the end of January. Maurice Couve de Murville, the French Ambassador and a future prime minister, was, as a matter of form, allowed in for the accompanying political talks, but, on the military side, the Americans kept their French colleagues well out of the way.[68] The task that the staffs faced was a very delicate one, since they were supposed to simulate western military intervention both on the Arab side and on the side of Israel. The Declaration was repeatedly confirmed in public as proof to the Israelis that, if attacked, they would get such powerful support that there was no necessity for them to purchase arms. In private it had always been assumed that the Israelis were the likely aggressor.

On the American side, Admiral Arthur Radford, the intellectually gifted but restlessly activist chairman of the Joint Chiefs of Staff whom Eisenhower, as a former victorious Supreme Commander, always kept on a very short rein, was incisive about a naval blockade of Israel. Its effect, he said, would be immediate and quite complete. He sounded less confident when talking of effective action against Egypt or other Arabs. The British were struck by the emphasis Eisenhower put – rather more, Dulles was to feel, than was necessary – on Congress's sole prerogative over action involving the United States in war. What particularly worried Dulles about the Tripartite Declaration was the danger of fighting breaking out in ambiguous circumstances.[69]

A dramatic British switch in priorities can be seen most vividly in reading two telegrams sent on successive days in mid-March by Sir William Dickson, the Chairman of the Chiefs of Staff Committee, to General Sir John Whiteley, the head of the British Joint Services Mission in Washington. In the first, of 15 March, Dickson said that Ministers were extremely anxious to receive a combined military plan soon. Whiteley was instructed to send urgently the plan to confront Israeli aggression. He added that 'for tripartite [i.e. French] reasons' it might be desirable to put in a reference to possible action against the Arabs, provided that this avoided any appearance of the West fighting on the same side as Israel.[70]

The very next day, 16 March, Dickson sent another telegram. As the result of speaking to Ministers, the entire thrust of the message had been transformed. The plan should assume 'the probability that Egypt is now more likely to be the aggressor'. The response to Egyptian aggression should provide for 'a combined US/UK operation to seize Port Said and other key points on the Suez Canal. The object of such an operation would be to paralyse Egyptian army operations in Sinai and to safeguard international use of the Canal.' Whiteley was told that he 'should not be deterred by the magnitude of the possible implications'. All the same, Dickson insisted that American forces must play a major part in any actions, including that on land. 'It would also be important', he concluded optimistically 'to feature such operations as anti-Egyptian as opposed to anti-Arab or pro-Israeli.'[71]

Fussed by press reports that Washington staff talks were going slowly, Eden rushed off a personal message to Eisenhower, urging utmost despatch. Sir Roger Makins, not for the first time, persuaded him that it would be a mistake to appear over-anxious.[72] An Anglo-American draft planning paper was considered by the British Chiefs on 20 March. What worried them was that the Americans wanted to stop Egyptian aggression by air action alone across the Egyptian lines of communication. But that would not stop the Egyptians from closing the Suez Canal in the meantime. The Americans, said the British Chiefs, must realise the drastic effect that such closure would have on Britain. There must, therefore, in their view, be a landing of some three or four divisions in order to secure the Canal. It was in connection with these exchanges that the Americans found out from the British about their shortage of tank landing craft (or any other landing craft, for that matter), which was to have a major influence on the Suez campaign.[73]

The British had one other major demurrer to the draft plan. They thought it underestimated the opposition in that 'volunteers' from the Soviet Union and Eastern Europe might well be found to be flying the planes and operating the tanks that the East had supplied. It was, after all, only five years since General MacArthur had met his Waterloo in Korea at the hands of such 'volunteers' from communist China. In April this fear was fuelled from an authoritative source when Sir Anthony Eden, in the guise of proponent of détente, was acting as host to the post-Stalin leaders of Russia, a two-man act known to the western public as 'B. and K.' – Marshal Bulganin, the Prime Minister, and Nikita Khrushchev, the General Secretary. At one point Eden told the Russians that, if he were an Israeli, he would be much tempted to 'have a go' at this stage when, though with fewer arms than the Egyptians, they would probably win. Khrushchev riposted, with that adroitness of repartee for which he became famous, that 'it would be unwise of the Israelis to count too much on their prospects of success since, if fighting started, the Arabs might get the help of volunteers, skilled in the use of modern weapons'.[74]

Aside from the military problems over action under the Tripartite Declaration there were also political problems. 'The difficulty still remains', wrote one British diplomat, Barbara Salt, after one round of Washington discussions, 'that under international law there is no justification for military action by third parties to restore peace between States in armed conflict *except* by request of one or other of the belligerents.' It was unclear whether either party would make such an appeal, the Arab States, for instance, being extremely suspicious that the Western Powers might pick some Israeli move as an excuse to inflict their unwanted presence on Arab soil. But, wrote Barbara Salt, 'in default of UN cover, the three Powers will be *ultra vires* in resorting to force under the Tripartite Declaration'.

British and American officials therefore sat down to work out what was called 'a satisfactory manoeuvre' in the UN which would provide coverage for tripartite intervention. They found it impossible. Either one waited until the breach of the peace actually happened, in which case 'Israeli forces would be in Cairo long before a finding was made', or one sought authority in advance, in which case the Soviet Union would either use the veto or demand the right to join in.[75]

One person who was worried very much by the prospect of action being planned 'outside the UN' was the world organisation's Secretary-General, Dag Hammarskjöld. The Swede, whom the Permanent Members had agreed to appoint to that office because they thought they were choosing a good, grey bureaucrat, was gradually emerging as one of the most remarkable men of the age. He was, writes Sir Brian Urquhart, who worked closely with him, 'the most unusual and striking personality I have ever encountered in public life', austere, somewhat aloof, supremely well qualified in law, economics, diplomacy and politics, a mystic (as his strange posthumous book *Markings* revealed), a driven character combining an intense intellect and a real talent for administration. Although, as Urquhart concedes, he was difficult to work for, he inspired intense loyalty among members of his immediate international staff.[76] If any one man could transform the effectiveness of the UN, Hammarskjöld might well be that man.

His speciality lay in inserting the UN into the interstices of difficult situations, often by using the device of 'the Secretary-General's personal auspices' and, after intense intellectual analysis, identifying particular directions and linkages by which progress could be made. Always, however, his actions were governed by a pervasive sense of the UN Charter. Hammarskjöld's reputation was to be made in many quarters by the Suez crisis, but he was not to emerge from it without critics and enemies. His methods, often admirable, could also be exasperating. Although capable if need be of expressing himself with unnerving clarity, his more normal form of expression was one of intricately constructed sentences, implied meanings and circuitous and qualified assurances. Operating during a crisis virtually without sleep, with what seemed to a national Minister or bureaucrat an exceedingly small personal staff, he was a phenomenon on no account to be ignored.

Hammarskjöld entered the Middle Eastern scene in a major way only in 1956. In February he toured the area to become acquainted with its leading personalities. In contrast to his view of Mahmoud Fawzi, whom he always found attractive, subtle and trustworthy, his first impression of Gamal Abdul Nasser was distinctly unfavourable. He told a British diplomat whom he met a little later on that 'he had found Colonel Nasser (whom he obviously did not like and whom he compared to an intelligent junior Nazi officer) pathologically suspicious of everybody, including the West, Russia, Israel, the International Bank, and the Secretary-General himself'.[77] By April Hammarskjöld was, according to Selwyn Lloyd, comparing Nasser rather incautiously to 'Hitler in 1935' and conveying his impression that the Soviet Union did not want him to become too powerful.[78] The Secretary-General's conclusion from his February trip was that a three-Power approach using the UN merely as an instrument would be quite unacceptable in the area. He was also disinclined to agree to a US idea for a special Agent for the Middle East. On the other hand he thought that he himself 'would be swallowed by the USSR and tolerated by the Arabs'.[79]

This meant for Hammarskjöld an early return to the region since the situation both on the Gaza and on the Jordanian fronts was again deteriorating. This was primarily due to the activity of the Palestinian *fedayeen*. According to a report sent to General Glubb the previous September from the Jordanian Military Attaché in Egypt, four hundred volunteers had been trained to undertake highly dangerous missions inside Israel, though at the time that he wrote only sixty were being used. The missions, personally assigned by General Hakim Amer, included the demolition of roads and buildings and 'the assassination of notable personalities such as Ministers, Members of Parliament and leaders of the Zionist Organisation'. The aim was said to be to create such an atmosphere of fear and loss of security inside Israel that immigration would be discouraged and existing residents encouraged to leave. In practice assassinations did not run to notable personalities but to soft targets in vulnerable settlements. Incidents of sabotage were from time to time celebrated in the Egyptian press. Two key figures in these operations, marked down by the Israelis for punishment, who worked at opposite ends of the gap between Gaza and the West Bank, were Colonel Mustafa Hafez, the intelligence chief at Gaza, and Glubb's old enemy, the Egyptian Military Attaché in Jordan, Colonel Salaheddin Mustafa.[80]

Until April 1956 the *fedayeen* had been used only on a small scale, but their existence meant that Nasser also now had available an instrument of reprisal. On 5 April Egyptian gunfire across the line, often caused, according to UN observation, by deliberately provocative Israeli patrolling right up to the edge of the border, invited a disproportionate response. When heavy Israeli mortar-fire was directed on the crowded shopping centre of Gaza town, nowhere near the Egyptian gun position from which firing had been reported, fifty-six civilians were killed and one hundred and three wounded. By way of reply Nasser sent the *fedayeen* across the demarcation line in large numbers, causing extensive incidents of grenade throwing and demolition, killing a dozen Israelis including school children at prayer.

This was the precise moment at which Hammarskjöld arrived on the scene. By a burst of intense negotiation he succeeded in halting for the time being what had seemed like a rapid deterioration into war. Lifting the 'cease-fire clause' out of the armistice agreements (with Syria and Jordan, as well as with Egypt) he persuaded the parties to reaffirm their acceptance of this feature irrespective of the state of observance of the rest of the agreements. He also gained assurances by Jordan and Egypt of vigorous measures to prevent crossings of the demarcation line. For a brief moment the impact of the Secretary-General seemed to lighten the scene. He was, however, under no illusion that the improvement would last as long as so many inflammable issues were unresolved. He would have to return soon to attempt a series of off-setting arrangements about issues of substance.[81]

Already relations between Israel and Jordan were disintegrating. Hammarskjöld wrote to Lloyd on 11 June that Jordan was permitting far too much unrest to continue along the armistice line. He had had to make a serious *démarche* to the man who, after an interval, had just been appointed to Glubb's old post, the King's former ADC, Major-General Ali Abu Nuwar.[82] At the end of June there was a serious breach between Israel and the UN; the Israelis walked out of the Mixed Armistice Commission with Jordan and paralysed its activities. The issue was a major one. The UN was insisting that the side claiming to be the victim of an incident had no right to shoot back over the armistice line or organise subsequent reprisals. David Ben-Gurion told General E. L. M. ('Tommy') Burns, the Canadian head of the Truce Supervisors (UNTSO), that the Government of Israel could not stand by and see its people murdered. If the UN could not stop attacks from Jordanian territory, Israel would take steps to do so. When Burns attempted to impress Ali Abu Nuwar with an unvarnished description of Ben-Gurion's intemperance, Nuwar replied that he was convinced that the Palestine question would only be settled by force of arms and that he would welcome the day.[83]

On 18 July Hammarskjöld returned to the Middle East to resume the dialogue with Ben-Gurion and to test the chances of a new peace initiative which Fawzi had just suggested. In advance of his arrival, the Secretary-General had received a secret message from Dulles. It told him of a scheme that he and the President had been pushing forward since April, against almost total scepticism from the Pentagon, to try to make the promises of the Trilateral Declaration seem more credible. The original idea was that a single stockpile of arms should be held 'in escrow' somewhere in the Middle East, to be delivered promptly in the event of war to whichever side was deemed the victim of aggression. When refined this became two stockpiles; 24 F-86s which would be turned over to Israeli pilots on Cyprus; and an attack cargo ship full of tanks, recoilless rifles and rocket launchers attached to the Sixth Fleet for delivery to Egypt or another Arab state.[84]

What Hammarskjöld thought of this scheme when he was told about it is uncertain but he was assuredly relieved to hear that nothing was to be said about it in public so long as he was in the Middle East. On 26 July Dulles, away in Peru, was enquiring when Hammarskjöld was to leave the Middle East, so that he might at the first possible moment unveil the principle of this ingenious two-way deterrent. But something else was to happen in the Middle East on that very day, as a result of which nothing more was ever heard of 'Operation Stockpile'.[85]

Hammarskjöld's trip began in Jerusalem with an eight-hour intellectual and philosophical encounter with Ben-Gurion of the type which both men enjoyed. Ben-Gurion insisted with a wealth of example that methods of violence should always be condemned and punished; Hammarskjöld with equal erudition condemned force used as a reprisal both on moral and practical grounds. Ben-Gurion argued on behalf of Israel that a long succession of incidents, small in themselves, could in the aggregate constitute a full-scale act of aggression against which a country was entitled under

Article 51 of the Charter to use her right of self-defence.

Hammarskjöld felt when he left Jerusalem that he had won from Ben-Gurion a little time free of reprisal raids in which to do his best to resolve the border problems. They had agreed that, if he failed, the situation would immediately be referred to the Security Council. It seems likely that to himself and to his immediate circle Hammarskjöld overestimated the extent to which this epic encounter represented a personal breakthrough. It is true that the two men continued to exchange letters that were polite though not cordial, true perhaps that what the State Department's secret history of the Suez crisis refers to as 'the apparent mutual dislike existing between Ben-Gurion and the Secretary-General' may have been somewhat abated. But during the next months the Secretary-General was to complain bitterly about Israel's unresponsiveness and her truculent diplomatic style and Ben-Gurion, on the last day of the year, told the American Ambassador that, as far as he was concerned, Hammarskjöld's good faith and impartiality were seriously in question.[86]

It was now time for Hammarskjöld to move on to Cairo and to assess the chances of a new initiative for peace. When he did so he flew right into the new crisis of the Aswan Dam and the Suez Canal. No one had time to talk about peace with Israel now.

6

Code-Word 'De Lesseps'

What we now saw in North Africa was the alliance between Pan-Slavism and Pan-Islam. All this was in the works of Nasser, just as Hitler's policy had been written down in Mein Kampf.

Guy Mollet to Anthony Eden, Chequers, 11 March 1956.

I started to look at Mr Black, who was sitting on a chair, and I saw him in my imagination as Ferdinand de Lesseps.

Gamal Abdul Nasser, Alexandria, 26 July 1956.

There was a structural anomaly in Western policy towards the Middle East in the 1950s: whereas the form was mostly tripartite, the reality was an affair of Britain and the United States. The *tertium quid* was France. Where cultural interest was concerned everyone was ready to acknowledge France's presence in the region.[1] There was a French business community in the Delta cities of Egypt and larger ones in Port Fuad, on the opposite bank of the Canal to Port Said, and Ismailia. The one big investment was the Suez Canal Company, with its dominantly French ethos. France's claim to political importance formerly relied on Syria and Lebanon, but towards the end of World War II she had been effectively bundled out of there by local nationalists encouraged to a marked extent by British political and military influence.[2]

Regardless of any evidence to the contrary, the British believed that they were basically loved in the Middle East and, where not loved, respected; they were certain that the French were hated. When constrained to work with them they did so, but still tried fastidiously not to be confused with them. Often they were conscious of what might easily have been (though it was not) termed 'the halitosis factor'. The French seemed to them to be acting out a mime in which Syria and Lebanon were still client states or, at any rate, as if certain political factions in them were still responsive to French manipulation. Thus, it was the opinion of the British Ambassador in Damascus that the French preferred the state of near-anarchy and incipient collapse to which Syria had been brought by her political system because 'their pockets of influence can exert that marginal pressure which is all that is necessary when contending forces are evenly balanced'.[3]

The British alternative was the Baghdad Pact and general support for the idea of the Fertile Crescent to give stiffening and purpose to the Asian Arab states. The French, disliking Nuri and his perpetual scheming which they associated with Hashemite ambitions to erode the independence of Syria, enrolled themselves among the diverse and well-filled ranks of the Pact's enemies. These, in addition to France, included Israel and Egypt, the Soviet Union and Saudi Arabia. To the British Foreign Office the French seemed infuriatingly indifferent to the larger issue of communist penetration which, it feared, had gone very far in Syria already. 'The French are so powerless in the Middle East now that any fingerhold has to be exploited', wrote a cross Whitehall official in February 1955, and Eden's minutes on French behaviour are peppered with irritation. 'Cheek! ... More cheek! ... Thoroughly unsatisfactory. French are double-crossing' was written over a telegram from the British Ambassador in Paris, Gladwyn Jebb, in March.[4] To the Quai d'Orsay (the French Foreign Ministry), the British were very naïve about the Baghdad Pact: it was a militarily valueless arrangement that had succeeded in nothing but attracting Soviet interest to the region while tying Britain to Nuri's destabilising conspiracies.

The 'special relationship' between Britain and the United States never worked so effectively as when it was concerned with excluding the French. They were left out of the 1954 Middle East Defence talks, left out of Alpha, left out of the Baghdad Pact and left out of the High Aswan Dam offer; they had even been left out of the staff talks held in the first half of 1956 on the implementation of the Tripartite Declaration of 1950 itself. Whenever a new policy line was under discussion the question of whether to ask in the French invariably featured high on the agenda. Invariably the decision was negative. Partly this was a general verdict on French political and military standing in the Eastern Mediterranean; more specifically it was because the French were held, especially in the Pentagon, to be insecure, both in the general sense of having a propensity to leak and in the specific sense that, by 1955, the existence of a special link between the French defence establishment and that of Israel had become known.[5] All told, at the beginning of 1956 two more unlikely co-conspirators in the Middle East than Britain and France would have been difficult to find.

By contrast with the Levant France's presence in the Maghreb was real enough, but here too it was under severe challenge. In two of France's three North African territories political settlements had been arrived at. Morocco and Tunisia achieved their independence in March 1956. But Algeria was a very different matter. One and a half million white Frenchmen lived there. The three northern *départements* of Algiers, Oran and Constantine, which contained most of the population, were not a colony but a juridically integral part of France. To the surprise and dismay of France, an armed rebellion broke out on 1 November 1954 among the majority Arab and Berber population, led by the FLN (*Front de Libération Nationale*) against French rule.

Egypt supplied some munitions and training to the FLN. Weapons from Egyptian stocks were stored at Sollum, in the Western Desert, and delivered either by boat or overland. General Franco, anxious to embarrass the French, allowed the Egyptian Military Attaché, Colonel Abdul Mun'im al-Nagar, to organise a supply line through Morocco and a training mission for Algerian fighters, while Colonel Nasser sent one of the former royal yachts as a personal contribution to the arms run. Cairo Radio became a daily propaganda voice for the Algerian cause. But the degree to which the rebellion was run from Cairo was much exaggerated. There was a sharp difference in outlook between the French Ministry of Defence, for whom the elimination of Nasser became the central factor in the war in Algeria, and the diplomats of the Quai d'Orsay which was well aware that, France having invested a considerable amount of her talent and skill in developing her relationships with the Arab world, had much to lose by any crude confrontation.[6]

One striking exception to the pro-Arab nature of French diplomacy was provided by Pierre-Eugène Gilbert, a flamboyant and unorthodox personality who, when sent at his own request as ambassador to Israel, quickly turned an academic knowledge of classical Hebrew into a very fluent command of Israel's contemporary national language. It was entirely with his approval that important links came to be formed between the Defence Ministries of France and Israel. On behalf of the Israeli Defence Ministry, Yosef Nachmias ran a brilliant lobby operation in Paris and was frequently joined by the thirty-one-year-old Director-General of the Ministry, Shimon Peres. Towards the close of 1954, the French Defence Ministry (in spite of objections from the Quai d'Orsay) provided the Israelis with their first jet fighters, a consignment of Ouragans. In the summer of 1955 France promised to follow this up with a squadron of the latest swept-wing jet fighter, the Mystère II. This, the British observed when they first heard of it, would 'very much enhance the Israeli Air Force' not only against the Egyptians and other Arabs but also against themselves who, under the Anglo-Jordanian Treaty, might well be the Israelis' opponent in air battle.[7] In the end Israeli pilots rejected the Mystère II because of tail wobble but this merely enabled Peres, at the moment when Nasser was acquiring Ilyushins and MiGs, to set his sights on the more advanced Mystère IV. The complication was that American approval would be required to interrupt the off-shore procurement flow of deliveries of this plane for use within Nato. 'France's very lack of real political responsibility permits her, if she chooses', grumbled Britain's Ambassador in Tel Aviv, 'to offer the Israelis palatable rather than sound advice; and, as over the supply of arms, to take irresponsible action to secure Israeli goodwill'. Sir John Nicholls added that the French were undoubtedly guilty of supplying arms beyond the quantities agreed to in the secret committee in Washington.[8]

The Mollet Government

On 2 January 1956, after a bleak winter campaign, a general election took place in France. Following it a new government took office under Guy Mollet, the working head of the Socialist Party organisation. This was the Government that was to take France into the Suez conflict alongside Britain. The Cabinet was drawn exclusively from the members of the *Front Républicain*, which had been formed on the initiative of a journalist, Jean-Jacques Servan-Schreiber, on the eve of the election in order to concentrate the forces of the non-communist left. It consisted of two important parties, the Socialists and the Radicals led by the dynamic ex-Prime Minister Pierre Mendès-France, and two smaller ones, the UDSR led by François Mitterrand (which did so badly at the polls that the British Embassy analysis of the result wrote that 'François Mitterrand has led his party to the slaughterhouse'), and the Social Republicans of Jacques Chaban-Delmas, whose origins lay in General de Gaulle's disbanded political movement.[9] Altogether the *Front* commanded only 170 seats in a National Assembly of 595, which made it all the more remarkable that Mollet's Ministry was to prove, at eighteen months, the longest-lived of the Fourth Republic.

According to a public opinion poll at the end of the campaign, twenty-seven per cent favoured Mendès-France as Prime Minister, two per cent favoured Mollet. The first was charismatic, the second was not. Before the election they had promised to take office only together. The President should make the choice; each would be prepared to serve under the other. President Coty chose the duller man, partly no doubt because the Socialists were the larger partner, but mainly because Mollet was considered much the better 'European'. It has to be remembered that 1956 was expected to be (and in fact was) a key year for deciding whether the drive towards European unity would be resumed with such fresh instruments as the European Economic Community (EEC) and Euratom, or whether it would just peter out following the defeat of the Defence Community. The new Ministry would need the outside support of the pro-European Christian Democrats (MRP) if it were to survive.

Mollet, who thus became only the second socialist Prime Minister in the country's history, was a Protestant of working-class origins. As a teacher of the English language (on which subject he had written a text book) he had been the Secretary-General of the Teachers' Federation. Until the war he had been a strong pacifist, but wartime occupation converted him to the cause of resistance, which led to his being elected Mayor of Arras after the Liberation. His takeover as Secretary-General of the French Socialist Party in 1946 occurred after a rough battle against the incumbent. The result was interpreted wrongly as a move to the left and, since the defeated incumbent was a Jew, gave rise to unfair whispers of anti-Semitism. Guy Mollet was not a very striking speaker or a particularly colourful man. His main preoccupations appeared to be two: the organisational development and discipline of the Socialist Party and the European cause, especially the Council of Europe's Consultative Assembly at Strasbourg, that body of which Anthony Eden said, 'Strasbourg was always a misfortune; it is now nearly a calamity.'[10] Mollet had been elected its President. Apart from two short periods when he had been a Minister of State (Minister without Portfolio) he came to the premiership without previous Cabinet experience.[11]

The two Ministers who with Mollet made up the team that directed French policy at the time of Suez were the Foreign Minister, Christian Pineau, and the Minister of Defence, Maurice Bourgès-Maunoury. Pineau, unlike Mollet, came from a middle-class intellectual background. The stepson of the writer Jean Giraudoux, he started his working life at a bank, where he became active in pushing white-collar trade unionism, while pursuing a second career as a successful author of children's tales. In the war Pineau had been active, like Mollet, in the Resistance, had spent eighteen months at Buchenwald and had been awarded the CBE by the British. He was Minister of Food under de Gaulle; since then he had been out of office, although in 1954 he had been called on to form his own government. He failed only because of the rule, shortly afterwards repealed, that his initial vote of confidence should come from over half the total membership of the Chamber. Christian Pineau was, like his chief, considered reliable on the European issue. It was made clear to him by Mollet from the outset that his and the Government's absolute priority in the international field must lie in the completion and ratification of the Community treaties. He was to need reminding of this several times during the ensuing months whenever his pronounced tendency to resign began to overtake him.[12] For all of this, Pineau's approach was that of an optimist and a loner. His performance in the international field was awaited with some curiosity.[13]

Under the *nom de guerre* of 'Polycarpe', Maurice Bourgès-Maunoury, now forty years of age, had played a leading, indeed legendary, role both within the Paris Resistance and in establishing liaison with de Gaulle and the Free French outside France. He was a radical and since 1947 had been in almost every government, of which there were a great many, either as Secretary of State (Minister of State) or as Minister; but, lest anyone should suppose he was a mere place-seeker, he had twice resigned through disagreements over policy. No orator, he was essentially a man of action, preferably of the covert variety. He and François Mitterrand, whose electoral misfortunes were rewarded by the third ranking position in the Cabinet as Minister of Justice and leader of the Senate, supplied some of the ministerial experience lacking in their fellows. But essentially this was a ministry of new men.

The impression abroad after the election, in which the most spectacular gains in seats had been by the Communists and by Poujardists, the new anti-tax and small shopkeepers' party, was that France was in a remarkably bad way. Jean Chauvel, the French Ambassador in London, remarked brightly to the Permanent Under-Secretary at the Foreign Office that it was clear that now no government could be formed in France. Recording the remark, Sir Ivone Kirkpatrick was led to comment, 'Like all good Frenchmen Chauvel evinced not the slightest misgiving about the precarious condition of his country'.[14] Two months later, Bourgès-Maunoury was telling Sir Gladwyn Jebb, the British Ambassador in Paris, that the present Government would probably last for quite a long time. In existing circumstances socialist support was absolutely essential if any ministry were to last; this was unlikely to be forthcoming unless the Socialists were in control. Jebb reported that the French political system thrived on paradox: resting on a smaller assured support than any of its predecessors, Guy Mollet's Government enjoyed the most enormous majorities in the National Assembly, winning communist votes because it was 'of the Left' and Christian Democrat ones because it was 'European'.

What upset the British and American Governments about the new French Government was what Jebb called 'M. Pineau's curious attempt to give the misleading impression that he is following a foreign policy different from that of his precedessors'.[15] His supreme performance on 2 March was given off the cuff (so that no one was able subsequently to produce an authentic text) before the Anglo-American Press Association, when he characterised the cold war policies of the West as 'an enormous error arising from an exclusive preoccupation with security'.[16] This hit Anthony Eden hard when he was already in the doldrums over the sacking of General Glubb.

The following day Eden suggested to Mollet that he might like to come to Chequers for a weekend to talk over foreign policy matters quietly. Mollet leapt at the idea and the meeting on 11 March would seem to have been good-tempered enough. Mollet's main message was that Britain and France should join forces to put issues across to the uncomprehending Americans. But what must particularly have struck Eden, since it came from a socialist Prime Minister, was what he said about Colonel Nasser.

In North Africa, said Mollet, what France was facing was an alliance between Pan-Slavism and Pan-Islam. 'All this [is] in the works of Nasser, just as Hitler's policy [was] written down in *Mein Kampf*. Nasser [has] the ambition to recreate the conquests of Islam. But his present position is largely due to the policy of the West in building him up and flattering him.'[17]

This friendly encounter at Chequers was followed by a series of overwrought exchanges which left Anglo-French relations in a very threadbare state. On his return to Paris Mollet said in reply to a press question that at Chequers he had 'recalled our reservations' about the Baghdad Pact which had remained undiminished. Eden demanded that Mollet should be told that he was 'gravely disturbed' at this poor return for loyal British support in North Africa; it should be put right in Mollet's next speech. Agitated exchanges followed on the exact words that Mollet should use. Dissatisfied, Eden reluctantly accepted advice that the Frenchman could not be pressed further than to say that his Government must accept the Baghdad Pact's existence as a fact.[18] No sooner had that banality been uttered than the American weekly *US News and World Report* came out with the text of a Mollet interview in which the French Prime Minister repeated his original view. Jebb was instructed over the telephone by Eden to 'express to him strongly my own resentment'.[19]

Meanwhile Pineau had been, with Selwyn Lloyd and Foster Dulles, at the Karachi Ministerial meeting for SEATO, where he was barracked by Lloyd for his attack on the Baghdad Pact and offended by Dulles's identification of Christianity with free enterprise. Afterwards Pineau went on to India where he debated the philosophy of neutralism with its high priest, Pandit Nehru. As he was about to leave, Nehru shot his visitor a question: 'Why don't you go and see Nasser?' In no time the Pandit, who perhaps had spotted in Pineau, as Tito undoubtedly had, a future recruit for the non-aligned movement, had everything organised. The next morning, without warning his Prime Minister, Pineau was on the plane for Cairo.

Christian Pineau found that Nasser in no way resembled Hitler, except for a sudden burst of anger against Israel and against Britain for the creation of Israel. He says in his memoir that he found nothing of the fanatic in him, nothing of that total certainty in his own star that was characteristic of the Nazis. Nasser denied that he was the soul of the Algerian rebellion or its secret chief. 'On his word of honour as a soldier' he asserted that no Algerians were currently being trained in Egypt and offered to facilitate talks – much desired by Mollet – on a party-to-party basis between the French Socialist Party and the leaders of the FLN.[20] Pineau's Prime Minister, though apparently very forgiving of his colleague, was not impressed with what he had to say in favour of Nasser. The colonel, Mollet told Jebb at the end of March, 'is a monument of duplicity', and the two countries should combine forces against him.[21]

Towards the end of May there took place an incident which indicated where things stood in Paris. Finding himself unable to attend the annual Ex-Servicemen's Congress, the Minister of Defence, Bourgès-Maunoury, delegated the task of giving the principal address to Louis Mangin, a reserve officer and son of a famous military figure in World War I. The text, somewhat toned down from the original, was passed by the Minister's *chef de cabinet*, Abel Thomas, on condition (a fruitless one) that Mangin deliver it 'in his personal capacity'. It was a violent polemic against Nasser and all his works. Dictators, Mangin said, announce their plans in advance and it was apparent from Nasser's writings that he had determined to rule not only the Middle East and North Africa but large parts of the Sahara, including territories that 'live in community with France'. It was for ex-servicemen to make their fellow-countrymen aware of the compelling reasons for resisting such a challenge.

Mangin's speech was quite naturally everywhere attributed either to the Minister or to the Government as a whole. Bourgès-Maunoury, taken sharply to task by both Mollet and Pineau at the next Cabinet meeting, covered his staff and offered to resign. This Mollet could not face and the incident was closed.[22] From that moment onwards Abel Thomas and Louis Mangin were the effective instruments of French policy in the Middle East. They had in common with Bourgès-Maunoury a strong pro-Israeli sentiment based on experience in the Resistance and a belief that success in North Africa would only come with the wrecking of Nasser.

Working with Pierre Boursicot, the Director of the SDECE (*Service de Documentation Extérieure et de Contre-Espionnage*), Mangin set up the first of the secret Franco-Israeli conferences, crucial to the Suez operation, near Chantilly on 23 June, making use of false passports, a special aerodrome and a private house. Moshe Dayan headed the Israeli delegation which included Colonel Harkabi, Peres and Nachmias. The meeting represented a watershed in the relations between the two sides. Above all, it represented in both capitals the triumph of Defence Ministry over Ministry of Foreign Affairs. In Paris there had been much wrangling, as the result of which the first twelve Mystères IV for Israel, contracted for on 26 December 1955, had been delivered on 11 April 1956.[23] In mid-April Bourgès-Maunoury had signed a contract for another twelve. When the Quai d'Orsay objected that it was one thing to participate in a joint Western decision to re-arm Israel, quite another to step out ahead as the sole re-armer, its officials, primarily Henry Roux of the Africa and Levant Department, were told by Bourgès-Maunoury that the new contract had been personally authorised by Pineau. Roux, who had not seen any such document but who, like his colleagues, was becoming rapidly aware of the personal style of his new master, spelled out in an acid minute the consequences for French policy in the whole region and in relations with the United States, Britain and Italy, of having foreign policy determined by the personal staff of the Minister of Defence.

However, on 6 May the Americans, who were under immense pressure at home to release modern jets to Israel but still did not want to supply their own, agreed to the interruption of the Mystère IV line of supply to enable France to complete quickly the delivery of what were described as the 'final twelve' aircraft to Israel. Pineau confirmed to Lloyd and Dulles that these would indeed be the last and this was said publicly in *Le Monde* on 15 May. Whether or not Pineau ever intended to stick by this firm departmental view, it was a line that was to be rapidly breached.[24] In June Mollet came down decisively on the side of Bourgès.

On the day after the Chantilly conference opened, Moshe Sharett, who had not been happy with the heavy reliance on special deals with France or Ben-Gurion's practice of conducting diplomacy through officials of his own Defence Ministry, was suddenly and brutally forced to resign. Abba Eban compared it to 'a couple who had been living together for forty years and suddenly decide to divorce'. Sharett did not understand, wrote Ben-Gurion, that 'our foreign policy must serve our security needs'. Following his departure (and replacement by Golda Meir), 'we were freed from the official, departmentalized approach that was so deeply ingrained in Moshe'.[25]

After four days of talks agreement was reached on what Israel required to match the newly equipped forces of Egypt. The arms contracts – for seventy-two Mystères, one hundred and twenty AMX tanks, forty Super-Sherman tanks, eighteen 105mm mobile guns, ammunition and radar – were signed by Boursicot and Harkabi, the two intelligence chiefs; the transaction would thus avoid parliamentary scrutiny in the Palais Bourbon.[26]

'I must retract what I said about M. Pineau getting sillier and sillier every day,' Gladwyn Jebb wrote to Eden on 13 June. In a public lecture the French Foreign Minister had given a *tour d'horizon* which 'succeeded for the first time since his advent to power in getting round a course of Grand National size without crashing at a fence or even seriously stumbling'.[27] There was no more socialism or even radical chic. By mid-year French policy had become more and more dominated by the situation in North Africa. To those who were directly handling it, such as Robert Lacoste, the Minister Resident in Algeria, there was no question, as he told Julian Amery, but that Nasser was the main enemy. The Egyptians were not only supplying the rebels with arms, they were also responsible for the military direction of the rebellion.[28]

Jebb wanted Britain to back France far more openly in North Africa. Such backing might well be of decisive importance in persuading the French to continue the struggle. Otherwise the French people might lose heart and, once they withdrew their troops, this would be followed by a mass exodus of French settlers, opening the way for the extension of Egyptian and perhaps Soviet influence as far as the Atlantic.[29]

Mollet and Pineau were now anxious to see their British counterparts and pressed for them to come to Paris on 26 or 31 July. When Eden talked of September for the formal visit, Pineau proposed to dash over to London by himself to see Lloyd on urgent business before the end of July. This did not suit the British Ambassador at all. 'It would be better', he cabled, 'for this rather foolish fellow to be received in the presence of the much solider M. Mollet – which is exactly, of course, what he is trying to avoid.' Pineau persisted and Lloyd felt that he could not refuse. He should come on 29

July and the agenda for his visit was headed: 'Adoption of a common policy towards Nasser'.[30]

The Suez Canal: Towards 1968

From the days of its French founder onwards, the Universal Suez Maritime Canal Company had wanted to enjoy the benefits but to suffer none of the disadvantages of Egyptian nationality. It took for granted that no one could conceivably have intended that, for example, Egyptian statutes relating to company law, labour law, exchange control, patriation of overseas earnings or, still less, the law making retirement compulsory for all company directors at the age of sixty – which would have lopped off at one blow all except four of its thirty-two directors – should apply to a company with its 'unique international status'.[31]

As it entered 1956, the company's thoughts about the future were dominated by the approach of 17 November 1968, the day on which its concession was due to expire and the entire control and management of the Canal to pass into the hands of Egypt. Until recently top management had given every appearance of believing that, since the Egyptians would be manifestly unready by 1968 to run things on their own, it would be possible to work out some arrangement whereby the company would remain substantially in charge. The Scandinavian Shipowners' Association had called for the internationalisation of the Canal after 1968 under the United Nations with Britain as the political Mandatory Power and the company as economic administrator. In July 1955 Jacques Georges-Picot, the company's Managing Director[32], outlined to a British Treasury official, William Armstrong, a possible route-map for arriving at the desired goal of internationalisation. The Canal would soon need to be widened and deepened if it were to cope with the rising demands of the international oil industry. For work on that scale American finance would be needed, covering a period which would last beyond 1968. So, an international conference would be summoned in 1960 at which the Egyptians would find themselves swamped, whereupon a new international body could emerge to run the Canal after 1968.[33]

This was precisely the type of clever manoeuvre that the Egyptians suspected and were determined to resist. Speaking of this period, Engineer Ezzat Adel, at the time of writing Chairman and Managing Director of the Canal Authority, said in 1986 that nationalisation was imperative because the 'ex-company' and other countries were doing their utmost to avoid handing over in 1968. Company officials, he alleged, were in the United States to build up commercial pressure for that purpose. If despite everything they were to be faced with having to hand over, Adel said, they were going to run down the business, scrap equipment and, by giving Egyptians insufficient training, force Egypt to confess her inability to cope without international management.[34] Nor were the Egyptians alone in their suspicions. Eugene Black, the President of the World Bank, thought it very unwise for the company's officials to be so obviously soliciting American business alliances without first taking the Egyptians into their confidence.

Colonel Nasser began showing an interest in the future of the Canal as soon as the Canal Zone agreement had been signed with Britain. In a broadcast on 17 November 1954, he spoke of the next fourteen years as a period of preparation during which Egyptians must strain every nerve to be ready to run the Canal, and in the following February he set up a Suez Canal Committee presided over by the Deputy Prime Minister.[35] There are some indications that even then Nasser had an earlier takeover in mind. Marshal Tito of Jugoslavia, in a speech at Pula on 11 November 1956, referred to his first meeting with Nasser in February 1955, when the Marshal had passed through the Suez Canal in his yacht. Nasser, he said, had then told him 'that he would have to nationalise the Suez Canal since Egypt, an independent country, could not tolerate foreign administration of its own country'.[36]

There was also a reference in Nasser's speech of 12 August (1956) to his having been thinking about the problem of Egyptianising the Canal for the last two and a half years. What is certain is that the preparatory paper work, the legal and historical justification, must have been done in advance of the actual crisis. But that is not to say that Nasser was working to a definite timetable. What he clearly was doing was scrutinising with pedantic care the overlapping transactions that would determine Egypt's future relationship with the West, with the overriding concern that he would not show himself as naïve as Said and Ismail. If there was any danger of his being cheated he wanted to be ready to take over the Canal.

In this connection, two sets of discussions were directly relevant in 1956: one, already referred to, and to which Egypt was not yet a party, about the financing of the Canal's widening and deepening, and the second a negotiation that took up the first half of 1956 between the Egyptian Government and the company to resolve the Government's accumulated grievances against *la Suez* and in return to remove the block on visas for fresh non-Egyptian Canal pilots. The initial contacts between the two sides were very sticky. As late as February 1956, François Charles-Roux, the company's President, on his annual visitation, sternly put the Egyptian Minister of Commerce in his place for making the suggestion that there should be two Egyptian members on the 'Inner Cabinet', the ten-man *Comité de Direction*, so that they could gain experience of the top management of the Canal before the end of the concession. Members of the *Comité*, he was told, must represent only shareholders since it had to discuss not only the operation of the Suez Canal but 'other affairs' of the company.[37]

It was in keeping with this attitude that the company fought hard to have the new agreement being discussed in 1956 termed a 'convention', as pacts with earlier governments of Egypt had been, so preserving the quasi-diplomatic tradition. But the Egyptian leaders were exceptionally well-briefed on the history of these past negotiations, thanks to the doctoral thesis which a young ex-diplomat, Mustafa al-Hefnaoui, had researched in the archives of the rue d'Astorg. There was going to be no convention. It seems in retrospect highly plausible that, given the distinct possibility of a break-down in these negotiations, the documentation for a nationalisation crisis was prepared for such an eventuality.[38] However, they did not break down and on 8 June 1956 an agreement was announced.

The terms made it absolutely clear that the Egyptians would not contemplate any extension of the company's concession beyond 1968, but they also made detailed arrangements on the apparent assumption that it would continue until then. The principal grievances had been that the company was keeping the whole of its reserves outside Egypt and that it was not employing sufficient Egyptian pilots. The agreement was that £10 million building up to £20 million should be invested in Egyptian securities and that thirty-two more Egyptians should be taken on as pilots, with the company finishing off their training. In return Egyptian pressure was relaxed to the extent that twenty-six more visas would be available for the recruitment of foreign pilots. The existence and wording of the agreement seemed to promise a smoother ride for the Universal Company in its remaining years.[39]

This, however, in no way solved the longer-term problem for western governments and shipping companies. If the company looked safe until 1968, it was more than ever apparent that after 1968 there would be no one but the Egyptians to carry out the Constantinople Convention of 1888. Unless some new international instrument were drawn up in advance, the huge commercial interests involved would be confronted with the unpredictable. In 1955 sixty-two million metric tons of crude oil and another five million metric tons of oil products passed northwards through the Canal, over twenty million tons of it headed for Britain. By 1968, it was predicted, oil traffic would have gone up to 254 million metric tons and by 1972 to 335 million. A paper drawn up in the British Cabinet Office in May stated bluntly: 'Our position concerning the Canal is fundamentally weak and that of the Egyptian Government conversely strong. Not only will the Canal revert wholly to Egyptian control in 1968 but the Constantinople Convention is no longer an effective instrument. Moreover, when Egypt acquires full control, it is to be expected that she will seek to force up the Canal dues and possibly to indulge in flag discriminations at our expense.'[40]

The British and French Governments had in fact for some years been attempting to promote a conference of maritime powers to bring the 1888 Convention up to date and reinforce its safeguards. It was the Americans who dragged their feet, in the first place so as not to 'gang up' on Egypt during the Suez base negotiations. Afterwards, they still hesitated because, it was suspected, of the fear of creating precedents that might be used against them over the Panama Canal. Early in his peacetime administration Winston Churchill had fought hard though ineffectively to secure that, as he said to the American Congress in January 1952, 'the whole burden of maintaining the freedom of the famous waterway of the Suez Canal' should become 'an international rather than a national responsibility'. He had had in mind an international syndicate of the United States, France, Turkey and Britain. Then it had been Eden's role repeatedly to call attention to the fact that the base was Egyptian sovereign territory and could not be thus casually transferred.[41] But Eden had secured inclusion in the Treaty of 1954 of an exquisitely balanced clause which recognised that the Canal 'which is an integral part of Egypt' was also 'a waterway economically, commercially and strategically of international importance'.

In the exchanges in the House when the terms of the 1954 Agreement were announced, Attlee queried from the Labour front bench whether reaffirmation of the 1888 Convention would suffice. Referring to the anti-Israel blockade, he went on, 'It is not much good just affirming a Convention which is not observed by one party, yet this is "our great Imperial lifeline".' Eden may not have cared much about Israeli commerce, yet he was determined to be taken in deadly earnest about oil. When Bulganin and Khrushchev were in Britain in April 1956, he told them that without regular supplies Britain would have unemployment and would slowly starve to death. He must be 'absolutely blunt about the oil because we would fight for it'.[42]

Still, examination of the records leaves the impression that those Conservative politicians who felt that Eden could have pushed the future regulation of the Suez Canal onto the international agenda more vigorously were not entirely wrong. It is probable that late in July this was something which would weigh upon his conscience.

The Tory backbencher who raised the matter, first at Question Time on 7 May and then, because he deemed the Foreign Office replies unsatisfactory, on the adjournment on 15 May, was John Peyton, a future Minister of Transport. Describing Nasser as 'behaving like a buccaneer', he asserted that the colonel's conduct had given 'nobody any grounds for confidence in him as custodian of an international waterway'. It was intolerable that either now or in the future the body in control of the Suez Canal should fall entirely under the hand of Egypt. It was no use waiting until 1968. In terms guaranteed to needle the government and its head, Peyton declared: 'I think that a clear approach and a clear lead – I know that this is a painful word nowadays – is called for from this country to lay down, in the name of international law, the conditions for the future of the Suez Canal.'[43] Peyton drew support not only from Captain Waterhouse and his group but from the Opposition benches where Members demanded to know what was being done about the five-year-old Security Council resolution against the blockade of Israel. These exchanges not only spoke to Eden about the temper of his own party but were carefully noted in Cairo. Anwar Sadat, for example, made much play in *Al Gumhouriya* ('The Republic') of which he was the Editor, with Peyton's term 'buccaneer' in relation to 'British piratical policy throughout the world' and declared that Egypt would not allow the Canal to be a threat to her sovereignty and independence.

The Cabinet Office paper already quoted showed that the backbench arguments were finding an echo inside Whitehall. Britain, the paper argued, must seek to put the Canal on a new and permanent footing at an early date when bargaining counters yet remained. Perhaps Britain should use a stick by organising a blockade of capital for Canal development; perhaps she should use a carrot by offering an earlier end of the concession in return for safeguards. Whatever was done should be done with the United States 'since the problem of the future of the Canal is fundamentally political and the support of the United States in future negotiations with Egypt will be essential'.[44]

It was at this point that the United States made a decisive move triggering off the future sequence of events. The move was made in relation not to the Suez Canal but to the High Aswan Dam.

Dam Out

After the tremendous rush to get the terms of the Anglo-American offer to Egypt on Aswan agreed before Christmas (1955), there was an awkward pause while Nasser scrutinised the small print. There was to be a letter of intent from the World Bank to Egypt coupled with *aides-mémoire* from the two governments. These drafts were sent in advance for approval by Cairo. Nasser did not like the proposed letter of intent. It seemed to give the World Bank, with its American president, total control over Egypt's economy on the grounds of ensuring that Egyptian resources were not squandered on other projects, and of keeping the rate of inflation caused by so large a scheme under control, yet without guaranteeing that even then Egypt would get a completed project at the end. Eugene Black flew out to Cairo to resolve the difficulties only to find Egyptian officials disposed to reopen many matters that he thought had been decided in Washington. The State Department, alerted to the danger that negotiations were 'on the verge of collapse', with Black getting ready to give a 'take it or leave it' ultimatum to Nasser, entreated the banker to consider that 'vitally important considerations of highest interest to [the] entire Western world' were at stake. Dulles and Hoover were aware that at that moment Operation Gamma and the Anderson mission had reached the critical stage.

Black responded and by early February, in place of Egyptian drafts that would have offered only a borrower's good intentions in exchange for the

Bank's total and immediate commitment for the full loan, had brought about an exchange of letters that both Bank and Nasser considered reasonable. It had been an exhausting experience and not one without the fraught moments that Nasser was to recall during his Alexandria speech of 26 July.[45]

But then there were the *aides-mémoire*. Nasser trusted western governments less than he had now gradually learnt to trust the World Bank. He wanted there to be no reference to Egypt having asked Britain and the United States for grants and he wanted these paid into the Bank, so that Egypt would in future have to deal with the Bank rather than with governments about complying with stipulations. He did not like the reference to subsequent grants being dependent on 'circumstances then existing', by which was meant Egypt's financial and economic good behaviour.[46]

In February the Egyptians submitted their alternative drafts to Britain and the United States and let it be known that they had changed their minds about forging ahead without waiting for prior Sudanese consent. Sudan, now independent, had protested vigorously against being ignored over a project which would flood a part of her country. Exaggerating the difficulty Egypt would have in reaching such an agreement, the West now assumed that there was plenty of time. That, however, ran the risk of ignoring the congressional appropriation cycle in the United States. If the money set aside for the Aswan initial grant was not committed to that purpose by the end of the fiscal year on 30 June, there would be a political problem about raising fresh money from Congress for the following year.[47] It was true that under the Mutual Security Programme economic aid money was not voted for particular items, but Congress was growing increasingly critical of the programme as a whole and constantly attempting to limit it in detail. The High Aswan Dam was hugely unpopular with a number of overlapping political categories – with Southerners from cotton states because they thought it would enable Egypt to increase her competing cotton crop; with Southerners and Westerners because the Eisenhower Administration was not being commensurately helpful to public works projects at home; with the growing number of Senators and Congressmen who could be reached by the increasingly effective Zionist Lobby and with politicians in general because of the mounting perception that Nasser was becoming anti-West.

While the initial slackening of pace was due to Nasser, Dulles was, from the end of March, contributing his own delaying tactics according to the Omega Memorandum. On 16 May Nasser hardened the congressional line-up against Egypt by announcing recognition of the People's Republic of China. On 25 May the Egyptian papers reported that Nasser would be visiting Peking. 'Red China' was a subject about which, as Eisenhower and Dulles had graphically spelled out to Eden in January, it was not possible in the United States to hold rational discourse.[48] The effect, therefore, was to harden immeasurably political opposition to the Dam. Dulles had to take seriously (though he did not think that it was constitutionally binding on him) the Senate Appropriations Committee's resolution that 'None of the funds provided in this Act shall be used for assistance in connection with the construction of the Aswan Dam.' He promised to consult the Committee before taking any action.[49] There was some danger of the prohibition being written into the Act itself, creating a precedent which Dulles was most anxious to avoid.

At the beginning of June the Minister at the American Embassy informed Sir Ivone Kirkpatrick that in the altered climate of American opinion there was no chance whatever of inducing Congress to put up money for the Dam.[50] With some exceptions this was not unwelcome news to the British. Ministers had in the past few months been made more conscious of the acute strains on the country's economy. This giving of £5.5 million to a government that was not even friendly and appreciative sounded like the sort of open-handed, free-spending gesture that Britain was now telling herself that she could no longer afford. Between January and May a press war between Britain and Egypt was going full tilt, though a few British journalists kept out of it. Both Nasser and Eden were, unfortunately, avid readers of press clippings from the other's country, a habit deprecated by Churchill. Nor were British Foreign Office officials immune from the new mood. They talked of 'educating' Robert Stephens of the *Observer*, one of two British journalists who were said to meet with Nasser's approval, about the consequences of his 'little Bo-Peep philosophy'.[51] They portrayed Nasser's ambitions in Africa and the Arab world as so opposed to Britain's real interests (and not just to her formal positions) that 'it is difficult to see how Egypt's friendship would profit us. We could as easily have had Hitler's friendship.' To this the Foreign Secretary appended the comment: '[I]t isn't Hitler that Nasser should be compared to; it is rather Mussolini or Peron, who gets involved with a bigger, wickeder (& more anti-British) power.'[52]

It was, therefore, with the feeling that '[T]his American approach gives us a good opportunity to push them to the fore and we should seize it' that officials greeted news of the negative slide in Washington's view of Aswan. This was indeed a contrast to the British panic of a few months back about the danger of the Russians getting the Dam. Officials like Adam Watson, who had recently taken over as head of the African Department, were claiming that Soviet aid for Aswan was not the only alternative to American aid. The Egyptians could go back to the original German conception of the scheme, before this was expanded by the World Bank; this only required £130 million in foreign exchange, some of which might be forthcoming from suppliers' credits.

The Foreign Office reaction deeply disturbed the Treasury official dealing with the Aswan Dam, Michael Johnston, who was not at all impressed by the idea that withdrawal of the offer would stick the Americans in the line of fire. 'Nasser will undoubtedly be appalled by the apparent breach of faith by the two Governments', he wrote on 6 June, 'and will seek to revenge himself. There is not much he can do against the United States but a lot he can do against us. Obvious examples are renewed pressure on the Suez Canal Company or stirring up trouble in the Gulf.'[53]

Some people, including Humphrey Trevelyan and Eugene Black, were getting seriously disturbed at the discourtesy of not replying to the Egyptian amendments to the proposed *aides-mémoire*. On 22 June Black called on Harold Caccia, the Deputy Under-Secretary of State, at the Foreign Office to tell him that the two countries must now make a final decision. There were only two courses open: to go ahead with negotiations with Nasser or to drop the project once and for all. Nevertheless Archibald Ross, who had taken Shuckburgh's place as Assistant Under-Secretary for the Middle East, pointed out in a memorandum that Nasser had a reputation for quick reaction and that, by withdrawing the offer abruptly, Britain could 'jeopardise our considerable financial and economic interests in Egypt and particularly in the Suez Canal'. There might, therefore, be a case for playing Nasser along still further, 'unless, of course we intend the decision to drop the project as a prelude to effective action to get rid of Nasser'.[54]

Henry Byroade was making a last attempt to make Washington see things his way in a series of long, hot, sometimes repetitive and involuted cables. On 26 May he complained that the original vision of the Aswan Dam scheme as a dramatic demonstration of America's commitment to helping underdeveloped countries to raise their standard of living had been submerged by irrelevant criteria such as Nasser's ability to deliver a Palestine settlement. Disillusionment had come, Byroade accused his fellow-countrymen, just because Nasser was 'honest enough to tell us frankly and bluntly what he felt he could do, rather than play us along in the typical manner of the Middle East'. On 16 June he described the close parallels he saw between the case of arms supplies, over which Nasser had tried repeatedly to arrange matters with the United States and had turned to the Soviet Union only when he got nowhere, and the question of the High Dam.[55]

But John Foster Dulles was no longer so sure that it would be a bad thing for the Russians to take on the Dam. He was filling his yellow legal pads with these fresh thoughts which he shared with the Senate Foreign Relations Committee in executive (secret) session on 26 June and with the British Ambassador on 13 July. Would it really be of benefit to the West to retain such a tight hold on the Egyptian economy for ten to fifteen years as the scheme required? Would not the Egyptian people blame the West for the resultant austerity and object that Britain and America were trying to run their affairs? On the other hand, if the Soviet Union took up the scheme, the Russians might well find that they had a white elephant on their hands, which in the end would earn them no gratitude from the Egyptian people.[56]

The Master Chess Player

On 23 June 1956 Gamal Abdul Nasser became the President of Egypt, the first native ruler of Egypt (if Neguib counts as a Sudanese) in 2,500 years. In a national election all except 2,857 votes went to the sole candidate. All political detainees were released. The regime was somewhat civilianised, in that the Revolutionary Command Council ceased to have any constitutional function. There were some new civilian Cabinet members, including no less than three highly qualified engineers, and such Free Officers as remained Ministers dropped their military ranks, except for the Minister of War, Nasser's one really close friend, Major-General Hakim Amer.[57] A National Assembly was to meet in November, after party-less but contested elections in which for the first time women were to have the vote.

The new President had waited to effect these changes until Egyptian soil was clear of British troops, the last contingent of which left Navy House in Port Said at fifteen minutes past midnight on 13 June. The end of seventy-four years of 'temporary occupation' was marked by three days of celebration at which the most prominent overseas guest was Dmitri Shepilov, invited as editor of *Pravda* but turning up as the new Soviet Foreign Minister whose name was associated with the wholesale rejection of Stalinism and with the policy of extending support to non-communist nationalists. Although the West rather expected a dramatic new Soviet offer during Shepilov's visit, the Aswan Dam was the subject of only brief discussion between him and Nasser. According to British sources, Shepilov introduced the issue by saying that since he had become Foreign Minister he had reviewed Nasser's objections to the last Russian offer. This offer had stipulated that only Russian materials, machinery and technicians were to be used and that, Nasser had said, would be seen as tying him too tightly to the East. The Soviet Union was now willing to offer aid without any strings attached.

The American account, passed by Allen Dulles to his brother on 27 June and forming the basis of the National Security Council briefing of the next day, went further in listing in detail proposals Shepilov was said to have brought. If true, the offer must have seemed what the probable source of the CIA report later called 'frighteningly good' (though the unremitting Treasury Secretary Humphrey said he was glad to hear of the Soviet offer to build the dam, that he hoped the Egyptians would accept it and that this was the best thing that could happen to the United States). Both accounts have Nasser moving rapidly off the topic, telling Shepilov that he would prefer to discuss the matter again in August, when he was to visit Moscow.[58]

The question was tensely debated in Nasser's circle, the most passionate advocate of a 'western solution' being Ahmed Hussein, the Egyptian Ambassador in Washington, who was currently in Cairo. He put it to the President that it was folly, having just escaped the political dominance of

Britain, to submit to that of Russia. Nasser was personally convinced that the United States was no longer interested in helping his regime, but decided to put this to the test by authorising Ahmed Hussein to return to Washington with orders to withdraw the Egyptian counter-proposals altogether, to accept the Western *aides-mémoire* without amendment, and to confirm a previous undertaking that there would be no Soviet participation whatever. In the course of a full day spent with his Ambassador, Nasser predicted that the answer would be 'No', but this would not necessarily mean that he would have to accept Russia's terms. He might, instead, nationalise the Suez Canal and finance the dam himself. Ten years later, he recalled to an American journalist the impact on Ahmed Hussein of this piece of lateral thinking. 'He looked at me strangely,' Nasser said. 'You know, such people don't imagine such things.'[59]

The Ambassador was not slow to spread the good news of his new mandate to, among others, Henry Byroade. Word of it reached Washington and London on 11 July. The two Governments now knew that they could not put off a decision much longer. The British press had no doubt what that decision should be. 'Does anyone in his right mind really want to give a £5 million present of British taxpayers' money to Colonel Nasser?' demanded the *Sunday Express* of 15 July, under the headline 'Not One Penny'. 'If the Dam does not go up, he may fall down,' ran the leader. 'But why should we help to maintain him in power?' Selwyn Lloyd told the Cabinet on 17 July that the American Government was 'likely to share our view that the offer of financial aid for the building of the High Dam should now be withdrawn'.[60]

This statement is important because it has been often said that Dulles's unilateral action in withdrawing the offer to Egypt was taken without warning to the British and contrary to their wishes. Eden himself wrote subsequently that it was 'a major calamity for us both in fact and in timing. However Dulles did not consult us about the latter.' For that reason the sequence of cables needs setting out in some detail. On 14 July the Foreign Office had received from Sir Roger Makins an account of a Dulles monologue indicating the way his mind was moving. It was quite clearly moving towards withdrawal. Eden indicated in the margin that he agreed. Dulles also spoke of holding out hope to the Egyptians that 'they would receive economic aid in some other form'.[61] Lloyd told Makins on 17 July rather surprisingly that he had not succeeded in arranging the full Cabinet discussion he had hoped for that day. He hoped for a further exchange between himself and Dulles before anything was said to Ahmed Hussein.[62]

At 3.40 a.m. (London time) on 19 July a warning arrived at the Foreign Office from Makins that Dulles was seeing Ahmed Hussein at 4 p.m. (9 p.m. London time) that day. 'My impression is that Mr Dulles will leave the Ambassador in no doubt that the offer of last December is withdrawn.' Sir Roger added that the Americans had not decided whether to leave the door ajar for some future economic assistance.[63] The reply to this message was not sent until 6.50 p.m. (1.50 p.m. Washington time). 'It will suit us very well if Mr Dulles speaks as you foresee.' On only one point did the British show anxiety: 'We should rather he said as little as possible about "some future assistance".' As Lord Sherfield (formerly Sir Roger Makins) points out, there had been ample time for a vigorous British demurrer to be sent.[64]

During the morning of 19 July Dulles told Makins what he had decided to tell the Egyptian. Makins commented that this had not been finally considered by the British Government, which had hoped for further consultation. The British point of view on substance was much in line with the United States but Britain would have preferred to 'play it very much longer and not give a definite refusal'. Dulles said he would have liked to have done that too but Congress was giving him no choice. The account of this talk arrived in London at 7.49 p.m. (2.49 p.m. Washington time).[65]

Ahmed Hussein, in a happy mood, walked straight into the trap that had been set. Dulles spoke slowly and plainly though not unkindly. The various arguments that he had been rehearsing before different audiences over the past month rolled out in succession – the number of riparian states that were entitled to be consulted about the Nile waters, the weight and duration of the economic obligations which would grind down the Egyptian people and turn them against the United States, the impracticability of a close working relationship with a government that was developing intimate ties with those who sought to injure American interests.

But what was decisive, said Dulles, was the state of American public opinion. No single project, he told the shattered Ahmed Hussein, was as unpopular in America today as the Aswan Dam. He concluded with the hope that tranquillity would return to US-Egyptian relations and expressed the belief that, considering their other economic burdens, the Egyptians should get along for the time being with projects that were less monumental. Scarcely able to credit his ears, the Ambassador asked if he had understood correctly that there was to be no assistance whatever for the Dam project. Dulles replied that was right.[66]

A press statement was at that moment being distributed to members of the State Department press corps. The document had been worked over several times before the decision had been finally made that, for public consumption, the offer's withdrawal should be attributed almost exclusively to the supposed overloading of the Egyptian economy and its consequent inability to sustain such a large undertaking. Dulles and his advisers imagined that this would be more acceptable than any other explanation – and, to judge from the telegrams from London, the British would not have advised otherwise – but this was to prove very mistaken psychology. There was also an unfortunate briefing of journalists from which arose misleading press reports that Dulles had very properly resisted a crude attempt at economic blackmail by the Egyptian Ambassador. Instead Ahmed Hussein, who was genuinely alarmed at the prospects of Russia's 'very generous' offer now being accepted, had sought to convey his personal feelings about the corner into which Egypt was being driven.

'Mr Dulles has taken the decision for us,' reads a hasty handwritten note in the Foreign Office files. 'We were not absolutely in step at the last moment but the difference between us was no more than a nuance: refusal outright or refusal implied, and it should not do us any harm.'[67] That urbane view was not to be taken by all British officials at all times. On 23 November, by which time much else had ensued, Sir Harold Caccia, by then the Ambassador in Washington, told Herbert Hoover Jr that he would be lacking in frankness if he did not say bluntly that the whole Suez crisis had been started by the way in which the United States had turned down the Aswan Dam project without any consultation.[68] Nevertheless, a British statement promptly endorsed the American move and withdrew also the British grant. With the grants absent, the World Bank loan automatically fell.

On 20 July, the day after the loan was withdrawn, Dulles sat down to lunch with Henry Luce, the celebrated owner of *Time* and *Life*, and his colleague C. D. Jackson, who had spent some time on the White House staff as an expert in psychological warfare. Dulles was happy and animated. He declared that his decision over the Aswan Dam had been 'as big a chess move as US diplomacy has made in a long time'. Nasser, said the Secretary of State with evident relish, 'is in a hell of a spot and no matter what he does can be used to American advantage. If he turns to the Russians now and they say "No", this will undermine the whole fabric of recent Soviet economic carpet-bagging all over the world ... If the Soviets agree to give Nasser his dam, then we are working up plans to lay it on thick in the satellite countries as to why their living conditions are so miserable with the Soviets dishing out millions to Egypt'.[69] *Time* magazine, in its next issue, loyally trumpeted Dulles's move as the work of a master chess player.

Only Couve de Murville in Washington saw anything wrong with this proposition. He told State Department officials that the abrupt withdrawal was stupid because it would inevitably drive the Egyptian Government to a reaction. 'What can they do?' asked the triumphant officials. 'They will do something about Suez,' Couve said. 'That's the only way they can touch the Western countries.'[70]

Nasser Replies

Nasser heard of the American decision in an incomplete radio message that reached the plane in which, with Pandit Nehru and his daughter Indira Gandhi, he was flying back to Cairo from Marshal Tito's home on the

Jugoslav island of Brioni. He had been on a state visit to Jugoslavia culminating in a 'summit of the non-aligned' with Tito and Nehru. Just as his attendance at the original non-aligned conference at Bandoeng in 1955 had first given Nasser's career an international projection, so he looked to this meeting to reinforce that image. *Al Gumhouriya* proclaimed: 'Tito, Abdul Nasser and Nehru represent the voice of reason in international politics. They stood firm in face of the tide of war which almost swept the whole world ... Nasser was selected by the people of Africa to speak for them ... The Brioni conference does not represent Nehru, Abdul Nasser and Tito, but Asia, Africa and Europe.'

From these heights Nasser was brought down with a bump by the message he received. It was the full publicity, the emphasis on Egypt's economy not being up to the job, rather than the decision itself, he said afterwards, that he found 'so insultive [*sic*]'. 'There is no end to their arrogance!' exclaimed Nehru when told of the news.[71] Neither then nor in the course of the next two days during which the Indian Prime Minister was his guest in Cairo did Nasser give him any indication of what in reality he was planning to do next. He rightly guessed that Nehru would have advised against it.

What Nasser wanted, apart from a spectacular demonstration of the fact that he was not to be put down, was some economic base from which he could negotiate anew for the Dam, but not as a mere suppliant to the Russians. There was not much choice: Egypt was not over-endowed with bankable assets. The idea of still building the Dam even without the Russians was not quite so absurd a proposition as the British Government was to make out. Sir Frank Lee, the very able Permanent Secretary of the Board of Trade, thought it was possible, with a combination of the more modest German scheme, suppliers' credits and some government guarantees. As there were several famous British firms in the original consortium, Peter Thorneycroft, the President of the Board of Trade, agreed to take the idea to Number Ten. Eden's reaction seemed to him quite disproportionate. Thorneycroft thought he had never seen anyone so angry in his life. He left protesting that he had only offered a departmental view and was not presuming to challenge a judgment of foreign policy.[72]

The Egyptian President, being an ex-staff officer, set down an appreciation of the likely reaction of three men to a sudden takeover of the Suez Canal Company: Eden, Pineau and Ben-Gurion. There was no American in this group. Ben-Gurion, interestingly enough, was dismissed in two lines. Nasser remembered his feverish efforts to gain admittance to the Non-Aligned Conference at Bandeong; he would surely not wish to have his new country associated with the old imperialists. (He was right to this extent that, throughout the crisis, Ben-Gurion showed himself to be curiously indifferent to the issue of the Suez Canal itself.) Eden, he assumed, would want to use force – he was not deceived by descriptions of him as 'an appeaser' – and France would support him. But, with the Canal garrison gone, had he the men and the materials near enough to hand for the purpose? Nasser sent out Free Officers to Malta and Cyprus, where there were Egyptian consulates to provide cover for military intelligence, to bring back the latest assessments of British deployments and state of readiness. If he nationalised, he calculated that there would be a ninety per cent risk of armed attack if the British and French could mount it before 10 August; down to sixty per cent for September, forty for the first half of October, twenty after that.[73]

Nasser had two speech deadlines for giving his answer to the West: 23 July, the anniversary of the Revolution and 26 July, the anniversary of Farouk's abdication. The first anniversary came and went. The envoys were not back from Malta and Cyprus. The President had to offer his disappointed audience only a raging against the tide. 'Let them choke in their fury, for they will not be able to dominate us or control our existence.' That day he told Major Mahmoud Younes, the army engineer whom he had picked to take over and run the Canal, to prepare in deadliest secrecy the small squads of men who were to move into the offices in Ismailia, Port Said and Cairo.

At Alexandria on 26 July, a few hours only before he was due to deliver his speech, Nasser briefed the Egyptian Cabinet as to what he intended to do. Mohamed Heikal has described the consternation that ensued. 'The Cabinet Ministers were stunned. Many of them were graduates of western universities and this was not at all the sort of political game they had expected to take part in.' When President Nasser finished speaking only one Minister applauded; the others asked nervous questions and suggested less absolute alternatives. He turned them aside, including those who had made reference to the fate of Mossadeq. Outright nationalisation would not involve any more risks that other paths suggested, such as taking a half-share. Success or failure, said Nasser, would depend on whether they could actually make the Canal work. He turned to one Minister – Engineer Said Marei, the Minister for Agrarian Reform – who had not spoken and asked him if he would say something. 'This decision means that we shall become directly involved in a war with Britain, France and the whole of the West', replied Mar'i. Nasser paused and then replied, 'I did not ask you to fight. If war breaks out it will be Abdul Hakim Amir who will be fighting, not you.'[74]

Nasser spoke at Manshiya Square. His speech was long, unscripted, not a little rambling, spoken no longer in the stiff formal manner that he had formerly used but in the Arabic of the streets, addressed directly, with a flavour of complicity, to the people. He started by paying tribute to Colonel Hafez and Colonel Mustafa, at the two ends of the *fedayeen* run, who had each been killed by a letter-bomb from Israeli Military Intelligence. 'We shall all of us defend our nationalism and our Arabism', Abdul Nasser said, 'and we shall all work so that the Arab homeland may extend from the Atlantic Ocean to the Persian Gulf.' Then he gave a brief history of the occupation since 1882 when the British had only succeeded 'with the help of their supporters in the Suez Canal', but at last that was now over. Talking to his audience as would a storyteller, Nasser told of encounter after encounter with the envoys of the West when he had sought arms but had been told to pay a political price. 'Israel's requests must be granted, they said. Israel's frontiers exist. But when you ask: "What about the people of Palestine?" they say: "That is a subject which we shall talk about later."' Afterwards, Egypt had been able to buy arms from Russia – 'I say from Russia and not from Czechoslovakia' – and then there was 'a big hullabaloo'.

Then came the story of the Aswan Dam, the long story of financial negotiations told in circumstantial detail, round by round, made to fit popular memories of how Egypt came to be subordinated to the British. Only this time our hero was in charge. 'I told them that we had had experience of this ... The result was that Cromer came and sat here in Egypt ... We said we would not accept this method.' The World Bank had wanted him to start building the dam using British and American grants for foreign exchange but also large amounts of Egypt's own money as well. Then when the time came the World Bank could confront him with a choice: 'stop halfway, after throwing $300 million down the drain, or accept our terms – the sending of someone to occupy the Finance Minister's seat, of another one to occupy the seat of the Minister of Trade and of yet another to occupy my post, while we sat in this country unable to move without their instructions and their orders'.[75]

The evening was wearing on, but still Nasser spoke, playing on the responses of the crowd, touching their emotions. It was America's turn for a roasting. What Dulles had meant by saying that he did not want any change in the cordial relations with the Egyptian people was that American measures were directly solely against Gamal Abdul Nasser. 'They are punishing Egypt because it refused to side with the military blocs ... This is conceit and the arbitrary domination of peoples ...' He reverted to the subject of the World Bank and the story of his encounter with Eugene Black, its President. 'I started to look at Mr Black, who was sitting on a chair, and I saw him in my imagination as *Ferdinand de Lesseps*.'

That was the trigger, the code-word going out over the radio that unleashed Major Younes and the troops in waiting. The takeover of the company's office was immediate and effective. Nasser, meanwhile, continued to speak long into the night, rehearsing the story of the Canal, mentioning the name of de Lesseps fourteen times for fear that the code-word had been missed. De Lesseps had pretended to be Said's friend but 'instead of the Canal being dug for Egypt, as de Lesseps had told the Khedive, Egypt became the property of the Canal'.

One hundred and twenty thousand Egyptians had died building the Canal, Nasser alleged – a figure he may have picked up from Herodotus who was writing about a rather earlier canal[76] – and all Egypt had to show for it was an annual income of $3 million, while the company collected a (gross) revenue of $100 million. 'Why shouldn't we take it ourselves?' Egypt would finance the building of the High Dam herself thanks to the restoration of her full, sovereign rights in the Suez Canal. 'Today, O citizens, the Suez Canal Company has been nationalised . . .' Instantly as the President spoke a law was promulgated providing for an independent body, the Suez Canal Authority with its own budget, which would 'retain the services of the officials of the nationalised company and of its employees'. These (including the expatriates) 'must continue their work and are forbidden to leave their employment . . . for any reason whatsoever', on pain of imprisonment and deprivation of any right to pension or compensation. This was the feature, with its severe human rights implications, which caused the most offence internationally and was the only major miscalculation by the Egyptian planners. By contrast the shareholders of the company were promised compensation on the basis of the closing prices on the Paris Bourse of the previous day, to be paid when all the assets of the nationalised company (many of them held abroad) had been fully handed over.

'At this very moment, as I talk to you,' Nasser perorated, 'some Egyptian brethren . . . are starting to take over the Canal Company and its property and to control shipping in the Canal, the Canal which is situated in Egyptian territory, which is part of Egypt and which is owned by Egypt.'[77] The Suez conflict had begun.

7

Plotting Nasser's Downfall

From the strictly legal point of view, [Nasser's] action amounts to no more than a decision to buy out the shareholders.
British Cabinet Minutes, 27 July 1956.

This has been a deliberate, unilateral seizure and people around the world are expecting some reaction now.
Dwight D. Eisenhower, 27 July 1956.

The Iraqi elite – young King Faisal, his uncle the Crown Prince, the deaf but for Westerners ever-fascinating Prime Minister, Nuri es-Said – was dining at Number Ten on the evening of Thursday, 26 July 1956. The state visit was over but, as no one who mattered would be in Baghdad at that time of the year, the visitors intended to stay on privately until well into August. Eden was being host to his favourite Arabs, the Iraqis, and especially to Nuri, whom he had counted as his friend since he had first visited Iraq in 1925. Several of the leading Cabinet Ministers – Selwyn Lloyd, Salisbury (the Lord President of the Council), Home (Commonwealth Relations Secretary) – were present, as well as Sir Dermot Boyle, the Chief of the Air Staff, and the Leader of the Opposition, Hugh Gaitskell. At 10.15 a private secretary passed a message: the Suez Canal Company had been taken by *coup de main*.

As Gaitskell was talking to the King, Eden came up with the news of Nasser's speech. There was mention of going to the Security Council. Gaitskell asked: 'Supposing Nasser doesn't take any notice?' To which Selwyn Lloyd responded, 'Well, I suppose in that case the old-fashioned ultimatum will be necessary.' Gaitskell noted in his diary: 'I said that I thought they ought to act quickly whatever they did and that, as far as Great Britain was concerned, public opinion would almost certainly be behind them.'[1] The call was already going out for other Ministers, for Earl Mountbatten of Burma, the First Sea Lord, and Sir Gerald Templer, the Chief of the Imperial General Staff. Also summoned to Number Ten were the French Ambassador, Jean Chauvel, and the American Chargé d'Affaires,

Andrew Foster. The Iraqis left and a rather disorganised meeting went on until four in the morning.

No official minutes were kept but from the cable Foster sent to Dulles and a diary entry by William Clark it is apparent that Eden dominated the meeting, setting its tone from the very beginning with his 'very strong feeling' that Nasser 'must not be allowed to get away with it'. The actual act of expropriation, it was conceded even then, might not of itself have violated the 1888 Convention. But one thing was certain: the Egyptian dictator was not to be permitted 'to have his hand on our windpipe'. That night, too, Eden expressed himself as being strongly of the view that British staff of the Canal Company should be advised not to go on working 'even though they might go to prison and the Canal might have to close down'.[2] Turning to Mountbatten, who in Dickson's absence through illness was the senior Chief of Staff, he asked him what the Services could produce as an immediate response. As Philip Ziegler, Mountbatten's official biographer, has explained, there has been some confusion as to exactly what was then said. To the ordinary fallibility of memory there has to be added, in the case of Mountbatten, a great man's well-attested habit of improving the historical record.[3]

What seems most likely is that the First Sea Lord addressed himself at one point directly to Eden's precise question. The Mediterranean Fleet was already, as it happened, assembled at Malta to await the First Sea Lord's inspection, the ships at four to eight hours' notice for sea. Mountbatten offered to send an immediate signal and by the next morning they could sail. A couple of days' fast steaming could get them to Port Said and they could pick up 1,200 Royal Marine Commandos from Cyprus on the way. Port Said and its causeway could then be occupied in a flash before the Egyptians got round to organising the defences. Such an operation, carried out with dash, would certainly make a large political impact. Admiral Sir Guy Grantham, the Commander-in-Chief, Mediterranean, continued to argue in its favour long afterwards.[4]

There were, however, two snags. It would not give Eden the control over the entire Canal that he wanted; and, if the psychological effect were not decisive, the Marines would be in real trouble once the Egyptians realised that they were without any possibility of early reinforcement. If this were the only thing that could be done immediately, then nothing, it was argued, could, 'within reasonable prudence', be done immediately. It appears from an account that Mountbatten recorded in September that, at some time in the discussion, he himself expressed that conclusion quite precisely. The other Chiefs of Staff in turn produced their answers to the Prime Minister's question. General Templer said that an adequate force for an invasion could not be put together in under six to seven weeks, information that was an obvious shock to Eden. The RAF, said the Chief of the Air Staff, could be ready in half that time.[5]

It became obvious that, to Nasser's dramatic move, Eden was not going to find an overnight response. He had always had a shrewd suspicion that the forces, largely occupied in training, absorbing and replacing large numbers of conscript troops, standing guard for Nato and fighting colonial rebels, were not well disposed to meet emergencies. A major defence review was actually in progress; the future role of the navy had been under intense scrutiny the preceding week. Now he knew the worst. It was going to be a long crisis. But he was nevertheless quite determined. Sir Dermot Boyle told an Air Ministry colleague in the morning: 'Eden has gone bananas. We may have to mount some invasion of the Canal Zone.'[6]

Next morning was a Friday. Then and on succeeding days the sense of national shock and indignation at what had happened was not to be understated. The nationalisation of the Canal had come to Government and people as a bolt from the blue. It affected all walks of life and most shades of opinion. 'In the manner of [Nasser's] nationalisation of the Suez Canal Company only one thing was lacking,' declared the *Daily Telegraph*. 'It should have been announced late on Saturday night, as was the way in Hitler's and Mussolini's day.' 'GRABBER NASSER' was the *Daily Mirror*'s phrase and it stuck to it for several issues. In a breathless front-page leader on Monday, 30 July, the left-wing tabloid declaimed: 'Col Nasser is the Boss leader of Egypt ... But he has chosen a crude and dangerous method to demonstrate that he is a Big Shot. Remember Benito Mussolini? Mussolini ended up hanging upside down by his feet in a square in Milan ... Remember Adolf Hitler? He ended up burning in a petrol soaked blanket outside his bunker in the heart of devastated Berlin ...'

Only the *Manchester Guardian* was an exception to this general tone. 'It would be a mistake,' it thought, 'to lose our heads with vexation over Col. Nasser's latest move or to underestimate its adroitness.' Thus was set, under the leadership of a great and dying editor, A.P. Wadsworth, a pattern of editorial comment that consistently opposed the use of force throughout the crisis. This line, which was developed by the young foreign editor, Alastair Hetherington, who took over as editor before the crisis was over, was to infuriate and disturb Anthony Eden; for him it meant a daily refutation before the world of the impression he sought to create of a united and resolute Britain.

Politically, what had happened threatened to prove a severe blow to Anthony Eden's personal position, since, despite the evidence now available from his minutes, his public reputation had been bound up with the controversial policy of trusting Nasser. Now he became in a sense a late convert to the Suez Group and sometimes appeared to have adopted, in addition to their personal view of Colonel Nasser, much of their general outlook. The Group in turn felt about Eden much as the anti-appeasers had felt about Neville Chamberlain in 1939, that he was now on the right track but was still a prisoner of his past. As he paused to enter the chamber of the House, Julian Amery felt a tap on the shoulder from Aneurin Bevan, the left-wing socialist, who remarked, 'I'm sorry to say, Julian, you've been right, after all'.[7]

A Cabinet Willing to Act

To judge from the minutes, the Cabinet on the morning of Friday, 27 July faced up immediately to the fact that Britain would 'be on weak ground in basing our resistance on the narrow argument that Colonel Nasser had acted illegally'. Ministers had to admit to each other that, with the company registered as Egyptian and subject to Egyptian law and with Nasser undertaking to compensate shareholders at ruling market prices, 'from the strictly legal point of view, his action amounts to no more than a decision to buy out shareholders'.[8] That, at the outset, in the light of all the bluster in public about illegality, was quite a concession.

Nevertheless, since the dictates of respectability required some legal cover, a document was later put together and circulated under the rubric 'Legal Opinion of the Lord Chancellor, Law Officers and Legal Adviser to the Foreign Office'. It contained six points which were meant to add up to an Egyptian breach of international law. Subsequent correspondence was to show each of the signatories except the Lord Chancellor, Viscount Kilmuir, repenting at leisure what he had agreed to in haste. But Kilmuir alone was in the Cabinet, and throughout the Suez crisis it was from that high luminary that Eden was to seek his legal guidance.

It was impressive how much had been prepared in detail for the Cabinet to endorse on 27 July. The case Britain resolved to present to the world was that the Suez Canal 'was not a piece of Egyptian property but an international asset of the highest importance [which] should be managed as an international trust'. The Government was not concerned merely with what happened until 1968: they wanted to settle what was to happen afterwards. Discussion of restoring the Universal Suez Canal Company was notably absent. They were going to promote, instead, management by a new international commission made up of the principal maritime powers, on which Egypt would be given 'suitable representation'. 'Colonel Nasser's action', the Prime Minister declared, 'has presented us with an opportunity to find a lasting settlement of this problem and we should not hesitate to take advantage of it.' The Egyptians – and this was one of the basic assumptions on which the whole British case turned – did not possess the technical ability to manage the Canal effectively. Furthermore their recent behaviour – meaning their defiance of the Security Council's 1951 resolution about Israeli ships and goods and Nasser's proposal to direct the profits from the Canal to the financing of the Aswan Dam – did not give any confidence that they would recognise their international obligations. They would not be able or willing to provide the resources for widening and deepening the Canal to cope with the increasing volume of traffic.

These changes were not to be brought about without pressure. The Egyptians would not yield to economic pressures alone. There must be political pressures as well from the maritime and trading nations; 'and, in the last resort, this political pressure must be backed by the threat – and, if need be, the use of force'. A military expedition against Egypt would be no small matter. It would require three divisions whose equipment would have to be transported by sea and would take several weeks to mount. A ring of bomber forces should be built around Egypt – a nice ringing phrase which, when it came to political and technical reality, was to amount to just Malta and Cyprus. Selwyn Lloyd said that diplomatic moves, to be concerted with the French and the Americans, would take two weeks at most; they must be ready to act then or very shortly afterwards.

The question of going to the UN Security Council, already raised in the Commons, was brought up only to be rejected by the Prime Minister. He did not favour this course because it would bring in the Soviet Union and also because he was not certain of the United States. He formulated two fundamental questions to be decided by the Cabinet: whether in the last resort they were prepared to threaten and, if needs be, use military action; and whether, should the United States and France default, they were willing to take action alone. The Cabinet, lacking only one member, R. A. Butler who was ill, without dissent answered both these questions in the affirmative. A Cabinet Committee, which was called the Egypt Committee, was set up – consisting of Eden, Salisbury, Macmillan, Selwyn Lloyd, the Earl of Home and Monckton – to manage the crisis; to be, as it were, the 'War Cabinet'.[9] The Chiefs of Staff were told to prepare a plan and timetable for military operations against Egypt. Eden was to ask Eisenhower to send over a representative to London since what Jebb had called 'that foolish fellow' Pineau, whom Eden was to take to with enthusiasm, was in any case coming over on Sunday, (29 July) for his prearranged meeting.[10]

Eden's cable to Eisenhower the same day told him that Ministers and Chiefs of Staff were all agreed that they could not allow Nasser to seize control of the Canal 'in defiance of international agreements'. A firm stand would have all the maritime powers behind them. Otherwise, 'our influence and yours throughout the Middle East will, we are convinced, be finally destroyed'. If the Canal were to be closed the United States would be asked to reduce the amount of oil she drew from the pipeline terminals in the Eastern Mediterranean and also to send oil from the Western Hemisphere. He went on to tell the American President that the British had decided, in the last resort, to use force to bring Nasser to his senses. 'I have this morning instructed our Chiefs of Staff to prepare a military plan accordingly.'[11]

Eisenhower immediately agreed to the request for an American representative. Dulles was in Peru, and Herbert Hoover was in charge of the

State Department, a man with a bullet head and an exceedingly prominent hearing aid which contributed to an impression of personal remoteness. It was decided to send the Deputy Under Secretary of State, Robert Murphy, who had had an adventurous diplomatic career beginning as a consul in Munich during Hitler's 1924 *putsch* and including political work with Eisenhower and Macmillan in North Africa during the war. He was told simply to 'see what it's all about'.

Records of meetings at the White House on 27 and 28 July do not at all convey the degree of cool detachment that Murphy's later account, which so irritated Selwyn Lloyd, was to suggest.[12] The President, for instance, said that 'this has been a deliberate, unilateral seizure and people around the world are expecting some reaction now'. He thought it would not take much for the West to go in and operate the Canal but the problem would be to justify such action in the light of world opinion. Hoover said that it was necessary to move strongly in the Middle East if they were to avoid the whole Western position being endangered. He warned, however, that the British wanted to move drastically; for the present, British and French suggestions of early action should be discouraged. The Americans focussed on the single most objectionable feature of Nasser's decree, the threat of imprisonment for pilots and other Canal staff who refused to continue working under the changed conditions. Eisenhower said that, if the Egyptians tried to seize or hold the pilots, Britain would undoubtedly use force and would undoubtedly be justified in the eyes of the world.

The President also talked of the possibility of legal action, with Britain and France putting the tolls into escrow until the International Court of Justice had passed on the matter, and with their also making it clear that if in the meantime Egypt were to stop their ships by force they would respond with force of their own. 'Such a line of action would probably be justified before world opinion.' The President even talked about the US and Nato possibly joining in some such statement. 'He did not consider that the western world could sit and do nothing, waiting to see whether the operation of the Canal deteriorates.' Eisenhower referred to the clause in the 1888 Convention that provided for warships to be stationed by the maritime powers at each end of the Canal. Why not activate this and perhaps even use the warships to escort traffic, if threatened, through the Canal?[13]

Eden's cable was found by the Americans to be rather cryptic, with its assumption of all Canal traffic suddenly ceasing and the whole pattern of world oil movements needing to be rearranged in consequence. The State Department experts were telling the President that Egypt had acted within her rights and that, unless her operation of the Canal was proved to be unjust and incompetent, there was nothing to be done. But to the President, Hoover expressed his personal frustration; action of some sort must be taken, otherwise the western position in the Middle East would be cut down.[14]

Ominously enough, on 28 July Admiral Arleigh Burke, the Chief of Naval Operations, deflated one of the White House's assumptions of the previous day: that, if the British and French were to pull out their Canal pilots, insurance companies would not cover ships in passage through the Canal. This was certainly what the mystique of the Suez Canal Company and the exceptional qualifications and remuneration of its captain-pilots would have led one to expect. But Burke was quite definite. Piloting through the Canal was not difficult. Insurance would not be cancelled if the European pilots were to leave.[15] On Sunday, 29 July Murphy flew over to London to see what was going on.

Interlude on the rue d'Astorg

The scene at the rue d'Astorg on the morning of Saturday, 28 July was one of much commotion. Sir Francis Wylie, a British government director, entered the headquarters of the Universal Suez Canal Company to find the elderly President, François Charles-Roux, and his Managing Director, Jacques Georges-Picot, with a 'sheaf of draft pronunciamentos that they wanted to put out immediately ... in addition to the less than cautious statements they had put out the day before'. These were all, in the quasi-sovereign style established by the Founder (as de Lesseps was known), bidding defiance to the usurper and demanding an immediate test of loyalty of the company's non-Egyptian staff. These should decline to recognise the new Canal Authority and, if required to do so, should come home.

Georges-Picot had wanted to go further and pull out the foreign staff at once, thereby confronting Nasser with an immediate and major crisis. The press had been liberally briefed about what the company had a mind to do, on the assumption that the two governments would be behind it.[16] That, indeed, was the way that the British Prime Minister had reacted on the night of 26 July. Four days later Lord Salisbury added that British employees might usefully sabotage the Egyptian oil pipeline into Cairo.[17]

What sobered opinion was anxiety about building up oil supplies, once it was realised that there could be no overnight countercoup. Britain had three weeks' reserves of petrol, France only eight days'. Both governments wanted to rush as much oil as they could through the Canal during the interval while their forces got ready. The company, therefore, was constrained to put out a communiqué characterising the form of compensation promised by the Egyptians as 'sheer robbery of the shareholder', calling on the banks to ignore instructions from the Egyptian Government, and warning that payment of dues direct to Egypt would not discharge a shipowner's obligations to the company – but not saying one word about the functioning of the Canal. After the sounds coming out of the rue d'Astorg the day before, this was sheer anti-climax.

Sir Francis Wylie had not been there long when the offices were invaded by four of the French directors. 'The Duc d'Audiffret-Pasquier, the Comte de Lesseps, Emmanuel Monick and Pierre Fournier entered *en trombe* and very aggressive. They said the whole of France was upset at the pusillanimous way the company was behaving and that the communist press was jubilant over our ineptitude. They wanted a whole heap of things done, most of them vastly imprudent.'[18]

A message was eventually drafted to the complete non-Egyptian staff, claiming that both governments were behind them, telling them to apply at once for repatriation and conjuring them to do no work in the meantime except under compulsion. Anybody voluntarily working for the Egyptian authorities would be considered to have broken his contract. Senior staff were to set an example and be the first to apply for repatriation. Those who thus proved themselves faithful to the company would be guaranteed one to three years' leave on full pay. By this time Wylie was being told to intercept these instructions since there could be no question of the British Government agreeing to them. The Canal must be kept open. The Egyptians nevertheless heard of the financial offer, which had been transmitted without comment by the French Embassy, and made much of accusations of bribery.[19]

Nevertheless, the wild triumphalism of Nasser's Alexandria speech was rapidly succeeded by plain statements from Ali Sabri, the head of the President's political office, that of course foreign staff could, if they wished, resign, provided they did not just desert but give in the normal contractual notice, and from Abu Nosseir, the Minister of Commerce, to the effect that arrangements had been made to compensate shareholders on the basis of the 26 July stock market price. Company shares, he said, were now in the category of promissory notes. The Egyptians had their hands on £8 million newly deposited in Canal Company accounts with foreign-owned banks in Egypt under the arrangements for investing some of the company's surplus in Egyptian development. But two-thirds of the company's liquid assets were abroad and steps were immediately taken by Britain, France and, shortly afterwards, the United States for them to be frozen and placed beyond the reach of the new Canal Authority.[20]

With Eden having now thought twice about immediately disrupting the Canal, the pilots and foreign ground staff were instructed to stay on for the time being at their posts. Shipowners were told they should pay their dues normally, which would mean that about sixty-five per cent of the revenue, including all from British and French traffic, would be paid into the old company's now frozen accounts in London and Paris. For a time Eden was under the impression that this meant that the Egyptians were having to run the Canal at a loss and wished for much play to be made of this in propaganda broadcasts, until it was pointed out to him that, even with that thirty-five per cent of the income normally paid to the company's account in Egypt, Nasser could still manage to break even.

A clash, it was thought, would come soon, since the Egyptians would not tolerate this method of financing. Indeed, some Egyptian officials did speak of ships which had not paid the new Canal Authority in advance being refused entry. On the whole, British liners wanted in those circumstances to go round the Cape, the tankers to pay under duress. So urgent was the need to build up reserves of oil that British officials were working out ways in which their own shipowners could manage to beat the British exchange control regime.[21] It was all unnecessary. Abdul Nasser placed such priority on creating an impression of ordinariness that he ordered that no ships should be stopped, even including two vessels sailing through under charter to the Israeli Navigation Company with cement for East Africa. Thus the next three months saw a dramatic contrast between the turbulence everywhere else concerning the Suez Canal and the extreme absence of drama on the stretch of water itself, where ships with great regularity transited through the desert from sea to sea.

But there had been one episode on that first night at Downing Street that carried a message. Jacques Georges-Picot had been by accident in London at the time of the seizure of his company and was brought to Downing Street by the French Ambassador. He was not admitted to the meeting or in any way consulted.[22] Whichever way the crisis was to work out, no one from the Conservative Government in London or the Socialist Government in Paris seemed to think of putting the Universal Company of de Lesseps together again.

The Tripartite Talks

The party to the London talks with fewest hesitations or doubts was France. It is true that her socialist Foreign Minister Christian Pineau had spent the night of 26/27 July debating whether he should resign. He was (like Lord Salisbury in Britain) a great resigner. But he was troubled not by any reluctance to act against Nasser but by mortification at having put faith in him. The news about Suez reached Paris at a dramatic moment for Mollet's two-track policy on Algeria. French Ministers were taking part in a night session of the Assembly at which supplementary military credits were being voted while, at the same time, in tightest secrecy, talks at party level were taking place in Jugoslavia with the Algerian FLN, a meeting which had been set up with Nasser's help.[23]

The impact of the Suez news on the French political world was immediate and, with the exception of the Communists and, in a rather muffled way, of Mendès-France, unanimous. Those who did not want to crush Nasser for the sake of Algeria, says the French writer Henri Azeau, wanted to crush him because of Israel.[24] In the morning, Pineau, bitter at the sneers he had been obliged to take, left Abdul Nabi, the Egyptian Ambassador, standing up while he launched into the reading of a polemic against Egypt, only departing from the text to reproach Nasser for violation of his personal honour as a soldier in breaking his pledged word to him. Abdul Nabi angrily walked out. It was the last act in the story of Pineau's unauthorised *démarche*.[25]

Despite Couve de Murville's perception of the link between the Aswan Dam and the Canal, Pineau had no warning of what was in prospect. He had analysed Nasser's Pan-Arabism as froth and rhetoric. In his memoirs he says he did not take seriously the hints in *The Philosophy of the Revolution* of an Arab empire, thinking the Algerian rebellion stemmed from its own roots and was not, save to a superficial extent, attributable to Nasser. In all these respects his perceptions differed from those of his Prime Minister and differed also from the impression he himself often left at the time as to his own views. What placed him as being as implacably opposed to Nasser as the rest of the French political leadership was the issue of the blockade of Israel. Also as a socialist Foreign Minister attempting to use his incumbency to tilt western foreign policy decisively towards economic development in the Third World, Pineau was outraged at what seemed to him Nasser's feckless undermining of investors' confidence in developing countries.[26]

Like many people critical of capitalism, he took for granted the capitalist's expertise. Georges-Picot asserted authoritatively Nasser's absolute inability to run the Canal without the Company's European pilots and technicians. It took years, he said, to train a new pilot. Egypt had neither qualified candidates nor the means of training them. Pineau afterwards reproached himself for his credulity.[27]

It was with Guy Mollet, as with Eden, more a question of learning the lesson of 1936. In this his reactions mirrored those of the majority of Frenchmen across the political spectrum. It was that which safeguarded the position of his government. Almost all the attacks that were made upon it during the course of the crisis were from people on the political right and centre who doubted that a socialist administration was psychologically equipped to act firmly or quickly enough. Mollet, however, was able to convince an impatient nation that his heart was in the right place.

Nasser, Mollet told the owner of *Time-Life*, Henry Luce, was 'somebody we created'. It was right to want to see Farouk replaced, but not to go overboard for Nasser. 'Everyone seemed to have to go on a pilgrimage to Cairo. Dulles went. My Foreign Minister went. M. Pineau now knows what a mistake that was ... We were certainly responsible in part for the fact that [Nasser] got a swelled head.' Mollet brought out his well-thumbed copy of *The Philosophy of the Revolution*. 'This is Nasser's *Mein Kampf*.

If we're too stupid to read it, understand it and draw the obvious conclusions, then so much the worse for us.'[28] The French press was hard at work on the historical analogies. The idea was in the air of reviving the *entente cordiale*. The main difference between 1936 and 1956, it was stressed, was that in 1936 the lead would have had to have been taken by France; now, for geo-strategic reasons, it was the turn of Britain.

Already, on the morning of Sunday 29 July, the French Ambassador was conveying to Lloyd the mood in Paris of extreme urgency: the impact of Nasser's spectacular coup was expected to be so serious in Algeria that, unless measures against him were taken immediately, the whole position might well collapse. The French, Chauvel said, were willing to put their forces under British command and would be ready to take troops from Algeria for use against Egypt. On the other hand they were very much afraid of the influence Robert Murphy would exercise in London.

The French were beginning as they intended to go on, conducting the alliance in a mood of hectic despatch. At ten o'clock on the Saturday evening Chauvel had found the tall and impressive figure of Admiral Nomy, the Chief of the French Naval Staff, on his hands. Bourgès-Maunoury, the conspiratorial Minister of Defence, had sent him over at the end of a Cabinet meeting to act on his own initiative and without regard for the English weekend to convince prominent Englishmen up to and including the Prime Minister of the earnestness of France's determination to have done with Nasser. Afraid, mistakenly, that Eden would be concerned only with the limited issue of regulating the Suez Canal and would in any case be restrained by American reactions, Nomy was to make clear that, if Britain were not willing to go all the way, France was ready to strike at Egypt in alliance with Israel. Confronted with unusual problems of protocol Chauvel telephoned the First Sea Lord, Admiral Mountbatten, at his country estate at Broadlands, where he was entertaining the Queen and his nephew the Duke of Edinburgh for the weekend. Told of the scope of Nomy's mission, Mountbatten rushed up to London on the Sunday morning, having first taken the precaution of alerting the Defence Minister, Walter Monckton. Nomy offered them the full support of the French armed forces to smash the Egyptian President. On Chauvel's advice he had omitted the part of the message that concerned Israel.[29]

Couve de Murville had reported gloomily from Washington about the disquieting atmosphere there: the Americans seemed to be adopting the same attitude as they had done over Abadan, threatening to appear in the dreaded role of mediator.[30] Makins had sent a similar telegram. He had been told by Hoover that, in default of some further overt act by Egypt, such as rioting against foreigners or imprisonment of pilots, military action could not be justified. Hoover seems to have suppressed the strong feeling he had displayed in the White House and left the British Ambassador with the impression that he and his experts were 'weak and irresolute in the face of this crisis and tepid about taking any vigorous action'.[31]

Pineau reached the Foreign Secretary's official apartment in Carlton Gardens slightly ahead of Murphy at 5.45 on the Sunday evening. He had time to tell his host that the position of the French Government was that one successful battle in Egypt would be worth ten in North Africa. The French had most confidential information that from 1 August Nasser planned to drop arms by parachute in the Aurès district of Algeria. Pineau pleaded that it was essential that Britain and France should not be seen as fighting only for the shareholders of the Canal Company. Lloyd swiftly outlined his strategy for co-opting the Americans. There would be trouble with them over military measures but they would actively back the principle of international control. The steps taken towards this would happily fill the gap until Britain and France were prepared militarily.[32]

Robert Murphy now joined the other two and the Foreign Secretary presented his case. He pitched it high: Nasser must not get away with it, otherwise Western control of each section of the oil supply network in the Middle East – oilwells, pipeline, the Canal – would be under attack. That would mean that Nato and Western Europe would be at the mercy of one irresponsible and faithless individual. They should go for international control with the support of as many countries as possible, particularly the neutrals. For that purpose the new authority should be established under the auspices of the UN.

In reply and treading water, Murphy had no difficulty in deploring Nasser's violent and reckless language (which was, after all, largely deployed against the United States), but he made it absolutely clear that for the United States the question of military intervention did not arise. It was essential that the West should carry world opinion with it; the maritime states, broadly defined, should bring their case before an impartial tribunal.

This was not at all the language which Lloyd and Pineau had been using to each other; it confirmed the worst that Makins and Couve had led them to expect. He was not entirely clear, said the British Foreign Secretary, exactly what Murphy meant by an impartial tribunal. Murphy replied he meant something like the International Court of Justice or the United Nations – not reassuring news for a British Cabinet that had already accepted that it did not have a strong legal case. Pineau protested more fundamentally against the whole American approach. It was not a legal problem, but a political problem and it had been caused by a United States decision not to finance the Aswan Dam. Like Hitler, Nasser made no secret of his intentions. If a legal decision went against Nasser, he was no more likely to take any notice of it than he had done with the Security Council resolution about Israeli transit of the Canal.

Lloyd and Pineau then sought to supply Murphy with a respectable context for the references to military force that were being exuded by Whitehall. There was no intention, he was told, of sending any kind of ultimatum to Nasser at this stage. But the Canal must remain an international waterway and the free transit of cargoes must as a last resort be upheld by force. Moreover Nasser had threatened the company's employees with imprisonment.[33]

Later the same evening the Ministers went on to consider the relation of all this to Israel. Pineau said that his immediate reaction to the seizure of the company had been to make use of the Israelis, but he had now thought better of it. Lloyd was quite definite: he had consulted Nuri earlier in the day and from him the word was that all would be well provided the tripartite powers were united and Israel was not in any way involved. 'Hit Nasser', Nuri had said, 'and hit him hard.' Pineau said the French Government wanted to supply twenty-four more Mystères to Israel; the other two men felt that any whisper of publicity about this would suggest that this was a tripartite action and would play into the hands of Nasser. Washington had already asked the Canadians to hold up the delivery, which it had formerly sponsored, of F-86 fighters to Israel.

Pineau then raised the idea of a complete blockade of Egyptian trade and a boycott of traffic throughout the Canal. Nobody else was keen. The immediate impact of a blockade on the underdeveloped economy of Egypt would not be great, and Britain had now decided that she wanted to keep the oil moving until the last minute. However, under the exchange control legislation she was removing Egypt from the sterling transferable account area which meant that from now on Egypt could not, without the British Government's permission, conduct any transactions in sterling whatsoever.

The British Minutes then record that it was agreed that it would be possible to operate the Canal without pilots – risks would be increased but masters could manage on their own – a statement which appears to be at complete odds with Pineau's self-reproach in his memoirs for being so credulous as to have accepted without question Georges-Picot's assurance to the contrary. In his own book Lloyd picks on this as proving that both he and Pineau had doubts from the beginning about the Company's contention that the pilots were essential to the working of the Canal. It must be said that, if so, the doubts were increasingly well concealed.[34]

The evening of the next day, Monday, 30 July, the differences, which had emerged clearly enough in the discussion, were emphasised by the attempt to draw up a communiqué. Murphy had in the meantime seen Eden and had lunch with him. The Prime Minister was on top form, obviously enjoying the chance to make major decisions in the way to which he had been accustomed during the war, taking for granted that Americans would endorse his policies, and saying that there was no thought of asking the United States for anything, 'but we shall rely on you to watch the Bear'![35] Although in the event President Eisenhower was not to be found wanting in this respect, this blithe assumption is what a superpower most dreads:

that allies should take it upon themselves to judge risks which, if they are mistaken, may result in superpower confrontation.

Aim: Nasser's Overthrow

The same euphoric spirit had entered into a session of the Egypt Committee that was held the same day, 30 July. Here Britain's policy priorities were unambiguously stated in a manner that they were not in the Cabinet itself: 'While our ultimate purpose was to place the Canal under international control, our immediate purpose was to bring about the downfall of the present Egyptian Government.' This was an ambition which perhaps came easily to the tongue of Ministers like Eden and Macmillan who had handled weak and unstable regimes in the Second World War and, in the case in point, would have had in mind politics under King Farouk. But Egyptian politics had changed. At crucial junctures in the past, in 1882, in 1942 and in 1952, Khedive or King were available to be bullied into doing Britain's will. There was no Khedive or King available now.

What the Egypt Committee presumably meant was that the psychological impact of a swift and impressive diplomatic and military line-up against Egypt might in itself be enough to dispose of Nasser. This might, the Committee concluded cryptically, require less elaborate operations than those needed to gain physical possession of the Canal. On the other hand, where world opinion was concerned, Britain must be seen to base her case on the need to establish international control of the Canal.[36]

Thus there was to be an agenda within an agenda. The more formidable the line-up against Egypt could be made to seem, the greater the chances that something might snap in Cairo. Nasser could be overthrown or murdered; his nerve might break and, by coming to heel after all his bombast and vitriol, he would rapidly lose credibility among the Egyptian people and the wider Arab masses. If that were the case, negotiations could be allowed to conform to a longer rhythm.

A question that does immediately arise to which there is still no very clear answer is what role covert operations in Egypt were expected to play in this scenario. It is clear from the periodic checks that had been made within the Foreign Office and with the embassy in Cairo that, while, as before, various names were dredged up from past political life, there was no alternative to Nasser that rang many bells.

Some of the military names that might be suggested might very well turn out to be worse. Ex-King Farouk was such a grotesque and discredited figure that his restoration was out of the question. The advice Ministers were getting from Nuri and the Crown Prince of Iraq was to go for the most presentable member of the former royal family, Prince Abdul Monheim, the son of Khedive Abbas Hilmi II, deposed by the British in

1914. 'The mob in Cairo is ultra-volatile and would cheer anything new,' said the Crown Prince.[37] The Prime Minister under the new King would be Ahmed Mortada al-Maraghi, the former Minister of the Interior, who had left Egypt in June and who eventually settled in Beirut. Trefor Evans, the Oriental Counsellor at the Cairo embassy (subsequently Professor of International Politics at the University of Wales) made a flying trip to Whitehall with a list of names from which the 'acquiescent' government would be formed.

How wide or active the conspiracy inside Egypt was during the Suez crisis one cannot be sure. The main account that is available about it comes from an Egyptian intelligence officer, Squadron Leader Isameddine Mahmoud Khalil, Deputy Chief of Air Force Intelligence, who was recruited into the plot while on a trip to Rome by a young member of the Egyptian royal family, Mehmed Hussein Khairi, who was a grandson of the Sultan who ruled Egypt from 1914 to 1917.[38]

At a second meeting between the two at Beirut, Khairi introduced Khalil to 'John Farmer' of MI6, who made a bargain with his Egyptian counterpart. Khalil would be given valuable intelligence items about Israel, which he would collect from abroad, thereby justifying frequent travel, in return for which he would establish a secret organisation of army officers in Egypt. Khalil stipulated that he should be the sole channel between the British and the conspiracy and that he should have substantial sums for expenses.[39] Retelling the story in his book *The Arab Secret Service*, Yaacov Caroz, who was at the time Deputy Chief of the Mossad (the Israeli Secret Service) cannot forbear from remarking, 'Harming Israel's security by handing over secret information about her did not apparently trouble the conscience of the British'.[40]

Whatever the original intentions of MI6 in August, the idea of actively pursuing a coup against Nasser in the short run was either dropped or pursued through other channels. Probably the disaster that befell an important part of MI6's network in Egypt at the end of August – which will be described later – caused abandonment of the idea that anything could be done prior to the inflicting of a military defeat (or possibly a severe diplomatic humiliation). Certainly Khalil was surprised not to be approached again for four months, after the Suez crisis was over. Then the 'Restoration Plot' was reactivated, Saudi money was involved and, according to Khalil, a plan was made to assassinate Nasser and his leading colleagues. The whole conspiracy was revealed by Nasser in person in a speech at Port Said on 23 December 1957 when he handed to the port's reconstruction fund the total of £166,500 that had supposedly been paid over by British agents. Khalil who turned out to have been a double agent, was awarded the Order of Merit.[41]

At least one other conspiracy was alive in August 1956. It started within the army and, unlike the Khairi–Khalil plot, when it too was exposed during 1957 no evidence of contact with British agents was produced. The originator was Lieutenant-Colonel Hassan Siyyam, commanding officer of 3 Artillery Regiment, who during the summer of 1956, before nationalisation, had recruited two other officers, including Brigadier-General Ahmed Atef Nassar. Siyyam's line seems to have been that bad conditions in the army were due to army officers being in the government. What was wanted was a civilian Cabinet and an elected National Assembly. They proceeded to form a group of retired and serving officers, 'The Partisans of Right'.

Once nationalisation was announced they decided to contact civilian politicians who could form a government after the coup. An employee of the Ministry of National Guidance, Abdul Mohamed al-Islambouli, was recruited as a go-between. During August a meeting was arranged between General Nassar and the former Wafdist Foreign Minister, Mohamed Salaheddine, at which the latter was offered and accepted the premiership. Although nothing is known of connections between this group and the British, it is perhaps significant that its programme included the improvement of Anglo-Egyptian relations and the cancellation of trade agreements with the Soviet Union, China and Czechoslovakia.[42]

Since there were close links between the British and American intelligence services and American policy too had been moving against Nasser, Eden may have counted on receiving the degree of partnership in covert action that produced the Iranian countercoup. In a paper which he wrote in January 1957, when he had reached the end of his part in the story, he recalled an agreement between Britain and America that they 'should work out alone and in the utmost secrecy a means of bringing Nasser down'. There is confirmation of a sort in *The Game Player*, the hugely irreverent memoirs of the CIA's Miles Copeland, which tells of the farcical nature of that Agency's share of that enquiry. Eden says that the talks were held in Washington over many weeks, with Britain sometimes being represented by Patrick Dean, who was the Foreign Office Chairman of the Joint Intelligence Committee.

Nothing came of all this. A document was eventually produced, not an impressive one, Eden says, but one at least that was headed, 'Means of Bringing about the Fall of Nasser'. 'Dulles asked that the title should be changed to something more innocuous.' A friendly American warned his British opposite number, 'Don't think the change is just one of title alone. It represents much more. It is in fact a change of policy.' In the intelligence battle as elsewhere, the British were (except for the French) to be on their own.[43]

In a 1985 television interview, George Kennedy Young, the then deputy director of MI6 in control of British agents in the Middle East, denied that Nasser's murder, which after all would have been the most direct way of carrying out the Egypt Committee's priority requirement, was ordered or considered justified. On the other hand, the internal overthrow of Nasser was considered; if the opposition had been effective, he said, it was easy to see that Nasser might have been killed. Morally British Intelligence would not have felt this amounted to the same thing as directly engineering his death.[44]

Peter Wright, at that time a scientist with MI5, says in his book *Spycatcher* that plans to assassinate Nasser were considered on two occasions during the Suez crisis. It is not clear how early on in the story the first episode he describes occurred. According to Wright two members of MI6, the separate and often rival intelligence service, sought his scientific opinion about the use of nerve gas for the purpose. Their idea apparently was to have an agent in Cairo place the canisters inside the ventilation system of the Revolutionary Command Council building. Wright says he pointed out that this would have required a large amount of gas and that it would cause a lot of casualties. The idea was eventually dropped.[45]

Black radio was much favoured. Since Abdul Nasser had issued the challenge of the soundwaves by turning Cairo Radio into a weapon levelled at Western interests, it seemed appropriate that his downfall should be contrived by the same agency. Less than forty-eight hours after the Alexandria speech and the nationalisation of the Canal Company, a powerful transmitter opened up, broadcasting in Arabic on a wavelength close to that of the *Voice of the Arabs*. Directional tests by the BBC Monitoring Service pointed to a station in the south of France. It opened up with a popular song, Abdul Wahhab's 'I Desire a Life of Freedom', followed by three mysterious code messages (such as 'Ali asks Salaheddine to wake up the seven sleepers in the magic cave'), and continued with two alternating announcers projecting strong innuendo, polemic and straight subversion.

'Gamal Abdul Nasser is the foremost traitor of Egypt and the Arab East. Egyptians want to get rid very soon of this madman' – this was the essential message from 28 July, the first day, onwards. The radio announcer argued that the Egyptian President was personally corrupt: 'the leader of the thieves who steal the people's money'; as a social reformer he was a fraud – 'Have you really liberated the *fellah* from feudalism? No, the inspectors of agrarian reforms still treat the *fellahin* in Egypt worse than in July 1952'; he had betrayed Arab unity through his attacks on the Iraqis, who 'have been and still are the foundation stone of Arabism', and he had betrayed Islam through his co-operation with the godless Soviet Union. He had 'liquidated the free nationalists who dared to raise the voice of truth, the patriotic voice of Egypt'. All this led up to the conclusion that, 'This Abdul Nasser is a traitor who betrays the Arab cause and is worthy of immediate death. His hour is very near and all of you will witness it.'

Referring directly to the nationalisation crisis the anonymous radio proclaimed: 'The tyrant Abdul Nasser is trembling from fear, after committing his greatest mistake two days ago . . . You must know that Britain has sent her fleet to patrol the sea before the shore of Alexandria . . . Sons of the Nile, wake up, beware, be on guard against the results of this raving madman's actions. Egypt will be in no position to oppose the fleets of the western states should they decide to occupy Egypt.'

Subsequent broadcasts day after day repeated or developed these themes. 'Who is going to defend the Canal when the guns begin firing at the sons of Egypt? Is it to be Gamal Abdul Nasser? He will run away like a rat to hide. The destruction of Nasser is the only way to rescue Egypt.' The announcers began dubbing their target *Fashil* (meaning 'the unsuccessful one') and Gamalov ('the communist hireling working on Moscow's orders'). They portrayed him as a buffoon and a poltroon, while conceding that he possessed a certain low cunning. 'Yes, Comrade Gamalov succeeded in skilfully hiding his Communism for a period of time. He used to pretend that he was a religious man and carried a book in his car in an attempt to impress the people that this book was the Koran. This book was in fact the bible of Lenin. You tyrant dictator, do you know the Queen of Britain? She is the Queen of the greatest Empire in the world. This Queen moves from one place to another quietly and without announcing her destination!'[46]

As the series got into its stride, a new theme became dominant – that of Nasser as the agent of Zionism. Certain news items were severely strained to fit this pattern. Israeli attention was alerted; an investigation was begun in the *Jewish Observer and Middle East Review*, a British weekly edited by Jon Kimche. 'It is the duty of the Egyptian people to destroy this minion of Zionism', the radio said, 'and to display his head in the biggest square in Cairo, so that the Egyptians may see the deserts of every traitor'. The yacht *Panaghia* had been allowed to stay three months in Port Said because it had been used for secret meetings between Nasser and the Zionists. 'Honest General Mohamed Neguib' should be recalled to lead Egypt back to constitutional life. The killing of Nasser was declared to be 'permissible'. The radio called for 'a hero' to do it.[47]

8

A Matter of Timetables

A way had to be found to make Nasser disgorge what he was attempting to swallow.
John Foster Dulles, London, 1 August 1956.

Please let us keep quiet about the UN.
Sir Anthony Eden, Minute, 7 August 1956.

It was necessary to co-ordinate timetables, to relate the real priority of overthrowing Nasser to the public purpose of achieving (or, as it was put, 'restoring') international control of the Canal. The Egypt Committee's intention was that the conference of maritime powers for which the Americans were pressing should be allowed one function only, that of endorsing a declaration of policy in the form of a Note to the Egyptian Government 'which we would be prepared, if necessary, to despatch on our own responsibility and which would be a virtual ultimatum. If Colonel Nasser refused to accept it, military operations could then proceed.'[1]

This was the authentic style of the Austro-Hungarian Note to Serbia in 1914. During the crisis the British leaders did not use euphemisms among themselves. Ultimatum, pretext, collusion, all were at times employed.

Eden reported on the afternoon of Monday, 30 July, to the House of Commons and to the Egypt Committee. To the House, he was the brief and businesslike technocrat: Egypt's sterling balances had been brought smartly to order; Egypt had been pitched out of the transferable account area; tripartite talks with Pineau and Murphy had begun and were continuing. Gaitskell dutifully announced that he was refraining from putting questions. An ex-War Minister asked about two former British destroyers which were being refitted for the Egyptian navy and were about to be delivered. Eden answered grandly, 'I think we can leave it to the Royal Navy. It will take care of them wherever they are.'[2]

In the privacy of the Egypt Committee, Eden admitted that Murphy was not empowered to make decisions. Lloyd revealed his brisk timetable for a maritime conference. It would open on 7 August and would close after three days. Its task would be to approve a plan for international control of the Canal. If possible, it would also explicitly condemn Egypt's action. The Baghdad Pact countries would be allowed a short time in which to endorse the plan. On 12 August it would be sent to Egypt. 'In the event of an unsatisfactory reply, action would follow.'

There was one other question, concerning the French, discussed at this Egypt Committee. Pineau had offered to provide a French division and a French parachute brigade for military operations against the Egyptians. The Chiefs of Staff had already been in touch, the French contribution could be ready in thirty days. This French offer did not find the British at first over-eager to receive it. As the Chancellor of the Exchequer, Harold Macmillan, remarked, French participation would be all right if the Americans were in too, but French participation by itself raised certain difficulties. The problem for the Egypt Committee was how to safeguard Britain's reputation with the Arab states as a whole. The 'halitosis effect' of the French weighed with Ministers still.

On the other hand, as one Minister pointed out, in view of the large share which the French held in the Suez Canal Company, it would be difficult to exclude them altogether from international arrangements for the control of the Canal. Macmillan and Salisbury were given the task of first working out what it was that Britain needed for the international control of the Canal and for a new regime in Egypt, so that a clear understanding could then be reached with the French before there was any commitment of French troops. In operational terms, the entente still lacked something in cordiality.[3]

By now, Dulles was back in Washington and was sending instructions. So long as there was no interference with navigation, he said, there were no grounds for military action. The basis of the conference should be the language of the 1888 Convention which was concluded in perpetuity, not the Canal Company concession which had been granted for a fixed term. Membership of the conference should be drawn not from users as such but from convention signatories, to which a few non-signatories who were major users, such as the United States, could be added. Article VIII of the Convention was a useful handle since it provided for a conference of agents of the signatories at the invitation of at least three of them. As for the date, more time would be required for preparation.

These (to the British) unwelcome views were conveyed by Murphy. As Lloyd put it candidly, it was Britain's aim to make the conference of maritime powers 'as reliable as possible'. That was why they wanted to exclude the Soviet Union (a signatory but not a big user) and Egypt. 'You can see', cabled Makins overnight, 'that Mr Dulles's attitude confirms the pessimistic impression that I derived from my conversation with Mr Hoover ... In prevailing conditions we can look for little help from Washington.'[4]

On the evening of 30 July, after a long private talk with Eden, Murphy dined at 11 Downing Street with his old wartime friends Harold Macmillan and Field-Marshal Lord Alexander of Tunis. Macmillan used the occasion to put the wind up the American. 'We certainly did our best to frighten him', Macmillan subsequently wrote, 'or at least to leave him in no doubt of our determination.' Both from Eden and Macmillan Murphy received the same message that was to be conveyed 'in utter secrecy' solely to Dulles and the President: Britain had decided to drive Nasser out of Egypt. The decision was firm; military action was necessary and inevitable.

Macmillan was the more graphic speaker. Pulling out all the stops in his Edwardian actor-manager's repertoire and indulging in the large generalisations from history which used to be considered particularly effective with Americans, the Chancellor declared that if, after her glorious past, Great Britain had to go down fighting, the British Government and the British people would rather go down over this issue than any other. He did not expect the Russians to come in. But, 'if we should be destroyed by Russian bombs now, that would be better than to be reduced to impotence by the disintegration of our entire position abroad'. Britain would then count as no more than the Netherlands. Three divisions would be landed in Egypt in six weeks' time; there would be little resistance. Over and over again, reported Murphy, Macmillan insisted that, 'whatever conferences, arrangements, public postures and manoeuvres might be necessary, in the end the Government were determined to use force'.[5]

Eisenhower, on reading Murphy's urgent and vivid cable, asked Dulles to go at once to London to let the British know 'how very unwise their decision is'. Dulles thought there was a better than even chance that a conference of all the relevant nations, including the Asian states, would give unanimous backing for the international operation of the Canal. It might then be possible to take armed action if need be with broad support. He also thought, contrary to his brother Allen of the CIA, that Nasser would probably come to such a conference. The military advice received by the White House at this time and subsequently was incisive and unambiguous. Given on this occasion by Admiral Arleigh Burke, it was that Nasser must be broken, by economic and political means if possible but, if not, by public backing of the British use of armed force.

The President brushed this aside, saying that too much emphasis should not be given to Nasser as a person, more to his embodiment of the emotional demands of the area for 'slapping the White Man down'. Action against him might array the world from Dakar to the Philippines against the United States. Dulles set off on his mission, saying that there was a chance, just a chance, that he could dissuade the British from their course of action, perhaps a bit at a time, gradually deflecting them.[6]

Meanwhile in Paris Guy Mollet was receiving embittered reports from Pineau of Murphy's negative attitude to the use of force and his refusal to accept the view of French intelligence that the Soviet Union was masterminding the whole affair. On 31 July Douglas Dillon, the American

Ambassador in Paris, on being summoned urgently to the Hotel Matignon (the French Number Ten) found the French Prime Minister 'quiet but obviously in a highly emotional state'. The present moment, he insisted, was as critical as the beginning of the Berlin blockade and the invasion of Korea and he was clearly scandalised that America was not treating it as such.

France, said Mollet, had the sense of being abandoned by the Americans even though it was the Americans who had started the whole affair by withdrawing the Aswan offer. He went on to complain that the reason France now found herself at a disadvantage in bombers compared to Egypt, with Soviet planes and Polish and Czech pilots, was her loyalty to a Nato decision that she should concentrate on fighters and leave the bombing role to others. The final turn of the screw he left to the end, as Dillon was about to leave. Recalling his visit to Moscow earlier in the year, Mollet informed him that it had been made clear then that Soviet Russia was prepared, with Nasser's help, to bring about an acceptable peace in Algeria provided France would come some of the way towards meeting Soviet views in Europe – nothing drastic like leaving Nato but just being less faithful to the West and in general semi-neutralist. Dillon was told, in as many words, that Mollet's stalwart rejection then of that temptation had earned him the right to firm American backing now.[7]

The Response from the Commonwealth

Next to the reactions of the United States, Eden was most anxious to learn what responses there were to the new crisis in the Commonwealth, whose leaders had recently been in London for a Prime Ministers' conference, at which by all accounts Eden had been at his most impressive in expanding on the new prospects of East–West détente. He now fired off messages to them putting his case with considerable urgency, placing the main emphasis on the danger of concerted action against the supply of oil from the Middle East. Thus appealed to, the Commonwealth gave off an uncertain sound.

'The Canadian reaction ... hasn't been very satisfactory from our aspect,' wrote General Sir Archibald Nye, the British High Commissioner, on 1 August. '[T]heir reaction – instinctive and perhaps sub-conscious – was "How do we keep clear of this mess?" and *not* "what can we do to help?" ' Louis St Laurent, the Canadian Prime Minister, had, said the High Commissioner, been tempted to reply to Eden with a homily on the danger of provocative action but 'was persuaded that it was hardly his business to do so'.[8]

The Australian Prime Minister's response was the most eagerly awaited. Robert Menzies's John Bull image and presence at sessions of Churchill's War Cabinet made him a counsellor whose judgement was naturally sought.

Unlike Canada, Australia was dependent for much of her trade on the Canal. Menzies, who was visiting the United States when the crisis began, started his analysis of the problem by dismissing out of hand the possibility of making use of force to resolve it. In days gone by, Menzies said, military action would have been the appropriate reply to Egypt. But, in present circumstances, it would split the western world. He advised that Pandit Nehru of India would be worth approaching because he thought he was feeling considerably embarrassed, having been with Nasser in Brioni. His silence on what had happened was eloquent evidence. A private message might bring him in person to the conference, where he might be helpful.[9]

Menzies was correct in his supposition that the Indian Prime Minister was feeling angry and hurt by Nasser's act. 'I feel the Egyptian Government is undertaking more than it can manage and is being pushed by some extremist elements,' Nehru cabled his sister, who was High Commissioner in London.[10] He was being sharply attacked in the Indian press either for having known in advance of Nasser's plans and having failed to stop him, or not known and thereby shown what little influence he had with his non-aligned partner. Indian opinion, aware of the prime importance of the Canal for Indian trade, feared increased tolls and interrupted navigation. The Pandit, according to Dr Sarvepalli Gopal, 'liked Nasser as a person but, judging by his pamphlet *The Philosophy of a Revolution*, did not think highly of his intellectual capacity; and now he felt that Nasser had acted in anger and in haste. In contrast, at this time Nehru was much impressed by Eden.'[11]

In a cold, formally worded letter to Nasser on 3 August, after a week of silence, Nehru underlined heavily Nasser's pledge to abide by the Convention of 1888 and proposed that Egypt take the diplomatic initiative herself by calling together an international conference to achieve conciliation. Mohamed Heikal says that Nasser found this letter from Nehru extremely worrying. He thought it was a bad harbinger of the opinions of the non-aligned.[12] In this he was perfectly correct, to judge by the remarks made two months later by the Jugoslav Foreign Minister Koča Popović to Selwyn Lloyd at the UN. Popović said the Jugoslavs disapproved of the way Nasser had nationalised the Canal Company without even warning his friends. Tito had exchanged telegrams with Nehru and they were both as shocked as anyone in the West. Nevertheless the Indians, like the Jugoslavs, acknowledged Nasser's legal right to nationalise.[13] Nehru's views mattered both because of the historic significance of the Canal for India and because he had considerable personal influence in important circles in the West. He was his own Foreign Minister, but was often influenced on international issues by the Minister without Portfolio, Krishna Menon, whom many in the West took to be his evil spirit.

A long-time resident in London, where he was once a Labour councillor in St Pancras, Menon was the first High Commissioner there after independence. He lacked any domestic political base, his influence depending entirely on his personal hold over the Pandit. He flitted restlessly about the international scene in a self-regarding way, exasperating many professionals beyond measure by his tantrums and his poses, but he was not without a certain shrewdness and diplomatic ability. Anthony Eden thought more highly of him than most and found him quite useful on a couple of occasions at the 1954 Geneva Conference on Indo-China.[14] Menon now told Malcolm MacDonald, the British High Commissioner, that it would be politically impracticable for India to come out publicly against Nasser. So long as India retained some influence with him she would make use of it at a later stage to modify his policy. Menon thought that the United States and the Soviet Union should be brought into agreement over the future of the Canal and that this could best be arranged without benefit of an international conference.[15]

In Pakistan the press and political reaction were generally favourable to Nasser. One leading politician for example thought that the 'curt and imperious manner' in which Britain and the US had announced their refusal to finance the Dam could not but wound Egypt's self-respect. Nasser had 'done no more than pay America and England in their own coin' and small nations naturally felt gratified that Egypt had not taken it lying down.[16] The President, General Iskander Mirza, waved all this aside when he received the Acting High Commissioner, Morrice James. No notice whatever was to be taken of the Pakistan press; it was quite irresponsible. The seizure of the Canal could prove Nasser's greatest mistake and might bring him down provided the powers did not allow him to 'get away with it' and western countries did not give way to the temptation to use Israel against Egypt. The Acting High Commissioner felt able to reassure the President that that point was well taken in London.[17]

The most heart-warming response came from the Prime Minister of New Zealand, Sidney Holland, whom Suez found in Los Angeles. He knew what was expected of a good Commonwealth man. In response to Eden's cable, 'I was able to tell Sir Anthony Eden ... that Britain could count on New Zealand standing by her through thick and thin ... [I]t was a very great man who coined the sentence, "Where Britain stands, we stand" ... I believe that that is the mood of the people of New Zealand. Where Britain stands, we stand; where she goes, we go; in good times and in bad.' A spokesman for the Labour Opposition declared: 'It is good at times that the roar of the British Lion should be heard.'[18] Eden had it in mind that loyal New Zealand, alone among the Commonwealth members, should play an active role in the chastisement of Egypt. The New Zealand cruiser *Royalist* was attached for training to the Mediterranean fleet. Holland was asked on 4 August whether, subject to his own final political decision, she could be used for bombardment and anti-aircraft defence should it come to force. The first hint of a chink in the loyalist armour came with Holland's reply. The *Royalist* could stay with the fleet. But 'Mr Holland is most anxious that this offer should not be known on any account and, if challenged, intends to deny it'.[19]

The Commonwealth mattered, but its members were not major actors. They waited to see how the three western powers were going to react to Gamal Abdul Nasser.

Dulles in London

John Foster Dulles joined the London negotiations on 1 August. It was a cold summer day and in his thin suiting the Secretary felt the chill. Lloyd told him that Nasser was a paranoiac and had the same type of mind as Hitler. He was being inflated by going from one success to another and the West was diminishing in power as a result. If shipping were to be stopped, the right of free passage must be asserted, if need be by force. Pineau was more scary and even more bellicose. According to him, only a few weeks were left in which to save the whole of North Africa; then all black Africa would rapidly slide out of Western influence and control. (There was nothing in the colonial and immediate post-colonial age like the map of Africa for creating geopolitical nightmares). French conviction on this point was so strong, Pineau said, that even if the Americans withheld their moral support and the British their practical co-operation, France would act militarily. How much less would she hesitate if she had Britain by her side. Still, the French Foreign Minister was ready to consider any alternative, provided it was a good one, one that would lay Nasser low.[20]

Dulles agreed that it was intolerable that the Suez Canal, which had been designed as an international waterway from the beginning, should come under the domination of one country without any international control. Lloyd asked him whether he was inhibited from advocating international control by the analogy that might be made with the case of the Panama Canal. Dulles replied that he was not, so long as the argument in the Suez case was firmly based on the 1888 Convention. That established its international status, whereas the Panama Canal had been built as a United States waterway, on United States soil, in the interests of the United States. If the conference was held on any other basis the Government of Panama, encouraged by Nasser, might try taking over that canal.

At this point Dulles, to the gratification of his British counterpart, launched off into a denunciation of the Nasser dictatorship and its abuse of the Canal in pursuit of national ambitions. The performance was highly unwise in view of what the Americans had already found out about the volatile state of feeling among their allies. As though wanting to ignite that feeling, Dulles started off by saying that while it was unacceptable that any one nation should dominate the Canal, it was far more unacceptable when that one nation was Egypt. Using language which, Eden later wrote, 'rang in my ears for months', he said that 'a way had to be found to make Nasser *disgorge* what he was attempting to swallow'.

There followed a rather long passage, to which much less attention was paid by his audience, in which Dulles spoke of the disastrous results that would follow the use of force against Nasser if not backed by world opinion and of the dangerous potential of Soviet intervention. Even if the Russians did not openly intervene, they would send 'volunteers' and supply weapons. The American Government would not be able to associate itself with an operation involving force which had not been preceded by genuine efforts to reach a solution by negotiation. Dulles openly characterised the difference between American and British attitudes to the crisis: 'While the United States considered that all possible efforts should be made to reach a satisfactory solution by international consultation, the United Kingdom regarded such efforts as a matter of form.'[21] In the light of what we now know of the Egypt Committee's conclusions, it was a shrewd summation.

Lloyd, in his memoir *Suez 1956* makes a distinction between the views of Dulles and those of Eisenhower, which were revealed in a letter from the President to Eden that Dulles had brought with him. It is clear that this letter cast a chill on the Anglo-American scene. After an affectionate opening, Eisenhower began by describing his alarm at receiving Murphy's cable 'telling me on a most secret basis of your decision to employ force without delay or attempting any intermediate and less drastic steps'. 'This was a strange letter,' commented Selwyn Lloyd twenty-two years later. 'The Cabinet had not approved the immediate use of force.' His comment strikes one as disingenuous. The use of force that was being approved was only 'not immediate' in so far as this had been found to be impossible. But the Egypt Committee was engaged in forging an instrument of war which would take six weeks to get into position and the only 'intermediate and less drastic steps' that the Ministers had in mind were either ones that would serve to fill the unavoidable time gap or ones that would anticipate military action by dethroning Nasser beforehand.

The President's command of syntax was notably erratic but his meaning was usually plain. So it was in this case; what Eisenhower wished to convey was 'the unwisdom even of contemplating the use of military force at this moment'. He pointed out that 'the employment of US forces is possible only through positive action on the part of the Congress', which was now adjourned, with its members about to engage in an election campaign. If force were used without every peaceful means having been genuinely exhausted, 'there would be a reaction that could very seriously affect our people's feeling toward our western allies. I do not want to exaggerate but I assure you that this could grow to such an intensity as to have the most far-reaching consequences.' When Dulles apologised for not having had the time to edit the letter, which Eisenhower had personally dictated just before the Secretary's plane left for London, he meant literally what he said. The British, who in general adhered to the view that Dulles was the effective originator of American policy, chose to interpret the remark as meaning that it was to be discounted. They could not have been more wrong.

'The President did not rule out the use of force' – that was the message that Eden drew from this keenly felt outpouring, which should have been given the more heed in that Dulles obviously had not drafted it. It is a comment to which Eden's biographer Robert Rhodes James calls special attention: the assessment was 'technically true', he writes, but the whole tenor of the letter was in the opposite direction.[22]

Pedantic and legalistic though he sometimes sounded, there was something of the risk-taker about Dulles. It was partly this which drove him on in London, partly something that linked him not only with Eden but also with much moderate opinion in Britain: the feeling that internationalisation of the Canal made an enlightened middle option in between exploitation by Anglo-French capitalism and exploitation by Egyptian nationalism. This was the high ground that Eden had swiftly seized with that tactical instinct that had often stood him in such good stead and that Dulles, now that he had rooted the case in the 1888 Convention and in the holding of a conference of maritime powers, persuaded himself that he was entitled to share.

In this connection it is instructive to read a feature article called 'Suez Choice' on the leader page of the *Observer*, the house magazine of the high-minded, on the Sunday after Dulles's visit. 'First,' it stated magisterially, 'we must ensure that operational control of the Canal – the power to grant or withhold passage to ships – is removed from the hands of an irresponsible dictator and placed under international authority'; similarly with provision for improvement of the Canal and adequate compensation. 'But how are we to achieve these aims?' the paper asked. It did not underestimate the problem. 'To be effective the International Authority will need to have *greater* powers of physical control than were at the disposal of the old company'. In addition to force and to acceptance of Nasser's deed there was a third course. 'Don't recognise Nasser's "Authority", pay dues into blocked accounts, offer Nasser the shareholders' slice of the profits. If that should lead to deadlock, build supertankers, put a pipeline through Israel, and give Israel arms for self-defence.' Then, if Nasser retaliated against British ships, 'he would be breaking the international convention and would also bring forcible action upon his head'.

So the *Observer*'s scenario also ended up at the use of force, though with more ports of call on the way and requiring a second overt act from Egypt. As Eden gradually allowed himself to be enmeshed in Dulles's tactics, the closer to the *Observer*'s strategy he would appear to be moving, to the uneasiness of sections of his own party and to the concurrent indignation of the French.

Selwyn Lloyd, in cheerful mood, reported to a meeting of the full Cabinet held on the evening of 1 August his impressions of a day's working with Dulles. The picture he gave was, on the whole, a reassuring one of a United States Administration anxious to help and support Britain. Dulles had said that Egypt must 'disgorge'; the final communiqué was to include a strong condemnation of Egypt and a commitment to international control. But there must be no 'premature' use of force and the Maritime Conference must be 1888-based, which therefore meant the Soviet Union as an 1888 signatory must be invited to attend. It was this last point that the Cabinet found very difficult to take: there would be a risk of Russian manoeuvres on behalf of Egypt, which would take up time and thus cause loss of momentum. The Soviet presence would be repugnant to British public opinion. Perhaps, though, provided the West made it sufficiently clear that the purpose of the conference was internationalisation of the Canal, the Russians might not turn up. In the end, the Cabinet decided that since the Soviet presence meant so much to the United States (because it was supposed to safeguard the American legal position over Panama), she should be allowed to have her way in return for a firm undertaking, preferably in writing, of continued American co-operation with Britain and France.[23]

In the course of persuading Lloyd on the Soviet presence, Dulles had made a little disquisition on the manner in which he had triumphantly stage-managed the Japanese Peace Conference despite Soviet participation. Provided there was sufficient preparation, nothing would go wrong. Having swallowed this, the Cabinet insisted that the conference should meet in London and no later than 13 August, instead of the end of the month as Dulles would have preferred.

Next day (2 August) Dulles argued for a longer period of diplomatic preparation, say three weeks; and he did not want the conference in the capital of any interested power. Lloyd answered very firmly that two weeks was the maximum – it was in fact convened for 16 August – and that it should be in London. Dulles said that the conference must be so orchestrated that, if Egypt were to reject its decisions, she would find herself on her own. The effort to reach agreement must therefore be a genuine one. Pineau observed gloomily that there would be a danger of making the resolutions too easy to accept and then the Egyptians would get away with a victory.[24] Dulles agreed that the conference should last no longer than a week. He said he wished to bring about a situation where Egypt would be under such moral pressure that she would be prepared to surrender.

'We do not want to meet violence with violence', declared Dulles publicly on returning to Washington on 3 August. For that reason twenty-four states, which were either parties to the 1888 Convention or else entitled to its benefits, would meet together to provide their 'sober opinion'. Nasser's Alexandria speech had made it absolutely clear that his seizure of the Canal Company was an angry act of retaliation against fancied grievances. 'Some people' had suggested an immediate use of force, but that would have been against the principles of the UN Charter and have led to widespread violence. At London, they had decided upon a different approach. 'By the conference method, we will invoke moral forces which are bound to prevail.'[25]

Eden Triumphant

The twenty-four nations which were to receive their invitations from Britain consisted of three groups of eight: eight parties to the 1888 Convention, including the Soviet Union and Egypt, eight countries whose citizens owned most tonnage using the Canal (that qualified the United States); and a third group of eight whose pattern of international trade showed a special dependence. The selection was to a certain extent arbitrary despite the apparently neat balance. The sponsors had to spend diplomatic time explaining to various states why they were left out, the Americans telling the Saudis that it was the only way of keeping out the Iraqis, the British telling the Iraqis that it was the only way of keeping out the Saudis. Marshal Tito was furious that Jugoslavia was not regarded, from a maritime point of view, as being the successor state to the Austro-Hungarian Empire; Israel put on a display of hurt and indignation that she, the maritime power with the greatest grievance against Egypt, was not present. But all who were asked were to accept, except Greece and Egypt.

Although Eden and Dulles did not take to each other as human beings, Eden was unquestionably exhilarated by Dulles's visit. The type of language that the Secretary had used during the talks in London gave him the feeling that the weight of the United States was swinging round to back British policy. A few extra days for the conference, some changes in the cast of characters who were coming, apart from that all was going ahead just as he had wished. 'I felt a great sense of relief that evening,' Eden said when he had seen Dulles.[26]

The House of Commons was about to break up for the summer holidays with 2 August the last day before the recess, when MPs were to go away until 23 October. Eden had been waiting until the conference with the Americans and the French was over before making a statement to the House. While the Cabinet met in the morning with Rab Butler in the chair, he laboured upstairs over the speech which he would have to give at noon. Receiving a message that Dulles was unwilling to sign the communiqué setting up the conference quickly enough to enable him to announce it to the House, he muttered irritably, 'Trouble about Foster, he is not straight.'[27]

The low-keyed speech that the Prime Minister delivered to a packed and deeply attentive House was well-suited to its mood and undoubtedly enhanced Eden's reputation. He laid out the main arguments, using Nasser's inconsistent and arbitrary behaviour towards the Canal Company – making agreements with it on 10 June acknowledging that the concession would go on until 1968, and roughly seizing it only six weeks later using language that set the world at defiance. There was the violation of the human rights of the pilots; and there was the threat to divert revenues from the development of the waterway to the building of the Dam. Nasser's figures would not add up. The annual revenue from the Canal would not, at the same time, compensate the shareholder, build the Dam and develop the Canal.

Eden announced to the House what he described as 'certain precautionary measures of a military nature', the movement of certain units to the Mediterranean and the call-up of a limited number of reservists. Being unable to say exactly what the three Foreign Ministers were fixing up, he ended with a brief announcement that nothing less than an international authority would be acceptable.

Thus, quietly and unemotionally, he had nailed his colours to the mast. There was to be no more appeasement; he had chosen where to make his stand. It was a popular position, attractive to internationalists and former right-wing critics alike. After the debate, wrote Hugh Massingham, the famous political diarist of the *Observer*, 'Sir Anthony Eden was to be observed in the centre of an admiring group which included quite a few Socialists. It was a remarkable demonstration.' But, in many ways, the most memorable speech was made by the Leader of the Opposition. In clear, penetrating tones which contrasted with Eden's rather throw-away manner, Hugh Gaitskell indicted the Egyptian leader before the world, starting with the persistent defiance of the UN Security Council over Israeli shipping, coming to the seizure of the Canal Company – 'it was done suddenly, without negotiation, without discussion, by force, and it was done on the excuse that that was the way to finance the Aswan Dam' – and concluding with the Pan-Arab boasting and the threats to destroy the State of Israel. Guy Mollet was right: Colonel Nasser's speeches were like only one thing – the speeches of Hitler before the war.

The Labour leader dilated on the importance of prestige in the struggle for mastery in the Middle East. 'Nasser wanted to show the rest of the Arab world – "See what I can do". He wanted to challenge the West and to win ... He wanted to make a big impression ... It is all very familiar. It is exactly the same that we encountered from Mussolini and Hitler in those years before the war.' If the Western democracies had simply accepted this and done nothing, dangerous consequences would have followed. The first thing was to get a conference and prepare a plan for international control.

Up to this point – and his speech was nearly over – Gaitskell might as well have concerted his presentation beforehand with the Prime Minister, so closely did the public positions coincide. The only difference was Gaitskell's emphasis on Israeli interests. But then came a passage at the end, suggested by two colleagues. After saying that he would not criticise Eden's military precautions he reminded the House of the UN Charter, 'and how, for many years in British policy, we have steadfastly avoided any international action which would be in breach of international law or, indeed, contrary to the public opinion of the world'. Britain must not run the risk of being denounced in the Security Council as the aggressor or of being in a minority in the General Assembly.

These two speeches left little for Captain Waterhouse, leader of the Suez Group, who was the next speaker, to add, beyond saying that, 'We have now got [Nasser] on the run and he must be kept on the run.' It was not until Denis Healey spoke from the Labour backbenches that the Government's record in the Middle East was sharply – and accurately – attacked for its contradictions and incoherence. But the interesting thing about this speech is the fact that even Eden's shrewdest critic endorsed the making of military preparations. Forceful action, in conjunction with others or if necessary alone, would be fully supported, Healey said, if Nasser tried to interfere with transit of the Canal. Moreover, Healey was sufficiently impressed by Eden's internationalism and his decision to base his case on the rights of transit rather than opposition to nationalisation as such that he complimented him on standing apart from all the 'tremendous shouting and screaming in the press about the insult to our national prestige'. A later speaker, the former Labour Foreign Secretary, Herbert Morrison, compared Nasser to Mossadeq and reproached the Eden Government with the failure of an 'excessive policy of appeasement towards Egypt'. He was in favour of taking the issue to the United Nations, so long as the UN would be expeditious and effective. But if, after elaborate and proper consideration, the Government were to come to the conclusion that use of force would be justified it might well be the duty of Members, including himself, to give them support.[28] The eighty-one-year-old Winston Churchill told his wife that he had 'even contemplated making a speech', but that all had gone so well that it would have been 'an unnecessary hazard'.[29]

The Government came away from the debate feeling that they had nothing immediate to fear and no parliamentary restraint in the weeks just ahead. There had been just a few markers put down to suggest to Eden that he needed to have a care about the United Nations. Sir Pierson Dixon, the British Permanent Representative at the UN, a dapper, academically gifted classicist with great rapidity of mind and pen, a former Private Secretary to Eden and by him much trusted, was on leave in England and had been consulted on three occasions by the Foreign Secretary. Not merely in the House but also in the Cabinet – in the prestigious and personally sympathetic form of Lord Salisbury – Eden encountered those who felt that there were in New York international proprieties that should be observed. Dixon, in conversation with Salisbury, on 1 or 2 August, suggested 'a form of reference to the UN which may turn out to have advantages over anything we have thought of yet', by which he meant, very probably, either a letter to the President of the Security Council or the possibility under the rules of holding a debate without a formal resolution.[30] Anthony Eden's real thoughts about the organisation of which he was a founder were conveyed a little later in a pithy minute. 'Please let us keep quiet about the UN', he scrawled across the top of a cable on 7 August.[31]

Apart from the treacherous shoals of its procedures, the UN embodied a paradox. It was the symbol of internationalist aspirations; at the same time it encapsulated a very uncompromising notion of national sovereignty. Inside 10 Downing Street, William Clark personified the contradictions that underlay much that was spoken or written by reflective British people at that time. 'The sad fact', he wrote in his diary, 'is that in the present state of international law and order, nationalism, which may destroy the world community's interest, is sacrosanct and Nasser could get away with theft before the UN. Equally, if Nasser does get away with it – in fact if Nasser is still dictator of Egypt next year – the Eden Government is doomed and British (and probably Western) influence in the Middle East is destroyed.'[32]

9

Musketeer

The English made the condition that Israel would not take part in this action and would not even be informed of it at this stage.

Shimon Peres, quoted in Ben-Gurion's Diary, 3 August 1956.

Dear Harry, Like millions of others I have been stewing about Suez and Nasser and the Middle East and, with recurring distress, I keep hearing a voice saying, 'Was Foster's chess game really so brilliant after all?'

C. D. Jackson to Henry R. Luce, 14 August 1956.

A plan had now to be made for military action. It was one which must conform to the two priorities of the Egypt Committee – that Nasser should be overthrown and that the Suez Canal be entrusted to international management – though, to be sure, by the time they came to be dealt with by the joint planners they were expressed slightly differently, as 'to seize and operate the Suez Canal and restore law and order in Egypt'. Eden had discovered that the type of war, which he needed the forces to be able to fight, was not one for which they were at all ready. The appropriately dramatic response to the seizure of the Canal Company which he would have liked to see would have been a series of paratroop landings next day at key points along the Canal. But the parachutists available in Cyprus had done no parachute training for upwards of a year, having been engaged in tracking down Greek Cypriot 'freedom fighters' in the Troodos mountains. In any case, even if they had been trained, there were no transport aircraft on hand. Even if this deficiency were remedied, there was an extreme shortage of the landing-craft required to carry in sea-borne reinforcements for the parachute drops. In the years since the Second World War the Combined Operations organisation, with whose wartime heyday Mountbatten's name was so closely associated, had been allowed to wither away. The Amphibious Warfare Squadron at Malta, for instance, had sufficient capacity to lift rather less than one Royal Marine commando.[1]

Nor did the crisis catch the RAF at a particularly happy moment. The modern bombers available were the Valiants and the Canberras, both fine aircraft but neither quite prepared. The Valiant squadrons, the first of the V Bombers, were so brand new that they were still in the process of forming at the end of July, which meant that they had not had sufficient training as units. Moreover, owing to production delays their proper bomb-aiming system had not yet arrived, so that a substitute visual sight had to be hastily installed. This was to prove less than wholly reliable. The famous Canberras, intended for service in Nato, were renowned for their very accurate blind bombing aid. Unfortunately that would not work in the Eastern Mediterranean since the device depended on the planes being within range of two separately located radio beacons. Worse, it had been decided a few months before Suez to disband the specialised target marker squadrons that would now be needed when Canberra crews would have to revert to World War II techniques. These techniques in turn were found to have fallen somewhat into abeyance.[2]

By 31 July the Chiefs of Staff had got from their joint planners an outline plan. At this stage the planning was strictly a British operation, though the planners had been told by Admiral Nomy that they could count on the French contributing. Nevertheless they assumed that, if necessary, Britain must be prepared to carry out the operation alone. They also assumed that, while nuclear weapons would not be used, 'no other restrictions would be placed on attack on military targets'. There would be a limited call-up of reservists but not general or partial mobilisation; shipping and civil aircraft could be requisitioned. They reckoned to have available thirty-one Valiant dual-purpose bombers, which were said to have a particular psychological effect as 'potential nuclear weapon carriers', and 200 Canberras with a high international reputation as medium bombers. But these could not all be deployed because of the shortage of airfields within striking range of Egypt. There would have to be a considerable reliance on carrier-borne aircraft. The Mediterranean Fleet, normally with one carrier, was to be built up to three. In fact, at the last minute in November there were five, with the French contributing two more.

Elements of the Royal Marine Commando Brigade were to be poised for an amphibious assault on Port Said; the Parachute Brigade Group would strike from Cyprus. A brigade group of 3 Infantry Division including armour, would be sent out from Britain and kept afloat in the Mediterranean ready to land at Port Said once the harbour was seized; 10 Armoured Division, which was stationed in Libya, should be concentrated near the Egyptian frontier to divert Egyptian attention from the Canal. Other troops were to be assembled at home ready to follow up the initial assault. It would be necessary to use parachute troops simultaneously with the marine commando landings because, on account of the extreme shortage of landing-craft, the punch that was to be landed on Egyptian soil would amount at its point of first contact to 'about 500 men in the first wave'. The minimum turn-round before the second wave could be brought in would be at least thirty minutes.[3] It was, therefore, extremely good to know that the French had offered 2,000 paratroops, most of them, moreover, seasoned in France's colonial wars and considerably better equipped than their British equivalents. The superiority of much of the French equipment and training was to be a recurrent theme of the Service reports of the expedition.[4]

All discussion of the potential campaign had to start from geography and here there was a tantalising feature. At first sight, the British island of Cyprus might seem an ideal asset. Conveniently placed off-shore from Turkey and Syria, it was frequently described as Britain's permanent aircraft-carrier in the Middle East. Lent to the British by the Turks in 1878 for their use as a *place d'armes* for the protection of Turkey, it had never in fact been treated seriously as a base until now. On inspection, its virtues were distinctly limited. It was only a day's sailing from the Egyptian coast but it had only one small harbour, Famagusta, with a quayside capacity quite unsuited for the launching of a major expedition and so silted that ships of more than 5,000 tons had to remain outside the reef. Moreover, the ordinary commercial life of the island could not simply be superseded. Limassol, the only other port, had no wharf, so that lighters were needed.

As for its use as an air base, Cyprus had only one airfield, Nicosia, in full use when the crisis began and even that was undergoing extensive reconstruction. There was a relief field at Tymbou which was very underdeveloped and liable in wet weather to become waterlogged. It was assigned for use by the French. Heroic efforts were expended to rush 800 tons of bitumen by airlift, by tank landing-craft and by commercial vessel from Benghazi in Libya to make its surface tolerable. The RAF base at Akrotiri (one of the two base areas to remain British after the independence of Cyprus in 1960) was due for completion in the autumn of 1957, as part of the programme for replacing the Suez Canal base. But the main runway was ready in August and the station was occupied and used with the builders still at work all around.[5]

The traffic management required to keep these very limited facilities in maximum use had to be of a high order. And there was to be constant anxiety about security. While no one held Egyptian airmanship in much esteem, it was a well-publicised fact that the Egyptians had up to forty-five IL28s on the Cairo West air base which might be flown by Soviet or East European 'volunteers'. The Cyprus airfields would offer a very crowded target; the radar protection was not of the best. Moreover, the majority of the population of the island was in a state of disaffection with its British rulers and would certainly not help to keep secrets. It was only a few months since Makarios had been exiled and the EOKA campaign was still on. Given the shortcomings of Cyprus, most of the expedition would have to be based on Malta, which was 936 miles away from Port Said and the Suez Canal.

The question which caused most discussion from the very beginning was whether, as the Joint Planning Staff put it on 31 July, 'the aim could be achieved by unseating the present Egyptian Government by bombing alone'. The advantage of such a course would be that it could start relatively quickly – the bomber force could get into position within a fortnight and start full bombing operations in a further week. But the Chiefs of Staff decided that they were not sufficiently confident that Egypt would capitulate to air attacks alone to advocate that bombing should start before the landing operation was ready. However, great stress was laid on psychological warfare on whose potential high hopes were placed, though one bright suggestion, by the Air Minister, Nigel Birch, that rumours should be spread that an atom bomb might be dropped on Cairo or Alexandria, was not followed up.

A study was ordered of the chances of enticing Egyptian armour to the east bank of the Canal and blowing the bridges behind them.[6] This would call for some co-ordination with the Israelis and, for this, political approval was required at the highest level. This approval Harold Macmillan, then the most hawkish of Eden's Ministers, wished to supply. On 2 August he raised the question of Israel at the Egypt Committee. Then again on 3 August, at a meeting of the Chancellor and Lord Salisbury with Treasury and Foreign Office officials, Macmillan argued that the disadvantages of Israeli participation in the military action did not outweigh the disadvantages of failing in the enterprise. Israeli assistance should, if possible, stop short of active intervention in order not to undercut support of the 'acquiescent Egyptian Government' which was to replace Nasser. But the Israelis should perhaps be persuaded, as the Chiefs of Staff Committee had recommended, to arrange some diversion (what Macmillan called 'making faces') a few days before the Anglo-French operation was to begin. That should tie down considerable Egyptian forces.[7]

Eden and Lloyd were consulting Nuri, who was still in London, about what Arab opinion would take. He again recommended a blow that would fell Nasser but effectively warned Eden off any hint of collusion with Israel. It would be, he advised, in the Egyptian character for Nasser to give up and resign as soon as he realised the strength of the forces against him. The Egyptians seemed to be nervous already. Nuri said he had already had two indirect approaches suggesting that Iraq come forward with an offer to mediate. Selwyn Lloyd told him that was the last thing the British required. The best thing the Iraqis could do to help was to kill mediation attempts stone dead.[8]

When their preparations were sufficiently far advanced, the Chiefs of Staff proposed to issue an ultimatum to Egypt. If rejected, this would be followed by maritime blockade and air assault to 'neutralise' the Egyptian air force with its new Russian aircraft. Then, 'if necessary', an assault would be made on Port Said with a feint towards Alexandria. These were the only two Egyptian harbours where military hardwear could be unloaded on the docks. The poverty in landing-craft made the landing of a substantial force on the beaches impracticable. Because the initial assault force was to be small, the air offensive and accompanying naval bombardment had to be heavy enough to see that the assault did not meet serious opposition. After the marine commandos and the paras had seized Port Said, forces would be landed there sufficient to break out from the narrow twenty-seven-mile causeway that links it to the mainland and then to take possession of Abu Sueir airfield fifty miles inland. Control would be gradually extended throughout the Canal Zone and, if necessary, elsewhere in Egypt. The timetable that was produced would enable all the intricate force movements to be completed in time to launch the operation on 15 September. Great pressure was exerted to reduce this by a week by cutting corners in the requisitioning and loading of shipping. The first, paradoxical move was to call the paratroopers who were already in Cyprus back to Britain, so that they could be retrained at dropping by parachute.[9]

As for the Strategic Reserve in Britain, the summer crisis caught it in a state of cumulative disadvantage: dispersed, disaggregated, undertrained, on leave, with obsolescent equipment well below strength. Brigadier J. C. de F. Sleeman, called on to improvise an armoured brigade with only two regiments and no headquarters staff, burst out: 'In BAOR [British Army of the Rhine] a whole year of concentrated training is required to train an armoured regiment in a National Service army – yet in the UK, where units are understrength, posted with ineligibles for overseas and woefully short of stores and equipment, they are expected to spread themselves all over the countryside providing training facilities for the Territorial Army; and yet go to war, fit to fight, as part of the Strategic Reserve at short notice.' The infantry had to leave behind their new anti-tank guns because they did not have enough ammunition to use them, and had to be re-issued with old 17 pdrs despite their known ineffectiveness against the heavier Russian tanks supplied to Egypt. 6 Royal Tank Regiment, the only armoured unit that actually saw action, was 'scattered here and there at various TA camps', says Major Kenneth Macksey, the RTR's historian, with 'no mobilisation role and, therefore, no mobilisation plan'. Brigadier Sleeman decided that, as the less unprepared unit, 1 RTR should go first into battle, but, without notice to the Brigadier, 6 RTR were shot off by the navy to Malta; 1 RTR and brigade headquarters were left behind.[10]

The decision was taken not to have a Supreme Commander but to work through the same collegiate system of three Service commanders that already existed in the Middle East. It was understood from the outset that the French had agreed to serve under British command. The three allied task force commanders were now appointed – for land, Lieutenant-General Sir Hugh Stockwell, who currently commanded 1 (British) Corps in Germany; for sea the existing second-in-command of the Mediterranean Fleet, Vice-Admiral Sir Maxwell Richmond (subsequently to be replaced, when his regular tour in the Mediterranean expired, by Vice-Admiral Robin Durnford-Slater, whom Mountbatten had wanted in the first place) and, for every type of air operation, Air Marshal Denis Barnett, who like Richmond was a New Zealander.

Stockwell and Richmond were able to bring their own staffs, enabling them to get off to a head start; Barnett, who was Commandant of the RAF Staff College at Bracknell, had to recruit his individually, although he was allowed to have the pick. The forces were to come under the three Commanders-in-Chief until the operation was ordered, when the task force commanders were to take over. As second-in-command to Admiral Sir Guy Grantham, the Commander-in-Chief, Mediterranean, Richmond was in any case the logical person to prepare to organise a landing or intervention. Barnett and his staff, on the other hand, were inserted awkwardly across the lines of the existing structure of Middle East Air Force and Levant Commands. This chaos was to become more acute in that, when preparations for action against Egypt were decreed, these did not supersede preparation for Levant Command's operation *Cordage*, directed potentially against Israel. The two co-existed uneasily, with the same planes (largely) and aircrews but different commands and very different enemies.[11]

The operation against Egypt was to be codenamed *Musketeer*;[12] information about it was put on a specially restricted circulation list designated *Terrapin*. *Terrapin* was a great excluder. Sir Frank Cooper, who was head of the Air Staff Secretariat at the time, has given a vivid description of what life was like in the Air Ministry for the next three months. 'We had several Air Ministries. There were what I call the troglodytes who, though not strictly part of the Air Ministry, were good healthy airmen living in the basement [of the Montagu House Annex] and emerging into the light of day bearing plans of various kinds on which they asked sometimes for comment and rarely received any constructive advice. There were a limited number of people on the Air Staff and in one or two other places who were reasonably privy to the military planning; and there were one or two people in the outer parts of the Air Ministry who were bullied by Whitehall to do things which they didn't know anything about . . . without any legal backing of any kind whatsoever. Then there was the great majority of the Air Ministry who knew absolutely [nothing] of what was going on.' For the greater part of the time the Secretary of State for Air, Nigel Birch, the civilian in charge of all this, could be included among the latter. An acerbic man, his private secretary recalls, this did nothing to improve his temper.[13]

The new force commanders looked at the plan and did not like what they saw. Alexandria seemed to them a far more suitable port of landing than Port Said. For one thing it had three times the capacity. Ships could berth alongside, and more rapid build-up would be possible. Alexandria's airfield, Dikheila, was close to the port while Abu Sueir was fifty miles from Port Said. Port Said's limited facilities would impose a slow discharge of stores by lighter. There was the danger of the Canal's installations being damaged by any fighting around them; the Egyptians might use blockships in the Canal's mouth. Also the space was limited in which to deploy troops. 'Port Said', said Sir Hugh Stockwell, 'was like a cork in a bottle with a very long neck.'[14] The narrow and easily sabotaged causeway between port and mainland was crammed with vulnerable items like the Canal, the railway, two roads and the Sweet Water Canal, the only source of fresh water in Port Said. It would be natural to suppose that a determined defender could make use of this topography to cause considerable embarrassment to the invader. The break-out from the exit to the causeway at Qantara – and thus the capture of an operational airfield at Abu Sueir – could in this way be seriously delayed.

More fundamentally, General Stockwell and his colleagues saw that a purely local action on the Canal would not of itself solve the Nasser problem. While it was true that the Tel al-Kebir campaign of 1882 showed that it was possible to dominate Egypt from the direction of the Canal, Alexandria offered a more direct route, starting 200 miles nearer to Malta. 'An advance on Cairo by the desert road,' Stockwell wrote, 'would menace the seat of government and the Egyptians would be forced either to capitulate or to stand and fight us to the north-west of Cairo where their army could be annihilated.'[15]

The force commanders' views were shared by Winston Churchill, who was being well supplied with papers, and by Harold Macmillan, who went to dine with him on 5 August and stimulated him to action. Macmillan told him that 'unless we brought in Israel, it couldn't be done'. The following day Churchill personally delivered at Chequers a note on the operation that was mirrored on 7 August by another note from Macmillan. The old war leader was worried by the month's delay during which 'it should be possible for at least 1,000 Russian and similar volunteers to take over the cream of the Egyptian aircraft and tanks'. He also thought that censorship should be imposed. As for the objective, 'the more one thinks about taking over the Canal the less one likes it . . . We should get much of the blame for stopping work, if it is to be up to the moment of our attack a smooth running show'. On the other hand, 'Cairo is Nasser's centre of power'.[16]

Macmillan completely agreed. 'I think it is doubtful whether the purpose of the plan is the right one,' he wrote on 7 August. 'The object of the exercise, if we have to embark upon it, is surely to bring about the fall of Nasser and create a government in Egypt which will work satisfactorily with us and the other powers.' Occupying the Canal was gravely insufficient. 'What shall we do next? After all, we were in the Canal Zone with 80,000 men and yet we were unable to prevent the rise of a government hostile to us leading to a permanent source of trouble.' It was doubtful, in any case, whether sufficient force was being made available. Only fifty Canberras and twenty-four Valiants were to be used. The weight of bombs to be dropped would be far less than had been needed to make German airfields unusable.

Macmillan favoured invading from Libya, with also a landing to the west of Alexandria from which that city and harbour could be seized and 'we can seek out and destroy Egyptian forces and government'. Of course, he conceded, such a plan could hardly be represented as 'merely taking the Canal as trustees for the nations of the world', but it would have the advantage of being effective if it came off. He briefly reverted to the Israelis. He wanted further thought given to their participation.[17] Churchill also favoured a role for the Israelis, saying, in the paper he read out to Eden at Chequers, 'We should want them to manage and hold the Egyptians and not be drawn off against Jordan.' Eden was not amused by this coincidence of opinions. 'As I expected', Macmillan wrote in his diary, 'the Prime Minister was in a very bad mood', when he next saw him at the Egypt Committee. 'He had refused to allow my paper to be circulated and I have no doubt that he thought that I was conspiring with Churchill against him.'[18]

Both Eden and Lloyd were flatly opposed to any arrangement, even a tacit one, with the Israelis. Abel Thomas, Bourgès-Maunoury's man, told Shimon Peres that 'the English' had made it a condition of joint action that Israel would not take part and would not even be informed at this stage.[19]

On one matter, that of using Libya for an attack on Egypt, the force commanders were in complete disagreement with Macmillan. They dismissed even the Chiefs of Staffs' idea of immediately concentrating 10 Armoured Division on the Egyptian border 'to demonstrate the seriousness of our intentions'. The move would be slow, logistically difficult and expensive, and politically unacceptable. When the acting divisional commander had told the British Chargé in Tripoli in strictest confidence that, according to instructions, the division was being put on twenty-four hours' notice to carry out training exercises in Eastern Cyrenaica, and would stay indefinitely in the area of Tobruk, the Chargé shot off a telegram, which was taken straight to the Cabinet, predicting a strong and unfriendly reaction from the Libyan Government and people. Britain was treaty-bound to seek permission for such exercises, 'and if and when I do so, no one will be deceived by this story'. The prospect, if a move were made against Egypt, would be of having to restore military administration in Libya. 'If "autumn manoeuvres" in Cyrenaica are to be held now in order to impress Nasser,' said another cable next day (3 August), 'they will not fail to impress the Libyans also but in the opposite sense. We shall have a major security operation on our hands ...'[20]

An entirely new plan drawn up by General Stockwell and his two colleagues for concentrating all resources on an assault on Alexandria was presented to the Chiefs of Staff on 8 August and agreed to by them. It provided for two to three days' bombing to knock out the Egyptian air force followed by an assault landing at Alexandria and an advance of some 80,000 men to the Suez Canal via the neighbourhood of Cairo.[21] Once Eden and the Egypt Committee had agreed to the plan, which they did on 10 August, all the intricate loading of stores which went into the newly requisitioned ships was related to the precise requirements of this particular operation, a circumstance that was to cause difficulties later.

Despite the open-handed French offers of collaboration, the planning had up till now been run in national compartments. When two French admirals, Admiral Nomy representing the French Chiefs of Staff, and Vice-Admiral Pierre Barjot, the short, stout, hyperactive officer who was to command the French forces assigned to *Musketeer*, presented themselves in London on 8 August they raised a number of awkward and embarrassing questions. For one thing, they told their Ambassador, Chauvel, that British planning was running a fortnight (in scenario time) behind the French, so that it seemed that the British were contemplating an interval of some three weeks between the end of the Maritime Conference and operations against Nasser, which was surely not possible. The Admirals asked if there were not something they could do to speed up this leaden-footed schedule – air transport perhaps or sea transport, anything Britain wanted. Chauvel passed on the spirit of Barjot's importunity to Lloyd, who replied tartly that he 'suspected the limiting factor was assault craft, of which I understand the French have none'.[22]

The Ambassador, likewise, hoped that Britain was going to bring in the French on the important decisions. He had detected, he said, the feeling that this was to be a British operation about which the French were not going to be consulted. In fact, though Eden had genuinely decided to work with the French, the sudden alliance disclosed many ambiguities. Admiral Nomy, for example, proposed the maximum publicity for Anglo-French joint military activity in order to impress French public opinion that something was happening. An immediate and obvious move might be made of French parachutists to Malta and a very public visit of the British task force commanders to Paris could take place on their way to the Middle East. Eden had an ambivalent attitude towards publicity. He was much in favour of unattributable briefings that built up a war psychology but very nervous of press reports of actual war preparations. 'Nothing could put us in a worse position in the eyes of international public opinion', the Foreign Secretary told Gladwyn Jebb, 'than to accompany our preparations for the conference with ostentatious military moves.'[23]

With the French decision to serve under British command – a decision lamented by General de Gaulle, who was consulted by Bourgès-Maunoury and approved otherwise of the operation – French deputies were now appointed to the task force commanders. In each case they also commanded directly the French forces involved. Major-General André Beaufre, an intellectual soldier whom General Stockwell was to consider better fitted to be the French representative at the UN, was the land deputy; Rear-Admiral Lancelot was for the navy, and Brigadier-General Brohon for the air. The last two worked without serious friction with their British counterparts. Generals Stockwell and Beaufre were something else again.

Sir Hugh Stockwell, with his clipped military moustaches and somewhat hearty manner, might correspond at first sight to the French stereotype of the Englishman at war. But those Frenchmen who were to work with him over the next five months were to find him disconcertingly lacking in English sang-froid and phlegm. Jacques Baeyens, who was to be the French political adviser to the expedition, described what he was like to work with:

> Extremely excitable, gesticulating, keeping no part of him still, his hands, his feet and even his head and shoulders perpetually on the go, he starts off by sweeping the objects off the table with a swish of his swagger cane or in his room using it to make golf-strokes with the flower-vases and ash-trays. Those are the good moments. You will see him pass in an instant from the most cheerfully expressed optimism to a dejection that amounts to nervous depression. He is a cyclothymic. By turns courteous and brutal, refined and coarse, headstrong in some circumstances, hesitant and indecisive in others, he disconcerts by his unpredictable responses and the contradictions of which he is made up. One only of his qualities remains constant: his courage under fire.[24]

According to the French, they handled this odd character with a stiff upper lip, but there was clearly much that jarred with Beaufre's superior intelligence and cool, analytical front. All the same, Stockwell who in 1948 had got the British troops out of Haifa, not perhaps with much glory but in safety, was to concern himself less than his French colleagues with such abstract considerations as honour and prestige.

For the first week, there was some embarrassment. French security being notoriously leaky, there was a sudden alarm about the dangers of disclosing to them the latest plan. Minutes before the French planners, accompanied by General Beaufre, were due to arrive, General Stockwell told his Chief of Staff, Brigadier Darling, that he had just received orders not to let on that anything about the plans had changed. 'There was not time to warn the assembled British commanders and their staffs of this development,' Darling recorded later. 'So the best I could do when the joint meeting started was to pass round a note, surreptitiously, saying no surprise was to be shown at whatever General Stockwell said, and then hope for the best. General Stockwell then gave a brilliant exposition which left the impression that our plans were to land at Port Said rather than Alexandria.' For a week, until the security question had been resolved between the two Governments, the British team, seeing documents marked 'UK Eyes Only', were obliged to mislead their French partners about the plan to which they were working. It was a policy, wrote Stockwell, that was 'both distasteful and foreign to British principles'.[25]

Patrick Dean, chairman of the Joint Intelligence Committee, was sent to Paris as the Prime Minister's personal representative to brief Mollet in person about the secure handling of *Terrapin* material. The French force commanders would be informed in detail but this information must be shared with Mollet and Bourgès-Maunoury only. Papers and signals should not be passed from Britain disclosing the details of the plan.[26] Dean eventually reported almost complete success in his mission; he had only had to agree that Pineau, not on behalf of his department (that was to be completely excluded) but in his capacity as Mollet's personal adviser on foreign affairs, should also be admitted to the secrets. But it was not until 16 August (the day of the opening of the London Conference) that the lines were cleared for totally candid co-operation.

With a D-Day on 15 September, preceded by two days of air and sea attack on the coastal defences, the proposed operation was to take place in three phases. In the first, following a raid by the Special Boat Squadron on the mole to open the harbour boom defences, there would be a direct entry into Alexandria harbour by marine commandos supported by naval gunfire. They would seize the dock area and harbour, while the French, landing across difficult beaches, would take the airfield at Dikheila. Two parachute operations, one French and one British, would occur south of the vital causeways across Lake Maryut. Phase II, lasting until D + 8, would see the landing of 3 (British) Infantry Division, the extension of the bridgehead and the operation of the Dikheila airfield, ready for the break-out from the bridgehead. With a certain optimistic vagueness 'capture of Cairo-West airfield and threat to Cairo' were put down for D + 10, while, under Phase III, further build-up was taking place of 10 (British) Armoured Division, now to be brought by sea from Libya, 7 (French) Light Armoured and 2 (British) Infantry Division from Germany.

'The whole essence of this plan was aimed at the centre of Egyptian resistance, the Government in Cairo,' according to General Stockwell, 'for with its collapse the control of the Suez Canal would fall easily into place. It also aimed at bringing to battle the Egyptian army in the open; for with its destruction the advance and occupation of the salient points on the Canal would present no difficulty.'[27]

It soon became apparent that the initial time calculations for such a campaign – eight days to get to the banks of the Canal – were far too optimistic. The 'new Battle of the Pyramids', as the French called it, was now to take place by D + 14. Then either the Cairo bridges would be found intact or an assault crossing would be conducted of the Nile Barrage, with the use of French paratroops. According to Sir William Dickson, no firm decision was made about what to do with Cairo. General Stockwell said afterwards that he had had no intention of occupying it, but the big city could hardly have been left in hostile hands. Foreign Office briefs spoke of going in for a couple of days, sorting out the Government and then leaving, a procedure that was perhaps better not put to the test.[28]

The reactions of the French to this change of plan varied. Beaufre was distinctly favourable, insisting only that the French must have a distinct role in securing the southern routes out of Alexandria. Rather worryingly, the French Deputy Commander-in-Chief, Admiral Barjot, began to develop other ideas which he expressed in the barely intelligible English that was to be quietly ridiculed by Beaufre (whose own English was impeccable). For the Admiral, Port Said remained the indispensable 'gage', an overused word that he introduced into Suez discourse.[29]

One thing to be noted about *Musketeer* was that it was not very adaptable. It had been put together by men who had been given to understand that the Task Force, most of it starting from Britain, had to be delivered in Egypt in the quickest possible time. The sailing day from Britain could, it was true, be changed but, once this had passed, not much else. Fourteen days after the ships sailed the assault landing would begin. But were the political leaders resolute that, come what may, the diplomatic and parliamentary prologue would be run in punctually to coincide with the military timetable?

Nothing could better illustrate the ambiguities of Britain's political stance than Gladwyn Jebb's instructions for political discussions with the French. 'We do not regard the London Conference as a formality which has to be observed before we can proceed to effective action,' they ran, 'but as a sincere and serious attempt to secure our objectives by peaceful means.' The rest of the document assumed that this attempt was foredoomed to failure. The resulting military operation might involve the occupation of the whole of Egypt and it might also bring the downfall of Nasser. But nothing was to be said about that in the political directive which should be drawn up. It was most important from the point of view of public opinion, especially in the United States and Asia, that the objects of any operation should appear to be limited. 'It follows that the leakage of a document appearing to define our objective in wider terms could be disastrous.'

Next it was essential to mitigate Arab resentment. This raised two problems: the problem of Israel and the problem of France. It was 'essential that our quarrel with Egypt should be isolated as completely as possible from the quarrel of Israel with the Arab States'. Therefore, there must be no large-scale arms deliveries to Israel for the duration of the crisis. Then, there was the French 'halitosis factor'. 'France is at present the most unpopular country in the Arab world. We must try to minimise the additional burden of French unpopularity to the greatest possible extent.' The French must be set a tight deadline for cleaning up their Algerian act. Before the joint action against Egypt was to be launched, France must have her new policy in place, a policy that recognised Algeria as an autonomous entity as opposed to an integral part of France.[30]

In public, the British took pains to limit their objectives, but Eden made no secret of his feelings to Eisenhower. 'I have never thought Nasser a Hitler, he has no warlike people behind him,' he said in a message to the President, 'but the parallel with Mussolini is close ... The removal of Nasser and the installation in Egypt of a regime less hostile to the West must, therefore, also rank high among our objectives.' Eden then loyally endorsed the hope expressed by the President that the coming conference would prove sufficient to induce Egypt to agree to an efficient operation of the Canal. He went on, 'Moreover, if Nasser is compelled to disgorge his spoils, it is improbable that he will be able to maintain his internal position. We should thus have achieved our secondary objective.'

But, Eden insisted, they must prepare to meet the contingency that Nasser would refuse to accept the outcome of the conference (he, no doubt, having also noticed that to do so would be to encompass his ruin) or perhaps would seek, 'by stratagems and wiles', to divide Britain from the United States so that the conference would yield no result. 'I really believe that the consequences of doing so would be catastrophic and that the whole position in the Middle East would thereby be lost beyond recall.' Eden concluded this message with a sombre warning: 'You know us better than anyone, and so I need not tell you that our people here are neither excited nor eager to use force. They are, however, grimly determined that Nasser shall not get away with it this time because they are convinced that if he does their existence will be at his mercy. So am I.'[31]

10

The First London Conference

In the Suez Canal the interdependence of nations achieves perhaps its highest point.
John Foster Dulles at the London Conference, 16 August 1956.

If my son were to come to me to volunteer to fight for Egypt, I would encourage him to go.
Nikita Khrushchev, Moscow, 23 August 1956.

The American President had been ruminating, as he had done earlier in the year when he had thought of inviting Ben-Gurion and Nasser to Washington, about the idea of some dramatic, personal intervention by himself in the Middle East scene. This time, it was a question of Eisenhower going to meet Nasser, not in Cairo but perhaps in Rome, and their both attending the London Conference. He was anxious for Egypt to be represented and was thinking of ways the Egyptian President could come into the lion's den without this involving a rebuff to his pride. It mattered to him whether Pandit Nehru was coming in person: then they could both act as mediators. Since Eisenhower was himself a candidate for re-election, it would not have escaped his attention that such a move might be a popular one at home, reminiscent of his pledge, when he had been a candidate before, to go to Korea. James Hagerty, his Press Secretary and prime advocate of such a course, pointed out that there would just be time to fit in a few days at the conference in London before attending the Republican Nominating Convention. 'Your prestige is enormous and you can do much on a personal basis.'

Dulles on 8 August, with a mixture of unction and admonition ('remember how Woodrow Wilson had dissipated his prestige at the Paris Peace Conference'), set himself the task of talking his master out of the idea. In the end, Eisenhower said that clearly the London Conference was no place for him; more especially since, Dulles told him, India was probably going to mean not Nehru, but Krishna Menon.[1]

The Pentagon was proceeding on lines which diverged from the Department of State; it predicted the need for force and was ready for the United

States to lend a hand. For the time being, Eisenhower temporised. At the National Security Council on 9 August, where the mood was sympathetic to the feelings of Britain and France, the President said that Egypt had gone too far. How could Europe be expected to remain at the mercy of the whim of a dictator? Admiral Radford said that Nasser was trying to be another Hitler. Dulles referred to Nasser's book, which laid down a long-term programme for Arab power. He said he felt that the United States simply could not ask the British and French to accept dependency on 'fanatical Egyptian control of the waterways'. Messages from Nuri es-Said had warned that Syria was planning to get the Arab League to call for a complete stoppage of oil production or at least of pipeline operations. America's whole investment in the future of Europe by means of the Marshall Plan might be at risk.

On the other hand a cable from the Supreme Allied Commander, Europe, General Gruenther, 'came as a revelation'. It reported that there was no question but that the British Chiefs of Staff would recommend military action. But if the British and French started military action, how was it that they were so confident that they could finish it quickly, when the presence of 80,000 troops in the Canal Zone a short time before had not done Britain any good? The Pentagon and the State Department were told to establish a joint planning group to study all possible contingencies.[2] Admiral Burke told Dulles quite plainly: 'The British can't do it. And the reason why the British can't do this is because they are totally unprepared.'

The Americans knew, from their talks with the British on how to implement the Tripartite Declaration just how short of assault landing craft the latter were. 'For God's sake, let's give them the craft,' Burke said to Dulles. 'Give them ours. They're over there. They've got to make things successful.' According to the Admiral's recollection, Dulles replied that he did not think that that was quite proper.[3]

But the United States had to face the issue of principle at this early stage. On 9 August Dulles received a phone call from Gordon Gray, the Assistant Secretary of Defence in charge of International Security Affairs, who was worried that, if he complied with a British request that their expeditionary force be allowed to take some radio electronic equipment assigned to Nato, this would amount to endorsement of the expedition. On this particular matter, Dulles advised him to go ahead; on another, a telegram sent that same night to London and Paris warned that for such transactions there must be no publicity and especially nothing which connected them with the Middle East. At the same time Bourgès-Maunoury was having extremely frank talks with Dillon, who was told that current plans called for sending one hundred and twenty French aircraft to Cyprus, including ninety F84Fs, and was asked for top priority assistance in obtaining the necessary spare parts for the latter. On 12 August came Washington's go-ahead. Bourgès-Maunoury was not exactly fantasising when as late as 1986 he was asserting that he thought he had covert American approval for military action.[4]

On 10 August Dulles went to New York to confer with Hammarskjöld who told him that, on the concrete issues which had been discussed on his trip to the Middle East, Israel was almost totally in the wrong. As to Suez, he did not see how the British and French could possibly justify the use of force. As an immediate, 'hot blooded', reaction it might have been understood, but it would never do after this much delay and deliberation. Dulles agreed that the more delay the less likelihood there was of force; that was one reason why he had advocated the London Conference.[5]

With the invitations to the conference Britain had enclosed a proposal which she, France and the United States had agreed to place before it to establish an International Authority which would operate the Canal, conform to the Convention, pay fair compensation and ensure to Egypt an 'equitable return'. Failing agreement on the last two points, the matter would go before a three-member Arbitration Commission. The Authority, working through a Council of Administration nominated by the Powers chiefly concerned and various technical organs, would decide the level of the tolls, all necessary works, all questions of finance, and 'general powers of administration and control'.[6]

Twenty-two of the twenty-four governments invited accepted the invitation, among them Soviet Russia and India, the two exceptions being Egypt and Greece. The Americans, as has been seen, had been courting the Russian presence. On 3 August a remarkable cable was sent to Chip Bohlen, the highly expert American Ambassador to Moscow, telling him to let the Russians know that the Americans were having a very tough time in restraining 'our friends' from taking quick, direct action in the Middle East and in making certain that Moscow was on the invitation list to the conference. Bohlen, a man whose confirmation in his post had been delayed by suspicions that he might not be hostile enough to his hosts, was horrified at what he took to be this disloyalty to allies and strongly queried the wisdom of confirming serious divisions in the western camp. Dulles persisted and on 7 August, in conversation with Marshal Bulganin, Bohlen carried out the repugnant task. Possibly as a result, the Soviets agreed to come but they made no great effort to comply with the Americans' second and more important request: to deliver the Egyptians.[7]

In accepting Britain's invitation the Indians made clear that they rejected its enclosure. The proposed Authority under the tripartite plan would 'have a status and extra-territorial powers which the Company never had . . . and which cannot be effected without Egypt's agreement or by an act of force'.

Behind the scenes Nehru had been trying to pacify Nasser and to persuade him to avoid any appearance of intractability. 'I would like to express the hope that your attitude would remain firmly conciliatory in spite of provocation,' he wrote to him on 5 August. The following day Nehru sent him detailed suggestions for a reply to London, which would indicate that

Egypt would be willing with Britain to issue a joint invitation to an agreed list of states, without requiring from the participants any prior abandonment of position. The conference so constituted would either execute a new treaty on freedom for navigation and the security of the Canal or update the existing convention.

Interestingly enough, Nehru expressed the view that he did not think it wise for Nasser to refer the problem to the UN. 'In the present state of the world the alignment of forces there may not be favourable. Further it can also lead to the interpretation of prior acceptance of international control.' But he thought Nasser could safely offer to take part in a later conference to be convened by the UN to consider the internationalisation of all international waterways, including Suez.[8] This of course was code for the internationalisation *inter alia* of the Panama Canal, which the United States, and especially Eisenhower, could be relied upon to refuse.

Nasser's first instinct was to go himself to London, inspired, Mahmoud Fawzi wrote in his memoir, 'by self-denying patriotism and the enthusiasm of youth'.[9] It would have been a dramatic move to make and it would have taken the argument into the enemy's camp. It also showed, the Minister of the Interior later told Trevelyan, that the President was not a man to be frightened of risking prestige.[10] But Fawzi joined the majority of the Cabinet in opposing the action as undignified. Egypt should not be 'a mere invitee or a party to be cross-examined'. The venue, the composition and the agenda appeared to be rigged by the other side; and attached to the invitations was the tripartite plan for international operation.

Nasser was still of two minds. He told Byroade on 4 August that he could not at present see how he could attend: 'the Egyptian case would not even be considered; the proceedings would be purely formal; a paper would be put up and everything would be completed in a rush'. It was clear, Nasser said, that not only was the agenda already fixed but the decisions were already made. In a conference made up of satellites of the great western powers, Egypt would end up alone with Russia, a point which worried him greatly because he who placed such a high valuation on propaganda war could see the outlines of a violent campaign against himself. Still, he said these views were tentative and he was clearly at that point reaching for an alternative.[11]

This, with their formula of a dually sponsored conference, the Indians attempted to supply. Following Nehru, Nasser overruled advice to go to the UN to complain about British and French military moves. He was tempted by the Indian plan. But there was tough opposition to it among his colleagues and Trevelyan had heard from Nawab Ali Yavar Jung, his Indian colleague, that the Cabinet by a majority vote had turned it down.[12] Any chance of Nasser's overriding his Cabinet over the British invitation was decisively ruled out by Eden's address on radio and television of 8 August.

This address had been most carefully drafted and then edited for hours round the Prime Minister's bed with official speechwriter, Conservative Party speechwriter, Secretary of the Cabinet and Parliamentary Private Secretary in attendance, as the press secretary William Clark put it, like a TV panel team. 'All act as if it were a legal document', wrote Clark, 'while I inform the press that he will speak merely from notes.'[13]

'The Suez Canal is a name familiar to everyone,' Anthony Eden began. He explained how for Britain it had always been 'the main artery to and from the Commonwealth, running through Egypt but not vital for Egypt,' how Colonel Nasser had seized it 'for his own ends', how oil supply had taken on a life and death meaning for the whole of Europe. 'Without it, machinery and much of our transport would grind to a halt.' Wasn't Britain used to the idea of nationalising industries? 'Colonel Nasser's action is entirely different. He has taken over an international company, without consultation and without consent.'

But, Eden went on, some people said Colonel Nasser had made promises about the passage of shipping. Why not trust him? 'The answer is simple. Look at his record. Our quarrel is not with Egypt, still less with the Arab world; it is with Colonel Nasser. When he gained power in Egypt we felt no hostility towards him. On the contrary, we made agreements with him. We hoped that he wanted to improve the conditions of life of his people and to be friends with this country. He told us that he wanted a new spirit in Anglo-Egyptian relations. We welcomed that. Instead of meeting us with friendship Colonel Nasser conducted a vicious propaganda campaign against this country. He has shown that he is not a man who can be trusted to keep an agreement . . . The pattern is familiar to many of us, my friends. We all know this is how fascist governments behave, as we all remember, only too well, what the cost can be in giving in to Fascism.'[14]

Sir Anthony had now publicly drawn the battle lines. He had openly laid his reputation as a principled opponent of Fascism on the line, thereby appearing to rule out, so long as Nasser was in power, a negotiated settlement. He had made it a personal issue, one of Eden or Nasser, but not both. Although in the rest of the broadcast he referred calmly and constructively to the coming conference and used language such as 'the broadest possible international agreement' to suggest a peaceful outcome, clearly the only way this could be reconciled with what had gone before would be on the assumption that an acceptance of the conference's terms would involve President Nasser's fall.

Rhodes James, Eden's official biographer, finds it difficult to comprehend how this 'measured statement' by the Prime Minister could have been treated by some Labour MPs as 'hysterical' and a prelude to invasion.[15] But it certainly dismayed by its tone some members of the Conservative Party, who expressed their views in letters to their MP or to Ministers. 'So to condemn a man who had just been invited to be a guest of this country at a Conference (where no doubt every effort would be made to induce him to see reason) clearly made it all but impossible for him to accept the invitation,' wrote one of them. 'The reference also to Dictators in general seems likewise out of place.'[16]

Nasser's mind was now made up. He told Nehru that he intended to reject the invitation because 'It is against our sovereignty and dignity that three Powers should without consulting us at all issue invitations, we being one of the invitees, and lay down future methods of controlling part of our territory.' Nasser grasped at the idea of a UN international regime for all waterways, saying he would be willing to take it up whenever the UN wished. He asked Nehru to reject the British invitation also, since for India to accept 'will seriously affect us and weaken our stand'. He complained of Eden's last speech and the announcement of Anglo-French military preparations, and concluded, 'Force is threatened because we are comparatively weak and an oriental people.'[17]

Greece joined Egypt in the rejection because of her quarrel with Britain over Cyprus. The small group of Greek pilots was to be a useful part of the team when the British and French pilots left. But the Soviet Union accepted and even sent a cordial message from Marshal Bulganin expressing his conviction that friendly relations between Britain and the Soviet Union would continue to develop and recognising Britain's vital interest in the Canal. The merits of having a British Prime Minister like Eden who was liable to take quite a different line from the United States over Vietnam did not escape the Russians. Still, Bulganin made it clear that they dissented from the tripartite draft; it was a step back from agreements of eighty years before.[18] The tone was one which the Russians kept up throughout the conference – one of looking after Egypt's interests but remaining on civil terms with the British.

Nevertheless the Jugoslav Ambassador in Moscow reported the irrepressible Khrushchev as having said, in the hearing also of the British and French envoys, at a Romanian Embassy party: 'Don't forget that, if a war starts, all our support will be with Egypt. If my son were to come to me to volunteer to fight for Egypt, I would encourage him to go.'[19]

As Britain was the host state and the general pacesetter, much preliminary work for the conference was completed in London in the days leading up to 16 August when the conference was to assemble. This work showed signs of the erosion to which the stark simplicity of the Foreign Secretary's original timetable was already being subjected. Take the case of the Marquess of Reading, one of the Government's resident grandees, an ex-Liberal and currently Minister of State for Foreign Affairs, who had the ability to drop his monocle onto its string at precisely the correct moment to punctuate his conversation. In a memorandum to Lloyd on 13 August, he remarked on the very general distaste, not confined to Asia, at the idea of the use of force to coerce Egypt. 'I assume at the outset', he said, 'that it is our genuine desire and purpose that the conference should achieve its object and that, as you told me recently, we do not regard it merely as a time-consuming device until a military operation can be effectively launched.' In that case 'the proposals must be such that Nasser himself, even if only under massive and combined political pressure, can ultimately be brought to accept them'.[20]

Similarly, an official inter-departmental committee – the Suez Canal Subcommittee of the Cabinet's Official Committee on the Middle East, meeting under the chairmanship of the Foreign Office's leading arabist, Harold Beeley – resolved on 13 August to amend the main policy brief for the conference 'to bring out that our principal aim, which must govern the pursuit of all our objectives, should be to secure those objectives without resort to military action'. The officials stressed that 'it was clear that military action in present circumstances would not only prejudice our political relationships over a very wide field, including serious damage to the Commonwealth, but might well also fail to achieve secure passage of the Canal'.

The brief listed only five other countries as being absolutely certain supporters of the tripartite plan – Australia and New Zealand, Holland, Portugal and Turkey. The legality of the act of nationalisation should not be conceded but neither was it to be at any length contested. The fixed assets essential to the Canal's operation were due to be transferred to Egypt in 1968 anyway in return for fair compensation, so this raised no great matter of principle. 'The essential factor on which no compromise is possible is the need for an international authority which will ensure the efficient functioning of the Canal.'[21]

As Selwyn Lloyd had put it very candidly when talking to a group of Suez Canal Company directors on 10 August: 'There are many advantages in this situation having arisen now rather than later. If the Egyptians had waited until the concession expired in 1968 they would have been in a very much stronger position.'[22] Ali Sabri, the Director of the Office for Political Affairs in the Egyptian Presidency, had made essentially the same point when he had said on 3 August that the uproar created in London over nationalisation only proved that the British Government would not have intended to let Egypt own the Suez Canal even after the expiry of the concession.[23]

Lloyd told a full meeting of the Cabinet on 14 August, including those Ministers who, not being members of the Egypt Committee, had not shared in the very explicit discussions about the deployment of force, that questions were likely to be asked at the Conference about how anything that was to be agreed was to be implemented. He proposed to duck the issue, saying that agreement to the principle of an international authority did not commit a country to any particular method of enforcement. 'It was important to avoid giving the impression that the Conference had been called merely to endorse decisions already taken to employ force against Egypt.'

Eden then said that there was a difficult question of timing: military preparations were now being completed and there would be a French contribution, but the forces could not be maintained in a state of readiness for any protracted period. That this was indeed a problem was confirmed by the discussion, since some Ministers clearly held that there would be insufficient public support for the use of force in the absence of some further provocation provided by the Egyptian Government.

The Prime Minister broke in with the idea that if Nasser were deprived, once the conference was over, of those transit dues – about 30 to 35% of the total – that were currently being paid to Egypt direct (mainly by American-owned shipping lines), this might cause him to lose prestige and drive him to retaliate. If he stopped ships from using the Canal or took action against company servants, then Britain would have her *casus belli*.[24]

When the Egypt Committee met later the same day the Cabinet Secretary, Sir Norman Brook, presented a timetable which sought to integrate three elements: the international conference and its diplomatic aftermath; the recall of Parliament, which Eden had accepted as a necessity, and the military action against Egypt. The Conference was to take a week, from 16 August; Parliament was to meet for two days on 27 August to endorse the conclusions of the Conference; and after it had again adjourned, Egyptian counter-proposals would be received and after six days (presumably for decent consultation) rejected. The assault force, having sailed from Britain on 7 September, was to land in Egypt on 20 September, the air bombardment having commenced three days before. Eden, faced with such a procrustean bed and having to carry colleagues with him, declined to commit himself straightaway. Once the military operation had been started, he said, it would be found practically impossible to call it off. It also would be impracticable to maintain the force at a high state of readiness in the Eastern Mediterranean for more than a day or two.

The military wanted a fresh call-up of reserves on 31 August and a decision in principle to go ahead with the expedition on 2 September. The transports would sail from home ports with vehicles and equipment on 3 September and the troops of 3 Infantry Division, which was to undertake the main assault, would follow on 5 September (two days earlier than in Brook's scheme). The final decision to land would be on 10 September and the landing on 17 September.[25] But at the Egypt Committee Ministers started voicing political possibilities that would not fit in with these deadlines. Supposing, it was said, that the upcoming conference, with full American support, decided on economic sanctions against Egypt. Supposing the Egyptians took the case to the International Court of Justice without physically interfering with the passage of ships. Then again, if the timetable were adhered to, the visible military steps that would have to be taken in advance even of 31 August – the requisitioning of the entire Bustard fleet which was used in carrying commercial vehicles to and from Northern Ireland to provide the bare minimum required of tank landing craft, the tactical loading of the transports during the last ten days of the month – might not seem compatible with the presence in London of some of the world's leading statesmen to settle the issue peacefully.

The reason for this shift in tone was that public opinion in Britain, unlike that in France, had not remained at that same high temperature which it had recorded immediately after the seizure of the Canal Company. Time, as Nasser had calculated, had degraded the pure atmosphere of intemperance.

Clark, anxiously watching the newspapers on his master's behalf, noted on 7 August that 'the first fine careless rapture in the press has almost entirely died away and the weasels are at work asking whether we should be so bold'.[26] But, as was pointed out in the Egypt Committee on 14 September, if it was to be decided that a further act of 'aggression' by Nasser was essential to support an act of force, then the Government would have lost control of the timetable altogether. The initiative would lie with the Egyptian President. The West could start a course of action such as cutting off the transit dues, but it would depend on Nasser whether he was to respond swiftly by stopping ships which had not paid.

There was one way in which most people thought matters could be brought to a head in the Canal. The British and French pilots were still being most reluctantly constrained by the Suez Canal Company, at the behest of the two Governments, to stay at their posts at least until the end of the Conference. If they were then withdrawn, it would soon be seen that Nasser was no longer competent to ensure that the world's shipping had free passage. Interestingly enough, at the Egypt Committee on 14 August somebody again warned against expecting too dramatic a halt to shipping movements if this were to happen. There would be some ships, it was said, which would still be able to navigate the Canal without pilots and the existing corps of Egyptian pilots might be reinforced from behind the Iron Curtain. But this thought does not seem to have made a lasting impression.[27]

Public Opinion Shifts

The shift that had taken place over the period of time since the snap-shot of a united public opinion in Britain immediately after 26 July was, as Clark had noted, very apparent. Some opinion – and that included important sections of the Tory party – was hardening in a way that spelt major political trouble for Eden should he weaken. But both Gaitskell himself in private and his political associates like Douglas Jay and Denis Healey in public were taking steps to distance themselves from any impression that the Opposition had given *carte blanche* to the Government for a hawkish policy in the Middle East.

The strong letter that Jay and Healey sent jointly to *The Times* on 7 August repudiating the use of force had Gaitskell's strong support. As early as 3 August, fearing misunderstanding as the result of the previous day's debate and having heard to his astonishment that journalists were being told at the Foreign Office that, if the conference's solution was not accepted by Nasser, there would be an ultimatum followed by an invasion, Gaitskell wrote to the Prime Minister. He pointed out that in the House he had deliberately refrained from asking certain questions in order not to weaken Eden's hand, but he wanted to make his views clear on the use of force. 'If Nasser were to do something which led to his condemnation by the UN as an aggressor, then there is no doubt, I am sure, that we would be entirely in favour of forceful resistance. But I must repeat . . . that up to the present I cannot see that he has done anything that would justify this.'[28] A meeting of the Shadow Cabinet on 12 August put particular emphasis on that final section of the Labour leader's 2 August speech, which had lingered on the necessity of going to the UN, and on 14 August a Labour deputation, headed by Gaitskell, saw Eden, Salisbury and Lloyd. The encounter was not a great success. Rhodes James quotes Eden as saying in his diary: 'Gaitskell gave us a donnish lecture about the situation of inordinate length but of unremarkable quality.'[29]

At the same time much of the press, once overheated, had gone off the boil. Most remarkably the *Daily Mirror*, which on 30 July was saying, 'Remember Benito Mussolini? Mussolini ended up hanging upside down'. was saying on 14 August, 'Eden cannot talk to Nasser in 1956 as Churchill talked to Mussolini in the 1940s.' The style of Eden's broadcast offended and embarrassed some, though it is also true that it evoked ardent expressions of support. 'What right have we to assume that Nasser will close the Canal to our shipping? So far he has made no attempt to do so,' wrote a doctor from Hornchurch to Downing Street. 'And if all these military preparations are intended to impress, they show a very bad knowledge of psychology . . . (When Hitler did this we used to call it "negotiating at the pistol point".) Have the British and French Governments lost their heads completely?'

'Why has the machinery of the UN not been used?' asked another correspondent. 'Of what value is the movement of troops to the Mediterranean?' A third declared: 'To threaten force by military action against Egypt is quite immoral. To hold an international conference to consider international control of the Suez Canal under military threat of force is again immoral. Do I assume correctly that if the conference you have called should fail (as it must *surely* do), the Government intend to launch British forces on Egyptian soil to enforce their wishes?' The answer to that last correspondent, as written by a civil servant in the Foreign Office, began: 'The Government are not threatening to use force or military action against Egypt, nor are they holding an international conference under such threats . . .'[30]

Some blank opposition to Eden's policy had existed from the beginning. The authentic voice of the radical left was to be found in Michael Foot's *Tribune*, which had been dismayed by Gaitskell's initial reaction. Its view can be summed up in the headline 'Labour Must Order the Government: Halt! About Turn!' On 17 August Foot wrote in an editorial: 'Returning sanity has even soothed the moist brow of the Labour Party leader who, when the crisis broke, leaped to applaud Sir Anthony Eden's panic measures.' But even *Tribune* had its moments of embarrassment. Every issue contained a column contributed by the idol of the Left and rival to Gaitskell, the great Welsh orator Aneurin Bevan. He was anti-Eden all right, but also anti-Nasser. This did not make for a neat polarisation of the issues. 'When [Nasser] could not get what he wanted from the West he got it from Russia, thus permitting himself to be exposed to the charge of the most dangerous form of international blackmail,' Bevan wrote. He accused the Egyptian ruler of 'treating the Canal like a medieval caravan route and levying toll for right of way'; as an underdeveloped country 'Egypt has the right to come into her own but not into someone else's'. In a later column, Bevan said: 'It must not be all "take", Colonel Nasser ... An absolute assertion of nationalistic values is not consistent with the belief that the better-off nations should help the worse-off.' A *Tribune* reader wrote in: 'As a disciple of Mr Bevan, it was most disappointing to see "Our Nye" climbing on to the Eden–Gaitskell bandwagon of hate against Nasser and Egypt.' And another wanted Foot to 'insert this caption before each of his articles: "The views of Mr Bevan are not necessarily those of *Tribune*"'.

According to Gaitskell's diary, 'To my particular astonishment, Nye Bevan himself was very much in agreement with me' at the Shadow Cabinet which reviewed the 2 August debate. 'He was in no doubt about Nasser being a thug.'[31] But there was another radical tradition that would have no truck with the jingoism of the Left. 'We allow ourselves to be hypnotised by the blessed word "Internationalism",' wrote the great radical historian A. J. P. Taylor in the *Tribune* on 21 August. 'No war for national interests! That's easy. But war, or at any rate sanctions, for the international control of the Canal. How idealistic and romantic that sounds! ... If we want to practice internationalisation we should do it with our own property not with that of others.'

Sir Norman Brook, the Cabinet Secretary, warned the Prime Minister on 9 August that the idea of using force was growing increasingly unpopular. 'How do you do it in this age? Call together Parliament, send in the troops, and get a positive vote of perhaps forty-eight in Parliament and a vote against you in the UN? It just isn't on.' He told Clark, as they went home from Number Ten after midnight, that bluff was all very well till the armada sailed; then they were committed because it could neither turn back nor sit offshore. 'Our Prime Minister is very difficult,' Brook told Clark as he left him. 'He wants to be Foreign Secretary, Minister of Defence and Chancellor.'

Eden remained clear about his priorities – rightly or wrongly he perceived the Middle East as the overriding issue for Britain and was impatient with those who were distracted by other considerations. Clark noted on 15 August that at one one point Eden remarked: 'People still talk about the danger of our alienating India or worrying Africa, but the fact is that if we lose out in the Middle East we shall be immediately destroyed.'[32]

This sense of 'life and death' emergency was difficult to convey in that hot lazy summer, when ships were passing through the Suez Canal without let or hindrance, when Nasser was not doing anything new that was outrageous, when relations with the Soviet Union were rather better than usual, when America was absorbed in her election campaign. On the eve of the London Conference Clark was assiduously seeking to stoke up the sense of tension in the press while trying to deflect the Prime Minister's instinct to censor the BBC. The Corporation was in dire trouble because of the crumbling consensus on foreign policy. Feeling guilty about having so far put across nothing but the Government's viewpoint on Suez, it chose the eve of the Maritime Conference to stage an item on the mass-audience Light Programme that reflected more diverse opinions, among others that of Egypt.

That the public should have been exposed, unprotected, to the voice and argument of Major Salah Salem was something which Tory Ministers found it very difficult to forgive. Eden wrote a strong letter to the Chairman of the BBC, Sir Alexander Cadogan, who was both a former Permanent Under-Secretary at the Foreign Office and a director of the Suez Canal Company. Other Ministers were even more outspoken and talked about ways of bringing the BBC to heel. No one was fiercer than Alan Lennox-Boyd, the Colonial Secretary, who thought it 'an outrage that a body widely believed to be in part at least associated with the British Government should broadcast at such a moment a speech by a notorious enemy'.[33]

On the eve of the conference Eden was buoyed up by a highly optimistic intelligence report indicating that Nasser was in serious internal trouble and thus would find it difficult to resist pressure. He was less impressed by a cable from Trevelyan on Nasser's plans for total war. This type of guerrilla action, said Sir Humphrey, could cause prolonged and serious disturbances after the end of formal hostilities and make things very difficult for a new Egyptian Government which in the circumstances would have to 'face the odium of compromise with foreign occupation forces'. 'Foreign Secretary. Tell him to cheer up!' minuted Eden.[34]

The Maritime Conference

Foreign Ministers and their advisers were now streaming into London for the Maritime Conference on Suez beginning on 16 August. The most important figure there was John Foster Dulles. As Lloyd pointed out to his Pakistani colleague, in the course of denying American press reports of differences between the US and Britain, 'the power of the United States both in the economic and military fields was overwhelming'. Dulles was absolutely firm, he said, on having an international authority and would put the whole of the United States' prestige behind it. On the Sunday before the Conference (12 August), Dulles, together with Admiral Radford and other advisers, had been at the White House with the President. The discussion brought out how differently Eisenhower and Dulles approached the Suez problem. Ultimately Dulles would always defer to the President but, in the meantime, the Secretary of State was liable to create an impression of the extent of American commitment on Suez that could not be sustained.

In this discussion, Eisenhower showed a grasp of the realities of the problem. He said that he thought Nasser would probably be able to keep the Canal open and functioning (Eisenhower knew something about canals, having done some of his early military service in Panama; he did not think that it was that difficult to steer a ship through Suez). He expected Nasser would make very firm promises about the way he was going to operate it. He could say that he would have had clear title to operate anyway after 1968. Dulles replied in terms which could have been a paraphrase of the Anglo-French case that Nasser, both in his writing and in his speeches, had indicated a very clear intention of using the Canal in a manner that was contrary to its international status. It was this threat to the international status of the Canal that 'provided the British and French with a solid foundation for possible action'. Dulles concluded that it was necessary to convey to Egypt and to other Arab nations the impossibility of the western world tolerating the situation arising out of Nasser's action.

This was a very strong statement and, if the President dissented, as he appeared to do, from its implications, it seems odd that he did not insist more forcefully on his viewpoint before Dulles's departure. The answer lies principally in the high regard in which he had come to hold Dulles's knowledge and judgment of international affairs and also in the care which Dulles took to cater for his chief's likely anxieties. At the same time as promising a firm line with Nasser, Dulles told Eisenhower that he must lead the British and French away from any kind of precipitate action they might feel like taking. 'If the London Conference does present a reasonable policy to Nasser and he rejects it and the British and French then feel that it is necessary to act in order to protect their interests, it would seem to be clear that the United States should give them moral and economic support.'

The British and French were quoted as saying that they would not expect the United States to commit any of her armed forces. The whole tone of the discussion, apart from the President's perceptive remarks at the outset, was one of backing for Britain and France, up to and including their use of force, provided only that their posture was 'reasonable'.[35]

Dulles, with this mandate, came to London on 15 August where he found a great desire that he should take the lead and thus put himself into a position from which it would be difficult to retreat. 'The atmosphere', he reported back to the President at one o'clock in the morning after the first day, 'on the whole is much more composed than two weeks ago.' He sensed on the part of the British and French a greater understanding of the scale of military intervention required and of 'the inadequacies of their military establishments to take on a real fighting job of this size.' He added that, according to Douglas Dillon, the American Ambassador in Paris, the French were beginning to be quite sobered by their military inadequacy. One interesting point was the unexpectedly positive impression made by the Soviet Foreign Minister, Shepilov. 'He made a very frank and orderly presentation of the problem and of his country's position. It was the best statement I have ever received from any Soviet Minister.'[36]

Talking to Selwyn Lloyd, Dulles tried to persuade him that although the conference was in London and Lloyd was the host, it would be a better idea if someone less committed took the chair. But the British Foreign Secretary, with a military timetable in mind, was not having that. Dulles reported defeat. 'Probably Selwyn Lloyd will be permanent chairman because he seems desperately to want it and because no one wants to seem discourteous in opposing it.'[37]

Out of this conference two propositions emerged; one, proposed by Krishna Menon of India and backed by the Soviet Union, Ceylon and Indonesia; the second advanced by Dulles alone, though it obviously had the backing of Britain and France, and in the end endorsed by eighteen of the twenty-two members. Curiously, in his first assessment to the President, Dulles estimated that the former had the support of the majority and certainly, from the tentative way in which many of the Foreign Ministers expressed themselves in the initial contacts, it may have seemed so. Menon's approach was essentially that of one paying heed to the psychology of the new nationalism. He made plain to Lloyd that India did not approve of Nasser's manner of nationalising the Canal and said the same thing, not quite so bluntly, in his conference speech. He proposed a series of principles, which (Nehru told Malcolm MacDonald the British High Commissioner), were designed to get Egypt to negotiate. Once she was engaged in the process of negotiation it might be possible to get Nasser to make further concessions.[38]

Starting from the recognition of Egypt's sovereign rights and of the Canal as a waterway of international importance, Menon's resolution called for the 1888 Convention to be reviewed and updated to include new provisions for just and equitable tolls and charges and for the proper maintenance of the Canal with a consultative body of user interests to be associated on a regular basis with the Egyptian Canal Corporation. The annual report of that Corporation to be transmitted to the UN.[39]

This plan, when they received news of it, did not exactly thrill the Egyptians. Suspicious of Menon's patronising manner, they considered him too anxious to accommodate the West. At the moment when the British thought that Menon was egging Nasser on, he was in fact sending reproachful cables to Ali Yavar Jung in Cairo and to Pandit Nehru complaining that the Egyptians did not give him sufficient freedom of manoeuvre or any sign that India had influence in Cairo.[40] Nehru did urge Nasser to show more flexibility but in his reply to Menon he suggested some sympathy with the Egyptian reaction. Menon was directed to find a 'more constructive' scheme. Feeling unappreciated he suggested that he walk out, a manoeuvre which he was capable of executing with great éclat, but which was vetoed this time by his chief.[41]

The resolution which expressed the requirements of the West called for a Convention to be negotiated with Egypt which would set up a Suez Canal Board, on which Egypt would always have a seat, but whose other members should be a mix of states chosen according to use, pattern of trade and geographical distribution. It should have the necessary authority to operate, maintain, develop and enlarge the Suez Canal. The operation of the Canal should be 'insulated' from the politics of any nation; Egypt would get an 'equitable and rising' financial return which was designed to offer her, for no extra responsibilities, an immediate and tempting increase in her income from the Canal; and, except for Egypt's share, there would be no profit. An Arbitration Commission should settle any disputes, including differences over the amount of the 'equitable return'. There would also be 'effective sanctions' for any violation of the Convention, and any threat to interfere by force with the use of the Canal would constitute a threat to peace, in the sense used in the UN Charter. (Once this point was conceded any Egyptian interference could legitimately trigger the Charter-sanctioned right of self-defence.)[42]

The speech with which Dulles introduced this resolution was remembered by those present as having been a particularly brilliant forensic achievement. He marshalled his case with much lucidity and skill in sharp contrast to the long, rambling, repetitive, though insightful speech of Krishna Menon, who immediately preceded him. Backed by purposeful lobbying, especially of Asian delegations, Dulles's presentation resulted in a notable firming up of opinion behind the United States' proposal. Nevertheless, reading it now in the light of what was to happen, it is clear that it contributed greatly to the dangerous breach, the baffled and bitter misunderstanding, that was to occur between allies. This was the reverse of Dulles's intention. His words read like a first-class lawyer's recital of the Anglo-French case; his identification with that case and all its implications was henceforth assumed, in the face of much evidence to the contrary, to represent the 'real, underlying' American position. It was a performance that was not universally admired even among his own team. The American Ambassador in Moscow, Chip Bohlen, who was one of them, thought it was Dulles at his worst. In his opinion, 'he shaded the edge of downright trickery and even dishonesty'. To the British and French he sounded as if he favoured them; in his private talks with the Russians he sounded anti-British and anti-French.[43]

'In the Suez Canal, the interdependence of nations achieves perhaps its highest point,' Dulles maintained. 'The trading nations of the world know that President Nasser's action means that their use of the Canal is now at Egypt's sufferance. Egypt can in many subtle ways slow down, burden and make unprofitable the passage through the Canal of the ships and cargoes of those against whom Egypt might desire for national, political reasons, to discriminate ... The international confidence which rested upon the convention of 1866 with the Suez Canal Company and the treaty of 1888 has been grievously assaulted.' His case rested on the phrase used in the preamble of the 1888 Treaty about the establishment of 'a definite system designed to guarantee at all times and for all powers the free use ...' He asked: 'Does such a plan infringe upon Egypt's sovereignty? The answer is, it does not. Egyptian sovereignty is and always has been qualified by the treaty of 1888 which makes of the Canal an international – not an Egyptian – waterway.'

Shepilov for the Soviet Union, having noted that 'bellicose cries are now much less in evidence' and that not a single argument had been put forward in defence of the Suez Canal Company, which had only a short time before been spoken of as the only agency capable of operating the Canal, declared that there was no legal basis for removing the operation of the Suez Canal from Egyptian hands. Under the American draft, Egypt's rights were to be recognised provided she relinquished them. 'Egypt is kindly allowed a place in her own home. If we really wish to observe the principle of sovereignty, then clearly Egypt cannot merely be one of the parties administering her own property.' Shepilov suggested that a Preparatory Commission of Egypt, India, the United States, Britain, France and the Soviet Union clear the ground for a conference of all states who signed the 1888 Convention (including all the legal heirs of the Austro-Hungarian Empire) and all states that used the Canal so that they could adopt a new convention or a supplement to the old one.[44]

This must have been a disappointment to Dulles who, warming perhaps as much as his nature permitted to the experience of working with a polite and approachable Soviet counterpart, had entertained the hope after an hour and a half's talk with Shepilov on 18 August that 'the Soviets would be open to making some kind of arrangement with us and perhaps join to impose it upon Egypt ... if ... we would more or less make it a two-party affair with some downgrading of the British and the French'. He told the President that Soviet agreement might not be worth having at the price 'but I shall do everything possible, short of disloyalty to the British and French, to get Soviet agreement'.[45]

Shepilov on his side may have expected more than he was to get from Dulles. At least he told Pineau on 20 August that the Dulles plan was a letdown after the apparent flexibility of his opening speech. Speaking as the ex-journalist, he insisted that over the last year he had spoken to all conditions of people in the Arab states and he knew that it was not just a question of the personality of Nasser but a fundamental determination not to put up with what they considered to be colonialist solutions. 'I had hoped, listening to the declaration of Dulles, that the United States was going to propose a flexible formula. Thus, for the first time in history the USA and the USSR would have been able to propose the same solution.'[46]

When Eisenhower received the text of Dulles's proposal he immediately queried the functions of the proposed board. 'Nasser', he said, in the understatement of the year, 'may find it impossible to swallow the whole of this as now specified'. He then went on to say that he saw no objection to a board with supervisory rather than operating authority. Operating authority could reside in someone appointed by Nasser. Having suggested fundamental changes which would switch the United States from a text gone over in detail with the British and French to something approaching the Indian draft, the President concluded with a bafflingly cheerful 'Your document looks extraordinarily good to me.'[47]

Dulles responded firmly: 'It is felt very strongly here by most of the countries that, if all the hiring and firing of pilots, traffic directors and other technicians and engineers is made by the Egyptians with only some right of appeal, then in fact Egypt will be able to use the Canal as an instrument of its national policy.' It would be very difficult, if not impossible, to shift the British and French in this direction. He concluded: 'It is to be borne in mind that we are not here negotiating with Egypt, for Egypt is not present, and I doubt whether we should make at this stage concessions which we might be willing to make as a matter of last resort in order to obtain Egypt's concurrence ... With your approval I shall at this stage defer use of your suggestion.'[48]

Dulles had indeed touched on what was the principal remaining problem. Ali Sabri was in London being briefed every day by Krishna Menon and Shepilov. But he was not a delegate. How were the majority conclusions of the conference to be conveyed?

Eden clearly did not visualise this taking very long. In the Egypt Committee on 16 August he was talking in terms of a small committee of two or three persons who could notify Egypt of the agreed formula for international control. The Conference could adjourn during the two or three days needed to wait for the Egyptian reply. A rather different scene was visualised by the Baghdad Pact group, led by the Turks, who had been energetically lining up as many Afro-Asian votes as possible behind Dulles's scheme, subject to five mostly cosmetic amendments. The main item of substance in their list was a proposal to set up a Committee 'to negotiate with Egypt on the basis of this declaration for the purpose of reaching a satisfactory settlement', the results to be reported back within a stated period. Chaudhry Mohamed Ali, the Pakistani Premier and Foreign Minister, explained that the stated period he had first thought of had been four months, but that, on reflection, three weeks had seemed preferable.[49]

This was not at all what the British had in mind. They argued that three weeks was too long for merely establishing whether the Egyptians were willing to negotiate; too little for actually working out a treaty. Eden told Dulles that delay would be fatal. He had, he said, suspended military preparations while the conference was going on but further action could not be long delayed. Dulles drily observed that since he had been in London he had encountered a general feeling that the British public would not support such action, a remark which he would not have made more palatable by adding that Shepilov had also expressed it. (Actually, Dulles sharply disapproved of the Labour Party's newly critical attitude on the ground that bipartisan unity would give Britain the best chance of retrieving her position peacefully.)

Eden lightly brushed Dulles's objection aside. Supremely confident of being in mystical tune with the British people, he assured the American that he was quite wrong. Criticisms were only heard because for the time being he had refrained from working on public sentiment but, when it came to the test, the Government would have full backing for any military operation. Hugh Gaitskell, after all, was in favour of fighting to protect Israel. The British public would be much more united in fighting to protect Britain. As a late night meeting at the American Ambassador's residence ended, Eden drew Winthrop Aldrich aside and urged him (not for the first time) to convince his Secretary of State that Eden was completely satisfied that Gaitskell would stand by the Government if force were to be used.[50]

The British, it was becoming very clear (as well as, for opposite reasons, the Scandinavians), wanted John Foster Dulles to serve in person on the committee to bring the news to Nasser. Its function would be a difficult one: Dulles had ruled out an ultimatum, the Anglo-French would not consider a negotiation. The British at one point floated the idea that the Secretary of State should be the sole emissary. They had detected his personal distaste for the Egyptian ruler and felt that they could rely on direct contact sharpening the antagonism and serving to align the United States with Britain and France.

Dulles was not going to be caught in this kind of trap. He realised that the British were manoeuvring to commit him further than the United States and the American President were prepared to go. Harold Macmillan told him over dinner on 18 August that there were only three choices: that Nasser voluntarily accepted Dulles's scheme, that he was compelled to accept, or that they accepted Nasser's refusal. 'In the last event,' said Macmillan, 'Britain is finished and, so far as I am concerned, I will have no part in it and will resign.'[51] 'I can see that I may be subjected to very strong pressure to carry forward the negotiation with Nasser', cabled Dulles. 'I am disinclined to do so as this might engage me for a considerable time.'[52]

In his reply Eisenhower made his wishes known as plainly as with courtesy he could. He said that he thought 'there would be more chance of success with you in a situation where you deal with Nasser than if some lesser individual should undertake the work ... We cannot afford to do less than our best to assure success ...' He left a narrow way out. 'By no means', he said, 'should you become involved in a long wearisome negotiation, especially with an anticipated probability of negative results in the end.'[53]

As soon as he saw that escape route Dulles bolted down it. He was elated by the number of states – eighteen out of the twenty-two – that he had got to endorse his plan. It was true that Shepilov was a great disappointment to him. He had been a pleasure to deal with and to compare notes with over the problems of containing Britain and France, but his final 'very inflammatory' speech had seemed deliberately calculated to make it difficult for Nasser ever to accept the eighteen-nation scheme 'unless it is heavily disguised'.[54] Still, as his last trick, Dulles had neatly separated three of the four minority states, India, Indonesia and Ceylon, from the Soviet Union by endorsing an emollient final communiqué drafted by Indonesia but rejected by Shepilov alone.[55] After achieving so much, Dulles was not about to risk his reputation either with his Western allies (if he were obliged to retreat) or with the world in general (should he draw a blank) by engaging in negotiation with Nasser.

In the end, by a consensus announced by the New Zealand Foreign Minister, the eighteen chose five of their number – Australia, Ethiopia, Iran, Sweden and the United States, with the Prime Minister of Australia, Robert Menzies as the chairman – to approach Egypt to explain their scheme and find out if Egypt would negotiate on its lines. The United States was to be represented not by Dulles but by a senior Middle East expert, Loy Henderson.

When the conference petered out without any communiqué on the afternoon of 23 August, no special arrangements had been put in train for its being reconvened. Pineau, it is true, had buttonholed Dillon at the reception given by the Edens to argue that they ought to be making arrangements ahead of time for the conference that would be needed to sort out the future status of the Suez Canal after the troops had gone in.[56] Eden was going round telling everyone 'what a wonderful job Foster has done here' but, on hearing from one of Dulles's senior advisers that much depended on public opinion, Sir Ivone Kirkpatrick snapped back that he did not care about public opinion: it was the business of informed leaders to lead in what they thought was the right direction.[57]

On the evening of 23 August, with the conference over, one of those informed leaders, the British Foreign Secretary, sat apart after dinner with the American Secretary of State and, showing 'obvious emotional strain', poured out his unhappiness with the nature of the military plans. As things stood, he explained, there would be a button pushed in early September and, after that, everything would happen automatically and irrevocably. Dulles was the only person who could do anything to change these plans, which failed to take account of pledges to the UN or 'set the stage' for military action so that it should not be made to seem 'open aggression' of the kind that was not in keeping with the times.[58]

Next morning at Number Ten Eden confirmed to Dulles that present military plans were to move in a week or ten days unless the situation had definitely cleared up. Dulles's (partially censored) account shows that he did raise some points about the UN but not, apparently, with the desperate urgency that Lloyd had aimed for. The effect must have been further diminished when, the Prime Minister having spoken of having received an 'embarrassing' request from the Pentagon for information about Britain's military plans, Dulles told him to 'forget it'.[59]

None of this seemed, on the surface, to diminish John Foster Dulles's optimism that, having triumphed in the conference arena, he had accomplished something in the real world. If Egypt handled the matter wisely, he advised Ruslan Abdulgani, the Foreign Minister of Indonesia, who was about to call in on Cairo, she could gain a great victory – far greater revenues from the Canal than before, foreign money to finance the Canal's expansion attracted by a permanent settlement, even the possibility of Egypt being able to finance the Aswan Dam from Canal revenues.[60] On the night that Eisenhower received his second nomination at the Republican Convention by wild acclamation, Dulles happily assured him that, so long as Nasser agreed to receive Menzies' committee, 'the chance of a peaceful settlement will, I think, be considerable'.

11

Keightley in Command

I remain firmly convinced that, if Nasser wins or even appears to win, we might as well, as a Government (and indeed as a country) go out of business.
Alan Lennox-Boyd, British Colonial Secretary, to Eden, 24 August 1956.

I can only see the consequences of choosing force rather than negotiation as establishing a second and more dangerous Cyprus.
Admiral Earl Mountbatten of Burma, First Sea Lord, in letter drafted but not sent, 1 August 1956.

Duncan Sandys, Winston Churchill's son-in-law and a man who had had access in wartime to matters of utmost secrecy, was now Minister of Housing and Local Government in the Eden Cabinet. He asked the Prime Minister what was the truth about all the reports about military action. He got a pretty ruthless brush-off. 'I feel I should explain to you before the next meeting of the Cabinet', wrote Eden on 22 August, the day before the London Conference closed, 'the limits within which the Cabinet can discuss the possibility of a military operation in the Eastern Mediterranean.' If, in the last resort, when all other attempts to achieve a settlement had failed, force should be contemplated, the Cabinet as a whole would be asked to take the 'final decision'. Knowledge of details 'must, for obvious reasons of security, be confined within the narrowest possible circle'. Such political guidance as was needed 'must continue to be given by me, in consultation with a small number of my most senior Cabinet colleagues . . .'[1]

Sandys rather tartly replied that 'I do hope that we shall be consulted as soon as possible about the broad lines of the military plan which is being prepared.' He recognised that operational detail must be kept within a restricted circle but, on the other hand, 'the extent of the territorial objective of the operation, the manner of initiating it and, above all, the grounds on which we should justify it to the world are obviously matters of major political importance'. Sandys, whose personal outlook was hawkish, acknowledged that it was for the Prime Minister to decide the right moment to consult the Cabinet, but 'I hope that you will take us into your confidence before it is too late for any views we may have to be taken into account'.[2]

In the meanwhile, such matters were discussed more candidly in the Egypt Committee. About its membership there was one remarkable feature: the man with the most misgivings was the Minister of Defence, Sir Walter Monckton. To be sure his opposition to the use of force was not absolute. 'I must say', he wrote in a subsequent note, 'that I was not fundamentally troubled by moral considerations throughout the period for which the crisis lasted. My anxieties began when I discovered the way in which it was proposed to carry out the enterprise.' He was led on unhappily from one point to the next, seldom finding the ground on which he should make a stand. He voiced his unhappiness to Clark, telling him that the senior civil servants were against the policy. That was certainly the case with Monckton's own Permanent Secretary, Sir Richard Powell. Clark records him on 13 August as seeing present plans ending up in a massive invasion that would turn world opinion against Britain and be violently unpopular at home. Monckton was also aware of the doubts of his Chiefs of Staff, most strikingly those of his most celebrated professional adviser, Lord Mountbatten.[3]

As soon as he had had time to reflect on Eden's unexpected leaning towards the use of force, Mountbatten had become increasingly uneasy. On the strength of his claim to be an old and trusted personal confidant of the Prime Minister's, he thought himself entitled to treat a personal remark of Eden's over the telephone as encouragement to express himself candidly to him in writing. On 1 August he drafted the first of two letters that he never sent. 'I can only see the consequences of choosing force rather than negotiation as establishing a second and more dangerous Cyprus,' he wrote. Even during previous disputes the Egyptians had never tried to sabotage the Canal, but if their country were now invaded they might find it a sacred duty to make the Canal unworkable. The absolutely paramount consideration for the next six weeks (when force could not be used in any case) should be to marshal world support. To do this the surest way was to offer terms to Nasser 'that it would be patently unreasonable and provocative for him to reject'.

He showed the letter first to his political chief Lord Cilcennin, the First Lord of the Admiralty, who was emphatic about the constitutional impropriety of a service chief addressing the Prime Minister, even if he were a personal friend, on such a matter. 'I naturally', says Mountbatten, 'had to bow to his directions.' He spoke to the Minister of Defence and found him to be of the same opinion. However, it was some consolation to discover that both Ministers shared much of his general outlook. 'We all felt', Mountbatten subsequently noted, 'that an armed amphibious assault against opposition in a built-up area (since there are practically no landing-places in Egypt which are not built over) would cause the death of thousands of innocent women and children since we obviously had to bomb and bombard the coast defence gun positions.'[4]

Under the curious protocol concerning service chiefs and politics there was one avenue open to Mountbatten for the expression of his opinions. Within limits the Chiefs were at liberty to raise what would otherwise be regarded as political factors in the frequent sessions of their Committee. On 14 August for example, the minutes show that the First Sea Lord asked what steps were being taken to ensure that, in the event of successful operations leading to the downfall of Nasser, a new government could be found in Egypt which would both support Britain's policy for the operation of the Canal and would also have the support of the Egyptian people. He said he feared that the Egyptian people were now so solidly behind Nasser that it might be impossible to find such a government.[5] On 21 and 23 August the First Sea Lord was expressing the view that Operation *Musketeer* would result in serious and continuing disorders in the Middle East. He pointed out that, on the one hand, they were building British forces up for operations against Egypt, while at the same time they were engaged, as part of the defence review, in reducing them in the same area.[6]

On 22 August the first postponement of military operations occurred. It was only for four days; if the initial timetable were to be adhered to, the violation of Egyptian airspace for the purposes of photographic reconnaissance would have had to be authorised at once and Eden did not think that this would be a very good idea with the London Conference still in session. The vital threshold on which Ministers had been hovering had now been crossed. Instead of diplomacy and politics serving the military timetable, Eden had begun to allow the reverse to happen.

On 23 August, the same day on which Selwyn Lloyd confessed to Dulles his anguish about the UN and the plans of the military, three senior Ministers – Macmillan, Salisbury and Butler – gathered with the Chief Whip, Ted Heath, in 11 Downing Street, the Chancellor's residence, to continue with Sir Pierson Dixon, who was still on leave, the discussion which had started that morning in the Egypt Committee, on how it might be possible to dress up British and French military action for the sake of world opinion. Any Security Council resolution that seemed designed for that purpose would be certainly vetoed by the Soviet Union. To use force immediately after a resolution had failed might smack of hypocrisy. Even worse, there was the risk of a resolution attracting 'embarrassing compromise proposals' or even an amendment ruling out the use of force.

Butler as Leader of the House and Heath as Chief Whip had to take into account that the UN had its strong supporters among sections of the parliamentary party, let alone among the Opposition. Lord Salisbury, as a hawk over Suez but a strong UN man, was in a genuine dilemma. As he wrote to Eden the next day, 'My difficulty is that I feel we must act firmly but that there are no possible means by which we can do that within the terms of the Charter to which we have solemnly adhered.' He felt committed by a 'definite undertaking' to refer a problem to the Security Council before resorting to force, but if they did that where would be their timetable? He was even ready to suggest that Britain and France should be prepared to leave the UN altogether if they received no adequate response to their bringing on Suez before it. Such a threat might even bring the UN 'up to the jump'.[7]

The Ministers at Number Eleven grasped eagerly at one idea of Dixon's. Britain and France would come before the Council without a resolution to inform it officially of the outcome of the London Conference and this would enable them to say, when later they would be hauled before the Council by Egypt for using force, that previous discussion had already demonstrated that the Council was too divided to act.

But, if they were to do this, Ministers worried that it meant slotting a Security Council debate into a timetable that already had to accommodate the timings of military planning, diplomacy and Parliament. If Parliament were to be recalled before the Security Council session, that would place the Government under political pressure to put the matter more fully into UN hands than it would wish. If, on the other hand, the Security Council were to meet before Parliament, there might well be strong and embarrassing criticism of the 'very modest' nature of the reference to the UN. The best plan, they decided, would be to synchronise the two exercises so that the Security Council debate would start while Parliament was in session. Dixon assured Ministers that, if necessary, it should be possible to spin out the New York debate for at least a week, so that it should still be going on when Parliament again rose.[8]

'Outburst' in the Egypt Committee

An Egypt Committee session on 24 August endorsed these ideas. Eden, summing up, said that the sequence should not start until a reply had been received by Menzies from the Egyptian Government. If that could be expected by 30 August, Parliament could be called for 3 September and the necessary steps could be taken for an announcement of a Security Council meeting on 4 or 5 September.[9] That, he thought, should take care of Opposition criticism.

At one point in this discussion Macmillan's cynicism in speaking of the military operation as a foregone conclusion, became more than Walter Monckton could stand. To the horror of a small group of Ministers and civil servants around the table, he created 'an outburst' which Salisbury described in a letter to Eden as 'both painful and rather disturbing'. The Minister of Defence, fortified no doubt by sessions of conscience with the First Sea Lord, spelled out the moral implications as well as the practical obstacles to the course on which they appeared to be set. The weakness of his position was that, as the outspoken Colonial Secretary Alan Lennox-Boyd wrote to Eden after the occasion, 'all these difficulties stood out miles when we first embarked on our policy'. Thus Monckton had been committed to the end result by the Cabinet's initial decisions on 27 July and by his active participation in the preparation of means to implement it.

Eden was evidently put out by this degree of opposition from within the inner circle. A number of those present – Lennox-Boyd, Salisbury, Home and the Cabinet Secretary, Brook – found it necessary to write to him afterwards to reassure and to warn.[10] Salisbury, in some respects a hard-liner, had himself observed in the Committee discussion that reference to the Security Council would be seen as a hollow sham if Britain had already started out on the military operation. Assuring Eden that 'I need not say that I am absolutely at one with you', Salisbury wrote of Monckton: 'I think that both you and I knew that he had for some time had doubts about a firm policy over Suez.' He warned the Prime Minister that there would probably be a measure of support for Monckton's views when the Cabinet next met on 28 August. 'Rab is clearly not happy and I gather from what he said to me after the meeting that he had been making enquiries and finds there are quite a number of others, especially among the younger members of the Cabinet who have not yet made up their minds.' Salisbury went on: 'I thought you might like to know this as the case for force will clearly need to be closely and cogently argued by those of us who agree with it.'

Norman Brook, writing to the Prime Minister the following day (25 August), ventured his own tally of those who would want to postpone the use of force 'until *all* else has been tried or until Nasser provides us with a good occasion, whichever happens earlier'. He wrote down the names of Walter Monckton, R. A. Butler, the Earl of Selkirk (Duchy of Lancaster), Heath, Kilmuir, Macleod (Labour), Heathcoat Amory (Agriculture), putting question marks after Kilmuir and Amory. (Salisbury had referred to the Lord Chancellor as being 'very sound on the whole thing', while Amory was definitely to prove himself to be a dove.) The Cabinet Secretary marked three Ministers as 'unknown quantities': James Stuart (Scotland – who in fact was very pro-use of force), Patrick Buchan-Hepburn (Works) and David Eccles (Education). 'The rest I would expect to be pretty solid.' Still, as Lennox-Boyd put it, 'if there really is uncertainty in the Cabinet, we can't be surprised if it exists in the country'.

Home also wrote to warn Eden that 'I see a definite wavering in the attitude of some of our colleagues towards the use of force . . . I had expected a cleavage of opinion in H of C and possibly a few of our supporters dissenting, but this, I think, represents something more serious.' The important thing, Home advised, was that Ministers should get their feelings off their chests so that Eden would know where he was. 'Derry Amory, for instance, who is one of the most stable of our colleagues, feels the deepest anxieties but I think would be ready to face up to it if all the processes of UNO had been exhausted. Others, I think, feel that it would divide country, party and Commonwealth so deeply that we should never recover . . . The anxieties of some, Rab for instance, might be removed if we didn't have to go on thinking in terms of button-pushing and dates and had plenty of time for diplomatic manoeuvre. All this is disturbing.'

The trouble was that the particular plan proposed by the Task Force Commanders and accepted by the Egypt Committee depended very heavily on 'button-pushing and dates'. Appeasement of the wing of the Cabinet that was troubled by such things would play havoc with the plans. Nevertheless, Brook urged Eden to build on the basis of the consensus that included Monckton and Butler. All the members of the Cabinet, without exception, were solidly in agreement that Nasser should not get away with it – 'for if he succeeds we lose our oil and, with it, our standard of life in this country, not to mention our position in the Middle East and our influence as a World Power'. Here Brook was very right; Monckton and Butler had shared in the emotional spasm that followed on Nasser's unexpected act. That had made them willing partners with Eden, Salisbury and Home in their determination to stop him, which meant that, if all other methods failed, they must be ready to use force. 'To this they have all assented including W.M.'

But as yet they did not know whether Nasser would reject the proposals outright. 'If he was clever,' Brook put it, thinking of the advice he would be offering if he were the Egyptian Cabinet Secretary, 'he would send a reply somewhere between acceptance and rejection – and offer to negotiate a new Treaty.' Some Ministers, he said, were less certain than others about the extent to which 'middle' opinion in the country would support forceful action in the absence of some clearer occasion for it. 'All this leads me to the view that it would be a mistake to put the Cabinet at the final fence too soon. At least until we have Nasser's reply I would not ask them to take the final decision.'

The correspondence arising from what Brook termed Monckton's 'ill-judged and ill-timed' intervention revealed that Eden's more hawkish Ministers were not given to understating what they thought to be at stake. It is in relation to such estimates that one must judge their readiness to contemplate drastic and devious methods. 'I remain firmly convinced,' said Lennox-Boyd, 'that, if Nasser wins or even appears to win, we might as well as a government (and indeed as a country) go out of business.' 'For myself', said Home, 'I have no doubt that if we cannot make anything of the Security Council – and that largely depends on Dulles – we have no option but to go through with it. I need not say more but I am convinced that we are finished if the Middle East goes – and Russia, India and China rule from Africa to the Pacific.'

In the circumstances it might seem odd that Eden kept on Monckton as his

Minister of Defence for the better part of the next two months. Monckton in turn never spoke out again so strongly as he had done on 24 August; he told his confidant, William Clark, of his unhappiness and of his determination to leave office once the crisis was over, but he never screwed himself up to the point of resigning from the Cabinet while the crisis was on because of his rather strange conviction that, if he did so, the Government would fall.[11]

Harold Macmillan, the man who had precipitated the clash, was operating on a very different plane from both Monckton and Eden. A man who, rather uncharacteristically for a British politician, liked to think in large tides and forces, he had now in his mind fitted the Suez question into a bigger scene. He had already rather startled Dulles, who had a high opinion of him, by calling him into a private room as they left Eden's reception on 20 August to ask him most earnestly whether he planned to stay on as Secretary of State in Eisenhower's second term. The reason he needed to know, Dulles reported him as saying, was that he was thinking of taking over the Foreign Office again in the reasonably near future and that his decision whether or not to do so would be influenced by whether Dulles would be his counterpart since their relations together had been so happy. All things considered, that was rather an extraordinary way to put it, and one to which Eden, unless he had said something, hitherto untraced, about a possible reshuffle, would surely have contributed a pungent oath.[12]

Shortly after this bizarre episode Macmillan sent the Prime Minister a memorandum. It was conceived on the grandest scale. Britain's return to the Middle East should not be confined to overthrowing Nasser and taking over the Canal. It must not be like Louis XVIII creeping back to France but like Napoleon bursting upon the plains of Italy. Britain should not merely occupy Egypt; she should summon a conference to which should come the oil states, oil transit states and those which were neither. There should be a plan which would benefit the whole region. Then they should settle boundaries. Jordan should go; there should be, in an indelicate choice of phrase, a 'final solution' for Israel. Macmillan saw a picture of another Churchillian settlement like that of 1921 in which a British Cabinet Minister determined the frontiers of the Levant. It was a strange fantasy, though not one in which Ben-Gurion would, as we shall see, have been reluctant to join.[13]

To Go or Not to Go to the UN

Since the Egypt Committee had not reached any conclusion about going before the Security Council in the event of a Nasser rejection, Selwyn Lloyd spent the weekend (25/26 August) puzzling the issue out. 'I have been strongly warned of the risks involved,' he wrote in a memorandum. 'It might result in a call to the parties to settle their differences by discussion, a call to the London Conference to resume, a reference to the International Court or the appointment of a committee of the Security Council. There might be an inclination to refer the matter to the General Assembly or to despatch a peace observation commission to the area. It would be impossible to extract from the Security Council a resolution justifying the use of force without further reference to the UN. It would not be possible to get, even if we wanted to, a resolution in favour of economic sanctions passed by a satisfactory majority, if at all.' Herman Phleger, the State Department's legal counsel, had thought it extremely dangerous to take the initiative in the Security Council. It was like quicksand; once one got in, one could never be sure how deep it was or whether one would get out.

But, nevertheless, Lloyd made up his mind in favour of going early to the Council. Otherwise, the clanking of the military preparations as time inexorably advanced towards D-day would mean that, somewhere between D−7 and D−4, Britain would find herself arraigned before the Security Council, if not by Egypt, then by the Soviet Union, Jugoslavia or even Iran. This was a prospect which throughout the crisis caused the British dismay to a remarkable degree. There would also be major political repercussions because of the interplay between debates in New York and in Westminster. 'If we had just begun a Security Council debate,' reckoned Lloyd, 'I should regard it as very nearly politically impossible to proceed with the assault on D-Day.' In a significant deletion (here italicised) he noted that 'moderate opinion at home and abroad would be outraged if we were to attack Egypt without having made some gesture towards the UN, the support of which body is *supposed to be* the foundation of our foreign policy'. Therefore, it was necessary to get a move on.

Lloyd's plan was that at the moment Nasser said 'No' to the London proposals, he should ask for a meeting of the Council. In accordance with French wishes, there would be a resolution endorsing the Eighteen-Power scheme. Pineau and Lloyd should lead off in person in order to 'infuse into the debate the atmosphere of crisis'. If, nevertheless, the proceedings became bogged down in procedural wrangles and innumerable amendments, 'the Foreign Ministers should withdraw saying that the proceedings were futile and that the UN had shown itself incapable of dealing with the matter'. Lloyd proposed to be very candid with the Americans. It should be pointed out to Eisenhower and Dulles that 'the object of the exercise is to put us in the best possible posture internationally over the action which we propose to take ...'[14]

The note was put before the Egypt Committee on 27 August with a bleak coda: 'Our choice therefore is a choice of evils. To go to the Security Council is full of risks; not to do so would be *certain* to have consequences of the greatest gravity.' The Committee endorsed the Foreign Secretary's conclusion and the following evening the Washington Embassy was instructed to pass a personal message to Dulles. ('It is most confidential.

Much damage would be caused if any idea of its contents were to leak.') It ran through Lloyd's weekend arguments before ending with this appeal: 'I cannot emphasise too strongly that your active help is essential to the success of this plan. I think that moderate opinion would be shocked at forcible action by us without any reference at all to the UN.' Lloyd included flattery of Dulles for his 'masterly' management of the London Conference and ended with a plea that the Security Council should be tackled as 'a combined operation in the same way'.[15] The object of this invitation was unmistakable: American collusion in the use of the processes of the UN to prepare for the pursuit of war.

When Dulles discussed this crucial message with John Coulson, the British Charge, on 29 August, he confined himself largely to asking various technical questions about the method of raising the matter in the Security Council and the chapter of the UN Charter under which Britain might hope to find redress. But when he saw Eisenhower the next day – to make sure, he said, that his mind was working on the same lines as the President's on the Suez matter – it was clear that on the central issue he was turning thumbs down on the British proposition. He told Eisenhower that, 'regrettable as it might be to see Nasser's prestige enhanced even temporarily, I did not believe the situation was one which should be resolved by force'. The reason was that 'I could not see any end to the situation that might be created if the British and French occupied the Canal and parts of Egypt. They would make bitter enemies of the entire population of the Middle East and much of Africa. Everywhere they would be compelled to maintain themselves by force and, in the end, their economy would be weakened virtually beyond repair and the influence of the West in the Middle East and most of Africa lost for a generation if not a century. The Soviet Union would reap the benefit.' Eisenhower agreed with him entirely: this was not the issue on which to downgrade Nasser. The Suez dispute and the question of Nasser's prestige in the Middle East were not to be confused.[16]

Earlier in the day Dulles had reported more formally to members of the National Security Council. He told them that the British and French had gone along with the American Canal plan very reluctantly and in the obvious hope that Nasser would not accept it. His refusal would permit them to resort to military force with a better grace. Assessing the British leaders, Dulles identified Macmillan and Salisbury as the strongest-minded elements in the Cabinet, 'thoroughly imbued with the tradition of British greatness'. By comparison Eden 'had shown himself to be somewhat vacillating'. Nevertheless he had informed Dulles that on or about 10 September decisions would have to be made which would be irrevocable. Dulles added that he had found it extremely difficult to take a strong stand against the British and French views, 'since, after all, the British and French would be finished as first-rate Powers if they didn't somehow manage to check Nasser and nullify his schemes'. On the other hand, to achieve their objectives they might have to try to reestablish colonial rule over the whole area of the Middle East. All this constituted a morass from which it was hard for him to see how the British and French could ever hope successfully to extricate themselves.

Admiral Radford then summarised several papers prepared by the Joint Chiefs of Staff which analysed eight possible courses of action for the United States. Of these, four were recommended as acceptable. The first choice was 'to endorse publicly and support politically, economically and logistically UK and French military action without direct participation by US forces and to guarantee publicly that the US . . . will take appropriate action, including direct military action by US forces as necessary in the event of significant military intervention by third parties . . .'

This was all that the British and French wanted. If this recommendation had been accepted and acted upon by the President, Eden and Mollet would have enjoyed the same degree of American support as was received twenty-five years later in the Falklands campaign. Two of the other acceptable courses represented the two parts of the preferred course considered separately; the fourth was to participate in military action with the British and French from the outset, with the aim of placing the Suez Canal 'under a friendly and responsible authority'. The four 'militarily unacceptable' courses included that of abstaining from providing any form of military support and of limiting such support to a public endorsement.

The President did not make much comment in that forum beyond observing that the Suez situation was so grave that it must be watched hourly. But it is clear, however, from his remarks to Dulles that he was never tempted to adopt the Joint Chiefs' advice. As a victorious general he was more than normally immune from being impressed by professional military advice where he disagreed with it politically.[17]

Keightley Takes Over

British and French planning was now, to all appearances, fully integrated. That there were later to be some exceptions on the French side was subsequently to appear. But now that security rules were understood, warm personal relations were rapidly established between servicemen of the two nationalities.

On 9 August, the day that the Force Commanders had presented their outline plan for *Musketeer*, the Chiefs of Staff had recommended that there should be an Allied Commander-in-Chief and that, in view of the short time available, the appointment should go to the existing Commander-in-Chief of Middle East Land Forces, General Sir Charles Keightley. This was approved on 11 August.

Sir Charles Keightley was a large man, his imposing frame making him appear out of scale in group photos of the expedition's commanders. His natural courtesy and charm were undoubted assets, much stressed by French writers, in helping cement an authentic *entente cordiale*. He possessed pronounced strategic views which he managed to impose on reluctant military planners and politicians alike. By appointing him the Government severed the link between Task Force Commanders and the political factors which were to play such a dominant role in the campaign. This was accentuated by the fact that Sir Charles was a rather remote figure throughout, what the French journalists, Merry and Serge Bromberger, who liked him, described as 'God-the-Father-Sitting-on-a-Cloud'. Despite his calm manner, his cables and assessments during and after the campaign were to show him to be a pessimist, and, at times, an alarmist.[18]

As Vice-Admiral Sir Maxwell Richmond put it in the naval report on *Musketeer*, Keightley 'was faced with taking over a running concern in which he had not had the opportunity of giving any higher direction'.[19] He was supplied with a deputy in the person of the French Commander-in-Chief, Vice-Admiral Pierre Barjot, and a political adviser, Ralph Murray of the Foreign Office. He had to get a grip on the military operation, whose concept he soon wanted to change, while in other parts of Whitehall attempts were being made to wrestle with the problem of what he should do politically once he had got to Egypt.

On the evening of Friday, 24 August, a group of senior Whitehall officials assembled in Sir Norman Brook's room in the Cabinet Office. They consisted of representatives of the Treasury, the Foreign Office, the War Office and the Ministry of Defence, with Brook in the chair; they constituted the first meeting of the Egypt (Official) Committee. Their task at this and subsequent meetings was to consider the extent and character of the military control to be established over civil affairs in Egypt.

The objectives were briskly restated: to destroy the Egyptian army, to bring down the Nasser Government and to control the Suez Canal. Once these had been achieved and a successor Government installed, the Allied forces would withdraw to the Canal Zone, pending the establishment of an International Canal Authority. To cater for the interim, a scratch military body, the Suez Canal Operating Agency, would take over from the Egyptians. At the end of August it was agreed to place this under French leadership, but the British representative was instructed to insist that anything that implied the restoration of the Universal Suez Canal Company would be 'politically unacceptable'. A 50/50 division of the controlling staff should be aimed at.

There were said to be 'good reasons to believe', given the defeat of the Egyptian army and the collapse of the Nasser regime, that a successor government could be formed, which would be able to maintain law and order throughout the country. True, a memo from the Foreign Secretary did acknowledge that 'it will be an ungrateful task to assume office on British bayonets and some difficulty may be experienced in finding competent Ministers'. However, since a 'large number of formerly prominent and able figures, not necessarily of marked party affiliations' were extremely dissatisfied with Nasser, some of them might be expected to come forward. Once a new government was in control, the Delta cities were no place for the allied forces. 'We might hope to stay in Cairo no more than a day or two and then withdraw to the Canal Zone,' wrote Selwyn Lloyd with astounding optimism, though he added that it would be necessary to see that 'no Nasser clique returns to power and overthrows the Government in Cairo'.[20]

The identification of the 'embryo government' was the work of Intelligence. Ahmed Mortada al-Maraghi, its leading personality, was in Beirut; some of its members were in Egypt and said to be in touch with Nahas, by now an elderly and decayed figure who was living in Cairo under close surveillance. Julian Amery, who had been for months one of this Egyptian opposition's points of contact with the British political world, flew out to France on 27 August with two MI6 officers to meet its representatives.[21] They were not going to move until Britain and France were advancing on Cairo; those who were in the city would then come out to meet them. One thing they heavily stressed was that the allies should not make any attempt to occupy Cairo. That was not unwelcome advice.

Just as Britain would not 'declare war', so she would not impose 'an occupation'. 'Although, whatever we say,' to quote the Foreign Secretary, 'we shall be instituting a temporary military occupation, we should, if possible, avoid establishing anything openly entitled an Administration of Occupied Enemy Territory, which would, incidentally, carry with it a legal and moral obligation to feed the population.'

Effective guerrilla action seems, at this stage, to have been, despite Trevelyan's warnings, fairly thoroughly discounted, although as a precaution it was said to be very helpful if the headquarters of such Nasserite agencies as the Army Intelligence, the Liberation Rally and the National Guard could be eliminated by military action at an early stage. What was known in the Second World War as Amgot (Allied Military Government, Occupied Territories, also known as Ancient Military Gentlemen on Tour) should be held ready for use only in the Canal Zone, for which purpose a strictly limited cadre was recruited, but even here wider administrative responsibilities were if possible to be avoided. Otherwise, 'on the basis of past experience', the Egyptian administrative machine was expected to function 'with something approaching its normal state of efficiency despite a change, or even a temporary absence, of government'.

The risk should, therefore, be taken that, if the machine should collapse, it would take some time to improvise a remedy. Although no provision was made for feeding the population as a whole, one ship (later increased to two) filled with food supplies and a tanker with kerosene would be held at

Cyprus in case of temporary famine in some areas. Two interesting touches indicated how far the planners expected to have to go to avoid making the task of a new Egyptian government completely impossible. They reversed an initial decision to go for an international zone for the Canal; the new Canal Authority would have to operate on Egyptian-run territory. And, secondly, they assumed that, if Nasser had nationalised British firms and investments in anticipation of military action, it would be politically impossible to ask a successor government to rescind that act.[22]

In the course of a memorandum for the Egypt Committee dated 20 August the Foreign Secretary addressed himself to the question of what was to be done with Nasser and the members of his Government. Some, he speculated, would doubtless go to ground, some might escape abroad. 'If, however, they fell into our hands, it is probable that we should eschew ideas of deportation ourselves. A better solution might be to work to hand them over to the successor Egyptian government to deal with, or possibly try to arrange for their residence in a sympathetic country (? India) on an undertaking not to indulge in political activities.'[23]

Delay and Doubt

The attack on Egypt now had to wait for the Menzies mission which had secured an invitation from Cairo. The British and French viewed the proceedings of the five-power group of which they were not members with nervousness and impatience. It seemed to them that they asked too many questions before they left and were being too accommodating to their hosts in accepting leisurely arrangements after their arrival.

Loy Henderson, the American Middle East expert to whom Dulles had deputed the task of serving on Menzies's Committee, declared himself far from impressed by the competence of his colleagues (except for the Swede) and was distinctly disconcerted by the attitude of the British and French towards their mission. Lloyd, in particular, kept firing abrupt questions at the American. 'What will you do if Nasser says "No, but –"?' 'How soon will you have an answer for us?' 'If your committee is to be of any use to us we must have an answer without delay and the answer must be clear-cut'. Chauvel was even more unhelpful, displaying a rigidity which Henderson found not in keeping with realities.[24]

On the evening of 28 August, Henderson was summoned to Number Ten where he told a 'worried and perplexed' Prime Minister that the party, forty strong and therefore fit for a prolonged negotiation, was not leaving until 31 August. 'He clasped his head and groaned, "Oh, these delays! They are working against us. Every day's postponement is to Nasser's gain and our loss." He needed a prompt reply so that he could go straight to the Security Council.' Henderson said that if it was delays he was worried about, the Security Council could hold him up indefinitely. No, replied Eden brightly, a Soviet veto would give Britain her freedom of action.[25]

The Egypt Committee now had to be told that, Nasser having agreed to meet the Menzies group, it was necessary to reconsider the date for D-Day. A possible sequence was: receipt of Nasser's reply on 6 September; meeting of Security Council on 13 September; proceedings to be complete on 19 September. Militarily, the crucial date by which a decision on D-Day was required was D – 18; the longest period that the operation could be delayed once the forces had arrived in the Mediterranean would be seven days. The members of the Committee were then briefed by General Keightley on the outline of the operation and there was some inconclusive discussion as to whether there should be a formal ultimatum. It was pointed out that with plenty of neutral shipping and aircraft around and a peacetime press, the security of the operation would be liable to be blown by preliminary moves as early as D – 8.

The full Cabinet on the same day (28 August) discussed the economic consequences of the Suez crisis. The Treasury paper offered a preliminary assessment of the financial and economic factors. In a sense the outlook was quite bullish. Military precautions presently in hand would not seriously disturb the economy and if there were operations the cost would not be heavy on the Budget in relation to the current level of defence expenditure. But – and this was the crux – the Suez Canal might be closed as the result of conflict, in which case the dollar cost of obtaining oil from the Western Hemisphere would place a serious burden on the balance of payments and a drain on the reserves. If the pipelines were closed as well, industry would be dislocated and Britain could not sustain for long the burden of paying for dollar oil supplies in replacement. If the whole of the Gulf oil was shut off, the British economy would cease to be viable.

One could draw many conclusions from this report but Harold Macmillan was quite clear where he stood: Nasser's ambitions threatened everything. The experience of Mossadeq demonstrated that, with these countries, one could not rely on policy being governed by commercial self-interest. Success by Nasser would damage Britain's relations with the oil-producing countries.

After this call to action from the man in charge of the currency, sobering cold water came from the Minister of Defence. Monckton agreed that Nasser should not be allowed to succeed, but the Cabinet should take note of some of the disadvantages of using force. The action would be condemned by much of world opinion, including many members of the Commonwealth; opinion at home would be divided. Oil installations in the Middle East would be sabotaged. Once Britain had sent troops into Egypt, how was she going to get them out? She might find herself saddled with a costly commitment. The Defence Minister was prepared to use force as a last resort, but all other means of curbing Nasser's ambitions must first be exhausted.

It was Salisbury who took Monckton up on this occasion. No course was now open to Britain that was free from serious risks. Britain would require the maximum possible international support. Before any military measures were taken, she should have recourse to the procedures of the UN. But they should remember that the UN was a means; the end was not merely peace, but the observance of law and justice. In this Salisbury was giving voice to what has been the cry of the Greek over Cyprus, the Arab over Palestine, and every dissatisfied petitioner to New York since the UN began to the present time of writing.

Kilmuir weighted the emphasis further towards action. Yes, of course, force was the last resort, but it was a weapon which Britain should not shrink from using if the need arose. Taking advantage of the fact that, as Lord Chancellor, he was the principal legal authority in the Cabinet, he weighed in with his own old-fashioned and highly controversial interpretation of the current law (from which, had they been present, the Law Officers, the Attorney-General and the Solicitor-General, would have dissented). Certainly, the Lord Chancellor conceded, it would be wrong to disregard the UN, but, apart from self-interest, Britain had a strong case morally and in international law. She was entitled to see that it prevailed. If it could not be made to prevail by peaceful means, the Cabinet should be resolved to impose it by force. He cited, with great satisfaction, the authority of Professor Arthur Goodhart's letter to *The Times* of 11 August, which argued that there was no foundation for the view that, under modern international law, force must be used only to repeal a direct territorial attack. A state might properly use force to protect a vital national interest which had been imperilled; and, in such a case, it was the state altering the *status quo* which was guilty of aggression.

Butler pointed out, as Leader of the House of Commons, that the Government would in practice be unable to act without having Parliament and the country behind it. A substantial section of the Government's supporters in the House would want to be sure that all practicable steps had first been taken to secure a settlement by peaceful means. The parliamentary situation would be difficult because there were some elements in the country who were completely opposed to any use of force to settle this question. Eden summed up by agreeing with everybody – a course that remained possible since, to take the two extremes, Monckton had said that force should be used in the last resort and so, with utterly different emphasis, had Kilmuir. It must, the Prime Minister said, be made clear to the public, at home and overseas, that no effort had been spared to get a satisfactory settlement by peaceful means. But they could not afford to allow these efforts to impose an undue delay. 'Our French allies, whose public opinion is less divided than our own, would be quick to place an unfavourable interpretation on anything which could be construed as hesitancy on our part.' So the pressure on Nasser must not lessen.

In his departmental persona, Monckton then delivered a brief military report, starting with the flat statement that the Cabinet would not wish to be informed about the details of the military plan. Military planning, he said, was still based on the original assumption that operations should be launched at the first possible moment. Up to now nothing essential had had to be postponed on political grounds. 'A stage would soon be reached, however, at which it would become difficult to preserve any large measure of flexibility in the military plan.' The efficiency of the operation must be endangered by any long postponement of the date on which planning was being based. These were arguments which in loyalty to the Services the Defence Minister needed to put forward, but they tended to be at the expense of his diplomatic and political case.

Although the Cabinet was not in a position to discuss the plans in detail, some Ministers did ask questions. What would be the scope of the operation? Enough to overwhelm any likely opposition. Would there be any preliminary bombardment? The preliminary *air* attack would be kept to neutralisation of military airfields, which would be carried out with due regard for civilian life and property. No word was apparently said about any preliminary naval bombardment and what effect that would be likely to have on civilians. Was there going to be any specific *casus belli*? That point was under consideration. Apart from the French, what chance was there of help from allies? There was the New Zealand cruiser *Royalist*, token help from Australia and moral support from Belgium and the Netherlands. The Cabinet departed, leaving things to the Egypt Committee until Nasser should have replied to the Menzies mission.[26]

One of the Service Chiefs in attendance at this Cabinet was the First Sea Lord, who for over a week, as he brooded on the nature of the enterprise in which he was becoming involved, had been contemplating resignation. In Mountbatten's private archives there is no complete resignation letter but various undated handwritten drafts, the earliest evidently of 20 August, the latest of 28 August just after the end of the Cabinet meeting. 'I have just received news that you have given the order for the bombing and military assault of Egypt to go ahead,' Mountbatten wrote. 'At this most critical moment in the history of our country I wish to send a last-minute appeal to you to countermand this order before it is too late.' He referred repeatedly to 'aggressive war', which threatened to lose the oil, antagonise world opinion and open the gates to Communism in the Middle East. 'I beg you to reconsider your decision. We are on the point of taking the risk of precipitating a thermonuclear war which may destroy civilisation as we know it.' Even if the war could be localised, Britain would be taking 'a retrograde and absolutely indefensible step'. It had been 'precisely in order to prevent actions like the one we have now embarked on' that we had helped to set up the UN. If Eden felt unable to 'countermand the fateful order', Mountbatten would have told the Prime Minister that he would no longer feel able to serve him.

The letter was not sent. As before, the writer went to Cilcennin and offered to resign. 'It would be fatal that this should ever be known if the button is *not* pressed', Cilcennin wrote.

On Saturday 1 September, when Mountbatten returned from a short stay at Balmoral, he, Monckton and Cilcennin met in the First Lord's bedroom. Both civilians were sick. Cilcennin was laid up after an injection for his back. Monckton 'was in a bad way with gout'. They had an hour and a half of candid discussion. The Ministerial invalids told the First Sea Lord that he must inform no one of his intention to resign because there was still a chance that the operation could be avoided. Monckton said that after his own 'outburst' in the Egypt Committee (when Mountbatten had not been present), followed by his more reserved intervention in Cabinet, his colleagues could be in no doubt that, if they were to order the operation, he would have to resign. But, while a Minister might resign, it was unheard of for a Service chief.[27]

Mountbatten drew their attention to the principle established at the Nuremberg trials (which were in the process of being set up when Monckton had been Solicitor-General) that a senior officer could not escape guilt for war crimes because his Government had given him orders. An armed assault against opposition in a built-up area such as Alexandria would require a preliminary air and naval bombardment that would cause the deaths of thousands of innocent women and children. According to Mountbatten's subsequent account, Monckton and Cilcennin took the view that only if *Musketeer* in its present form were ordered would Mountbatten be entitled to resign. Even then, said Monckton, it would be a most difficult decision. But if his mind was really made up, he should wait until the Minister of Defence had handed in his own resignation first, then see the Prime Minister alone to tell him his thoughts. If on the following day Monckton's resignation had been accepted, only then would it be proper for Mountbatten's letter to be sent.[28]

12

The Birth of SCUA

I showed the President the draft outline of a plan for a Users' Association. The President went through this and said that he thought it was interesting but was not sure that it would work. I said that I was not sure either.
John Foster Dulles, 8 September 1956.

Our relationship with the Americans in this crisis is following the pattern which has appeared on previous occasions ... We press for immediate action, while the Americans are inclined to move with greater phlegm and deliberation. This is the opposite of what our natural temperaments are supposed to be.
Sir Roger Makins, 9 September 1956.

That same weekend of 1–2 September, Anthony Eden, who had gone to his Wiltshire house at Broadchalke for a few days' holiday, was raging over the telephone about press coverage and stimulating from the Foreign Secretary a 'for your eyes only/burn after perusal' telegram to Humphrey Trevelyan in Cairo. 'We are concerned at the delay in the Menzies mission getting face-to-face with Nasser,' it said. 'The Prime Minister and I have done our best to warn Mr Menzies that the Egyptian tactics will spin out these negotiations while they strengthen their hold on the Canal.' Sir Humphrey was asked to take every opportunity to spur on the Australian Prime Minister.[1]

Three other events heightened the atmosphere in Cairo for the coming encounter. French troops started arriving in Cyprus; the British and French advised their subjects to leave Egypt if they had no compelling reason to stay, and the Egyptians announced the rounding up of a ring of British spies. The French had asked that they be allowed to station some administrative troops of 10 (French) Parachute Division and a nucleus of French Air Transport Force staff at Tymbou, the underdeveloped and easily flooded airfield that was to be theirs during *Musketeer*. The British did not feel able to refuse, but the arrival of this advance guard of the combined operation was delicate under two heads: it might seem clumsily provocative at the moment when attention was being directed to the peace option, and it injected yet another element into the already overcrowded Cyprus domestic scene. The Americans responded sharply. Linking the French move to Cyprus with the warning to civilians in Egypt, they strongly disapproved of what they considered as escalation in the psychological war.[2]

The French were, at the same time, making one further move which, if the Americans had known of it, would have disturbed them greatly. On 1 September the Israeli Military Attaché in Paris sent a telegram to Moshe Dayan, informing him that Admiral Barjot, still no doubt furious at the switch to Alexandria, felt that Israel should be invited to take part in the operation, though in what capacity was not at all clear. It was arranged that the Israeli Chief of Operations, Brigadier Meir Amit, who was already in Europe, should talk with Barjot to find out what he had in mind. The Israelis wished to appear obliging because from 30 July to 27 September a stream of French landing-craft was delivering the tanks, planes and guns which the Israelis desperately needed in secret landings at dead of night, often attended by Ben-Gurion and a few especially privileged observers. The Israelis calculated that it would be 1 January 1957 before the armour and 1 March before the planes would be fully absorbed. Amit was instructed to be extremely cautious; he was to clarify and not to undertake commitments. He found Barjot, too, was only at the exploratory stage.[3]

Meanwhile the British had suffered a severe blow in their supply of intelligence information from Egypt. On 27 August Lt-Col. Abdul Kader Hatem announced at a press conference in Cairo that a dangerous espionage ring had been exposed and that James Swinburn, the business manager of the Arab News Agency, who had been arrested and had promptly confessed, was at the head of it. Three other Britons were also arrested, of whom two were eventually acquitted and the third, James Zarb, a Maltese owner of a porcelain factory, convicted with Swinburn in May 1957. There were eleven Egyptians accused, including a headmaster, Sayed Amin Mahmoud, who was later executed, his naval officer son, and a royalist (and militantly anti-communist) Jugoslav, Colonel Milovan Gregorović. Two British diplomats were expelled.

The recent information passed in this way was said to have included details of military dispositions, secret political developments, purchase missions to communist countries. Colonel Gregorović, nephew of a wartime Prime Minister in exile, who seems to have made a career out of blackguarding Communists (he called himself 'the number one enemy of Communism' and 'Tito's greatest enemy') was, according to the prosecutor, a factor in 'inciting' Britain against Egypt since his reports were designed to show that Egypt was 'heading towards Communism'. At the time of Shepilov's visit in June 1956, Gregorović was said to have reported that, on Russian advice, the Arabs had proposed to form a united front which should not only oppose the Baghdad Pact but would draw up plans to nationalise Middle Eastern oil. The effect of these reports, it was alleged, 'was to drive the British mad to the extent of interfering militarily against Egypt'. In view of the nature of this indictment and of Nasser's friendship with Tito it is interesting that, in the end, Gregorović was acquitted and allowed to leave the country.

Two charges that were not made were perhaps more significant than those that were. Sayed Amin Mahmoud's son had for a period been the naval attaché to General Neguib when he had been President. As with the Muslim Brotherhood cases in 1954, there were reports that Neguib was compromised and would be ruined, but all reference to that aspect of the affair was deleted at the trial. Even more remarkable is the fact that the English-language *Egyptian Gazette* of 29 August contained, alongside Colonel Hatem's briefing about the arrests, an obviously inspired article revealing further details, such as that very important instructions were about to be delivered to the British network in Cairo, that a special plane was due to fly in from Cyprus and that meetings had already been held with some well-known Egyptian personalities. The article went on: 'But what is more important is that Swinburn confessed that they were planning a *coup d'état* on the lines of the Zahedi coup in Iran.'

Yet on 2 September Nasser himself shot down this story. In an interview with Martha Rountree, an American TV personality, he said: 'The case did not constitute a plot, as the accused were only gathering information.' Nasser's confidant, Mohamed Heikal, has written that the two diplomats involved, J. G. Glove and J. B. Flux, had been in contact with 'student elements of a religious inclination' with the idea of encouraging fundamentalist riots that could provide an excuse for military intervention to protect European lives.[4]

Menzies in Cairo

Menzies's arrival in Cairo was preceded by frequent news stories in the western press, all carefully culled for Nasser's inspection, representing the Australian as a particularly rugged, blunt fellow. Nasser prepared himself to withstand the impact. After two world wars 'Aussies' were not an unknown factor in Egyptian experience. He told the American Ambassador that he presumed the Menzies mission would take two days to give him their views. It would take only one hour to give his.[5] This mission, which besides Menzies and Loy Henderson consisted of the Foreign Ministers of Sweden, Ethiopia and Iran, reached Cairo on the evening of Sunday, 2 September, and saw Nasser the next day.

The previous evening Henderson had gone with Byroade to see the President. Nasser, who had already received the minutes of the London Conference from Ali Sabri, said that the mission was apparently the bearer of a resolution which he would be told either to accept or reject. 'I don't work in that way', he told the American. 'I want to reach an agreement. Instead you sent this Australian mule to threaten me.' Henderson defended Menzies. 'Menzies is a blunt man and he is not here to dictate terms. He is a man you can talk to ... His mission can amount to very nearly the same thing as negotiations and he wants to make a success of it.'[6]

While this did indeed represent Menzies's attitude, though it was on his power of oratory rather than on his diplomacy that he plumed himself, he was not in any real sense a negotiator or nearly the same as one. Only very grudgingly had Eden and Lloyd allowed him the time he required to work up answers to questions that the Egyptians were thought liable to (but did not) ask. They preferred to get the mission over with in the shortest available time. Menzies showed considerable skill in holding his diverse delegation together. At the first meeting with the Egyptians (Mahmoud Fawzi and Ali Sabri, as well as the President) on the evening of 3 September Menzies was evidently at his rhetorical best. 'He has on several occasions indicated his admiration for Churchill whom he loves to imitate,' reported an admiring Loy Henderson. 'His voice took on Churchillian tones and his discourse was interspersed with a Churchillian type of humour.'[7] It was not an association that would have been expected to commend him to the Egyptians.

Mahmoud Fawzi's judgment of him in the Suez memoir which he wrote in English was this: 'Tall as Abdul Nasser and distinctly heavier, with gruff eyebrows, glaring eyes and a sharp voice, Menzies represented physically the principal protagonists of the London Conference who were bent on retrogression and imposition.'[8]

Henderson thought that Menzies 'showed considerable tact in presenting the more unpalatable passages [of his exposition] in the best possible light'. It was all to no avail. Nasser and his advisers got the message behind the repeated emphasis on respect for Egyptian sovereignty and on the proposed system being as much to Egypt's benefit as to that of the users. Menzies, wrote Fawzi, 'saw nothing amiss in asking Abdul Nasser to accept two premises for negotiations: (1) the incompetence of Egyptians and (2) the untrustworthiness of Abdul Nasser himself. He was so far from understanding the raw sensitivities of Afro-Asian nationalities that he thought it a sufficient inducement to assure Nasser that the proposed international board would do all the work on the Canal while Egypt would get all the profits.'[9]

At the end of the first session Menzies asked for a few minutes alone with Nasser. He then warned him solemnly, while insisting that he meant no threat, not to assume that the strength of British and French public feeling had in any way abated, or that the London Conference had removed the option of force if no peaceful solution were found. Nasser was not likely to take such a message kindly and he did not. Menzies, however, was confident that he had made an impression. Ever afterwards he complained to Eisenhower himself and to anybody else who would listen that the American President had 'pulled the rug completely from under him' by a thoughtless answer at a press conference the same day, which was reported prominently in the next morning's Egyptian papers. The answer reads mildly enough to the effect that the United States was 'determined to exhaust every possible, every feasible method of peaceful settlement', though there was an implication that these efforts would continue even if the London proposals did not succeed. 'How could the West deal with a man like Nasser,' the Australian Prime Minister spluttered, 'if they throw their trump cards into the wastepaper basket?'[10]

Both at his first meeting with Nasser and at a later banquet in the mission's honour Menzies made a considerable effort to get on friendly terms with the Egyptian President. It was not a great success although Nasser put himself out to appear courteous. 'He is in some ways a likeable fellow,' Menzies conceded in a later letter to Eden, 'but, so far from being charming, he is rather gauche, with some irritating mannerisms such as rolling his eyes up at the ceiling when he is talking to you and producing a quick, quite evanescent grin when he can think of nothing else to do. I would say that he was a man of considerable but immature intelligence ...'[11]

The mission saw Nasser again on 5 September. The President took up the central thesis at the heart of his visitor's case: the need for insulation of the Canal from politics. 'But how is this to be done?' demanded Nasser. 'The Canal is part of Egypt ... Was the London Conference a technical one? Are the proposals that you are bringing me technical proposals? No: both the conference and the proposals are political ... You talk about the need for trust, but trust is a two-way traffic. I have read a statement by Sir Anthony Eden, or it may have been Mr Dulles, that he didn't trust Gamal Abdul Nasser. I must confess that I don't trust them either ...' Menzies then repeated in this more open forum part of what he had said in the private encounter about the high feeling in Britain and France. Nasser (showing heat for the only time) snapped back that if the Australian Prime Minister was trying to convey the idea that rejection of the proposals would lead to trouble, he was quite prepared to let it come at once.

Members of the mission got increasingly impatient at the frequency with which Nasser reverted to the phrase 'collective colonialism'; the protests of the Ethiopian, Iranian and Swedish Foreign Ministers seemed to be of some temporary effect. Henderson laid America's anti-colonial credentials on the table. The contradiction remained: the mission (or at least its head) was trying to compel Egypt to negotiate of her own free will a derogation of her national sovereignty.[12]

The mission was now agreed that they had come up against a brick wall. Nasser had said that he was prepared to make agreements with the user states about rates and non-discrimination, but within a framework of complete ownership, management and operating control of the Canal by the Egyptian Government. The development programme of the former Canal Company would be continued, together with other programmes of wider scope and longer range. The Suez Canal Authority was to be an independent entity with its own budget and all necessary powers outside the normal government structure. An adequate percentage of the revenue would be earmarked for future development and could not be raided for other purposes. The Egyptians did not do what Brook had suggested that they might do: produce ambiguous replies to the conference, documents that would tie everybody up in weeks and months of negotiation. They did not even announce acceptance of the Krishna Menon plan. Menzies, who was determined that he was 'not going to get into a bog', pushed his colleagues towards winding up the proceedings quickly, accusing Loy Henderson of wanting to 'play a separate game' by encouraging Nasser to produce counter-proposals. This, thought Menzies, would only 'leave the results of our mission obscure and land us into a wilderness of debate in respect of which we have no mandate whatever'.[13]

The Menzies mission drew up a final *aide-mémoire* which restated its proposals and placed their advantages to Egypt in an attractive form. It then recorded that these proposals had been rejected. On 9 September its members had a farewell meeting with Nasser. The previous day Anwar Sadat wrote in *Al-Gumhouriya*: 'It has now become quite clear that Eden wants nothing but war ... He has no other course open to him than either to declare war or to resign.'[14]

As soon as the five-power mission had left Egyptian soil, the Egyptians issued their own proposals. These took the form of a re-statement of Egyptian interest in freedom of navigation, the development of the Canal to meet future requirements and the establishment of just and equitable tolls together with a readiness to discuss these matters with all states using the Canal. To this end Egypt suggested the formation of a 'negotiating body' which would be 'representative of the different views' to review the Constantinople Convention. But first there would have to be talks about talks to decide the composition, venue and meeting date of this body. Archibald Ross at the Foreign Office dismissed the proposal as being 'designed to waste as much time as possible in preliminaries' and not to be accorded the dignity of comment.[15]

Nasser could not have expected much else. He told Byroade, who was being re-posted to South Africa, 'The British and French are going to stay out there in the Mediterranean until they find a pretext to come in.'[16]

Duck Island Thoughts

While Menzies was in Cairo he was under pressure from Lloyd to bring the talks to an early end in order to fit the timetable for going to the Security Council.[17] Otherwise, it was feared, Egypt might get there first with a complaint about the mounting evidence of hostile military preparation. Also, the Security Council could not be held too late in the sequence because, as Lloyd put it, it would be a mistake to have bombs falling 'out of the blue' during the actual debate. As the Menzies mission proceeded the realisation gradually spread that the Americans were dragging their feet over the UN.

John Foster Dulles had withdrawn over the long Labour Day weekend to his inaccessible Canadian retreat on Duck Island.[18] There, thinking through the Suez crisis without other distractions, he began writing as was his wont on a yellow legal pad.

On returning to Washington on 4 September, he summoned the British Chargé, and said it seemed to him that the West were at present in a weak position juridically. They were asking the Egyptians to accept a new treaty and threatening them with the use of force if they refused; yet all the while they had the rights they wanted under the 1888 Convention. It was a fatal and unnecessary weakness to assume that, if Egypt did not voluntarily accept, she should be compelled. There was another way: the signatories or the users could club together and run the Canal themselves from a ship at anchor at either end. This was possible because the Canal itself was an open waterway, devoid of physical barriers along its route. There was no reason why ships had to hire pilots through the agency of Egypt. Nasser would thus see the money slipping out of his hands, a much more likely deflator than the threat or use of force.[19]

At the same time Dulles shared his brainwave with Loy Henderson in Cairo. He did not think much of it. The institutional arrangements required would be even more unpalatable to Egypt than the proposals currently falling on barren soil while the effort to put them into effect would serve to increase international tension and the danger of a resort to force. It was precisely this feature that attracted the attention of the British and brought a positive reply from Lloyd on 6 September. He assumed, he said, that the plan would require an interim authority with its headquarters outside Egypt and that, for a start, all transit dues would in future be paid to it. Eventually it could take over all the functions that had been intended for the International Board.[20]

In a separate message Lloyd explained to the Ambassador, Sir Roger Makins, the grounds for his enthusiasm. 'The great tactical advantage of Mr Dulles's proposal is that, if the Americans were to participate in the actual setting up of an international body after Nasser's refusal, they would have committed themselves much further towards a policy of compelling the Egyptian Government by some means or other to accept international control'. Sir Roger was given to understand that, in the Foreign Secretary's mind, this consideration far outweighed the juridical flaws, which he acknowledged.[21]

For Dulles, the CASU (Co-operative Association of Suez Canal Users) as his idea was originally called (it was only later known as 'SCUA'), was a means of derailing the Anglo-French drive to war or, at the least, of gaining some time. For the British, it was a fresh opportunity to co-opt the Americans in a process which would end in the forceful compulsion of Egypt.

This development in Dulles's thinking was the more welcome in that the Americans were creating a great deal of worry during the time that Menzies was in Cairo. There was, for one thing, the contribution of President Eisenhower. On 3 September he wrote to Eden: 'I must tell you frankly that American public opinion flatly rejects the thought of using force.' He went on to point out that the British economy would not be able to sustain prolonged military operations or the loss of Middle East oil which would probably follow. Once more Eisenhower argued that Eden should segregate the long-term problem of the Canal from what was properly a short-term problem of dealing with the Egyptian dictatorship. 'I found this most disturbing,' wrote the Prime Minister, who rushed up from a short break in the country specially to deal with it. The message was clearly and forcefully worded and it seemed to place an absolute ban on British use of force. From the time that he received it, if not before, Eden should have been in no doubt whatsoever of the American President's firm standpoint.[22]

'A Very Noble Bit of Prose'

Sir Ivone Kirkpatrick prepared 'a very noble bit of prose' in response to Eisenhower which Eden then worked on with 'much care'.[23] The body of this pronouncement worked out at some length the analogy between 1936 and 1956. 'In the 1930s Hitler established his position by a series of carefully planned movements ... His actions were tolerated and excused by the majority of the population of Western Europe. It was argued that Hitler had committed no act of aggression against anyone or that he was entitled to do what he liked in his own territory or that it was impossible to prove that he had any ulterior designs or the Covenant of the League of Nations did not entitle us to use force and that it would be wiser to wait until he did commit an act of aggression ...' In more recent years Russia had tried the same thing, starting with the Berlin blockade. Now the seizure of the Suez Canal was 'the opening gambit in a planned campaign designed by Nasser to expel all Western influence and interests from Arab countries'. If he succeeded he would mount revolutions of young officers in Saudi

Arabia, Jordan, Syria and Iraq; the new governments would be 'Egyptian satellites if not Russian ones'. 'They will have to place their oil resources under the control of a united Arabia led by Egypt and under Russian influence. When that moment comes, Nasser can deny oil to Western Europe and we here shall be at his mercy.'

'You may feel that even if we are right it would be better to wait until Nasser has unmistakably unveiled his intentions,' Eden's message concluded. 'But this was the argument which prevailed in 1936 and which we both rejected in 1948 ... I agree with you that prolonged military operations as well as the denial of the Middle East oil would place an immense strain on the economy of Western Europe ... But if our assessment is correct and if the only alternative is to allow Nasser's plans quietly to develop until this country and all Western Europe are held to ransom by Egypt acting at Russia's behest, it seems to us that our duty is plain. We have many times led Europe in the fight for freedom. It would be an ignoble end to our long history if we accepted to perish by degrees.'[24]

The next morning (7 September) Dulles phoned Eisenhower to tell him that he thought Eden's statements were intemperate and the concepts not thought through. The President said that the British had got themselves into a box in the Middle East by choosing the wrong places to get tough – as in the case of Buraimi where they had only succeeded in incurring the hatred of the Saudis. It was pretty hard, he said, to attack Egypt so long as Egypt did not get in the way of running the Canal. Dulles had been talking to members of Congress and found them eager to see the Canal shut down so that Americans could sell more oil. 'With the British using what for money?' Eisenhower asked.[25]

In his reply to Eden the President warned him of the danger of 'making of Nasser a much more important figure than he is'. They should be thinking in terms of more supertankers, the building of new pipelines, finding other sources of oil. 'Nasser thrives on drama'; so the answer to him was to drain the situation of drama. Dulles coaxed the President into bolstering the message with references to his new idea of a Users' Association. He showed the President his draft plan. Eisenhower's immediate reaction was that he did not think it would work. Dulles said that he was not sure either, but it was essential to keep the initiative because there was no chance of getting Britain and France not to use force unless they were offered the prospect of something strong to do.[26]

When Eisenhower's reply reached Whitehall, Sir Ivone Kirkpatrick sent Sir Roger Makins a note of his immediate and personal reactions.

> I wish the President were right. But I am convinced that he is wrong ... [I]f we sit back while Nasser consolidates his position and gradually acquires control of the oil-bearing countries, he can and is, according to our information, resolved to wreck us. If Middle Eastern oil is denied

> to us for a year or two, our gold reserves will disappear. If our gold reserves disappear, the sterling area disintegrates. If the sterling area disintegrates and we have no reserves, we shall not be able to maintain a force in Germany, or indeed, anywhere else. I doubt whether we shall be able to pay for the bare minimum necessary for our defence. And a country that cannot provide for its defence is finished.[27]

This is what Britain's leaders thought was involved in the Suez conflict.

British public opinion was giving off an uncertain sound. Eisenhower and Dulles were continually making reference in their conversations about Suez to the ever-mounting indications of opposition within Britain to Eden's policy. 'The fact is', the Conservative Party chairman Oliver Poole wrote to Eden on 29 August, 'that the majority of people in this country want the best of both worlds. They want negotiations with Nasser to end in a diplomatic victory for this country with as much loss of face to Nasser as possible ... and at the same time they are unwilling to take the final step of military intervention, particularly if this is to be done by Great Britain on her own.' Still, the Gallup Poll in the *News Chronicle* of 31 August showed that fifty-nine per cent of the people (including seventy-seven per cent of Conservatives) approved of the Government's handling of the Suez crisis as against twenty-five per cent who did not.

A more detailed poll taken on 10 August had shown that whereas only ten per cent thought that Egypt could be trusted to keep the Canal open to all shipping, only thirty-three per cent were in favour of military action if Egypt would not accept conference decisions, including twenty-seven per cent who would go ahead even without America. Poole felt by the end of the month that, as time went on, there had been a 'noticeable softening' among active supporters of the Conservative Party about the idea of using force without further conversations, particularly at the UN.[28]

On 10 September Clark told the Prime Minister that, in reply to questions asked by Gallup when the conference was still in progress, eighty-one per cent of the public had favoured going to the UN if Egypt would not agree to the plan being put to her. If the UN failed, thirty-four per cent were in favour of a military ultimatum and forty-nine per cent against. The most significant figures in the separate *Daily Express* poll published on 10 September showed the contrast in Labour voters' opinion of Eden's handling of the situation compared with the previous month. In August he had the support of forty-three-and-a-half per cent with thirty-three per cent against him; in September it was twenty-five per cent pro and fifty-seven per cent con.[29]

At the British Cabinet meeting of 6 September there was confirmation of Eden's decision, taken two days before, to recall Parliament for 12 September. Eden, having put this move off for as long as possible, was now anxious to have a stage on which to deploy his case, instead of having to suffer its steady erosion from criticism in the papers. The misgivings attributed both to Pineau and to Bourgès-Maunoury by the Paris embassy that a parliamentary session would merely advertise Britain's disunity the more widely were tartly rejected. Assuming that the Menzies talks were going to fail, Selwyn Lloyd told his Cabinet colleagues that the next steps were to persuade as many nations as possible to withhold payment of Canal dues and to refer the dispute to the UN Security Council.

There were, however, some delicate matters of timing. The Cabinet was told that the request for a Council meeting ought to be made within the next few days if the build up of the military preparations were not to overtake the debate and make an unfortunate impression. But the French did not want to go ahead in New York without first getting two guarantees from the Americans: that they would give no support to any departure from the Eighteen-Nation plan and that they would not back any amendment ruling out the use of force.

It was also noted that although the Americans had promised to make good any shortage of oil should the Canal be closed, nothing whatever had been promised about paying for it in dollars. Then again, unless military action was swift and unless British troops could then be immediately withdrawn, the use of force would probably involve a run on sterling. Macmillan and Salisbury insisted that even this was to be preferred to the 'slow strangulation' that would surely follow from Egypt extending her control over the oil-producing countries of the Arab world. But, with an eye to the need for public support, it was agreed around the Cabinet table that 'the fullest possible use' must be seen to have been made of the international machinery that was available.[30]

UN or SCUA?

When Hervé Alphand arrived in Washington as the replacement for Couve de Murville, he told Makins candidly that, in the minds of the French, action in the UN was generally regarded as an alibi for failure to act outside it. But Lloyd had talked his ally round, subject to their getting the two guarantees. He asked Dulles point-blank whether he agreed to give them. Dulles said that he could not commit the United States to vote against an amendment calling on the parties to refrain from the threat or use of force, as this, after all, was the declared purpose of Chapter VII of the Charter under which Britain and France were proposing to introduce their resolution. Alphand in his blunt way asked Dulles whether he had any definite date in mind for the Security Council. He replied that he had not, since he was still doubtful of the wisdom of going to the Council at all.[31]

There was a desperation creeping into Selwyn Lloyd's tone. Dulles was getting him dangerously rattled. 'We seem to be further apart than at any time since 26 July,' he said to Makins on 8 September. 'I cannot accept the present US thinking that the two problems of settling the Canal issue and deflating Nasser can be separated either as to timing or method. Please convey to Mr Dulles my grave anxiety at the present state of our consultations and seek to impress upon him the absolute necessity for effective action urgently. Any further dawdling will be fatal.' He could not, he said, understand how Dulles, having himself suggested the Users' Club scheme, could now argue, as he appeared to be doing, that it was doubtful if the users had the right to refuse payment to the Egyptian Authority. 'I feel at the moment that I do not know where the US Government stands on any of these matters.'[32]

Lloyd was not the only one. Shortly afterwards Douglas Dillon was reporting from Paris that he had never seen Christian Pineau so upset. The Foreign Minister had complained to him that there was no US policy on Suez and that, apparently, there was no means available in the State Department for arriving at one. During the past week the Department had turned down all positive suggestions on one excuse or another. This left only war.[33] 'We are wasting our time talking to the Americans', Pineau told the British Ambassador. They would *never* authorise any action likely to provoke the fall of Nasser, at any rate until after the American election. 'Our two countries should now go firmly ahead on our chosen path.'[34]

That was all very well but the financial implications for Britain, as banker of the sterling area, of action unsupported by the United States were likely to be severe. Sir Edward Bridges, the Permanent Secretary to the Treasury, in a memorandum to Macmillan on 7 September, referred to 'the vital necessity from the point of view of our currency and our economy of ensuring that we do not go it alone and that we have maximum US support'. The Chancellor minuted: 'Yes, this is just the trouble. US are being very difficult.' He seems to have adopted a fatalistic attitude, writing in his diary, 'The more we can persuade [the Americans] of our determination to risk everything in order to beat Nasser, the more help we shall get from them ... We shall be ruined either way; but we shall be more inevitably and finally ruined if we are humiliated.'

Macmillan does not seem to have felt the need, in the light of this analysis of the prospects, to take such precautions as drawing down the gold tranche from the International Monetary Fund, as the French did in October, or strengthening the Treasury's powers over capital movements. Instead he plunged into an orgy of leisure reading, gobbling up novel after novel by George Eliot and Villari's *Lives* of Machiavelli and of Savonarola.[35] He told the Cabinet on 11 September that speed of settling the issue by all necessary steps, including the use of force, was of the essence. If the minutes are to be trusted, the Treasury view that American support was the only chance of avoiding imminent financial and economic disaster was not conveyed.

The American election was now very close and the President, in his latest letter to Eden, had made his own views very clear. But Sir Roger Makins, who was on the eve of his return to Whitehall as Permanent Secretary to the Treasury, warned Lloyd in a personally directed telegram on 9 September not to attribute too much to the election climate. 'It is true, as the President says, that there is no support in the United States for the use of force in present circumstances and in the absence of further clear provocation by Nasser. This is not due to the imminence of the elections but is a normal manifestation of American public opinion. The election atmosphere merely has the effect of distracting the attention of the American public from the Suez issue.'

The Ambassador went on to urge the British Government to look on Dulles's new approach positively. 'The fact that the legal basis of his proposal for a users' committee may be a little shaky does not seem to me to be important. What is important is that Mr Dulles is willing to sponsor it. It does not represent any backsliding from the proposal of the Eighteen. As Mr Dulles said to me, "We made Egypt a fair offer which they turned down; we now proceed to something which they will like much less."'

It was essential, Makins continued, that responsibility for breakdown in the operation of the Canal should lie squarely on the Egyptians.

> I do not really know what your innermost thoughts are as regards military action but, as it looks from Washington, to attempt it without full American moral and material support could easily lead to disaster. There were times perhaps (they are surely very rare) when we must take our own line because our national interest transcends even the need to uphold the Atlantic Alliance. But this, I think, is true only when there is an issue of profound substance dividing us. Here it is a case of our wanting to perform an operation (cutting Nasser down) one way and the Americans another. Ours may be better, but if we can keep their immense power working in our favour, is it not preferable to try theirs?[36]

The American way did not make much sense to Jacques Georges-Picot, the Managing Director of *la Suez*, when British Ministers – Lloyd, Nutting and Harold Watkinson, the Minister of Transport – discussed the future with him and the French Ambassador, Chauvel, in London on 8 September. His main interest remained that of getting his pilots and shore staff out. The British and, at their behest, the French Government had hitherto urged them repeatedly to stay at their posts. Now Pineau was definitely in favour of the Company being instructed to recall them. Lloyd did not wish the British Government to be seen actually doing that; he preferred to abstain from offering them any further advice. He also tried to sell Georges-Picot on the idea of the Users' Association.

Georges-Picot was not impressed. Too much emphasis, he said, was being put on the function of the pilots. In fact, the operation was as much to do with the ground organisation as with them. Ships had to be marshalled in convoys; pilots needed to be in constant touch with the shore. The Egyptians would not be doing nothing. With such pilots as they would still have, they might be able to manage forty to fifty per cent of the present traffic. So there would be two different organisations trying to control traffic, one based in Egypt, the other based outside. The result would be chaos.

Watkinson, the British Transport Minister, made the shrewd observation that the trouble was that they had two conflicting objectives: they wanted Nasser to lose face by revealing his inability to operate the Canal, but they also wanted this to happen without interrupting the flow of oil to Europe. Nutting's reply was that the real pressure on Nasser would be financial because of the denial of Canal revenues. Georges-Picot was again unhelpful. Withholding dues, he said, would not affect Egypt's economy for a long time. Nutting said that the pressure would be moral rather than economic: if Nasser acquiesced in the non-payment of the dues, he was bound to lose prestige. Watkinson said that what he feared most was that the Egyptians might, by various measures, such as organising convoys with a qualified pilot only in the leading ship, manage to run the Canal at seventy-five per cent efficiency with the promise of gradual improvement.[37]

Only events could demonstrate the accuracy of these fears and calculations. The decision was taken by Ministers and the Company that the Company's foreign staff should be free to withdraw by a deadline of Saturday, 15 September. The supreme test of wits and nerve for Egypt was approaching.

Also, at the same time, the diplomatic climate was being set by a still earlier deadline, Wednesday, 12 September, the day the British Parliament was due back in Westminster in emergency session. It was a deadline, moreover, that was being put to use by the British in the hope of netting the elusive American Secretary. Two days beforehand Lloyd put Eden's speech-writing problem bluntly to Dulles in a letter which Makins handed over to him. If Nasser's summary rejection of the Eighteen-Power proposals was not to strike the House as yet a further blow to western influence in the Middle East, the Prime Minister must be in a position to proclaim a clear and decisive western policy in the light of it. But what was that policy to be? If it was to be the Users' Club when the House was expecting the UN, he must in the same breath announce full Anglo-American agreement that all dues must be payable forthwith to the new Club only and that, in case of Egyptian interference or non-co-operation on land, the users would be free to take whatever steps that seemed fit to them to enforce their Treaty rights. Otherwise, the Prime Minister would 'be unable to withstand pressure for an early debate in the Security Council at our initiative'.[38]

On the same day, 10 September, Mollet and Pineau arrived for a two-day summit at Downing Street which discussed Menzies's report and (as will appear in the next chapter) a major alteration in the military plan, but also the nail-biting questions of the Users' Club and the recourse to the Security Council. Pineau began by asking the key question, 'Is the Dulles proposition put forward to gain time until the election or is it serious?' Lloyd, who clearly shared some of his doubts, said that what really counted was whether American ships paid or did not pay all their tolls to the new Association. He added that it would not be necessary to negotiate with the Egyptians, who would be told about the new arrangements but not asked. In practice 'incidents would arrive quickly' under the scheme as Dulles had expounded it. 'That is precisely why I am sceptical about the determination with which Dulles is going to pursue it,' said Mollet. Eden was that day more buoyant. 'It has always been Franco-British firmness that has brought Dulles along,' he said. 'Why not set up our Users' Club?'

The talk turned to the Security Council. Pineau pronounced himself against going. The risk was too great of the West being paralysed by an amendment condemning recourse to force. Selwyn Lloyd agonised that if they waited any longer they could be forestalled by Nasser.[39]

The following day (11 September) was the eve of the return of Parliament. The reply from Washington to the British representations had been at least partially reassuring. Dulles was disposed to acknowledge that any Egyptian interference with or refusal to co-operate with the Users' Association would rank as a violation of the 1888 Convention, in which case each Power would 'regain its liberty of action'. What he was not prepared to do was give a blanket endorsement in advance of any retaliatory measure to which Britain and France might choose to resort. Lloyd commented that it was very important that the users' organisation should be known as a Dulles Plan because it was up to him to make it work. 'If this were to appear to be our idea and the whole thing misfired we would suffer the consequences.'[40]

Eden, thinking of the expectations there would be in the House next day, said that he could not see why they should not have both the Users' Club and a Security Council resolution at the same time. 'If the rules of the UN oblige us to go there before using force, why not go now?' Mollet objected that, if they were going to create the Users' Club, what pretext could they have for going to the UN? By way of answer Selwyn Lloyd started reading out the text of a letter to the President of the Security Council that he had prepared for possible use some time previously. The longer he read, the more it dawned on everyone, according to the French account, that this wording would no longer do. Pineau tried his hand at the phraseology but Mollet interrupted him. Why should they commit themselves to go to the UN when the Users' Club was going to create incidents as the result of which Dulles's formula about everyone regaining his freedom of action would suit them much better? At this stage of the discussion a note was passed up to Eden from Harold Watkinson who (having no doubt reflected on what Georges-Picot had told him) reported that the idea of pilots operating from ships stationed at the two ends of the Canal would be unworkable; a land staff was indispensable.

Eden insisted that he must have a formula ready for tomorrow about reference to the Security Council. Everything else was well prepared. The Security Council was 'the thorn in my flesh – is it to be today or later?' The two Frenchmen seem overnight to have acquired fresh enthusiasm for the 'Dulles Plan'. 'Doesn't it show a want of confidence in our plan to envisage its failure and to anticipate an appeal to the Security Council?' Mollet asked. But Eden, evidently shaken by Watkinson's message, gave prompt evidence of such a want. 'I doubt whether this organisation will work,' he said. 'And what do we do if the United States does not accept suspension of paying dues to Egypt?' Mollet was now keen to press ahead with the club. 'It will be taken by international public opinion as being a kind of sanction against Egypt,' he said. 'And, in any case, it would look like an energetic measure.' 'To be a sanction', snapped Lloyd, who was a lawyer too, though not perhaps as celebrated a one as Dulles, 'it would have had to go before the Security Council.' Mollet said he did not mean a real sanction, merely one that would pass as such with public opinion.[41]

Lloyd continued to express misgivings about the danger of Dulles 'slipping through our fingers' if they went ahead with the plan. But for Mollet the capital point was that the 'Dulles Plan' would constitute a *rapprochement* of Britain and France with the United States at a time when Egypt had thought she had driven a wedge between them. Whatever his misgivings Eden summed up the session: they would back the plan provided the United States shared equal responsibility; failing that they would go to the Security Council.

Still unhappy, the Foreign Secretary cabled to Sir Roger Makins on 12 September, 'There seems to me a risk that Mr Dulles, having rejected the idea of a Security Council debate, having refused to deny dues to the Egyptians, having reached the conclusion that further economic pressure is impossible, will find that his own scheme is impracticable.'[42]

13

Musketeer Revise

It is . . . of the greatest importance that this invasion of Egypt is launched with our moral case unassailable and the start of the war clearly and definitely Nasser's responsibility and no one else's . . . [T]he problem is whether it appears likely that this moral case can be achieved within the next few weeks and, if not, whether some other plan which can be launched at a much later date is not required.

General Sir Charles Keightley, Allied Commander-in-Chief, 7 September 1956.

Perhaps I do not understand, perhaps it is my fault, but if, for example, I am asked: what did we decide [on the Egyptian proposal], I have to say – 'Nothing'.

Dr Paulo Cunha, Foreign Minister of Portugal at the Second London (SCUA) Conference, 21 September 1956.

General Keightley, the Allied Commander-in-Chief, was getting increasingly uneasy. *Musketeer* was not originally his scheme. It involved a large number of intricately related deadlines and implied a degree of precision that married ill with the habits of international diplomacy and debates in Parliament and the Security Council. D-Day was getting repeatedly postponed. First it had been 15 September; next it was 19 September; now because of the Menzies mission, it was 25 September. On 4 September the Egypt Committee was told that the maximum postponement possible was until 6 October. After that the plan must be recast. This meant that, since the earliest entry on the lengthy calendar of triggers was D – 18, it followed that the last possible decision date would be 18 September. To Keightley each new development seemed to make it less likely that this deadline could be counted upon. What was required instead was a scheme that was flexible, tied up fewer resources in indefinite waiting and could be ordered up at short notice. On 7 September Eden received from Monckton a report from the Chiefs of Staff which incorporated Keightley's appreciation and included a separate note from the general.[1]

The apparent precision in talking about 6 October as *Musketeer*'s latest allowable D-Day had, it appeared, been arrived at by aggregating a number of imprecise factors such as security ('We have already had leakages over certain matters with the French which we stressed must remain secret'); the building up of Egyptian preparations in the Alexandria area (mines and blockships in the harbour, dug-in tanks and heavy mining on the beach-heads) which might break the dash which the initial operation required; and the increasing opportunity for Russian and East European 'volunteers' to make the Egyptian air force a real threat to the airfields on Cyprus, with their out-of-date radar and desperate congestion. 'We have had information from intelligence sources that a tie-up between the Egyptian and Syrian air forces is in fact taking place,' Keightley wrote. 'We also believe that given time an increasing number of Russian volunteers will be obtained to fly their aircraft.' The General worried about the effect on morale of the men if units were held for long periods without their own equipment and on the state of readiness of much of the equipment itself after being on shipboard for six weeks. What if the vehicles would not start when they were being unloaded onto docks, probably under shell-fire?

There was also the question of weather. On this the Prime Minister, on reading Keightley's appreciation, wrote 'Not at all' against the General's observation that it was 'somewhat unpredictable in the Mediterranean at this time of the year', with the possibility of storms over Cyprus. Eden reacted even more impatiently to the passages where Keightley touched on the political sphere. It was, said the General, of the utmost importance that the Arab countries and, even more so, the rest of the world should not be against British military action. The invasion must be launched 'with our moral case unassailable and the start of the war clearly and definitely Nasser's responsibility and no one else's'. 'Yet he won't delay to strengthen it,' protested Eden. Keightley answered the objection, if rather naïvely, in the next two paragraphs. It would require, he said, 'a great deal of money and effort spent' to ensure that Britain's case really got over to the people of the Arab world. 'Following this, the problem is whether it appears likely that this moral case can be achieved within the next few weeks and, if not, therefore, whether some other plan which can be launched at a much later date is not required.' Against this Eden wrote the single word 'French'. Britain's one ally had made it abundantly clear that, as far as she was concerned, she could not endure much further delay.

But there was another, stronger reason why opinion was hardening against the Alexandria plan. Many of those few Ministers and Service chiefs including Keightley who knew the plans were deeply disturbed by the scale of civilian casualties and urban destruction that would be caused by the air and naval bombardment which landing in the harbour at Alexandria would make necessary. On 3 September, by a long-standing arrangement, Lord Hailsham entered the Government (having turned down the post of Paymaster-General at the December reshuffle) and took over from Lord

Cilcennin as First Lord of the Admiralty. Cilcennin warned the First Sea Lord that the omens were not good. Mountbatten's new political chief had already made little secret of his conviction that force was the right way to deal with Nasser. Yet when Hailsham was briefed about *Musketeer* he was horrified. He had a personal reason for his distress. During the Second World War, when he was serving in the Middle East, he had come across two old-fashioned flat-bottomed Monitors. He had been told that they had once been equipped with eighteen-inch guns and used in close-range bombardment, firing on a virtually flat trajectory. The destruction they could cause was massive and its description had been so vivid that it had remained with him. He told William Clark: 'There is one thing in this that I simply cannot stomach and that is the bombardment from the sea by the British fleet of the open city of Alexandria.'[2]

On the other hand, General Keightley was determined not to be caught underestimating the courage of the Egyptian soldier. For the defence of what would be a comparatively small front, the Egyptian forces available would be very adequate. 'We are certain', he said, 'to have some very bitter fighting.' With the small number of assault landing craft available the margins of safety for a landing operation in Alexandria harbour would not be such that the attackers could manage without a preliminary display of massive firepower.

It was against this background that Keightley considered that what was needed, in stark contrast to *Musketeer*, was a plan that 'must be capable of being held until our moral cause is unassailable' and could be put into action at short notice. In a scheme that bore an obvious relationship to the one being planned in case of war with Israel, he spoke of relying almost entirely on the RAF, the Fleet Air Arm and the French equivalents to impose the Allies' will on Egypt. D-Day would, therefore, mark not the landing of the first troops but the opening of a sustained though selective air offensive, to be ordered 'when Egypt gives us a *casus belli*'. The landing when it eventually came would be at Port Said rather than Alexandria and would involve, in the first instance, only troops that were already stationed in the Mediterranean. 3 (British) Infantry Division would still be required from home but it would be sufficient to embark it only after the operation had started; 2 (British) Infantry Division from Germany would not be required at all. Thus the preliminary build-up for an attack could be very considerably simplified.

Almost jauntily, General Keightley claimed large merits for this scheme, the first and foremost being that it was an operation which could be put on at short notice and would not be affected by postponement. It would also, it was confidently claimed, cause far fewer casualties to the civilian population and less damage to property than an assault landing followed by an advance through Egypt. There would be no withdrawal of an infantry division from Nato duty in Germany, all reservists could be released at the end of October, and a large number of ships (including five or six passenger liners) would not need to be requisitioned or, if already requisitioned, could be released.

Musketeer Revise

It sounded too good to be true and General Templer, the CIGS, thought that it was.[3] On 6 September, when the Chiefs of Staff discussed Keightley's note, Templer said that he doubted whether this combination of economic, air and naval action could achieve such disintegration of the Egyptian army as would make any land fighting whatsoever unnecessary. According to an entry in his diary Eden read the paper late that night and 'was not at first much enamoured of it'. After only five hours' sleep ('at least, uninterrupted', he noted wrily), he plunged into a two-hour session with the Chiefs of Staff and Keightley, in which he sharply queried the wisdom of such a radical change of plan. He wrote that in course of discussion he 'became more reconciled'. Having granted a request from the First Sea Lord to be allowed to raise a political matter he received the full force of Mountbatten's message about the political effects of a naval bombardment followed by a prolonged land campaign. Eden, according to Mountbatten, said that he had been given the impression that British forces landing at Alexandria could be in Cairo within five days. Templer said that that was only if the Egyptians did not fight. If they did, it might take up to twenty-three days to reach Cairo and cross the Nile. When Eden replied that the Egyptians were yellow and would crumble immediately, Mountbatten referred to the bitter resistance put up in the Ismailia police barracks in 1952. Keightley, too, thought the Egyptians would now fight well.[4]

During a long session of the Egypt Committee in the afternoon of 7 September Eden acknowledged that two features of the existing military plan caused him grave concern. First, it was now apparent that the devastation and loss of life caused by the assault on Alexandria would be much greater than envisaged earlier. Secondly, and even more seriously, there was the lack of flexibility. Indeed, unless D-Day was again postponed, the sailing to the Mediterranean of seventeen store ships and ten tank landing ships as well as the requisitioning of four or five passenger liners would have to be put in train during the next two days. The new concept, it was decided, was to be examined in detail with great urgency by the Chiefs of Staff, the sailings were to be suspended, and Mollet and Pineau should be invited over on Monday, 10 September on the pretext of hearing Menzies's report but in reality to be told that *Musketeer* would have to be changed.[5]

Eden, in the privacy of his diary, pronounced himself 'still not entirely convinced'. He felt he was in a false position, being sold by the military a plan whose advantages were 'largely political'. But he ended the day with another long talk with Keightley alone. To him after all had been entrusted the supreme responsibility for the operation. 'It was clear', he wrote rather sadly, 'that he much preferred the second plan,' and closed the entry tersely, 'Tired'.[6]

When the French arrived, Mollet, in the mood to make something special of the new spirit of *entente cordiale*, astonished the British by asking whether Sir Winston Churchill's 1940 offer of an Anglo-French union with one common citizenship could not be revived.[7] The initiative was a personal one. Even Mollet's *chef de cabinet*, Emile Noël, had not worked on it, let alone the Quai d'Orsay.[8] Eden, embarrassed but game, set up a committee. On military plans it was agreed that *Musketeer* should be changed; the principles of *Musketeer Revise*, Keightley's new concept, were endorsed. The French Chief of the General Staff, General Paul Ely, records that the French had in any case been none too keen to get involved with a possible urban guerrilla war in the dense streets of Alexandria and welcomed the switch of attention back to the Suez Canal, which would offer improved possibilities of liaison with the Israelis.[9] Admiral Barjot, to General Beaufre's disgust, had been of that mind all along.

When worked out in detail the new plan, which provided the basis of the actual Suez operation, had three phases. Phase One was the neutralisation of the Egyptian air force; Phase Two was the aero-psychological campaign, lasting ten days or more: Phase Three the unopposed landing. The air offensive in Phase Two, accompanied by the most carefully directed psy-war, would be 'a systematic and graded application of pressure ... on certain carefully selected economic and military targets', with the aim of producing 'ever increasing disruption of Egyptian economy, morale, administration and armed forces and *eventually* destroying the will to resist'.

The principal economic target was to be the oil supply to Cairo, its pumping stations, pipelines, and storage tanks. (This was considered to be the one way in which the rather primitive civilian economy could be quickly crippled.) Military installations on the outskirts of Cairo, Alexandria, Port Said and Suez would be destroyed and all communications between them wrecked, thus 'showing the impotence of the Egyptian army, air force, and navy to the civilian population'. Only when this open-ended exercise was complete would come Phase Three: the movement into Port Said of a land force designed to 'restore order in the Canal Zone and to assist in the reopening of the Suez Canal'.[10] The timing for this would depend on when it could be 'assumed our land forces could move in without much organised opposition'. 'D-Day' being now air attack day, 'L [for Landing] Day' was to be a moveable feast.

In an accompanying note, General Keightley insisted that the opening two phases depended for their success on the firmness and ingenuity of the psychological warfare measures. Should the opening phases result in the fall of the Nasser Government, organised resistance was expected to cease, but the allies must be prepared to cope with disorganised resistance during the third phase, which could be sufficient to require landing against opposition at Port Said, 'with possible heavy damage to the city and civilian casualties'.

The dubieties of the scheme stand out from the Chiefs of Staff memorandum that commended it: 'The new plan is based on the assumption that the air offensive will break the Egyptian will to resist and bring about the disintegration of the army. The validity of this assumption is impossible to check.' On this point Keightley's note was none too hopeful. 'The Egyptian army can be attacked most profitably when concentrated in the open near the Israeli frontier or where its lines of communication converge to cross the Canal. Elsewhere it may be difficult to attack effectively.'[11]

The Psy-War

Since the new concept depended so heavily on the success of the 'psychological phase', Cairo Radio was placed among the first targets of the air offensive. Once eliminated, the commercially-run but MI6-owned Near East Broadcasting Station in Cyprus – *Sharq al-Adna* – should occupy the wavelength. A carefully prepared propaganda campaign should then be put into effect, using leaflet drops including thousands of cartoons by Ronald Searle showing Nasser and his cronies in unflattering postures, voice aircraft (such as were being used in Kenya to talk to the Kikuyu in the jungle during the campaign against the Mau Mau) and the best of 'black' radio. It was apparent later that General Keightley had entertained certain illusions about the potentialities of psychological warfare, derived no doubt from the legend that this was one of Britain's special successes in the Second World War. Looking back after the operation, he was to recall that he had 'endeavoured to get a really high grade man to run psychological warfare from among those who had experience in the 1939–45 war' but for various reasons each of these was disallowed in turn. 'In the end, I got the best man I could, a serving Brigadier with imagination, initiative and originality.' This was Brigadier Bernard Fergusson, later Governor-General of New Zealand (as had been his father) and Chairman of the British Council. But for all Fergusson's flair, Sir Charles Keightley concluded sadly, in this field and in the influencing of world opinion the Egyptians had it all their own way.[12]

It was not that the Brigadier did not throw himself into the task with characteristic zest. The softening up process, he noted in a paper circulated among the senior commanders, had begun already by way of broadcasting. Israel, too, had noticed this. Golda Meir was in a continual lather about the Near East Broadcasting Station and the anonymous anti-Nasser station, both of which, the latter much more crudely, attempted to smear Nasser as an agent of Zionism. 'Why does the traitor Nasser not occupy Palestine?' the anonymous radio asked on 3 September. 'And so it goes on day by day, preaching hate and war against the Jew and trying to tar Nasser with the Zionist brush,' complained the *Jewish Observer and Middle East Review*.[13]

In response to Anthony Eden's repeated queries about the publicity campaign in Egypt, the Foreign Office sent him the latest script of 'the SCANT radio station, run by a national freedom group' as an example of 'covert broadcasting'. 'The beacon is flashing for the third time! O Egyptians! O Arab brothers! Listen to the truth about the grave situation into which the regime of semi-literate half-colonels has plunged our nation and region!' SCANT opened up. After a little more of this, its announcers got down to Eden's favoured theme: 'Already Egypt has been losing money fast ... Now with the setting up of an association to protect the interests of Canal Users, fewer and fewer countries are paying dues to Egypt ... It will mean that Egypt's receipts from an international waterway which costs some £2 million a month to maintain will fall to the ridiculous figure of around £120,000 a month ... O Brothers! Nasser's Canal venture costs the people £1.5 million a month. This is the pass to which Nasser's self-conceit and infantile policies have brought us all!' There was a reference to 'our former friend' Nehru having 'sternly criticised Nasser's method of taking over the Canal', a suggestion that Nasser's inept statesmanship would leave no option but to 'benefit the Jews by allowing free passage of Israeli shipping through the Canal', and a conclusion that 'even the old Egyptian statesmen were better patriots than Nasser!'[14]

Great emphasis after D-Day was to be put on undermining the morale of Egyptian forward troops. For this reason Fergusson urged the rapid transmission of local information picked up in the field, so that messages could be transmitted such as: 'Colonel X, your commanding officer, is the man who distinguished himself by the speed with which he ran away from such-and-such a battalion in the Palestine war.' Civilians would be addressed thus: 'To the townspeople of Z. No doubt your Governor, A, is shivering in his shoes. No wonder, after the dirty trick he played in B and C.' Tape-recordings would say 'The British and French are your friends. Nasser is dead.' Or alternatively, 'Nasser has fled. Surrender now.' The ordinary Egyptian would be urged, 'If any Russians or other Communists are with you, disarm them and bring them with you. They are your enemies and mean to swallow your country.'

'At present', Fergusson briskly confessed, 'there is no overt opposition and no indications of any covert opposition of any strength.' But he drew comfort from his supply of general oriental knowledge. 'The Egyptian character will not have altered fundamentally in the past few years and at heart he is a materialist ... [He] is unlikely long to sustain the rigours of wartime economy or the actual experience of battle and remain faithful to the regime. It seems less likely to be a question of *if* there is a collapse of the public morale and support for the regime as of *how* quickly that will take place.' That process would be speeded up, in his opinion, by encouraging, at an early stage of the battle, the emergence of a potential Opposition leader. Having read this paper, the Air Task Force Commander was to comment on 3 October that it 'demonstrates (if indeed any confirmation were necessary) how lukewarm has been the determination at the top to pursue the original stated aim which was to use air/psychological warfare to secure the push-over.'[15]

Keightley's Critics

The new concept *Musketeer Revise* was not popular with the Task Force Commanders, as General Sir Hugh Stockwell made abundantly clear in the report which he wrote after the operation. Phase Two, he says, produced considerable apprehension in the minds of the commanders. 'Our sources of intelligence in Egypt were slender. Short of a fall of the Nasser Government or an Egyptian request to treat for terms, it would be almost impossible to judge exactly when the country's will to resist had in fact been broken or was showing signs of collapse.' Not only that, the Task Force Commanders 'considered that it would be difficult to justify their position in the eyes of the world if they persisted in a long, continuous and remorseless bombing of Egypt, even if every safeguard against causing civilian casualties were taken and fully advertised.' They also did not think that the Egyptian Army, the National Guard and armed civilians could be destroyed or subdued solely by air attack. A properly mounted, balanced force would be needed to assault and occupy the Canal Zone.[16]

The New Zealander in charge of the Air Task Force was even more blunt in his report. 'The plan for *Musketeer Revise* was dictated to the Force Commanders as the result of political limitations,' declared Air Marshal Barnett, 'and was never considered by them to be a sound military operation.'[17] This was an extraordinary degree of no-confidence in an operational concept by the men most concerned with putting it into effect. With complete uncertainty about when the Egyptian will to resist would collapse, it was impossible to say in advance when the assault convoys of over a hundred vessels were to leave Malta and Algiers. The voyage from Malta would take six days and for logistic reasons the convoy could not be kept at sea for longer than seven or at most eight days. If collapse were clear on D + 4, it would be D + 10 before the Malta force arrived. If, on the other hand, it had set out prematurely, the armada, at a cost of considerable chaos, would have to take refuge in the inadequate shelter of Cyprus.[18]

As the days passed, Air Chief Marshal Sir Dermot Boyle, the Chief of Air Staff, and his staff advisers became increasingly conscious of the dangers of a scheme which one of them described, in a brief for Boyle on 24 September, as 'essentially a compromise between an all-out air plan and an assault landing leading to occupation'. The danger was of 'being neither the one nor the other and having within it the seeds of failure in both Phase II and Phase III'. What really worried the airmen was that, at the very moment when a major defence review was in progress that everyone knew was going to effect the shape of the British Services for years and decades to come, the concept of air power might be discredited by a half-hearted display of what it could do. They had in mind the widespread criticism that had already been generated by the failure to achieve decisive results from the air in Korea. Requirements of logic, flexibility and economy of effort, according to Boyle's staff, all argued for an air plan in the current case, but the great weakness was the danger of having Ministers lose their nerve under pressure of public opinion while the bombing was actually on. 'To put the matter in its bluntest form, would they authorise bombing targets in the centre of Cairo and Alexandria if all other air action had failed?' Now that so much of the air plan had been adopted, the air staff urged in vain that, while it was clearly too late to change the Commander-in-Chief, he should be surrounded by air force officers.[19]

At a meeting of the Chiefs of Staff Committee on 19 September, at which General Keightley gave a long description of the revised plan, Air Chief Marshal Boyle went so far as to say that it would be unnecessary to land at all provided that the bombing went on long enough – a period which on examination turned out to be 'up to a month', to which for political reasons his colleagues strongly demurred.

Meanwhile *Musketeer Revise* having, with whatever reserves, been adopted as the plan, the Task Force Commanders sought ways of making sense of it. The French Land Commander, General Beaufre, knowing that it was essential to preserve the possibility of acting more quickly than the plan provided, extracted authority to keep the nucleus of a quick-reaction force, its amphibious shipping loaded with vehicles and equipment, off Cyprus. Called 'Plan A' this allowed for the floating *matériel* to be joined from Algeria with great rapidity by French assault troops aboard the brand-new battleship *Jean Bart*. It was supposed to be operated only if Egyptian resistance were certified as 'negligible'. But, being in effect under French command, this plan gave Beaufre the sense of having another option. Not a man to let politicians do all the political thinking for him, he found it reassuring that, if world pressure built up fast, he would be capable of moving into Port Said without delay.[20]

Plan 'B', however, was the one which the British expected to use. It moved to the slow rhythms of the aero-psychological phase; air- and seaborne forces from Cyprus, Malta and Algeria were to land simultaneously. The new scheme, misleadingly labelled a 'revise' of the old one, required a new deployment of forces over a wide area, still without unloading or reloading the ships – some of them packed for the original Chiefs of Staff plan before *Musketeer* – for fear that, in conditions of peacetime news reporting, the wrong political signals should be given. In the case of those ships in home ports there was also anxiety, now that the unions were showing hostility to the whole venture, that there would be trouble with the labour force. It was not forgotten that in August the small change of cargoes that had followed from the decision not, after all, to send units to Libya had 'created a very marked impression amongst the dockers'.[21]

One further contribution to strategy was on offer in mid-September from two men who had been used to making strategy a dozen years before: Winston Churchill and Field Marshal Montgomery. Churchill was coming to see Eden after talking to the Field Marshal; and Brigadier Head, the Secretary of State for War, took care to rubbish his views ahead of the visit. For one thing 'Monty' had a poor view of Keightley, in whom the Chiefs of Staff, according to Head, had complete confidence. Then, the Montgomery plan of campaign was completely impractical. It proposed a landing on the open beaches towards Mersa Matruh which would require large numbers of landing craft which Britain and France did not possess. It also provided for the capture of Cairo. 'We have always thought, rightly in my opinion,' Head wrote, 'that we should avoid entangling ourselves by fighting in, and the subsequent occupation of, Cairo.'[22]

SCUA: Instrument of War or Peace?

After Mollet and Pineau had gone home on 11 September the full British Cabinet met to decide what to do next. It was told that the Menzies mission had failed, that the US was strongly opposed to both the military action and to reference to the United Nations. Instead Dulles was offering the users' club, CASU, which would both get the United States involved in action to enforce users' rights and deprive the Egyptians of more than eighty per cent of their remaining revenue from the Canal. The Egypt Committee had, therefore, decided to go forward with the scheme but strictly on the condition that United States full participation should be announced in the Commons the next day.

Some members of the Cabinet did not neglect to point out that a traffic control organisation working from warships at either end of the Canal would have no control over bridges and the signalling system. The confusion that was likely to follow was, however, considered to be worthwhile as the price to be paid for America's public involvement. The President of the United Nations Security Council was to be notified, putting Britain on record as not overlooking the United Nations while avoiding the inconveniences of a debate.

At this point, Macmillan powerfully intervened. He said that it was unlikely that effective international control over the Canal could be secured without the use of force. CASU, therefore, was to be welcomed not as, in itself, a solution but as a step towards the ultimate use of force. It would not work. But it would serve to bring the issue to a head. This was highly desirable from the viewpoint of the national economy. A quick decisive solution would restore confidence in sterling. But, if a settlement were long delayed, the cost and uncertainty would undermine Britain's financial position.

He was directly answered by Monckton. The Minister of Defence said he hoped the plan would not be regarded solely as a step towards the use of force. 'Any premature recourse to force, especially without the support and approval of the United States, is likely to precipitate disorder throughout the Middle East and to alienate a substantial body of public opinion in this country and elsewhere.' (When William Clark read the minutes two days later, he remarked, 'There really is a severe split in the Cabinet.') Butler reported that the Conservative Party in the House of Commons would support the use of force but only if they were satisfied that all practicable steps had first been taken to secure a peaceful settlement. Eden summed up by saying it was clear that they were agreed that Egypt's disregard of her international obligations could not be tolerated, that every reasonable effort must be made 'to re-establish' international control by peaceful means, but, if these should all fail, they would be justified in using force to restore the situation'.[23]

On the morning of 12 September, the date intended to be that on which Parliament's return would dovetail with an appeal to the Security Council, agreement with the Americans at last took place on the wording of the CASU announcement. But confidence in London in American solidarity was immediately shaken by news of two answers that Eisenhower had given at his press conference the preceding day. Asked by one correspondent whether, if Britain and France eventually resorted to force, America would back them, the President replied:

> I don't know exactly what you mean by 'backing them'. As you know this country will not go to war ever while I am occupying my present post, unless the Congress is called into session and Congress declares such a war. Now, if, after all peaceful means are exhausted, there is some kind of aggression on the part of Egypt against a peaceful use of the Canal, you might say that we would recognise that Britain and France had no other recourse than to continue to use it even if they had to be more forceful than merely sailing through it.

In answer to another reporter who asked whether Britain and France would be justified in using force to restore a management acceptable to the non-Egyptian employees, he said that the 1888 Treaty gave them rights but that did not entitle them to use force. 'I think this. We established the UN to abolish aggression and I am not going to be a party to aggression if it is humanly possible.'[24]

Having read the text of this and after a sleepless night wrestling with Dulles's plan, Selwyn Lloyd went round to Number Ten where the Prime Minister was working on his speech to tell Eden that he had changed his mind, that CASU would not work and that Britain should go straight to the Security Council, which was both the course which the Opposition and many Conservatives wanted and expected and the one which the Egypt Committee had accepted as a necessary preliminary to the use of force.[25] Eden said later that he was a great deal shaken at hearing this. The speech notes were laid aside. There was an earnest exchange, after which he decided to leave the speech unaltered: Eden would gamble on the Americans.

SCUA Launch and Mis-Launch

As the Prime Minister slipped into his seat on the Treasury bench his Chief Whip, Ted Heath, whispered: 'There will be no division if you announce that you are going immediately to the UN.'[26] Knowing that this was just what he could not do, Eden plunged into his account of what had happened since the beginning of the recess. For this first part of the speech, he got a good hearing. He dwelt on the degree of consensus in the earlier debate, the impressive amount of international support received at the London Conference, and the unanimity that had prevailed among Menzies' Committee of Five at Cairo, including, as it did, the Foreign Minister of Sweden whom, the speaker said, his opponents would not count as bellicose in comparison with the present Prime Minister of this country. Colonel Nasser had rejected these proposals without weighing their merits or listening to reason.

This was the point at which everyone expected the announcement about the UN. Instead came the surprise news about a Users' Association. Intended to lay particular stress on American involvement with Britain and France, it came across as a proposal both implausible in itself and belligerent in intent. Many doubted whether it would fly. Ironically, Eden was in most trouble when he read out the agreed wording that was released simultaneously in Washington and Paris. Shouts of 'Deliberate provocation!', 'Resign!', 'What a peacemaker!' and 'You are talking about war!' built up as he uttered the carefully rehearsed sentences: 'I must make it clear that, if the Egyptian Government should seek to interfere with the operations of the Association or refuse to extend it the essential minimum of co-operation, then that Government will once more be in breach of the Convention of 1888. In that event HMG and others concerned will be free to take such further steps as seem to be required, either through the UN or by other means, for the assertion of their rights.'

Eden finished on a personal note which enabled his speech to end with a genuine display of enthusiasm from his own side of the House. 'In the last few weeks', he said, 'I have had constantly in mind the closeness of the parallel of these events with those of the years before the war. Once again we are faced with what is in fact an act of force which, if it is not resisted, if it is not checked, will lead to others.' However the impression of the speech which crossed the Atlantic was that, as Dulles put it over the telephone, 'Eden kind of knocked the whole plan down.' He might, he said, have to 'put some qualifications in'.[27]

In the House Eden was followed by the Leader of the Opposition, who found it necessary to insist that he had not changed his views since 2 August. But nothing Eden had said to the House in August had given the impression that the Government had determined on the use of force. Only the lobby briefings for several days after had created a climate of war preparation. 'If those statements were authorised, as I think they must have been, they should have been made publicly by Ministers; and, if they were unauthorised, I think it is a major scandal that civil servants should be given such dangerous powers.'

As Gaitskell staked out the grounds of his departure from bipartisanship, he sharpened them. 'I dare say that the Government may believe ... that it is a matter of landing a few parachute brigades, seizing the Canal, overthrowing Nasser in Egypt and then they will have got control. Control over what? Exactly how is one then to proceed? ... Are we to leave there the troops which the Government themselves withdrew only very recently or are we to withdraw again?'

As for the Users' Association, it depended what it was for. If it were a bit of machinery for negotiating with Egypt, Gaitskell would not object. But many of the purposes attributed to it sounded dangerously like provocation. What did the Government mean by reserving the right to take further steps through the UN or *by other means*? What other means? 'Force is not justified as a solution of this problem. Force is justified in self-defence and that is a totally different matter.'

The following day the speech which gripped the House and was the talk of the lobbies was made by the former Conservative Attorney-General Sir Lionel Heald. At the time it was treated as a major and courageous challenge to the Government's policy by one of its leading supporters. In fact Sir Lionel's was not an anti-Government speech so much as an attempt to build a new basis for consensus around British respect for her international obligations. He reckoned that she had acted correctly so far under Article 33 of the Charter (prior obligation to settle a dispute by negotiation). The Users' Association fell under the same heading. Only if that failed was she under any obligation under Article 37 to go to the Security Council. Sir

Lionel said that 'if a reasonable and proper plan is put forward to the UN *and approved there*, then I personally will be perfectly willing to support the Government in any measure they then think it necessary to carry out'.

This was wrongly treated by the House as being in conflict with the Government, since Ministers, wishing to conceal their policy split with the United States, did not disclose that their own desire to go to the Security Council had been frustrated by Dulles. Heald never said what he thought should happen if 'a reasonable and proper plan' was not approved by virtue of a Soviet veto.[28]

As the debate moved towards an acrimonious conclusion, the news agency tapes brought in news of yet another 'terrible' Dulles press conference. The Secretary of State had walked into the conference late, having responded to a 'most urgent' request from the Egyptian Ambassador, Ahmed Hussein, to see him before it should begin. The message from Cairo which Hussein conveyed was plain spoken. 'The scheme which Prime Minister Eden wants to impose is an open and flagrant aggression on Egypt's sovereignty and its implementation means war. If the United States desires war it may support the scheme, but if its desire is to work for a peaceful solution the scheme has to be abandoned.' As he came out, Hussein told members of the press that 'User's Association means war'.[29] It was with this message ringing in his head that Dulles offered himself to the media.

First he made the agreed announcement about the Users' Association. What, he was asked, would he do if Egypt resisted this plan? 'If physical force should be used to prevent passage,' said Dulles, 'then obviously, as far as the United States is concerned, the alternative for us, at least, would be to send our vessels around the Cape ... But it is not our purpose to try to bring about a concerted boycotting of the Canal. I think under those conditions each country would have to decide for itself what it wanted its vessels to do.' Later he said: 'We do not intend to shoot our way through. It may be we have the right to do it, but we don't intend to do it as far as the US is concerned.'[30]

Eden says in his book *Full Circle* that 'it would be hard to imagine a statement more likely to cause the maximum allied disunity and disarray'.[31] There is no doubt that it struck him very hard. He had taken the parliamentary risk, which he admitted he had underestimated, of accepting Dulles's judgment against going to the Security Council; his reward, while the debate in which he was so frequently reproached for failure to go to the UN was still on, was this wanton display of weakness and lack of alliance solidarity. The Dulles text came through just before the eloquent young Labour backbencher Tony Benn rose to speak, and he cited it briefly, declaring: 'This debate changes its course as it proceeds.' But it was Gaitskell who was able to make the most use of Eden's discomfiture during his summing up by quoting Dulles's words and demanding a pledge that Britain also would not shoot her way through the Canal. The right way to see that Nasser did not 'get away with it' was to do what the Opposition had again and again pressed the Government to do: allow Israel to purchase arms.

Did Gaitskell really think, came back Eden in his reply, that if Nasser got away with it, Britain's position would still be such that she could do as much to help Israel if she were attacked as she could today? 'My own forecast is that ... then there will be such a rush of power, such a haste and hurry to get on the bandwaggon of the Egyptian dictator as has not been seen in our generation in respect of any country at all.' Eden insisted that he was in complete agreement with the United States on what to do if the Egyptians obstructed the Users' Association, though what exactly that was was not a little obscured by the turbulence in the House. However, the impression was left that Eden had bound himself to go to the UN before using force apart from a sudden emergency calling for immediate reaction. At this point Macmillan noted he 'thought that all was lost'. But the Prime Minister, not unduly fazed by the roar of applause that this 'concession' had evoked from the Opposition benches, ploughed on through the tougher concluding passage that the Chancellor had drafted for him.[32]

The Opposition divided and the word went out to the world that the Government was backed only by 319 votes to 248, though to be sure the Liberals under their new young leader, Jo Grimond, voted on the Government side; this afforded Eden some consolation. But he was 'quite exhausted' at the end of 'two difficult days'.[33] 'I was saddened', Eden wrote in a note to a backbencher, 'by the depth of party division which seemed to me inexcusable at such a time.' Worse, Heath as Chief Whip was reporting 'a good deal of trouble in the Party'. Specifically, the Tory group opposed to the use of force might be large enough, if the matter came to a head, to put the Government into a minority in a division. Eden told Macmillan that it was 1938 and Munich all over again and he could not be a party to it.[34]

This was a view which had some resonance in the country at large. It was, after all, only eighteen years after Munich. David Owen, who was born three months before Munich, was spending the summer of 1956 digging in the waterlogged trenches of a new sewage plant to finance himself at university and, incidentally, to make the acquaintance of the working class. 'The *Daily Mirror* backed Gaitskell but these men were tearing up their *Daily Mirrors* every day in the little hut where we had our tea and sandwiches during our break,' Owen found. For the future Foreign Secretary this was a seminal experience. He later told Kenneth Harris: 'My mates were solidly in favour of Eden. It was not only that they taught me how people like them think; they also opened my eyes as to how I should think myself.'[35] Consequences in British political history were to flow from this three decades later.

Eden was buoyed up by his confidence that his instincts were in tune with the masses. In a message to his pre-Suez biographer, William Rees-Mogg, who was standing as a Conservative at a by-election at Chester-le-Street in the Prime Minister's native county of Durham, he declared that the uninterrupted passage of ships through the Canal 'is a matter of daily bread for all of us in this island'. If it were to be interrupted, 'there would quickly be unemployment and higher prices in Britain'.

At the same time as the Commons debate there was a parallel debate in the Lords, which served to highlight the legal issues. Lord McNair, with all the authority of a recent President of the International Court of Justice at The Hague, declared flatly that during the last fifty years there had been a complete transformation in the attitude of the law towards resort to armed force, starting with the Kellogg-Briand Pact of 1928 renouncing war as an instrument of national policy (which was judicially enforced at Nuremberg) and coming on to the Charter of the United Nations. By Article 51 the member states must 'refrain in their international relations from the threat or use of force'; only the 'inherent right of individual or collective self-defence' in the case of an armed attack was allowed and then only until the Security Council had taken the appropriate measures. 'The combined effect of these Treaty provisions', concluded Lord McNair, an authority whom the Government were very pleased to cite when he had been one of the few lawyers who supported their case on the illegality of the seizure of the Canal Company, 'has completely transformed the legal position of armed force. It is no longer a discretionary instrument of policy but its use is regulated by law'.

The Lord Chancellor replied to what he at once recognised as a dangerous attack on the position which he was upholding. According to him, two ends were served by the UN Charter – not only to save succeeding generations from the scourge of war, but also to establish conditions under which justice and respect for international obligations were maintained. These two were interdependent. International entities like canals or land corridors were the landmarks of international achievement. If another part of the world machinery (i.e. the Security Council) failed to work, the duty remained of preserving their international character. For some obscure reason, the analogy of John Hampden refusing to pay Ship Money to Charles I came into the Lord Chancellor's mind. Like him, Britain would not be found wanting in responding to the call of moral duty. The *fait accompli* must not be allowed by the most glaring use of force to acquire 'prescriptive right over ... the slothful hearts of men'. The argument was delivered with such great force that it moved the Marquess of Aberdeen and Temair to leap to his feet with the cry: 'My Lords, in these last few moments may I propose a hearty vote of thanks to the Lord Chancellor.'[36]

The Ships Pass – Egypt's Silent Victory

The most dramatic moment of the whole crisis was approaching. All attention was switched back from world capitals to the stretch of water in question, the Suez Canal. The deadline of 15 September had been fixed by the rue d'Astorg for those British, French and other non-Egyptian staff of the Canal Company who wished to quit. In the event two hundred and twelve foreigners, including ninety pilots, were issued with exit visas without any of the anticipated difficulty.[37] The Greek consul announced that the handful of Greek pilots would stay. *Al Ahram* reported that twenty-two fresh foreign pilots – including fifteen Russians, four Jugoslavs, three West Germans and a Norwegian, had arrived to take up employment. More Greeks and Jugoslavs were on their way. Thirty-six new Egyptian pilots had been recruited since 26 July. The world held its breath: everyone waited and watched to see what would happen.

'The Suez Canal started yesterday functioning without any help from foreign pilots,' declared President Nasser at a passing-out ceremony of air force cadets at Bilbeis on 16 September. 'Do you know to what level the West have sunk? Yesterday, for the first time in living memory, fifty ships arrived at Port Said and Suez wishing to transit. But we managed to direct them safely through with the help of the seventy Egyptian pilots and the Greek pilots who refuse to be bribed.'[38]

It was, indeed, the case that by Operation *Pile-Up* the British had arranged to bundle together the maximum number of ships at the moment when the system might be most expected to break down. The Minister of Transport, Harold Watkinson, told the Egypt Committee that it was his object to 'establish a sufficient pile-up of shipping at each end of the Suez Canal to show that Egypt could not operate it successfully under present conditions'.[39] His Ministry had drawn up detailed instructions. All offers of compromise methods of transit – such as experienced captains being authorised to take their own ships through or ships following a 'lead ship' with an experienced pilot on board – must be refused as unsafe. A barrage of complaints to Nasser and to the world about the unavailability of transit and unsafe conditions must be organised. As soon as Operation *Pile-Up* had brought about chaos, Operation *Convoy* could clear it up. Britain and France, acting in the name of the yet-to-be formed Users' Association would put Suez Canal pilots on every ship that had been held up. As soon as the convoy was organised, demand should be made to Nasser for its free and unobstructed passage. If this were not granted, warships might lead the convoy.[40] A cruiser and a destroyer would be positioned at each end of the Canal 'to give assistance to our shipping if this should be thought necessary'. No such necessity arose.

Since the end of July the Egyptian staff had been studying with the utmost care what was done by the high-priced foreign experts. They found it was not so difficult. 'We have emerged from this experience triumphant,' rejoiced Nasser, 'I bestow the Order of Merit on every pilot who took part in this operation.' On 17 September Watkinson was forced to admit that the Egyptians had managed all right so far by working long shifts and taking ships in single convoy without the usual change of pilot at Ismailia. He still thought that, provided the number of ships requiring transit could be kept as high as possible, efficiency would then deteriorate because of the long hours; then delays would result.[41] The Egyptians kept up the pace.

Nasser, happy enough that for the first time in its existence the Canal was running smoothly without the least trace of the 'ex-Company', was not proposing to allow the Users' Association to force his hand. Slade-Baker of the *Sunday Times* asked him on 15 September whether he would stop a British ship trying to get through the Canal with an ex-Suez Canal Company pilot under the auspices of CASU. Nasser replied that he would let all CASU ships through as they came. Sooner or later there would be an accident, the Canal would be blocked, and CASU could take the responsibility for the breach of free navigation. He then spoke of his plans for guerrilla war in case of a British attack on Egypt. If people in England thought that the war would be over in forty-eight hours, he said, they were very mistaken. The subsequent guerrilla campaign was already organised throughout the Delta. Each group had a secret headquarters and no one knew who the others were. If he were killed his successor was already nominated. If the British put in a new Egyptian President or Prime Minister he would be murdered within twenty-four hours.[42]

At this moment the Soviet Union, after a considerable period of silence, gave forth on the subject of Suez. In notes to Eden and Mollet and in a published statement dated 15 September, the Russian authorities described the Users' Association accurately enough with respect to two of its three sponsors, as designed for 'the artificial creation of incidents which could be used as a pretext for the use of force against Egypt'. The Soviet statement then went on to interpret the UN Charter in a way that was generally in line with Lord McNair.

'There can hardly be any doubt', it added ominously, 'that a military attack on Egypt and military actions in that region would lead to immense destruction on the Suez Canal and also in the oilfields ... and to the oil pipelines.' Russia announced her acceptance of the Egyptian invitation to a conference and proclaimed, 'The USSR, as a Great Power, cannot stand aloof from the Suez question ... because any violation of peace in the region of the Near and Middle East cannot but affect the interests and the security of the Soviet State.'[43]

Egypt, in a letter to the President of the Security Council, announced on 17 September that her own invitation to a conference on the Suez Canal had been accepted by twenty-one countries. This conciliatory procedure was contrasted with the Users' Association, which 'will lead to a complicated and contradictory situation as a result of the creation of two opposing authorities, one legal and the other illegal, one a rightful authority and the other a usurper'.[44] The puzzle for Nasser was the United States. British and French enmity he understood and he looked for nothing else. But, 'I really do not know what the Americans are after!' Nasser told the air force cadets at Bilbeis. 'We have reminded [Dulles] that the American President professed peace and we have asked him why on earth America supported the formation of an Association which was in effect an Association for waging war.'[45]

Precisely that impression had been left in the Scandinavian capitals. Importance was attached to their views in London, Sweden's because of the support given to Menzies in Cairo and Norway's as a major Suez Canal user. Sir Ivone Kirkpatrick saw Östen Undén, the Swedish Foreign Minister, in London on the morning of 12 September as he was about to leave for Stockholm. 'I am sorry to say', he said, 'that I found him in a rather flabby mood. He seems to feel that, having failed to put across the views of the Eighteen, he should now try to cast about for some compromise between this standpoint and that of the Egyptian dictator.' Sir Ivone had no time whatsoever for such an attitude. 'But the fact is', he went on, 'that there is no room for compromise. We have had one experience of entrusting a vital highway to the caprice of a single Power: the administrative delays devised by the Russians brought about the blockade of Berlin. We should be foolish to repeat that experience.'[46]

By the time he had got back to Stockholm, Undén was in no mood to endorse publicly what Eden had just said in the Commons about CASU. He told the British Ambassador sharply and firmly that this was a plan to create incidents and to justify the taking of the forceful measures that Britain and France had in preparation.[47] In Oslo, at the same time, the British Ambassador was informed that the Norwegian Government's views were more likely to be in line with those of the British Opposition than with those of the British Government.[48]

The delegates of the eighteen states – thirteen of them Foreign Ministers – were now gathering in London for the opening on 19 September of the conference summoned to decide what to do now that their scheme for international control had been flatly rejected. There were already signs that, as R. G. Casey – the Australian Foreign Minister – had supposed, 'if and when the first round is fired ... the eighteen powers would dwindle to a very few'. It was the general impression of the American Secretary of State 'that the British and French have quite isolated themselves even from what are naturally their closest friends'. Gaetano Martino of Italy had written to Selwyn Lloyd that the superiority of the western world was due to its respect for the principle of peaceful regulation of controversies even when that principle went to the West's disadvantage. In Whitehall this piety came over like a lead balloon. The Foreign Office, whose officials were in an increasingly truculent mood, reacted (in a minute by Archibald Ross): 'This is a sorry performance, due to endemic suspicion and jealousy of Great Britain, desire to cut a figure with the Arabs and tendency to side with the Americans rather than with ourselves.'[49]

Meeting first at Stockholm, the three Scandinavian Foreign Ministers jointly declared that the dispute must go to the United Nations: in the meantime they would turn up in London but preserve an agnostic approach to CASU. From the 'white' Commonwealth, Lord Home obtained the same message. The four High Commissioners were unanimous in thinking that the matter must be brought to the UN. The Canadian, Norman Robertson, was as usual the most outspoken: he said emphatically that the UN Charter prevailed over obligations in conflict with it. They could, therefore, not rely on the 1888 Convention to support the use of force.[50]

The whole world seemed to want Britain and France to go to the UN – except its Secretary-General. Dag Hammarskjöld told Pierson Dixon that at the beginning of the month he had really thought that it might be Britain's intention to use force. But he was now reassured and so felt that the moment was not ripe for Security Council action. All that could happen now would be an attempt by one side or the other to use the Council to mobilise support for its point of view and put the other side in the wrong. This would be unfortunate. The time for Council action was when the two sides were ready to talk and the Council could provide cover for negotiation.[51]

The Second London Conference

The first item on the conference agenda was the reporting back of the Committee of Five. The Iranian made it plain that, in his opinion, the main reason the Five had failed had been their restricted terms of reference, preventing them from entering into any form of negotiation. The Swede and the Ethiopian were more concerned to blame Nasser for not formulating any counter-proposals while they were in Cairo. Even so, Ato Aklilou Habtewold of Ethiopia added that, badly as Nasser had behaved, other countries had behaved worse on account of their ostentatious military preparations.

John Foster Dulles then again took the lead in relaunching the new western plan and in securing for it a much more favourable reception than had at first seemed likely. 'If the Government of Egypt', he argued, 'insists that ships' masters be in the position of suppliants who can never pass through the Canal except under such conditions as the Government of Egypt may from time to time impose, then there is no guarantee of free and secure passage such as the Convention of 1888 prescribed.' Basing himself, therefore, on the concepts of the existing treaty rather than seeking to impose a new order of ideas, he proposed practical machinery designed to avert the danger of discrimination. He wanted to set up a small operating staff under an Administrative Agent knowledgeable in shipping matters who would handle the traffic and try to work out an *ad hoc* basis of co-operation with the Egyptian authorities.

For many of the delegates the effect of Dulles's handling of the proposal, combined with various amendments to the text, removed from it its patina of menace. The Pakistani and the Ethiopian declared that the final declaration that emerged on 21 September was quite a different proposition from the original draft. 'As it has emerged,' said Malik Firoz Khan Noon, the Foreign Minister of Pakistan, 'it emphasises co-operation with the Egyptian Government.' 'There is no thought on the part of the US', said Dulles in reply to a series of very pointed questions asked by Haruhiko Nishi of Japan, 'of trying to impose any of the facilities of the Association upon Egypt by force.' The British and French became increasingly uneasy at the tone of accommodation that seemed to prevail. 'One thought running through some speeches has disturbed me,' said Lloyd. 'It seems to me that we should not abandon what we consider fair and reasonable because at the first time of asking the Egyptian Government does not accept it. Otherwise, he will go on saying "No" until he has got unconditional surrender.'

Christian Pineau was becoming more and more unhappy about the whole idea, calling particular attention to the fact that payment of dues to the Association was to be voluntary. 'If thirteen or fourteen of us have already decided not to pay dues to it, this will make our Association quite useless,' he broke out at one point and called for pledges from his colleagues to do everything possible to see that their countrymen paid up to CASU and not to Egypt. At this, the Italian Foreign Minister explained that his country had a clearing arrangement with Egypt which obliged Italian shipowners to pay the Egyptians direct. Change would require parliamentary action and Gaetano Martino did not think a discussion in the Italian parliament on this matter would be in the best interests of the Association. This episode left the French in particular with a very sour taste in the mouth indeed.

Two matters remained. The Conference discovered only on the last afternoon, when in the process of preparing the final communiqué, that Item (2) on the agenda – the Egyptian proposal of 10 September for a method of settlement – had not been discussed at all. Dr Paulo Cunha of Portugal, who discovered this omission, said the problem of how the Association should establish contact with Egypt could not be ignored. Pineau replied, roughly, that he could not accept that CASU, with its limited powers, could become a negotiating body. Cunha said: 'Perhaps I do not understand, perhaps it is my fault but if, for example, I am asked: what did we decide on [the Egyptian proposal]? I have to say – "Nothing!"' Alberto Martin Artajo, the Spanish Foreign Minister, was blunt: Spain had already accepted the Egyptian invitation. Dulles was dismissive. The

Egyptian proposal was so vague that he did not know what it meant. It might be useful for the conference to discuss it another day but, in that case, he would ask to be represented by a deputy because he had to leave in half an hour.

There remained only a matter of the acronymn of CASU itself. 'This may be a silly remark but I do not like very much the word CASU,' interposed Joseph Luns, the Dutch Foreign Minister. 'It suggests an easy and not very funny joke – *in casu belli*. What about CASCU?' Cunha rejoined: 'In Portuguese CASCU is something which really is not mentioned.' 'For those of our colleagues who do not know French', said Pineau, 'the term CASCU in French is extremely derogatory and I would ask you not to compel us to use it.' The Chairman, Selwyn Lloyd, contributed ASCU. 'Mr Chairman', it was Cunha again, 'I regret that in Portuguese and in Spanish the implications of ASCU are equally regrettable.' Martino finally came through with SCUA, which was thereupon adopted, suggesting associations that were unflattering but not obscene.[52]

There was on the last day of the conference, Friday, 21 September, a mood of depression in Number Ten and of disillusionment with the United States. As William Clark saw it, 'Dulles pulled rug after rug from under us and watered down the Canal Users' Association till it was meaningless. Tony Moore (of the Foreign Office) came in halfway through the afternoon almost in tears about the whole thing – how could we prevent it all seeming a total disaster? Then Pineau came in and seemed almost on the edge of dissolving the alliance.'[53] The plain fact was that Britain and France needed a fresh *casus belli* before they could act and Nasser was far too clever (and Major Younes's team too skilled) to give them one. The word was put out through the lobby and through ministerial speeches that Suez was to be 'a long haul'.

Selwyn Lloyd had a long talk with Dulles after the conference was over. As was his habit when dealing with allies, Dulles laid initial and sometimes misleading emphasis on common ground. It was imperative, he said, that, as a result of Suez, Nasser should be made to lose. The only question was, how? War would only make him a hero. He must be made to wither away. He suggested that the two Governments should set up a political warfare group which could subject Egypt to an economic squeeze, undermine her political relationships and destabilise the Nasser regime. The directive to the new group should be to get rid of Nasser in six months. Lloyd pressed for an immediate session of the Security Council, citing a luncheon party of Eden's at which representatives of Iran, New Zealand, Norway and Portugal had all argued vehemently in its favour. Not only did British public opinion demand it but the Scandinavian countries and perhaps some others would be unlikely to join SCUA if the UN were further neglected. Dulles, worried that the British would use the UN debate (ending probably with a

Soviet veto) only as a means of pleading 'UN impotence' before resorting to force, still argued against undue haste.[54]

But Dulles no longer carried conviction. At the weekend, operating from his official flat and with the assistance only of a private secretary, Lloyd hurriedly launched the much sought-after and much-agonised-over move to the United Nations. By telephone he mobilised France's association with his bid for one meeting in New York on 26 September to inscribe on the agenda an item labelled 'Situation created by the unilateral action of the Egyptian Government' and for a further meeting on 2 October (thus allowing time to concert tactics) at which the Egyptians would be invited to attend. It was not certain whether the French Ambassador in London, who had been by-passed, was more put out by the abruptness of this procedure or the (to him) alarming imprecision with which the Foreign Secretary referred to matters of substance. There had been no time to draft fresh language to justify the application, so that the dead words of several weeks ago were made to serve as if, Jean Chauvel remarked, it was the day after the nationalisation. Nor was there any sign, he noted severely, of Lloyd having given fresh thought to the next stage, the resolution that they might want the Council to adopt.

Acting on previous instructions Chauvel spoke, when he was brought in, of the necessity for 'international *management* of the Canal', only to find the Foreign Secretary disturbingly elusive on that very point. He kept using the word 'control' which, in English usage, the French find ambiguous, and even tried a Selwyn Lloyd joke – that he preferred 'international control over an Egyptian management' to 'international management under Egyptian control' – which Chauvel correctly took to be a worrying sign.[55]

Nevertheless Pineau had decided to make the best of a bad job and had committed France to join in with the British application. While Dulles was on the flight back to Washington and unknown to him the request for the Security Council meeting was on its way to New York.

14

The Israeli Factor

I made three negative assumptions: (1) We shall not be the ones to open. (2) We shall not participate unless there is British agreement . . . (3) That no action will be taken contrary to US opinion and without it being informed.
David Ben-Gurion, Diary, 27 September 1956.

I know Ike. Ike will lie doggo.
Harold Macmillan, on returning from seeing Eisenhower, September 1956.

John Foster Dulles felt distinctly ill-used when, on landing in Washington, he was told for the first time of the sudden rush of Britain and France to the Security Council. He did not conceal his feelings when he saw Harold Macmillan, who was in Washington on Treasury business, and Sir Roger Makins on 25 September. The British Note had given three reasons for the decision: intelligence sources had said that the Russians were planning to get in first and 'we cannot accept the diplomatic defeat which would be involved if we were taken to the Council as defendants'; the precarious position of the French Government with their public opinion being very upset at the results of the SCUA conference, and, 'finally, we must dispel the appearance of indecisiveness'.[1] To these, Macmillan added the further argument that there had been plenty of evidence in London that recourse to the UN would make a great many states happier about signing up for SCUA.[2] Dulles broke out into a stream of complaints, partly in refutation (American Intelligence had been able to find nothing to confirm the idea that the Russians intended to forestall), but mainly on the lines that he did not know what kind of UN action the British had in mind, under what chapter or article of the Charter they were taking it or what type of resolution they were contemplating. As often happened, Dulles did not think that others took these questions of UN procedure sufficiently seriously.

He was, however, prepared to make an offer on a matter of importance to London. The American Government would, as Britain had been pressing since the end of July, make it unlawful for American registered vessels to go on paying their Canal dues to Egypt. That would mean that they would have to pay into SCUA. But, before acting, he wanted it clearly understood that the economic impact on Egypt would not be great since American flag vessels were only 2.7 per cent of the total tonnage, two-thirds of American owned ships using the Canal being registered as Liberian or Panamanian and being therefore unreachable by American regulation. He also wanted to be sure that the likely economic consequences for Britain and France were fully grasped. Nasser was at present conniving at those two countries not paying dues to him because they were going into the blocked accounts of the old company, which he had undertaken to compensate. These moneys, Nasser assumed (correctly as it eventually turned out), would be reckoned in the final accounting. Dulles wanted the British and French now also to pay into SCUA, so that, if one western power was hit by retaliation, they all three would suffer. Before starting down this path, he wondered whether Britain and France felt able to face the consequences in foreign currency loss of having to divert oil from the Canal, which had been reckoned for Britain alone as $500–600m on the balance of payments. He quite clearly did not want to be faced with a choice of having either to reduce Britain's extra exchange needs or to endorse her military.

Macmillan told Dulles that, while Britain would pay dues to SCUA, the detour around the Cape was not for her a practicable possibility for any length of time. She could not afford to borrow more money. She was already suffering strong pressure on her reserves as a result of lack of confidence due to Suez.[3] But, as he told Eden, he did not pursue the argument as 'I did not wish to be drawn into a discussion of what our British reaction would be if Nasser refused passage to our ships'.[4] Macmillan, after all, was the foremost advocate of the *casus belli*. To quote Brendan Bracken, his 'bellicosity was beyond all description'; he was 'wanting to tear Nasser's scalp off with his own fingernails'.[5]

After the formal interview was over, Dulles took Macmillan into a small private room and said that, although hurt by the UN business, he would put the matter out of his mind and discuss alternative methods of getting rid of Nasser. This, he assured his visitor with great earnestness, was as much America's objective as it was Britain's. New plans, which involved economic pressure and covert action throughout the region, for example in Syria, might, he thought, prove successful. 'But', he warned, 'of course they would take six months.' The Chancellor, full of a telegram from Baghdad, in which the British Ambassador, Sir Michael Wright, had urgently conveyed the conviction of Nuri and the court circle that time was working in Nasser's favour and that if he could avoid accepting international control he would have won the game, said that they could not wait for six months unless Nasser was obviously losing face all the time.

Dulles, then as so often, proceeded to display the other side of his nature. Having accurately reflected Eisenhower's priorities – against armed intervention, for deniable subversion – he used words safeguarding his hawkish flank that contributed to the miscalculations about America's position. He quite realised, he said, that Britain might have to act by force. In any case, he thought that the British *threat* of force was vital, whether they used it or not, to keep Nasser worried. According to Macmillan's account of the conversation Dulles reminded him how he and the President had helped Eden in May 1955 by agreeing to a Four-Power summit, which had undoubtedly been of great benefit to the Conservatives in the General Election. The Americans now wanted something in return. Could not Eden and Macmillan try to hold things off in the Middle East until after 6 November? Dulles in his account of this delicate exchange is understandably more coy, having Macmillan begin the exchange by hoping devoutly that the President would be re-elected and Dulles choosing the opportunity to get in a dig by way of reply to the effect that he hoped the British would do nothing drastic that would spoil his chances. Then, according to the American, it was Macmillan who recalled that the Americans had been helpful at the time of the British election and said he would bear that thought in mind. He added that Britain's new military posture did not any longer involve heavy shipping charges so that action could be more easily held in suspense.

In answer to the Chancellor's attempt to get grant aid from the United States to meet the dollar costs of reorganising Britain's oil supply, should this be required, Dulles repeated that Congress did not like voting aid for Britain and France, who after the Marshall Plan were now expected to stand on their own feet, but that, once the election was over, the severe conditions of the Anglo-American Loan Agreement, which made it practically impossible to use the clause permitting a waiver of interest payments, might be relaxed. 'But', said Macmillan, 'Dulles asked me specially to keep absolutely secret all that he said,' on account of the election.[6]

Macmillan had also gone in by the back door to the White House to see Eisenhower. They appear to have had a chat as old wartime friends more about electioneering than about Suez. It led the President to telephone Dulles that nothing had been said that need worry him in any way. 'As is usual with Ike,' Macmillan wrote to Eden, 'it was rather rambling and nothing very definite.'[7] He drew from the President's reserve about Suez the wrong conclusion. The very fact that the White House meeting had taken place lent authority to the assurance which Macmillan was to give to his colleagues over Suez: 'I know Ike. He will lie doggo!' It was a costly misjudgment.[8]

Italian Entr'acte

The Italians were greatly put out at the threatening clash between two of their Nato allies and the Arab world. Their discomfort was apparent at the SCUA conference and it was not surprising to find them active in trying to promote mediation. The initiative was taken by a prominent politician, Amintore Fanfani, a former Prime Minister and now Political Secretary of the Christian Democratic Party and known to Eisenhower as the right-hand man and political heir of the leading post-war statesman Alcide de Gasperi. At the end of September he sent an envoy, a professional diplomat named Raimondo Manzini, to see Dulles. Manzini had had an interview in Cairo with President Nasser and other leading Egyptians. Everywhere in Cairo he found lack of experience and a desperate desire to prove 'independence'. Nasser had expressed to him his desire for a quick settlement of the Suez crisis before he found himself forced into dependence on the Soviet Union. At the same time he expressed bitter resentment of Britain's anti-Nasser radio transmissions which were clearly worrying him.

He told Manzini of his reluctance to go to the UN Security Council because he did not want to find himself only supported by the Communists and did not like or trust Krishna Menon, whom he suspected of having some link with the Russians. What Nasser wanted was a direct negotiating channel with the United States through some secret emissary. If there were a Suez settlement Nasser would offer his services in working out a settlement in Algeria also. The Italian brought a letter from Fanfani, offering to help set up such a channel.

Dulles was doubtful about 'the embarrassment of secretly negotiating with Nasser while working with the British and French', while Eisenhower was quite clear that 'we should not negotiate behind their backs or without their knowledge and acquiescence'. However, with Dulles's encouragement Manzini was twice in Cairo during the first week of October to find out exactly what Nasser was willing to offer. Nasser gave him the gist of a plan for permanent links between the Egyptian Canal Authority and a Users' Association.[9]

French Moods

The French had returned from London in a sullen mood to find the Socialist Government under scornful attack from the right-wing press. Mollet had to fight hard to maintain the unity of his Cabinet. Acquiescence in SCUA was only announced grudgingly after Ministers had returned to Paris and then subject to the unamended Eighteen-Power scheme for international control being implemented. Pineau was said to have told Eden before he left that, if Britain felt unable to attack, it seemed that the French had no choice but to work hand-in-hand with the Israelis. Eden reputedly responded in a flaccid tone that he was not opposed to this provided Israel did not attack Jordan.[10]

In these circumstances Bourgès-Maunoury sent for Shimon Peres, the young Israeli civil servant who had wormed his way into the centre of the

French power structure. As it happened, he had just left France for the United States, after exploiting France's desire for an adventurous ally in an exceptionally daring way, and to the alarm of his own bureaucratic colleagues, by persuading the French to agree in principle to the installation in Israel of a small 100 kwt atomic reactor.[11] This was the beginning of the Israeli nuclear programme. On hearing of Bourgès's summons, Peres instantly flew back to France to be told that the French Government had 'decided that it cannot accept the [SCUA] plan and is prepared to act against Nasser – with the knowledge and consent of the English'. When Ben-Gurion noted Peres's report in his diary, the essential entry was the statement that, 'A three-man Israeli delegation including at least one Minister should come to Paris to hold discussions with Mollet, Pineau and Bourgès, working together *as equals*'.[12] This was the essential consideration as far as the Israeli Prime Minister was concerned. The initiative should come from France so that Israel was not the *demandeur* and the arrangements should be such that she should avoid the status of a ward, subject to the custodial will of the Tripartite Declaration Powers.

At this stage, however, the French were thinking of the Israelis only as part of a contingency plan if the British were to prove impossible allies. They still preferred the British connection partly because of its implications for the 'making of Europe'. The French did not yet know it but in a Friday meeting on 14 September, just the day after the end of the two-day debate on Suez, the British Cabinet had debated 'Plan G', the notion of a European Free Trade Area which was supposed to link Britain decisively to the continent.[13]

Not being able to reveal, until the Commonwealth had been consulted and the Cabinet had made up its mind, that Britain was on the verge of this major commitment to Europe. Eden and Lloyd had to respond graciously but meaninglessly to Mollet's talk of Franco-British union. This and a suggestion from the same source that France should join the Commonwealth had been referred to a Cabinet committee, presided over by Butler, which received and co-ordinated uniformly dismissive reports from successive government departments.[14]

Entente Cordiale

It was not therefore with an immensely enthusiastic brief that Eden and Lloyd set out for Paris on 26 September on what had been advertised before Nasser's *coup* as a wide-ranging review of Anglo-French relations. Their French hosts were determined that the visit should be a success. Nevertheless, when they first arrived, Mollet and Pineau led their two guests, into 'a very difficult discussion' about Suez.[15]

Pineau in particular was in suspicious mood. Going to the UN meant, in so far as he was concerned, taking a stubborn stand by every syllable of the Eighteen-Power proposals, accepting no amendments whatsoever. Eden and Lloyd, on the other hand, in the Egypt Committee and Cabinet meetings before they left, had been showing a new openness to alternative suggestions including what seemed to be a constructive interest in the compromise arrangements being promoted by Krishna Menon of India, provided only that one principle was upheld: the Canal must not be left in the unfettered control of one country. 'Provided this requirement were satisfied', Eden had summed up the discussion in the Egypt Committee, 'it would still be possible to maintain other pressures which in the longer term should achieve the downfall of Colonel Nasser's regime in Egypt.'[16] This sounded like Dulles talking and, in a sense, it was. It made a lamentable impression on the French, who were scornful at America's failure to do anything about the dues paid by American ships of Liberian and Panamanian register. In a burst of exasperation Pineau declared that the net result of the Second London Conference was that the Italians were paying all their dues to Egypt whereas previously they had paid only part of them. Meanwhile every week lost made military action more dangerous; Russian tanks and aircraft were reaching Egypt in a continuous stream.

'My own feeling', concluded Eden, 'is that the French, particularly M. Pineau, are in the mood to blame everyone, including us, if military action is not taken before the end of October.' The French were no better than General Keightley over the weather in the Eastern Mediterranean. If the allies did not get on with the job, winter would cut it out. Eden contested this. He was left at the end of two hours with the conclusion that, whereas Mollet would like to get a settlement on reasonable terms if he could, 'I doubt whether M. Pineau wants a settlement at all.'[17]

One paradoxical feature of the visit was that, despite the awkwardness of the conversations both about Suez and about Franco-British union, the Anglo-French entente visibly blossomed. Partly this was because the French were so determined that it should be so. Mollet in no way indicated in public the stickiness in the collaboration that is apparent in Eden's account. The British visit, he declared, was designed to show that 'Franco-British solidarity is total'. Pineau also, speaking at a meeting of the Foreign Affairs Commission of the National Assembly immediately before Eden's arrival, asserted that solidarity had survived in difficult circumstances. Pineau did not fail to add that, thanks to Suez, the British had understood that they had been wrong not to have identified themselves more with Europe.[18] But it was also Eden's doing. His relaxed charm and his fluent French put him at ease with a company whose youth and vigour left a lasting impression on him.[19] At least as far as Mollet was concerned, he inspired complete confidence.

At one stage of the discussions, Mollet, who had military advisers with much more recent experience of paratroop operations than the British, asked whether they could not seize the Canal by surprise *coup de main* from the air. Pineau muttered that this was the Suez Canal defended by Egyptians, not the Kiel Canal defended by Germans. When Eden enlarged on the danger of exposing paratroopers to counter-attack, especially with tanks, before reinforcements were to hand, Pineau (according to the anonymous French source cited by the Canadian writer Terence Robertson[20]) again injected the idea of Anglo-French action being co-ordinated with that of Israel. Selwyn Lloyd, who was not visibly stimulated by French company as was his chief, was becoming increasingly abstracted. He did not take kindly to the notion. But it registered with the Prime Minister.

When Eden and Lloyd went home the mood was distinctly up-beat, greatly assisted by an obliging French press.[21] Jebb reported afterwards that the visit, coming at a moment when French morale was low after a conference generally regarded in France as the nadir of Western policy, had been 'an outstanding success'. Only François Mauriac, the intellectual columnist in *L'Express*, warned his readers that in the last resort Britain would always sacrifice Anglo-French to save Anglo-American solidarity. Britain was committed to working with the French much closer than before. A royal visit to Paris in 1957 was announced – the only survivor from Gladwyn Jebb's short list of possible Francophile gestures[22] – and parallels were being dreamed up with Edward VII's visit in 1904.

On the same day as Eden travelled to Paris, Dulles held a press conference at which the limitations of SCUA as an instrument of short-term diplomacy became embarrassingly public. It included one of those disquisitions on the nature of foreign policy in which Dulles liked to indulge. He was asked what would happen if a Users' Association ship, equipped with its own pilot, having paid dues to the association, presented itself at the Canal and was refused entry. This was precisely the situation visualised by the British as a *casus belli*, though, to be sure, they could scarcely have supposed that the Americans would treat it as such for their own ships. Nevertheless, the impression of tripartite solidarity required keeping up if Egypt was to feel under pressure. Dulles explained that it depended what one meant by something 'happening'. 'If by that you mean that we would try to shoot our way through, there is no reason to think that we would shoot our way through. I have excluded that . . .' Would such ships then go round the Cape? Dulles thought that some would, some would not. Each vessel would decide for itself.

Dulles insisted that, since the revenue that Egypt got from the Canal was not a major factor in her economy and since there would in any case be plenty of boats of other registries to go through, 'if you try to hurt Egypt to the extent of $1 at the cost of $10,000, that isn't a very profitable enterprise in the long run . . .' It seemed to most of the journalists present as if Dulles, aided by the line of questioning, had rather neatly demolished his own artefact. However, he appeared not to think so and earnestly expounded his central thesis: that a nation like Egypt cannot usefully stand alone in defiance of the main trading nations. Western tourists were being repelled by the fiercely anti-Western nature of Egyptian pronouncements, Western investors would opt for supertankers, new pipelines and alternative sources of fuel such as nuclear power, rather than invest in the deepening and widening of the waterway. The pressures for interdependence 'which gradually grow up, not artificially stimulated but quite natural and inevitable' would assert themselves 'if we are patient, resourceful, persistent'. That, he maintained, was the only way under the Charter of the United Nations of achieving results.[23]

That was all very well. It did not help to repack Britain's military equipment that had been months on seaboard; it did not solve the problem of the bored and sometimes restive reservists, hanging around in Malta, Cyprus, Libya and in Britain, usually separated from their specialist equipment, in inferior accommodation and with nothing to do. The six months mentioned by Dulles to Macmillan would seem a low estimate of the time it would take for these long-run factors to work. It had taken years to remove Mossadeq; and the oil was a far more central part of his economy than the Canal was of Nasser's. The clash of time scales was becoming critical.

Jordan in Danger

Meanwhile, the centre of attention in the Middle East was switching away from Suez, where the danger of Anglo-French war against Egypt seemed to be receding, and over to Israel's borders with Jordan. The situation had been building up since 10 September, when an untrained Israeli army unit on a map-reading exercise was fired on by Jordanian National Guards in the Dawaima area; six Israelis were killed and three wounded and the bodies of the dead men dragged across the Jordanian border. The Mixed Armistice Commission eventually found against Jordan. But Israel did not wait for the Commission to complete its investigation. An Israeli unit of battalion strength crossed the Jordanian frontier west of Hebron on the night of 11 September, assaulted the police fort at Rahwah, killed six policemen and ten soldiers and then totally demolished the building and also a UN school. An Arab Legion party coming to reinforce was ambushed, and another four soldiers were killed and three wounded.

'Quite apart from its effect in confusing the Suez and Arab-Israel affairs, another such raid would carry the risk of embroiling us in conflict with Israel at the very moment when we should be striving to keep Israel on our side with an eye to the future,' moaned the Foreign Office, as it issued a critical press release and suspended action on current Israeli arms requests. On the night of 13/14 September Israeli troops inflicted the same medicine on Gharandal, where once again the police post and the UN school were blown up, with this time eight Jordanians being killed and others wounded. It was pointed out, on the one side, that the police posts which had been destroyed were the main inhibition to Arab infiltration of the Israeli border and, on the other, that during the last six months twenty-nine Israelis had been killed and thirty-three wounded as the cumulative result of border crossings.[24]

The Foreign Office repeated its formal warnings to Tel Aviv about the continued validity of the Anglo-Jordanian Treaty, and under Operation *Cordage* British naval and air forces to be used in support of Jordan were kept at the ready. Land reinforcements, Britain was told by Jordan, would not be welcome because of Suez; to fulfil that function Jordan now turned to Iraq. In a report to the Security Council dated 12 September but not published till 28 September, Hammarskjöld declared that, 'If the cease-fire is permitted continuously to be challenged by actual events, it will lose its sanctity and become a dead letter.'

Because of the Israeli 'reprisal' raids, a very worried King Hussein visited Habbaniya base on 14/15 September to concert with King Faisal and Nuri 'the immediate measures that should be taken in accordance with the Jordanian-Iraqi Defence Treaty'. An Iraqi military mission was sent to Jordan to discuss the stationing of Iraqi troops on Jordanian soil. Following the clashes on the borders, the Jordanians withdrew the Arab Legion from the job of frontier control and regrouped them tactically further back, leaving the border posts, including the Old City of Jerusalem, exclusively manned by the far less well disciplined Jordanian National Guards. If the Israelis meant war, it made a great deal more sense not to have the best troops strung out along the frontier, but the possibility of incidents was much increased.[25]

On 23 September machine-gun fire was opened – the Jordanians said by a crazed National Guardsman – on a congress of eminent archaeologists who were inspecting a site just yards from the border. Four of the archaeologists were killed and sixteen wounded. On the following day there were two more incidents, in each of which an Israeli civilian was killed. On 25 September Ben-Gurion called a special Cabinet meeting to decide on military action against the Arab Legion by way of retaliation.

Before the meeting began he met Shimon Peres who had just flown in from Paris with his news that the French were willing to work with the Israelis as equals. 'This is the birth of the first serious alliance between us and a western power,' said Ben-Gurion. 'We can't not accept it.'[26] The limits of permissible retaliation had to be fixed with an eye to this information. Peres says that Ben-Gurion was very anxious to avoid a war with Britain over Jordan; it would certainly not be a happy way to inaugurate a new alliance with France. But this was not going to make him abandon the policy of reprisal. He authorised an attack on the Arab Legion post at

Husan, in the Jerusalem hills near where the previous incidents had occurred. He then appointed the delegation to go to France – two politicians, Golda Meir and Moshe Carmel, a former General who was now one of the Ministers from the Achdut Ha'avoda party, the left-wing hawks in the coalition, and two technicians, Peres and Dayan.

They were told to make sure in Paris that France realised in advance that Israeli forces would be less than totally ready and to establish that the operation which the French had told Peres they wanted to launch on 15 October had the active backing of Britain and would be done with the knowledge of the United States. Ben-Gurion's instructions were that 'we shall not be the ones to open' the hostilities. Israel's war aims were to be to obtain control of the west coast of the Gulf of Aqaba and the entrance into the Straits of Tiran at Sharm al-Sheikh. Then the Straits would be open; Eilat would be a great port; the 'hinterland' of the Negev would be developed. Some of Ben-Gurion's Cabinet colleagues expressed anxieties – Russia would send 'volunteers', the 'English' would betray them, the Arab states would all enter the war against them – but Ben-Gurion pressed ahead with the mission. At last Israel was going to obtain an ally. Just before Golda Meir and the others left via Bizerta in an exceedingly uncomfortable French anti-submarine aircraft, the last contingent of French arms, twenty Super-Sherman tanks, had been unloaded at night.[27]

During the night of 25/26 September Husan was attacked by the Israelis in the presence of Moshe Dayan. They met fierce resistance from the Arab Legion and only succeeded in demolishing the post after bloody hand-to-hand fighting. Ten Israelis were killed and sixteen wounded. Thirty-seven Jordanian soldiers and police and two civilians, one a twelve-year-old girl, died and another eleven had wounds. It had been a costly operation.[28]

In a letter which he wrote the next day to Hammarskjöld, Ben-Gurion reverted to his arguments based on the complete text of the Armistice Agreement, complaining that Israel was being expected to acquiesce in a 'double standard, one for Israel and the other for the rest of the world'. Quite contrary to the Charter, Israel was being subjected to 'continual, open threats', which filled the press, the radio and the public speeches of the Egyptian dictator, the Jordanian King, the Syrian President and the King of Saudi Arabia individually and in chorus. Access to the Wailing Wall was denied, the Canal blockaded; why then should Israel allow UN observers to wander around such critical areas of contact as the Al Auja zone with Egypt and the Tiberias zone with Syria? 'Even the present British Prime Minister, who can hardly be suspected of any bias in favour of Israel against the Arabs, has publicly stated that he did not care to take the Suez problem to the UN because Egypt has been able to ignore with impunity the Security Council's decision regarding the passage of Israeli shipping through the Canal.' Hammarskjöld had been wondering whether a further visit to the area would be worthwhile; Ben-Gurion told him that he must decide for himself but he would always be a welcome guest. Though personally courteous, the letter was in substance unpromising.[29]

On 27 September Ben-Gurion reviewed with Dayan the danger of a full-scale war with Jordan. Would Britain be involved? Ben-Gurion was evidently worried at the possibility. The British might want to take the opportunity to demonstrate their friendship for the Arabs. Would Iraq? Ben-Gurion sounded uncompromising: if Iraqi troops came anywhere near the Israeli border, Israel would occupy the West Bank. But Dayan was not quite certain that he had in reality made up his mind.[30]

Jordan was now approaching a major crossroads. The King had dissolved Parliament and called for elections for 21 October. It was not as if contested and frequently disorderly elections had not taken place before, but they had been between independents. This was to be the first (and, so far, the last) contest of parties.[31] There was a feeling that anything might happen and that feeling created an air of expectancy in the region. Influenced by Israel's destabilising policy, Egyptian and Saudi propaganda and the surge of Arab nationalism associated with Templer's rebuff and Glubb's dismissal, the victory of the pro-Nasserist National Socialists under Suleiman Nabulsi was a highly possible result and that of the revolutionary Ba'ath Party the most feared.

It was these conditions of mounting complexity that sharpened the anomalies of British policy towards Israel and her neighbours. 'There really seems to be no end to the contradictions we involve ourselves in,' wrote Sir Gerald Fitzmaurice, the Foreign Office Legal Adviser, to Sir Ivone Kirkpatrick, drawing his attention to the Foreign Office News Department's latest denunciation of Israel's policy of reprisals. 'Is it wise', he asked, 'for the British official spokesman to be condemning in such round terms action of the type which we might very well be led to take ourselves, and have indeed, as the whole world knows, made extensive preparations for taking?'[32]

The Conference of St Germain

Between 30 September and 1 October Golda Meir's delegation met secretly with French civil and military leaders in Paris at the Montparnasse home of Colonel Louis Mangin, Bourgès's adviser. (The Israelis always called it the Conference of St Germain, after the district where their own delegation was housed.) They sat down in a room dominated by the imposing portrait of the General, Mangin's celebrated father.

The impression left by this meeting rather varies, depending on whether it originates from Peres or from Dayan. Conscious that Golda Meir was not among his greatest admirers,[33] Peres was anxious to stage-manage the formal offer by the French of a full-dress military alliance. Accordingly, he felt rather let down by what followed. For one thing, Guy Mollet did not turn up at all, to the young Israeli's deep mortification and Mrs Meir's visible offence. Next, the French plans seemed rather unfocussed and Pineau's statement of willingness to go ahead if necessary without the British carried less than complete conviction. It emerged that the French very much preferred the Israelis to start the war independently, thus enabling the French and (possibly) the British to join in later. Ben-Gurion's instructions on this point had been categorical: the two allies or the three must attack simultaneously.

Dayan was not put down: he was sure that in what the French said there was enough to build on to make an effective partnership. But Matti Golan, Peres's biographer, says that other members of the delegation shared the feeling that, in his enthusiasm for the French connection, Peres had exaggerated the prospects of reaching an accommodation and had surrendered to a state of unfounded optimism.[34]

Pineau began the work, which had to be pursued throughout the next month, of persuading the Israelis that Anthony Eden was a man who could be trusted. He explained that the British Prime Minister remained solid for action but he had to have a pretext and was being hard pressed by his political critics. The decision to go to the UN would occupy a certain amount of time; the British Cabinet would be unable to reach a decision until about 15 October. If, then, the British dropped out and the French wanted to act alone, the latter would have to act immediately while the weather in the Mediterranean was still calm and the United States was preoccupied by the presidential election. Therefore they needed to know what were the alternatives open before them, whether an Israeli attack with French assistance or a joint Franco-Israeli offensive.

Pineau thought that, before the election, Eisenhower would not want to be seen as abandoning his allies; after it, he would probably do a deal with the Russians about the Canal. But the French were emphatically against telling the Americans, as Ben-Gurion had wished, what they were planning to do. Dulles would be certain to interfere because of his deference to the oil lobby.

Answering in turn a sequence of difficult questions put to him very directly by Golda Meir, Pineau ruled out the possibility of an American military intervention against Israel, France and Britain. As for economic sanctions against Israel, about which Mrs Meir described Israel as highly sensitive, the United States would not act before the election because of the Jewish vote. It was another reason for moving fast. General Maurice Challe, an air force officer who was present, a man of some ingenuity and address who was to play a major part in the eventual plan, intervened to say that the Americans were already conniving at French action since American officers at Nato headquarters in Paris (France had not yet left the integrated command system) had willingly responded to requests to release Nato equipment for use by the French contingent already in Cyprus.

It was clear that France much preferred Britain to be in from the outset. For one thing, the French and British forces were already mixed up together in the current planning; it would be difficult to disentangle this. For another, the French had no equivalent of the Canberra bomber which was thought to have outstanding qualities for use against the runways of airfields, so as to paralyse the potentially powerful Egyptian air force. No one was worried about Russian planes flown by Egyptian pilots. It was 'volunteer' pilots that concerned the Israelis and the French. Neither did the French have any air bases in the region while the British had Cyprus. On Israel's side, if she got involved in any operation against Egypt she would need to know where Britain stood if Jordan attacked Israel in support of Egypt or invited the Iraqis into her own territory, which Israel was resolved not to tolerate.

Even Dayan confessed himself none too happy with the political phase of the talks. The one point that emerged clearly, he said, 'was that the situation was unclear'. It would have to remain such until the end of the Security Council meetings.

At the personal level the Israelis, and especially Dayan, went over well with the French military. He was supremely confident that the Israelis could take Sinai even without allies. But they were not interested in establishing a bridgehead on the west bank of the Suez Canal. The French were open-handed in responding to Dayan's requests for more American-made Super-Sherman tanks, tank transporters, bazookas and, most important of all, trucks with four-wheel drive to tackle the rough challenge of the Sinai desert. Bourgès-Maunoury let them go without immediate payment, on a basis rather similar to 'lend-lease'. The Israelis now had sixty Mystères IV either in Israel or on the way and did not ask for more. They had learnt little about French military plans and they had not been called on to make any decisions. They were aware both that the French Government thought that there was no escape from the use of force and that it was still worried about the *casus belli*.[35]

The Israeli party returned home in considerably more comfort than they had come, since the French had put at their disposal the specially equipped DC-4 which President Truman had presented to General de Gaulle. With them came a military delegation under General Maurice Challe in order to assess the military capabilities of the Israeli forces and the technical possibilities of basing the French air force on Israeli bases if the British did not come in and Cyprus were not available.

On the evening of his return, Moshe Dayan called a meeting of the General Staff and gave them an Early Warning Order. He told them that a campaign was probable against Nasser, although the actual decision had not been taken. He thought it would begin on 20 October and last three weeks. Preparations for mobilisation should be explained as precautions in the event of an Iraqi entry into Jordan. He emphasised the supreme importance of surprise and speed.

At the same time as Dayan was completing this briefing, Ben-Gurion was writing a memorandum on the result of the Paris talks. It reflected acute anxiety, born of personal memories of the London Blitz, about Tel Aviv and Haifa being bombed and heavy casualties inflicted. The danger would, in his estimation, be very much increased if the British bombers were not available, and especially so if French planes were to be based in Israel, which would thereby become the sole target of counter-attack. He also remained strongly opposed to Israel standing before the world as the sole aggressor. Nevertheless, the memorandum ended with no firm conclusion other than that the French should be told of his reactions. It showed characteristic ambiguity. He might be preparing the ground for a blank refusal. Or he might be concerned to have it recognised by France that no small matter was being expected of the State of Israel.[36] Dayan persuaded him not to write to Mollet immediately. The chance of gaining France as an ally after the years of isolation was not to be missed. The French and Israeli air forces could perfectly well deal with the Egyptians.

The French military delegation was not immediately enchanted by what they saw and heard of Israel's untidy, improvising, citizen army and its dramatic war plans. Their first reaction to the latter was that Dayan's notion of a whirlwind Sinai campaign seemed like an 'irresponsible adventure'. There was an embarrassing exchange between Challe and Dayan, when Challe, very sceptical that Israelis could reach the Suez Canal as fast as they claimed, declared: 'Let us assume you do make the Canal bank. For how long can you hold it?' Dayan sought to evade the question, on the grounds that it was 'for the political echelon'. Challe insisted. 'I guess it would be some 300 years,' Dayan replied. The angry look in Challe's eyes suddenly vanished as he burst out laughing. The Israeli officer who was interpreting says that, as between these two men, the chemistry was strong from that moment.[37] But there were still some sticky passages. 'I didn't know you had any of these,' said a French officer, passing members of a reserve unit reporting to base and taking them to be a tribe of gypsies.

When Ben-Gurion met the French delegation he asked what was a fundamental question: how did the contemplated military action, the seizure of the Canal Zone, relate to the principal declared aim of the operation, the overthrow of Nasser? There followed much discussion but no one produced a real answer to it or to a related question: how was the campaign to be kept short if Nasser succeeded in waging guerrilla warfare? The French left full of enthusiasm for the standards and leadership of the Israeli citizen army. But Dayan records that Ben-Gurion's impression after the talks was that the operation would not take place.[38] Nevertheless, the planning of what was now described as 'Operation Kadesh'[39] went rapidly forward.

All the emphasis was on speed and depth of penetration, by-passing enemy positions. There are three classic invasion routes across Sinai. At this stage, the major attacks were to be on the two more northerly axes; the southern attack was only to be a feint. Gaza, which many Israelis thought of as the main threat to Israeli settlements, was to be cut off and left till later. The initial target was to be Al Arish, the administrative capital of Sinai on the Mediterranean coast, which would be assaulted by air drop of two battalions of paras from Sharon's brigade while a third landed from the sea. They would be reinforced by a swiftly manoeuvring armoured brigade (the 27th) which had been freshly formed from the French-supplied tanks. At the same time the Egyptian defensive lines at Rafah would be under assault, while lower down on the Nitzana(Al Auja)–Ismailia axis (the central route across the Sinai) deep outflanking movements by the Israelis would permit them to attack the most formidable of the fixed defences, the Abu Agheila/Umm Qataf positions, from both east and west.

Once they had been relieved, Colonel Sharon's paras were to be withdrawn from Al Arish and re-used in what was in some ways regarded as the most important operation of all: the seizure of Sharm al-Sheikh at the southern tip of Sinai. As for Suez, it was Dayan's intention from the beginning of the planning of Kadesh to drop some small forces at the outset, perhaps thirty or forty men in all, in the Canal area to set up ambushes and roadblocks to disrupt Egyptian supply lines, and interfere with the flow of reinforcements. The Israeli army, as such, was not expected to reach the Canal until four to five days after the attack.[40]

Following gloomy reports from the French Ambassador, Chauvel, and his Defence Attaché, Admiral Amman, in London about the state of British morale and the extent of the pressure to which Eden was being subjected, Admiral Barjot issued his 'Secret and Personal Instruction' outlining 'Hypothesis I' for Israel, which provided for a purely Franco-Israeli offensive. All that would be needed from Britain was that she be neutral, would keep America quiet and would allow the use of the Cyprus bases.[41] But then the doubts began. The word from Dayan in secret staff talks that started in Paris on 12 October was that the most that the Israelis could do for a French para landing at Port Said would be to send 'light detachments' through the desert to make a token contact at Qantara (where the Suez causeway opens out). General Ely was becoming increasingly opposed to such a risky effort and he was fortified by the anxieties of President Coty, who feared the intervention of Russian flyers and wanted to move, if at all, with the British and without the Israelis.

Challe, returning to Paris from his visit to the Israel Defence Forces an ardent missionary for the Israeli cause, was sent off to New York in considerable secrecy to brief Pineau, who was at the Security Council. The opinion was again hardening in Paris in favour of only moving with full British participation.[42] As to that, everyone knew that nothing could happen until the end of the Security Council debate.

15

Taking it to the UN

Could it be that the ruling circles planned to reply to public demands for a peaceful settlement: 'You have urged us to appeal to the UN. We have done so, but, as you see, it is powerless. It can do nothing. Other steps must be taken. Egypt is guilty. Crucify it!'?
Dmitri Shepilov, Soviet Foreign Minister, UN Security Council, New York, 8 October 1956.

I have an announcement, I have got the best announcement that I could possibly make to America tonight . . . [I]t looks like here is a very great crisis that is behind us.
Dwight D. Eisenhower, 12 October 1956.

On 1 October in Whitehall the Egypt Committee met to plan the strategy for the UN Security Council. Eden said that the Americans must be made to feel issues in Africa and the Middle East in terms of straight 'cold war' confrontation. That was why he had sent a cable to Eisenhower stating flatly that: 'There is no doubt that Nasser, whether he likes it or not, is now effectively in Russian hands, just as Mussolini was in Hitler's.' The message had gone on to talk of 'accumulating evidence', of Egyptian plots in Libya, Saudi Arabia and Iraq.[1] Anglo-French solidarity must be maintained. That lent special importance to the French conviction that their forces could not be kept at the ready for long.

The Foreign Secretary, on the other hand, was now giving the impression that he had become more hopeful of a settlement and that, as he had hinted earlier, he was ready to accept something short of international management. The onus should be placed on the Egyptians to produce counter-proposals which must contain clear provision for any future Egyptian interference with the rights of users to be visited with effective sanctions. In the case of a future Suez crisis Britain should not find herself in the present embarrassment: full of grievances but not permitted to do anything by the UN Charter.

Lloyd professed himself perfectly willing to take up the latest proposal that was being floated by Krishna Menon. This was a detailed document which proposed to bind Egypt over maximum tolls, non-discrimination and the precise and timely execution of existing programmes for the development of the Canal. It also provided that there should be joint sittings, periodically or at the request of either side, of the (Egyptian) Canal Authority and a Users' Association rather differently composed from SCUA (which was formally coming into existence at the Third London Conference at the start of October) and including Russia and India among its permanent members. The Foreign Office reacted that, if this was going to be any good for Britain, decisions in the Users' Association would have to be by majority vote. The difficulty would be to define the sanctions to be available in case of violations. Menon had proposed reference to the International Court, but that did not seem quick enough; yet it was hardly possible to insert into an international agreement explicit provision for the use of force in case of its breach. The other problem was how to cram this sort of negotiation into the time-frame required by the French.[2]

Lloyd's task was not made any easier by the fact that Dulles tripped over his tongue during a news conference on 2 October. He was asked about reports widespread since the ending of the Second London Conference of a split between the United States and the British and the French over the content of the SCUA proposal and especially the sanctions that were to go with it. Dulles set off on a long, ruminative reply which took him way beyond the question asked. As far as SCUA was concerned, he denied that there had been any watering down of the original plan. 'There is talk that the teeth were pulled out of it. There were no teeth in it.' That was bad enough. It was immediately seen in France and Britain as a brutal kick in the face for their diplomacy. But Dulles ploughed relentlessly on. There was some difference in the approaches to the Suez problem. One difference related to the fact that the United States, France and Britain were not treaty allies the whole world over, only in parts of it. 'Other problems relate to other areas and touch the so-called problem of colonialism in some way or other. On these problems, the United States play a somewhat independent role.'[3]

Howls of resentment and indignation were unleashed in Britain and in France by this curiously innocent formulation. The anti-Americanism of the right, always potentially more lethal than the anti-Americanism of the left, was released from its usual inhibitions. The feeling that 'America is going to do us down', from naïve anti-colonialism, from sinister oil interests or from sheer inability of a superpower to tolerate other world interests, was widespread. It was not created by Dulles's blunder, but coming so soon after repeated warnings about 'not shooting a way through the Canal', it was mightily assisted by it. 'If the Suez crisis has taken a bad turn,' wrote Roger Massip, the foreign editor of *Le Figaro*, 'it is because the support of our American friends has been completely denied to us from the beginning.'

Iverach McDonald, the foreign editor of *The Times*, found Eden the next morning 'immeasurably angry and shocked'. He despaired of ever being able to work with the Americans. 'It was I who ended the "so-called colonialism" in Egypt. And look at what Britain has done all over the world in giving the colonies independence,' he declared. 'How on earth can you work with people like that? It leaves us in a quite impossible position. We can't go on like this.'[4]

Dulles realised that he had blundered. He initiated an apology to Eden, acknowledging that he had been drawn into a line of discussion which was in itself undesirable. 'The most dishonest policy I ever read!' was Eden's reaction to an article by Chalmers Roberts of the *Washington Post* which expanded on Dulles's long-evolving thoughts about colonialism and concluded that the only thing that was surprising in his remark was that he had made it in public.[5] There is no doubt that this event, which seemed to betray so much about the American Administration's association of ideas, deeply influenced the Prime Minister's judgment. It filled him with the sensation that Britain's position was being constantly eroded from the direction of what should have been her firmest friend, and was particularly galling in that Eden regarded himself as a proponent of decolonisation. Dulles seemed to be confusing Colonial behaviour with the necessary projection of a nation's power. Something was clearly amiss in the special relationship.

Another consequence of this crisis in transatlantic confidence, which was much noted in the press, was the boost in the sentiment for European unity. American press correspondents all confirmed that, on account of Suez, the climate for an assertion of Britain's European identity had been immensely improved. The paradox did not escape them that, whereas European union had been a cause sponsored by the United States, it was only acquiring a real momentum as the result of the anti-American mood. 'American policy-makers', wrote the Alsop brothers, Joseph and Stewart, in their regular column in the *New York Herald Tribune* of 2 October, 'are now reaping a bitter harvest of Allied anger and ill will. This country's chief world partners, Britain and France, are feeling emotions and making charges that are without precedent in the last ten years.' The brothers, while they had a reputation as prophets of doom, were extremely well connected socially and professionally in Washington and abroad. Their column was closely followed by political leaders, often for the political signals of others that they thought were being sent through it. In this piece the Alsops essentially took the side of the Europeans against Dulles, describing the way in which the Secretary of State had 'put on an imposing display of righteous determination' when he had met and briefed a French parliamentary delegation in Washington, making it seem as if a tough boycott of the Suez Canal was to be organised and financed by the United States while what had emerged from the SCUA conference was a 'pious sham'. In these circumstances, the Alsops concluded, it was easy to see why the British and

French Governments thought that they had been bamboozled and why the present soreness in Paris and London would lead to even graver strains in the alliance in the very likely event of the Middle East situation getting worse.

This sore state of transatlantic relations, the departure from a feeling of confidential partnership, caused anxiety at the State Department and set the Secretary of State thinking about the long-run nature of the relationship. In an 'eyes only' despatch to the Ambassadors in Paris and London, Douglas Dillon and Winthrop Aldrich, on 4 October, Dulles lamented: 'I know the British and French want us to "stand with them", but we do not know where they stand nor are we consulted.' The British had said that they wanted negotiations to begin at the UN but it was impossible to find out what kind. Was the move to the UN genuine or was it designed by the British and French to put a Soviet veto 'in their pocket', so giving them 'liberty of action'? 'Both British and French embassies seem to be completely in the dark and we cannot get guidance from them. We do not know and cannot find out whether they want peace or war.'

The uncomfortable experience thus described led Dulles on into an intellectual exercise about European union. 'The Western European nations', he said, 'have been preserving their political divisions, which keep them weak, partly because they have felt that they could afford this luxury so long as they had more or less a blank cheque on the US for economic, military and political support everywhere in the world.' The Suez matter was teaching them that this was not true outside the Nato area. Their remedy was to unite to form a powerful force in the world comparable to the Soviet Union and the US. 'Unfortunately it is the fact that great movements such as the federation of separate sovereignties rarely occur purely as a result of logic ... The knowledge of such countries that they cannot count on such support irrespective of our independent judgment will naturally irritate them and create a measure of anti-US feeling. But that may be the only atmosphere in which the momentous step of European union will be advanced.'[6]

The real difference of analysis between Eden and Eisenhower over Nasser was brought out by an incident that occurred at the White House on 6 October, when Hoover mentioned to the President that he had had a visit from the CIA group that had been instructed to plan ways of toppling the Egyptian. Eisenhower's reaction was that for a thing like that to be done it was essential to choose 'a time free from heated stress holding the world's attention'. According to a CIA note attached to the State Department's secret reconstruction of the history of Suez, it was at this time that, immediately following a British official mission to Washington headed by Patrick Dean, 'CIA representatives concluded that estrangement' between the two normally closely aligned countries 'was becoming dangerously acute'.

When the British and French Foreign Ministers arrived for the Security Council session they had called, Foster Dulles received them in his New York apartment on the morning of 5 October. He told them that he must know where he stood. Was this move to the UN a genuine attempt at a peaceful settlement or was it an exercise in going through the motions to get freedom of action for stronger measures? America's position was that a peaceful solution should be sought by all possible means and that war would be a disaster. Lloyd insisted that their purpose in going to the UN was genuine and that they were ready to accept a week for negotiations so as to get an agreed settlement. If this method failed, they could either apply economic sanctions, which would be fine if they produced results in a week or two, or they could use force. This, he conceded, had certain dangers, such as how to get the troops out once they had gone in and how to justify the use of force to public opinion.

He thought that the way they would do it would be to denounce the 1954 agreement and go back into the Suez Canal Zone. Effective action must be taken without delay because the whole position in the Middle East was rapidly deteriorating. In Libya the Egyptians had brought in arms and there was a plot to kill the King; King Saud was threatened; Syria was virtually under Egyptian control; in Iraq there was dissatisfaction with Nuri among the younger officers. Matters could not be allowed to drift. In the last resort force would be the lesser evil.

Pineau then added his contribution to Dulles's misery. He would, he said, put his cards on the table. French opinion was very strained. Nothing less than the existence of Nato was at stake. If Nasser succeeded over Suez, the Sultan would be thrown out of Morocco, extremists would take over in Tunisia, everywhere the West was losing out by the appearance of weakness. Pineau, who by the rule of monthly rotation held the current chairmanship of the Security Council and had made it quite clear that he had no intention of standing down for this item, said he was ready to 'play the game' so long as debate did not drag on too long. But if it was not possible to get negotiations on the basis of the Eighteen-Power proposals, 'we must recover our freedom of action or we shall be led into capitulation'.

Dulles, also, was playing for high stakes. He did not hesitate to bring to bear the dire threat of American isolationism. He said that if force were used in violation of the UN Charter, the United Nations itself would be destroyed 'with incalculable consequences not least in the United States'. Nor did he agree that the situation was deteriorating. Instead, developments were going against Nasser; his prestige was declining. Egypt had had to take troops out of the Gaza Strip and the Negev area on account of the Suez crisis and manifestly could not help Jordan. Jordan was turning to Iraq, not to Egypt or Saudi Arabia, and there was an Iraqi–Saudi rapprochement. He fully agreed that the *potential* use of force must be kept in existence; that would keep up pressure on Egypt to settle in the UN. But, if it had to be used, the West could write off Pakistan, Iran, Ethiopia.

Lloyd insisted that press stories of Britain and France being held back from headlong action by American influence were quite unfounded. Unlike Pineau he said that he was prepared to look at an alternative to the Eighteen-Power declaration but speed was of the essence. 'We think that to take a week is not rushing it.' 'If you have ever argued in an Egyptian bazaar in Cairo you will know that they don't work like that,' Dulles responded glumly. He reported to the President that the next few days would be 'make or break' and he observed that, 'If we can put into it the spirit which seems to have animated the Dodgers in the game today, then there is a chance we can make it.'[8]

'We must never forget', commented Eden when he read the telegrams from New York, 'that Dulles's purpose is different from ours. The Canal is in no sense vital to the United States and his game is to string us along at least until Polling Day. I can imagine what the buzz of mediators is like. I shall shortly have the Hornet [Krishna Menon] here myself.' This rather jaunty cable concluded on a sombre note: 'I have been struck down by a tiresome virus with a high temperature but hope to be about again in a day or two.'[9]

This was sinister news. The Prime Minister, as Robert Rhodes James has explained, had suddenly felt freezing cold and had begun to shake uncontrollably with fever when he was visiting his wife in hospital. His temperature was 106 degrees. It was a return of his old problem with a vengeance. However on this occasion he appeared to bounce back quickly. But his biographer writes that, although in a few days he felt surprisingly well, these fevers were profoundly weakening and caused bouts of lassitude, against which Eden fought irritably. Nor was this the first time that he had felt unfit since the crisis began. On 21 August, after a wretched night largely spent awake with abdominal pain, he had been talking with his medical advisers about a 'final decision' on whether to have another operation or a drastic change of treatment. It was put off then until he could take a holiday. He had had another reminder in early September.

In view of what was to happen during the succeeding month there will always be speculation about the extent to which Eden's failing health influenced his judgment. There can be no firm answer. Rhodes James, who has looked into the medical record carefully and has dismissed the more sensational extrapolations from the history, says that 'perhaps wrongly' the doctors decided after 5 October that he was well enough to carry on.[10]

In New York, Lloyd and Pineau rejected the Soviet suggestion of a negotiating committee of the three western powers plus Egypt, the Soviet Union and India. Nor would they tolerate the notion of a small mediating committee. But they did favour direct private discussions under the auspices of the Security Council. This method was agreed, with Mahmoud Fawzi, the Egyptian Foreign Minister, talking to Pineau and Lloyd in the active presence of Dag Hammarskjöld. The idea represented an important innovation in UN procedure, setting a precedent for informal and private negotiation within the Council that was only taken up again after an interval of some twenty years.

The American newspapers on 8 October spread despondency in the British ranks. They were full of evidently inspired talk of a rift in the Security Council between the United States and Britain. Lloyd learned that Dulles himself had told leading correspondents privately that Britain would have to accept the Indian proposals for 'organised consultation' in the end. Having been given a rough ride by representatives of the British press, Lloyd determined to have this out with his American opposite number before the debate began. He told him in a quaint reversal of roles from three days earlier that he wanted to know just where he stood. 'Was Dulles preparing some plan behind the backs of the French and ourselves? Where did we disagree?' Dulles denied the remarks attributed to him, promised to impose some discretion on the members of his delegation and said that they were in agreement about everything except the wisdom of the ultimate use of force. Britain and France were absolutely right to make preparations and to maintain the threat. They could rely on him to make 'a very powerful speech' in their support. Eden strongly endorsed Lloyd's stand. 'We have been misled so often by Dulles's ideas that we cannot afford to risk another misunderstanding.'[11]

It was in fact Eisenhower rather than Dulles or the State Department who was becoming impatient with the policy of allowing the British and French to call the shots. On 2 October the President had repeated his conviction that the Canal issue was not the one on which to undermine Nasser. When Dulles mentioned MI6 plans for his overthrow, he replied at once that 'we should have nothing to do with any project for a covert operation against Nasser personally'. He wanted the Eighteen-Power proposal to be treated as the opening bid in a bargaining process and was eager for the United States to take 'possibly dramatic . . . possibly dramatic' action. In a list of questions that the President sent to the State Department on 8 October he wrote, 'If therefore we can think of any plan that we could accept, even though it falls somewhat short of the detailed requirements listed by Britain and France, we might, through some clandestine means, urge Nasser to make an appropriate offer.' He talked of issuing a White House statement that the United States would not support a war in the Suez area and he wanted to summon a new international conference possibly with the help of Pandit Nehru. It was the State Department which replied that it would be a mistake to be more specific with the Indians in case 'we give an erroneous impression of willingness to compromise and thus undermine the general US–UK–French discussion with the Egyptians in New York'.[12]

Still propped up in his hospital bed, but with his temperature down, Eden was reading the *Sunday Times* and particularly a despatch by its Cairo correspondent, J. B. Slade-Baker. This spoke of a 'spirit of fatalistic defiance and determination as Egypt approaches the hour when she must make good her case against the West'. Noting that there was no change whatever in the Egyptians' attitude to foreigners towards whom they remained individually friendly, Slade-Baker quoted a senior official for the view that the crisis had burned itself out and that the problem of who was to control the Canal no longer existed. The Security Council meeting was welcomed as a chance to show how strong Egypt's juridical case was. As for force, the attitude was: 'You will need a million men to protect your interests [in the Arabian peninsula] and more to protect the men. You will lose your oil and have to buy from America with dollars. We know who will win in the end.'

On reading this the Prime Minister cabled Lloyd that it reinforced his own belief that, in the last resort, military action would be necessary. 'It is, therefore, very important that, while appearing reasonable, we should not be inveigled away in negotiation from the fundamentals to which we have held all along and that we should not be parted from the French!'[13] Selwyn Lloyd regarded that last as a most binding instruction and, at considerable cost in nervous strain, adhered to it to the end.

Ten weeks into the quarrel, there was now to take place the first substantive confrontation of the parties and the arguments. Fawzi, who had been told by Dulles that 'my credit is almost exhausted' with his two allies, had the distinct impression that the American Secretary of State was embarrassed at his own part in setting the trail of gunpowder alight. His approach to his Egyptian counterpart was to say that, in withdrawing the Aswan offer, he had never meant to insult Egypt or damage its economy, and he would not object if the Russians participated in the Dam. Fawzi said Egypt preferred to try to work out a system involving neither Superpower, under which she in effect built the Dam herself. Dulles, Fawzi was happy to report, did not insist on the Eighteen-Power formula. He urged the Egyptian to work out with the British and French agreed guidelines and principles.[14]

Egypt's problem throughout was that most nations, including India and probably the Soviet Union, felt distinctly uncomfortable at Nasser's abrupt and abrasive manner of proceeding. The nationalisation coup had been the type of gesture that raises the hearts of emerging peoples but does not appeal to governments of any brand. Fawzi, with his quiet, elliptical manner, had the task of making rough policies acceptable to official world opinion. Shepilov gave him advice. The West had to be shown an honourable means of retreat from their ideal of internationalisation. Would Egypt wear a consultative body which would give the West the impression that they were involved in running the Canal while Egypt would retain all the essentials of control? At the same time the Soviet Minister gave Fawzi a sharp warning not to let the Americans in; once in they would not prove easy to get out.[15]

Krishna Menon, meanwhile, had been commuting between London and Cairo, believing himself, in his self-dramatising way, to have been assigned the key role of chief peacemaker. Though all – including Fawzi and Hammarskjöld – tended to run him down and he was, indeed, a severe trial of everyone's patience, a surprising amount of time was devoted to humouring him and discussing his suggestions and ideas. He could take credit for spreading word that there was an area of potential compromise that Nasser was willing to discuss. It was only at the following stage, during negotiations in New York, when, in Fawzi's words, Krishna Menon suddenly appeared at a Security Council meeting 'wearing a Kashmiri headdress round his shoulders and seeming to expect everyone to applaud his entrance', that he came to be treated as a fifth wheel to the carriage.[16]

The Security Council started off with a traditional public debate. On Friday, 5 October, Lloyd and Pineau presented the Western case against Nasser's action. They emphasised such links as there were (and there were not many) between the wording of the concession to the Company and that of the 1888 Convention, which, in the words of its preamble, 'completed the system'. Lloyd said that an inter-governmental regime would have been a novelty in the nineteenth century; a company possessed of an international character served at the time the same purpose. Pineau referred to the fact that the Egyptian government had for a hundred years negotiated with the Suez Canal Company 'as it would have done with a foreign power'. The question of the manner by which the nationalisation deed was done, conducted as if it were a *coup d'état* and presented in Nasser's speech as an act of national retaliation, was relevant because it destroyed all confidence that the whole flow of trade between Europe and Asia would not be endangered by sudden measures taken in a nationalist tantrum.

Pineau went on to defend the military preparations made by Britain and France. 'If we had been acting with aggressive intent we would not have shown the patience we have shown ever since 26 July.' The military precautions could be thanked for the better tone of Nasser's more recent speeches, for the large number of ships that were passing through the Canal without paying tolls to the Egyptians and for the fact that, despite the threats levelled at them, the Company's foreign pilots had been allowed to leave. 'We had to remove the Suez Canal from the atmosphere of passion and violence into which Colonel Nasser's words and acts had plunged it.'

After the weekend, Fawzi gave his reply. He saw the new *entente cordiale* between Britain and France as aiming, as had the original one, to recapture the methods of the nineteenth century 'when time was slumbering and the sky was dark'. The 'system' which the 1888 Convention 'completed' was clearly not the concession to the Company but the previous *firman* of the Turk which had proclaimed unilaterally that there should be free navigation for all. Historically it had been Britain which had always upheld the purely Egyptian character of the Company. Proper compensation had been offered to the shareholders, together with strict adherence to the Convention. Egypt had never refused negotiation, only dictation. 'We were not offered a conference but a trial; we were not invited to a meeting but assigned to a court.'

Then Shepilov set about SCUA. It was a closed body with a limited membership set apart from the scores of other countries using the Suez Canal. It would be difficult to imagine what would remain of freedom of navigation on the Canal if various groups of countries were to start setting up such associations, instituting their own arrangements and acting in any way they saw fit. Could it be that 'the ruling circles' had ready this reply to public demands for a peaceful settlement: 'You have urged us to appeal to the UN. We have done so, but as you see it is powerless. It can do nothing. Other steps must be taken. Egypt is guilty. Crucify it!'? But, Shepilov said, he liked to think the best of Lloyd and Pineau and proposed an updating of the 1888 Convention based on co-operation between Egypt and the users, to be negotiated by a six-nation committee and confirmed by a broad international conference.

After other members of the Council had spoken, Dulles wound up with a short speech on the morning of 9 October which did not disappoint his allies and in which he emphasised, not without, one cannot help feeling, a certain irony, the number of moves by Britain and France that had constituted options for peace. After a short secret session the Council then adjourned while Lloyd and Pineau were launched on four days of private talks with Fawzi in Dag Hammarskjöld's room and in his presence. Fawzi had agreed to this procedure, which might seem less favourable to Egypt than Shepilov's committee, only when Hammarskjöld gave him his personal assurance that he considered Selwyn Lloyd genuinely wanted a peaceful solution. The personal rapport between Hammarskjöld and Fawzi was very marked – and caused a certain reserve towards the Secretary-General among some British officials[17]; that between Hammarskjöld and Lloyd was perhaps more unexpected, since Lloyd did not obviously display those qualities of intellect that Hammarskjöld sought out among his friends. Nevertheless he had cultivated Lloyd's friendship when the latter was Minister of State and they kept up a personal correspondence. He felt he knew Lloyd well enough to certify that he was working for a settlement.

The Six Principles

In the private talks Lloyd conscientiously adhered to Eden's admonitions to keep in line with Pineau. That this was not achieved without pain is apparent from a memorandum that he wrote shortly afterwards. Pineau, he said, 'behaved in a rather extraordinary manner. In the first three days of the private talks he appeared utterly unreasonable. He came late, went early, made difficulties about long meetings and spent considerable time at the beginning of some of the meetings arguing about some obviously false point.'[18] Pineau, to be sure, had a heavy cold while he was in New York. He also had, unknown to his British ally, a personal liaison with Ben-Gurion in the shape of Colonel Yehoshafat Harkabi, the Israeli Chief of Army Intelligence. He met Pineau every morning in his hotel and sent daily reports of the Foreign Ministers' private discussions by special code to Ben-Gurion.[19]

Fawzi said Egypt was quite willing to update the signatories or the content of the Convention and to negotiate agreements setting aside an agreed portion of the revenues for development and fixing the tolls for a number of years. She would recognise a Users' Association which could not, Fawzi said, simply be amalgamated with the Egyptian Board as Pineau had asked. The Egyptians were not prepared to make what Pineau had termed 'an omelette'. But Board and Association could, however, hold combined meetings to discuss the operation of the Canal. What if there was disagreement?, he was asked. There would have to be some procedure, perhaps an arbitration tribunal with one member from each side and an impartial chairman (apparently Krishna Menon had got this out of Nasser at the last minute). How about enforcement? To this there was no reply.

Lloyd asked whether a certain percentage of foreign nationals on secondment to the UN could be involved in the running of the Canal. Fawzi said they would be welcome but they must take orders from the Egyptian Board. He did not think it impossible for SCUA to provide its own pilots, but then the Board's pilot would have to have the last word. Lloyd told Eden that he and Pineau had been extremely guarded, and Fawzi was similarly imprecise about many important aspects. In one highly important matter, over the payment of dues, they may have misunderstood one another. The question was raised of whether dues could be collected by SCUA. Fawzi reports himself as saying that that would be very strange, a remark he no doubt made at one stage of the discussion. But Lloyd's report, without mentioning this, quotes the Egyptian as saying that he did not think there would be any objection to dues for SCUA ships being paid through the Association.[20]

News of this remark excited the interest of the Egypt Committee meeting in London on the morning of 10 October. Here was the chance for which they had been searching to exercise leverage over the Egyptian management of the Canal. If all dues were to be paid into SCUA, then the withholding of payment from SCUA to Egypt could be used as a sanction. The purposes for which the dues might be used, including compensation to the former shareholders, needed to be defined; then Egypt should be handed over her agreed share. In this way she would be prevented from using income received from the Canal for other purposes.[21]

With an eye to future Soviet and Indian membership of SCUA, the Egypt Committee stipulated that a decision to withhold the dues should be taken by majority vote. It also laid down that, while this ability to withhold dues was a sufficient safeguard against minor infractions, sterner measures would be needed in the case of something really serious such as discrimination against the ships of any one country. Ministers did not seem too certain how this was to be achieved but, somehow, Britain must be free under the Charter to take action in such a case. Lloyd was to be told to seek Dulles's help urgently to work something out, possibly on the lines that SCUA was to be considered a regional body with rights of self-defence. Eden's telegram emphasised speed and the importance of clinging to the partnership with Pineau.[22]

That day the private talks were resumed. Fawzi seemed to agree that the operation of the Canal should be insulated from the politics of any one government. He also offered no objection to the idea of SCUA having complete access to the books of the Egyptian Board. Lloyd asked Fawzi a number of questions which, Hammarskjöld thought admiringly, 'put him right against the wall ... [but] in such a way as not to break any bridges'. Fawzi's positive replies made Pineau turn 'greener and greener', especially as he had, not for the first time, exaggerated his grasp of English and had tried to function without an interpreter. Hammarskjöld told Lodge that the real worry was over Fawzi's power to commit the Egyptian Government.[23] Fawzi in his turn made a number of pointed enquiries into what exactly was the current status of SCUA, which much of the Western press was writing off as an empty shell. There was inconclusive talk about the collection and payment of dues, concerning which Selwyn Lloyd, for all his good resolutions about Pineau, did not fail to antagonise his French colleague. In the course of a somewhat sour cable to President Coty, Prime Minister Mollet and the Quai d'Orsay, Pineau attributed to his British colleague the 'very unfortunate proposition' that, 'We could not give up international management without a counterweight which we could present to our public opinion.' Since the Frenchman did not want to give up international management at all, he cabled Chauvel telling him to let Eden know of his anxiety that the British Foreign Secretary was being 'drawn away into unsatisfactory waters'.[24]

The would-be mediators outside the doors were getting restive. Shepilov was reportedly very angry that he was not playing a larger part; the Jugoslav was irritated, while Menon was mortified at being cold-shouldered by both sides. He was firmly told by Fawzi to stop saying authoritatively that various things were Nasser's last word.[25] In London Eden was clearly by now in two minds as to how to proceed. For the next few days, sensing that the chances of a *casus belli* were fast receding, he appeared to warm to the prospects of a compromise settlement.

Lloyd reported an extremely baffling conversation with Pineau, who began as if on a conciliatory tack to say that the Ministers would be able to report to the Security Council that the outcome of the talks had not been entirely negative, since, if there was co-operation between the Egyptian Board and the users over the next few weeks or months, a basis would emerge for a permanent settlement. When Lloyd remarked, 'That means resort to force would be ruled out,' Pineau objected that that was not so at all; once the Security Council discussions were over, Britain and France would reserve their full liberty of action. Lloyd was beginning to be anxious about his French partner. He cabled Eden: 'I doubt whether Pineau really believes that a peaceful settlement is possible and I am not entirely convinced that he wants one.'[26]

The second day's talks were considered the next morning not by the Egypt Committee but by a meeting at Number Ten attended only by Eden, Monckton, Harold Watkinson, the Minister of Transport, and three civil servants. Most of the Conservative leadership had left London for Llandudno, where, since it was the party conference season, the ruling party was displaying its wares.

There was no Foreign Office Minister in Downing Street on 11 October, because Anthony Nutting was quite unexpectedly to make the big speech in the opening debate at Llandudno. It was to be about Suez and Lord Salisbury, who should have spoken in place of Selwyn Lloyd in New York, was ill. The motion made much of the Government's 'resolute policy', of the sanctity of international contracts, the dastardliness of the Opposition in dividing the country, and the Government's devotion to 'a peaceful solution according to the principles of the United Nations Charter'. The mover, a Welshman, set up a contrast between Nasser with his 'act of piracy', as the result of which 'the vast industrial world could collapse', and Sir Anthony Eden, 'the greatest preserver of peace we shall know in our time'.

The task, in that setting an immensely satisfying one, of plunging the knife into Hugh Gaitskell, was left to the seconder, Peter Walker, the voice of Young Conservatism on the party executive. Although not a Welshman, he was a future Secretary of State for Wales. To Walker the attitude of the Opposition 'must surely rank as the most treacherous action of any political party in the history of our country'. When put under pressure, Labour had bowed to 'that group of frustrated journalists and barristers who are always eager to applaud the actions of foreign nations and to decry the actions of their own countrymen'. Peter Walker's advice to Gaitskell was 'to leave public life and enter some sphere of activity where his personal ambition would do less harm to the country'.

Captain Waterhouse and Julian Amery, by a prior arrangement which had had to be tenaciously striven for, thereupon introduced an amendment that replaced bland generalities with a specific requirement for international control of the Canal 'in accordance with the proposals of the London Conference'.

It was to this debate that Nutting replied in a speech which Lord Salisbury had written but which was not attributed to him ('Make no mistake', the Minister of State was heard to say, 'This is to be Nutting's day').[27] The speech, which won rapturous applause for the speaker, was divided between the attack on Nasser ('he has debased the whole currency of international good faith') and the attack on Gaitskell ('How far the Labour Party have moved since August! And how fast they have run!'). The speaker distinguished a domestic act of nationalisation from what Egypt had done, which was 'to remove from the 1888 Convention the international guarantee that was written into it by the recognition, under the Convention, of the Company as the effective operator'. Confronted by this challenge to international law and order, Britain and France had behaved, as Nutting told it, like model UN members, conscientiously seeking a solution under Article 33 of the Charter, first by the London Conference, then by SCUA. Having exhausted these possibilities, the two countries had thought it right and timely to bring the matter before the Security Council where even at that moment Selwyn Lloyd now was striving for peace but peace with justice.

It was a smooth if selective presentation of Britain's case as it was publicly known and it was pungently delivered. But, alas, the Minister lamented, the days of a truly national approach to foreign policy were gone – the days of the Berlin airlift, and of Marshall Aid, the days of Ernest Bevin. After dilating on the change of tone between the Labour leader on 2 August and the same man on 12 September, Nutting firmly declared: 'If, however, unhappily, the UN were to find itself unable, for one reason or another, to do its duty ... this would not absolve us from doing ours. Should that hard test come upon us ... I do believe this country will not flinch from it today any more than it has done in the past.'[28]

This was stirring stuff. Nutting later described his embarrassment when he first saw the speech written in this vein and how he had tried to tone down one or two of its expressions, though Eden in retirement refused to accept the explanation.[29] It must be said that, while it certainly was a partisan presentation which served to identify the speaker emotionally with all that Eden was doing, it was not actually inconsistent with a future opposition in principle to what in the event was done. To all appearances the day was a political triumph for Nutting: Eden's Eden had become the conference's darling.

When the three Ministers and their civil servants met that day at Number Ten the mood was one of hope for the chances of negotiation. True, the Prime Minister chose to emphasise the absence so far of agreement about major sanctions. Monckton and the others gave Egypt credit for accepting the principle of the insulation of the Canal from one nation's politics. SCUA was now being effectively set up; if Fawzi could be relied upon, it looked as if it would, after all, be a virile and effective organisation. Eden cabled Lloyd stressing the importance of making SCUA an effective instrument of financial control. He also injected into the negotiation the highly emotive question of Israeli shipping which had not hitherto figured largely in the negotiation, urging that it be stipulated that, for the purposes of the Suez Convention, the armistice should be deemed to be a state of peace. On the other hand, Lloyd was told that, as agreement now seemed on the way, he should not feel that he needed to shut off negotiations and come home by the end of the week.[30]

Pineau's cold had now reached fever point and his capacity for tiresomeness redoubled. He found fault with Hammarskjöld who had been playing an active and helpful role, preparing notes and papers which, without being minutes, advanced the discussions. Now, on the third day, Pineau queried so much that Hammarskjöld had to withdraw his notes.

Fawzi reported that Hammarskjöld had told him that it seemed that, every time Lloyd was making a tentative step forward, Pineau was hauling him back.[31] In the afternoon, Pineau proposed that Britain and France should submit a list of written questions to Egypt requiring written answers. It turned out that he had not got the list ready. Fawzi objected to questionnaires; he was not, he said, a defendant in the dock. He also protested against Pineau's reversion to the original Eighteen-Power proposals; no agreement was to be reached along that route.

At that point Lloyd articulated the essence of the West's position, in the form of 'Six Principles'. These were: free and open transit without discrimination, overt or covert; respect for the sovereignty of Egypt; insulation from the politics of any one country; dues to be decided between Egypt and the users; a fair proportion of the revenue to go for development; and points at issue between Egypt and the old Canal Company to be settled by arbitration. Fawzi accepted the principles thus expressed, though he seemed to have some scruples over the meaning of the insulation of the Canal from politics. Later the Egyptian submitted a paper about 'recourse', as users' sanctions were now politely termed, but it was clear that more time was required for detailed negotiation. Lloyd was worried about how to 'pin the slippery Egyptian down' and 'deeply disturbed' by Pineau's general attitude.[32]

The agitated faces were more pressing outside the closed doors of the secretariat. Speaking in his capacity as President of the Security Council, Christian Pineau abruptly announced that he was calling the Security Council into public session in the immediate future when France would insist on the Eighteen-Nation Proposal and nothing else. Aware of the Conservative Conference's explicit stand and of his instructions to maintain solidarity with the French, Lloyd accepted that the resolution must include an endorsement of the proposal. That would mean automatically that there would be a Russian veto but a good vote in favour should carry moral force. The Egyptians, on the other hand, who had until now been pleased by Lloyd's attitude, were alarmed at this development. Ahmed Hussein, who was in New York as a member of Fawzi's delegation, told William Rountree, the US Assistant Secretary for Near Eastern Affairs, that they wanted a settlement, wanted to mend their relations with the West, and wanted to avoid a situation in which the Soviet Union would be portrayed as the champion of Egypt.[33]

For Sir Anthony Eden, the concluding rounds of the negotiation coincided with the most partisan occasion in his political calendar: the Leader's address to the Tory 'representatives' after the end of the annual party conference. On the morning of Saturday 13 October, having moved to Llandudno, he received in bed his blunt-spoken Local Government Minister, Duncan Sandys, who, reflecting the views of those who had detected and been dismayed by a softening of the British approach, insisted that there must be no middle ground. Either there must be complete and unqualified agreement by Egypt with the Eighteen-Nation Plan or they must fight. Sandys left the bedroom with the impression that Eden had agreed with him and would telephone Lloyd to that effect before making his big speech. Eden did telephone Lloyd but, after an anxious exchange, authorised him to continue the search for a compromise.[34] Then he rose in an intensely emotional atmosphere, to deliver his address. In it the patriotic notes were struck but in a restrained, at times defensive, fashion. An impression which he was most anxious to erase was that of indifference to the UN Charter. Reminding them that he was one of the UN's founders, he took pains to recall that, whereas the first draft of the Charter had said simply that international disputes must be settled only by peaceful means, the final version had stipulated that the settlement should be 'in conformity with the principles of justice and international law'.

'I know', said Sir Anthony, 'there are some who argue that we should have acted more promptly by striking back the moment Colonel Nasser seized the Canal [*sic*]. I do not agree. By going through every stage which the Charter lays down, we have given an example of restraint and respect for international undertakings.' Were the military precautions excessive? They had already induced a measure of caution in some minds. 'What would anyone in this country have said if we had not taken these precautions? And if there then had been a repetition of the massacre in Cairo in 1952? Better to be safe than sorry.' Britain was showing 'the most absolute restraint', but she would not shift from the principle with which she began, that no arrangement for 'this great international waterway' should leave it in 'the unfettered control of a single Power'.

One happy result of the crisis had been the unity with the French – 'stage by stage we have been in close agreement' – and the increase in the sense of partnership between the nations of Western Europe (though even in this context Anthony Eden could not forbear to add, 'For us in Britain the Commonwealth must always come first.') A graceful tribute to Selwyn Lloyd whose report from New York that morning had seen 'some progress but still wide differences of opinion', and the representatives went away refreshed and reassured that the unresolved crisis could not be in wiser and firmer hands.[35]

Back in New York, Lloyd was not finding partnership with the French at all easy. The unfathomable Frenchman had chosen to put on a new face on the last day of the private talks. Before he had told Harkabi, and hence Ben-Gurion, 'There is no hope for an arrangement. What has to be taken from this is war.' Now his view apparently changed. He told Lloyd that the talks had been most useful and ought to be resumed. 'This', minuted the Foreign Secretary, 'was a *volte face* with a vengeance.'

According to the book he wrote twenty years later, Pineau had decided, in apparent defiance of his instructions from the French Cabinet, to try to make a private deal with Fawzi under which Israeli rights of navigation in the Canal and the Gulf would have been established in return for concessions to Egypt over the handling of dues. He was willing for this to involve his own resignation.[36] If this was, indeed, his process of thought, it could perhaps have explained the mysterious discontinuities of conduct which Selwyn Lloyd noted privately at the time.

'A Crisis Behind Us'

President Eisenhower was now only three and a half weeks from his Election Day. When word came to him that the three Foreign Ministers were agreed over the Six Principles, he reached for the television networks to share the great news with the nation. 'I have an announcement, I have got the best announcement that I could possibly make to America tonight. The progress made in the Suez dispute this afternoon in the United Nations is most gratifying. Egypt, Britain and France have met through their Foreign Ministers and agreed to a set of principles on which to negotiate and it looks like here is a very great crisis that is behind us.'

Next night, Saturday 13 October, when the full Security Council met in public session, the atmosphere was not so ecstatic. Lloyd declared, 'It would be wrong to delude ourselves by supposing that great strides have been made.' What they had got was 'the framework within which to find a basis for negotiation'. The Anglo-French resolution was voted on in two parts. The first, setting out the Six Principles, was adopted unanimously, Fawzi observing with regard to 'insulation from politics', this could best be achieved by rejecting the second part of the resolution.

This second part would have put the weight of the Security Council behind the London proposals and placed on the Egyptian Government the onus of producing promptly its own ideas for a system that would meet the Principles and provide the Canal users with guarantees which were 'not less effective' than the London ones. SCUA would have been acknowledged as 'qualified to receive the dues payable by ships belonging to its members' and 'the competent Egyptian authorities' instructed to co-operate with it. This was defeated by nine votes in favour and two against, including that of one permanent member (the Soviet Union).[37] Talking to Eisenhower over the phone Dulles expressed the belief that, with some minor modifications, the Americans could have got a resolution the whole of which would have gone through but that the British and French could not live politically with anything that the Soviet Union would approve.[38]

Lloyd cabled London the credits and debits of the week. He thought the results were better than expected before coming to New York. The UN atmosphere toward Britain and France had changed much for the better and the suspicion that they were using the UN simply as a formality had been dissipated. With the changed atmosphere, he assured Eden, they ought to be able to count on a more understanding reaction if they became obliged to take extreme measures. Lloyd's exasperation with his French colleague came across when he said that, but for Pineau's earlier attitude, 'I believe that we might have got agreement by Friday [12 October] on a basis for negotiation.' He congratulated himself on emerging from the week without any resolution enjoining Britain and France against the use of force or one setting up a negotiating committee. On the debit side it might be said that they were committed to further talks with the Egyptians without a time limit so that the Egyptians might think that, since they were no longer in danger of armed attack, 'they have therefore won'. Lloyd wondered whether 'the Secretary-General may have been given too prominent a role' but, then, 'if only in virtue of his office he is as keen on internationalisation as anybody'.[39]

Eden, who was at Chequers for the weekend after the party conference with two crucially important French guests, cabled back that the French and British should ask the Egyptians to ignore the veto and come to Geneva to wind up the talks as if it had never been cast. 'If they say no . . . a new situation will arise.'[40] The tone of these exchanges was still that of Ministers engaged in a reasonably hopeful negotiation.

Over the weekend Pineau was making his freelance effort with Fawzi and Hammarskjöld. He wanted the Egyptians to accept formally that the use of the term 'without discrimination' in the first of the Six Principles included Israeli shipping. Despite several references to Nasser on the telephone, Fawzi failed to obtain the necessary instructions. Pineau returned to Paris and immediately offered to resign on account of his unauthorised attempt. Mollet refused: 'We will leave together or we will stay together

... Don't forget, you are in the Quai d'Orsay to make Europe, only incidentally to regulate the problem of the Suez Canal.'[41]

Selwyn Lloyd had one more disagreeable duty to perform before coming home. Until the last stage his relations with Dulles had been friendly enough, although he had spoken sharply to him about Eisenhower's premature celebration of peace.[42] The important clash between them came at the end over SCUA and caused a profound loss of confidence in American leadership.

Throughout the SCUA conference and the subsequent negotiations at the UN, Britain had looked on the ability of the Association to raise and control the revenue from the Canal as the counter to Egypt's physical possession of the Canal itself. Originally Dulles seemed to hold that view. 'The users would run the Canal themselves', he had said on 4 September. 'Nasser would thus see the money slipping out of his hands.'[43] Then just after midnight on Sunday, 14 October, following the Saturday debate in the Security Council, Dulles and Lloyd had an unwitnessed and unminuted conversation, in the course of which Lloyd was flabbergasted to hear that Dulles had in mind that something around ninety per cent of the dues collected by SCUA would then be made over to the Egyptian Canal Authority. This would very much increase Nasser's existing income from the Canal.'I cannot believe', he wrote immediately afterwards, 'that it is what you really intend.'[44]

The two men wrote long formal letters that crossed each other on the day after this traumatic encounter. Dulles produced ample quotations that were supposed to indicate that the British should have been quite clear what he had in mind. They did document that Dulles was offering the Egyptians practical co-operation pending an agreement and indicating that they would be paid for it, but there had been no mention of a figure of ninety per cent. This seems to have slipped out in Dulles's conversation. It seems an extraordinary indiscretion – perhaps tired leaders should not be allowed out to meet unchaperoned at the end of an exhausting day – and still strange that he did not see to it that the formal reply to the British note was not more openly reassuring. As it was, an analysis of the text that was made by British officials suggested to them that there was nothing amiss that could not be handled in detailed (and lengthy) talks during which dues could be withheld, but among Ministers the damage was done, the percentage figure had lodged in the mind, and Selwyn Lloyd had been rendered psychologically less equipped to cope with the severe test to which he was to be put immediately on his return to London. 'I have done my utmost', he wrote to the American Secretary of State, 'to prevent exaggeration of our differences of approach to the Suez Canal problem in recent weeks ... But we must face the fact that revelation of so grave a divergence between us on the purposes of SCUA would have serious repercussions in Britain.'[45]

16

Two Frenchmen at Chequers

I will not allow you to plunge this country into war merely to satisfy the anti-Jewish spleen of you people in the Foreign Office.
Sir Anthony Eden to Anthony Nutting, 13 October 1956.

Perhaps that was a real night – perhaps a night of dreams.
In the dream: steel, much steel, new steel,
Bearing long tubes, thundering on steel chains,
Arriving from afar, mounting the beach and – all fantastic – becoming all real.
And on its first contact with the soil becoming Jewish power.
Nathan Alterman, quoted in the Knesset by David Ben-Gurion, 15 October 1956.

Relations between Britain and Israel at the beginning of October were to all appearances at their very worst, although during that very time – on 3 October – Sir Anthony Eden observed cryptically to his colleagues that: 'The Jews have come up with an offer.'[1] While the UN Security Council debated or staged private talks over Suez, the crisis around Israel's borders seemed to be heading for an explosion. It was a crisis that threatened to pit Britain as the ally of Jordan and Iraq against France as the ally of Israel. 'If we do get involved with hostilities against Israel, owing for instance to their performing some *limited* act of aggression against Jordan,' Gladwyn Jebb wrote to Anthony Nutting from Paris on 2 October, 'the situation here is likely to get pretty ticklish.'

The following day the Ambassador followed this up in a long letter to the Permanent Under-Secretary. Britain was encouraging the Iraqis to send troops into Jordan (admittedly to hold the line against Nasser) and promising that, if the Israelis were to react to this by aggression, 'we should immediately declare war on Israel and notably proceed to bomb Israeli bases from the air'. Predictably from a professional diplomat, the next sentence read: 'I am not of course saying this decision was wrong.' But the French, with their troops in Cyprus from which the bombing raids on Israel would start, might surely be asked for their view. 'Apart from anything else, they would rightly come to the conclusion that we could hardly be at war with the Israelis and in a position to impose our will on Colonel Nasser at one and the same time.'[2]

Since Husan on 25/26 September, there had been a period of calm on the Jordanian border until the afternoon of 4 October when, in broad daylight, two vehicles on the S'dom–Beersheva road were ambushed by a party of Arabs well dug in in prepared positions some nine miles from the Jordanian border. There was no immediate reprisal; the Israelis were deliberately trying to hold off until the Security Council session should indicate to Ben-Gurion whether or not Britain and France were going to war with Egypt. Peter Westlake, who was British Chargé d'Affaires in Tel Aviv, was attempting to prepare the ground with the Israelis for an Iraqi move into Jordan to add strength to the King during that country's election. On 27 September he reported that Golda Meir was in 'a very unreceptive mood'. The reason, he thought, was that the policy of using reprisals as a deterrent was clearly not being very effective.

The Israelis were also working themselves up over two manifestations of British policy to which they took particular exception: the anti-reprisal briefings by the Foreign Office News Department and the news output of *Sharq al-Adna* in Cyprus.[3] On 27 September the Israeli Ambassador in Paris, Jacob Tsur, told the Quai d'Orsay that relations between Israel and the British Government had never been so bad. Britain was trying to distract the attention of the Arab world from the Suez affair by inciting Iraq to send troops to Jordan and to supplant Egypt as the champion of the Arab cause against Israel.[4]

On 3 October Dulles had some good news for the British. Abba Eban, the Israeli Ambassador, had just brought him word from Ben-Gurion that Israel would not react sharply to Iraqi troops entering Jordan, on four conditions: that the Israelis were given good advance warning; that no heavy equipment moved in; that no unreasonably large numbers were involved; and that the Iraqis stayed on the east bank of the Jordan. The conditions did not seem onerous; the news was most welcome in Whitehall. The object should be, wrote the Assistant Under-Secretary responsible, Archibald Ross, to urge Nuri to move into Jordan without delay. Now was the time to bring in Paris. 'We want to consult the French', said Ross, 'if possible in such a way as to show that it was always our intention to do so and without revealing that we have already been in touch with the Americans. All we want of the French is that they should make no difficulties . . .'[5]

This, to judge from Ben-Gurion's diary, was to ask too much. On 9 October he records a conversation between an Israeli Foreign Ministry official and a French diplomat. The French were said to be worried by Iraq's entry into Jordan. 'They fear that the English want to conquer Jordan [and] Syria with the help of the Iraqis. They do not trust the British partnership. They expressed their astonishment that we would let the Iraqis enter.'

The issue was complicated by the appearance in *The Times* of 7 October of an interview with Nuri es-Said in which he repeated in public his frequent line that Israel's existence should be recognised but with frontiers based on the 1947 partition plan. The Foreign Office News Department promptly came out with a welcome for Nuri's initiative, as a break in the circle of non-recognition. Mrs Meir was beside herself. She demanded to know what was the relationship between the proposed Iraqi troop movements and these plans to truncate the State of Israel. Were the British dreaming old dreams, she demanded of the American Ambassador, of the merger of Iraq, Jordan and Syria? The Israeli Government's 'conditional acquiescence' in the Iraqi move was withdrawn, under circumstances that immediately prompted Whitehall suspicion of what officials termed 'collusion' between French and Israelis against Britain. In the Foreign Office the Levant Department speculated as to whether Pineau was playing a different game from his officials and little thought how soon the same could be said of them.[6]

Israeli forbearance on the Jordanian front was coming to an end. On 9 October, two Israeli farm labourers were murdered in an orange grove in the narrow waist of the country between Tel Aviv and Haifa and their ears were cut off. The next day Ben-Gurion issued a statement accusing King Hussein personally of releasing men under arrest in Jordan for previous murders of Israeli Druzes. That night (10/11 October) an unusually large-scale reprisal raid was undertaken against the police fort outside the Jordanian town of Qalqilya. Unlike previous attacks it was preceded by an artillery bombardment with Israeli planes flying over the scene and all the appearance of a major military initiative. It was the more so in that it did not go off entirely as planned. The unit sent to set up ambushes from Arab Legion reinforcements ran into severe trouble and was only, at the cost of major casualties and intense effort, extricated back across the border by daylight.[7] The casualties and the mishandling were not taken at all well by the Israeli public; the policy of reprisals would have to be completely rethought.

In the middle of the night King Hussein called for assistance from the RAF bases in Jordan under the Anglo-Jordanian alliance. At 4.15 a.m. on 11 October, immediately he became aware of this, the British Consul-General in Jerusalem telephoned the Israeli Governor of the city and told him that, if the Israeli attack was not called off immediately, there was grave danger of Britain and Israel finding themselves at war. This personal initiative was warmly commended by Eden,[8] and it had its impact on Ben-Gurion's thinking.

Later in the morning, the King sent for the British Ambassador, said that it looked as if a major Israeli attack was imminent and asked for all British help possible, including the immediate strengthening of the RAF in the country. On 12 October the Foreign Office cabled Amman that flights of Hunter aircraft were being quickly organised between Cyprus and Jordan as a public show of strength and commitment. It was not possible, it was explained, to base them permanently in Jordan so long as there was the quarrel with Egypt.[9] King Hussein had also cabled his cousin King Faisal and asked him to send a division immediately.

On the same day the British Embassy notified the Israelis that units of the Iraqi army were about to enter Jordan and would be stationed there for an indefinite period. Mrs Meir did not receive the news well. The assurances offered were not nearly specific enough; the entry of Iraqi troops was part of a scheme to support Iraq's expansionist drive to the Mediterranean; it amounted to a direct threat to the territorial integrity of Israel which the Government of Israel, in fulfilment of its obligation to its people, was determined to meet. Westlake made clear that any military move by Israel to counter the entry of the Iraqis would activate the Anglo-Jordanian alliance. This Mrs Meir described as an ultimatum. Did that mean that the RAF would in these circumstances bomb Israeli territory? Westlake replied, 'Yes.'[10] Meanwhile in London Eliahu Elath, the Israeli Ambassador, was lamenting to Sir Ivone Kirkpatrick about how bad Anglo-Israeli relations had become.[11]

The impact of the two crises now began to be felt on each other. Sir Charles Duke in Amman questioned Whitehall's judgment that the pattern of Israel's reprisal raids was inconsistent with the idea of an all-out attack. He recommended that Britain state publicly that Israel's deliberately organised and large-scale military operations against Jordan amounted to an act of war, which, if repeated, would cause Britain to feel bound to intervene. Britain would need to be prepared to strike swiftly and effectively the moment another such attack occurred. Otherwise no explanations would serve to save her reputation in Jordan or in the Middle East.[12]

The answer came back swiftly and hard on Sunday, 14 October, the day Anthony Eden was entertaining two special French guests at Chequers. 'It is manifestly not in our interest and not in Jordan's interest to treat raids as an act of war and intervene. The situation is that Jordan by an act of her own volition has dismissed Glubb, diminished the efficiency of the Arab Legion and expressed a wish to dispense with British assistance on land. There is no prospect of any help from Egypt. In consequence, Israel can at any moment destroy the Jordan army and occupy the country.' The Jordanians seemed to think they could rely on the RAF to win the land battle; that was a lethal illusion and it was no use hankering after a policy based on an illusion. Even air support on the largest scale and delivered at once together with naval measures could not possibly of itself halt the Israeli army and save Jordan if full-scale war broke out. If Britain treated a raid as war and deployed the RAF against Israel, the consequence would be Israeli air attacks on the airfields in Cyprus and Jordan, 'which would be highly inconvenient at the present juncture', and the occupation of Jordan.[13]

King Hussein was given renewed assurances at this time that Britain would fulfil her obligations but his precise questions were not answered. Rather understandably, though a little late, Kirkpatrick wrote a memo asking whether the value of the Jordan treaty was so great 'that it justifies us in getting into these difficulties'. All the British would be able to do for Jordan in the case of Israeli aggression, the Chiefs of Staff Committee noted, was 'to inflict such losses on the Israeli air force that Israel would stop the war before they reached a state of serious inferiority to the Arab states'. Also the British at Aqaba would immediately occupy Eilat.[14]

The Chief of the Imperial General Staff took a firm line on 10 October. General Templer said that it should be brought home 'very forcibly' to Ministers that 'we could either go to the aid of Jordan against Israel with sea and air power or we could launch *Musketeer*; we could not do both'. He thought *Musketeer* served as a deterrent to the Israelis, which was another reason for keeping it in readiness, but once it was launched, 'Israel would be certain to take advantage of the situation' and Britain would not be able to do a thing about it. Marshal of the RAF Dickson, the chairman of the Chiefs of Staff Committee, had already pointed out that Israel 'had the capacity seriously to interfere with our *Musketeer* operation'; hence any fresh assurances made to Jordan that 'we would honour our Treaty obligations' should not go into any details, particularly as to timing.

It was left to Mountbatten to bring up another danger: the United States might not play a passive role. 'If, during *Musketeer*, Israel attacked Jordan and the US went to Jordan's aid against Israel, then we and the US would be fighting on opposite sides. We should be the unwilling allies of Israel and our forces in Jordan would be hostages to fortune.'[15]

The French, as can be imagined, were highly concerned at these complications. They repeatedly warned the British that the Israelis were in a dangerous mood. Any time they might fly off the handle. The results would be extremely grave. Gladwyn Jebb was urged by Albert Gazier, the French Minister for Social Affairs, who was in charge of the Quai d'Orsay while Pineau was in New York, that Britain should screw four more assurances out of Nuri. He should be made to say that Iraqi troops in Jordan would be very few, that they would not be well armed, that they would not come very far and, most important of all, that they should go away quickly. Gazier seemed deeply worried that the Israelis could not be stopped from occupying the West Bank. He sent for Jebb both on the Friday (12 October) and on the Saturday.[16] Also on the Saturday, Mollet telephoned to ask Eden to receive Gazier at once with a very special message from himself. It was arranged for him to have lunch at Chequers on the Sunday.

There was considerable speculation as to what the French had in mind. Jebb had picked up information in Paris that they were stacking up the numbers of Mystères IV in Israel (which was true though the number his informant supplied, seventy-five fresh planes, was an exaggeration). An early Israeli attack seemed likely, but against whom? Nutting and Eden discussed over the telephone whether the victim might be Jordan. Nutting suggested that it had perhaps been a mistake to hold Nuri back; he should be told to move his troops in quickly as a deterrent. In his book, Nutting recalls that this aroused Eden's wrath and the conversation ended with the Prime Minister shouting: 'I will not allow you to plunge this country into war merely to satisfy the anti-Jewish spleen of you people in the Foreign Office.'[17]

The visitors flew in on the Sunday (14 October) morning by military plane. They consisted of Gazier and a companion who was introduced as 'M. Challe of the Prime Minister's personal staff'. The French Ambassador's instructions were to greet them on arrival, but not to accompany them to Chequers. Gazier explained to Chauvel that, since his mission was to complain to Eden about the attitude taken in New York by his Foreign Secretary, the Ambassador's presence was considered unsuitable. Only later Chauvel was told by a junior attaché that he had recognised in the second visitor General Maurice Challe of the General Staff.[18] Jebb, although in London, was not invited either. The practice had begun, of excluding key figures from the civil service.

At Chequers with Eden and Nutting, Gazier immediately launched into a discussion of the problem of Iraqis going into Jordan. The French were in close touch with the Israelis and knew what a highly nervous state they were in. Eden agreed at once to a temporary postponement while the extra undertakings were obtained from Nuri,[19] whereupon Gazier asked what Britain would do if Israel attacked Egypt. Eden, at first, gave the standard answer about consultations under the Tripartite Declaration but, when pressed, conceded that he could not see himself fighting to save Nasser. Gazier argued that, since the Egyptians had said that, not being a party to the Declaration, they did not recognise it, Britain and France were under no obligation. (This, although it was, henceforth, adopted by the British as a part of their case, was an exceptionally weak argument. Apart from the fact that the Israelis had in the past taken up exactly the same position towards the Declaration as the Egyptians, the Declaration was by its very nature a unilateral commitment which did not call for any recognition from the Middle Eastern states.)

At this point Challe was called on by Gazier to outline an additional option of his own. Under this new French proposal, the Israelis should be encouraged to attack Egypt. The general, with the zeal of a new convert, had enthusiastic words in which to describe their capacity to occupy at top speed the whole of Sinai up to the line of the Canal. Britain and France should thereupon order both sides to draw their forces back from the Canal to save it from war damage. They should then send in a police force 'to separate the combatants', which should occupy the complete length of the

Canal from Port Said to Suez. (Challe spoke of a simultaneous seaborne landing at Port Said and paratroop drops at other key points such as Ismailia.) In this way the two western powers would find themselves in control of the whole operation of the Canal; they would thus be able to install international management and break the blockade of Israel.

In his book Nutting writes that the Frenchmen avoided saying whether the Israelis had agreed to this scheme, but the indication was that preliminary soundings had been made. It is possible, though not likely, that something had been said to them in Paris, but Ben-Gurion was certainly not informed until two days later and the idea was then served up to him as a British plan.

Sir Anthony Eden was struck with the novelty and daring of the new scheme. Although formally non-committal – he said it would be studied and that Nutting would come over to give Mollet his answer on the Tuesday (16 October) – he left both Nutting and the two Frenchmen with the impression that he was a convert. In fact, Challe said on his return to General Paul Ely, the French Chief of the General Staff, that he was rather taken aback to discover from Eden's reaction that the British had apparently not thought of the idea before. 'If M. Gazier had not been present and if he had not gathered the same impression, I should have wondered if M. Eden were not making fun of me.'[20]

Still, Eden did not commit himself to anything on the spot. Nutting was instructed to discuss the idea with only two civil servants, Sir Ivone Kirkpatrick and Archibald Ross. Knowledge of it was to be kept very much in a tight inner circle. The security was even tighter in France. Planning centred on Bourgès-Maunoury and his sharp, young political advisers in the Ministry of Defence, Abel Thomas and Louis Mangin. The Quai d'Orsay, except for its Minister, was, as had become usual, cut out of the circuit. Nutting had been told to put Nuri on hold. 'For your own very secret information', he cabled Sir Michael Wright in Baghdad, 'there are reasons which cannot be divulged but which make it essential that [the Iraqi] move [over the frontier] should not take place for forty-eight hours ... You may tell Nuri for his own information that the Prime Minister personally attaches great importance to this.'[21]

The Poetry of Weapons of War

On Monday, 15 October Ben-Gurion spoke to the Knesset. The first third of his speech was a re-formulation of his case against Menachem Begin's openly advocated policy of preventive war. After speaking of his deep grief at the losses of 1948, he said: 'In place of war, whose sacrifices are certain and whose historic advantage is doubtful, we said: "Let us make an effort to strengthen the Israel defence forces with defensive arms."' Although not yet fully satisfied, they had acted according to 'the imperative command of our human and political conscience'.

France and Canada were thanked for supplying jet planes whereas Britain (who had sold heavy tanks to the Egyptian dictator although she knew they were to be used against Israel) was rebuked for stubbornly refusing to sell them to Israel. Ben-Gurion then recited to the Knesset the whole of a very long poem by Nathan Alterman in praise of the hitherto secret arrival of the new weapons, streaming in from France at night, linking them with the great days of ancient Hebrew history. 'In my poor prose', the Prime Minister added, 'I can only say that a considerable change for the better has occurred in the strength of the IDF.'

He reviewed the history of the *fedayeen* and then waded into Britain. The plot that was hatched either in the Guildhall or in Baghdad for the purpose of tearing up Israel could never be carried out. Britain forgot to invite Israel to the London Conference on Suez, but after all the Israeli Government was not moved very much by the change in the Canal's ownership. Ben-Gurion went on to complain about the Alpha plan, though not by name and though he continued to attribute it exclusively to Britain, before declaring that the entry of the military forces of a hostile state (Iraq) even into eastern Jordan would violate the *status quo*. 'The Government of Israel will reserve its freedom of action.'[22]

In the ensuing debate the most significant speech came from Israel Galili, who before independence had been head of the Haganah High Command and now sat in the Knesset for Achdut Ha'avoda. Galili doubted that peace could be maintained. 'Eilat is our Suez,' he said and no one was going to blast the way open through the Straits for Israel if she did not do it for herself. The General Zionists who had tended to flirt with the Herut warmongers earlier in the year agreed this time with the Government in not undertaking military adventures during the Suez crisis. Only Begin and his supporters argued that 'this is our last chance to act'.

On 17 October Ben-Gurion was told for the first time about the Challe 'scenario' and hit the roof, all the more because the French apparently left the impression on his representative, Joseph Nachmias, that it originated not with the French general but with the British. The Israelis had known that Challe and Gazier were going to see Eden with a series of options: tripartite attack, British attack, Franco-Israeli attack based on Cyprus, Franco-Israeli attack based on Israel. Now they were told that these had all been rejected, the last one because 'if France were to go to war without England it would bring down Eden's fall'. But, Ben-Gurion wrote in his diary, 'The English propose that we should start on our own, they will protest, and when we reach the Canal they will come in as if to separate and then they'll destroy Nasser.'[23]

Ben-Gurion always subsequently referred to 'the British' or 'the English plan' (which it was only in the sense that it was invented to overcome

British inhibitions). Shimon Peres has described the volcanic nature of the 'old man's' spontaneous reaction to it, seeing in it only 'the best of British hypocrisy'. It reflected, Ben-Gurion thought, 'the British desire to harm Israel more than their resolve to destroy the Egyptian dictatorship'. His suspicion of the British was intense. He wrote in his diary on 17 October: 'The English plot, I imagine, is to get us involved with Nasser and bring about the occupation of Jordan by Iraq.'[24]

Nevertheless the cable from Paris included an invitation to Ben-Gurion to come secretly to Paris to examine the options. If necessary a British Cabinet Minister would also be asked. He did not wish to refuse this totally and sent a reply saying that 'the British proposal' was unacceptable but if, knowing that, Mollet still wanted him he would come after the usual Sunday Cabinet meeting on 21 October from which he did not wish to be absent. Already Moshe Dayan had begun working on him with the alchemy of his capacity for lateral thinking. Why not, he asked, use the occasion for making a political agreement with the British about the Middle East? Nasser should be destroyed and Jordan disappear, Israel would take the West Bank, Iraq the East; and Iraq, an underpopulated oil state, could well absorb the Palestinian refugees. 'The enormous difficulty,' reflected Ben-Gurion, 'even if we thought that England would consent (and it is hard even to think about it), is what to do with all the Arab population' of the West Bank.[25] But he did not discard the idea on that account.

Golda Meir struck Nicholls on 18 October as being 'tired and emotional'. He 'found it difficult to deal with one grievance before she passed on to another'. The whole Iraq project seemed to Mrs Meir to be so provocative and so dangerous that she found it very hard to take it at face value. Nuri's peace plan and Britain's prompt endorsement of it all pointed to an attempt to impose an unacceptable peace.[26]

On the other side of the border, King Hussein was saying that the troop movements and violent statements of the Israelis could not be regarded as bluff; they must be preparing for a major attack on Jordan. The Chief of Staff, Ali Abu Nuwar, was arguing that, by the ground rules held to distinguish an incident from a war, Qalqilya should have qualified as war because the Israelis had used weapons such as aircraft which the Jordanians did not possess. In future the RAF commander in Jordan should be given prior authority to intervene if the situation recurred. Otherwise, he asked, what was the use of having the British air bases? This was precisely the question that the British hoped that the Jordanians would never ask.[27]

The UN chief, General Burns, was driven by the prevailing atmosphere to make a practical suggestion to the British which they found too embarrassing to adopt. He thought that the Jordan Government should be advised to issue a public statement in advance that people in areas attacked by Israel must not try to get away but should stay to offer passive resistance.

In this way the Israelis would know in advance that there was not going to be another 'miracle'.[28]

In Washington the CIA representative was telling the National Security Council that Nasser had advised Jordan not to become embroiled with Israel. So long as the Suez crisis was preoccupying Egypt, there was little likelihood of Arab-Israeli trouble. Dulles was not so sure, now that Israel might well take advantage of the Suez opportunity to seize the West Bank. Eisenhower suggested that Nasser might want to unite the Arab world by provoking Israel. Dulles said, No, Nasser would not run that risk at the present time. The view of the Joint Chiefs of Staff, expressed by Admiral Radford, was that the Jordanian army was in an extremely exposed position, being concentrated in a small area of west Jordan and offering to the Israelis a tremendous temptation to surround it and wipe it out in a single, swift operation.[29]

America's window on the Middle East was at this moment being provided by the new U-2 high altitude reconnaissance aircraft, flown by civilian pilots including Francis Gary Powers, which were intended for intelligence use over the Soviet Union. It was only in 1960 when Powers was shot down by the Russians, causing a Khrushchev explosion, that the existence of this remarkable plane became public knowledge. Now an ultra-secret project, the plane, representing a technological breakthrough, was tightly controlled on Eisenhower's insistence by a small civilian group meeting at the White House in whose proceedings the President took a personal interest and often a direct involvement. The U-2 was ready for action in May 1956 but the President was, for the time being, banning flights over Russia. On 27 September Powers and his fellow-pilots were ordered to fly over the Eastern Mediterranean and map Egypt, Israel, Jordan, Saudi Arabia and Cyprus. The photographs were considered to be of very high definition: with pardonable exaggeration it was said that the U-2 could pick out 'every blade of grass'.[30]

It is fascinating to note how much and how little the Americans knew, equipped with this very special eye. Before it was known that the U-2 was used during the Suez conflict, America used to be described as if blundering about in an intelligence fog. Since the use of the U-2 has been known, the assumption has been that Washington must have known everything. That was not so, either, as events were to show. But on 15 October Eisenhower noted in his diary that pictures from the U-2 clearly showed that Israel had acquired sixty Mystère pursuit planes when she was supposed to possess only twenty-four. The Israeli jets seemed, Eisenhower remarked wrily, 'to have a rabbitlike capacity for multiplication'.[31]

The President told Dulles to speak very sternly with Eban; he was to be told that the Israelis must stop these 'savage blows'. Otherwise, if there were to be a UN resolution condemning Israel, Russia would be able to bring in considerable forces under the guise of carrying out the UN mandate.

She would end up by Sovietizing the whole region, including Israel. Dulles was instructed to see that Ben-Gurion did not 'make any grave mistakes based upon his belief that winning a domestic election is as important to us as preserving and protecting the interests of the United Nations'. Even if Israel got an immediate advantage by aggression, the President said, she could not in the long term fail to bring catastrophe on herself, 'and such friends as she would have left in the world, no matter how powerful, could not do anything about it'.[32]

Following Qalqilya there was a period of calm on the Jordanian border, a fact which the Israelis naturally saw as proving that the Jordanians were capable of keeping the armistice line quiet when they wanted to. Immediate attention was diverted to the Egyptian border. On 14 October, just before Ben-Gurion's Knesset speech, four Egyptian *fedayeen* were encountered by the security forces very near to the Prime Minister's desert *kibbutz* at Sde Boqer. Two were killed and the others captured. Ben-Gurion referred to this 'ominous' incident in the course of his speech, using it to bolster his assertion that Israel's greatest danger remained that of an attack from Egypt.[33]

Building Up a Scenario

The British Foreign Secretary had been told to take his time in New York; he was now urged by Eden, full of fresh thoughts from the French, to come home at once. Lloyd preferred not to cancel some important appointments and did not return until the morning of Tuesday, 16 October.[34] In the meantime, Nutting, with the two Foreign Office officials whom he was allowed to consult, was assembling a formidable brief listing multiple objections to the proposed policy. Practically everything, it would seem, was wrong with it. The promising signs of Selwyn Lloyd's diplomacy in New York would be thrust aside, the many-times-reaffirmed Tripartite Declaration ignored. America would be against it, the UN would condemn it, the Commonwealth be divided, the stability and perhaps survival of all the pro-Western regimes in the Middle East put into peril, and the security of British and French oil installations and oil deliveries at once endangered. All this was at the behest of a French scheme designed to protect French interests in Algeria, without for a moment taking Britain's multiform Middle Eastern interests into account.[35]

It was the summation of Foreign Office wisdom and Nutting deployed it eloquently at an unminuted ministerial meeting at Number Ten on the Tuesday morning. Eden, who knew the Foreign Office as well as anybody, had decided in advance to reject it. For him, *gouverner, c'est choisir*. Foreign Office formulations, cleverly though they were argued, in fact led nowhere. One must not dither any longer.

At this point, after the meeting had started, Selwyn Lloyd arrived back. His initial reaction to the French plan was hostile. 'I thought that the idea of our inviting Israel to attack Egypt was a poor one,' he later wrote in his book.[36] But he was also, no doubt, still choking with indignation about Eisenhower, Dulles and the Canal dues. Over lunch he was, with however many reservations, enlisted by the Prime Minister, who had decided that they both should go back to Paris at once with the British answer, instead of sending Nutting, as had originally been planned.

Once in Paris they conferred with Mollet and Pineau without officials and dined together alone. 'It is, I believe, a novel arrangement for diplomatic business of the highest importance to be conducted by the principals without any official being present,' protested Jebb afterwards, who was much put out. Eden told Lloyd to say firmly to the Ambassador that he will have read the telegrams. 'Beyond this, by arrangement with the French, there is nothing we can say. We are sorry ... In fact, in the war it often happened that we had talks with no officials present ... in Washington, London and Moscow.'[37] Eden was now dealing with great affairs at the level at which he felt himself uniquely qualified. The words 'in the war' often passed his lips in the weeks to come.

However, Lloyd wrote down an account two days later. (There was no other official record.) Sir Anthony Nutting, who read it thirty years afterwards, describes it as 'a shocking attempt to mislead future historians'.[38] At any rate, it represented Lloyd's assessment of how Eden intended the meeting and the plan to be eventually explained. Nutting, who was not present at Paris, says that he demanded to be briefed by the Foreign Secretary on his return. 'Under cross-examination', Nutting says, Lloyd agreed that from the outset Eden had confirmed his complete acceptance of the whole French scheme, including co-ordinated pre-arrangements with the Israelis. The French said that the Israelis would be coming to Paris and asked for senior British representation at a tripartite conference. Lloyd said that he was still attempting to resist this but did not sound confident that he would succeed.

'I have seldom seen', Nutting has written, 'a man more confused and unhappy than Lloyd was on that occasion.' Nutting told his chief that he would resign if the plan went through.[39]

Lloyd's more circumspect record starts with the Foreign Secretary, plausibly enough, arguing the possibility of some sort of agreement on the lines discussed with Hammarskjöld and Fawzi. Both Mollet and Pineau reject the idea. They then look into the question of Dulles's behaviour over SCUA. The French Ministers say they feel that they have been double-crossed. SCUA was brought forward as a means of putting pressure on Nasser. Once Dulles achieved his purpose of preventing Britain and France going to the Security Council, he gave up any attempt to make it an effective instrument. The four men decide to bring home to Dulles with the utmost vigour this reproach of breach of faith in the hope of changing his attitude.

The French then ask what actions are to be expected from Israel and how Britain will react to them. (Lloyd makes the conversation read like a virtual rerun of Eden's exchange with Gazier at Chequers.) Britain will fight for Jordan and will not fight for Egypt. Between them the French and British leaders decide that their public opinions would regard a government that proposed fighting against Israel on account of Nasser as having taken leave of its senses. What is to happen in the UN if Israel attacks? ask the French. Lloyd says that, after repeated threats by the Egyptians to exterminate the Israelis and the State of Israel, it will be very difficult for Britain to brand Israel as an aggressor.

The likely course of a war between Israel and Egypt is looked at. It is agreed that the Egyptian force in Sinai will be rapidly destroyed. Eden says that the Israelis will probably not stop at the Canal but will try to seize bridgeheads on the other side. That will present Britain with a serious problem because she has many millions of pounds' worth of ships and cargoes in the Canal at any one time. With that thought in mind, they go on to take a look at the American constitution, in the light of Dulles's frequent statements that nothing can be done by the American forces without congressional authority. 'It was agreed', says Lloyd's record, 'that, if Israel were to act before the end of the American election campaign, it was most improbable that Congress could be re-summoned or, if re-summoned, would give this authority.' Afterwards Bourgès-Maunoury told the Americans that Britain was the 'prime mover' in the choice of an eve-of-election date for the operation.

It becomes extremely important to know who had access to how much information in the ensuing days. Even now one cannot be quite certain. But it seems unlikely that, for example, the Chiefs of Staff or General Keightley were told in a direct way that action against Egypt was being co-ordinated with the Israelis. It seems that they were given information in line with the Lloyd version of what happened in Paris on 16 October. Others below the rank of Chiefs of Staff or allied Commander-in-Chief were not to be 'in the know' including, supposedly, the Vice-Chiefs of Staff and the Task Force Commanders, though not, apparently, Iverach McDonald, the Foreign Editor of *The Times* whom Eden personally briefed in extraordinary detail. The Prime Minister was right in assuming that 'the gentleman from *The Times*' could keep a secret, but he turned out to be quite wrong in supposing that this signal mark of confidence would oblige the paper to support his actions. Sir William Haley, the Editor who rushed back from leave, was repelled by what he was told and prepared himself to keep his distance.[41]

The British Ministers had said in Paris that, after conferring with their senior colleagues, they would send early confirmation of their answers to two questions that the French had formally put to them. There were whether, in the event of hostilities in the neighbourhood of the Canal,

Britain would join France in calling on the belligerents to halt and withdraw from the immediate vicinity, intervening forcefully if one or both parties refused; and whether, in the event of hostilities between Israel and Egypt, Britain would agree not to come to the assistance of Egypt under the Tripartite Declaration.[42]

Such confirmation was speedily forthcoming (no meeting of Ministers at which it was given being minuted); the British declarations after being sent to the French were conveyed by Pineau to Ben-Gurion's defence representative, Nachmias, for forwarding to Ben-Gurion. Selwyn Lloyd's mind, said Pineau, was not easy about either declaration, but Eden's opinion had been decisive. With the British all options had been rejected except one – an Israeli attack, with French and British guarantees. The Americans would be angry, Pineau said, but if the Israelis went before Election Day (6 November) no action would follow.[43]

The outline of the Suez affair was becoming clearer. On 18 October Eden at last provided himself with a Minister of Defence who believed in what he was doing and had the energy to set about it. This was Antony Head, a former brigadier, who as War Minister had been actively involved from the start in the war preparations. Eden, astonishingly, had kept the unwilling Monckton in office long after he had indicated that he had neither the health nor the conviction for the task, and he persuaded him even now to stay on in the Cabinet as Paymaster-General,[44] thus preserving the appearance of solidarity. Monckton ceased attendance, however, at the crucial meetings of the Egypt Committee.

Although Monckton had since 24 September been indicating a wish to resign, tempered only by a scruple about rocking the boat, it seems likely that his final insistence on leaving the inner circle occurred the previous day when he realised that Eden was intent on linking Britain's actions in some way with Israel. 'I did not like the idea of allying ourselves with the French and the Jews in an attack on Egypt,' he said afterwards.[45] He continued to grumble and agonise to those of like disposition, such as Anthony Nutting and William Clark, but the fall of the Government which, surely mistakenly, he feared might follow from his departure from it, always loomed as a bigger catastrophe than any Eden was brewing.[46]

Two days before the resignation took effect, Monckton put his initials on his last memorandum to the Egypt Committee. This outlined the Winter Plan by which military preparations to coerce Nasser could be put on 'hold' during the winter months. It was a very important reminder of the extent to which the mechanism of the policy of negotiating from strength was being eroded.[47]

The third military plan, it will be remembered, had been designed to accommodate the strategy to the imprecisions of the political and diplomatic timetable. Even so, it had been made clear by General Keightley that there would have to be a further adjustment if no orders had been received to go ahead with the use of force by the end of October. The reasons were the deteriorating weather conditions and the need to unload, re-sort and service the vehicles and equipment if they were to remain operationally effective. Brigadier Fitzroy Maclean, the Junior Minister at the War Office, had already reminded the Egypt Committee that it had decided not to try to unload the ships gradually, at the cost each time of showing 'weakening of resolve', but to unload all of them as quickly as possible if nothing had happened by late October. It was this deadline that was approaching. Watkinson, the Minister of Transport, was also 'becoming increasingly anxious' about his ability to keep the requisitioned ships in a state of readiness. The crews had been completely idle for over six weeks, were not earning any overtime and were showing definite signs of boredom and dissatisfaction. There was a limit to the number of times extra cigarettes and beer would do the trick.[48]

Monckton now proposed as his parting shot that the forty-two merchant ships should be stood down and shortly thereafter that the reservists also should be sent home, subject to recall. The reservists were indeed an important part of the problem. Pulled away at a moment's notice from civilian jobs that were in the majority of cases better paid, and often considerably so, than a conscript army, many of them left behind families who were before long in financial difficulty. The hire purchase culture had recently become well nigh universal and it was impossible to keep up payments on cars and television sets when family income had dropped from £17 or £20 a week to £5 or £6. The maximum that was paid out in National Assistance grants was £5. Men in Malta with nothing to do were getting letters from home saying, 'The money runs out tomorrow.' Restless and inactive, they were often unable to spend the time in technical training because their equipment was immunized afloat. Even when, as with 6 RTR in Malta, there were Centurion tanks available, some of the men let off high spirits by playing dodgems with the tanks on the polo ground at midnight, the music coming over the intercom. 'The sound of two Centurion tanks hitting each other at full tilt', said one ex-reservist, 'is quite dramatic.'[49] Quite often men had been called up on a scale that was inappropriate to their reorganised unit – five-man crews, for instance, for Centurion tanks, which took only four – or to carry out skills they had forgotten or never known.[50] None could be released, because that would look like backing down.

As time went by, the sense of urgency had drained from the situation. The popular press had a field day with individual grievances and hardships. There were a few incidents which, although they came to nothing, would in an earlier age have been treated as mutinies and which gave rise to a sharp reminder that servicemen could not expect to be able to have recourse to the remedies of 'civvy street'. In Malta 200 Grenadier guardsmen responded to an irregular notice advertising that, 'For anyone who dislikes bull there will be a meeting tonight at the Naafi at 7 p.m.' Incensed at talk of a full-scale peacetime kit inspection the guardsmen advanced in procession on the officers' mess. As a method of registering complaints, this was distressingly incorrect. In Cyprus twenty-one junior NCOs and men were placed under close arrest following a noisy and undisciplined meeting on the roof of their hotel high up in the Troodos mountains. They too had gathered in the Naafi and had engaged in disgruntled conversation. When the serjeant-major turned out to hear their complaints, their nominated spokesman said to him: 'It's not you we're getting at. It's the Government.'[51] There was a growing feeling, reflected in Monckton's farewell paper, that it would not be politically acceptable to leave men hanging around much longer.

To that paper there was an accompanying memo from the Chiefs of Staff and an appreciation by Sir Charles Keightley. Since the Winter Plan never came into effect, there is no point in describing it in detail beyond saying that it retained the structure of *Musketeer Revise* almost intact, while making its controversial features even more pronounced. There had to be longer notice (fourteen days) before the air offensive could start, because of the need to re-requisition ships that had been stood down; therefore, greater delay in landing and, as General Keightley pointed out, still more need for political resolution and public support to withstand pressure for a cease-fire.

Finally, Plan 'A', the quick option, dear to General Beaufre, of snatching Port Said from Cyprus if the chance arose, did not appear in the Winter Plan. Keightley had an additional reason besides the weather for wanting to get rid of it. He was terribly worried by Nasser's evident lack of worry and thought that this must be due to firm assurance of help from the Russians. In view of the 'extreme vulnerability of our airfields' in Cyprus, Sir Charles thought that the extra risk of attack by Russian pilots integrated as volunteers into the Egyptian air force would become too great during the launch of airborne operations.[52]

In the course of drawing up this latest project the three Directors of Plans had put in a paper, which they were later obliged to withdraw, in which they had invited the Chiefs of Staff to challenge head-on the political premises on which the planning was based. They had been told by General Keightley, they said, that he had had a personal assurance from the Prime Minister that there would be no lack of political resolution, and this had become the tenet of faith upon which the plan was based. 'We consider', they contended, 'that HMG will embark on this operation with a fund of resolution. The amount in the fund will depend directly on the degree to which our nation commands national and international support. Should Nasser have carried out a hostile act, for example an air attack on Cyprus, there will be ample in the fund ... But should opinion in general remain as at present, the fund will be half empty. As the days go by after D-Day and pressure builds up, resolution will dwindle until eventually it might disappear.' A protracted Phase II – and it would be even longer under the Winter Plan – would mean hostile opinion increasing in tempo and volume with every day.

The only way to deal with this, the planners argued, would be to carry out an assault landing on D+2 (that is, directly after the two days' neutralisation of the Egyptian air force) to establish a bridgehead on Egyptian soil. Then foreign opinion would treat it as a *fait accompli* and pressure would relax, military success would boost morale at home and the fact of casualties would stifle criticism. HMG would have become so committed that they would be less susceptible to pressure to call the whole operation off. With the bridgehead established, an air offensive on military and economic targets could then force the Egyptians to negotiate or, failing that, there would be an advance from the bridgehead.[53]

These serious doubts by insiders about a major premise of the military planning were suppressed. Keightley wanted the Winter Plan to come into effect on 21 October and the Prime Minister must have had little doubt that it would be difficult after this to mobilise support for military action, once so much of the preparation had been stood down. Furthermore the French were insistent that they could not hold their forces in readiness for much longer.

It was with these military time factors very much on his mind that Anthony Eden met a somewhat reduced Cabinet of eleven other Ministers (plus Ted Heath as Chief Whip) on 18 October.[54] Before Eden spoke of the Paris visit, Lloyd reported on New York. The summary in the Cabinet minutes gives a rather upbeat impression, highlighting what had been achieved at the United Nations in winning support for the Eighteen-Nation Plan and avoiding being ensnared by 'the appointment of a mediator or negotiating body'. The way was clear for the Egyptian Government to come up with its alternative scheme and the Foreign Secretary called on it promptly to do so. However, in the note he made at the time, Selwyn Lloyd's emphasis is on 'my doubts about the possibility of getting the Egyptians to put forward proposals which we would find tolerable', and in his later book he was much more negative. There he is very anxious to refute as 'absolute nonsense' the thesis that he had nearly reached an agreement with Fawzi and Hammarskjöld before he had left New York.[55] Nevertheless the Cabinet showed its awareness of the widespread pro-UN sentiment in the country by urging that the positive tone of Lloyd's report should be conveyed in all speeches and public statements.

But the main business that day was the Prime Minister's report on Paris, and on this Eden's handling of the Cabinet from the chair was absolutely crucial. There were signs, he said, that the Israelis might be preparing to make some military move. An Israeli attack on Jordan would really put the British on the spot. If the Israelis were going to attack someone, it would be far better if they attacked Egypt and, he added, he had 'reason to believe that if they made any military move it would be in that direction'. He mentioned the formal assurances to be passed on by the French to the Israelis. The decision to ignore the Tripartite Declaration was to be grounded on three considerations, none of them, in truth, very substantial. First, Egypt was in breach of the Security Council resolution on Israeli shipping, a situation which had existed for the past four years, during the course of which the Declaration had been repeatedly reaffirmed. Second, Egypt was in breach of international law through the seizure of the Canal Company. Third, the Egyptians 'had repudiated Western aid under the Tripartite Declaration'.

The Prime Minister then asked whether the Cabinet differed from his analysis. 'There was', wrote Lloyd at the time, 'no adverse comment.' Eden next said that in his view they must, at all costs, prevent fighting over the Canal and damage both to the Canal and to the ships passing through it. He added that he had already discussed this with some of his senior colleagues and they had agreed. Around the Cabinet table, there was no dissent.[56] Quite how much was said at this stage about the mechanism for carrying out this policy is not clear, but it seems likely that the 'all costs' which would be involved were not closely examined. The crucial answers to the French had been sent the previous day after discussion with 'senior colleagues'.

These did not include Butler, who might be thought to be the most senior of all (since he presided over the Cabinet in Eden's absence), but who had been performing duties out of town. But Eden had taken special trouble to square him just before the Cabinet meeting when, glancing at handwritten notes he had jotted down on a dinner menu, he had outlined the chain of events that had been foreshadowed in Paris. Butler says in his memoirs, *The Art of the Possible*: 'I was impressed by the audacity of thinking behind this plan but concerned about the public reaction.' After a limited discussion between the two men, the Prime Minister indicated that 'things were now moving in the direction he had described and in all the circumstances I said that I would stand by him'.[57] Politically this was an extremely important moment. Eden was assured that there would not be effective opposition from the one of his major colleagues from whom it might have been expected. Butler, having been kept to the outer edge of the inner circle, had accepted the *fait accompli*.

For the next few days the Prime Minister was driving forward with a plan known only to a very narrow group, while, outside that group, policies that clashed with it maintained a momentum of their own. Thus Eden winced when, at the UN Security Council debate on 19 October about the incident at Qalqilya, Dixon sharply attacked Israel. 'I am really concerned about the effect of this on Israel,' Eden complained to the Foreign Secretary. 'The French warned how suspicious of us the Israelis are.' He deplored the way Dixon 'aligns himself with the Russians', and asked whether 'we could not for once take a back seat and say very little'.[58]

On 18 October certain military instructions went out from Whitehall. Vice-Admiral Davis, the Vice-Chief of the Naval Staff, suggested that Mountbatten alert Admiral Grantham to the fact that 'the real danger time' in the Middle East was 'between now and the date of the American elections on 6 November'. The suggested signal continued: 'The Jews may well think that now is their last chance to square matters up with the Arabs and that they will confront everybody with a *fait accompli* before the Americans are geared to do anything effective.' Consequently Grantham was to be told that he should 'unobtrusively bring your *Cordage* forces to about 72 hours' notice by the middle of next week'. Davis was not one of those supposed by the Prime Minister to be privy to his inner secrets. At some point Mountbatten decided to violate this crippling inhibition and take Davis completely into his confidence, but this was probably later. By now Mountbatten would have known more. He edited Davis's text slightly – replacing 'Jews' by 'Israelis' and cutting out 'unobtrusively' – and added a further paragraph which referred to the 'extremely serious view which we now take of [the] likelihood of having to intervene in [the] Arab/Israel conflict'.[59]

The effect of the signal was to order the concentration of all three aircraft carriers then in the Mediterranean at Malta on short notice by 24/25 October. The declared purpose may have been *Cordage* (war with Israel); but the same dispositions would be right for *Musketeer* (war with Egypt). Mountbatten, who kept Grantham as well informed as he could during the crisis, sent him a personal message 'by secure means' on 19 October: 'It is in fact *Musketeer* which is being held in readiness over and above *Cordage* plans.' At the same time Grantham was told that Keightley (then still in London) wanted the command ship *Tyne* in Cyprus for use by all three *Musketeer* Task Force Commanders. She should leave with the minimum of press speculation.[60] Most conveniently, a command and communications exercise called *Boathook* had been set up for 1–3 November.

But, in a signal as late as 20 October, Sir Guy Grantham showed that among the Services in the Mediterranean there was still uncertainty about whether they were going to fight the Arabs or the Jews or quite possibly both. As part of his argument for the *Musketeer* Task Force Commanders to come out early to Malta, the Admiral urged that this would keep the staffs involved clear of Cyprus, 'where the HQ might be involved with *Cordage* at the same time'. Grantham's signal ended with the classic thought that, 'If *Musketeer* [against Nasser] is likely to be ordered closely after *Cordage* [against Ben-Gurion], it will be necessary to withdraw the carrier effort from *Cordage* once the Israeli air force has been neutralised.'[61]

Also on 18 October Air Marshal Hubert Patch, the new Commander-in-Chief, Middle East Air Forces, was notified that authority had been given for the immediate but unobtrusive deployment of the remaining bomber forces allocated both to Cyprus and to Malta. It would be completed by 26 October. Again Patch asked whether these were to come under *Cordage* or *Musketeer* because different command structures were involved. Finally a week later he was appealing to Sir Dermot Boyle, the Chief of the Air Staff: '[The] state of readiness is now half at six and half at twelve hours. I would like guidance as to what operation this state of readiness is related to?'[62]

Finally on 18 October General Keightley abandoned the switch to the Winter Plan which was to have taken place on 21 October. *Musketeer Revise* was extended and said, rather oddly in the circumstances, to be operable at ten days' (covert) notice.[63] On 19 October Barjot, the French Commander-in-Chief, and Beaufre decided to load the ships at Algiers immediately and to airlift three regiments of French parachutists from Algiers to Cyprus.[64]

Preoccupations of the Superpowers

It was not long before the United States got some inkling – but not enough to be effective – of what was happening. The day after the British Cabinet meeting on 18 October, Douglas Dillon, the American Ambassador in Paris, was being seen by Jacques Chaban-Delmas, a man who in the four decades since the Second World War has been the leading politician of Bordeaux and who at this time sat in the Cabinet as the Government's liaison with General de Gaulle. He now told the Ambassador that the French and British were planning early military action and were for this purpose in touch with the Israelis. Chaban-Delmas however was not privy to the latest moves; consequently he told Dillon, no doubt sincerely enough, that the military action in question was scheduled to begin a few days after the American election. He passed on the information because he hoped it would make the Americans realise that, if they wanted to head off war, they needed to take a strong and open position against Nasser. On receiving it, Eisenhower resolved to announce a new Middle East peace initiative the moment that his re-election had been proclaimed.[65]

Meanwhile, events in Eastern Europe were also affecting the context. The overthrow of Stalin's cult of personality seemed likely to lead to the crumbling of Soviet hegemony in Eastern Europe. This is what Dulles had predicted when, to considerable scepticism and some ridicule, he had announced that the Soviet system was having to confess the total failure of its economy. The Republican Party had always talked about 'rolling back' Soviet imperialism from Central and Eastern Europe as opposed to 'containing' it. Had not Dulles said during the 1952 campaign that he wanted to 'shift from a purely defensive policy to a psychological offensive, a liberation policy ... to give hope and a resistance mood inside the Soviet

Empire'? And had not Averell Harriman, the experienced Democratic diplomat and politician, in replying to him said that 'nothing can be more cruel than to try to get people behind the Iron Curtain ... to try to revolt and have a new tragedy and a massacre'?[66] For most of the Republicans' first term Dulles's electioneering words had been made to look like empty rhetoric. But now, just as the Republican President was seeking re-election, events were appearing to bear him out. In Poland there had been tension since mid-summer, marked especially by the Poznan riots at the end of June. This was followed by widespread agitation which focussed on demands for the removal of a Soviet citizen, Marshal Rokossovsky, from the position of Minister of Defence and for the restoration to power of a nationalist-minded Communist, Wladyslaw Gomulka. Excitement built up, with the Russians on the verge of sending in the Red Army, until 19 October when Khrushchev suddenly decided to give in on both points.

There were already signs in mid-October that dissent was spreading from Poland to Hungary. Hungarian students were making detailed demands, first about university problems and progressing to a call for the restoration of Hungary's own congenial Communist, the former Prime Minister Imre Nagy. Once started, there was no knowing when the dominoes would cease to fall. There was a problem of credibility for Khrushchev: if he were to settle at Warsaw, where else might he not settle? Coming a decade after the end of the war and so shortly after the CIA's publication of Khrushchev's devastating Twentieth Congress speech against Stalin, this movement released a surge of hope that the days of the 'Iron Curtain' were passing and that a real community of Europe could be re-established.

All this seemed more important to many people even in Britain and certainly in the United States than the Suez Canal, especially since the Canal continued to run normally and to the satisfaction of its users. American policy remained, as Eisenhower had expressed it at a National Security Council meeting on 12 October, to keep the lid on a little longer and then work out some kind of compromise plan.

The truth was that the British felt very acutely that time was being actively employed to undermine their position. They saw its strength ebbing away. If they were anxious, so were the French. In Paris, the only threat to the Government came from the suspicion that, being largely socialist, it would be too soft. Most of the Ministers were as much in the dark as everybody else. *Foreign Report*, the 'confidential' weekly newssheet published by *The Economist* but sold separately to a select but influential circle of subscribers, ran this headline over the issue of 25 October: 'Has M. Mollet a secret?'

The story, which was unattributed as usual but emanated in fact from Jacques Fauvet of *Le Monde*, featured the latest Cabinet leak. At a meeting the previous week Gaston Deferre, the Socialist Party boss of Marseilles who was Minister for France Overseas, had not concealed the feelings which he said he shared with most of France. 'Where are we going?' he had wanted to know. 'We seem to be straying from the firm position we once took. We know nothing of what is going on.' Mollet was represented as calming him down with these words: 'You must have confidence in me. Something is going to happen before the end of the year. I cannot say any more. *There is a diplomatic secret to be kept!*' In a few days, the 'blue *Economist*' (*Foreign Report* is printed on blue paper) was being waved around in the State Department by Walter Robertson, an Assistant Secretary of State, as circumstantial evidence of collusion.

The Security Council excursion might have enabled Britain and France to present a more acceptable face to the world but there was still no definite date for the resumption of the talks with Mahmoud Fawzi. Before Fawzi left New York, Hammarskjöld had tentatively arranged with him that the three Foreign Ministers and the Secretary-General should resume their talks on 29 October at Geneva. But the British and French would only make their acceptance of this or any other date conditional on their first receiving an Egyptian proposal that would implement the agreed Six Principles just as effectively as the rejected formula of the London Conference. Without such a draft on the table they feared being 'bounced into a conference on an unsatisfactory basis'.

From Fawzi, now back in Cairo, there was no direct reply until under the very different circumstances of 2 November. However, on 18 October Hammarskjöld sent Lloyd and Pineau a summary giving his impressions of what Fawzi was willing to accept. As Britain and France appeared to be holding out for 'something in writing' from Egypt before they would agree to turn up on 29 October, Hammarskjöld tried to crystallize the issue on 24 October by himself drafting and sending to Cairo the sort of document to which Fawzi might with a bit of luck be expected to agree. He described it as trying to 'spell out what are my conclusions from the – entirely noncommittal – observations made in the course of the private talks'.

This three and a half page draft suggested that the area of convergence was quite considerable, covering revision of the Constantinople Convention to deal with tolls and charges, maintenance of the Canal, a set-aside of funds for development and recognition of the principle of 'organised co-operation between the Egyptian Authority and the Users'. This would require joint meetings, involving a recognised Users' Association, which could raise any matter for discussion or complaint and have guaranteed access to the necessary information, without however having the right to interfere with the functions of administration. Safeguards were to include remedies of the sort debated by the Foreign Ministers in New York – arbitration, International Court, Security Council. The only passage that read as though Hammarskjöld might have gone over the mark from the Egyptian point of view was the one in which he suggested that, where the appropriate organ certified non-compliance with its award, the aggrieved side might 'be entitled to a certain limited "police action"' on its own behalf.[67]

This rather positive foundation for future negotiations which was designed to tease out of Fawzi the piece of paper which would deliver Lloyd and Pineau at Geneva, was wrapped up in a typically Hammarskjöldian outer covering of tentative expression and conditional clause. Nobody wanted a mediator. This, therefore, was the Secretary-General's manner – resolute of purpose, tentative of form – of ratcheting matters towards a conclusion without raising the issue of his credentials for doing so. Later on, after the storm, Selwyn Lloyd was to quote in the Commons one of these serpentine sentences as if to refute the suggestion that agreement was close. This was hardly fair. He understood Hammarskjöld and he knew the code. On 29 October, the putative day for the talks to open, Fawzi was telling the new American Ambassador, Raymond Hare, that he would have been in Geneva at that time had not the unreasonable demand been made for a detailed Egyptian plan in advance. Egypt could not accept the principle that SCUA should collect tolls regardless of the portion turned over to Egypt.

President Nasser, meanwhile, had decided that the time had arrived for him to play the personal role in Suez diplomacy for which he had hankered since August. The Geneva talks, he said, could take place in a fortnight's time and he himself would represent Egypt, provided that Eden and Mollet would also attend personally. Egypt would have proposals to make on tolls and for dealing with all users, not just with members of SCUA alone. The military danger, he thought, was now over. He would present himself on the international stage.

17

Sèvres, Conference of Collusion

Well, why are you here altogether? If you can settle it with Nasser, go ahead and do it.
Moshe Dayan to Selwyn Lloyd at Sèvres, 22 October 1956.

It is known that [Nasser] is already plotting coups in many of the other Arab countries; and we shall never have a better pretext for intervention against him than we have now as a result of his seizure of the Suez Canal.
Sir Anthony Eden to his Cabinet, 24 October 1956.

Distrust of Britain's motives and policies was one of the features that brought the French and Israelis together. National stereotypes present themselves with surprising regularity in the course of international relations. Now it was British hypocrisy, unreliability and, in relation to the Foreign Office, visceral pro-Arabism that were invoked. All the same, Mollet was convinced that Eden was one British political leader who could be trusted; Ben-Gurion, having in mind particularly the Guildhall speech of the previous November but also the hostile nature of the recent communications about the Jordan border, thought the opposite. Peres wrote in his diary for 16 October of 'the deep mistrust which Ben-Gurion harbours towards the British Government and to Eden in particular. He sees in him not only the progenitor of antagonism to Israel, but also a weak leader whose deeds do not match his declarations.'[1]

Ben-Gurion had accepted the invitation to Paris but rejected the 'English' scenario. The idea of a division of function between Israel as the sole aggressor and Britain and France as the two umpires with clean hands did not appeal to him. It was, he growled, 'out of the question'. He had left it up to Mollet whether, in view of this, he still wanted to see him. He now received a warm renewal of the invitation.

Ben-Gurion's young advisers began working on him, most especially Moshe Dayan. He argued that the only contribution that Israel was in a position to make to the Anglo-French operation was to provide the pretext. Everything else could easily be managed without Israeli help. That ability to supply the pretext was Israel's historic opportunity. As for Israel's being considered an aggressor, she need not fear that charge. She had ample justification: Egypt's insistence on a state of war existing between them, the *fedayeen* raids, the naval blockade. Provided Israel had French planes for the defence of Israeli cities, the plan should be agreed.[2] Ben-Gurion had received word of Eden's two declarations with which Lloyd's mind 'was not easy'.[3] As between the French and the Israelis, the time had come for a political decision to be made if the staff talks, which were going forward in Paris, were not to jam. Brigadier Meir Amit, who was conducting these talks with Barjot and his planners, was complaining that the French were already working to the assumptions of the 'British proposal', which contradicted Ben-Gurion's directives. He bristled at a sight of the French planners' written directive – 'to assist Israel in attacking the Egyptian army' – and asserted proudly that Israel was not in the business of 'receiving aid' but instead would act by way of 'mutual assistance'.[4]

Ben-Gurion, his mind fertilised by the thought of conferring with an ally, was off on a different tack. On 19 October he exposed to the sympathetic ears of the French Ambassador, Pierre-Eugène Gilbert, Dayan's plan (now become his own) for reconstructing the boundaries of the entire Levant. Gilbert remarked only that the interest of Britain must be enlisted since, without her support, no such ambitious plan would have a chance.[5]

On the morning of Sunday, 21 October, de Gaulle's comfortable plane, intended for Ben-Gurion's use, landed in great secrecy at a military airfield in Israel, carrying General Challe as well as Louis Mangin. They understood that they had a job of persuasion still to do. In a mood of complicity they put it to Dayan that the British required to be humoured, that their action must be seen publicly as that of an intermediary and the scenario written accordingly. Dayan records that he lost his temper at this 'perhaps as much for the tiresome word "scenario" as for the reasoning'. Just for the sake of sticking to a scenario, he said, Israel was not going to leave Tel Aviv wide open to Egyptian bombing while Israeli planes were being employed in a campaign that was shaped to Anglo-French ends and not those of Israel. Challe suggested that French squadrons stationed in Israel could provide an answer. The first breach in the scenario had been suggested and by its author.[6]

Given Ben-Gurion's unpromising mood Dayan thought it better to keep the Frenchmen away from him until the point of take-off in the late afternoon. He was right. When Ben-Gurion heard that they had been there, still peddling 'the English plan', he talked of cancelling the trip. But, in view of the generous arms supplies from France, he was not really going to discountenance an ally. Instead, he settled down in the plane over a volume of Procopius in the original Greek, remarking simply to General

Challe: 'If you intend to suggest to us the English proposal, the only use of my trip to France will be that I shall make the acquaintance of your Prime Minister.' In a diary entry written on the plane he commented on Challe's enthusiastic chatter about deposing Nasser and forming a new Government: 'I fear that in this there is a great deal of wishful thinking. How do they know that Nasser will fall – even if they do take Cairo and defeat his army? He will organise a guerrilla.' He went on polishing his master plan for the Middle East, but most of the long flight he spent with Procopius, confirming his previously expressed conviction, extremely convenient if the decision was for war, that the ancient Jewish kingdom of Yotwat was to be identified with the island of Tiran in the Straits of that name.[7]

The delegation was an interesting one. Apart from Ben-Gurion himself there were no politicians. There were Dayan and Peres, Ben-Gurion's military secretary, and the head of Dayan's office, Colonel Mordechai Bar-On. Dayan was the sort of general who thought politically as well as strategically. He was a future Foreign Minister, just as Peres was a future Prime Minister. Bar-On was to serve in the Knesset. None of them ranked as a politician at the time. Dayan played an extremely active role in the conference, but no one was in any doubt that the decision would be taken by Ben-Gurion alone.

After an exhausting flight, prolonged by very poor visibility, they made an emergency landing at the small, deserted aerodrome at Brétigny and were taken to a secluded villa at the end of the rue Emanuel Girot in the fashionable Parisian suburb of Sèvres. It belonged to the Bonnier de la Chapelle family, whose son had been shot after assassinating the Vichyite Admiral Darlan in Algiers in 1943, and it had been used by Bourgès-Maunoury as a safe house during the Resistance. At the beginning, the talks were bilateral, Guy Mollet, Christian Pineau and Maurice Bourgès-Maunoury representing France. They crowded in together among the plants in what was a kind of conservatory.

Ben-Gurion began his first international summit with a review which opened with Plato and took in the general re-ordering of the Middle East. He outlined the ideas he had given to Gilbert, adding that he did not know who could stabilise Syria. The Israeli border with the Lebanon would be the Litani River (an old Jewish ambition, which would have incorporated into Israel proper part of what was thirty years later to become known as 'the security zone'). The Suez Canal would be internationalised, possibly with Egypt holding one bank and Israel the other. Sharm al-Sheikh and the island of Tiran – Yotwat – would go to Israel.

The French insisted that time was of the essence. They could not talk now of such things. Guy Mollet was quiet and courteous, concerned with creating a cordial atmosphere, Pineau more bluntly pragmatic, Bourgès-Maunoury, the dynamo, constantly stressing the extremely tight deadlines to which they needed to work if anything was to be done.

Ben-Gurion repeated his objections to the 'English plan'. He said that Israel was not in a hurry to hit Egypt; if she consulted her pure self-interest, she could take care of Nasser at a later date when Israel's new weapons had been fully absorbed. Since the French were urging her to bring forward the action, Israel was willing to help her friends but there had to be a proper plan. He was very unhappy at merely doing a limited service for the British, who were not willing to recognise Israel as an ally. Israel must be a full party to any joint plan. Mollet gently explained the problem of timing: Nasser was daily getting stronger, the Russians were consolidating their hold over him and the Americans, as always, were late in taking action. Anthony Eden was now ready to fight, but he was surrounded by a 'swamp of hesitation' and one dared not assume that he would agree to another plan. To reject the present plan meant scrapping the whole thing for good. 'The English', said Pineau, 'are incapable of acting without a pretext.' Israel could supply the 'detonator for *Musketeer*'.

Bourgès-Maunoury turned on the pressure: the time-gap between the Israeli attack and the Anglo-French intervention could be fixed at less than the seventy-two hours currently proposed; France would undertake to use her veto on Israel's behalf in the Security Council; the Russians would be wholly absorbed by their own problems in Poland and Hungary; American attention would be quite taken up by their elections. In any case France could wait no longer. She had requisitioned fifty merchant ships and mobilised reserves; it was impossible to hold these inactive. 'The beginning of November is to be the last possible date.' Ben-Gurion replied: 'If there is a war with full co-operation, we are ready to start it tomorrow.' Dayan then introduced what he described as his personal opinion, although it had been cleared with Ben-Gurion though not yet endorsed by him. If the Israelis were to launch in the afternoon what would appear to be a deep reprisal raid taking them close to the Canal, the Egyptians were not likely to attack Israeli cities from the air. France and Britain could then execute diplomatic manoeuvres ('need to safeguard Canal', etc.) and go into action twelve hours later at dawn.

While they were talking, the French received confirmation that the 'Number Two' of the British Cabinet had arrived secretly in Paris. There were guesses, Ben-Gurion wrote, as to whether this was Lord Salisbury, Rab Butler or Selwyn Lloyd. The last would be the least welcome. Guy Mollet had already made the observation that, while Eden was insisting on an operation, Lloyd was looking for a compromise with Fawzi. Ben-Gurion grumbled that a British Prime Minister could remove a Minister quite simply if he wished. The mystery was solved when, at about 4 p.m., Selwyn Lloyd, accompanied by his junior private secretary, Donald Logan, reached the rue Emanuel Girot. He had been warned at Chequers by Eden only the preceding day and his travel arrangements were made with the utmost concern for security.

It was the intention that the Foreign Secretary's presence at Sèvres should never be known. There are no papers about it in the 1956 records in the Public Record Office; only a very few elusive hints.[8] Pineau and Dayan having first described the proceedings at Sèvres in their memoirs and on BBC television in 1976, Selwyn Lloyd wrote his own account shortly before his death in 1978. Shimon Peres's diary has been drawn on by himself and other writers. (Sir) Donald Logan, the only British person present on both days of the trilateral part of the conference, made his detailed and vividly expressed recollections known on the BBC 2 *Secrets of Suez* programme and in the *Financial Times*, in 1986. Minutes were not supposed to be kept but Ben-Gurion, alive to the need, as he frequently said, to win battles a second time in the history books, authorised Dayan's bureau chief Bar-On to keep extensive notes, despite periodic mutterings of disapproval from Pineau. These will shortly be published. Ben-Gurion himself, as usual, made entries in his daily diary. Nevertheless, the wishes of the principals were to a limited extent respected, in that Mollet and Ben-Gurion were dead when the first two memoirs appeared – Dayan having explicitly deleted material about Sèvres at the request of the 'Old Man' from his earlier volume, *Diary of the Sinai Campaign*, – and likewise Eden died before Selwyn Lloyd wrote. The principal plotters of Sèvres had sought to carry their secret to the grave.[9]

The word 'collusion', with its pronounced association with fraud, to describe what Eden had authorised and Lloyd was now doing requires some explanation. In the first place, it appears quite often as a term of art in the usage of British diplomacy to describe something which other people do, most characteristically the French. The whole French diplomatic performance in the Middle East was usually portrayed through Foreign Office eyes as a kind of utterly perverse intrigue. When it took on a more sinister shape it became 'collusion' and, in the circumstances of 1956, French collusion meant, above all, collusion with Israel. Thus 'British collusion' conveyed the sense that Britain, contrary to her normal practice, had joined in that sort of game.

But as used in the wider world, when suspicion grew over what had been going on, collusion had a deeper resonance. It was not simply that the Sèvres meeting was held in secret (that was an accepted device of diplomacy), nor that it was with the Israelis (in 1956 a popular cause in many quarters in Britain and especially with the official Opposition), nor even that the policy that it inaugurated was unsuccessful. The case against the proceedings at the villa in the rue Emanuel Girot has always been twofold: that the British presence was an essential ingredient in the launching of an aggressive war, and that it was the subject of a major misrepresentation to the British public of what British troops were being called upon to do.

After a briefing by Pineau, Selwyn Lloyd was brought in to meet the Israelis. They looked, he remembered, exhausted. 'One young man [Bar-

On] was snoring loudly in an armchair. Ben-Gurion himself looked far from well.' (He had 'flu.) But for them this was a great moment in the history of their state: to be meeting as equals and potential allies the power on whom they had formerly been dependent and with whom, as recently as a fortnight before, they had been on the verge of war. A tripartite discussion was convened in another room; Ben-Gurion and Dayan represented Israel. 'Ben-Gurion', says Lloyd, 'seemed to be in a rather aggressive mood indicating or implying that the Israelis had no reason to believe in anything that a British Minister might say.'[10]

The Israeli Prime Minister, now that he had a British audience, opened up once more with the grand design for the Middle East. It would have gone down a treat with Macmillan. Selwyn Lloyd ignored it. He explained, as he had done in Paris, that, following the talks in New York, it was evidently possible to make an agreement with Nasser in the space of a week about running the Canal. Important sections of public opinion in Britain, some Commonwealth countries and Scandinavia set much store by peaceful settlement. British forces which had been mobilised to enforce international control could not remain much longer in a state of alert. If it really was the intention of Israel to attack – and he listed the drawbacks of such a course, not least in the United Nations, with a depressing thoroughness – he confirmed that this would supply a basis on which Britain and France would intervene to avert the threat so created to the operation of the Canal.

Ben-Gurion explained that a two-day delay before the allied intervention was unacceptable because of the danger of an Egyptian blitz on Israeli cities. His counter-proposal for an intervention the next morning ran into equally stiff objections. Lloyd said that Britain would be condemned throughout the Arab world, but also in many European states, as an aggressor. Why then should Israel take such odium on herself?, Ben-Gurion shot back. Selwyn Lloyd said that Israel had good reasons. Nasser had denied her her rights. A compromise idea was suggested under which France should bomb Egypt the next morning and Britain should join in twenty-four hours later. Pineau liked the idea but said he had no bombers and no air base, except in Cyprus. Ben-Gurion's diary continues, 'I said: "England will loan bombers and pilots [to the French]". There was a precedent for such a loan when Roosevelt lent England fifty battleships. Lloyd derided the battleships as not having been worth anything.'

The tone of this exchange and its cold manner, in marked contrast to the camaraderie of the French, alienated the Israelis. Dayan said of Lloyd afterwards: 'I had the impression that he just hated the whole thing. He didn't like it, like he was trying to hold something that was not quite clean and you want to wash your hands afterwards.' To Bar-On, the Foreign Secretary gave the impression of having a dirty smell under his nose.[11]

This did not look like the foundation of a famous alliance. According to Dayan the Israeli line was: 'Well, why are you here altogether? If you can settle it with Nasser, go ahead and do it.' Lloyd explained that 'from the perspective of the British Cabinet, a UN-type agreement has one important drawback, namely that Nasser remains in charge' and the British Cabinet was intent on his removal. Ben-Gurion had already displayed to the French his scepticism about whether Nasser's fall would follow automatically from loss of the Canal. What concerned him now, as Lloyd plodded on through the scenario, was the inequality of treatment between the parties, one 'offender' and 'two policemen'.

Bar-On, then a young man in his late twenties who was observing Ben-Gurion closely, has written: 'The roguish smile on Ben-Gurion's face throughout the talks with the French had completely vanished. His face was pale and his expression had narrowed into a bitter one. He is not making any effort now to hide his disgruntlement and his profound contempt for the despicable diplomatic manoeuvres of Great Britain. He is speaking in short, sharp sentences and gives a negative reply to Selwyn Lloyd's conditions.'[12] Israel was not willing to declare war against Egypt. Israel did not want to be declared an aggressor and to be served an ultimatum. If they were attacked, Israelis would defend themselves and they would prevail, even if they were forced to stand alone against Egypt.

The French faces fell. They had struggled to bring the parties to the plot into the same room; now it was all going to fall apart. Ben-Gurion, however, switched to a more positive theme. He picked up Dayan's 'private' scheme of a large scale reprisal raid in the Sinai launched late one afternoon with the Anglo-French joining in the following day. Dayan explained that he would arrange for a paratroop drop in the vicinity of the Canal. It would do no harm to call on Israel not to advance beyond the Canal since she had no intention of doing any such thing.

Lloyd insisted that it would be essential for Britain that Israel carry out a '*real* act of war', so as to avoid any danger of Britain being thought an aggressor by Commonwealth and Scandinavian friends when she took action in response. The pretext must be credible. Pressed both by Pineau and Lloyd, Ben-Gurion named the evening of Monday, 29 October, as the date for the operation, provided that its other features were agreed.[13] The French and the British would be expected to convene Cabinet meetings immediately, present their ultimatum and start bombing Egyptian airfields in the early morning. But Selwyn Lloyd was talking about the interval of seventy-two hours being possibly reduced, at most, to forty-eight.

They adjourned for dinner at 10 p.m. and continued talking afterwards till midnight. Ben-Gurion could not escape the memory of the five months he spent in London during the 1940–41 blitz. If Israel was to go to war, she must do so in safety, not leaving Haifa and Tel Aviv for days insufficiently protected. General Challe tried to convince him that Mystères would bring down any Egyptian bombers that might try to get through to Israel. For Ben-Gurion this was not insurance enough; the Egyptian airfields must be attacked. When Bourgès-Maunoury suggested that in an emergency the French could give fighter cover from Cyprus, Lloyd interposed that they could not.

Dayan gave some not very precise assurances about the nature of his proposed attack. Lloyd was urged by the French to reduce the gap from forty-eight to thirty-six hours. The discussion petered out, leaving the Foreign Secretary with the impression that the *casus belli* (or strictly speaking, the sufficient cause for impartial intervention) for which Eden sought was just not there. Logan remembers that Ben-Gurion looked depressed. He says himself in his diary that there was renewed discussion about the possibility of a 'loan' to France of fifty British bombers which should be painted in the French colours and that 'the conversation concerning this matter did not end with a definite conclusion'. Lloyd left near midnight to fly back for the morrow's Cabinet meeting and the resumption of Parliament after the summer recess.

The impression which Lloyd took away from the villa in the rue Emanuel Girot was not a positive one. Nor were the feelings that he left behind. Pineau announced that he would not rely on Lloyd to convey their plans in the right spirit but would fly over to London himself on the following evening. 'We'll see what happens tomorrow,' Ben-Gurion wrote. 'I fear that Pineau's trip will be in vain.'

It remains unclear what the Foreign Secretary really in his heart wanted and it probably was unclear to him at the time. He seems to have felt himself still bound by the initial decision in the Egypt Committee to go for the overthrow of Nasser as a priority or, at any rate, sufficiently bound by it to point out whenever policies and negotiations were not likely to lead to that end. He had, after all, felt very strongly about Nasser himself earlier in the year. On the other hand, he contrived to give the impression to quite a number of people that he wanted the Security Council negotiations to succeed and that he was ill at ease with the exercise at Sèvres. It must be remembered that he felt that he had been over-promoted and that he shared the feeling, which was widespread, that Anthony Eden (whatever drawbacks he might be thought to have as a domestic Prime Minister) had in foreign affairs the golden touch.

In the end, Lloyd felt it was for him, as it would be for a civil servant, to present analyses and choices and for the Prime Minister to decide. In his book he makes one main self-criticism: he says that he might well have been wrong to have opposed joint planning with the Israelis. 'I had in mind the mobs coming out in Cairo in 1952 and their mass-murders. I hated the efficacy of Radio Cairo – as powerful as Goebbels. My preoccupation was to safeguard Britons in Arab countries from massacre and our strategic assets from destruction. I believed that an alliance between Israel and ourselves would produce exactly this feared result. I may well have been wrong.'[14]

Lloyd left Sèvres, not to return. The next morning the Cabinet met. Eden reminded his colleagues that, at the last meeting on 18 October, 'there had been reason to believe' that Israel was about to bring the matter rapidly to a head by attacking Egypt. But now he had concluded *'from secret conversations which had been held in Paris with representatives of the Israeli Government'* that the Israelis would not alone launch a full-scale attack. The Cabinet thus knew that there had been direct contact with the Israelis about the *casus belli*. It is the only direct reference to the Sèvres conference to be found in the British records so far released. Exceptional steps were taken to prevent the knowledge spreading. Of the various versions of the Cabinet Minutes for 23 October to be found in the Public Record Office only one contains the passage that has been italicised here.[15] All others have Ministers being told mysteriously that 'it now seemed unlikely' that the Israelis would, in effect, oblige by setting off the fuse.

The Cabinet were told, therefore, that the initiative was once more in their own hands. The French, Ministers were informed, were hot for early military action; they had just produced specific proof of provocation by Egypt through the interception of a Sudanese-owned ex-British mine-sweeper, the *Athos*, in the act of carrying seventy tons of arms from Alexandria to a Moroccan port – for the FLN with six Egyptian-trained Algerians on board – and had consequently recalled the French Ambassador from Cairo. Eden said that, if the French considered that this gave them sufficient grounds for going to war, they were bound to ask for British facilities to operate from Cyprus.

The Foreign Secretary reported that the Egyptian Government had now declared that it was ready to put forward alternative proposals for the control of the Canal of a kind which, in Dag Hammarskjöld's opinion, would make a basis for renewed discussions. Lloyd said, as he had done at Sèvres, that he did not exclude the possibility of reaching a negotiated settlement 'which would give us the substance of our demand for effective international supervision of the Canal'. But he then listed 'three serious objections' to what might otherwise have seemed a positive recommendation for peace. The first was that the French would not have it. The second was the danger that switching to the Winter Plan would weaken the negotiating position. The third (and presumably the most telling) was that he could see 'no prospect of reaching such a settlement as would diminish Colonel Nasser's influence throughout the Middle East'.

Eden then told the Cabinet that it would be called upon to take grave decisions in the course of the next few days. For the moment nothing could be done until the French attitude was clearer and, for that purpose, Pineau was coming over that evening. It could have been that an unwavering Prime Minister remained confident that, despite Lloyd's report, he would be able to arrange everything with Pineau, but there is some evidence that points the other way: towards an Eden coming to terms with frustration. During that morning, Eden told Sir Charles Keightley personally that the 'hot' news had gone cold, not that it had not been true in the first place, but that 'the people concerned' had had second thoughts and cancelled this 'D-Day'.

Tipped off by Keightley, Mountbatten wrote 'by secure means' to Admiral Grantham although strictly speaking even he, in charge of the Mediterranean Fleet, was not supposed to be 'in the know'. Mountbatten spoke of 'this fantastic degree of secrecy' which 'made us all, Charles and the three Chiefs of Staff, look pretty silly', although, he conceded, 'We'd have seemed very clever if the "hot" news had remained "hot".' General Templer had said that he was expecting his Vice-Chief 'to bring in two doctors and a straitjacket for me any day now!' The First Sea Lord added: 'I'm very sorry for the mess we've got into – I've now had to take [the Vice-Chief of the Naval Staff, Admiral Davis] into the secret to help me disentangle it. I'm cancelling *Daring* and *Defender* and will not send out any more of the Home Fleet.'[16] Meanwhile General Stockwell's 2 Corps Headquarters was given the codeword *Relax* 'which', the general said, 'it did'.[17] It seems improbable that, if the Prime Minister had been confident of going ahead, he would have allowed such rapid and unsettling reversals of mood in the top command.

That afternoon the Government had, for the first time since 14 September, to face the House of Commons. It is interesting to compare Lloyd's statement and answers to questions with his report to the Cabinet that morning. On the one hand, the statement did not refer to Egypt's readiness to make proposals or Hammarskjöld's opinion. Nor, however, did his answers reflect the belligerent implications of his three reservations. 'In such a matter', he said, 'for the British people, force will always be the last recourse. Of course, we want a peaceful settlement and we have done our best to work through the UN.'[18]

Entr'actes

External events were again having their effect. In Poland and in Hungary the popular feeling against Soviet-style Communism continued to gain expression, though events in the two countries moved to different rhythms. In Poland, Gomulka was consolidating his position in a way that showed some successful defiance of Moscow but an acknowledgement of the practical limitations imposed by *raison d'état*. On 23 October, inspired by the Polish example, a large student demonstration in Budapest built up into a mass revolt against the system. Overnight, the Government and party, which had shown themselves fatally indecisive, tried to buy time by installing Imre Nagy, the people's favourite, as Prime Minister. The Soviet Union might well be preoccupied for a considerable while.

In the Middle East, the Jordanian election had taken place and brought the opposition leader, Suleiman Nabulsi, to power. The new Prime Minister declared: 'We respect Colonel Nasser and consider him the saviour of Arab national interests and welfare.' His purpose, he said, was to 'liberate Jordan from foreign and imperialist influence'. It had all taken place with remarkably little fuss; Sir Charles Duke reported that it was the quietest election Jordan had ever had.[19] Nabulsi lost no time in building up links with Egypt and Syria. On 22 October, before he had even taken office, it was announced that the three Chiefs of Staff of those countries would meet in Amman.

Also on 22 October, Ben Bella, the external leader of the Algerian rebellion, with several of his colleagues was skyjacked by the French secret service SDECE when flying under the King of Morocco's protection, but with a French pilot, to Tunis. The operation, though 'covered' by a junior Minister, was a shock to Mollet and his colleagues, who were trying to open negotiations with whoever was the authentic voice of the rebels but seemed rather at a loss to know what use to make of such an unexpected coup. President Coty's instinct was to release the prisoners, a sentiment which Pineau shared, but the surge of approval for their seizure from the public at a time when criticism was mounting over Mollet's apparent inaction over Egypt made that impossible. Pineau submitted one of his periodic resignations: he was told once more by Mollet to 'remember Europe'.[20]

Moshe Dayan spent the morning of 23 October at Louis Mangin's house discussing the bilateral aid that the French would supply for an Israeli offensive against Egypt. The French were ready to station two or three fighter squadrons at Israeli airfields to provide an aerial umbrella for Israeli cities. In addition they would send French pilots to fly those Israeli Mystères for which there were not yet trained Israeli pilots. They would airdrop supplies in the Sinai and provide some off-shore naval support. And they would write off many loans for previous weapons purchases. The British were told of none of these arrangements.

A 'Real Threat' to the Canal

The basic problem remained that, despite Dayan's buoyancy, the French military could not see how it was possible to span the gap between the British and Israeli concepts of the campaign. Dayan's task remained to persuade Ben-Gurion that he could launch an operation that would at the same time look to the Egyptians like a stepped-up reprisal raid and to the British like a major threat to the Suez Canal. He was spurred on by the blunt reminder by Bourgès-Maunoury over lunch that, while France would continue to give Israel such military assistance as she could, a joint enterprise was now or never.

Ben-Gurion had what proved to be a more realistic grasp of the American attitude than did the French. He argued strongly that they should wait for the American elections to be over and then tell Eisenhower frankly what they planned to do. He was also, says Dayan, disappointed by the French unreadiness to talk about the Middle East plan, a concept which, perhaps, he would have expected to appeal to the French mind. As a politician, he had been affected by the strength of Israeli popular reaction to the scale of the losses suffered at Qalqilya and this made him hesitant about adventurous strategies. At the same time, as he noted in his diary, the in-coming news all told of mounting Egyptian pressures – France's diplomatic break over the *Athos*, the pro-Egyptian nature of the new nationalist regime in Jordan, the capture of two *fedayeen* who had been sent over the Lebanese frontier by the Egyptian military attaché.

Could a *casus belli* not be found that would make Israel the victim of aggression in British eyes? Shimon Peres suggested running an Israeli ship through the Canal, since this was the issue on which the Security Council had already found in favour of Israel and which had now at last been picked up as an argument by Eden? General Challe, that fertile source of *ruses de guerre*, had an idea. It could be arranged for bombs to drop on Beersheva, which should make it natural that Israel go to war. Ben-Gurion exploded. He wrote in his dairy, 'I announced in my own name – as a Jew – that I could not participate in a deception against the world.' His line was straightforward: Israel already had legitimate reasons for fighting; exercises of this kind were uncalled for.

In the afternoon Dayan checked through the details of the revised and still unauthorised plan with his Prime Minister with, this time, a thirty-six-hour gap between Israeli attack and allied bombing. He sketched in the changes, some quite substantial, in the operational orders for *Kadesh* that could accommodate Britain's requirements and at the same time enable Israel to hedge against possible British betrayal. Before Pineau left for London on his mission to counteract the negative report he felt sure Lloyd was going to deliver, Dayan dictated to him his plan's seven main points. They resembled closely the outline which was to be known as the Protocol of Sèvres.

Pineau arrived in London and, as he had expected, did not gain much satisfaction when he dined with Lloyd. They agreed that they would not go to Geneva to meet Fawzi and Hammarskjöld on 29 October unless the Egyptians themselves had put forward firm proposals that fulfilled the Six Principles. But where they differed was over the nature of the international regime for which they were looking. To Pineau's discomforture Lloyd was attracted by Hammarskjöld's approach of an Egyptian authority managing the Canal with international restriction and control. This, Lloyd thought, was better for the long term than having a 'state within a state', an international company conducting the whole management itself. He made no headway whatever with Pineau, who found Eden very much more congenial company when the latter paired them after dinner.

The three men discussed the issues raised in the Dayan plan, which, because it now embodied the central feature of an Israeli attack thirty-six hours ahead of the others, enlisted the Prime Minister's keenest interest. When Pineau left he was basically convinced of Britain's consent. However a letter was written to him after the meeting by Selwyn Lloyd who, worried lest the French had misunderstood the eagerness with which Eden had joined in the discussion, wanted it put on record that there was no question of Britain asking Israel to undertake anything. Rather, 'we were only asked what would be our reactions in certain contingencies'.[21]

Ben-Gurion, whose decision for war had not yet been made, had had a troubled night of decision. On the morning of 24 October, however, his 'young Turks' noticed a changed mood. He had prepared a list of questions, but their character was different from those asked before. Whereas the previous day the questions and arguments were of a man sceptical about the whole operation, these ones assumed the operation was going forward. He confirmed this, indirectly, by remarking at lunch time that there must be drawn up a formal protocol setting out the obligations and signed by all three parties. He added: 'All the time I have been wondering how a Jewish state was able to survive at Yotwat without a proper water supply.'

The British Cabinet met again on 24 October. Lloyd reported that because of the *Athos* affair the French did not favour an early resumption of negotiations with the Egyptians. On the other hand they too required a sufficient pretext and one, moreover, which unlike the *Athos* involved the British equally. Head, the new Defence Minister, then said that the present level of readiness for *Musketeer Revise* could not be held for many more days. The reservists were restive; the vehicles were deteriorating. They must be released and unloaded unless something happened soon. All this, it was underlined, could not fail to weaken Britain's bargaining position.

There followed a misleading discussion about military action against Egypt, which assumed that the Israelis might jump into a war which had already started. This would apparently now be welcome since it might serve to reduce quite considerably the gap between the phases of the Anglo-French operation. The motive for sowing the idea of this hypothesis only became apparent the following day.

To the objection that Israeli involvement would unite the entire Arab world in support of Egypt, Eden said that this was a serious risk but it must be weighed against the greater risk that, unless early action were taken to damage Nasser's prestige, his influence would grow so much in the Middle East that it would become much more difficult to overthrow him. They would never again have as good a 'pretext' to do so as 'the seizure of the Suez Canal'. 'If . . . a military operation were undertaken against Egypt, its effect in other Arab countries would be serious unless it led to the early collapse of Colonel Nasser's regime. Both for this reason and also because of the international pressures which would develop against our continuance of the operation, it must be swift and successful.'

If that indeed was the absolute priority, as the Cabinet might have been forgiven for thinking, either the Suez expedition should have put to sea ahead of the ultimatum so that it was just 'over the horizon' when this was delivered, or, as Selwyn Lloyd thought afterwards, there should have been joint planning with the Israelis from the beginning. Anglo-French paratroop drops down the full length of the Canal could then have been supported on land.

The Cabinet on 24 October also went on to consider how the Suez issue could be brought to a head diplomatically. Should not a time limit be given to the Egyptians to produce their promised alternative system for running the Canal according to the Six Principles? But the trouble was that 'if such a demand were made, the Egyptians were likely to comply with it'. They would produce within the specified time proposals which, though unsatisfactory, would appear to offer a basis for discussion. So the British and French had to make up their minds.

> They could frame their demands in such a way as to make it impossible for the Egyptians to accept them – being resolved on an Egyptian refusal to take military action designed to overthrow Colonel Nasser's regime.
>
> Alternatively, they could seek the sort of settlement of the Canal issue which might be reached by negotiation – recognising that, by accepting such a settlement, they would abandon their second objective of reducing Colonel Nasser's influence throughout the Middle East.[22]

The Prime Minister adjourned the meeting until the following day saying that there must be further discussions with the French.

Protocol of Sèvres

Selwyn Lloyd decided that he had had enough of functioning underground. On 24 October Patrick Dean, the chairman of the Joint Intelligence Committee who had recently been on leave and had not been privy to recent political planning with the French (or the Israelis), was despatched after a short briefing from the Prime Minister to take Lloyd's place at Sèvres. Dean noticed that Eden seemed tired, worried and over-strained, though not more so than people in the Foreign Office had known him be at times in the past. He told Dean that he wanted him to go at once to Paris to emphasise that British forces would not participate unless there had developed a clear threat to the Canal. It is evident that Dean must also have been authorised to meet the Israelis to the extent of agreement to a thirty-six hour gap. Eden told Dean nothing about the political arrangements and he did not enquire because he assumed the whole plan was a contingency military plan which had the backing not only of the Prime Minister but also of other Ministers.

Donald Logan was also sent out by Lloyd to provide continuity with Lloyd's visit and to fill Dean in on the preceding talks. It is not the case that Dean was either present with Lloyd at 22 October at Sèvres or was the mastermind behind the conferences of collusion. He was instructed to undertake a specific and limited mission and has always maintained that Eden was under no obligation to tell him more than he did.[23]

Before this pair joined the company at Sèvres, Pineau had arrived back from London, reporting success with Eden and bearing news of an agreed six-point plan which covered approximately the same ground as Dayan's tentative proposal. Eden had accepted that the operation should begin on Monday, 29 October, as a raid rather than a full-scale war, but he had insisted that it be as near the Canal and as 'noisy' as possible. However, there was nothing from the British in writing. Shimon Peres made a note of what Pineau had said. As Ben-Gurion transcribed it in his diary two days later, it said that the Israelis would start on Monday, 29 October at 7 p.m. (This was, according to Colonel Bar-On, an almost certain error for 5 p.m. since it was at that hour that Dayan always planned to launch the attack.) Britain and France would present Egypt with an ultimatum the next morning and their joint air forces would bomb Egypt's airfields at approximately 4 a.m. on Wednesday, 31 October. Ben-Gurion, still ultra-suspicious of the British, insisted on the terms being extended in two respects, so that they should explicitly make the Anglo-Jordan Treaty inoperative and should endorse Israel's seizure of the Straits of Tiran.

Dean handed over Lloyd's distancing letter to Pineau. He saw his brief as being to probe Israeli intentions, but within a context of 'no threat, no intervention'. Dayan was intending to send a battalion to the Canal area on D-Day; he thought the British might hold out for a brigade. He was accordingly reticent about disclosing his military plans in any great detail. He said: 'We will carry out such an operation that you will be able, without any doubt, to claim that there is danger to the Canal. We won't make a declaration [of war]. We'll simply smash 'em'. Ben-Gurion announced that Israel's main interest in the campaign lay in the capture of Sharm al-Sheikh and the freeing of the Enterprise Channel through the Tiran Straits. Dean observed that that was a long way from Suez. Dayan drew sketch maps and called attention to the Mitla Pass, a steep defile some thirty to thirty-five miles east of the port of Suez. Dayan promised that there would be activity by proper military units in the region of the pass. Beyond that he would not go.

The two British civil servants recognised that this was as much as they were going to get. 'There followed', says Logan, 'a somewhat desultory recapitulation of issues already discussed during the week which did not clarify the intentions of the three parties any further and raised no new issues'. The Israelis, they felt, remained suspicious of their intentions. After they had adjourned they heard the sound of a typewriter working in the next room and Dean was, presently, to his surprise, invited to sign three copies, all in French, of a paper summarising what had been discussed. It was, Dean and Logan decided, an accurate summary. Nothing had been said before they left London about signing or not signing a document. They concluded that, because Eden obviously set such store by the detail of the commitments, there was an advantage in having them recorded. Dean placed his signature alongside those of Pineau and Ben-Gurion, making it clear as he did so that he was signing *ad referendum* (subject to the approval of his Government).

The Protocol of Sèvres lacks a preamble. Bar-On says that the drafters tried their hand at one, but abandoned the attempt and began the document simply: 'The results of the conversations which took place at Sèvres from 22–24 October 1956 between the representatives of the Governments of the United Kingdom, the State of Israel and of France are the following.' There are seven articles. The first simply announced the Israeli decision to launch a large-scale operation on the evening of 29 October 'with the aim of reaching the Canal Zone the following day'. The second article says that 'on being apprised of these events', the Governments of Britain and France were to issue two separate and simultaneous 'appeals' (a scrupulous substitute for 'ultimatum', to which Ben-Gurion had objected) to the belligerents to stop all military action and to withdraw all their forces ten miles to the east of the Canal in the case of Israel and to the west of it in the case of Egypt. But to Egypt alone would be sent the demand that she accept 'the temporary occupation of key positions on the Canal by Anglo-French forces to guarantee freedom of passage through the Canal by vessels of all nations until a final arrangement'. This newly-worded provision, which meant that the Egyptians would be required to accept occupation troops whether or not they accepted the other terms of the ultimatum, had been brought back from London by Pineau. It was intended to prevent any possibility of the Egyptians accepting the terms.

If either government rejected the appeal or failed to give its agreement within twelve hours, the Anglo-French forces would take the necessary measures. The Government of Israel would not be required to fulfil the conditions if the Egyptians failed to accept them. If Egypt did fail to accept, the Anglo-French attack on the Egyptian forces would be launched in the early hours of the morning on 31 October. Israel would be entitled to seize the western shore of the Gulf of Aqaba and the islands of Tiran and Sanafir. Israel would not attack Jordan during the period of hostilities against Egypt; Britain would not help Jordan if she attacked Israel. Finally, it was laid down that the provisions of the Protocol were to remain strictly secret and were to enter into force as soon as they had been confirmed by the three

Governments. The text bears signs of having been hastily drawn up, with some minor typing errors and inconsistencies of layout.[24]

The Protocol was signed by Pineau, Dean and Ben-Gurion. There were three typed copies, at least one of which, at the Ben-Gurion Archive at Sde Boqer, is still in existence. It is not available at the British Public Record Office at Kew. Ben-Gurion on that day took particular satisfaction in folding his piece of paper and placing it gently but with some ceremony into his pocket. For him this was the supreme achievement: to have an alliance with two Great Powers. There was an obvious paradox. The Protocol on its face pledged total secrecy for ever; Ben-Gurion looked to it for his vindication before history. But in his mind, no doubt, he was accustomed to think of long spans of time. He took considerable steps to be loyal personally to the secrecy clause, but he also took care to see that the history of these events was recorded.

Dayan has laid claim to a certain elegance and symmetry about the balance of obligations involved. In a way, from Israel's viewpoint, that is true. The two sides of the treaty of collusion look after their own objectives: the Anglo-French take care of the Canal, the Israelis of the Straits of Tiran. All that is co-ordinated is the timing. But, in other respects, it is a misshapen document reflecting the different aims of the negotiators or their principals and above all of those two who did not meet, Eden and Ben-Gurion. The original aspiration for the appearance of even-handedness as between Egypt and Israel has been knocked out of shape by negotiation with one of the parties. The façade does not stretch round the face of the building. There was no provision, for instance, for sanctions against Israel if she did not respond to the 'appeal'. In appearances Ben-Gurion wanted balance with Britain and France, not with Egypt. At least in the Protocol he got it.

But when all is said and done the fact remains that Ben-Gurion, having come to Paris swearing to reject the 'English scenario', in effect left the villa in the rue Emanuel Girot with what was basically the same scenario signed and neatly folded in his pocket. Bar-On, who despite the great disparity of age knew Ben-Gurion quite well, attributes this to three factors: the pressure of the French, to whom he felt warm bonds of gratitude, the flair and psychological skill of Dayan at working on him, and the piece of paper itself, signed by three Powers, arising from a face-to-face meeting with the British Foreign Secretary.[25]

There was, also, for the Israelis a second document, signed by them and the French alone and not shown to the British though they suspected that something was afoot that they had better not know about. It made detailed provision for French squadrons on Israeli airfields and French naval vessels with anti-aircraft guns in Israeli harbours, as well as last-minute war supplies (to be flown in in ten transport planes). After the Protocol had been signed, the first to leave the rue Emanuel Girot were the British. They left, writes Dayan, 'mumbling as they went words of politeness tinged with humour and not quite comprehensible'.[26] The Israelis and the French were still talking animatedly and Shimon Peres was improving the hour by discussing with his French comrades details of his next scheme, which was to transfer French uranium and nuclear know-how to Israel. Dayan was drafting operational orders for the campaign he had created.

When the two civil servants reported to Eden at 10.30 that night (24 October),[27] and told him of the Protocol, the Prime Minister made no attempt to conceal his dismay. Didn't they realise that there were supposed to be no documents whatsoever? They had heard nothing of this. Eden said that Dean and Logan would have to go back to Paris the next day to arrange with the French for all copies of the document to be destroyed. When they arrived at the Quai d'Orsay, 'Pineau seemed doubtful', Logan recalls, 'but said he'd have to think about this'. The two Britons were asked to wait and were shown into one of the grand reception rooms at the Quai. After a while, it being lunchtime, they tried to go out and found that the door was locked. Remembering that the entire Quai d'Orsay was cut out of the circuit of those who knew about Sèvres, they realised how embarrassing their presence was. They stayed under lock and key until 4 p.m. when Pineau informed them that Ben-Gurion, who was already in Israel with his copy of the Protocol, would not accede to the request. Pineau let it be known that he agreed with him.[28]

Dean and Logan returned to London empty-handed. Lloyd's private office was ordered to hand over to Number Ten all copies that had been made of the document and of the English translation. But Eden now knew that somewhere and at some time there would be a smoking gun.

18

A Parachute Drop at the Mitla

Something very strange is happening. The Israelis are in Sinai and they seem to be fighting the sands.
Gamal Abdul Nasser to Mohamed Heikal, 29 October 1956.

We must face the risk that we should be accused of collusion with Israel. But . . . it [is] preferable that we should be seen to be holding the balance between Israel and Egypt rather than appear to be accepting Israeli co-operation in an attack on Egypt alone.
Sir Anthony Eden, Cabinet Minutes, 25 October 1956.

By late October President Gamal Abdul Nasser was well satisfied at the way his plans were working out. Events, Mohamed Heikal has noted, were conforming very nicely to the appreciation that he had made in July. The Western forces were still present in strength in the Eastern Mediterranean but the political will and diplomatic backing of France and Britain had been drastically undermined, so that it looked in Cairo as though an attack was very unlikely. The Russians were proving satisfactory allies, while the Americans seemed unthreatening. A memorandum drawn up by the Egyptian Intelligence Department and quoted by Heikal was reassuring about the Israeli attitude to the Suez crisis. 'Criticism by Israel of actions by Egypt since nationalisation has been very restrained,' it ran. 'Many recent broadcasts have emphasised that Israel should not allow herself to be used as a cat's paw by the Imperialist Powers.' It noted by way of support the Israeli press campaign against Britain.[1]

While Nasser was certainly aware of the British efforts to isolate Egypt in the Middle East, and was particularly sensitive (as, in their way, were the Israelis) to British and French 'black' broadcasting, he was very active in countering their effects. He visited Saudi Arabia in late September to consolidate his rather curious and uneasy alliance with King Saud and Crown Prince Faisal, who expressed their concern to him at the encouragement he seemed to be giving to the mob.[2] But his most important accomplishment was his new triple alliance, the tripartite military pact with Syria and Jordan which placed all the forces of the front-line states opposed to Israel (except for Lebanon) under a united military command headed by the Egyptian General Abdul Hakim Amer. This finally accomplished in October 1956 what Nasser had been struggling to achieve since February 1955; it was made possible by the approaching assumption of office by Suleiman Nabulsi in Jordan. Egypt was now to be what she had often seen herself as being, the acknowledged leader and organiser of the Arab states.

The change of government and of direction in Jordan was everywhere being interpreted as another blow to British influence, but the dictates of prestige compelled Britain, nevertheless, to cling on to her guarantees to that country despite the hostility of much of the Jordanian (and especially the Palestinian) public. The fall of Jordan could not be permitted because it was thought it would lead to the downfall of Britain's friends in Iraq. The Jordanians themselves did not want to dispense with Jordan's relationship with Britain. They were concerned to convince Sir Charles Duke that this was perfectly compatible with a military alliance with Egypt.[3] Meanwhile the Israelis, seeing Nasser behind the trigger everywhere they looked, determined to smash the new alliance at its head before it had any chance to become operational.

The British Decide

On 25 October, while General Dayan drew up fresh directives and briefed his senior commanders about the attack which would now take place, the British Cabinet gathered for its most fateful meeting. Eden reminded his colleagues that two days before he had told them that 'it now seemed unlikely' that the Israelis would attack. Now there was different news. 'It appeared that the Israelis were, after all, advancing their military preparations with a view to making an attack upon Egypt.' Eden did not attribute this move to the need to dispose of the *fedayeen* but to the more fundamental rationale, more suited to a full-scale war, that Nasser's ambitions threatened Israel's continued existence as a state. The Israelis 'evidently felt . . . that they could not afford to wait for others to curb his expansionist policies'. The Cabinet were, therefore, called on to decide now what to do in the event of hostilities (date unspecified) between Israel and Egypt.

The French Government was strongly of the view, the Prime Minister went on, that intervention would be justified as a means of limiting hostilities. If Britain declined to join them in this, France might well act alone or in conjunction with Israel. Eden suggested that, if Israel were to launch a full-scale military operation, Britain and France should at once call on both parties to desist and to fall back ten miles from the line of the Canal. Israel might well accept. 'If Egypt also complied, Colonel Nasser's prestige would be fatally undermined.' But if she failed to comply, there would be 'ample justification' for military action against Egypt. Not since the reign of Henry VII had a Minister contrived such a perfect example of Morton's fork.[4]

Eden warned his Ministers that: 'We must face the risk that we should be accused of collusion with Israel.' But, he argued, this charge 'was liable to be brought against us in any event for it can now be assumed that, if an Anglo-French operation were to be undertaken against Egypt, we should be unable to prevent the Israelis from launching a parallel attack themselves'. The marker for this had been carefully put down the previous day. Given this predicament, Eden put it to his colleagues that 'it was preferable that we should be seen to be holding the balance between Israel and Egypt rather than appear to be accepting Israeli co-operation in an attack on Egypt alone'.

The Foreign Secretary followed up this remarkable definition of the options available by building up with thick layers of paint a picture of the whole Middle East riddled with Egyptian and communist conspiracies. It was true, he conceded, that from the point of view of Arab opinion Israel's intervention in Britain's dispute with Egypt would be unfortunate. (Lloyd could have described the lengths to which he had gone at the UN just a fortnight before to exclude Israel, precisely for this reason, from the Suez Canal debate which intimately concerned her). But there seemed to be 'little prospect of another early opportunity for bringing this issue to a head'.

In the Cabinet Minutes, in spite of the delicate way in which Cabinet secretaries list points made in a discussion without matching names to arguments (unless the individual Minister makes a formal request), there can be found evidence of formidable objections being raised to the remarkable course of action that had been proposed. The operation, it was said, might do lasting damage to Anglo-American relations, since there was no prospect of securing the support or approval of the American Government; Britain would be charged with failure to comply with the Tripartite Declaration which she had gone to such lengths to affirm and reaffirm. 'In seeking to separate the two belligerents we should be purporting to undertake an international function without the specific authority of the UN.'[5]

Although these ought to have alerted Eden to the extent to which his policies were causing doubt and unease, these objections in the short run led nowhere. The main doubters were Monckton, Heathcoat Amory (the Minister of Agriculture), and Iain Macleod (Minister of Labour), who was rated a political high flyer in the Cabinet and party. But none of them formally dissented from the agreement in principle to the scenario that was to be followed 'in the event of an Israeli attack on Egypt'. The Cabinet was deceived about the extent of collusion with the Israelis or, at the least, not addressed with candour on the subject. As a consequence, Eden later found himself obliged to preserve consistency with his cover story in respect not merely to the outside world but also to those of his Ministers who were not in the know. But Ministers were told in advance about the action contemplated and they had agreed to it though, in some cases, with a heavy heart.

They were told at the Cabinet meeting the following day about the economic background. This was already so serious that, unless all the country's financial resources were mobilised to maintain the fixed rate against the dollar, it was said that it would be necessary to move to a floating exchange. That would, in Macmillan's estimation, end sterling's role as an international currency and destroy the Sterling Area. The Chancellor warned his colleagues that he expected the loss of gold and dollars to be as high as $300m during the month of November; the shock to international confidence would be severe. Informal contacts with the Americans should be used to prepare the way for the substantial loans that would be needed if the existing parity were to be defended. It was in anything but a robust state of health that Britain was going into battle.

One last effort by the Chiefs of Staff, the men who would have to oversee the coming battle, was made on 25 October to call the Egypt Committee's attention to the wider defence consequences of what they were about to do. Assuming, they said, that Phase II of *Musketeer* had been carried out, they would expect to find the Egyptian economy 'seriously damaged, railways, roads and communications largely disrupted, civil administration considerably strained and disease more widespread than usual'. In these circumstances they could be certain, regardless of whether a new 'co-operative government' was forthcoming, that there would be a lot of hostility around. The British must be ready (and the Chiefs did not disguise their belief that the French contribution would soon diminish to token levels) not only to reoccupy the Canal Zone but, if needed, to enforce a change of government and maintain in power a new one, to occupy Cairo and possibly Alexandria as well.

The occupation force, therefore, would have to be of the order of three to four divisions, with this time a full civil affairs staff in support. To keep such a force in place, one infantry division would have to be withdrawn from Germany indefinitely, the UK Strategic Reserve would have to be committed (so making it impossible to respond to contingencies elsewhere), reservists retained, hopes of reducing or abolishing conscription abandoned.[6] All this was a very different story from the minimal occupation and avoidance of responsibilities that had characterised the civil service drafts in August.

General Keightley saw the Prime Minister alone before departing for Cyprus and expressed his anxieties. There was no question, he said, of his not being able to conduct the operation successfully but, before he did, he wanted to know if Britain was going to be any better off afterwards. According to the General's account to Mountbatten, 'Eden gave him a very severe dressing down and told him that these were questions with which military commanders should not concern themselves'.[7]

The ways were parting as the moment of action approached. Anthony Nutting, Minister of State and chief British spokesman at the UN General Assembly, was arriving at the agonising decision that his most promising career in office must suddenly come to an end. For him the issue had now been simplified. 'I knew that I could not defend the Government in Parliament or anywhere else.' He has described in *No End of a Lesson* how he had reviewed the arguments with Walter Monckton, now Paymaster-General. The latter, Nutting records, 'made no bones about his view that Eden was a very sick man. He had always been excitable and temperamental, but in the last few months he had seemed to be on the verge of a breakdown.' This was a disturbing impression for a Cabinet Minister, who had until recently been a member of the Egypt Committee, to convey.

Monckton then said he would like to resign himself but, since he was a member of the Cabinet, his departure 'might topple the Government, with incalculable consequences for all concerned'. Evidently considering that nothing could be worse than that, the objectors remained silent, nursing their convictions as a private grief. Nutting says that he suddenly felt, as he walked back to the Foreign Office, 'a sudden wild desire' to make for the US Embassy and tell all to Winthrop Aldrich, in the hope of averting disaster.[8] But the honour of the regiment, as it were, was not to be compromised. There were no whistle-blowers at Suez.

War on the BBC

By what may have struck him as an acute irony, Nutting was required as almost his final ministerial duty to execute the latest move in what had become a running battle between the Eden Government and the BBC. He was told by Rab Butler, the chairman of the Cabinet committee on overseas broadcasting, to present that committee's conclusions in person to the Director-General, Sir Ian Jacob, 'partly as a means of administering a shock to the BBC and inducing them to reconcile their independence with the need for greater care in conducting these [external] services in the national interest'. The Government were clearing the decks. It was difficult enough in all conscience to deploy the psychological weapon in the Middle East and elsewhere without being made at the same time to bear the self-imposed obligation of giving equal time to Hugh Gaitskell and the *Manchester Guardian*.[9]

The BBC's ideology on news required a seamless web: 'You cannot suppress news on one service and allow it on another', in the words of Harman Grisewood, the BBC's Director of the Spoken Word.[10] Much of the tension that existed in Broadcasting House, where the whole ethos of the BBC as an independent public service was felt to be in peril, arose, paradoxically, out of the efforts of William Clark as a former television

Nasser and Eden meet for the only time in Cairo, February 1955.

Ships travelling in convoy through the Suez Canal.

General Nuri es-Said, Prime Minister and Minister of Defence of Iraq, the favourite Arab of British politicians and diplomats, co-founder of the Baghdad Pact.

King Hussein of Jordan with the man he dismissed, Glubb Pasha, the commander of the Arab Legion.

Col. Ariel Sharon, head of Unit 101 and later of 202 Paratroop Brigade, briefs the Prime Minister of Israel, David Ben-Gurion.

Dmitri Shepilov, the new, young Soviet Foreign Minister, with President Nasser.

Right Krishna Menon, Nehru's favourite, Eden's 'hornet', India's loquacious and self-regarding mediator. He had good ideas but was trusted by none.

Below Christian Pineau, French Foreign Minister, Eden and Dulles at Downing Street during the London Conference.

Bottom Robert Menzies, the Prime Minister of Australia, brings the Eighteen Nation Plan to Mahmoud Fawzi, Egyptian Foreign Minister and President Nasser, who reject it.

Maurice Bourgès-Maunoury, French Minister of Defence and later Prime Minister; former resistance hero and chief promoter of the alliance with Israel.

Guy Mollet, the Socialist Prime Minister of France.

The narrow Enterprise Channel through the Straits of Tiran under an Egyptian gun at Ras Nasrani.

The Villa in the rue Emanuel Girot where the conference of Sèvres took place and the Protocol was signed.

Left Dwight D. Eisenhower, puzzled.

Below John Foster Dulles listens to Sir Pierson ('Bob') Dixon, Britain's Permanent Representative at the UN.

Above Dag Hammarskjöld, 'the amazing Swede', Secretary-General of the United Nations.

Left Henry Cabot Lodge, the US Permanent Representative, sitting in the UN.

Above The commanders. General Stockwell, General Keightley and General Beaufre.

Left above The second wave of British marines wade ashore at Port Said.

General Moshe Dayan, the Israeli Chief of Staff, with his men on the Sinai campaign.

Psychological warfare. Ronald Searle drew the cartoons but the R.A.F. declined to drop them on Port Said.

Bodies of Egyptians killed in the assault on Port Said dumped outside a cemetery. Probably about 750 were killed in Port Said and Port Fuad combined, but some said the figure was higher.

Vice-Admiral Pierre Barjot, the Deputy Allied Commander-in-Chief in a barge in front of the Suez Canal Company's offices at Port Said.

French troops escorting Egyptian prisoners at Port Said.

Right The fall of the Founder. De Lesseps blown off his pedestal in December 1956 when the British and French left Port Said.

Below The handshake. General Sir Charles Keightley, Allied Commander-in-Chief, greets Lieutenant-General E. L. M. Burns, the Canadian Commander of UNEF in Port Said. They wore the same cap badge.

Above One of the 51 wrecks in Port Said harbour and the Suez Canal.

Right The End. Anthony Eden leaves to go to the Queen to present his resignation, January 1957.

interviewer and presenter, to explain the tribal habits of Portland Place and Number Ten to each other. Alarmed by Eden's mounting irascibility about the BBC as the Suez crisis progressed, Clark seems to have repeated to the broadcasters some of the wild talk that could be heard in Number Ten about instructing the Lord Chancellor to prepare an instrument to take over the BBC and place it under government orders. This has now entered into the folklore of Suez. Clark later confessed that he might have exaggerated; his aim was to alert the BBC to the dangerous mood that he thought the Prime Minister was in.[11] Certainly there is no trace either among the records that have been released or in Clark's quite candid diary of the Lord Chancellor's proposed instrument.

There may well have been confusion between the BBC as a whole and the External Services. The latter depended on a government grant, and as early as 28 August Sir Ivone Kirkpatrick was making it abundantly clear to the Director-General that Ministers did not think they were getting their money's worth. The whole trouble, as he put it, stemmed from the BBC's fetish of attaching 'too much importance to impartiality'.[12] What Nutting had to do on 25 October was to crack the whip over Jacob and tell him to behave, without doing anything so radical as had been suggested. Now that bipartisanship in foreign policy had broken down, Nutting explained, the Government was determined, at least in the services for which it paid, to have its own case put over in a clear and unambiguous way, 'without having contrary views also carried to the confusion of peoples in certain parts of the world who did not understand our political system'.

It was all too late. The BBC was far too skilled a bureaucracy to be brought to heel by half-measures. General Jacob took off as planned for Australia; the External Services continued during the next weeks to put out balanced reports of parliamentary debates and press reviews, and the luckless Foreign Office 'nark' who was established in Bush House to keep these independent broadcasters in line arrived when the fighting was over. Presently he faded away.[13]

Israel Mobilises

The world's attention – or that part of it that was not fixated on the last two weeks of the American presidential election – was now captured by the spectacle of Hungary shaking herself free of Soviet imperial power. Like a crowd spellbound by some immensely dangerous spectacle, other countries held their breath with fascination and awe as one of the 'satellites' made a bid to be independent, pluralist and neutral and thus to disprove the widespread assumption that there was no going back on satellite status.

On the evening of Friday, 26 October, Hungary was the main topic of conversation between Dulles and Henry Cabot Lodge at the UN as they sought to promote action in the Security Council. But Dulles confessed to Lodge his sense of foreboding about Britain, France and Israel. 'We don't know what the British and French agreed to in their last talks,' Dulles said. 'I think they may be going in to fight.'[14]

The mobilisation of the Israeli forces had begun as soon as the Protocol of Sèvres had been signed but, for the first two days, the emergency call-up machinery was not used in order not to attract too much attention. Even so, it was impossible to conceal completely what was happening; accordingly, disinformation was pumped out by Israeli intelligence about the Iraqi army entering Jordan and even about King Hussein having been assassinated.[15] All attention was to be directed to that front and to the provocations of Nabulsi's new nationalist regime. News of the mobilisation had reached and deeply worried Washington and New York. The U-2 told part of the tale, and the Americans also deduced how comprehensive the mobilisation was from the fact that their military attaché's driver, who was three fingers short, had been called up.[16]

Already by the afternoon of Friday, 26 October it was apparent to Colonel Leo J. Query, the American Army Attaché in Tel Aviv, that this call-up was on a larger scale than had been ordered since 1948–9. At 8 p.m. on the Sabbath, the Ministry of Defence building and various military posts which would normally have been closed at sundown were seen to be in full operation. The newly mobilised troops were mostly in bivouac to the south of Tel Aviv. Colonel Query's sources told him that the French were working with the Israelis and that the target was probably the Straits of Tiran.[17]

On the morning of Saturday, 27 October President Eisenhower discussed the evidence with Dulles and Hoover. The most probable direction for an Israeli attack was still thought in Washington to be the West Bank while Nasser was preoccupied with Suez. Dulles, says the memorandum on this meeting, 'next referred to indications of possible developments in Syria'. The reference is without a doubt to the long contemplated and many times postponed 'Operation *Straggle*', the Iraqi-planned coup on which British and American intelligence were working together, designed to overthrow the Nasserist Government of Syria. It had been on the intelligence agenda since the CIA–MI6 conferences in March–April (and on that indefatigable conspirator Nuri's agenda for very much longer) and was at last coming up to the deadline. The necessary cash had been delivered to the leaders of the conspiracy inside Syria by the CIA's man Major Eveland. The target date had been switched from 25 to 29 October. The 301st Meeting of the National Security Council had been told by Allen Dulles on the morning of 26 October that a coup was likely to take place in Syria.

The memorandum on the White House meeting goes on to say that Secretary Dulles suggested that the Israelis might have information about what was about to happen in Syria and might be mobilising to take advantage of the opportunity on the West Bank.[18] What it does not do is reflect what Allen Dulles was later to claim was his first warning, given to the State Department by the CIA that morning (27 October), that 'a major Israeli attack against Egypt could be expected at any time after the close of the Hebrew Sabbath' that evening. Nor has any record been found of such a warning in State Department files.[19]

Eisenhower was talking about inviting Eden and Mollet over to Washington towards the end of November to discuss the Middle East, the invitations to be conditional on no prior use of force against Egypt. From London, Aldrich suggested that such an invitation should be broached privately at once, before the election; that he, Aldrich, should deliver the letter personally; and that he should watch Eden's face as he read its terms for any giveaway signs that early use of force had been planned. But 'I do not believe', Aldrich concluded, 'that either Eden or the British Cabinet is so wedded to the possible immediate use of force ... as to be unwilling to accept the invitation.'[20] Unfortunately Eisenhower did not follow through on the idea; instead he had a new offer of mediation drafted for him to launch publicly on the night of his expected election victory.

On the evening of 27 October, Dulles delivered at Dallas his only election speech of the campaign. It dealt mainly with Hungary, but the text of his brief passage on Suez was changed at the last minute on the advice of the CIA who, without any positive evidence, felt there was sufficient possibility of either French or Anglo-French collusion with the Israelis as to make it unwise for any passage to suggest afterwards that Dulles had been aware of this at the time and had approved of it.[21]

Exercise Embark

Such was the degree of secrecy that it is very difficult to tell even now who in the inner circle in Whitehall knew what and when. The Chiefs of Staff do not seem to have been told about the Protocol of Sèvres, all copies of this within Eden's grasp having been destroyed. They were given an indication, probably on the lines of Lloyd's memorandum on the Paris meeting of 16 October, that the Israelis were expected to attack Egypt. It is known that 29 October as a probable date was conveyed to Keightley, who had been present when Lloyd was sent on his clandestine journey. The Task Force Commanders had no official guidance, though the policy was different with their deputies who were French. Admiral Davis, in his unpublished autobiography, says that 'though the precise date never reached the Chiefs of Staff, we could guess'. Yet despite this he still did not, at the time of writing his memoirs, believe the allegations of collusion.

Davis does go on to say, however, that 'some days beforehand' he was advised in the strictest confidence that the Israelis might attack the Sinai peninsula on about 29 October. Without any authority to do so, the Admiral promptly warned the two leading shipowners 'in the strongest possible terms' that British merchant ships and liners should be kept clear of the Canal. The informal British system worked. Despite the extreme precipitancy of the crisis and in contrast to what was to happen in 1967, no British-owned ships were among those trapped in the Canal by the war. When Hailsham, the First Lord, was told by Sir William Davis after the event, he said that he was absolutely thankful it had happened and that by no stretch of the imagination could he or any member of the Government have authorised it.[22]

On 22 October General Stockwell received from the French staff integrated with his 2 Corps Headquarters the first intimation that D-Day was likely in the near future. Only three officers including himself were, he says, 'in the know' and only another three in the War Office itself. On 24 October the news which had 'gone cold' was 'hot' again. Sir Charles Keightley sent a signal reminding everyone that *Musketeer* (the 'revise' was now dropped) was still in force and said that it was to be held at ten days' notice. He must not then have known that D − 10 had already passed. On 25 October, on Admiral Grantham's warning that the weather had broken early in the Eastern Mediterranean and that it was no longer possible to keep loaded ships off the coast of Cyprus, Keightley cancelled Plan 'A' and adjusted the remaining Plan 'B' to allow for an eventual assault on Port Said against limited resistance. This was to be followed by a build-up with a view to breaking out and occupying the whole Canal Zone.[23] Thus was brought home to General André Beaufre, the Deputy Land Force Commander, the miseries and servitudes of an integrated command. A quick landing from Cyprus would no longer be possible.[24]

Thanks to Mountbatten's order of 18 October, the three aircraft carriers were now concentrated at Malta, and the communications exercise *Boathook* would involve moving *Tyne,* the destroyer/depot ship, which was to serve all three Task Force Commanders as their command post, the carrier group and the various headquarter groups to the Cyprus area by 30 October. Fortuitously, another exercise had been arranged for the following week to practise getting the soldiers down the narrow Maltese streets and aboard their landing craft.

In the Air Ministry files there is an unsigned note of 26 October headed 'Points for the Prime Minister'. It begins: 'The operations must now be run as required militarily. But we will not make any overt moves which are not essential. We will use the signal exercise [*Boathook*] as a cover plan.' The note goes on to say that the timings were dictated by not being able to make any overt moves before D-Day + 1. This meant no air offensive until the night of D-Day + 3 and no landing until D-Day + 10. It ends with a plea that Keightley, whose plans were now complete and issued, should be directed to go ahead and that further alterations could only cause confusion since the troops taking part were split three ways between home bases, Malta and Cyprus.[25]

Precisely at 5.30 p.m. on 26 October, as the Acting Quartermaster-General to the Forces, Major-General John Cowley, noted, he was sent for by General Templer, 'a splendid but not the most patient of men', to be given this Delphic message: 'The PM has decided that the landing at Port Said must take place as soon as possible but has also said that no one is yet to be told.' The message was passed on to Cowley's key subordinate, Major-General 'Robbie' Ewbank, Director of Movements, as follows: 'I am not allowed to tell you this but if I should state that the Port Said operation is on and that the troops waiting in Malta and North Africa must be alerted and embarked and sail as soon as possible to the Eastern Mediterranean, what would you do?' To which Ewbank's first response was, 'I would assume that you had gone off your head.' But nonetheless orders went out to collect all ships within reach so that, although officially still at seven days' notice for embarkation, units were ready for it within three days.

But actual troop movements were still controlled from the highest political level. A Guards regiment was under orders to sail for the Middle East from Southampton at midnight. It embarked at 4 p.m. and two hours later received orders from the Prime Minister that it was on no account to leave the country. Two hours later still, with the regiment safely disembarked, arrived a message 'from the same source' that it must set sail at midnight. On the evening of 26 October General Cowley drafted a message to the British civilians at the Canal Base, 'Get out with your families as quickly as you can.' The message was stopped on political grounds.[26]

General Stockwell, the Land Force Commander, with his Chief of Staff, Brigadier Darling, flew to Malta on 26 October before sailing on *Tyne* to Cyprus. They stopped off at the French military airfield at Villacoublay and were met by Stockwell's French deputy General Beaufre, from whom Stockwell learnt for the first time that Israel would probably launch an attack on Egypt on 29 October, which might well be followed almost at once by allied intervention. It was clear that the intervention was to be *Musketeer*, not *Cordage*. When Stockwell arrived in Malta he passed on the news to the four admirals (Grantham, Commander-in-Chief, Mediterranean; Durnford-Slater, the Naval Task Force Commander; Lancelot, his French deputy, and 'Lofty' Power, who commanded the carrier force). 'I can see Admiral Power now', Stockwell later recalled, on television, 'with a chart of the Mediterranean in front of him and dividers.' He said: 'My dear old boy, we'll have to start tomorrow.'[27]

Admiral Power was, in fact, not at all pleased with what he had heard. By his own account, his first reaction to Admiral Grantham was: 'The Government must have gone raving mad. If we are in any way mixed up with Israeli action we shall upset the whole Muslim world and I think we shan't have the rest of world opinion behind us either. It's daft.' To which

Sir Guy Grantham replied: 'I don't know about that. It will be a good show if we bring it off.' Power contented himself with the thought: 'Thank God I've only got to fight and not worry about the politics.'[28]

Sir Dermot Boyle, Chief of the Air Staff, sympathising with a Commander-in-Chief, Middle East Air Forces, who, under the strange command structure, had been left with large titular responsibilities but very little role, cabled him on 27 October, 'I appreciate the complexity of the present situation and the worry it must be causing you.' He added: 'When you have seen Hudleston, who is coming out tonight, situation will be much clearer.' Air Vice-Marshal Hudleston had what was, in view of the nature of the coming campaign, one of its most sensitive assignments: he was to select the targets whose elimination, without too much loss of life, was to bring Colonel Nasser low. He turned up with Boyle's directive that *Cordage* preparations were to be stood down for *Musketeer*.[29]

The commanders had been confronted by a drastic shortening of the expected notice just as life in Malta was moving into a peacetime weekend. On the Saturday (27 October), after a dash to London by Abel Thomas, Bourgès-Maunoury's *chef de cabinet,* the British at last agreed that some ships could leave Valletta harbour on the night of 28 October.[30] But 30 October was the earliest date that the forces could be alerted that they were going into action. They should be ready for D-Day on 31 October and landing day on 8 November. Although condemned by the world as leaden-footed, the allied forces in the event got there faster than that.

On the evening of Saturday, notices went out round the pubs and clubs of Malta for officers to gather for an urgent meeting on Sunday morning. The loading exercise was then brought forward twenty-four hours; it was to begin immediately 'as for war'. Those who could put two and two together, like the reserve officer Douglas Clark, who later published a lively memoir, *Suez Touchdown. A Soldier's Tale*, concluded from various bits of evidence that this was no exercise but the real thing.[31] Vice-Admiral Power sailed for Cyprus on 29 October to keep his *Boathook* rendezvous with three carriers, two cruisers and sixteen destroyers. But nothing could induce London to instruct the slow ships, the troop landing craft, to sail early. That would be to raise doubts whether the Israeli attack had really taken everyone by surprise. Even the Air Task Force Commander, Air Marshal Barnett, only uncovered collusion by chance. He went in to see Keightley. Someone came into the room and a paper blew onto the floor. Barnett saw written on it the note: 'Hooknoses' D-Day – 29 Oct'. He said to himself: 'Christ, you aren't in some awful bloody hook-up are you?'[32] But to Keightley he said nothing.

Countdown to Kadesh

The changes that Dayan made to the orders for Operation *Kadesh* on 25 October reflected his desire to confuse the Egyptians about the scale of the attack. His guiding principle was to put off for thirty-six hours any action that could be as well done after the intervention of the allies, so that the campaign would be a limited liability for Israel should the alliance break down. This required him to issue instructions that ran at almost every point counter to the ethos which he had spent three years instilling into the Israeli Defence Forces. His ideas, writes his bureau chief, Mordechai Bar-On, had penetrated deeply into the consciousness of all ranks. They were all ideas of speed, aggression, breakthroughs deep behind enemy lines, all from the very first moment of the war. It was something of a culture shock to find the high priest of the reprisal raid becoming the apostle of restraint and, while it was understood that his motives were political, Dayan was extremely discreet and sparing in parting with information. He was at the same time very insistent on the need for meticulous discipline in the carrying out of even strange orders.

The most dramatic change in the plans for *Kadesh* brought about by the Protocol of Sèvres was the switch of 202 Paratroop Brigade, commanded by Colonel Ariel Sharon, the veterans of so many night clashes on the Egyptian and Jordanian borders, from the star fighting role of capturing first Al Arish and then Sharm al-Sheikh to the star diplomatic role of providing the 'real threat' to the Suez Canal. At the opening of the campaign a battalion was to be dropped at the Mitla Pass and was to be reinforced by the rest of the brigade over the taxing lower invasion route (Kuntilla–Nakhl–Mitla) with only an unsurfaced road. A reserve unit, 9 Infantry Brigade, previously assigned to a diversionary attack along this axis, was to cross the border at Ras an-Naqb on the first night but, only when there was no longer any threat from the air and the rest of the campaign was well underway, was it to set out on what was now to be its main task: to tackle Sharm al-Sheikh, not by the air drop that had been previously assigned to Sharon, but by the extremely arduous overland route. Finally, the armour, Israel's shiny new weapon, two and a half brigades instead of the previous one thanks to the French arms deal, was not to be used in any impetuous, off-the-mark style. In fact it was not to be used at all until the allies were in the battle. Israel would not forfeit the option of treating the whole enterprise retroactively as a grand reprisal raid.[33]

The air force, too, was told to clip its wings. The pilots' instincts, as (the then) Major Ezer Weizman was to point out in his autobiography, were to go straight for the Egyptian airfields and smash the Egyptian planes on the ground, thus attempting without as much equipment what was to be achieved so dramatically in 1967. Now their orders were peremptory: they were not to cross the Suez Canal. 'In Sinai we'll act as if we own it, but

Heaven help us if we cross.' In accordance with the bilateral section of the Protocol of Sèvres, the two French squadrons – thirty-six Mystères and F84s – took up their position on Israeli airfields on the eve of battle. They were under the command of Colonel Maurice Perdrizet, who had been the top French air force planner in the Montagu House basement in London until he had suddenly disappeared without explanation for this new assignment.[34]

But France's main contribution to Israel lay in the supply of *matériel*. Just how narrow were the margins was revealed by Dayan when he published his *Diary of the Sinai Campaign* in 1966. The one aspect of Israel's famous Swiss-like mobilisation of a citizen army which very nearly came unstuck was the standard of maintenance of the civilian transport on which the Israeli army relied. Only sixty per cent of the registered 13,000 vehicles came in and many of them were in a shocking condition and in absolutely no state to face the Sinai desert. The indispensable rescue, a French shipment of two hundred 6 × 6 trucks with front-wheel drive, came in only on 27 October, two days before D-Day; they were instantly assigned, half to the Paratroop Brigade and half to 9 Brigade which was to pick its tortuous way to Sharm al-Sheikh.[35]

Reports reached Washington from Tel Aviv that the call-up of reservists and civilian vehicles had gone on throughout the night of 26/27 October and Eisenhower sent a special message to Ben-Gurion at noon (7 p.m. Israeli time) on 27 October. It had to wait for delivery by Edward Lawson, the American Ambassador, until eight the following evening on the grounds that the usual Sunday Cabinet meeting had lasted all day. By now the quiet method of mobilisation had been found to be less than satisfactory. Many reservists failed to receive their orders; in one brigade only fifty per cent had turned up. Israel therefore switched to the emergency – and therefore highly publicised – system, whereupon volunteers, suddenly aware that this was no routine test of the system, flooded in.[36]

By the time Lawson finally got in to see Ben-Gurion at his Tel Aviv home to deliver his pressing message, Ben-Gurion was, according to Dayan, 'very apprehensive about its contents'. Lawson found him looking tired, his voice weak and his temperature high. Obviously suffering from fever, he protested that he had only called up 'a few units' as a 'defensive precaution'. 'We don't know from what point of the ring around us we can expect attack . . . We shall be as happy as the President if things remain quiet.' Afterwards, scrutinising with anxious care the wording of the messages he had received, he concluded to himself with some satisfaction that the President dealt only in generalities and, where there was a specific reference, it suggested that American attention was still fixed on Jordan.[37]

The CIA's Watch Committee met at noon on Sunday, 28 October (5 p.m. London time, 7 p.m. Middle East time) to compile a special report. Their prediction, which was approved by the Intelligence Advisory Committee and circulated that afternoon and evening was that, 'Past Egyptian provocations, the key role of Egypt in the Arab threat and UK involvement with Jordan indicate the attack will be launched against Egypt in the very near future.' The scale of mobilisation was such as to enable the Israelis to occupy the West Bank and Damascus as well as Sinai if need be. The Watch Committee also sent Secretary Dulles a separate memorandum bearing, besides this conclusion, the 'highly sensitive information' that the British had brought up their strength in Cyprus in the last forty-eight hours to sixty-three (Canberra) medium bombers, doubling the previous strength, while eighteen French transport aircraft, capable of airlifting 1,500 men, had arrived within the past twenty-four hours, raising Anglo-French lift capacity to between 2,500 and 3,000 paras.[38]

These reports issued from the American intelligence community just in time to save Allen Dulles's face in the *post mortem* on Suez but in practice too late to influence the making of policy over a weekend at the commencement of the last week of a presidential campaign. With regard to Britain and France, the Americans had noted the exceptionally heavy cable traffic between Paris and Israel, the 'deliberate British purpose of keeping us completely in the dark' about Middle East policy pursued for a week by the Washington Embassy, the breaking off in the field of the normally intimate contact between the military attachés of the three western powers. Of French collusion with Israeli military plans the Americans felt almost certain. About Britain they were not sure and wanted to feel that it was not true.

On the Sunday night Dulles, telephoning the President, spoke to him about the Anglo-French build-up on Cyprus. Eisenhower's spontaneous reaction was that he just could not believe Britain would be dragged into this. Dulles told him of a conversation he had just had with the French Ambassador and the British Chargé, John Coulson. (Sir Roger Makins had gone home to become Permanent Secretary to the Treasury and his successor, Sir Harold Caccia, was coming the slow way by sea, an arrangement that did not strike the Americans as, and indeed was not, accidental.) Both Coulson and Alphand denied having any information of the sort possessed by the American Government about Israeli mobilisation, a form of ignorance that Dulles told the President was almost a sign of a guilty conscience. He had, he said, cautioned them severely not to assume that, because it was the eve of an election, the US was incapable of taking an anti-Israel stand should one be called for. Meanwhile, a White House statement had described the Israeli mobilisation as 'almost complete' and had added, as a way of testing the allies, that the President was going into immediate discussion with the British and French to find out what steps needed to be taken under the Tripartite Declaration.[39]

In Whitehall a most abnormal situation prevailed. Steps were being taken to ensure that no one who was likely to be unsympathetic to the operation that was being planned should be aware of what was going on. Even the head of the political section of MI6 was affected. When he noticed that there was a break in a numbered series of telegrams he was told that he was 'not on the list' to receive the missing items. Subsequently it transpired that these messages were a series cabled by Nicholas Elliot, who had been sent out from MI6 to establish liaison with Tel Aviv. Then there was the case of 'the mutilated telegram'. Harold Beeley, an Assistant Under-Secretary dealing with the Middle East, was alerted to something going on about which he had not been informed by reading an incoming telegram from Sir John Nicholls, the Ambassador in Tel Aviv, which carried the highest classification for an account of a conversation with Ben-Gurion that on the face of it could only be described as routine. When Suez was over it emerged that the passage that had been deleted from the copies circulated in the Foreign Office had Ben-Gurion responding to Nicholls's expression of gloom at the widening gap between Israel and Britain by the startling statement that the Ambassador, who had just returned from home leave, did not know all his Government was doing. 'Our relations are a good deal closer than you think.'[40]

Over lunch at the Reform Club or at tea time at the Ritz, where Nigel Birch, the Secretary of State for Air, who had been excluded from the planning, sought enlightenment from his senior officers, those who would expect to know what was going on discussed the strange sensation of being a part of the machine that had been disconnected. Coming back from leave on 29 October to Number Ten, William Clark found that he was being kept out of the Private Office. After lunch he ran into a meeting gathering outside the Cabinet Room including the Service chiefs and Keightley, who was supposed to be in the Middle East. Mountbatten took the occasion to remark: 'I don't envy your job in the next few days; this will be the hardest war to justify ever.'[41]

In the Foreign Office the number who knew would scarcely exceed the fingers of one hand – a few in the Private Office, Kirkpatrick and Ross, the two officials Nutting had been allowed to consult. One interesting discovery was that it was possible, for a short period at any rate, for a few senior Ministers to carry out a policy without the aid of most of the civil service. Foreign Office channels were dispensed with, for example, in communicating with the French about the operation on which the two Governments were about to embark. Presumably, as in the case of Tel Aviv, MI6 channels were employed.

The most delicate aspect concerned relations with the United States. On the Sunday evening Aldrich had entertained Lloyd to dinner together with the American Minister and Harold Beeley. On instructions from Dulles, Aldrich asked Lloyd if he knew the reason for Israeli mobilisation. The Foreign Secretary, with a perfectly straight face, confessed to being in the dark about this. But he said that Britain had warned the Israelis, using very strong language indeed, that, if they attacked Jordan, they would have Britain to reckon with. Aldrich asked him whether he did not think Israel might be planning to attack Egypt. Knowing from a previous conversation that Beeley was convinced that Jordan would be the victim, Lloyd turned to him for corroboration that this was unlikely. The Foreign Secretary kept on stressing how seriously Britain's position would be compromised by an Israeli attack either on Jordan or on Egypt. Aldrich left the table thinking that, 'Although he reiterated that he would like to see something happen to Nasser, his concern over the consequences of Israeli initiative carried sufficient conviction for me to conclude that any UK complicity in such a move is unlikely.'[42]

At the end of its prolonged meeting that Sunday, the Israeli Cabinet issued a statement attempting to show that the state was in sudden peril from a combination of dangers: the *fedayeen* activities of the past fortnight (which had been few and minor); the new military alliance between Egypt, Jordan and Syria; various threatening statements by Arab rulers; and 'the mobilisation of Iraqi forces on the borders of Jordan'. All this which, once granted Israel's permanently uncomfortable situation, did not really amount to very much, was said to have compelled the mobilisation of a 'number of reserve battalions' (instead of, in fact, virtually the entire available manpower). These battalions were going to take the initial shock of any enemy attack in order to 'afford us a sufficient breathing space ... to mobilise our reserve forces on which alone depends the defence of Israel'. The statement ended with a warning to pay no attention to 'flying rumours'.[43] That did not stop the Director-General of the Foreign Ministry, Walter Eytan, from using his regular weekly broadcast to give an extra spin to the flight of Israel's decoy. Jordan's action in creating an active alliance with Egypt and Syria, he said, amounted to a 'declaration of war'. It meant that 'the die has been cast'.[44]

The Israelis Attack

The British Embassy promptly next morning (Monday, 29 October) reported the 'two flying rumours' that appeared to the Americans to carry most credence. One was that Britain had agreed with Israel and Iraq to partition Jordan. (This was a piece of deliberate disinformation for which Colonel Query subsequently received an apology from his Israeli liaison officer Major Sinai.)[45] The other was that Britain had agreed with Israel and France to launch a concerted attack upon Egypt. The main support for these ideas, explained Sir John Nicholls, who like all British Ambassadors was not informed about Sèvres, arose from the lack of British reaction to the mobilisation compared with the very sharp reaction over the danger to

Jordan a fortnight before. That could only mean, said Israeli gossip, that some secret agreement had been reached.[46]

On the same morning Nicholls saw Golda Meir and had no difficulty in getting from her an assurance that hostilities against Jordan were not intended. He told her that, while he could readily understand some precautionary calling up of reservists, he was at a loss to explain the scale of the present mobilisation which would cause the kind of economic dislocation that Israel could ill afford. Mrs Meir told him Israel was not seeking military adventures, but must be prepared.[47] News was released during the day of what was supposed to be a *fedayeen* incident in the Negev, not far from the Strip. In fact it was a phoney 'provocation' arranged by the Israelis.[48]

At 7.15 p.m. the British and French Military Attachés were called to the Ministry of Defence and told that Israeli forces had entered Egypt. A force of paratroopers, of unspecified size, had been dropped about twenty miles to the east of the town of Suez and a light division was advancing on a broad front in order to link up with them. 'The object was to reach the Canal and only to fight if resistance was encountered.' There had been no air fighting and no action had been taken against Egyptian airfields.[49] In that modest fashion, in accordance with Dayan's prescription at Sèvres, the Sinai campaign was launched.

Two hours later the public were told that Israeli forces had penetrated Sinai and attacked *fedayeen* bases and had taken up positions 'towards the Suez Canal'.[50] A much longer statement from the Foreign Ministry rehearsed in typically rhetorical style the familiar case against Nasser's 'war of limited liability' against Israel. During the height of the Suez Canal crisis, incidents of murder, mining and sabotage had died down on the Egyptian border. Then, once the Security Council debates were over, Nasser had 'felt himself immediately free' to start them up again. Israel's leaders had declared their readiness, at any time and at any place, to meet their Egyptian equivalents. 'The proffered hand of peace has always been brutally and even derisively rejected.'[51] The tone of the statement matched the Israeli popular mood. After the raw-edged months of perceived isolation and exposure, the Israelis went willingly to battle.

'The Israeli attack on Egypt seems undoubtedly to be an act of aggression,' said the British Foreign Office the next day, in a circular to Arab capitals. 'On the other hand, Egypt has called this on herself, first by insisting that the state of war continues, secondly by defying the Security Council and thirdly by openly threatening to encompass the destruction of Israel.'

The first casualties of the new war were Palestinian Arab civilians. At midday on 29 October a curfew affecting them was announced on the radio to begin that evening at 5 p.m. When a unit of the Border Guard arrived at the village of Kafr Kassem, twenty miles north-east of Tel Aviv, to notify the village of the curfew and to enforce it, it was told that a number of farm workers, mainly olive-pickers, would come back to the village later than five. When they arrived in carts, lorries or on bicycles they were shot. Forty-three were killed, many of them women and young boys and girls. At first the Israeli censorship kept the news out of the press; when a communist member spoke out in the Knesset her speech was dropped from the minutes. Eventually the news came out. Nathan Alterman wrote another, reproachful poem, and eleven soldiers with their platoon and battalion commanders were sentenced to between seven and fifteen years' imprisonment. Three years later they were all free, their sentences reduced by military appeal or presidential pardon.[52]

The attack began at the prearranged zero hour of 5 p.m. with the dropping of 395 paratroopers at the Parker Memorial to the east of the Mitla Pass, forty-five miles from the town of Suez and 156 miles from the Israeli border. (It was meant to be closer to the Canal but photo-reconnaissance had shown shacks, tents and vehicles at the western end of the pass, which was the original target of the drop – later it was discovered that these belonged to road-workers and not to Egyptian soldiers.) Forty minutes earlier, the advance guard of the rest of the 202 Parachute Brigade crossed the Egyptian frontier near Kuntilla to cover the intervening 156 miles of Sinai desert and link up with their comrades. They had already been travelling for over nine hours, since the strategy of decoy required them to adopt a threatening posture along the Jordanian border until the latest possible minute. The only way to switch to confront Egypt was across the unmarked Negev desert. It was a punishing march, the desert was merciless to vehicles without front-wheel drive. Most of the brigade's tanks were out of action before they had even reached the Israeli-Egyptian border. At Themed and Nakhl, the latter an Egyptian battalion headquarters said falsely (over Israeli radio) to be a training base for *fedayeen* (but, Sharon writes, 'There were no terrorist bases in Sinai'), the Israelis took defended positions by rapid assault.

However, the main obstacles to Sharon's advance were organisational, the chief one being the shortage of suitable vehicles for movement across the desert. Dayan noted in his diary that the brigade had been promised 153 of the French 6 × 6 trucks. Twenty-four hours before H-Hour they were notified that they would be receiving ninety; when they went into action there were only forty-six, and they lacked tools. 'In the entire column there was not a single spanner to fit the wheel nuts of the vehicles with front-wheel drive, so that any truck with a punctured tyre had to be abandoned.'[53] As for tanks, they began with thirteen, lost six before they reached the starting post at Kuntilla and had only three left, one of which turned over, by the time that they encountered any organised resistance. Nevertheless, they arrived in time to prevent the battalion at the Parker Memorial from running into trouble. The link-up was at 10.30 in the evening of 30 October.

Two-thirds of the brigade's trucks were stuck along the route.

Also on the night of 29 October, the frontier was crossed near Qussaima on the central axis (Nitzana to Ismailia), while in the south the reserve brigade moved from Eilat into Ras em-Naqb. Nothing at all happened in the most visible sector, in the north, by the Gaza Strip and the Mediterranean shore.

Nasser Reacts

When the Israeli paras dropped, one of the first men to know should have been the British Prime Minister. He had ordered his Chief of Air Staff to maintain special high level reconnaissance flights above the Egyptian-Israeli frontier at the crucial hour. Every fifteen minutes Sir Dermot Boyle received Eden's feverish calls for news of the 'surprise aggression' which should precipitate British and French intervention. The *FLASH* signal was slow in coming and the tense Prime Minister was quick to anger. Sir Dermot Boyle's private secretary listening on the extension was astonished to hear the manner in which this distinguished airman was berated.[54] Selwyn Lloyd remained sceptical till the end that the Israelis would keep their deadline. Finally the news arrived; the fuse had indeed been fully lit.[55]

President Nasser was taken completely by surprise, despite previous reports of Israeli mobilisation. It is true that details of French arms supplies to Israel had been reaching him from the Egyptian military attaché in Turkey. At noon on 29 October a messenger from Colonel Tharwat Okasha, one of the original Free Officers who was Military Attaché in Paris, briefed the President about the story of collusion, as the colonel had heard it from a sympathetic French officer. Nasser commented: 'It is impossible that the French and British should degrade themselves to such a level.' But Amin Hewedy, who was Vice-Director of the Planning Section of the Egyptian General Staff, believes that Nasser's over-confidence rested on his theories about the force of the political deterrent supplied by the nationalist emotions of the Arab world. He was also sceptical, says Hewedy, of statements about Israel's desperation because the military balance was turning against them. Besides, he felt that Israel's self-respect as a new state would forbid her tying herself to the old colonial powers.[56]

Kadesh found Egypt's Sinai forces in a weakened condition. Since the summer there had been a substantial reduction in their deployment as units were called back for training in the new Eastern weapons. Egyptian intelligence had concluded that the danger of an Israeli pre-emptive war had passed. The Suez crisis had reinforced this trend, the Egyptians being anxious that their forces should not be caught by Britain and France on the wrong side of the Suez Canal. The Israeli writer Yonah Bandman has pointed out that the Egyptian Government had begun to behave very circumspectly towards Israel – the activities of the *fedayeen* were stopped, the Palestinian division which held Gaza was brought under strict control, and the radio instructed to be non-provocative. Altogether, one complete division of troops and two armoured brigades had been withdrawn from Sinai, leaving only one Egyptian infantry division and the Palestinian division, with a battalion of scout cars in the south and a reinforced infantry battalion at Sharm al-Sheikh.[57]

To protect themselves from attack, the Egyptians in north Sinai relied on a series of fixed defences which had been installed on the advice of the German General Frambecher, who, at the head of some eighty German military experts, began advising the Egyptian forces in 1951. The attack that they chiefly anticipated was not a drive down to Suez but a repetition of Ygal Allon's offensive at the end of the previous war, designed to take Al Arish on the flank and to cut off the main Egyptian forces in the rear. Fixed defences were, therefore, established at Rafah, near the coast, and at Abu Agheila, a tiny village which lent its name to a defensive system lying athwart the main, metalled road to Ismailia. It was at Abu Agheila, which has been described as 'a hedgehog of three successive, strongly fortified sand ridges', of which Umm Qataf was the most substantial, that the Egyptians would hope to stop the flanking attack. But the key to the mastery of north Sinai lay in the succession of low hillocks and earth ridges, little more than 150 ft high, which in totally flat countryside formed the commanding heights of Rafah. Both at Abu Agheila and at Rafah the emplacements were mutually supporting; the trenches and bunkers had, with German advice, been carefully sited.[58]

On 29 October the Egyptian Commander-in-Chief, Abdul Hakim Amer, was in Damascus where he had been attempting to co-ordinate the efforts of the new triple alliance against the expected onslaught on Jordan. He had deferred his flight home from the previous night, which was just as well since the Ilyushin transport plane he should have taken was shot down over the Mediterranean, with eighteen of his senior staff officers on board, by a single specially briefed Israeli Meteor jet. 'That's the first half of the war over,' Dayan is supposed to have told the pilot (whose exploit did not become public until 1989). General Ali Abu Nuwar, the Jordanian Chief, remembers that he had told Amer that in fact the Israelis were about to attack Egypt. He based this on information from General Burns of the UN that the Israelis were massing around Beersheva. The only Jordanian target to be reached from there would be Hebron. Why, he asked, should they want to attack Hebron? Amer was not convinced. Jordan it was which was in the sights. Egypt would supply air support in the case of attack. Syria would send in troops, and the Saudis would do what little they could.[59]

Mohamed Heikal recalls Nasser telephoning him during the evening: 'Something very strange is happening. The Israelis are in Sinai and they seem to be fighting the sands, because they are occupying one empty position after another.' The information he received did not make strategic sense to him. If the Israelis meant full-scale war they would surely use their air force to attack Egyptian airfields. Yet they appeared to have pushed troops nearly to the Suez Canal without providing proper air cover. Nasser and his closest advisers concluded that Israel believed that Britain and France were about to reach a settlement with Egypt over the Suez Canal. Therefore, Israel must have thought she would have to rush in with her attack before an agreement was signed and the Egyptians made free by it to station their complete force in Sinai. British intervention was discounted. Nasser calculated that Britain had altogether too much to lose from association with the Israelis: the size and economic influence of the British commercial community in Egypt; the reputations of Anglophile politicians like Nuri throughout the Middle East; the security of Britain's supply of oil. Moreover there was Fawzi's assessment that in New York Selwyn Lloyd had appeared to favour a negotiated agreement about the Canal. Britain would be unlikely to put the United Nations so blatantly at defiance.[60]

Nasser and Hakim Amer accordingly decided to risk committing additional forces to Sinai. Infantry was ordered to cross the Canal to destroy the Israeli paratroops, to be followed by 4 Armoured Division. General Mohamed Sidqi Mahmoud, the Air Force Commander, was urged to use his ex-Russian planes at the base at Cairo West to bomb and harass Israeli airfields and Israeli troops at the Mitla Pass. According to the memoirs of Wing Commander Abdul Latif Boghdadi, one of the Free Officers who was now Abdul Nasser's Minister for Rural and Municipal Affairs and Planning, Sidqi was 'uneasy and embarrassed' at receiving these orders and raised such unimpressive objections as that they were short of fuel at Cairo West.[61] A plan was made, but never carried out, for Egyptian parachutists to be dropped behind the Israeli battalion so as to cut it off from reinforcements.[62]

Even ahead of orders from Cairo, an infantry brigade had begun moving forward into Sinai, in what was to be a striking exception to the general Egyptian practice of absence of initiative in the lower commands. However, the priority given to the smooth passage of merchant vessels through the Canal was still so absolute that no interruption in the passage of convoys was permitted even for this military reason. Nevertheless Egyptian reinforcements – 5 Infantry Battalion and one company of 6 Battalion – having crossed near the town of Suez made their way, despite harassment from the Israeli air force, to the Mitla Pass. They took their positions in the caves and natural stone emplacements on both sides of the long, steep and winding pass. They were ready for Ariel Sharon's next move.[63]

19

Ultimatum

Nevertheless, we would not wish to support or even condone the action of Israel.
Sir Anthony Eden to Dwight Eisenhower, 30 October 1956.

I could not dream of committing this nation on such a vote . . . I have done my best. I think it is the biggest error of our time, outside of losing China.
Dwight Eisenhower, on telephone to Senator William Knowland, 31 October 1956.

When Dwight Eisenhower received news of the Israeli attack, he felt that a dramatic moment had arrived in his Presidency. He had all along entertained an image of himself as not behaving like Harry Truman under election pressure. Zionist influence was something a politician was supposed not to be able to resist at any time within range of the polls, let alone on their very eve. Eisenhower had promised himself and promised others that, if need be, he would prove that he was not in that sense a politician. Now the opportunity had come of making that demonstration in the most emphatic way, even to the extent of recalling Congress and announcing help for Egypt.

The British and French embassies had booked in advance an interview on the afternoon of 29 October with Dulles 'to discuss the Israeli mobilisation'. Dulles confronted Coulson and the French Number Two (whom Alphand sent along when asked to come himself), with the proposition that the three Powers should go to the UN Security Council that very night. He even had a draft resolution ready – he had taken from the drawer the appropriate contingency resolution drawn up by a tripartite working group a year before. The wording was as tough as possible, naming the aggressor, calling for hostilities to cease and Israeli troops to withdraw from Egypt immediately but also for 'all Members' to 'render prompt assistance to the UN' and to 'refrain from giving any military, economic or financial assistance to Israel'. Coulson and Charles Lucet stalled. They were without instructions. They thought the Tripartite Declaration was inoperable and that it would be impossible for Britain or France to take military action against Israel.[1]

At the same time Hammarskjöld was meeting in New York with the Western Three – Henry Cabot Lodge, Sir Pierson Dixon and Bernard Cornut-Gentille. Like Dulles, the Secretary-General called for a session that evening. The British and French brushed the thought to one side. It was now the middle of the night in London and Paris, they would have no instructions until the morrow, the Security Council was meeting in any case the next afternoon, that would be time enough. These delaying tactics were considerably assisted by the fact that, so long as October lasted, France would be in the chair.[2]

In the evening Eisenhower gathered his most immediate security advisers around him in the White House. Dulles speculated that the British and French might have concerted their actions with the Israelis. They might think America had no choice but to go along with them. The President declared that 'nothing justifies double crossing us' and that he could not permit it to be justly said that 'we are a nation without honour'.

Eisenhower asked if a blockade of Israel by the Sixth Fleet would be effective; Radford said, No, because the Israelis would be at the Suez Canal within two or three days. The President and his advisers had no doubt at all that France was deeply involved; they thought of a way to test whether Britain was also and, if she were wavering, to deter her. Eisenhower said he had sent for Coulson and that, by behaving with him as if he believed that France was playing a lone hand, he would solicit British partnership in really speedy action at the UN. The British would be allowed to know that if they backed the Israelis they might expect to find the United States on the other side.[3] 'Last spring when we declined to give arms to Israel and to Egypt we said that our word was enough,' Eisenhower told Coulson. 'If we do not now fulfil our word, Russia is likely to enter the situation in the Middle East.' Coulson did not know about Sèvres, but he knew enough of the views of his political masters to be distinctly uneasy as he heard the President say that if he had to call Congress back in the middle of the election to redeem America's pledge he would do so. He replied that surely the Americans planned to go to the Security Council first. The President said they planned to go there first thing in the morning, when the doors opened, before the Soviet Union got there.[4]

The next morning (30 October) Dulles told the President about Henry Cabot Lodge's encounter the previous evening with Pierson Dixon. It had begun at the first night at the opera, the two men, each in white tie, each in his box, Dixon with his new private secretary, Douglas Hurd, straight from Peking and destined thirty-five years later to be Foreign Secretary. All the while Callas was rendering *Norma*, the two boxes were exchanging notes. These were not to the mutual satisfaction of the occupants. Dixon, Lodge had told Dulles, was normally an agreeable fellow but 'last night it was as though a mask had fallen off. He was ugly and not smiling.' What Dixon had said was that the Tripartite Declaration was 'ancient history and without current validity'. When Lodge had spoken of the three Powers living up to their undertakings, the British response had been, 'Don't be silly and moralistic. We have got to be practical.' Dixon had gone on to describe the draft resolution as 'fantastic' and to add that he 'simply could not understand what the United States was thinking of'.

In the morning Dulles discovered that, in his eagerness to beat the Russians to the draw, Lodge had filed his request for an item on the Security Council agenda late the previous night, with copies put on every delegate's desk. That was 'a bad slip up', Dulles said. The President's tactic of trying to 'unhook' the British from the French must have priority. The copies of the letter were retrieved and efforts continued to get Dixon's signature to make it a joint request. Dulles told Lodge, who was much agitated by the delay, that the effort to carry the British was 'basic and goes to the heart of our relations all over the world'. Dixon was more accommodating in manner than the night before but, while willing, unlike the French, to ask for a debate, held out for changes in language that Eisenhower in the end was not prepared to accept.

At one point during the morning Dulles told Lodge over the phone that, according to the White House's information, British and French military units would have control of the Canal by that afternoon. This faulty impression had apparently been derived from a news agency flash that an Anglo-French landing was imminent.[5]

At 9.30 a.m. London time (4.30 a.m. Washington time and 11.30 a.m. Cairo time) on the same Tuesday morning (30 October) Aldrich went to the Foreign Office. Subsequently (in 1967) he published an account of his conversation with Lloyd which has become part of the Suez legend. According to this, the Foreign Secretary, asked what Britain intended to do about Israel, answered that he expected that Britain would immediately cite Israel before the Security Council as an aggressor. 'Believe it or not', Aldrich remarked, 'that's what he told me that morning that they were going to do.' If that was really what occurred, the Americans a few hours later had every right to feel grossly deceived. But was it? Since 1987 we have had access to the Foreign Office version of the same conversation, where the intention of citing Israel is attributed by Lloyd to the United States, while his own comment is that, 'In our view the issue is not so clear-cut as this.' Since May 1990, we have also had access to the cable that Aldrich sent at 11 o'clock in the morning (British time; 6 a.m. in Washington), the striking feature of which is its perfect compatibility with the British account. Specifically there is no reference whatsoever to what would have been a spectacular piece of disinformation.

Lloyd was agreeable, according to the Aldrich cable, to the Security Council discussing the matter at once but not to the treatment of Israel as an aggressor. Military assistance for Egypt would be politically impossible for the British. But it would have been available at once if Jordan had been attacked, and Israel had been left in no doubt on this point. Attempting to lay a base for difficult arguments to come, Lloyd remarked on how worried he was about the £75 million of shipping Britain had in or near the Suez Canal. The Israelis would, he assumed, want to seize the Canal bridges to prevent Egyptian counter-attacks. Mollet and Pineau were coming over to London later that morning and nothing would be decided until they met.

After solemnly repeating Dulles's warning against overrating Jewish influence in Eisenhower's Washington – and fending off a Selwyn Lloyd swipe about American anti-Semitism – Aldrich made it plain that there was a deep suspicion in Washington of a French prior arrangement with Israel. In that atmosphere any appearance of disharmony between the United States and Britain in the Security Council would create the impression of Britain and France having contrived the Israeli moves in order to get rid of Nasser. The effect on public opinion in the United States would be very serious indeed.[6] It cannot be said that the American Ambassador failed to make himself painfully clear.

Eisenhower had been drafting a long personal message to Anthony Eden. It began: 'Dear Anthony, I address you in this note not only as Head of Her Majesty's Government but as my long-time friend . . .' He appealed to him for help in 'clearing up my understanding as to exactly what is happening between us and our European allies.' First, there had been the French supply of arms, including planes, to Israel that exceeded by far the amounts authorised under the tripartite system. Then there had been the Israeli mobilization; the increase in the communication traffic between Paris and Tel Aviv, the sad story of Cabot Lodge's recent experiences with Pierson Dixon. All this 'seems to me to leave your Government and ours in a very sad state of confusion'. What if, the UN having found that Israel was the aggressor, Egypt were to ask the Soviets for help? It was of first importance that, come what might, Britain and America should concert their ideas and plans.[7]

This presidential cable reached the American Embassy at 4.30 p.m. GMT just as Eden rose to make a statement in the House of Commons. At 10 a.m. just after Lloyd had seen Aldrich, the Cabinet had met. This was the first meeting of which minutes were kept since the Israeli attack, although, according to Lord Hankey, who was still well-informed on such matters, the Cabinet in fact had met at 10.30 the previous evening (two and half hours after the news had come through of the drop at the Mitla) and had not dispersed until 2 a.m.[8] In the morning Ministers were told of the French leaders' impending visit. The terms of the notes to be addressed to Egypt and Israel, already mapped out at Sèvres, were approved by the Cabinet. Selwyn Lloyd reported the American determination to ask the Security Council urgently to condemn Israel as an aggressor and then made what in the circumstances was a remarkable suggestion. It was that, if the French agreed, action should be deferred for twenty-four hours, while an appeal was being made to the Americans to persuade them to back British and French efforts to bring an end to hostilities. This delay (which would have gone, of course, entirely against the pledges that were made to the Israelis at Sèvres) was defended on the grounds that there had been little fighting so far between Israeli and Egyptian forces.

The subsequent discussion showed that many Ministers, like Heathcoat Amory and Iain Macleod who had been uneasy about totally misleading the Americans, drew a little comfort from this gesture. The Cabinet minutes record a consensus that, 'even though it was unlikely that the United States Government would respond to such an appeal, we should do our utmost to reduce the offence to American public opinion which was liable to be caused by our notes to Egypt and Israel'. Then came ominous news supplied by Macmillan: 'Our reserves of gold and dollars were still falling at a dangerously rapid rate; and, in view of the extent to which we might have to rely on American economic assistance, we could not afford to alienate the US Government more than was absolutely necessary!'[9] On the eve of battle this was not encouraging, especially for Ministers like Lord Selkirk (who was Treasury spokesman in the Lords), who had never been able to see how Britain alone (or with France) could hope to carry the strain on sterling of such an enterprise and had always been puzzled by Macmillan's *insouciance*. Iain Macleod was making no secret of his view that the Cabinet had not been kept properly in the picture.[10] Either now or in the course of the next week, when Eden made use, as he was given to doing, of the phrase 'in time of war' when defending his reticence, Macleod riposted sharply: 'I was not aware that we were at war, Prime Minister!'

The message which now came in to the White House from the British Prime Minister would only have made sense if Eden had had a landing force just off the Canal entrance ready poised for instant action. He wrote: 'We cannot afford to see the Canal closed or to lose the shipping which is on daily passage through it. We have a responsibility for the people in these ships. We feel that decisive action should be taken at once to stop hostilities.' About the UN Eden displayed what must have seemed to the Americans a sinister ambivalence. 'We have agreed with you to go to the Security Council and instructions are being sent at this moment,' Eden said, as if searching for harmony. Then he added, 'Experience however shows that its procedure is unlikely to be either rapid or effective.' He would send a further message when he had had a chance to talk to Mollet and Pineau.[11]

Eisenhower and Dulles drew the natural conclusion from such language: that Britain and France had placed themselves in a military posture so that 'decisive action' could be taken 'at once' to ensure that the Canal would not be closed or the shipping in it lost. In mid-morning Dulles told Lodge, who thought the French and British were both bluffing, that according to information received British and French military units would have control of the Suez Canal by that afternoon. Considering the vast armada that was required to deliver the Suez expedition a week later at Port Said, it is surprising that, even though American intelligence-gathering facilities were only at their 1956 level, they did not know that Anglo-French forces were not within range of the Canal. Photographs from the U-2 showed the state of preparation in Cyprus and in Malta; it must have been clear on 30 October that the main expedition had not yet set sail from Malta. The Americans presumably thought that their allies would risk mounting a *coup de main* from Cyprus.[12]

First Pineau and later Mollet came over to London during the course of the morning. The idea of a twenty-four-hour pause to permit a last-minute effort to enlist the Americans did not survive their arrival. But no record whatever was kept of the process by which earlier scruples were overcome. At 2.50 p.m. a telegram was despatched to alert the faithful Australian Prime Minister to what was happening. It is of great interest both for what it reveals of Eden's mood on the brink of action and for what it conceals even from this recipient. After congratulating himself for having avoided a 'calamitous' war over Jordan, he disclosed that, 'Our latest information is that Israel has accused Egypt of aggression and is delivering a counter-attack.' But there was an explanation for Israel's restiveness; it was because she had a feeling that Selwyn Lloyd's negotiations looked as if they might succeed and that if they did Israel would have to pay the price in terms of enhanced prestige for Nasser. '[T]he nearer we have appeared to get to a negotiated solution the more apprehensive Israel has become.' Then Eden expressed his real thoughts: 'I would very much have preferred that the incident which has provoked this showdown could have been based on wider considerations which would have had a wider general appeal . . . We must take things as we find them.'

Having gone through their final editing, the ultimatums were presented jointly by Pineau and Ivone Kirkpatrick to the Israeli Ambassador at 4.15 p.m. GMT and to the Egyptian Ambassador at 4.25 p.m.

The notes start out in identical even-handed fashion. The outbreak of hostilities is noted in a mood of dry detachment and the threat recorded to the 'freedom of navigation through the Suez Canal on which the economic life of many nations depends'. The French and British Governments are portrayed as virtuously devoting themselves to ending hostilities and safeguarding free passage. Both notes then call on the respective sides to stop all warlike action and to withdraw all forces to a distance ten miles from the Canal. Then come the passages which show the unevenness in the treatment of the two sides. The note to Egypt requests her, in order to safeguard shipping and separate the belligerents, to accept the 'temporary occupation by Anglo-French forces of key positions at Port Said, Ismailia and Suez'. The Israelis are merely informed of the request made to the other side and are invited to perform no reciprocal act whatsoever. Moreover, as the first chapter of this book has indicated, the term 'temporary occupation' has a rather special meaning in the Egyptian lexicon.

The texts again converge at the end. An answer is 'requested' within twelve hours. Then comes the ultimatum: 'If, at the expiration of that time, one or both Governments have not undertaken to comply with the above requirements, UK and French forces will intervene in whatever strength may be necessary to secure compliance.'[13]

Eden sent a gloss on this handiwork to Eisenhower, worded as if the whole scheme had emerged out of Mollet's visit that morning. It is a masterpiece of prevarication. 'It may be', acknowledges the Prime Minister, 'that Israel could be accused of a technical aggression.' On the other hand, there was the case for saying Israel acted in self-defence. 'Nevertheless we would not wish to support or even condone the action of Israel.' Time was short and, since there appeared to have been very little fighting up to then, there was still a chance of preventing serious hostilities. He entirely agreed that this matter should go to the Security Council. But, 'as you well know', the Council could not move quickly in a critical situation, and 'we have felt it right to act, as it were, as trustees to protect the general interest'.

The rest of the message was worded as an imaginary debate with Eden warding off fancied thrusts from Eisenhower. He referred by implication to project Alpha and their shared ambitions for a Middle East settlement and professed to see in what he was now doing 'an opportunity for a fresh start'. But, in the last paragraph, imagining what Eisenhower and Dulles would be saying to each other, he went back on the defensive. 'I can assure you that any action which we may have to take to follow up the declaration is not part of a harking back to the old colonial and occupational concepts. We are most anxious to avoid this impression.'[14]

Eden Goes to War

The timing having been planned to ensure that there was no opportunity for the Americans to stop him, Anthony Eden rose in the House of Commons just after 4.30 p.m., on Tuesday, 30 October, on a motion to adjourn the House. He started his statement with the Joint Military Command between Egypt, Jordan and Syria, 'the incursion of Egyptian commandos on Sunday night', the sterling effort of Britain to urge restraint on Israel, the worthy tale of tripartite discussions in Washington on 28 and 29 October. Upon this scene had burst the Israeli penetration deep into Egyptian territory. Then there had come further reports of paratroops being dropped and of an 'Israeli spearhead' which was not far from the Suez Canal. Britain, true to her obligations, had proclaimed publicly and privately that she would stand by Jordan and had thereby secured an Israeli pledge that Jordan was safe from Israeli attack. But the urgent thing now was to stop hostilities, or the ships, passengers and cargoes actually in passage would be at peril. His first thought, Eden's statement was at pains to show, was of the United Nations. France and Britain had now instructed their New York representatives to join the United States in seeking an immediate meeting of the Security Council. It had begun just half an hour before.

The Prime Minister had come nearly to the end of his statement. His manner was calm, statesmanlike, consensual. Very briefly he summarised the 'urgent communications' which had been addressed to the Governments of Egypt and Israel and the undertaking to intervene if they were rejected. The House took the statement very quietly, perhaps stunned by the brisk decisiveness of the conclusion. Gaitskell, who had had fifteen minutes' warning of the content, said that it would be unwise to plunge into any lengthy discussion until it was possible to think over what had been said. He approved Eden's lavish references to the UN and hoped Britain would pledge support in advance to whatever decisions the Security Council might reach. He observed that Eden had made no reference whatsoever to the Tripartite Declaration, the keystone of Britain's proclaimed policy in the Middle East. 'Certainly', Eden replied, 'the spirit of the Tripartite Declaration and more than the spirit operates in our minds.' He apologised for the rush. Discussions with the French Ministers had finished only a few minutes ago. He had come to the House at once to give the information: 'I thought it was right that I should.'

There was some scepticism from the Labour benches at the new consideration suddenly being displayed by the Government for pro-Israeli arguments, especially those related to the blockade of Israeli ships. Members sought a pledge from Eden that he would consult the House again before taking any military action. With only twelve hours for Egypt and Israel to reply, action might be taken before dawn the next day. It would be a crime and tragedy if, at the very moment freedom and national independence were being suppressed by Russian tanks in Hungary, British tanks were shooting down women and children in the streets of Port Said. Other Labour Members, especially Reginald Paget, were concerned about the request addressed to Israel – 'really, to demand of her that she stop that action on our say-so is unrealistic'. The House turned its attention to fatstock prices, having decided to take a pause for thought before resuming in a couple of hours at 8 o'clock.[15]

The UN Security Council had met in New York just over half an hour before the Prime Minister rose. Henry Cabot Lodge opened the debate about Israeli invasion in the strongest terms. 'The Government of the United States', he said, 'feels that it is imperative that the Council act in the promptest manner to determine that a breach of the peace has occurred, to order that the military action undertaken by Israel cease immediately and to make clear its view that the Israeli armed forces should be immediately withdrawn behind the established armistice lines. Nothing less will suffice.' The Russian representative, Sobolev, came to the rostrum to say that Israel could not have made the attack without the help of those who were trying to find some pretext for moving their troops into the area. He then read out in English an Associated Press tape that had just arrived. It contained the essence of Eden's announcement in the Commons. It created a sensation. Pierson Dixon asked for time to consider Eden's statement and the debate adjourned until the afternoon.[16]

Aldrich, who had been promised a second interview with Selwyn Lloyd after his talks with the French Ministers, had instead been given Sir Ivone at 4.45, at a time when Eden was already on his feet. He was handed the two ultimatums. He immediately commented that Egypt could not possibly accept the conditions of the one addressed to her. Sir Ivone simply shrugged his shoulders. Dulles, after reading the texts over the phone to the President, said that the twelve-hour ultimatum to Egypt was 'about as crude and brutal as anything he had ever seen'. Eisenhower called it 'pretty rough', to which Dulles responded that it was 'utterly unacceptable'. The British and French would, of course, be in the Canal by the next day. The President sent identical (and coldly formal) messages to Eden and Mollet, making it manifest that he completely dissociated himself from their action and informed the press.[17]

At 8 p.m. GMT, one hour before the Security Council resumed, the House of Commons came back to the study of Eden's statement. The shape of this debate would determine whether the world was facing a united Britain. Eden's speech added little. He asked the House to defer judgment. There was a fair and reasonable chance that the terms would be accepted by both sides. Then only token forces needed to be landed in the Canal to supervise compliance. After that would come the real objective – a further attempt at a permanent settlement.

Hugh Gaitskell then defined the attitude which he was to take, with mounting confidence, during the extraordinary week that was to follow. His first criticism was that there was nothing in the United Nations Charter which justified a nation appointing itself as world policeman. If Britain could do this, so could anybody else. Secondly, he could not find any legal justification for what it was proposed to do. The Prime Minister's argument that Egypt had denounced the Tripartite Declaration read oddly since she had objected to it from the very beginning, while the British Government had repeatedly pledged itself to abide by it. The disrespect for the 1951 resolution of the Security Council was deplorable but it had been known for the past five years. 'I do not think anybody will accuse me of lack of sympathy with Israel,' Gaitskell said, 'but I am bound to say that a proposal which is intended to stop the fighting and which involves the withdrawal of the Egyptians ten miles further within their own frontier and a withdrawal of the Israelis ten miles from the Canal Zone – which still leaves them at some points 160 miles inside Egypt – is hardly one which would commend itself on equitable grounds.'

He warned Eden that, if he was not willing to defer action by the British armed forces until the end of the Security Council debate and until the Commons had discussed the matter again, the Opposition would have to divide the House. From an international point of view this was no idle threat at a time when Britain was on the brink of war, and a war, moreover, in which the psychological factors were to play more than their usual part.

The short wind-up speech by Alfred Robens, the Labour Party's chief foreign affairs spokesman, was notable for one thing: the beginning of the interplay between the UN debates in New York and those in the chamber at Westminster, which was such a notable feature of the succeeding week, with George Ivan Smith, the Australian who headed the UN information office in London, supplying transcripts at great speed to the House of Commons Library, where Labour members like Philip Noel-Baker saw that they were put to good use.[18] In the attempt to create an appearance of consensus Eden had seemed to co-opt the United States with his talk of tripartite consultations in Washington and 'close communication' with the American Government. That cosy picture was radically spoiled by Robens's citations from Cabot Lodge's speech in the Security Council's morning session and from the State Department spokesman who had put it on record that there had been no prior warning of the British and French threat to use troops.

Winding up the debate, Selwyn Lloyd denied that the British Government was trying to judge the rights and wrongs of the situation between Egypt and Israel. The Opposition seemed to think Israel had been guilty of aggression, a statement that produced opposition cries of 'Yes' and 'No' from different sections of the Labour Party. 'And the Foreign Secretary?' a Member shouted. 'This presents a matter which must be carefully debated and discussed,' he said. 'An ultimatum?' broke in a Member. That was because, the Foreign Secretary went on, Britain could not wait for such a debate of great, though necessary, length. 'We are faced with an actual situation. We are faced with a situation in which Israeli troops are within a few miles of Suez,' said the man who had insisted that General Dayan perform towards the Suez Canal a 'real act of war'. But Clement Davies, the Liberal, had information that they were getting no closer and perhaps even moving away. Lloyd produced one of his stuck-machine-gun effects. 'Israeli forces are within a very few miles of Suez. They are moving towards Suez. They have been moving towards Suez, they are moving towards Suez, and they are within very close distance of Suez.'[19]

The Opposition divided the House, the Government winning by 270 votes to 218. It was not a happy ending for the first day of the *dénouement* of the Suez crisis. Next morning Eisenhower told William Knowland, the leader of the Republicans in the Senate: 'I could not dream of committing this nation on such a vote . . . I have done my best. I think it is the biggest error of our time, outside of losing China.' As Eden's staff went back with him to Number Ten to await the responses to the ultimatums, a 'pleasant, cheerful Foreign Office character' said breezily: 'It's rather fun to be at Number Ten the night we smashed the Anglo-American alliance.'[20]

When the House of Commons voted, the Security Council was once more in session. Pierson Dixon, looking, according to Sydney Bailey who was present, 'white and drawn and speaking almost apologetically', said he feared that Britain's motives might be misconstrued. Making the best case he might, he rejected 'with contempt' Soviet insinuations that France and Britain were seeking to settle their differences with Egypt about the Canal by force or that they had prompted Israel to take action against Egypt. Unhappily neither Israel nor her Arab neighbours had seen fit to listen to Britain's advice, said Dixon, implying that they were as bad as each other. For the moment there was no action which the Security Council could constructively take which would contribute to the twin objectives of stopping the fighting and safeguarding free passage.

This hapless speech, to which the French delegate, who was in the chair, mumbled his assent, was swept on one side by Lodge, who tersely introduced his resolution calling for the complete withdrawal of the Israelis and the suspension of all military, economic and financial assistance from them until they should have complied. In addition, all members were called on to refrain from the use or threat of force in the area. If the draft resolution were adopted and complied with, he argued, the basis for the twelve-hour ultimatum disappeared. Lodge went remorselessly on: 'I wish to make it clear that we do not imply that in any circumstances this ultimatum would be justifiable or be found to be consistent with the purposes of the UN Charter.' The Soviet delegate, Sobolev, noted that the American resolution (in its final version) lacked a clause explicitly condemning Israel for her act of aggression but in the interests of time he would not submit any amendments. The Security Council was not behaving at all in the lethargic manner prescribed for it in the House of Commons.

The only lengthy contribution came from Abba Eban, an orator to whom grandiloquence came naturally. He spoke in paragraphs and exercised perfect control over exceptionally long sentences. Of British and South African background, he was (and still is) especially admired by Americans who feel that he speaks English in the way they like to think it should be spoken. A scholar and diplomat of great accomplishment, he was admired in Israel for his talents but yet was never really close to the centres of domestic political power.

With no incentive to conserve time, Eban now presented a comprehensive dossier of each and every *fedayeen* episode, with an anthology drawn from the most belligerent Egyptian broadcasts. The casualty figures over six years he put at 101 Israelis killed and 364 injured, as the result of attacks over the Egyptian-controlled border. There had been 1,843 cases of armed robbery and theft, 1,339 armed clashes, 172 cases of sabotage. He preceded this tale by asking what he described as the tormenting question his Government had had to face. 'Do its obligations under the UN Charter require us to resign ourselves to the existence of uninterrupted activity to the south and north and east of our country, of armed units practising open warfare against us and working from their bases in the Sinai Peninsula and elsewhere for the maintenance of carefully regulated invasions of our homes, our lands and our very lives, or on the other hand are we acting in accordance with an inherent right of self-defence when, having found no other remedy for over two years, we cross the frontier against those who have no scruple or hesitation in crossing the frontier against us?' Eban, therefore, rejected 'with vehement indignation' the charges of aggression against Israel and declared what he had been instructed to say, 'Israel is not out to conquer new territory.'

Dixon intervened again to speak of the imminent peril to the ships and cargoes in the Canal and of the thousands of British and French nationals whose lives were at risk without saying how either were to be assisted by the kind of action that Britain and France had in mind. 'This grave question is one for the Security Council to consider,' he agreed, adding unpersuasively, 'But I do earnestly suggest that this particular moment is not the moment for the Council to take up a position on this grave matter.' In view of the rapid approach of the time of expiry of the ultimatum – 11.30 p.m. (New York time) – Lodge hustled the Council towards a vote, disallowing the Australian's plea for an adjournment to enable him to consult his Government. Seven votes were cast for and two against the American resolution (Australia and Belgium abstained). As the two against were permanent members, Britain and France, the resolution failed.[21]

It was the first time in the history of the UN that Britain had cast a veto. She cast it over the Suez Canal, the very example which eleven years before, Winston Churchill had used with Stalin to demonstrate the great beauty of the Great Power veto when seeking to recruit him to the United Nations.[22]

Instantly Sobolev, in his new role as partner of the United States, responded with tactical subtlety. He reintroduced Lodge's motion, stripped of any element of sanctions, simply and solely ordering Israel to evacuate. Dixon, longing to drain the debate of some of its acrimony, wanted to avoid using the veto again and, since his French colleague's instructions did not leave him any discretion in the matter, he persuaded him to adjourn the session while they telephoned their political masters. Before the session resumed one hour later Bernard Cornut-Gentille, having endured the painful task of presiding over a forum before which he was the first of the accused, had himself become a casualty of the Suez conflict. He had arrived in New York from a West African proconsulship shortly before. With the Council about to resume, Dixon was sent for urgently by Louis de Guirangaud,

Cornut's deputy who was later Foreign Minister of France, and was led into the President's office. Cornut-Gentille was on a sofa, shaking with malaria, brought on by nervous strain, saying that, for the honour of France, he must continue to preside. A doctor was found to pronounce him unfit and the new session opened under the gavel of de Guirangaud.[23]

The answer had come over the telephone from Lloyd and Pineau, who were at the time sitting together in Number Ten. De Guirangaud and Dixon would veto the new text. The voting figures were the same as before. It had been, reported Dixon at midnight, a thoroughly unsatisfactory day's work. Accustomed to clearing tactics routinely with the Americans, he had found Lodge organising the Security Council against him. Ordered to stick by the French whatever happened, he discovered that this left no room for flexibility. He described feelingly the various signals that he had sent during the day to his American colleague; they were not merely rejected but produced the dead opposite behaviour to that which he had requested. Normally, when it encountered some difficulty the Security Council could be relied on to adjourn but, lamented Sir Pierson, this was ruled out by the twelve-hour ultimatum. 'The procedure itself of ultimatum, exploited to the hilt by the Russians and disapproved by the Americans, was greatly disliked by the Council.'[24]

The debate was not over with the two Western vetoes. The Jugoslavs were determined to sustain a momentum which, after all, had both superpowers behind it. There was still an Egyptian complaint against the ultimatum from Britain and France on the agenda. It is hard to see why the victim of aggression should receive such an ultimatum, said Omar Loutfi, the Permanent Representative of Egypt. Fifty-one ships had that very day transited the Canal in perfect safety. The Israelis were still far off. French and British subjects who had wanted to leave Egypt had been able to do so without the least interference.

There existed the procedure called 'Uniting for Peace', passed at the time of the Korean crisis but never yet used, whereby an emergency session of the General Assembly could be convened to take over a subject from the Security Council when, through lack of unanimity among its permanent members, that body was unable to act. It had been adopted to thwart the Soviet Union on some future occasion when the Russians should not be so obliging as to boycott the Security Council session. Only on the morning of 29 October, just before news of the Israeli attack came through to New York, Henry Cabot Lodge had been speaking to his French and British colleagues of using the procedure for the first time against the behaviour of the Soviet forces in Hungary. Now it was to be used, not against Russia but against Britain and France.

In Washington, the British Chargé d'Affaires surveyed the wreckage of the Anglo-American special relationship. Dulles told him bluntly that: 'We are facing the destruction of our trust in each other.'[25] This was before the two vetoes were cast. When they had been, John Coulson cabled that, 'All indications are that the Administration from top to bottom is both angry and dismayed. You were, no doubt, anticipating a serious reaction but it is even worse than I would have myself expected.'[26]

In the 302nd Meeting of the National Security Council which assembled at 9 a.m. on 1 November, Dulles described recent events as 'marking the death knell for Great Britain and France'. Treasury Secretary Humphrey said he believed Britain was the real aggressor and Israel only the pawn. But in this arena Britain had a champion in the form of Harold Stassen, who courageously and persistently took on the field, including the President himself. The Soviets were much to blame for putting arms in the hands of Egyptians, the Suez Canal was an absolutely vital lifeline for the British and Stassen could not see how it would serve the country's interests to strike now at Britain and at Israel. According to him, the United States should support a simple cease-fire and no more.

'With great warmth', the notetaker recorded, Dulles was compelled to point out to Stassen that it was the British and French who had just vetoed a proposal for a cease-fire. Of course, once they were lodged in Egypt, they would be agreeable to one. A cease-fire of that kind would be very much to America's advantage, said Stassen. Dulles shot back with 'an emphatic negative'. What the British and French had done, he said, was nothing but the straight, old-fashioned variety of colonialism of the most obvious sort. George Humphrey brought up the split in British opinion, including splits among Conservatives. He thought recent British action was 'primarily Eden's own creation'.

Stassen retorted that if the British public was divided so too was the American public. Turning to the President, he said that he would fail to get a united Congress in support of his foreign policies if he went on the erroneous assumption that Britain and France were going downhill. In response, Eisenhower stated his emphatic belief that those Powers were going downhill so long as they pursued their present policies. On the other hand he did not want Britain and France branded as 'aggressors' and use of American force against them was 'unthinkable'.

During Admiral Radford's subsequent military briefing the President asked his chief military adviser whether it was possible that the Russians might have 'slipped' Nasser half a dozen atomic bombs. The Admiral replied that he would hardly think they would, in view of the Egyptians' total failure to make effective use of the conventional weapons with which they had already provided them.[27]

President Eisenhower was not altogether unmoved by Stassen's arguments and remained extremely exercised about the possible impact of these events on the solidarity of Nato. During the day (1 November) he drafted a telegram to Eden, which in the end was not sent. Lacking all polemic or reproach it was written on the assumption of an early landing and aimed solely at damage limitation. With this in mind he intended to urge that, 'the very second you attain your minimum objectives', Eden should 'instantly call for a cease-fire', undertake to resume negotiations on the basis of the Six Principles, and 'state your intention to evacuate as quickly as the Israelites return to their own national territory' and the Egyptians agreed to negotiate. A somewhat similar line of thought, suggesting a preparedness to accommodate to a brief and preferably bloodless landing, was to underlie an equally unsent message of 5 November.

There is to this story of the worst day in the history of the 'special relationship' a curious codicil. The Intelligence services of Britain and the United States had now arrived at the moment which should have seen their much-discussed, much-postponed joint operation *Straggle*, the coup d'état in Syria, spring into action. The two Dulles brothers had a bizarre telephone conversation at 5.30 p.m. Washington time (10.30 p.m. GMT, 12.30 a.m. Middle East time) on 30 October about whether anything could be saved. Allen said he was sending the following telegram: 'If the assets can be held together for a few days more without taking action, we would much prefer it. If this is not the case, let us know and we will give a final decision.' As he told his brother, 'The British are pressing us to go ahead.' 'Naturally', Foster observed drily. 'What will happen if you get hooked in this and get friends in and fighting starts? It will put us in a difficult position.' Allen said: 'The argument on the other side is that it is good to have an anti-communist Government in ... But I am suspicious of our cousins and if they want a thing I think we should look at it hard.'[28]

Ben-Gurion Dismayed

In the Middle East, while the UN was debating, the Israelis were, though more slowly than might have been expected, coming to grips with the ultimatum addressed to them. At 11.30 p.m. local time (9.30 p.m. GMT and 4.30 p.m. New York time) Arthur Lourie of the Israeli Foreign Affairs Ministry, phoned the Third Secretary on duty at the British Embassy, Ronald Higgins, to say that although Mrs Meir had heard over the radio about Eden's House of Commons speech, no note had arrived from Britain or France. In fact, the ultimatum had been painstakingly translated into Hebrew and encoded before being transmitted. There had been difficulties with the radio transmission, and on arrival in Jerusalem it had to be decyphered. Then the black-out impeded its further transit to Tel Aviv. Five hours into a twelve-hour 'ultimatum', it was still on its way. Higgins was told to pass on to the Israelis the Embassy's copy, which had been received from London *en clair*, and beg for a quick reply. Though the scenario had been well rehearsed at Sèvres it took another hour before the

Israeli Foreign Ministry, most of whose staff had been kept in the dark, was able to muster the necessary acceptance.[29]

Sir Humphrey Trevelyan had already been to see Fawzi earlier on 30 October, to receive a vigorous protest against the overflights of Canberras on aerial reconnaissance and to announce that Britain wished to withdraw forthwith the civilian contractors who had, with such prolonged diplomacy, been inserted in the Canal Base in place of British troops. Arrangements were made the same day for Egyptians to take over the installations. Fawzi observed gently that the original day, 29 October, for the resumption of Suez Canal talks at Geneva had been allowed to pass. He objected, as before, to the British requirement that the Egyptians produce what was in effect a draft Treaty before the sides could meet again. But he thought the latest note from Dag Hammarksjöld would provide a basis for negotiation. Then, Fawzi mused, might begin the new era of co-operation and mutual understanding.[30]

Nasser sent for the Ambassador in the evening, at 9 p.m. local time. Trevelyan's appearance and manner left the Egyptians in no doubt that he had been completely innocent of the policy of the ultimatum which they had now received. When the President referred to it as an ultimatum, Sir Humphrey demurred. The note said it was a 'communication'. Nasser replied, 'We take it as an ultimatum.' It was a threat of unprovoked aggression without any justification. Trevelyan spoke of stopping the fighting and protecting the Canal. 'We can defend the Canal,' said President Nasser, 'and tomorrow we shall be defending it from more than the Israelis.'[31]

Later that night, Cairo radio was broadcasting Egypt's defiance of the two-Power ultimatum. For all of Nasser's self-possession at the interview with Trevelyan, he was astounded at what had happened, not because he had any illusions about Britain's standards of conduct but because the ultimatum violated his sense of Britain's self-interest. He still did not expect it to be followed by any action. 'When we received the ultimatum', he said subsequently on BBC television, 'we thought ... [it] was directed to keep our troops out of Sinai. By that time they would be able to give Israel opportunity to gain cheap victories. And until next day all our estimations were based on the idea that Britain would not participate in any attack.'[32] He thought Britain would be crazy to risk everything when she had so much to lose. Nasser did nothing whatever that night to halt the reinforcement of Sinai, which Amer was pressing forward with what his Cabinet colleague Abdul Latif Boghdadi thought was excess of zeal and nervous attention to small detail. One Egyptian lieutenant-colonel in command of a regiment was in receipt of four, quite different, movement orders from Cairo headquarters inside twenty-four hours.[33]

In Sinai itself, while Sharon's 202 Brigade was reassembling to the east of the Mitla Pass and Egyptian reinforcements were moving into the pass itself, the battle on the central sector for the heavily defended Abu Agheila complex of defences was building up during 30 October faster than Dayan had planned or desired. His politically motivated strategy was falling apart. General Simhoni, the GOC Southern Command, one of the few who had been told the political reasons for Dayan's orders, disregarded them on the first morning of the campaign. The reserve brigade assigned to capture Qussaima, in the central sector, encountered a series of logistical mishaps – the civilian buses, for instance, in which the men were riding out to battle, got repeatedly stuck in the sand – and, as a consequence, instead of attacking at 11 o'clock at night on 29 October it did not do so till 4 o'clock in the morning. Impatient at this slippage and, in any case, out of sympathy with the political logic of the orders, Simhoni ordered in 7 Armoured Brigade, which Dayan was deliberately withholding from the fight until the allied planes had joined in. The tanks arrived at Qussaima just after it had been captured and then surged on into central Sinai to tackle the strong Egyptian defensive position of Umm Qataf from the rear.

When Dayan arrived to visit the Qussaima sector he found the armoured brigade, which was supposed to be waiting, 'silent, motionless, unobtrusive' and twenty-five miles inside Israel, deployed in clouds of sand twenty-five miles inside Egypt. He expressed his fury with Simhoni on account of this insubordination but then, accepting what had been done, ordered the armour to move rapidly to the west, at the same time advancing other operations by twenty-four hours since the damage of disclosing the scale of the offensive had already been done.[34]

According to the theory of the campaign, this brashness was asking for heavy retaliatory raids on Tel Aviv and Haifa. Ben-Gurion, in bed with a high temperature, would remain anxious until he had heard news of the Anglo-French onslaught on the Egyptian airfields, due, he had been given to expect, early in the morning of 31 October. (The ultimatum was to expire at 4.30 GMT, 6.30 Cairo time). But that night he had heard reports that the allied operation would not take place until the following evening. Dayan found him in anguish, resolved to withdraw the paratroops from the Mitla forthwith lest they be cut off. In the circumstances the Chief of Staff did not think it prudent to tell the 'old man' exactly where 7 Armoured Brigade now was.[35]

Only a relatively few Egyptian pilots had been fully trained by their Czech and Polish instructors to handle their new Soviet-made planes. Nasser said later that he had 150 MiG fighters but only thirty pilots (plus ten trained to fly Ilyushins).[36] The Egyptian air force managed to fly forty sorties against the Israelis during 30 October and ninety on the following day. Fourteen air battles were reported, with the Egyptians losing four MiG-15s and Vampires for no loss by the Israelis. With the exception of two bombers, which caused no significant damage, they operated only within Sinai. But, at the end of the first full day of war, the Israelis were not out of the woods yet. The instructors might take over the controls; Soviet 'volunteer' pilots could appear; a massive air attack on Israel was still possible. Israeli intelligence was eagerly searching for any sign of British intention to act on what the Israelis had understood was the agreed timetable of Sèvres.

But Eden was not prepared to sanction so immediate an assault. In face of the opposition from the United States, from the Commonwealth, from the Opposition in the House of Commons which the news of the ultimatum had aroused, it would have seemed crassly brutal to have bombs dropping on Cairo the very next morning. Moreover, people would soon have been able to work out that the orders for the operation would have had to have been given before the ultimatum had been issued, let alone expired. Adequate notice to keep away from targets could not have been broadcast to the civilian population. Marshal of the RAF Dickson remembers saying to Eden that, when running air control on the North-West Frontier of India, they always allowed refractory tribesmen twenty-four hours' warning before a punitive bombing of their villages.[37] Eden knew that everything he did would have to be defended, in an atmosphere full of hostility, in terms of the separation of combatants rather than in those of the discharge of military obligations to an ally. He also had to take into account the strong preference of the air command to start the sequence with night bombing to be followed by ground-attack just after dawn.

During a restless night, lying in bed stricken with fever, with his mane of white hair spread out over the pillows, David Ben-Gurion received the reports of the absence of offensive activity on the part of the allies. Urgent enquiries pressed upon French officials produced unconvincing excuses about bad weather conditions. Finally Peres called up Guy Mollet on an open line. 'Would we use intelligence [channels], probably the Americans would know, the Russians would know,' Peres says. 'But speaking on the normal line nobody was following us.' Mollet asked if the weather seemed foggy and was told it was fair and fine.[38] The French Premier's military advisers had themselves been worried that Britain's resolution was already failing. Admiral Barjot had reported adversely on the absence of the sense of urgency which he had expected in Cyprus, General Ely had been haunted by the fear that the British were still considering the idea of a twenty-four-hour delay to lobby the Americans. But he had contacted Dickson and been reassured.[39] Mollet told Peres that the Israelis could count on an air attack in the evening. During all this uncertainty, Ben-Gurion seemed to his young assistants like an injured lion. 'And how he roared,' one of those present remembers. Britain was the main target. All the vehemence of the love–hate relationship came through without much sign of the love. 'The old whore!' Ben-Gurion said.[40]

20

The Die is Cast

The noble and learned Viscount referred to the attacking Power, against which we have to exercise self-defence. Who is the attacking Power?
Geoffrey Fisher, Archbishop of Canterbury, House of Lords, 1 November 1956.

The affairs of Britain seem now to be in the hands of a madman.
The Egyptian Gazette, 31 October 1956.

The great armada was now ready to put to sea. Because of the arrangements for Exercise *Boathook,* HMS *Tyne* had been able to sail from Malta on 27 October with General Stockwell and Admiral Robin Durnford-Slater aboard, reaching Cyprus, where Air Marshal Barnett already was, on 30 October. According to Durnford-Slater, in a draft report of the naval operation which was afterwards suppressed, Stockwell had said on 1 October that they should be ready for D-Day on 31 October and L [for landing] – Day on 8 November. The earliest day on which they would be allowed to alert the forces and sail the ships would be 30 October. By expanding the scope of *Boathook,* whose ships were to leave Malta on 29 October, Durnford-Slater was able, with some of the *Musketeer* vessels, to beat this deadline. The loading exercise already arranged was advanced by twenty-four hours.

Quite apart from the different levels of fiction according to which the departure was organised, which themselves gave rise to various imperfections, liaison with the French was less than smooth. At a meeting of the British and French staffs on 27 October it was found that the French ships, most of which had already managed to set sail, were working to a later landing date (9 November) than the British. This was put right but, when Grantham (who retained command until the actual start of the operation) and Keightley decided by exchange of signals on 28 and 29 October that the landing date would, thanks to the early start of the ships, be advanced to 6 November, that news failed to reach the French naval authorities. They continued to assume, until after the convoys had got to sea, that the assault would take place on 8 November.[1]

Anything, even reports for internal purposes, even after the operation was over, which created a suspicion that Britain knew in advance when it was to take place, was treated as poison. Not only were all copies of the Durnford-Slater report ordered to be held under lock and key and the first two pages destroyed by fire, but Air Marshal Barnett's report was also hastily recalled just after it had been circulated for the removal of a paragraph which suggested that some operational orders had been received prior to the time when everyone was supposedly taken by surprise by the sudden Israeli attack.[2]

In the case of the Air Task Force, some of the missing material can be found in the operational report of Group Captain G. C. O. Key, who was in command of the Bomber Wing, Cyprus. In a section headed (after Horace) *Nec Scire Fas Est Omnia* ('nor is it permitted to know all things'), the Group Captain shows that Air Task Force Headquarters at Episkopi assumed control over all offensive aircraft (a sure sign that *Musketeer* was lumbering into action) at noon (GMT) on Sunday, 28 October, the day before the Israeli attack. The Force Commander was then issued with an operation order for the bomber task under the plan and told that it was already D − 3 by the *Musketeer* timetable. This meant that Wednesday, 31 October must be D-Day. The worst chaos caused by this rushed timing was over photo-reconnaissance (PR) which was supposed to begin at D − 8. The thoroughness of the execution of this feature had been regarded as an essential condition of success because of something on which all commanders commented when *Musketeer* was over: the astonishing absence, considering the British had just left Egypt after seventy-four years, of reliable information about what was going on. High priority demands for PR flights flooded in.

During Monday (29 October) the Bomber Wings (in Malta, as well as Cyprus) were alerted that operations might begin earlier than 31 October. Four Egyptian airfields and the transmitters of Cairo Radio were then selected as the first targets. Although both Bomber Wings were brought to a state of six hours' readiness as of 9 a.m. on 30 October, the provisional H-hours were still for 31 October, starting with a 2.15 a.m. (midnight fifteen, GMT) strike at the first target. This was to be the airbase at Cairo West, where the Egyptians kept those Ilyushin bombers which so worried Ben-Gurion. At this stage, then, operations must have been contemplated that fitted the terms of the Protocol of Sèvres.

Alerted for possible take-off as early as 30 October, the Cyprus Wing, having as Group Captain Key's report explains not even yet received an official copy of the air plan, acquired enough information to apply with brush and distemper the operation's yellow and black aircraft recognition markings and, by working all night, to get its Canberras prepared on time. Throughout the day of 30 October, until news of the ultimatum arrived, both Bomber Wings were kept poised; they were told that the executive order, when it came, might give only one hour's notice of the take-off of the first raid. Meanwhile, frantic exchanges went on between the Air Ministry and Air Operations Centre, Episkopi (Cyprus) about whether it was possible or desirable to leave the final decision to bomb or not to bomb until the planes in the air were actually approaching the target. Feeling that this would be exceedingly rough on the crews, quite apart from the consequences of an error or a breakdown in the very imperfect communications, Air Task Force argued most forcefully that, while possible, this was most undesirable.[3]

Once the terms and timing of the ultimatum became known, it was evident that the Canberras and Valiants would not be attacking at 2.15 in the morning, but they were told to remain at six hours' readiness. At 2.40 p.m. GMT on 30 October the Chiefs signalled Sir Charles Keightley that he could expect full instructions at about five o'clock. 'Meanwhile planning should be completed for day air attack 31 October.' Promptly at five o'clock they followed this up with a brief summary of the ultimatums which were to expire at 4.30 a.m. GMT on 31 October. The message went on: 'You should be prepared to commence daylight air attacks on bomber airfields starting as soon as possible after receipt of executive order ... These operations should be followed during night 31 October/1 November by *Musketeer* Phase I air operations as planned.'

This message crossed a *FLASH* signal sent at 5.35 p.m. GMT from Keightley to the Chiefs of Staff. It reported that, to the aircrews' astonishment, four high performance recce aircraft had been intercepted, two of them at altitudes of 47,000 and 35,000 feet respectively, heights at which they thought themselves invulnerable. The recce planes escaped, but their having been challenged was taken as showing that 'the Egyptian radar control organisation is ... considerably better than was anticipated'. The top air commanders, Patch and Barnett, both wished Keightley 'to stress with all the emphasis possible the risks and disadvantages to engaging the enemy piecemeal by day'. The Allied Commander-in-Chief asked that he be allowed to hold the air offensive back until 5 p.m. (local time) on 31 October. He offered an earlier alternative but with palpable distaste.

At 1.45 a.m. GMT on 31 October the Chiefs, who had just emerged from a meeting at Number Ten with Ministers and, significantly, Pineau, cabled back that Ministers had agreed that Keightley should have his way about the timing of the air offensive. (Among themselves they used the reason, rich in irony, that there was no sign of Israeli air activity against Egypt.) However Keightley was required to be ready, if needed, to execute an attack during daylight hours on one of the Egyptian Ilyushin bases. This would be ordered by London 'if Israel suffers serious air attack [that] morning'.[4] With that exception, therefore, the air forces were after all to stick to their preferred sequence of bombing at night first, followed by ground attack at first light, twenty minutes before dawn. That meant that there would be no action until at least twelve hours later than the Israelis had been given to expect.[5]

One major reason for mounting the attacks at night was that this made less likely the risk of rapid Egyptian reprisal. This risk may appear in retrospect ridiculously slight but the allied commanders were not to know that Khrushchev was going to be so completely deterred in respect of volunteers. Air Vice-Marshal Crisham, the AOC Levant, who was responsible for the defence of the crowded Cyprus base, afterwards wrote: 'If only a few enemy fighter/ground attack aircraft had pressed home attacks, they would have caused damage and confusion out of all proportion.'

The sole provision that had been made to cater for Ben-Gurion's anxieties was, therefore, provision for an act of retaliation rather than, as Ben-Gurion had tried to stipulate, one of pre-emption. Six of Key's crews on Cyprus were briefed and standing by from 2 p.m. for an immediate day-time attack with fighter escort on Cairo West should there occur an 'air strike by the Egyptians on targets against Israeli territory'.[6]

Admiral Power was given to expect that his carrier-borne planes would go into action at first light on 31 October. Since so much stress had been put on the capital importance of ample briefing of aircrews and the studying of target material, he had decided that, for this first operation, the briefing could not be delayed beyond noon on 30 October. But as the ultimatum had not been published, nothing had been heard as this deadline approached. Despite previous orders, Power pressed ahead with the briefings, regardless. 'The situation in the Middle East is evidently so serious', he told his men, 'that we may be called upon to act at short notice.'[7]

Although the commanders did what they could to cut corners and anticipate moves, the overriding policy was that anything which could not be explained away as deriving from the communications exercise or from the four-day loading exercise had to wait for the ultimatum. The cover story had to fit not only here and now but also the history books of tomorrow. The three aircraft carriers, *Eagle*, *Bulwark* and *Albion*, being covered by *Boathook*, sailed from Malta between 7.30 and 8.45 a.m. on the morning of 29 October. Between them they carried 116 aircraft and were to join up with the French light carriers *Arromanches* and *Lafayette* with another 41.[8] But the marine commandos and the armour could not by the rules start embarking until late on 30 October and were not ready to take to sea until 31 October. Two additional light carriers, *Theseus* and *Ocean*, joined the force at the last moment and bore 600 commandos and twenty-four assault helicopters intended to pioneer the brand-new technique of 'vertical envelopment', a personal enthusiasm of Mountbatten's, embraced over the objection of some other admirals, involving the air landing of marines behind the enemy's lines.[9]

Once launched, the convoy moved forward at the maximum speed of the slowest vessels (the troop- and tank-landing craft) which meant that it must expect to take six days to cover the 936 miles to Port Said. The numbers increased as they approached their destination, until there were about a hundred and thirty warships (the actual size of the Spanish Armada of 1588), not to mention the numerous supply ships, commandeered merchant ships and other supporting craft, bearing the response of two Empires to the challenge from the banks of the Nile. Following on behind, destined to arrive when the war was over, British troops of 3 Infantry Division set sail from home ports on 1 and 2 November.

A telegram to Malta from the Prime Minister, anxious to sustain the new 'fire brigade' or 'neutral police force' role of the armed forces, instructed that naval bombardment was not to be used at all against Port Said to avoid civilian casualties. Admiral Grantham, feeling that this 'was the same kind of damn nonsense that happened in Dieppe', flew off to London to tell the First Sea Lord, 'We're not going to jeopardise the thing by putting on woollen gloves when the time comes. This kind of signal must be cancelled.' Mountbatten took him before the Chiefs of Staff, who decided that he should see the Prime Minister in the Cabinet room. He found Eden 'looking terrible . . . worn and worried and tired'. The Admiral insisted that 'we'd see very little damage was done', but that the operation could not be jeopardised by any absolute bans against the use of what force they wanted. Eden finally gave way; the signal was cancelled. 'It distressed me', Sir Guy Grantham said, 'to see Anthony Eden in such a mess.'[10]

This is not however the only image that we have of the Prime Minister at this time. His biographer William Rees-Mogg, who had just fought and lost a hopeless seat in a by-election, was in the days after the ultimatum engaged in helping him write his speeches and used to see him in the morning with three or four other speech-writers in a bedside conference. 'There have been many stories about Eden's exhaustion and irritability,' he has written. 'I saw no sign of it . . . He did show a rather boyish spirit, a sort of elated calm in crisis. That seemed natural. It is not every day of the week you invade Egypt, even if your name is Anthony.'

Rees-Mogg made one other observation that contained its own comment on the course of events. On 30 October, when the ultimatum had just been issued, he was told in Number Ten by Robert Allan, Eden's PPS, 'My understanding is that the paratroops will go in at dawn tomorrow.'[11] Such was the assumption so close to the seat of power. It was not so and had never been so. But at least something was happening. There had been so much waiting, so many changes of plan. Commanders were exercised both about the absence of notice when the order came and about the condition and appropriateness of their equipment. For the men, there was relief that the long boredom was over and, in the large, there was relish at the prospect of 'sorting out Johnny Gyppo'.

Hungary and Suez

The two days 30/31 October saw the Hungarian Revolution reach its turning point. On 30 October two representatives of the Soviet Politburo, Mikoyan and Suslov, were in Budapest; their approach was conciliatory. They apparently agreed to the establishment of a coalition, the prompt withdrawal of Soviet troops, and negotiations about Hungary's withdrawal from the Warsaw Pact, whereupon she would join her historic partner, Austria, in permanent neutrality. Some scholars regard this Soviet reaction as having been treacherous from the start.[12] Whatever the truth about 30 October, 31 October was certainly the day when the Soviet leadership, with Mikoyan and Suslov still absent, finally resolved to overthrow the Nagy Government. It is questionable how much difference the Suez question made to this process of decision-making; it should be noted that the Russians did not fail to crush the Prague Spring in 1968 when there was no comparable distraction for the West. The profoundly disillusioning effect that subsequent events in Hungary were to have on many Western Communists and their fellow-travellers took place regardless of what had occurred elsewhere. Yet there is no doubt that this precise coincidence of dates – of the apparent victory of the Hungarian Revolution with the launching of the Anglo-French ultimatum – enormously heightened the emotional content of the Suez affair.

The man who made the link between the two events of 30 October to most immediate effect was John Foster Dulles. It happened that on that very evening he was booked for one of his regular off-the-record dinners with a group of senior American reporters, organised by Chalmers Roberts of the *Washington Post*. This was one of the means by which he aimed to set the pace of public discussion of foreign affairs, since his unattributable views could be relied upon to seep into the open by the journalistic process known as 'compulsory plagiarism'. Dulles spoke that evening of the ways in which he had been let down by his allies: the freezing out of communication as between friends, the cold attitude of non-cooperation at the UN, the absence of a British Ambassador while Caccia was coming slowly by sea to replace the departed Makins. He also made it clear that it was not in assessing Nasser as a man to be 'dumped' that he had differed in judgment from Eden. It was simply a question of the methods used and the pace and the occasion of the undermining of the Egyptian ruler.

Dulles then related these things to what was happening in Hungary. The West was now on the point of winning an immense and long-hoped-for victory over Soviet colonialism in Eastern Europe, he said. Yet this was the very moment chosen by Britain and France to make the United States declare herself for or against western colonialism. Since the Second World War the United States had walked a tightrope between maintaining old and valued relations with Britain and France and securing the friendship and understanding of newly independent countries that had escaped from colonialism. Suez showed it to be highly doubtful that America could walk that tightrope much longer. The latest Hungarian development, the Soviet withdrawal from Budapest, suggested the chance arising of a middle band of neutral states emerging in Europe. In those circumstances, it might not any longer be so necessary to defer to the interests of European allies.[13]

Eden's mounting anti-Americanism was showing as he launched his statement to the House of Commons on 31 October with an attack on the motion which Lodge had proposed and Dixon had vetoed in the Security Council. It was, in effect, he said, a condemnation of Israel as an aggressor, whereas the reality was the growth of a specific Egyptian threat to the peace of the Middle East. Eden said it was his and Mollet's intention that their action to protect the Canal and separate the combatants should result in a permanent settlement which would prevent such a situation ever arising in the future. By entering the Canal Zone they would be holding the only line of division which was practicable; even if it would have been fair, it would not have been possible to have attempted to establish themselves on the armistice line.

This short speech was much interrupted, especially when Philip Noel-Baker, a former Labour Minister of State at the Foreign Office and future Nobel Peace Prize winner, attempted persistently to pin Eden down on why, given the advertised daily consultations with the Americans, including on 28 and 29 October, nothing had been said to them about the Anglo-French plan. Next, Hugh Gaitskell tried to get out of Eden whether 'Yes or No', on the expiry of the ultimatum, British and French forces were under instructions to occupy the Canal Zone at once. Understandably, the Prime Minister attempted a graceful evasion, which was roughly handled, especially by James Callaghan, who made a name during the Suez debates for highly audible interruptions delivered from a recumbent position. 'The Hon. Gentleman', said Eden, 'is a master at sitting and shouting. He seldom stands.' Brought to his feet Callaghan demanded: 'Are British troops engaged in Egypt at this moment? Have they landed or where are they?' The Speaker struggled to restore order amid the general uproar. Reginald Paget (Labour) was finally heard asking on a point of order: 'How can we debate a war when the Government will not tell us whether it has started?'

Gaitskell delivered a root-and-branch attack on the Government's policy which was described by many who heard it as the most brilliant speech from the Opposition benches for many a year. He accused the Government of abandoning at one blow the three principles governing British foreign policy since the Second World War – solidarity with the Commonwealth; the Anglo-American alliance; and adherence to the UN Charter – and he cited in some detail the doubting sounds from such normally loyal associates as Australia and New Zealand which were strongly suggestive of lack of consultation. But the UN was the centre of his case. The Government had complained throughout the crisis about its slowness of action and its impotence in the face of the veto. Who was delaying it, who was vetoing it now? The whole world looked on the present action as a transparent excuse to seize the Canal, to do at last what public opinion had prevented the Government from doing before. But, he said, there was an even worse story going round. 'It is the story that the whole business was a matter of collusion between the British and French Governments and the Government of Israel.' With this, any calculation of the Opposition's line that might have been based on Gaitskell's well-advertised pro-Israeli outlook was in an instant confounded.

After referring to what was happening in Hungary where 'the ideas of democracy and liberty had won a sensational and exciting victory', Gaitskell uttered words that would profoundly influence the events of the next seven days: 'I must now tell the Government and the country that we cannot support the action they have taken and that we shall feel bound, by every constitutional means at our disposal, to oppose it.' The first of these constitutional means (he emphasised that he would make no attempt to dissuade anybody from carrying out the Government's orders) was to introduce a motion of censure 'in the strongest possible terms' on the following day.

The House which had listened to the biting indictment for the most part in silence was deeply stirred to primal emotion by this conclusion. There were roars of 'Resign' from the Opposition and counter-cries from the Government benches. When order had been restored the next speaker, Viscount Hinchingbroke from the Tory backbenches, began: 'I entertain at this moment the most profound feelings of disgust and degradation. The country will judge of that speech . . . The conclusion will be that the speech represents the nadir of British fortunes, the most miserable depth to which this country has fallen.' Members of the Opposition had 'such a weak attitude to public policy that I can only suppose that they object to all physical exercise in any form'.

For the most part the debate was a dialogue of the deaf, as the following exchange bears witness:

> Captain Pilkington (Conservative): Are we not trying to stop war?
> Desmond Donnelly (Labour): No, we are not trying to stop war. Because we have started war.

At ten past six Sidney Silverman, a diminutive and extremely sure-footed Opposition backbencher, interrupted another member to supply the news from the tape that 'at this moment British bombers are bombing Egyptian territory'.

Selwyn Lloyd's reply did not lack ingenuity. If the Security Council resolution had been allowed to pass, Israel would have taken no notice of it so long as her grievances were unmet. The Security Council would then have been unable to stop the Israelis from reaching the Suez Canal and thus threatening the fatal disruption of traffic. 'We have said that we understand why Israel should regard her action as vitally necessary from her point of view, but that is not to say that we regard it as right and much less that we condone it.' (Israelis who had been present at Sèvres would have recognised the man and his way of putting things). Lloyd wondered how the Opposition would have reacted if the Government had come to the House to propose that British armed forces should be deployed under the Tripartite Declaration to defend Colonel Nasser's regime. The shortage of consultation was all to be explained by the extreme shortage of time. 'In an emergency, which this was ... it is not practicable to have prior agreement.' As for Gaitskell's raising the matter of collusion: 'It is quite wrong to state that Israel was incited to this action by HMG. There was no prior agreement between us about it.'[14]

The first of these last two sentences could presumably just be excused on the grounds that the incitement came from the French Government and was merely abetted by Britain. But one need go no further than the second to answer the question of whether or not the House was explicitly misled. It still remains astonishing that the man who spoke these words was subsequently elected Speaker of the House of Commons.

While the House of Commons debate was still on (at 3 p.m. in New York, 8 p.m. in London, and 10 p.m. in the Middle East), the Security Council reassembled and was stunned to hear what sounded like the offer of Dag Hammarskjöld's resignation in the face of this behaviour by two Permanent Members. His official biographer, Sir Brian Urquhart (himself a very distinguished servant of the UN, later becoming its Under-Secretary-General, denies that Hammarskjöld had any intention of resigning. Apparently it was to avoid this interpretation being placed on his words that he showed his statement to the permanent members in advance.[15] What he actually said was that, while the Secretary-General must usually avoid taking public stands on conflicts, nevertheless 'the discretion and impartiality thus imposed ... by the character of his immediate task may not degenerate into a policy of expediency'. He was the servant of the Charter and could not serve except under the assumption that all members meant to observe the Charter. The bearing of this, he said, must be obvious without any elaboration (the unspoken elaboration being that he could not in conscience be neutral or anything except hostile towards the acts of Britain and France). If members took a different view of the Secretary-General's task, 'it is their obvious right to act accordingly'.

In private, Dixon protested that this was not playing fair, and indeed it was true that there had been no hint of resignation whenever the Soviet Union frequently invoked her power of veto. But, publicly, the statement brought out on all sides expressions of confidence in Hammarskjöld. At this point Omar Loutfi, the Egyptian delegate, read out an agency bulletin similar to that produced by Silverman in the House of Commons saying that 'the city of Cairo' was under attack.

Pierson Dixon fended off these blows as best he could. His argument was that the action was strictly limited to military targets, primarily airfields, and that the civil population had been warned in advance. Surely, he said, nobody was going to take very seriously Soviet stories of a British plot with Israel. It was common knowledge that, over the past few months, relations between the two countries had been very difficult and even strained. As for the argument that, since Israel had now agreed to keep ten miles away from the Canal, there was no longer any need for the Anglo-French forces to land, Dixon pointed to Israeli acceptance being conditional on Egypt's positive reply. It was Britain's view that Israel should withdraw her forces from their present positions as soon as this could be satisfactorily arranged.

The Jugoslav later that evening moved that the matter be referred to an emergency special session of the General Assembly and this was carried by seven votes to two, with two abstentions. As this was a procedural resolution, there was no veto.[16]

The Bombs Drop

Sir Humphrey Trevelyan expected to wake up on the morning of 31 October with the Embassy surrounded by Egyptian troops or police, but instead all was normal.[17] The press carried Nasser's rejection of the ultimatum, and editorial comment as in *Al Akhbar* took the line that Israel had allowed herself to play the role of catspaw in what was primarily an Eden–Mollet plot to seize the Canal. Anwar Sadat wrote in misplaced triumph in *Al Gumhouriya*: 'What Eden and Mollet seem to have again forgotten was that the Israeli spearhead, which they expected would find no difficulty in ... reaching a point in the immediate vicinity of the Canal, was immediately annihilated.' The *Egyptian Gazette* began its editorial: 'The affairs of Britain seem now to be in the hands of a madman.' What was threatened was not so much directed to keeping the Canal open as to closing it down. The pipelines also would probably be cut, 'thus reaping the harvest of no Canal and no oil'.[18]

The atmosphere in Egypt seemed calm but determined. Arms were distributed to the paramilitary organisations: the National Guard and the National Liberation Army. Classes at universities and secondary schools were temporarily suspended so that students could enrol in the National Liberation Army. Owners of lorries were told to put them at the disposal of the military. There was no rioting against Europeans. Diplomatic relations were not broken off with the British until 1 November.

The civilian contractors' staff at the Canal Base were in the most vulnerable position. As early as 11 August it had been agreed at a meeting at

Chequers that the base and stores would have to be abandoned to the Egyptians and the contractors pulled out at some point after the London Conference. But at the end of October they were still there. The Egyptians, determined to be meticulously correct, allowed normal transactions, including the movement of war supplies out of Egypt while the build-up in the Eastern Mediterranean was going on. In the early hours of 30 October Trevelyan in Cairo and the Consul at Ismailia received signals advising British subjects to leave immediately by whatever means possible. Not exactly 'all' British subjects were to be so advised, since those of Maltese and Cypriot extraction, the majority, were to be 'discouraged from attempt at mass evacuation'.

The Consul was told, 'We must leave it to you to do what you can to help the contractors' employees to get away.' The contractors' leaders knew exactly what they wanted: they sent a signal asking for transport planes to be sent immediately to Abu Sueir, the Suez Canal air base, to evacuate 480 technicians; they also took the precaution of booking passages on a Greek ship due to sail from Port Said on 2 November. Two brothers asked and were given permission to make a 1600-mile run for it by road to Libya. They were the only ones who got away. On the night of 31 October, when the bombs had dropped on Cairo, the men were all rounded up by the police and interned in conditions of some discomfort in school rooms, not to be released until 20 December.[19]

Trevelyan, who until 2 November was able to move outside the Embassy, reflected on what had befallen his mission. His thoughts were recorded movingly in his book *The Middle East in Revolution*. What was happening did not make sense. His Government appeared to be making policy from motives and on assumptions that were unfathomable. 'It was, I confess', he wrote, 'difficult at that time not to come near to tears, not of self-pity, but of vexation and despair.'[20]

The reason that the Israelis had not arrived at the Canal was that that was not their aim. At the end of 30 October, Dayan once again told Sharon that his paratroopers were not to advance west into the Mitla Pass. This axis was of no interest. The 202 Brigade was intended later to advance south towards Sharm al-Sheikh to help to release the passage through the Enterprise Channel. But the next day (31 October), there occurred a second major act of insubordination among the Israeli assailants. Sharon, temperamentally unused to a passive role, and professionally uneasy about the unfavourable ground on which his unit was drawn up within striking distance of Egyptian armour, which might well have attacked, determined to move on. He managed to secure permission on 31 October to send a patrol unit into the pass on condition that it avoid battle. Instead of a patrol, he sent a substantial combat team which was promptly pinned down by the reinforced and heavily armed Egyptian troops cunningly positioned in the caves of the defile.

The Egyptian air force intervened to some effect while the Israelis were unable to bring up air support because of a breakdown in communications. The result was the most desperate fighting of the whole campaign, a seven-hour battle lasting until well after dark in which the Israelis finally prevailed after hand-to-hand fighting up and down the slopes of the defile, but at a cost of what for them amounted to heavy casualties – 38 killed and 120 wounded. Sharon, resenting no doubt the implication that his famous hard-fought victory had been a wasted one, later reproached Dayan for letting his strategic purposes be dictated by Britain and France.

In the central sector, the Israeli 7 Armoured Brigade was beginning the assault on the three-ridged defensive complex of Abu Agheila on 31 October. The brigade, which had the mortification of being attacked several times by its own planes because of the failure of the air support signal system, captured a number of key points including, after fierce fighting in the dark, the Ruafa dam. Although there were occasions when the Egyptians offered little or no resistance this was not the case here. The Israelis had a very tough fight and had then to dispose of a counter-attack that the Egyptians managed to mount.

Despite mishaps the targets had been achieved. But in another part of the Abu Agheila battle the Israelis were facing setbacks. Acutely conscious that the UN was acting fast, Dayan knew he had little time. He sent a reserve brigade, the 10th, into the attack on the stronghold of Umm Qataf, whose possession by the Egyptians was blocking Israeli convoys from using the only asphalt supply road. Here, Dayan says bluntly, 'the Egyptians fought extremely well and our forces extremely poorly'.[21] During the Sinai campaign generally the Egyptians gave a good account of themselves so long as they were fighting to a pre-plan; it was improvisation that caused them to come adrift.

At long last, during the evening of 31 October, came news that British and French bombs were dropping. Ben-Gurion had been raging and reproaching until the last minute. At 5 p.m. local time he cabled Bourgès-Maunoury: 'I am cast down and confused by the fact that at this hour we are still without news of an Anglo-French operation against the Egyptian airfields. We have parachuted battalions close to the Canal with the sole aim of serving your purposes, for this was not designed to serve ours. According to the Protocol, your operation should have started this morning.' Later, we were told it was to start at 3 p.m. GMT (5 p.m. Cairo).' The entire weight of the Egyptian air force, he said, was being directed at the Israelis in Sinai; the two French squadrons based on Israel were not doing anything to protect Israeli troops because they said they had received no instructions to do so. 'The members of the Government are asking me if we have been abandoned to our fate.'[22]

At 6.15 p.m. (4.15 p.m. GMT), the first bombs were being dropped by seven Canberras on Cairo, though on the wrong target. The original target was to have been Cairo West, to strike at the menace of the Ilyushins. Suddenly news had reached London from the Cairo Embassy, which could still transmit, that the American community, some thirteen hundred strong, was being evacuated by the road which bordered on that airfield. Eden, looking at an outdated map which showed the road running much nearer the airfield than it in fact now was, ordered the raid to be cancelled immediately. Since the *FLASH* signals in cypher were taking too long and that part of the bomber force that was flying in from Luqa (Malta) was already in the air, the Prime Minister's orders were conveyed personally by the Chief of the Air Staff over the open telephone to Group Captain Lewis Hodges, the commander of the Bomber Wing in Malta. After strenuous effort, the Valiants in the air were contacted 'in plain language' as they passed near the RAF's Libyan base at Al Adem on their long journey. They were under control of Task Force Headquarters on Cyprus, which had heard nothing. After an interval of confusion while they were receiving conflicting messages from the two islands, they turned. 'We had a situation', recalls (Sir) Lewis Hodges, 'where eight Valiants were returning to Luqa with full bomb loads and further waves were taking off to go to Cairo ... We had to have the bombs jettisoned ...'[23] The Canberras that were to fly against Cairo West from Cyprus then had their target hastily changed to the military airfield at Almaza. Some of the pilots had only ten minutes' warning of the change, navigators had to work out new flight plans in the air. For all the British familiarity with Cairo, the briefing material available for this last-minute work was poor; no attention was called to the close proximity of Cairo International Airport to Almaza. Tension on board was high as the crews were on the alert for the first sign of the dreaded MiG 15s. In the end, going for Almaza, they hit Cairo International.[24]

Cairo West was not the only high priority target that the allied crews were not allowed to attack. In what had been designated an aero-psychological campaign, Cairo Radio was arguably the most important target of all. But it too had been struck off the list because of London's last minute qualms about killing civilians combined with a lack of awareness that the all-important transmitters were not in the crowded city but out in the desert. Until later in the assault, therefore, the *Voice of the Arabs* continued to be heard loud and clear.

There were altogether eleven sorties that night. The Canberras and Valiants attacked five different airfields in the first raid. The results were not impressive to those who subsequently evaluated the operation – too few bombs, too much dispersal. The total load that the bombers dropped during the course of Operation *Musketeer* was 1,962 bombs (in eighteen attacks on thirteen targets), which was an amount that would have been considered adequate by the end of the Second World War if concentrated on one relatively small target. Neither the target marking nor the bombing came up to the expected standard. The result even after the second night of bomber operations (on 1/2 November) was that all airfields except Cairo West were still serviceable for operations. And Cairo West had been put out of action by the Egyptians themselves, after first using it to fly their Soviet machines either to Syrian or Saudi airfields or to distant Luxor in Upper Egypt. According to an Air Force Staff College lecture, 'photo reconnaissance showed that the potential of the Egyptian air force had not been materially changed and that the objective of preventing the immediate use of the airfields was not achieved'.[26]

However, results in war are properly measured in relation to the response of the enemy. Little seemed to go right with the bomber operations, the fulcrum of so much planning and diplomacy, yet as a whole the air offensive was a complete success. The Egyptian air force was grounded or took itself off. Of those planes which stayed, upwards of 200 had been destroyed on the ground by the British and French ground-attack aircraft by the end of 2 November. The high potential of the Egyptian air arm had been totally paralysed for minimal loss to the attackers. Nor, once the British and French had intervened, were the Israelis subsequently harassed. The weather was perfect, and except initially for some surprisingly accurate anti-aircraft fire, the enemy was totally inactive. Given these ideal conditions the British and French just made it. 'There is no doubt', wrote Air Marshal Barnett, the Force Commander, in his report, 'that, if we had been up against an enemy with even a modicum of fighting qualities with the modern aircraft and equipment the Egyptians had, the situation would have been different ... If enemy air opposition had been effective and had disrupted our plans, there is no doubt that communications would have been hopelessly inadequate.'[27]

The biggest chance taken was over the packing of the three airfields on Cyprus with 289 aircraft parked wing-tip to wing-tip with no dispersal or blackout and inadequate radar. However much in other respects the British could be accused of planning this operation as if they were going to land again on the beaches of Normandy, they took large risks with the safety of the air forces. They acted as if their enemy was a nullity and it turned out that he was. General Keightley, however, in his worst moments both during the operation and in the weeks after it, would visualise 'the effect of even a couple of MiGs, flown perhaps by Russians, flying once over Nicosia airfield with a load of rockets'.

One pilot only, Flying Officer Dennis Kenyon of Canberra WH 915, failed to take off and the squadron, on returning, found the bomber with its nose on the tarmac. 'Hello, Dennis, did you press the wrong button?' asked the commanding officer. Kenyon was subsequently court-martialled and given a year's imprisonment for not carrying out a warlike operation with the utmost exertion. It was thought that he would plead that the operation against Egypt was wrong, and that, because it was wrong, his orders were illegal. In fact, his position was rather confused; he said he had disagreed with the Suez operation but had pressed the wrong button by accident. Evidence was given that he had not eaten or slept for two days. The case did not become the *cause célèbre* the authorities had feared. No other case is recorded of individual resistance to taking part in the undeclared war.[28]

The die had now been cast. Following the 'communication' directed to both sides in the Middle East war, bombs had been dropped on one of them, the one which had been attacked and invaded. President Nasser was at home receiving the Indonesian Ambassador when the bombs started falling on the International Airport. He went onto the roof and realised, since they were jet bombers, that they were not Israeli. Now that he saw the mistake of his initial assessment, the important thing must be to prevent the reinforced Egyptian army being cut off in Sinai by a Franco-British landing on the Canal. He met his advisers in the office of Hakim Amer, the Commander-in-Chief. He insisted on an immediate and total withdrawal from Sinai. To this Amer was completely opposed, saying that it would demoralise fighting units which were locked in battle and fighting heroically against the Israelis. Nasser had himself to issue the orders over the telephone to the senior officer of the 4 Armoured Division, which had just moved into Sinai, to bring it back immediately.[29]

Towards midnight the second air raid on Cairo had begun. For a while the Egyptian leadership was in a state of paralysis and confusion. It seemed on the face of it impossible to resist Britain and France as well as Israel. This was the critical moment for the allies' aero-psychological strategy since they were not going to have the luxury of a ten-day assault on the nation's economy. Its impact must be made now, at the beginning, or not at all.

The description by Abdul-Latif Boghdadi of the mood at military headquarters both on the first night of the air attacks and at some points subsequently suggests that the chances of success were perhaps not so remote as has sometimes been suggested. There was some initial panic because the dropping of marker flares over the racecourse at Misr al-Jadida which is close to the military Headquarters and also to Nasser's home, was mistaken for paratroop jumps and thought to be a bid by elite troops to capture or kill the President. Nasser did not at first assert his leadership and seemed confused and preoccupied with the safety of his young children.

Boghdadi portrays himself as mainly concerned to ensure that Abdul Nasser should behave in these circumstances like an authentic hero. 'Our honour and the honour of this generation', he says, 'were dependent on him.' There was much animated discussion about whether to continue the war at the cost of much devastation and suffering or whether to arrange a surrender and continue the struggle underground. Nasser did not for the time being show his hand.[30]

The Anglo-American Breach

In Washington, Eisenhower was on the television screens to speak both about Hungary and the dropping of bombs on Cairo. As to the first, he promised that he would not look to Eastern European countries for potential military allies and that he would extend to them economic assistance, with no conditions attached about the nature of their social order; on the events in the Middle East, he was resonant and emphatic. 'The United States', he declared, 'was not consulted in any way about any phase of these actions. Nor were we informed of them in advance ... We believe these actions to have been taken in error, for we do not accept the use of force as a wise or proper instrument for the settlement of international disputes.' There would be no US involvement in the present hostilities – therefore there was no need to call Congress into special session. He ended with a ringing endorsement of the United Nations and an assertion that there could be no peace without law. The General Assembly, with no veto operating, would bring the opinion of the world to bear on the problem.[31]

The Americans expected the British and French to run into immediate trouble with their supplies of oil. They would need to get access to substitute supplies from the Western Hemisphere for which they would be short of dollars. 'They may be planning to present us with a *fait accompli*, then expecting us to foot the bill,' Eisenhower told Dr Arthur Flemming, the Director of War Mobilisation, on the evening of 30 October. He showed his feelings by the remark that those who began the Suez operation should be left 'to boil in their own oil'.[32]

Since the Israelis were the primary target of the Administration's wrath, and since so much had been made of the need to demonstrate the ineffectiveness of Jewish influence at election time, they in particular might have dreaded the lash of retribution. At this stage it was not so impressive. There was, it was true, an initial scurry to block Israel's bank balances in the United States until George Humphrey found out that these amounted to 'peanuts'. The effective thing, he told Dulles, would be to prevent private remittances, but on the other hand that would cause 'terrible political activity'. John B. Hollister, the man in charge of foreign aid, took the language of America's UN resolution literally and issued instructions to cease all aid to Israel at once. Banks were told to issue no more letters of credit, the Department of Commerce asked to refuse export licenses, the Department of Agriculture to send no more surplus food. Dulles was disconcerted at the rapidity of this action and took steps to reverse it. Hollister's memorandum was cancelled and all copies recalled. Down the line there occurred the well-known sequence of order, counter-order, disorder.[33]

Within the State Department William Rountree drew up a list of possible sanctions against Israel. Dulles decided to defer the most important one – a Treasury block on all funds, private and public and on their transfer to

Israel – and to obtain the National Security Council's approval for a package that he variously described as 'very mild' and 'nothing more than a slap on the wrist'. Still, he insisted against some opposition that sanctions there must be and the President seemed disappointed that they did not amount to more. At that particular moment they made an uncomfortable contrast with the treatment of Egypt, who, if there was 'aggression', had to be the 'victim' of it; her balances remained blocked, as a consequence of the nationalisation.[34]

Nevertheless, in Cairo the reports from Washington were sufficiently encouraging for President Nasser on 1 November to ask the new American Ambassador, Raymond Hare, for United States support against Anglo-French aggression. Hare's first reaction was to question bluntly whether this was not a mere gesture preliminary to a serious appeal to the Soviet Union. Nasser convinced him that it was meant.[35]

The breach was rapidly opening up across the Atlantic. In London, Rab Butler, in an 'off-the-record' speech to editors which reflected the mounting strength of anti-Americanism in government circles, bitterly attacked the Americans for their record of repeated failure to co-operate with their British allies. He coupled their unhelpful behaviour over long-term economic policies with that over the Suez Canal.[36] By contrast, the Americans were receiving warm praise from the leaders of the Labour Party. Aldrich reported that, 'without prompting and on their own initiative', Hugh Gaitskell and several of his colleagues, including Aneurin Bevan and James Callaghan, had expressed 'deep appreciation' of Washington's reaction to the 'Eden–Mollet folly'. Gaitskell declared that 'more than half if not three-quarters of the British nation' was opposed to this 'monstrous' policy. He called on the Americans to see that Britain and France be named as well as Israel in the UN resolution calling for the withdrawal of forces from Egyptian territory. Continued firmness by the United States was the only way to heal the injury being inflicted by Eden on the Alliance.[37]

'Is Britain at War?'

In Britain the public confusion spread to those quarters most inclined to award a Conservative Government the benefit of most doubts. 'Britain At War' was the headline that confronted *Daily Mail* readers on the morning of 1 November. In great solemnity its front page 'Comment' column began: 'Britain is at war with Egypt. That is the grim, inescapable overriding fact of this November morning.' The writer went on, perhaps a little grudgingly: 'Questions and criticisms there will be and must be. We may have some to proffer ourselves. But let them wait.' Next morning's tale was different. 'Comment' was headed 'A Police Action'. It ran: 'It seems we were wrong yesterday to head our Comment: "Britain at War". Britain is apparently not at war. She is engaged in a police action in the Suez area.' It may have been a mistake, reflected the *Mail*, for Britain and France not to have awaited the sanction of the UN.

Between the two articles lay Thursday's (1 November) astonishing scenes in the House of Commons when, before the debate on the Opposition motion of censure had even started, the Defence Minister had been brought up against the basic question: was Britain at war? In a statement after questions Head had reported four airfields bombed at night and nine in the morning, also that an Egyptian frigate encountered by the Naval squadron that had entered the Gulf of Aqaba to protect British shipping had been sunk. Since the General Assembly was meeting that day in New York, Gaitskell immediately asked that the Government should pledge itself to accept instantly anything recommended by a two-thirds majority and not to take any further military action until the Assembly had acted. But from the backbenches Sidney Silverman put the most fundamental question of all to the Speaker as a point of order. The Minister of Defence had just coolly spoken of the sinking of the ships and the dropping of bombs, the destruction of life and property, in a country with whom Britain was in friendly relations. There had been no declaration of war, no breaking off of diplomatic relations. Was there anything that the House could do, he asked the Chair, to prevent those who had taken the oath to the Crown being required to commit murder all over the world? When the Speaker, W.S. Morrison, demurred at having to answer this sort of question, Gaitskell in clear tones and with a mounting clamour of support then demanded of the Government whether there had been a declaration of war. Eden declined to answer in advance of the forthcoming debate on Gaitskell's motion of censure. Aneurin Bevan, who hitherto had played a strangely muted role in this affair (so that some Tories affected to see a contrast between his sense of responsibility and Gaitskell's lack of it), now came forward. 'The question put to the Right Hon. Gentleman simply amounts to this. Under the orders of the Government, British airmen, soldiers and sailors have been sent into action. If they are captured and no declaration of war has been made, what protection have they under international law?'

The House rocked with shouts of 'Answer'. Eden responded unconvincingly: 'The action which has been taken has been, as I explained yesterday, in accordance with the statement we made.' There was no holding the House. Bevan rephrased his question at greater length, the Speaker said it could all be dealt with in the debate and, led by Bevan, the Opposition side of the House contradicted him and shouted him down. Speaker Morrison suspended the sitting on account of 'grave disorder' for half an hour.[38]

An experienced witness in the Press Gallery, Iverach McDonald of *The Times*, described what had happened as 'quite the most shattering experience I've ever sat through ... the divisions, the uproar, the emotion were much worse than at the time of Munich'. It was, he said, like a Reinhart Production (a film extravaganza): 'You've got the Government benches mainly silent but at each word the whole of the Labour benches rose like a wall. No longer shouting, they were howling with anger and real anguish.' When the sitting was suspended, 'out the Members trooped, still shouting and shaking their fists. It really was a most terrible, terrible spectacle.'[39]

As often happens, when the House resumes after a big row, the debate on a motion of censure was somewhat of an anticlimax. It was not moved by Gaitskell and the Prime Minister was calm but uninformative, except to say that there had been no declaration of war but that troops in 'armed conflict' were covered by the Geneva Convention. The earlier release of anger seemed to have exhausted and perhaps shamed the House. Sir Anthony Eden with his calm manner and unprovocative language imposed himself on the debate, to the visible relief of the Conservative benches. He had bought a little time. Yet, in seeking to lower the atmosphere and blunt the shafts of his critics by his unsensational style, Eden supplied the means by which his whole policy would be unravelled. 'We do not seek', he said, 'to impose by force a solution of the Israel–Egypt dispute or the Suez Canal dispute or any of the disputes in the area ... The first and urgent task is to separate these combatants ... If the UN were then willing to take over the physical task of maintaining peace in that area, no one would be better pleased than we.' It was a challenge thrown out to the UN and it was one which the UN was very rapidly to answer.

The winding up speech for the Opposition was made by Bevan who compared the wording used in the ultimatum to Egypt with that used in the German ultimatum to Belgium in 1914 and the German ultimatum to Norway in 1940. He captured, too, in his speech the eerie feeling many people who were accustomed to admire Eden had, that he was acting out of character. 'I am bound to say that I have not seen from the Prime Minister in the course of the last four or five months ... any evidence of that sagacity and skill that he should have acquired in so many years in the Foreign Office. There is something the matter with him.'

Before Rab Butler could reply to the debate an unusual event occurred. From the Tory backbenches up jumped the young member for The Wrekin, William Yates (who was subsequently to be an MP in Australia and Administrator of Christmas Island). He had intervened once before in the debate, when a speaker had remarked that Israeli troops had not yet reached the Canal, saying 'The plan was that Israel would not reach the Canal in any case.' Now he appealed dramatically to the Speaker: 'I am a young Member of the House and I desire to have your advice. I have been to France and I have come to the conclusion that HMG have been involved in an international conspiracy ...' At this point the Speaker called him to order. Gaitskell intervened to say that Yates 'evidently has an extremely important communication to make to the House', but Yates merely managed to blurt out naïvely that he wanted advice as to whether, in these circumstances, it would be considered right and patriotic for a person deliberately to try to bring the Government down. It was the nearest brush the House of Commons was to have with the truth in these days of earnest and ferocious debate. At the end of the debate the motion of censure was lost by 324 to 255 votes. The Liberals, for the first time on this issue, voted with the Opposition.[40]

Meanwhile, in the House of Lords, the Government's legal position was being comprehensively defended by Lord Kilmuir, the Lord Chancellor. Lord Kilmuir rested his case on the doctrine that intervention is justified when there is an 'imminent danger of injury to nationals' through the failure or inability of the territorial sovereign to protect them. He extended this to what he called 'really valuable and internationally important property'. Therefore, there were three good grounds for intervention: the danger to nationals, particularly in Ismailia, one of the three points to be 'temporarily' occupied; the danger to shipping in the Canal; and the danger to the enormously valuable installations. How could the bombing be justified as being strictly confined to protecting British nationals? The answer was that measures of protection must be clearly proportionate to the resistance offered to them. The Egyptians had said they would resist intervention with all their land, sea and air forces; therefore the two allies were entitled to take the steps necessary to defeat those forces.

In any case, according to the Lord Chancellor, the right of self-defence was not at all limited to the circumstances specified in the UN Charter (Article 51). A wider inherent right remained. Nor did the Charter restrict such self-defence to cases where the attack had actually been launched. 'If that were done, it would be a travesty of the purpose of the Charter to compel a defending State to allow its opponent to deliver the first, fatal blow.' It was apparent that, if the British Government held to the Lord Chancellor's opinion, it would be challenging the whole basis on which Dag Hammarskjöld and others considered that the UN Charter had moved forward radically the concept of international law by outlawing the use of force and making pre-emptive blows especially unacceptable. In the debate that had been taking place between Hammarskjöld and Ben-Gurion, Kilmuir was coming down heavily on the side of the Israeli.

In the course of Kilmuir's exposition, the Archbishop of Canterbury, Geoffrey Fisher, repeatedly confronted him – Archbishop versus Chancellor, as if in a mediaeval court. The question, the Primate maintained, was a simple one. 'The noble and learned Viscount referred to the attacking power against which we have to exercise self-defence. Who is the attacking power?' Kilmuir spelled out his logical sequence: 'First [propose to], make a peaceful landing [to protect nationals]; then, if a power into whose territory we are going says that they will resist with all their force, the force which we have the right to use is automatically extended to that sufficient to repulse the force threatening'. The Archbishop was implacable: 'Which is the attacking power in this case?' The Lord Chancellor tried again. Then the Archbishop said: 'Here is the Canal; here are our nationals; here is our property. There is an attack on them which you have to resist. Who is making the attack?'

After first stalling, the Lord Chancellor said: 'The threat of force is made by the person who refuses to stop the hostile operations that are threatening the people and the installations.' 'Who is this attacking power in this case?' Crossly, Kilmuir said that the Primate might have guessed that for himself. 'It is obviously Egypt, who has refused to stop.' The Archbishop would not let up. Two rounds later, Kilmuir conceded that there were 'two situations', of which the first 'which attracted our peace-making intention ... was started when Israel crossed the border'. 'I merely said that there are two stages, one and two,' the Primate observed sweetly. 'You omitted to mention the first. I have now inserted it.'[41]

The Attorney-General, Sir Reginald Manningham-Buller, the Solicitor-General, Sir Henry Hilton-Foster, and Sir Gerald Fitzmaurice, the legal adviser to the Foreign Office, had not been asked about the Government's move and would not have supported it. They were considerably put out when the Foreign Office informed some foreign capitals that HMG 'are advised on the highest legal authority' that they could do what they were doing. Legally, said Sir Gerald in a memo to Kirkpatrick, it was impossible to see how the policy could be justified merely on the basis of an Egyptian refusal to clear out of a large zone of their own territory in face of Israeli attacks. He stood foursquare behind the doctrine that the UN Charter made all the difference. 'The plea of vital interests, which has been one of the main justifications for wars in the past, is indeed the very one which the Charter was intended to exclude as a basis for armed intervention in another country.' It would provide the ideal basis for justifying the Soviet occupation of the satellite states.

The doctrine, relied on by Kilmuir, that force may be used to protect one's citizens from imminent danger only applied, said Fitzmaurice, where the danger came from the Government itself or arose because the local Government had lost control and the mob held sway. It definitely did not stem from the ordinary dangers arising from the fact of war in the country concerned; otherwise any country would be entitled to intervene in any other which was at war. 'It will in any case be said, where is the danger to British lives in the present case, other than such as may arise from armed intervention? The Egyptian Government have made no move against British subjects as yet in the whole course of the Suez dispute.' As for the supposed right to protect property abroad, there was no such right under present-day international law. 'In any case where is the British property in question?'[42]

21

World Opinion Speaks

The one overriding lesson of the Suez operation is that world opinion is now an absolute principle of war and must be treated as such.
General Sir Charles Keightley, 11 December 1957.

We had not realized that our Government was capable of such folly and such crookedness.
Leading article in the *Observer*, 4 November 1956.

Criticism and questions had been expected: the sheer volume, universality and scale of adverse reaction to the British and French attack on Egypt shocked, sobered or scandalised the supporters of the policy. First of all, Britain looked to the Commonwealth for understanding and, if one looked hard enough, it was to be found – from Sir Roy Welensky in Central Africa, from New Zealand and from parts of Australia. 'There is no time for words,' wrote the *Auckland Herald*, 'but instead adherence to what is believed to be right.' 'People of British stock everywhere will admire [Sir Anthony Eden] for the stand he has taken – there is to be no retreat from principle,' loyally echoed the *Wellington Dominion*. Sir Roy, just taking over the Premiership of a doomed Federation, declared that, 'It was with a feeling of relief that I learned of Britain's decision to take some firm stand.'

Robert Menzies dominated the Australian political stage and in his public pronouncements eclipsed the misgivings of others, including his own External Affairs Minister, R. G. Casey, who was in London and complained that he could find no one amongst his friends, apart from senior Ministers, who was in favour of the policy.[1] In a major speech Menzies found it 'entirely reasonable' that action had to be taken with no delay for Commonwealth consultation. Above all, the Canal must be protected.

The complete absence of that special advance consultation about major foreign policy decisions which was always advertised as being such a special feature of Commonwealth status was not accepted in many places with such equanimity. Even in Australia there was sharp press criticism. 'The obvious doubts of the Australian representative on the Security Council, asked without warning to choose between Britain and the United States as sponsors of two radically different policies, will be widely shared,' wrote the *Sydney Morning Herald* on 1 November. 'Many, indeed, even of those who endorse Britain's policy will be dismayed at her Government's rough disregard of the other members of the Commonwealth and of her great American ally.'

In Ottawa that would have been regarded as an understatement. Lester Pearson, the Canadian Minister for External Affairs, told Norman Robertson, the High Commissioner in London, to express 'our feeling of bewilderment and dismay at the decision which they have taken ... while the Security Council was meeting in New York; decisions which came as a complete surprise to us and which had not been hinted at in any previous discussions'. A veteran already of Commonwealth and Nato diplomacy, 'Mike' Pearson was accustomed to confidential relationships among trusted colleagues. The harsh brutality of the unheralded ultimatum jarred. He told Robertson that Dulles had been on the phone to him 'in a state of emotion and depression greater than anything I have seen before in him'.[2]

Canadian public feeling was passionate in both directions. 'The explosion of bombs on Egyptian airfields had blown away the flimsy pretence of the British and French Governments', began the leader in the *Toronto Daily Star* of 1 November under the heading: 'Britain, France Defy World's Conscience'. But its rival, *The Globe and Mail*, supported British policy and denounced the 'pharisaic cant' of the 'New Commonwealth' leaders, 'the Nehrus, the Bandaranaikes and the rest of the shifty crew'. Many Canadians were glad that a stand had been made and telegrams of support flowed into the High Commission.[3]

The Prime Minister, Louis St Laurent, was in an uncharacteristic rage, though he composed himself to write a courteous reply to Eden's cable of 30 October, rather than the 'brutal and unfriendly' message that was rumoured at the time. Underlining that Eden's cable had arrived behind the press reports of the ultimatum and observing that he found its reasoning unpersuasive, he deplored the effect on the UN, of which Britain had been 'such a staunch and steady supporter', the splitting of the Commonwealth and the fracturing of the Anglo-American alliance.[4] St Laurent managed to hold in his real feelings, largely by refusing, often brutally, to give any press interviews at all until the latter part of November when, in a debate in the Canadian House of Commons, he rejoiced that 'the era when the supermen of Europe could govern the whole world has and is coming pretty close to an end'.[5]

That was a sentiment that would have caused some satisfaction in South Africa. In a frigid statement that produced considerable distress in Whitehall, Eric Louw, the South African Foreign Minister, noted what he called a major change of policy by Britain in the matter of Commonwealth consultation. The first time he had been officially informed about the proposed ultimatum had been some eighteen hours after Eden's statement in the House. Sir Anthony's mention of close consultation could have been true of Canada and Australia but it was certainly not so of South Africa. Louw went on, in typical National Party fashion, to express perfect indifference about whether he was consulted or not – 'these after all are matters for the UK Government to decide'; all he asked was that Britain ceased to give the wrong impression.[6]

This, then, was the white Commonwealth, from whom most support was to be expected. Only one of those countries actually had to make a decision about whether it was to go into battle at Britain's side; New Zealand, whose cruiser, *Royalist*, was still with the Mediterranean Fleet. Her ship's company had even signalled to the New Zealand Navy Board on 15 September, when there was talk of her going home, that 'to leave at this stage would be humiliating'. But, as the weeks went by, Sidney Holland, the New Zealand Prime Minister, already worried in August that he had perhaps gone too far in offering material support to Britain, was increasingly on the rack. There was a new reason for his misgivings. 'It is not straining possibility', he told Eden, 'that, in certain circumstances, New Zealand could, with the UK and France, be charged before the Security Council with aggression. This, you will appreciate, is a serious prospect for a small country.'[7]

One of the very few documents in the Public Record Office that provides evidence of collusion is an Admiralty briefing paper for Lord Mountbatten, which is undated but on internal evidence (about ship movements) was probably written at some time on 29 October. Since the First Sea Lord was to see the Prime Minister, it was suggested that Eden should be asked to tell Holland of the sudden emergency that called for *Royalist*'s use for a very few weeks, and that this message be sent 'immediately prior to the ultimatum'.[8]

Holland dithered throughout the crisis. When the High Commissioner went to see him he had just been listening to Eisenhower's broadcast and clearly did not fancy siding against the United States. Then he moved off to a lengthy Cabinet meeting which decided not to decide. In a tortuous personal message to Eden, Holland started out on the congenial theme of New Zealand's strong ties of blood and Empire and her traditional attitude of standing by Britain in her difficulties, before coming painfully to the reasons why this attitude might not be decisive in this case. There was the matter of the Security Council which is 'of special significance to New Zealand', the fact that 'this direct action was taken without Commonwealth consultation' and, finally, the seriousness of the breach between Britain and the United States.

'We now find ourselves', Sidney Holland declared candidly, 'in the distressing predicament of wishing to stand by the UK, however great our misgivings on the wisdom of the present course of action, and of not wishing to jeopardise our relations with the United States, upon whom our security in the Pacific largely depends.' The result was that, whereas New Zealand had no desire to embarrass Britain by a withdrawal, there was insufficient time for a decision not to withdraw. So *Royalist* would stay around but not take part in any operations.[9] For Eden it was something short of a ringing endorsement. Three days later the High Commissioner reported: 'I think Mr Holland is genuinely up against it politically over *Royalist*.'[10]

Given these moods among the white Commonwealth, it was not surprising to find 'new Commonwealth' attitudes openly hostile. 'In all my experience of foreign affairs, I have come across no grosser act of naked aggression than what Britain and France are trying to do against Egypt,' declared Pandit Nehru, the Prime Minister of India, in a public speech at Hyderabad. Who, he asked, had assigned the role of policeman to Britain and France? The nineteenth century was over now. He told Malcolm MacDonald, the British High Commissioner, on 31 October that instead of punishing the aggressor Britain was punishing the victim of aggression. Picking it up presumably from the *Economist Foreign Report*, Nehru cited Mollet's reported claim that he had 'a diplomatic secret' and that all would soon become clear.[11]

But a much more turbulent reaction was to occur in Pakistan, and there seemed to be a real danger of her flouncing out of the Commonwealth. News of the ultimatums came in just as President Iskander Mirza, a former army officer, was leaving, accompanied by his Foreign Minister, Malik Firoz Khan Noon, a veteran of the Indian Civil Service, for a state visit to Iran. Noon received the Acting British High Commissioner, Morrice James, an hour before he left and told him, privately and off the record, that he had felt all along that a satisfactory solution of the Suez question could not be obtained without the use of force. Only this could bring Nasser to negotiate. The Pakistan Government, out of Muslim solidarity, would probably be forced to voice some criticism. He hoped that Britain would not take it to heart. At this they departed for Teheran, leaving the problem to Hassan Suhrawardy, the Prime Minister.[12]

Suhrawardy, a former Chief Minister of Bengal under British rule, regarded the Anglo-French action as wholly irrational: it set the whole world against Britain, alienated the Commonwealth and the United States and all to no clear purpose. Speaking personally, he could not see why the Israelis could not have been allowed to carry on with their drive across the Canal, which would in practice have eliminated Egyptian sovereignty; after which the UN could have sorted out the problem of international control. James said that it would not have been morally right to sit back and do nothing; leaving it to the Security Council would have meant the destruction of the Canal. The Israelis would only respond to compulsion. To this, Suhrawardy replied that it might be so but not a soul in Pakistan would believe it.[13]

Eden and Mollet were not alone in finding contemporary leaders who put them in mind of Hitler. 'Hitler Reborn' was the headline under which the normally rather dull Karachi daily *Dawn* printed an unprecedented front page editorial on 1 November. The reincarnated Führer was Anthony Eden, who according to the paper 'throws his own country's honour and all cherished moral, human and international values, which it has itself fostered, out of the windows of the Houses of Westminster and into the Thames, and proceeds to shed innocent Muslim blood to dye red the Nile . . .'[14]

The campaign of resolutions, editorials and street demonstrations demanding that Pakistan leave the Commonwealth and break up the Baghdad Pact mounted. The Suhrawardy Government seemed daily less able to resist. 'It will be difficult to hold the position domestically for more than another forty-eight hours,' cabled James in the early hours of 3 November, having received at 1.30 a.m. a letter from the Prime Minister. Suhrawardy must satisfy his critics 'and, if we do not help him, the mullahs and neutralists may win the day'.[15]

The visible unhappiness, amounting in places to outright anger, caused in the Commonwealth by Suez served partially to explain the development of opposition to Eden's policy within a section of Conservative Party supporters, including about two dozen MPs. The Opposition naturally tended to play on this aspect since it visibly made the Government uneasy; there was, also, particularly on the left wing of the Labour Party and in many *bien pensant* circles, that additional tendency to regard Pandit Nehru as a guru of exceptional wisdom and enlightenment.

The Clerks Betrayed

On the evening of 30 October Sir William Hayter who, as Britain's Ambassador to Moscow, occupied the front line of the great ideological battle, attended a reception for the Prime Minister of Afghanistan at which Foreign Minister Molotov was telling everyone that Britain and France were behind the Israeli invasion. At the end of a hard-talking evening spent asserting that in the Security Council Britain would prove her readiness to restrain the Israelis, Hayter returned to the Embassy to read the text of the ultimatum. 'As I read it I could not believe my eyes; I even began to wonder if I had drunk too much at the Kremlin. I felt quite bewildered.' Hayter lay awake most of the night wondering whether he should send in his resignation.

From across the entire communist world were heard slogans of solidarity with Egypt and denunciation of colonialism. But by far the most colourful display was provided in Peking, where all round the immensely long walls of the British Embassy compound there marched the seemingly inexhaustible but well-disciplined battalions of Chinese workers from successive factories, each bearing 'big character' banners and each a petition to be handed over to whoever was considered in the Embassy sufficiently junior to receive them.

In New Delhi Malcolm MacDonald, an ex-Cabinet Minister and not a lifelong member of the Diplomatic Service, spent the evening of 6 November drafting a personal letter of resignation to Lord Home. It was never sent because early next morning he learnt that the battle was over.[16]

Inside the Foreign Office there were similar thoughts, the professional affront done to area specialists denied access to many of the crucial papers having to be set against the civil service principle that it is only advice that is being given to Ministers; theirs alone is the responsibility for its acceptance or rejection. In this atmosphere of despondency and resentment, Paul Gore-Booth, the new Deputy Under-Secretary (Economic) and a future Permanent Under-Secretary, whose job put him in contact with many different branches of the Office, took the initiative. On 2 November he wrote a confidential note to Kirkpatrick saying that after hearing from people at all levels he felt that 'Ministers should realise that the overwhelming majority at the Foreign Office considered our action to have been a bad mistake and that Britain should urgently extract herself from her untenable position by grasping the lifeline [support for a UN police force] offered by Lester Pearson'. No one senior resigned, but a handful of the younger members of the service did so, including Evan Luard, a future Foreign Under-Secretary and spokesman for Britain in the UN General Assembly, and Peter Mansfield, the author and journalist on Arabian affairs.[17]

The point of maximum anguish in the Middle East was Baghdad. On the morning of 31 October came an urgent cry from Sir Michael Wright, the Ambassador, to furnish him with hard evidence of Britain's impartiality. Parallel to landings on the Suez Canal, there must be a demand for immediate Israeli withdrawal to the armistice lines, followed by military action if Israel failed to comply. Later in the day, Wright saw Nuri after a Cabinet meeting at which consternation had been displayed at British action. 'Unless we can redress the balance today, we may be in for a very dangerous time,' said the Ambassador. 'I should be failing to give you an accurate picture of the situation if I did not underline this with strongest possible emphasis.' Nuri's position might quickly become untenable.[18]

The Foreign Secretary in his reply was at his most emollient. The action at Suez was 'merely an emergency and temporary fire brigade operation'. Military reports had indicated that, 'unless something is done quickly, Israeli forces will inflict crushing defeat on Egypt'. When hostilities had ceased 'we shall at once tackle the situation created by the Israeli advance'. As for Sir Michael's plea that the Israelis be sent back over the Armistice line, 'In the present situation it will not be enough to speak of armistice lines. As Nuri rightly said only recently, there must be a settlement. Our vital interests have too long been placed in danger by the perpetuation of the so-called state of war.'[19]

Wright hastened to see the King and his uncle to convey Selwyn Lloyd's message. Their answer was that it was absolutely imperative that air or other action be taken simultaneously against Israeli forces. 'Time is of the essence,' said Sir Michael at well past midnight. 'I should be grateful for guidance by *emergency* telegram . . .' Lloyd responded on 1 November that, militarily, action against Israel was out of the question.[20] The Crown Prince sent a personal appeal to Eden. Britain's action, he said, 'has put the friends of Britain, among whom I count myself, in a critical position towards Arab and Iraqi opinion'. Unless, within a day or two, the British could announce steps to force the Israelis to withdraw, Sir Michael doubted whether the Iraqi regime and government could hold out. A week was the very outside.[21]

Eden replied on 2 November, repeating Lloyd's arguments, adding that the Israelis had been stopped ten miles short of the Canal 'although the gates of Egypt itself are now wide open to them'. It should soon be apparent to the world that only Anglo-French action could have brought about this desistance. 'As soon as we have occupied the keypoints on the Canal, we shall ask the Israelis to withdraw from Egyptian territory.'[22] 'The situation here is so nearly lost', cabled the Ambassador on the morning of 3 November, 'that I am never sure whether, before receiving your replies to my telegrams, it may not have got completely out of hand.' The defeat of the Egyptian forces was everywhere being attributed solely to the destruction by Britain and France of the Egyptian air force. The time had gone by when such criticisms could be met by argument. Britain's friends were saying that not even a single bomb had fallen on an Israeli airfield, not a single action taken against an Israeli detachment. Sir Michael begged for the immediate and repeated announcement on the BBC Overseas Service, as the first item of news, that Israel was being urgently and forcibly called upon to withdraw.[23]

Later the same day (3 November), the exasperated Ambassador repeated his plea in even more strenuous language. The BBC continued to carry communiqués from Allied HQ, Cyprus, about the destruction of the Egyptian planes and sweeping claims of victory made by Tel Aviv. 'The presentation could not suggest more clearly that Israel and Britain are in collusion if it had been calculated to do so.' Where was the evenhandedness between the combatants? Sir Michael concluded his telegram: 'The position is now as nearly desperate as it can be and it will be nearly a miracle if we can hold on.'[24]

Nuri was by now in Teheran where the Shah and the President of Pakistan had summoned the Baghdad Pact members less Britain. It was a way of appearing to take action and thus winning time in the hope that something good would begin to emerge. According to what the Iranians told the British, Mirza, on leaving for his state visit, had coolly invited the Premiers of Turkey and Iraq to propose themselves as well.[25] The British, eager to save the Baghdad Pact, made the best of this development. The Ambassador in Teheran was fitted out with a kit of Machiavellian arguments to brief the visitors. 'The result of our present action against Egypt', he was to say (no question here of 'separating the combatants') 'will leave Egypt militarily weak and unable to cause further trouble'; as a result 'this will leave Iraq as the major Arab Power, to which, if the other Arab states are worried about Israel, they will have to look for protection'. That, in turn, would cause them to see that their interest lay in close association with the Baghdad Pact.[26] In answer to a straight question put to him through Sir Roger Stevens by President Mirza, Selwyn Lloyd authorised the Ambassador on 3 November to 'give him a categorical assurance that we did not concert with Israel in advance and are not associated with Israel in any attack on Egypt'.[27]

Operation Beisan

Just after midnight on 29/30 October, the first orders had gone out from General Hakim Amer's new Supreme Command. Jordan and Syria were to mobilise infantry and armour for Operation *Beisan*, the plan to slice Israel in half by striking across her narrow waist to Nathanya on the Mediterranean coast. King Hussein wanted to attack at once. Ali Abu Nuwar told him that he too wanted to attack but not yet; it was important to be effective. He had, he said, a plan for a surprise attack on two flanks which would result in Jerusalem being surrounded, in addition to the drive to the coast. But it would need a few days to absorb the expected Syrian reinforcements. Suleiman Nabulsi, for all his hero-worship of Nasser, did not want to attack at all. He afterwards told his biographer Suleiman Musa that he thought it his greatest accomplishment during his term of office to have kept Jordan out of the war.[28]

The Syrians came after three days but Abu Nuwar got a shock when he saw them. They arrived without any logistic base, the troops travelling in buses or in tanks they did not know how to drive properly. The tank units ran out of petrol and refused to use Jordanian fuel in case it fouled up the engines. Though the difficulties seem not wholly dissimilar from those the Israelis suffered from and overcame, Abu Nuwar might well have reflected glumly that Glubb's legacy was a genuine margin of efficiency for the Arab Legion.[29]

In the period before the Anglo-French ultimatum Nasser was already hesitating before he plunged the entire Arab world in a *Götterdämmerung* at a time not of his own choosing. He was particularly aware of the intelligence plot aimed at Syria through his contacts with Colonel Abdul Hameed Sarraj, the head of the *Deuxième Bureau* in Damascus, and did not want to set off the destabilisation of the Syrian regime. There seems to have been a genuine fear that if Syria became involved in the war she might be occupied by British and French troops.[30] During the course of 30 October, the H-Hour for *Beisan* was more than once postponed and was put off indefinitely in the early hours of 1 November. The Egyptians asked the Jordanian Government to prepare small bands of Palestinians and men from the army to harass the Israelis by means of sabotage. Nabulsi kept them waiting for an answer.[31]

Exactly as if it had been a more typical royal government, the parliamentary regime turned to Sir Charles Duke, the British Ambassador, for advice. It was categorical. If Jordan attacked Israel in present circumstances, the Anglo-Jordanian Treaty would not be brought into force. Nabulsi looked doleful, speaking of conflicting obligations. But the deterrent worked.[32] Following the delivery of the ultimatum, the bombing of Cairo, and his decision to evacuate Sinai, Nasser told King Hussein on the phone that he wanted Jordan to stay out of the conflict. There were not the uncontrolled anti-British demonstrations that had been feared from the experience at the beginning of the year.

Once Eisenhower's position was made clear, Nasser was anxious not to antagonise the United States by interfering with the flow of oil through the Syrian pipeline. In the absence of the Syrian President Quwwatly who, at Nasser's urging, had gone ahead with a pre-arranged visit to Moscow on the day after the Israeli attack, the Syrian Government did not at all favour such action. But Sarraj was determined to do it and make a thorough job of it. By the time the Cairo Supreme Command had transmitted a message 'not to destroy oil pipelines as this is injurious to the interests of other countries not implicated' it was too late. Sarraj's men had used massive dynamite charges on three pumping stations. According to Heikal's graphic account, the intelligence chief was summoned by the Prime Minister, who expressed anxiety in case Syria as well as Egypt should be invaded by the British and French. He wanted reassurance about the security of the pipelines. It was not the pipelines, said Sarraj, it was the pumping stations. 'According to our information, the three pumping-stations have flown away.'[33] Oil ceased to flow from the Iraqi oilfield at Kirkuk to the Lebanese port of Tripoli for some six months.

Meanwhile at a meeting with Khrushchev, Bulganin and Marshal Zhukov, President Shukri Quwwatly appealed for help, asking Zhukov to bring 'the great army which defeated Hitler' to help Egypt. Zhukov produced a map and pointed out some of the practical obstacles to such a course. Instead, Khrushchev promised vigorous support at the UN.[34] When Nasser received Quwwatly's report he put it away in his safe without showing it to any of his colleagues, so as to avoid damage to their morale.

Another Arab state directly affected by these events was Egypt's western neighbour. Libya, which shared with Egypt the Western Desert with which the British army had been so intimately concerned, had been independent only since the end of 1951. In return for subsidies from Britain she gave British forces base and training rights. When plans were made for *Musketeer*, it has been seen that the immediate assumption was made that 10 Armoured Division stationed in Libya would move in the tracks of Rommel up to and across the Egyptian border and that Libya's harbours and airfields would be at Britain's disposal. Any such illusions were very rapidly dispelled. That front was no sooner spoken of than it had been closed down. On 30 October the Libyan Government denounced Israeli aggression and reiterated that it would 'refuse permission to forces stationed in Libya to attack any Arab government and to prevent this by all possible means'.[35] The following day an urgent telegram arrived from Walter Graham, the British Ambassador in Tripoli, saying that he had learnt that Shackleton aircraft operating from Al Adem, in Libya, were covering the fleet from which the attack on Egypt was being made. If this were ever found out it would be certain to precipitate a wave of violence. 'I urgently request that all use of Al Adem for operations even remotely connected with present hostilities be discontinued at once.'[36]

'Uniting for Peace'

Arab and Commonwealth states were not alone in being shocked and dismayed by British conduct. At a private session of the Nato Council on 31 October the American delegate made it clear that his Government had no prior knowledge of the ultimatum and favoured a peaceful solution; others hastened to line up behind him, emphasising the lamentable effect of the absence of prior consultation and of the impact of Suez on events in Eastern Europe.[37] *Le Monde* did not fail to point out on the same day that the likely effect of the Soviet Union's new stated willingness to withdraw her troops on request from East European states would be *détente* between the Great Powers. They would then be liable to settle regional questions directly between themselves, without much regard for allies.

West Germany's attitude was thoroughly depressing for the British, with the single but extremely significant exception of Chancellor Konrad Adenauer, for whose support Eden was intensely grateful, and who told Maurice Couve de Murville, who was now French Ambassador in Bonn, that he thoroughly approved of the action but that, to ensure success, decisive results must be very rapid. For the rest, eleven years after the suicide of Adolf Hitler, Britain found herself the object of moral lectures in international behaviour from the Germans. Reports from consuls in the various *Länder* betrayed condemnation and reproach. The *Westdeutsche Allgemeine* and the *Bonner General Anzeiger* talked of the return to unrestricted power politics and of pursuing a policy of naked self-interest. The *Stuttgarter Nachtrichten* thought London and Paris had committed both a blunder and a crime, while the *Berlin Morgenpost* attributed to France the malign ability to press Britain into supporting an outdated colonialism. 'A mixture of fear, anger, disappointment and *Schadenfreude*', wrote the British Ambassador in his annual report, 'led to unmeasured condemnation of our intervention.'[38]

The Soviet Union produced on 31 October what was in the circumstances a rather odd statement, accusing 'the Western Powers' of invoking 'the colonialist declaration of 1950 . . . which has been unanimously rejected by all the Arab states'[39], whereas the whole point had been that Eden had repudiated that declaration on precisely those grounds. The Kremlin's attention was clearly riveted on central Europe; someone had reached for a formula from the bottom drawer. But apart from this statement and Sobolev's quite agile performance at New York there was not in the first few days much comment from the Soviet Union though, as early as 1 November, Pineau was showing symptoms of alarm to the American Ambassador at the savage remarks about French policy in the Middle East that were being attributed to the Soviet leaders.

The occasion on which all this moral rejection of the acts of Britain, France and Israel could be collectively expressed was the overnight debate on 1/2 November of the First Emergency Special Session of the UN General Assembly. It began with a crisp summary of developments by the Egyptian delegate, which did not fail to include a damning quotation from Hugh Gaitskell in the House of Commons to emphasise that Britain's position was not a united one. Dixon followed with an anti-communist tirade and the claim that 'by our swift intervention the Israeli advance has already been halted and this threat to the Canal has been averted'. He then made a point of repeating what Eden had said in the House: 'If the UN were willing to take over the physical task of maintaining peace in the area, no one would be better pleased than we.'

As Dixon came to an end, John Foster Dulles, who had been delayed in the air from Washington by the extremely rough weather that had grounded all commercial flights, walked into the chamber to make the speech for which this debate would be remembered. He spoke extemporaneously and with feeling. 'I doubt that any representative ever spoke from this rostrum with as heavy a heart as I have brought here tonight,' he began. 'We speak on a matter of vital importance where the United States finds itself unable to agree with three nations with which it has ties of deep friendship, of admiration and of respect, and two of which constitute our oldest and most trusted and reliable allies.' It was the first time that the Assembly had met pursuant to the 'Uniting for Peace' resolution for whose passage Dulles, then a member of the American delegation to the UN, had been responsible. He gave a concise account of the Suez Canal issue, saying of the exchanges between Egypt, Britain and France that, 'They did not continue, although I am not aware of any insuperable obstacle to their continuance.' Then he came to 'the resort to violence, first by Israel, then by France and the United Kingdom ... Surely I think that we must feel that the peaceful processes ŵhich the Charter requests every member of the United Nations to follo had not been exhausted.'

Dulles proposed a resolution that called for an immediate cease-fire, a halt to the movement of military forces and arms into the area and the withdrawal of all forces behind the armistice lines. On the cease-fire becoming effective, steps were to be taken to reopen the Canal and secure free navigation. The Assembly was to remain in emergency session pending compliance, on which subject the Secretary-General was to report. On the suggestion of Pakistan the vote was, because of its urgency, taken before the end of the debate, the remaining representatives making their speeches afterwards. The American resolution, in effect but not in name condemning the three Powers alike, was carried by sixty-four votes to five (only Australia and New Zealand joining the three in the dock), with six abstentions (Portugal, South Africa, Canada, Belgium, Netherlands, and Laos).[40]

'You should know', cabled Dixon from the chamber of the Assembly, 'that even our closest friends here are becoming intensely worried at the possible consequences which might follow if we and the French remain for long in open defiance of the UN. They point out that the Assembly, in its present emotional mood, will not easily be held back from moving to more extreme courses if we pay no attention'. Besides sanctions, 'our friends' were also said to be concerned that open defiance would result in there being no option for Britain but to leave the UN altogether. 'The effect of this on the Commonwealth and on the whole of the network of Western alliances might then be disastrous.' It was with this judgment in mind, from a diplomat of whom he had the highest opinion, that Eden was that day to face the House of Commons. But the business in New York was not yet finished.

Immediately after the voting had taken place at 2.30 a.m. on 2 November, the Italian delegate rose and called attention to a dramatic cable that had just been circulated. It was from Imre Nagy, the Prime Minister and Acting Foreign Minister of Hungary, stating that further Soviet units were entering Hungary, that he had protested most strongly to Yuri Andropov, the Soviet Ambassador, demanding their instant withdrawal and that he had notified him of Hungary's immediate repudiation of the Warsaw Treaty. Hungary turned to the UN to obtain its help in defending Hungarian neutrality. Thus the two crises, Suez and Hungary, remained interwoven.

Though the hour was late and the vote had been taken the Assembly remained in session till 4.20 in the morning so that delegates who had not spoken could explain their vote. By far the most important of these was an abstainer, Lester Pearson of Canada. He pointed out that the resolution, though adopted, was only a recommendation and if, instead of rushing to get a vote in the quickest possible period, a short delay and informal talks had been allowed, they might have hoped to get some response from those governments whose co-operation would be needed to carry it out. In particular, he regretted two omissions: a procedure for the permanent political settlement of the questions of Palestine and of the Suez Canal; and the setting up of a UN Force large enough to keep the borders at peace while the political settlements were being worked out. This latter was an old idea of Pearson's which he had raised with Eden a year before.[41] But it was now an idea whose time had come; it was seized on by Dulles. In another short intervention, he endorsed it with enthusiasm and invited Pearson to formulate and introduce a concrete proposal.

Britain Against Herself

The second of November was a Friday, so that the House of Commons assembled at 11 a.m., just an hour and forty minutes after the Emergency Assembly in New York had adjourned. Gaitskell at once asked Eden whether the Government was prepared to accept the General Assembly's recommendation. This now became the battleground on which the two sides were noisily, at times raucously, arrayed. Eden replied, defensively that he must have time to study the resolution and the speeches. The Opposition continually pressed to remain in permanent session throughout the weekend, since lives, including those of British soldiers, depended on the decision the Government was going to announce. The former rivals within the Labour Party, Gaitskell and Bevan, worked in tandem, Gaitskell with his sharp, incisive questions, Bevan, whose only formal role was as shadow spokesman on colonial affairs, playing more the elder statesman, the guardian of constitutional propriety. (Alfred Robens, the 'shadow Foreign Secretary', was nowhere.) 'We are at war', said Bevan. 'We now hear today that the vast majority of the UN Assembly has condemned our action in being at war . . . The only argument that we have, in my respectful submission, in order to keep peace in the country and to prevent action of a kind that we might all deplore, is to be able to say that Parliament has taken charge of the situation. If Parliament is not allowed to take charge of the situation, what answer have we got?' In the afternoon it was announced that the House would meet again the next day in a rare Saturday session.[42]

Bevan had been right about Britain. The country was roused, but in two directions. 'Military action has a clear motive which will commend itself to all the people: To safeguard the life of the British Empire,' said the *Daily Express* on 1 November; the *Daily Mail* was certain that 'so grave a decision was reached only in the deep, sincere conviction that, if we had remained quiescent, Britain and the whole world would have suffered irreparable damage', while to the *Daily Telegraph* the UN had proved itself useless in the Middle East. For the *Daily Mirror*: 'This is Eden's war. It can achieve nothing; it can settle nothing', and for the *Daily Herald*: 'One hope still remains of stopping Eden ... The voice of the British people must din in this Government's ears the demand to call off this lunatic aggression.'

From the Government's point of view, it was the 'extreme centre' (as Geoffrey Crowther once called it) that was not holding. *The Economist* wrote of Eden's 'splenetic isolation' and declared that: 'For an opposition officially to oppose a war after hostilities have started is, in modern times, unprecedented; but so too is what Sir Anthony Eden has done ... The manner in which the crisis has been handled suggests a strange union of cynicism and hysteria in [Britain's] leaders.' The paper ran a despatch cabled from Cairo (as was still possible for a day or two after the ultimatum) by its local correspondent, Tom Little. He said: 'Britain seems tonight to have embarked on a policy which should produce a local victory and ultimate defeat ... There is still a sense of unreality as though war were something disproportionate to any offence within Egypt's range of action.'

Nor did 'the gentlemen from *The Times*', an organ which Sir Anthony flattered himself he knew how to handle, justify the extraordinary confidence he had reposed in them. Rather its leaders reflected the first reactions of Sir William Haley and Iverach McDonald to the privileged information they had received. Their position was founded on the relationship with the United States, a reminder amid so many fashionable expressions of anti-Americanism that pro-Americanism was still a powerful tide. On 2 November, Haley used a Churchillian quotation with devastating effect: 'I hold it perfectly justifiable to deceive the enemy, even if at the same time your own people are for a while misled. There is one thing, however, which you must never do, and that is mislead your ally.'

Yet nothing quite equalled the shock that was administered on the Sunday to some of the patriotic, middle-class readers of the *Observer*, while some others just gulped and many overwhelmed their paper with praise. The anonymous leading article, written in fact by Dingle Foot, the ex-Chairman of the *Observer*'s Board of Trustees, was simply headed 'EDEN'. It began: 'We wish to make an apology. Five weeks ago we remarked that, although we knew our Government would not make a military attack in defiance of its solemn international obligations, people abroad might think otherwise. The events of last week have proved us completely wrong.' At this point the Editor, David Astor, inserted the sentence that was quoted round the world. 'We had not realised that our Government was capable of such folly and such crookedness.' Britain and France, Foot went on, had acted 'not as policemen but as gangsters'. The Conservative Party would only save itself from obliteration for a generation if it produced a parliamentary rebellion. 'In our view there is one essential: Sir Anthony Eden must go.' To that end this respectable paper called for a mass letter writing campaign and street demonstrations. The *Observer*, which was owned as well as edited by Astor, had that September passed its rival, the *Sunday Times*, in circulation for the first and, as it was to prove, the last time. Subscriptions were cancelled, advertisements withdrawn, two of the Trustees resigned.[43] But the middle ground, without which no government could speak in a truly national sense, had found its voice.

At the same time 335 members of Oxford University Senior Commonrooms, including ten heads of colleges led by Alan Bullock, the Censor of St Catherine's, signed a statement saying: 'We consider this action is morally wrong, that it endangers the solidarity of the Commonwealth, that it constitutes a grave strain on the Atlantic alliance and that it is a flagrant violation of the principles of the UN Charter.'

There were of course many people, perhaps most, who were confused by the issues and only on balance took one side or the other. Some felt strongly that Britain should not be kicked around any more, that Nasser richly deserved what was coming to him, that the UN was feeble and discredited, that the US had played a treacherous role and that it was wonderful to see Great Britain, for once, showing herself capable of pursuing an independent course of action. Others, while not sharing some or all of these sentiments, considered that Anthony Eden's record was sufficient guarantee that 'if only we could know what he must know, we would understand why he's doing it'. It was, after all, only just over a decade since the British had been living under the disciplines of war and Eden had been their second most celebrated civilian leader. They had been accustomed to trusting him then; many felt it natural to trust him now. To a certain extent the very fact that the Government's case sounded so bizarre and implausible provided added reason for that trust because, with such a seasoned statesman in charge, the undisclosed information must surely have been conclusive. (This view was to receive a severe setback on 5 November when the resignation was announced of Anthony Nutting, which had been submitted on the morning of 31 October. He had been Minister of State at the Foreign Office; if there had been any secrets he should have known them.) Others again, without having such complicated thoughts, felt that the country was in danger, that the troops were about to go into action and that it was the wrong time to debate the rights and wrongs.

On the opposite side of this great debate, which convulsed the country, tearing apart every party, every class, every family, opening up the kind of civil rift which occurs in Britain not more than two or three times a century, were to be found those who took their stand on the UN Charter and who believed that Britain's adherence to it had an exemplary force in the world. There were also those who instinctively felt a prime allegiance to the Anglo-American alliance and others who felt, to the contrary, that priority should go to the Commonwealth (and not just the white part of it), two feelings which in the case of Suez led to the same conclusion.

Both sides, in a sense, looked back to the Second World War for their inspiration. The conclusions that they drew differed according to their perceptions of it. Those who supported Eden either did so because they had been willing to sacrifice all for 'King and country' once and would do so again, or because they shared his particular insight that it was essential to strike early at a dictator who was threatening British interests before he built up his strength by repeated success. For those influenced more by the reasons Eden gave for the action taken, it was no new thing for Britain to stand alone (or with France), upholding principle and enduring misunderstanding until the United States and others in the course of time came round to the same opinion.

But there were many among those who had fought in the War for whom the UN Charter and the Nuremberg Trials more closely represented their sense of personal commitment. That commitment had been to one particular war; it had been unconditional because the evil against which it had been fought had been absolute. Two conclusions followed from this: hereafter, force should never be used again as an instrument of foreign policy (except by the UN, or in strictly limited circumstances of the most immediate self-defence); and superior orders, where war crimes and the crime of aggression are concerned, are no excuse. That a leader, acting alone on secret information or with a few ministerial colleagues, should be trusted absolutely to determine questions of peace or war, when the rationale sounded not quite right to one's own ears and radically flawed to practically the whole outside world, was unacceptable to this part of the war generation.

22

France's War

As seen from [Cyprus] there is little if anything covert about French close and active support of Israel.
Ralph Murray to Sir Ivone Kirkpatrick, 1 November 1956.

It was the action of the US which really defeated us in attaining our object.
General Sir Charles Keightley, Allied Commander-in-Chief.

France, from the beginning, was engaged in fighting a different war from Britain. Inhibited by her Commonwealth ties, her 'special relationship' with the United States, and that regard for appearances which both her domestic politics and her record at the UN required, Britain had gone to war publicly in order to separate combatants and to restore peace. Her every act must be made to conform to that prescription. France wanted to destroy Nasser and to help Israel and had no incentive, other than consideration for Sir Anthony Eden, to pretend otherwise. Aside from the Communists, who were outside the normal political system, the silent Mendésistes and the Poujadists who did not wish, as their leader put it, to 'die for the Queen of England', the operation had the approval of the entire political world.

There was trouble from the beginning over the Israelis. When Jacques Baeyens, the Quai d'Orsay's Political Adviser, was flying with Admiral Barjot, the flamboyant Deputy Allied Commander-in-Chief, to Cyprus overnight on 30/31 October, the admiral remarked with great satisfaction that the Israelis had asked for the assistance of the guns of the cruiser *Georges Leygues* during their advance down the Sinai coast. Baeyens politely enquired whether Barjot's superior, General Keightley, knew anything of this. Barjot was appropriately silent. The French were allotted their cramped quarters and supplied with a liaison officer, a major of the Brigade of Guards, who was perfectly bilingual but passionately anti-Israeli because of his experiences with the Haganah. It proved impossible to get rid of him when Louis Mangin, Bourgès-Maunoury's faithful Achates, turned up daily to report the fruits of his intimate liaison with the Israeli forces.[1]

A secret radio link, independent of the British, had been established two nights before between the French on Cyprus and Tel Aviv. From the first day of the Israeli attack, French planes (one squadron of F84 Thunderstreaks and another of Mystère IVAs) were stationed on Israeli airfields, overpainted with the Star of David, to be ready, if so ordered, which they were not, to defend Israeli cities. To say that this French private enterprise was unknown to the British was, however, as General Lucien Robineau has written, stretching the point a little far. 'To see without surprise thirty-six planes take off for the east after a brief stopover at the airfield at Akrotiri [in Cyprus] and not come back again speaks more of phlegm than of naïveté', he says. Ten Nord 2501 transports, some flying from Tymbou in Cyprus and some from Israeli territory, gave crucial logistic support to Israeli columns crossing the desert.[2]

Late on 31 October a notice went out from HQ Air Task Force that 'information has been received' (from where was never subsequently established) that 'friendly Mystère and F84 aircraft' (nationality unspecified) operating east of the Suez Canal might be found to have the three yellow and two black stripes round the centre of each wing and on the fuselage that were the telltale markings of *Musketeer*. A photograph of an Israeli aircraft wearing such markings was to be published in *The Aeroplane* magazine at the end of the month.

During the assault itself the most striking achievement of the F84s based in Israel was their success in eliminating all eighteen of the Egyptian air force's dreaded IL 28 bombers which had felt themselves safe in the remote air base at Luxor and had been untouched by Canberra attacks.[3] General Brohon, the French Deputy Air Task Force Commander, was, unlike his land and sea colleagues, exercising effective hour-to-hour control from Cyprus of all allied air forces, since his superior, Air Marshal Barnett, was isolated on *Tyne* with its woeful communications. At the same time Brohon was engaged in the un-allied activity of limited air support for the Israelis.

Three French naval vessels, under cover of an anti-contraband patrol, dropped in to Haifa for 'refuelling' on 29 October and were conveniently present when a formerly British frigate of the Egyptian navy, the *Ibrahim al-Awwal*, attempted to bombard the port in the early hours of 31 October. The French destroyer *Kersaint* opened fire on the *Ibrahim* two and a half hours before the expiry of the twelve-hour ultimatum. Although it was in fact Israeli planes and ships which disabled and captured the Egyptian vessel, the French had made a practical demonstration of whose side they were on at the beginning of the battle.[4] All this was very confusing for General Keightley who cabled the Chiefs of Staff on 31 October: 'I would welcome direction at what stage or in what degree it is visualised we fight as the Allies of the Israelis. The French are already doing a lot covertly and are proposing to increase their effort.'[5]

The next day Keightley's political adviser, Ralph Murray, was cabling Ivone Kirkpatrick: 'As seen from here there is little if anything covert about

French close and active support of Israel.' He listed the operation of French aircraft from Israeli airfields bearing allied force markings; the shelling of Rafah by the cruiser *Georges Leygues* in direct support of the Israelis; and the sending by the French navy to the British Commander-in-Chief, Mediterranean, of an apparently routine request that a French ship, the *Gazelle*, under his command should bring supplies to Israeli troops who were said (inaccurately, as it happened) to have already captured the southernmost point of the Sinai peninsula and fetch off their wounded. The signal had been intercepted by the Admiralty in London, referred for political guidance, and the request turned down. Later on the same day (1 November) Murray reported that two Israeli officers had turned up in uniform at headquarters. Keightley sharply ordered the French to bring this to an end.[6]

Eden cabled in some agitation to Mollet telling him about Murray's complaints and adding: 'Actions of this sort, which cannot possibly remain secret, are extremely embarrassing. I hope you will agree that in our common interest they must be discontinued. Nothing could do more harm to our role as peacemakers than to be identified in this way with one of the two parties.'[7]

On 2 November General Keightley told the Chiefs of Staff that 'the situation regarding Franco-Israeli cooperation is getting increasingly disturbing'. Barjot was personally understanding but had quoted his liaison officer with the Israelis as having said that 'an agreement was made for certain help between governments and, if it is not honoured, the Israelis will publicise and exaggerate the agreements made'. Keightley reminded the Chiefs that he was of course 'completely unaware of what, if any, arrangements were in fact ever made between the French and Israeli Governments'. He held that the only solution lay in the two Governments sending identical directives to himself and to Barjot.[8]

Murray reported to Kirkpatrick on the morning of 3 November that the French now said that all co-ordination of operations with the Israelis would cease, aircraft would be concealed and there would be no publicity about their presence. It was the aircraft which, Murray thought, were the biggest risk. They were said not to be needed any more for the Sinai campaign but were being held to support the Anglo-French assault. Murray left the French in no doubt that he would be happier to see them go altogether, and this feeling was reinforced during 3 November as he learnt that Syrian and Iraqi troops were moving into Jordan. He reacted to this news in the way in which a Foreign Office man with Middle Eastern antennae might be expected to react: it could only mean trouble with the Israelis. 'I do not know on what understanding [the French aircraft] are there,' Murray told Kirkpatrick, 'but, whatever it is, I doubt whether you should put much faith in its being rigidly interpreted.' There would, not to put too fine a point on it, be a 'severe risk of [the planes] being turned over to their hosts in some way'.

British air commanders to whom Murray had spoken did not think the French planes necessary for the coming assault on Port Said and entertained lively apprehensions of the problem they would present if Britain had to take action against Israel on behalf of Jordan.[9]

There was one other front on which France's war differed from that fought by Britain: the psychological front towards the United States. Towards the Americans the French (or, at any rate, one Frenchman, Christian Pineau) declined to remain with the hypocrisy of the ultimatum for very long. He preferred to shift the blame to the Israelis, though in a way that has no support in Israeli sources. On 1 November Pineau told Dillon that immediately after the Security Council meeting Israeli representatives had approached France and had declared that Israel, having reached the conclusion that the United States had decided to side with Nasser and allow the annihilation of Israel, was going to act against Egypt in self-defence. Paris had then approached London and general agreement was reached on 'the present course of action'. Final decisions were taken during the Eden–Lloyd visit to Paris on 16 October including a joint decision not to inform the United States. Only on the fact of Sèvres itself did Pineau preserve discretion, as he did a fortnight later when on 16 November he made slightly more detailed confessions to Allen Dulles and to Admiral Radford at the French Embassy in Washington. The CIA annex to the State Department's secret history of collusion dated 5 December was still able therefore to state that 'the evidence is not persuasive that the British did in fact connive directly with Israel, but is conclusive that the French did'.[10]

The Long Shadow of the Sixth Fleet

While the British were most anxious not to appear to be obliging to the Israelis, another of their preoccupations was the failure of the American Sixth Fleet to be obliging to them. Everywhere the pieces of the Great Armada that was assembling in the Eastern Mediterranean went, there they found units of the Sixth Fleet before them. The British and French sought to adopt the dispositions of war while their mighty ally sprawled peacefully around them, fouling their sonar and their radar, illuminating the warships at night with their searchlights. 'Sixth Fleet are an embarrassment in my neighbourhood', signalled Admiral Durnford-Slater on 31 October, 'We have already twice intercepted US aircraft and there is constant danger of an incident.' He reported to Grantham on 1 November: 'Have been continually menaced during past eight hours by US aircraft approaching low down as close as 4000 yards and on two occasions flying over ships'. Admiral Grantham replied to the exasperated carrier force commander, Vice-Admiral Power, on 2 November: 'Interference by Sixth Fleet ... must be wearying and frustrating, and it is clear that HMG are alarmed at the prospect of any untoward incident. US Admiral ['Cat'] Brown [Commander, Sixth Fleet] knows where you are operating ... [b]ut he seems incapable of keeping his forces well clear of yours.'[11]

Looking back afterwards on the entire operation Sir Charles Keightley wrote: 'It was the action of the US which really defeated us in attaining our object!' The movements of the Sixth Fleet 'endangered the whole of our relations with that country ... This situation with the US must at all costs be prevented from arising again.'[12]

As with everything else in the air and naval phases of this military operation, it worked out all right on the night because there was no opposition. If the Egyptians had been able to threaten the carrier group or any other part of the naval operation in any way, the counter-measures taken would have run an immediate risk of accidental clashes with the American forces, so closely did they keep the Anglo-French effort covered. It was an incessant anxiety. According to Admiral Power, 'I ... considered it quite feasible that an ultimatum to stop operations might be issued by the American Government, placing me in an impossible position. In addition, there was the ever-present possibility of our aircraft mistaking US aircraft for Egyptian, thus creating an international incident which might have seriously influenced American policy.' But there was room for an even more sinister interpretation. 'I considered it quite possible', wrote the Admiral, 'that they were obstructing us on purpose as their aircraft flying in the area rendered our air warning virtually useless.'[13] American ships remained in Alexandria harbour evacuating American citizens until 3 November. The Egyptians, who expected the allied landings to take place at Alexandria, deliberately contributed to the delay because the American presence brought them protection; all planned air attacks on Egyptian ships in the harbour were called off so long as they remained. But the Americans did not give the impression of being in a hurry.

According to Admiral Arleigh Burke, the Chief of Staff of the US Navy, the Sixth Fleet's orders were to keep in close touch with the British and French 'to make sure we knew where they were and what they were doing'. He had sent orders to Admiral 'Cat' Brown to 'go to sea with his bombs up, ready to fight anything. "Cat" Brown sent back: "Who's the enemy?" and I sent back, "Don't take any guff from anybody."' Dulles, once the ultimatums had been sent, asked Burke whether there was a way the Sixth Fleet could be used to stop the operation. 'And I said, "Mr Secretary, there is only one way to stop them. We can stop them, but we will blast hell out of them." He said, "Well, can't you stop them some other way?" I said, "No, if we're going to threaten ... then you've got to be ready to shoot ... We can defeat them – the British and the French and the Egyptians and the Israelis – the whole goddam works of them we can knock off, if you want. But that's the only way to do it.'[14]

On 3 November there were reports that the Sixth Fleet had moved off to the North-West. But on the night of the 4th/5th searchlights were shone on the blacked-out vessels; next morning dummy runs were made by American planes on French ships. Two American submarines had to be sharply ordered to the surface. On the morning of 5 November, when Antony Head asked Sir William Dickson what position the Americans could have been expected to take up if it were the intention to interpose the Sixth Fleet between the Allied convoy and Port Said, the answer was that its present position was ideal for this purpose. Mountbatten, told this by Dickson, backed it up; Admiral Brown had been asked if he could move but had replied that he had taken up his position on direct orders from his Government.[15] The long shadow of the Sixth Fleet, the ever-present symbol of American disapproval, fell ominously across the path of *Musketeer*.

'Abandon Sinai'

The military position in the Sinai in the early hours of 1 November was that the French cruiser *Georges Leygues* was bombarding the Egyptian positions at Rafah as the Israelis, now that their 'allies' were properly in the war, opened up the hitherto silent northern sector. In the central sector along the route running to Ismailia, although one of the three Abu Agueila ridges containing Abu Agheila itself and Ruafa dam had been taken, the Egyptians in the crucial Umm Qataf stronghold had repelled all Israeli assaults. In the south, Sharon's brigade, having at last won a costly and exhausting battle of doubtful necessity on the slopes of the Mitla Pass, had been pulled back to the Parker Memorial where it had been twenty-four hours before.

At this point Abdul Nasser's traumatic order was given to evacuate Sinai at once. The Abu Agheila 'hedgehog' was to become the rearguard of a fighting retreat. The troops at Rafah were to be the first to go. But their brigade commander, Brigadier Jaafar al-Abd, had just for the first time become engaged in battle. The Israeli assault had at last begun. The attackers had promised themselves a World War II style opening, with naval and air bombardment, as in war films, with no need for a serious land battle for the elaborate fixed defences of Rafah and Al Arish. They were to be disappointed. The Egyptian defences were not blown down by the naval support from the *Georges Leygues*. The air strike had to be called off when the Israeli air force, having landed the flares in the wrong place, seemed more likely to eliminate the attackers than the defence.[16]

The battle was hard fought. The Israelis showed tactical initiative and skill and understandably feel certain that they had all but won the battle. The Egyptians, equally understandably, lay stress on the fact that during the night of the attack Brigadier Jaafar al-Abd received Nasser's order to withdraw. Given the tactical situation, the Egyptian commander argued fiercely against this. But at 7 a.m. the order was peremptorily confirmed.[17] The Israelis stress in their accounts the large amounts of military equipment that were abandoned.

It should be remembered that the Israelis by now enjoyed total air supremacy. Yet the Egyptians did manage to conduct enough of that very difficult action, a fighting retreat, to ensure that the Israelis did not enter Al Arish until the following morning (2 November) and failed to cut off the entire Egyptian force. The National Guards and the Palestinian division that were manning the Gaza Strip were left to their fate. The Governor of Gaza surrendered in the afternoon of 2 November and with him the Israelis captured an archive of documents on the *fedayeen* campaign; a Palestinian brigade managed to hold out in Khan Yunis until 3 November.

In the central sector, the Egyptian defenders of the Umm Qataf and Umm Shihan portions of the Abu Agheila stronghold gave the Israeli attackers a very tough time indeed. According to the letter of Liddell Hart's strategy of mobility and the indirect approach, which Dayan claimed to be following in planning the campaign, these positions could have been by-passed and ignored till a later time. But the very need to maintain the mobility of the entire campaign in the face of the political pressures from abroad, of which Dayan was so conscious, made him impatient to open up a supply line along the one metalled road blocked by Umm Qataf. 10 Brigade failed there because it 'did not make the effort required'; 37 Brigade with plenty of dash and resolution did not do any better and lost its commander. After dark on 1 November, having received their orders, the Egyptians quietly stole away. Their departure was not noticed by the Israelis until the next day. The Egyptian regular troops withdrew in an orderly manner and made good their escape; the reserve battalion fell apart in the sand.[18]

The limited success which the Egyptians achieved at Abu Agheila and the circumstances in which the Rafah evacuation was ordered have led to the assertion that there was in fact no Israeli victory in the battle for Sinai and that the Israeli occupation of the peninsula was entirely won on the back of the Anglo-French intervention.[19] That is not a reasonable verdict. The Israelis had shown, prior to the allied bombing (since it was on the bombing that Nasser acted in Sinai, not the ultimatum), qualities of leadership, flexibility and dash which would in all probability have in the end scored decisively over the stolid defensive fighting qualities of the Egyptian soldiers. But they would not have produced so rapidly the appearance of a total and almost instant knock-out which seemed to give this campaign its decisive, almost miraculous stamp. When the story of actions in individual sectors became known, as opposed to the overriding initial impression of unstoppable Israeli triumph, it became clear that the Israeli performance was not always first-class and in keeping with their out-size reputation and that, though the Egyptian army command was certainly lacking in military flexibility and initiative, there was nothing shameful about the Egyptian soldier's record.

There was little more for the Israeli army to do except mop up. Yet the one thing that might seem to have been overlooked was the prime object of Israel's offensive – Israel's Suez, Sharm al-Sheikh and the batteries at Ras Nasrani. Capture of the batteries by the Israelis had been reported by the French on the evening of 31 October but that report had been untrue. 9 Brigade did not set out from Ras an-Naqb, close to Eilat, down the coast of Aqaba, until the early morning of 2 November. Dayan never said why he had waited that long to send it off. At first it was held back because it might have been exposed to Egyptian air attack and, besides, it could have been needed as a reserve in case the paratroopers got into trouble. But in view of Dayan's overriding emphasis on speed to beat the UN it seems strange that he did not feel able to release it twenty-four hours sooner than he did.[20] It had a rough task. The mountainous landscape with its coruscations of light, ethereal rock formations in multiform shapes is astonishingly beautiful. But, thirty years ago, it presented every possible obstacle to the progress of a fully motorised infantry brigade – deep sand, huge boulders, sharp slopes, deep ravines, no road surface. It was no terrain for a rapid strike or short deadlines.

Ben-Gurion continually urged haste over Sharm al-Sheikh. Dayan decided on reinsurance; on the evening of 2 November Sharon's paratroopers were moved from the Parker Memorial, some in vehicles down the western (Gulf of Suez) shore of the Sinai peninsula, others by parachute drop on the airstrip at Al Tor, to bring in support from an additional direction, should it be needed, to 9 Brigade sweltering its way down the eastern (Gulf of Aqaba) side.

The Anglo-French air strike had completed its work under Phase I of *Musketeer* by 2 November. Two hundred and sixty Egyptian planes had been destroyed on the ground for the loss by anti-aircraft fire or accident (for the whole operation) of seven aircraft and three pilots. The British Defence Minister, Antony Head, had discussed what to do next with the Chiefs of Staff in the Egypt Committee late the previous evening. Under *Musketeer* it had been intended at this stage to switch to attacking the oil installations, on the principle that, if the large oil storage tanks were destroyed, the civilian population would be affected in four or five days. But now there were doubts which were allowed to prevail. For one thing, if Egyptian oil installations were attacked, other Arab countries which had so far refrained from attacking British oil interests might well be impelled to do so. For another, attacks on oil installations would not look good for a peacekeeping fire brigade. Again, any serious damage done to the Egyptian economy would fall to the British to repair if they were going to be the occupiers of any part of Egyptian territory.[21]

Having just talked themselves out of the one blow from the air which they had previously decided could cripple Egypt, Britain's war leaders decreed that air attacks must only be directed against Egyptian army or 'army-related' targets, and Cairo Radio. The attack on Cairo Radio was the same kind of ambiguous success that marked so much of the air war. Made in broad daylight (the possibility of fighter interception being now totally discounted) eighteen Canberras escorted by French fighters failed in their task and yet achieved their objective. The target marking was inaccurate, the planes came in too low and too fast. 'The results were that the buildings were not hit. Three lots of bombs overshot the target whilst the fourth undershot.' Apart from one aerial mast which was destroyed only superficial damage was done.[22]

Yet Cairo Radio went off the air; and the *Voice of Britain* was at last able to home in on the same wavelength with its message from the impartial peacekeepers: 'O Egyptian people, your broadcasting station has been destroyed ... Why has this befallen you? First, because Abdul Nasser went mad and seized the Suez Canal which is of vital importance to the world ... Abdul Nasser did not keep his promise and betrayed Egypt. He thus brought war to the country ... He promised equality for the Egyptian people but instead he adopted dictatorship ... O Egyptians, accept the proposal of the Allied States ... Otherwise you will bear the consequences of Abdul Nasser's mad behaviour ...'[23]

Brigadier Fergusson was doing his best, under, it must be confessed, rather adverse conditions. The team which for years had assembled and presented the programmes for Sharq al-Adna, with offices in Beirut as well as in Cyprus, had broken up when the station had been taken over by the Allied Command. Many resigned, including the British director, Ralph Poston; there were four reported sabotage attempts; the remaining Arab staff conspired to put out a repeated announcement that they were not responsible for the content. As a result three 'known ringleaders' were served with restriction orders under the Cyprus Defence Regulation confining them to their homes. Feelings were so tense that the authorities at one time would have served Poston with the same order if they had been legally able to do so. Urgent appeals for replacements were sent to Bush House (headquarters of the BBC's External Service) and Beirut.[24] At the same time Fergusson's two million leaflets, including the Ronald Searle cartoons, were not being dropped; after one attempt, the RAF found that they would have to fly with them too slowly and too low to make the risk worthwhile.

'You have taken to hiding in the little villages,' said the *Voice of Britain* to Nasser's soldiers. 'Do you realise what that means? We shall have to come and bomb you there. Imagine your own village being bombed. Imagine your own wife and children, your mother and your father, your grandparents having to run away from home, leaving all their possessions ... [Y]ou have nothing to protect you – nothing – no air force – nothing.

We shall find you and bomb you, however much you hide ... You made only one mistake. You trusted Nasser ...' The Jewish Haganah at Haifa and in Galilee in 1948 had shown that in some circumstances such 'whispering propaganda' works, but these were not the circumstances of Egypt in 1956. There was something a little desperate about the neutral fire-brigade complaining about human rights offences against Egyptian Communists. 'When brought to trial for alleged Communist sympathies', the *Voice of Britain* said, 'Dr Sabri and Dr Shawi showed unmistakable signs of torture and had been mauled by dogs. Yes, the existence of these concentration camps is known to the world. Indeed the new Communist allies of Gamal Abdul Nasser's regime have protested against it constantly.'[25]

In practice even military targets were often ruled out during Phase II because of renewed orders not to cause civilian casualties. 'Attacks on Egyptian armour and road and rail communications from Suez to Tel al-Kebir and Suez to Cairo were severely hampered by the fact that these highways were clogged with refugees fleeing towards Cairo,' it was noted on 4 November. Indeed by 3 November, says Air Marshal Barnett, 'it was becoming increasingly obvious that it would be difficult to justify in world opinion the maintenance of an air offensive until the assault forces were available to land'.[26]

There had been no overt sign of Egyptian public morale giving way, although the disappearance of Cairo Radio from the air on 2 November was, according to subsequent confessions, treated as a signal for fresh activity by Nasser's opponents. When it happened, Colonel Hassan Siyyam, the principal military conspirator, was brought together by the ubiquitous go-between Islambouli with the Wafdist ex-Minister Abdul Fattah Hassan. Colonel and politician took turn and turn about in proffering the initiative to the other, Siyyam suggesting that the civilian leaders should act first by demanding a meeting with Nasser at which they would explain that the disasters befalling the country were due exclusively to the personality of its leader, and Hassan replying that civilians could do nothing until the army had first arrested Nasser and replaced him by another military figure – probably, because of his continuing popular appeal, General Mohamed Neguib.[27]

Nothing much more seems to have happened before the cease-fire, though another civilian leader, Suleiman Hafeez, who had been Deputy Prime Minister in the first Neguib Cabinet from 1952–3 and who still was performing official functions as a constitutional lawyer, persisted in demanding to see Nasser on 2 November and, when the President was unwilling, saw instead both General Amer and Wing Commander Boghdadi. Although evidently not of the Siyyam group (since he was not arrested later with the conspirators), he delivered a somewhat similar message to the effect that Nasser should return to his regiment and Neguib to the Presidency if they hoped to arouse a spirit of popular resistance.[28] Meanwhile Mortada al-

Maraghi and Hussein Khairi crossed over from Beirut to Cyprus.

President Nasser was following very carefully the reactions of the rest of the world, the attitude of the United States, the voting in the UN, the militancy of the Opposition in Britain. Moreover, the Egyptian people in Cairo and Alexandria were belying their reputation for volatility by their general calmness. On 2 November, just after the allied planes had been over, Nasser drove in an open car to perform Friday prayers at the Al Azhar Mosque in Cairo, a place of enormous resonance in the Islamic world. He was everywhere applauded by crowds who lined the route. After the Friday sermon, he addressed the crowd in the open air and explained why the troops had been withdrawn from Sinai, leaving, he said, suicide squads behind. The conspiracy to draw Egypt's army into the peninsula, so that Britain and France would be able to do what they liked with Egypt, had been foiled. In the first twenty-four hours of the fight, that army had inflicted disastrous losses on the Israelis, so that Israel 'could not, for two days, foolishly buzz and boast, as she had done previously'. The withdrawal from Sinai, he affirmed bravely, had been 'more successful than I ever imagined'. Then he hit the note the crowd liked to hear: 'Along the Canal were the stores of the British, worth £300 million. We have taken them to compensate for ...' The applause drowned out his words. When he could again be heard, he declared that vehicles and tanks had been allocated to the armed forces, small arms to the people. In Churchillian style he concluded: 'In Cairo I shall fight with you against any invasion. We shall fight to the last drop of our blood. We shall never surrender.'[29] The speech and the response were the answer to those who would claim that Nasser was not the man to rouse popular resistance.

Dilemmas of Two Serving Officers

Inspired by his great success with the crowd, Nasser had shortly afterwards to face a major problem of morale; the aero-psychological war had nearly claimed its most prominent victim. Boghdadi was called on the phone by Nasser in mid-afternoon to come immediately to the Prime Minister's office. There he found the President with the Commander-in-Chief General Abdul Hakim Amer. Told by Nasser to repeat before Boghdadi and another Free Officer what he had said to him already, Amer declared that, since the continuation of the war would only bring about the destruction of the country and the death of many civilians, they should ask for a cease-fire. Boghdadi describes himself as responding very emotionally. General Amer had said that the people would learn to hate the regime; but hate was much more bearable than scorn. They were going to lose the war but they must do so honourably. They should at least fight on until the capital had fallen.

Nasser did not comment. The group was joined at this stage by the impressionable Major Salah Salem. He repeated what Abdul Hakim Amer had said and declared dramatically that, since Sir Humphrey was still at the British Embassy, Nasser should, after broadcasting news of the surrender to the nation, go there and give himself up. Heikal who also tells this story (though he times it earlier) quotes Salem as saying: 'Now is the time for you to make one more, one last sacrifice. It is you the British want.' Nasser did not feel that this was the solution. He agreed that it was better to take poison than to surrender. It was decided that they would fight for Cairo until it would be madness to go on. Then Nasser would appoint a civilian (no name was mentioned but some think he had in mind Fathi Radwan, the Minister of Culture, a man on whose integrity he could depend) who would negotiate an end of the fighting. Nasser himself and his close military associates would go underground. Small arms were distributed among the people, the so-called Army of National Liberation, and preparations were put in hand for guerrilla warfare. For weeks now the entire country had been divided up into autonomous areas with a command structure and arms supplies; these were told that they must be prepared to conduct resistance on their own.[30] Orders were given for the assassination of any of the old politicians who would serve in a collaborationist government.

Rumours reached the French of the strains at the top in Cairo. Nasser was said to be on the verge of resignation and only remained in power on the urgent representations of the American Ambassador. That Pineau was saying this openly was reported to Washington and vigorously denied by the Deputy Under-Secretary, Robert Murphy. 'The United States', he told Alphand in the presence of other State Department officials, 'wants the success of your enterprise provided that it can succeed with the shortest delay.'[31]

All this time the 'hundred-ship' expedition moved at leaden pace across the face of the Mediterranean at landing-craft speed. The army targets for the Israelis (except for Sharm al-Sheikh) had run out. So had acceptable air targets for the allies. The volume of noise from world opinion was constantly rising. There were still three to four days to go.

Admiral Earl Mountbatten of Burma, the First Sea Lord, wrote a letter to the Prime Minister on 2 November to tell him of his 'great unhappiness' at what was in prospect. 'It is not the business of a serving officer to question the political decisions of his government,' he wrote, touching upon what was always the sensitive point about the ex-Viceroy's resumed naval career. He did not believe, he explained, that in any dispute a just and lasting settlement could be worked out under military threat. But he had done everything in his power to carry out Eden's orders loyally and to the full in making all the necessary naval preparations to build up to a position from which Britain could negotiate from strength. Now bombing had started, the assault convoy was on the way. 'I am writing to appeal to you to accept the resolution of the overwhelming majority of the UN to cease military operations and to beg you to turn back the assault convoy before it is too late . . .' Mountbatten closed the letter with a sentence that showed the agonies of divided loyalty. 'You can imagine how hard it is for me to break with all Service custom and write directly to you in this way' – the First Lord, Lord Hailsham, who was his political chief, was not to know for two days – 'but I feel so desperate about what is happening that my conscience would not allow me to do otherwise.'[32] This time the letter was delivered.

It was a moving statement of the dilemma of a senior civil servant or serving officer faced with the Nuremberg challenge. Since the appearance of his authorised biography made his position generally known,[33] Mountbatten has been criticised for not writing the letter sooner or for not pressing his opposition to the point of resignation. He did as a matter of fact offer to resign twenty-four hours later but that is said to have been so late as to make the offer unreal. He had been pressing persistently in the Chiefs of Staff Committee since August for clear political guidance about the aims of British policy in the Middle East and had asked, but not had answered, highly pertinent questions. He was aware more than anyone, because he had been several times reminded, of the boundaries over which, as a Service chief, he could not properly step. But having once exercised political power in a position of great responsibility and in a sphere (India) which made him acutely sensitive to the currents of opinion in what is now called the Third World, he also could not but be aware of the 'world-wide repercussions' of Britain behaving as she now planned to do. Despite these abnormal pressures, Mountbatten carried out his duties with great professional efficiency. He walked the narrow line between duty and conscience with difficulty but with honour. It was also highly characteristic of him, when sending the letter, to note that he was slipping down to Kent during the weekend 'to see my sister the Queen of Sweden'.[34]

On the evening of 1 November General Paul Ely had been summoned by Pineau to the Quai d'Orsay where, despite the absence of anything at all resembling the pressure from domestic opinion that existed in London, there was an atmosphere of acute disturbance because of world reactions. Since these reactions tended to bear out the Quai's professional predictions, the general noted drily, it was natural that the officials should emphasise them. They feared that the Russians would be able to identify themselves with the United Nations in the Middle East in the way that the United States had done over Korea.

When Pineau had mentioned these misgivings, Ely remarked that the Russian risk had always existed and that it had been decided to discount it. The operation had been launched and France was now committed. In any case, the Soviet reaction was much less than it might have been. Pineau said that, nevertheless, British agreement must be secured for the landing at Port Said to be hastened. Ely sent a message to Barjot in Cyprus:

'Information received from Israel gives the impression that the Egyptian army is beaten and routed. Even if there is some exaggeration, this success must certainly be exploited as fast as possible. Reports from Egypt indicate a deterioration of the political situation ... Consider especially a light operation, mounted very rapidly!'[35]

How Fast to Land and Where?

It was against this background that Ely and General Challe came over to London on 2 November for an urgent meeting with the British Chiefs, whose endorsement would be essential for any change of plan. The British were not too impressed by French ideas for meeting the difficulties by an earlier landing. The main complication, Marshal of the RAF Dickson explained, was the shortage of airfield space in Cyprus. If transport aircraft were put in there for an early assault by parachutists, the number of bombers and fighters would have to be seriously reduced. There could be a small air drop in two days' time, on 4 November, but then Egyptian opposition might be greater than expected and a lightly equipped and weak assault force might be repulsed. The political repercussions of that, Dickson said, would be very serious. A suggestion from Admiral Barjot that the battleship *Jean Bart* should simply steam into Port Said harbour on 3 November with 1,000 paratroops on board was rejected because of the danger of mines. Dickson, fortified by intelligence reports that had come, perhaps, from the new cypher-breaking technique known as *Engulf* which had, according to Peter Wright's book *Spycatcher*, been used by MI5 and GCHQ against the Egyptian Embassy in London so long as it was still in action and receiving relays from the Embassy in Moscow,[36] confidently dismissed French suggestions of possible active intervention by the Russians. He asked Ely to tell Mollet how much worry the French were causing British Ministers by their scarcely concealed co-operation with the Israelis.[37]

After the meeting Ely was received by Eden, whom he found reclining on a sofa, looking distinguished but somewhat distracted and speaking, the general noted appreciatively, in French. Ely urged him to land paratroops on the morrow on the Canal banks at a short distance from the Israelis, who would in effect cover the landings. Thus, he observed slyly, the French and British would indeed be placing themselves in between the Egyptians and the Israelis. He claimed afterwards, rather implausibly, that Eden was pleased by this concept and that only the anti-Israeli sentiments of the British generals stood in the way. In a telegram sent at midnight to Admiral Barjot, who was himself in a lather of impatience and needed no urging, Ely insisted on the absolute political necessity of having men on the ground in the immediate future. The main landing should be no later than 4

November; parachute landings should, if at all possible, be made on 3 November.[38]

Dickson tried his hand at hastening Keightley's proceedings. He told him by *FLASH* signal that he understood from the French that a parachute drop was now planned for 4 November. Assuming that was correct, Dickson said that it was of great political importance in relation to the UN Assembly that the men should have dropped before mid-day. Back came a doleful reply: Keightley had hoped to be able to do some such operation on Sunday, 4 November, but the photographs showed it to be completely out of the question. The combination of anti-aircraft guns, tanks and mines now installed made the parachute drop impossible. 'Such an operation', Keightley concluded in terms that must have frozen his French partners in Cyprus, 'could only be successful if there were indications of a weakening of the Egyptian will to resist, but, in fact, the converse is the case'. Nasser's strategy was working. By placing the priority on resistance to the Anglo-French, he was deterring them from acting in a time-frame that might have brought them success.[39]

Later on 2 November, Keightley revealed, to the dismay of the French commanders, just how bleak his revised estimation was of the prospects of an early and unopposed (or lightly opposed) landing. He now clearly felt, says Colonel Becq de Fouquières in his *Guerre des Six Jours*, that Nasser must have had sufficient time to carry out a retreat, the rapidity of the Israelis' advance being only explicable by the void which they had found. From this, de Fouquières wrote, the British concluded that Nasser now lay in strength along the Canal and that any instant strike by paratroops from Cyprus was consequently ruled out.[40]

Such news was exceptionally unpopular with the commander of the French paras, General Jean Marcelin Gilles, a man who had struck the British Military Attaché in Paris as 'the rudest, most unpleasant and most hostile French officer we have ever met'. With his one eye staring out from a rather coarse, battered face, he had gained the reputation in Indo-China of 'declaring to all and sundry that unless they wore a red beret and kept jumping out of aeroplanes they were useless as soldiers'.[41] He was not a man to take quietly to being grounded at Tymbou.

Keightley cabled the Chiefs of Staff in Whitehall that, 'The situation has now clarified and any chances of an easy entry into Port Said are removed. As a result of today's photo reconnaissance, the Egyptians are clearly going to resist our assault on Port Said with everything they have got.' The extremely unwelcome news coming through from the pictures amply confirmed that 'we have reason to believe [that] Nasser's contention that he intends to concentrate and fight the West first and leave Israel till afterwards is true'. Consequently, if they were going to pull off the assault without heavy casualties, the allies would have to put 'a really heavy naval and air bombardment on to Port Said' and, even then, they would still clearly be in for a battle in the town itself. What with tanks being dug in, a 'vast number' of AA guns spotted, mining operations taking place, gun positions being established even in houses, and the blocking of the port with four ships during the night, the enterprise promised to be a tough one.

The Allied Commander-in-Chief did not conceal his annoyance at the change that Israeli involvement had made in the plan he had originally worked out for *Musketeer Revise* with its promised ultimate reward of a virtually unopposed landing. 'As I think you know,' he told the Chiefs, 'this situation is no surprise to me. I never thought the Egyptians would do anything else and the devastation of Port Said is the price we must pay for changing our plans by elimination of Phase II. Psychological warfare is now also most complicated as Nasser has cleverly bound up our attack with the Jews – and that is the only rallying point on which, probably, the whole nation and the whole Arab world are solidly behind him.' In these circumstances, there were only three options open to Keightley: to carry on as before with the assault, only with a more devastating bombardment commensurate with the increased defences; to revert even at this last moment to *Musketeer Revise*, except that Phase II would now have to last as long as fourteen days before coming to the unopposed landing; and to land somewhere else, such as Gaza, when there would be no opposition and hence no damage.[42]

Confronted with these choices, the Chiefs of Staff split. In a Saturday morning session (3 November) with the Minister of Defence, Mountbatten took the view that, 'if we were at war', he would have no hesitation in supporting the landing at Port Said. They had the necessary resources to succeed. But under present conditions it would be extremely difficult to carry out the landing without very considerable damage to the town and loss of life. Since it was not possible to delay the operation he supported landing at Gaza, by-passing Port Said and advancing up the Canal. General Templer was beside himself at this suggestion. He had seen the Egyptians, he said, and he knew that when it came to it they would not fight. He was in favour of telling them at the earliest possible moment and in the clearest terms that 'we intend to land at Port Said and unless they evacuate the town or surrender it we will attack with all the weapons at our disposal'. If they landed at Gaza this would merely demonstrate to the Arab world that the allies were collaborating with the Israelis. Templer believed that, whatever Nasser wished, the Egyptians would not remain in the town once they had been made aware of the capability of the allied forces. But a demonstration of that capability would again mean putting off the landings for one or two extra days.[43] And it was days of which the allies were running out.

Head brought the issue in its yet unresolved state before the Egypt Committee. A parachute drop at Qantara, the exit from the causeway, on 4 November which the French and also Stockwell's Chief of Staff, Brigadier

Darling, had favoured was now clearly out. The wartime lesson of Arnhem, never to drop on 'a bridge too far', was held to apply, since the strengthened defences could seriously delay the arrival of reinforcements. Before the seaborne landing at Port Said on 6 November there would now have to be a preliminary naval bombardment of the new positions along the seafront, with all the political cost involved. What with the blockships now sunk in the harbour and the destruction in the port area that would now be unavoidable, was there something in the First Sea Lord's suggestion of an unopposed landing somewhere else? But where? Three places were now named: Haifa, Gaza and Al Arish. But Haifa was in Israel and the other two, though they might seem more naturally placed for separating combatants close to the Armistice line, would require open Israeli approval. Moreover, so long as the object was to capture Port Said, Ismailia and Suez, heavy equipment had to be landed and this could not be done at Gaza or Al Arish.[44]

Rhodes James says that Eden listened to these arguments 'with astonishment and anger'. It was certainly rather late in the day to be thinking of such changes. But then Eden was requiring the Service Chiefs, at scarcely any notice at all, to dress their work in an entirely fresh political guise, as if they were neutral peacekeepers. At the end of the discussion Head volunteered to fly out immediately to Cyprus to see whether it seemed likely that Port Said could be taken without heavy civilian casualties.

Nothing had been said at Sèvres about the anticipated pace of the Anglo-French advance on Suez. The Israelis, like everybody else, were expecting a landing shortly after the expiry of the ultimatum. There was increasing bewilderment as the days passed and allied communiqués spoke of air strikes but of nothing else. Mrs Meir spoke rather crossly to the British Ambassador in Tel Aviv 'as if our failure to occupy the Suez Canal Zone was exposing Israel's forces in Sinai to unnecessary risks'. To Nicholls's mind the implication seemed to be that, unless they were promptly screened from Egyptian reinforcements, Israeli forces would advance and occupy security bridgeheads across the Canal.[45]

23

Slow March to Suez

All my life I've been a man of peace, working for peace, striving for peace, negotiating for peace. I've been a League of Nations man and a United Nations man and I'm still the same man with the same convictions, the same devotion to peace. I couldn't be other if I wished.

Sir Anthony Eden, broadcast, 3 November 1956.

Make no mistake about it – this is war: the bombing, the softening up, the attacks on radio stations, telephone exchanges, railway stations, to be followed very, very soon now by the landings and the fighting between ground forces ... It is not a police action, there is no law behind it – we have taken the law into our own hands.

Hugh Gaitskell, broadcast, 4 November 1956.

Next to the Middle East itself, there was no place where the time factor counted for more than in the United States. Despite Eisenhower's genuine reaction of anger and frustration, there were many Americans whose first thoughts after the ultimatums, and even after the bombing, were more favourable to the British and French than were those of the Administration. For one thing, since the Presidential election campaign was in its last days, there was the Democratic Party opposition. Adlai Stevenson, the former Governor of Illinois, who was for the second time Eisenhower's Democratic opponent, altered his eve-of-poll speeches to concentrate completely on the Middle East. In a major speech in Detroit on 2 November, he lambasted the Eisenhower–Dulles policy for inconsistency and irresolution. 'The Administration first offered and then refused to help Egypt with the Aswan Dam. It refused to send Israel defence arms but then encouraged others to do so. It came forward with one proposal after another in the dispute over the Suez Canal but never really committed itself to stand firm on anything. And it acquired for itself ... a reputation for unreliability which is about as damaging a reputation as a Great Power can have ... [O]ne question which arises irresistibly out of the Middle Eastern crisis is this: has the President of the United States really been in charge of our foreign policy?'

John F. Kennedy, campaigning in Manhattan for a wartime naval comrade running for the House, hammered away at the theme that it was the Administration's fault that it had alienated America's chief European allies.

The high ground was occupied by Richard M. Nixon, the Vice-President, who bore the heat and burden of the Republican campaign. At Hershey, Pennsylvania, he spoke rhapsodically of America's 'second declaration of independence'. According to him, the sixty-four to five vote for the American resolution in the General Assembly had 'constituted a worldwide vote of confidence, the like of which has never been known before ... For the first time in history, we have showed independence of Anglo-French policies towards Asia and Africa which seemed to us to reflect the colonial tradition. That declaration of independence has had an electrifying effect throughout the world ... If the UN had failed ... it might have gone the way of the old League of Nations, which lost its moral influence in the world when it was unable to deal with the use of force by its members.'[1]

Among the leading Washington commentators, Chalmers Roberts (*Washington Post*) thought that the Suez crisis 'has destroyed the priceless ingredient of the Anglo-American alliance – America's trust in Britain's word'. According to the Alsop brothers, 'This city, which has seen a good many extremes in political behaviour, has never witnessed such an exhibition of pique and anger as the Anglo-French-Israeli action against Egypt has touched off.' But George Kennan protested that, 'We have fumbled on certain past occasions; and our friends have not turned against us. Moreover, we bear a heavy measure of responsibility for the desperation which has driven the French and the British Governments to this ill-conceived and pathetic action.'

In many ways the most interesting attitude and one that was representative of quite a number of Americans was that of Walter Lippmann, the doyen of American columnists. 'The American interest', he maintained, 'is to refrain from moral judgement ... The Franco-British action will be judged by the outcome – in the first instance whether the military objectives are achieved in a reasonable time and at not too great cost ... The American interest, though we have dissented from the decision itself, is that France and Britain should now succeed. However much we may wish they had not started, we cannot now wish that they should fail.' Lippmann was, during these days, and quite contrary to his usual custom, forever running out of his study to scrutinise the ticker-tape that was supplied to his house and which was normally torn off and handed to him at discreet intervals by an assistant, so anxious was he now to see if the allies had landed. He could not believe, as could few Americans, that the British and French could take so long.

Since the story of the even-handed police force or fire brigade was universally disbelieved, no one could understand why the landing force was not just over the horizon when the ultimatum was delivered. Many

Americans, feeling that the old European powers were 'slick operators' when it came to a Machiavellian stroke, were quite prepared to see Nasser neatly unhorsed provided it was done with speed and address. Allen Dulles, the director of the CIA, expected no such thing. He told a British journalist during the crisis that he had been reading Alan Moorehead's book *Gallipoli* and he knew better than to suppose that the British moved nimbly and speedily during such operations.[2]

'Life gets more difficult by the minute,' President Eisenhower wrote on 2 November to his old army friend General Al Gruenther, who had just retired as Supreme Commander, Europe; 'I really could use a good bridge game.' He had been talking with some of his old British friends in the last few days and they were truly bitter about the action of their Government. 'One man said, "This is nothing except Eden trying to be bigger than he is." I do not dismiss that lightly. I believe that Eden and his associates have become convinced that this is the last straw and Britain simply *had* to react in the manner of the Victorian period. If one has to have a fight, then that is that. But I don't see the point in getting into a fight to which there can be no satisfactory end; and in which the whole world believes you are playing the part of the bully, and you do not even have the firm backing of your entire people.'[3] Here Eisenhower's private thoughts stood for those of most Americans, except for that sneaking feeling among many that it would be splendid if, despite everything, the 'bullies' were to carry it off.

For the second time since the Suez dispute started, the idea was discussed of Eisenhower and Nehru jointly floating at cloud level above the scene and moderating Middle East disputes. The notion was appealing to a President with some idealistic urgings. Nehru had somehow manoeuvred himself into the position where he was regarded as a benchmark of moral stature, able to play the role that many Americans would wistfully prefer for themselves were they not plagued with the responsibilities of a superpower. The President discussed the possibilities with Dulles and Hoover at the White House on 2 November; after his wearing night at the UN, Dulles thought Lester Pearson might well suggest the Eisenhower–Nehru approach. A two-tier operation was discussed, with committees seeking solutions to the Palestine and Suez Canal questions and the two big figures looming over them as a 'board of appeals'. Dulles said that it was necessary to move quickly, maintain momentum and keep out in front of the rapidly developing action.[4]

It was John Foster Dulles's last significant contribution to the Suez crisis. He was stricken with pain during the night of 2/3 November and underwent an immediate operation for cancer. Herbert Hoover took over, in his place, as Acting Secretary of State.

World Opinion Hurts

In London there were two Cabinet meetings during 2 November, one at 4.30 p.m., the other at 9 p.m., both dealing with the same major problem, how to reply to the General Assembly resolution. At a meeting of senior Ministers in the morning there had already been agreement that, even after the conclusion of a cease-fire, it would still be necessary for Anglo-French forces, 'which are the only forces immediately available for policing purposes', to occupy certain key points to prevent a resumption of the conflict. However, if the UN were to put itself into a position to maintain an international force between the combatants, the Anglo-French police force would hand over to them, provided they were prepared to stay until a final peace treaty over Palestine had been signed.[5] The Cabinet strategy was to ignore the plain fact that Britain and France had in effect, if not technically, been overwhelmingly condemned by the UN, and to continue to act the part of a UN surrogate until the UN took over the job itself. It would follow that legitimacy would retrospectively be conferred on what the surrogate had done.

It was this plan that was discussed at the two Cabinet meetings, but for some undisclosed reason the entire set of Minutes of the first of them, the one that began at 4.30 p.m., alone among the Suez series of numbered Cabinet meetings at which records were kept, is to be withheld until the year 2007. It is known that the possibility of American oil sanctions against Britain and France was mentioned by Selwyn Lloyd, who also spoke grimly about the impact of the Suez war throughout the Middle East and the Gulf, his words influenced no doubt by the tone of high alarm from Baghdad. But, in addition, covert operations must presumably have been discussed.

Between the two meetings, Pineau came over to concert the terms of the reply. Nothing could more clearly illustrate the different attitudes of Britain and France towards the Israelis. Eden's attempt to make 'the impartial policeman' more credible was stamped on by the French. Pineau would not agree to the issuing of a formal requirement that Israeli forces should stay at ten miles' distance from the Canal. The Cabinet, on the other hand, put a stop to all further British arms exports to Israel.

The unhappiness of some Government supporters on the left of the party found an echo in the discussion when Macleod and Amory argued that a soft answer offering to transfer peacekeeping responsibilities to the UN was hard to fit in with an immediate assault on Egypt. The UN might, it was suggested, even feel that Britain's offer had not been made in good faith. Other Ministers represented other sections of the party who would be very dissatisfied indeed if the proposal to transfer responsibility to the UN were made into an excuse for premature abandonment of the enterprise.[6] It was not a harmonious session.

The agreed reply was read out to the Commons by Eden when the House assembled at noon for an exceptional Saturday session on 3 November. Britain and France, it said, stuck to their view that 'police action must be carried through urgently to stop the hostilities which are now threatening the Suez Canal' and to 'pave the way for a definitive settlement of the Arab-Israel[i] war', but they would most willingly stop military action as soon as three conditions were met. These were: that Egypt and Israel both accept a UN force; that the UN should keep the force there until both the Palestine peace settlement and the Suez Canal settlement had been reached; and that both Egypt and Israel should, pending the creation of the force, accept 'limited contingents' of Anglo-French troops between the combatants.

The occupants of the Tory benches were by now in an aggressive mood. They were determined not to let the Opposition get away with what they considered its lack of patriotic response. But Gaitskell had got the bit between his teeth. According to him it was no part of Britain's business to lay down conditions to the UN. It was her duty as a loyal member of the UN to accept the decision ('And sell Britain?' came the voices from the benches opposite). The Canal was blocked, Gaitskell said, the war was virtually over, Britain was engaged in wrecking the UN at the very moment that it was involved in taking a stand over Hungary. At one point the Labour leader appeared to stumble when he said that the Israeli-Egyptian war had been brought 'prematurely to an end', a phrase which invited a wave of ironic cheers from Government supporters. He recovered himself quickly and spoke directly to that section of the Tory party that was known to be disenchanted with Eden's policy. It consisted of upwards of twenty members, very loosely co-ordinated by Sir Alexander Spearman, though the best known public personality (for his television appearances) was Sir Robert Boothby. Others included Jacob Astor and Nigel Nicolson. 'Up to this moment', Hugh Gaitskell said, 'I, for my part, had hoped for a change in government policy . . . Alas, that is not so and we can draw only one conclusion. That is that, if this country is to be rescued . . . we must have a new Government and a new Prime Minister. The immediate responsibility for this matter rests upon the only people who can affect the situation – Hon. Members opposite. I beg them to consider in their hearts where we are being led at this moment.'

The Prime Minister replied with courtesy and calm. An Assembly resolution was a recommendation to governments, not a decision binding on them. Although the present crisis was supposed not to be about the Canal dispute, he justified the inclusion of a Suez settlement among the preconditions on the ground that 'we shall try to use this situation to deal with all the outstanding problems in the Middle East and it would be unwise to leave any one of them unresolved'. In answer to questions from Shinwell, he carried himself still further from international reality by observing that, if the UN force went in, 'we should naturally not expect to be excluded from it', and while the reply was being considered the Government would not stop bombing Egyptian targets since the combatants must still be separated and the position stabilised. Gaitskell made what he described as 'one last appeal' to the Prime Minister to cease further military action. It was without effect.

The debate ended in a shambles as the Foreign Secretary was shouted down with Labour Members on their feet howling cries of 'resign!' at the Government front bench, while Government supporters responded furiously by waving their order papers and roaring, 'We support you,' and similar expressions of encouragement. Time having run out, Eden, with his customary composure under fire, walked out of the chamber while the Opposition, caught in whorls and paroxysms of frenzy, continued to howl at him. From the Opposition Front Bench, the short, stumpy figure of George Brown, a future Foreign Secretary, could be seen, 'with outstretched arms and pointing a furious index finger' at Ministers whom he seemed to be 'consigning ... to a dreadful doom'.[7]

Politically and internationally this was Britain's first crisis to be fully reported on the small screen. Competition had only hit British television the previous year; no public issue was supposed to be discussed if the Commons was expected to consider it within the coming fortnight. Beginning with the mid-recess debate on 12 and 13 September, the infant Independent Television News broke new ground and conveyed to its viewers the sense and feel of these passionate encounters in brilliant verbal essays, that were both summary and sketch from its parliamentary reporter and newscaster Robin Day, who was laying the foundations of a highly successful media career.[8]

While the confrontational nature of party politics had detracted somewhat from the impact of Gaitskell's onslaught, much the same critique was being supplied in two private cables from Eden's highly trusted Representative at the UN. Sir Pierson Dixon began by citing a document that was being circulated by Dag Hammarskjöld as an annex to his report. It was an urgent cable from the Canadian Colonel David Ely, the UN Truce Supervision representative in Cairo, and three other senior UN officials. The cable reported that, whereas the bomb attacks had been directed till now at military targets, the *Voice of Britain* had announced 'an imminent switch to include communication centres, railway stations and telephone exchanges many of which are located in densely populated areas'. These were the 'army-related' targets on the *Musketeer* list; but on the ground they looked much more nearly related to civilians. The UN officials felt that, despite advance warnings to the civilian population, implementation would 'result in a terrific loss of life'. Ely's cable concluded – but this Hammarskjöld censored before circulating it – 'it is our opinion that this will be an act of barbarous brutality'. 'Can I deny that this is our intention?' Sir Pierson asked. 'If not I am afraid our position here will become untenable ... If we bomb open cities with resulting loss of civilian life or engage in battle with Egyptian forces, there is not the faintest chance of [our response to the Assembly's resolution] receiving any sympathy. On the contrary it would make our offer seem completely cynical and entirely undermine our position here. In these circumstances the only honest course for HMG and the French Government would be to withdraw their representatives and leave the United Nations.'

This was to define the issue raised for Britain by the Suez crisis in its most brutal terms and in a form that would be most telling for the Prime Minister. It placed in direct juxtaposition two methods of conducting foreign policy: that which used the traditional methods of 'the great game' of nations, moderated perhaps by the hundreds of years of customary international law to which Lord Kilmuir had appealed, and that which was conducted in terms which paid some deference to the norms of the UN Charter.

For France, the idea of leaving the UN in bitterness had already come up in 1955 over North Africa; for Britain never. While it is quite clear from his internal minutes that Eden was not an admirer of the UN, there is no doubt that an important part of his public persona was as a League of Nations man and by extension a United Nations man. In his broadcast to the nation that very night he was to draw heavily on that reputation to give him credentials for his present stand. By far the biggest emotional punch that was packed by the opponents of his Suez policy came from the large reservoir of support there was then to be found in Britain for the United Nations idea.

Lloyd spoke to Dixon over the telephone about the instructions for Phase II of *Musketeer* and suggested how they might be explained. Again and again he repeated over the open phone, 'We can accept anything from the UN – so long as it doesn't stop our troops going in.'

Dixon sent a further cable, reporting that the Assembly was going to have an evening session. 'It is my considered view,' said the Ambassador, 'which I urge with the greatest possible emphasis that, as things now stand, we have no chance of getting a fair hearing for our ideas unless my French colleague and I are in a position to announce, if possible at the outset of the proceedings, that Anglo-French forces are suspending all further military activities until we know whether the UN are prepared to deal with the whole situation effectively.'[9]

At a meeting at the White House with Hoover, the Acting Secretary of State, Eisenhower insisted that the United States must stipulate that she was not waiting for or accepting the entry of the British or French to the Canal area. The approach favoured by Eden, with the UN taking over from the two allies, as in a relay race, was utterly rejected. It was essential, the President declared, to remove any need or basis for Anglo-French landings.[10]

Peace Through War

That evening, 3 November, on radio and television the Prime Minister addressed the nation, including the troops waiting expectantly in their craft as they moved forward towards Port Said. 'All my life', he said, 'I've been a man of peace, working for peace, striving for peace, negotiating for peace. I've been a League of Nations man and a United Nations man and I'm still the same man with the same convictions, the same devotion to peace. I couldn't be other even if I wished. But I'm *utterly* convinced that the action we have taken is right.' He looked distinguished, sincere and emphatic. He referred to the mood of peace at any price and how much Britain had had to pay for it in the past. 'Between the wars we saw things happening which we felt were adding to the danger of a great world war. Should we have acted swiftly to deal with them, even though it meant the use of force, or should we have hoped for the best and gone on hoping and talking as in fact we did? There are times for courage, times for action and this is one of them.'[11] Eden had put into this speech the whole sum of his experience and the conclusion to which he thought it led. His career had come 'full circle' (to quote the title which he chose for his volume of memoirs dealing with the years 1951–6). The battle against Neville Chamberlain, lost in 1937–8, must be won at Suez.

A flood of letters and telegrams poured in to Number Ten, evidence that he commanded a large element of popular approval. To many people this was a worthy call to unity and sacrifice for old, familiar causes. Their fury against anyone at home who broke this mood of dedication and defiance of the uncomprehending world outside was often very great and very bitter. As 'our boys', regulars and conscripts, sailed on into danger, the controversy and noise provided by those who felt that Britain was being untrue to her finer self seemed to them positively obscene. But that was not the reaction of all patriots. As he watched Sir Anthony Eden on television Christopher Chancellor, the chairman of Reuter's, a proconsular figure of legendary impassivity, hurled his whisky glass at the screen, and Major-General John Cowley, the Acting Quartermaster-General to the Forces, told a senior civil servant that he wanted to resign his commission. 'My dear fellow', came the reply, 'it would not make the slightest difference if you did.'[12]

Gaitskell immediately claimed the right of reply. The Prime Minister's view was well known – once the forces were committed this was a national occasion and no time for partisan broadcasts. Edward Heath, the Tory Chief Whip, turned down the Opposition's request. Under the byzantine ground rules then prevailing, the final decision as to whether a Ministerial broadcast had been 'controversial', thus qualifying for a reply, lay with the BBC. It was an exposed position, with the Director-General away in Australia. Losing patience with the Corporation's careful observance of protocol, Gaitskell displayed his temper, threatening the Director of the

Spoken Word with public exposure for suppressing the Opposition unless he came quickly to the right decision. Given the strength of the BBC's ideology, which even reached to its maudarin chairman, Sir Alexander Cadogan, there was little real doubt what the decision would be.[13]

Hugh Gaitskell appeared on Sunday, 4 November, to give the Opposition case and to expose both to the nation and the world the extent to which Britain, going into battle, was a nation torn in twain. He held up to examination the justificatory language used for the action – police action, fire brigade, separating the combatants. 'Make no mistake about it – this is war: the bombing, the softening up, the attacks on radio stations, telephone exchanges, railway stations, to be followed very, very soon now by the landings and the fighting between ground forces. We are doing all this alone, except for France, opposed by the world, in defiance of the world. It is not a police action, there is no law behind it – we have taken the law into our own hands.' It was simple, direct, devastating. Or, if one saw it through different eyes, was it not treasonable, a betrayal of Britain's soldiers, sailors and airmen on the eve of battle?

Gaitskell then made what was probably an error: he repeated to a wider audience his appeal to Conservatives who backed him on this issue to vote according to their convictions. Speaking with great earnestness he undertook 'to support a new Prime Minister in halting the invasion of Egypt, in ordering the cease-fire and complying with the decisions and recommendations of the United Nations'.[14]

For many people, desperately unhappy at what was being done in their name and at what seemed to them to be the unacceptable level of hypocrisy which they had been invited to endorse, Gaitskell had found the language to embody their thoughts. They would have echoed the words of a letter to him from Lady Violet Bonham Carter, Asquith's daughter and a leading Liberal politician in her own right: 'It was not for your party only you were speaking – you "spoke for England" – for England's *real* and best self.'[15] But while, thereby, Gaitskell acquired fierce loyalties and affections that stayed with him for the remainder of his life, he became for other people quite simply 'the Traitor'. He administered the stab in the back on the eve of a great enterprise. He (together with Dulles and others) had betrayed Eden's gallant stand for everything that had made Britain great and had done so quite nakedly for motives of petty political manoeuvre.

On the troopship on which Anthony Howard, a young conscript subaltern later to be known as a talented editor, television broadcaster and biographer of R. A. Butler, was serving, the entire ship's company listened to Eden over the tannoy system with great reverence and appreciation. On the next night, when there was Gaitskell, nothing was said on the troop deck about any such broadcast. It was for the ears of the officers' verandah deck only. 'It was heard, I have to say,' Howard recalled on BBC television twenty years later, 'through such expressions of fury and disgust and revulsion as I have rarely seen among grown men; they hated it. Words like "traitor", "treachery", were bandied about, and various threats as to what they would do to him if they ever came across him were also expressed.'

Although this new role of a neutral police force protecting the Canal from both sides had been suddenly invented for British troops, they had no special training to fit them for these duties. Howard remembers daily pep talks on board ship of a very traditional kind, his own company commander saying, 'I want you to think of the Egyptian rather like a rat; he's a nasty customer when he's cornered.'[16] In fairness it should be said that there was no reason to suppose that the Egyptians would treat these men as peacekeepers when they arrived.

In Cyprus, urged on by Admiral Barjot, who himself was receiving a stream of increasingly urgent cables from General Ely in Paris, General Beaufre was attempting on the morning of 3 November to get his fellow-commanders to endorse a plan for three parachute drops on 5 November. These would be to the west of Port Said (at a small local aerodrome called Gamil), to the south of Port Said to secure the Raswa road and rail bridges and to the south of Port Fuad (which is on the opposite, eastern, side of the Canal). This would enable the strength of Egyptian resistance to be tested; the allied commanders could then have a better idea of the nature of the sea-landing that would be called for. Admiral Barjot, enthusiastically supported by the French paratroop commander, General Gilles, wanted to strike twenty-four hours sooner. He even attempted at one point to disentangle the French troops from the integrated command, mobilising political support in Paris for such a move.[17]

The commanders were soon confirmed in their suspicions that the politicians were getting extremely nervous. From London came the *FLASH* signal to Keightley that 'for very strong political reasons we may wish to make an announcement that the landing will be at Port Said, in order to save the lives of civilians, thus sacrificing tactical surprise. Can you accept this? And can we make the announcement at any time suitable to us?' Keightley was asked what targets he planned to knock out before he landed. Finally, and ominously for the generals and admirals, 'We assume you still have flexibility to postpone landing for up to 48 hours as before?'[18]

Keightley was understandably provoked. 'Since we were launched on this operation the whole emphasis has been on speed,' he replied over the direct circuit from Episkopi, 'and I must see whether the steps taken by commanders make a postponement now possible. Incidentally, it will cause a complete break with the French to whom we have given a solemn undertaking we will not postpone except for bad weather. What is behind this suggestion?' Vice-Admiral Richmond, who was in charge of the rear link in London, responded dubiously that he understood that the suggestion arose from the possibility that a longer aero-psychological phase might soften resistance in Port Said, 'though', he said, 'it is realised that this is a slender hope'.[19]

At dinner, General Stockwell had just told Beaufre that he had persuaded Admiral Barjot to drop *Telescope*, a modified version of the plan for three parachute drops, when a message came through to Keightley that, following a dash to London by Bourgès-Maunoury and Pineau, *Telescope* was now on.[20] Head and Templer arrived at 2 a.m. on 4 November from London to confer immediately with Keightley and Barjot. They confirmed the order to attack, but it was clear that the whole purpose of their visit was to make quite sure that, insofar as was humanly possible, performance matched international pretension. The operation, it was made plain, was to be confined to the Canal Zone. There was to be no veering off to Cairo to change the government of Egypt. No political directive to General Keightley was to be issued. The attack was to go ahead – *Telescope* on 5 November and the assault landing at Port Said, if necessary, on the next morning. The idea once entertained that 'vertical envelopment', or assault by helicopter, should form part of the drop on Raswa, on the southern approaches to Port Said, was abandoned on the correct assumption that Egyptian fire-power was now likely to be too great to try out this novel technique against active opposition.

Head laid out in stark outline the political stakes involved. The Soviets were in agreement with the Americans, the Afro-Asian world was united, including those Arab states which would have been glad to see Nasser fall. The pace of the Hungarian crisis imperatively required that allied action be seen not to mirror that of Khrushchev in Budapest. Keightley agreed to call on the inhabitants of Port Said to evacuate their homes twenty-four hours ahead of the operation and not to make use of the heavy-calibre naval guns in any preliminary naval bombardment. The mighty French battleship *Jean Bart* would not open up at all; the others would fire nothing above 4.5 in. guns, carefully targeted. Brigadier Butler, the British paratroop commander who would be landing on Gamil airfield, expressed confidence in being able, together with the French paras, to master Port Said on Monday evening, 5 November, so making bombardment in any form superfluous.

Head asked how long after the fall of Port Said it would take to get Ismailia, to which Keightley replied '48 hours', to the chagrin of Barjot who felt that the paras could manage it in half that time. They then discussed the condition of the Canal, along the length of which they could now see the Egyptians sinking bridges, barges, cranes, anything to multiply the obstructions, but they came to no conclusion about how long it would be out of action. The French Admiral Champion, who was to be in charge of getting the Canal working again, and his salvage experts would be in Cyprus in twenty-four hours.[21] Head left for London; all was now set to go, though a certain lack of communication must have explained the fact that when the carrier force commander, Admiral Power, received the directive to give priority support for Operation *Telescope* on Monday, 5 November, the name and nature of this operation were a puzzle to him.

All this agonising about how to win a war without inflicting casualties was closely related to what had been happening in New York. At 3 p.m. (in New York; 8 p.m. GMT and 10 p.m. Middle East time) on Saturday, 3 November, the Security Council had taken up the case of Hungary where a coalition Cabinet had now been announced by Nagy. All was quiet in Budapest but there were ominous signs in the rest of the country of the Russians taking over and sealing off the frontiers. At 8 p.m. the attention switched to the General Assembly and to Suez.

Since his early morning speech on Friday, 2 November, Pearson had canvassed Hammarskjöld over lunch about his idea. He got a very cool and pessimistic response. The Secretary-General, who seemed to the Canadian to be much put out by Israel's 'aggressive and acquisitive' style of diplomacy, said he thought Israel as a state would not last. UNEF, he feared, would be a very doubtful starter with the Israelis since Ben-Gurion considered even the present UN observers to be intruders. Not discouraged, Pearson then returned to Canada and began drafting with his staff. On Saturday morning the Canadian Cabinet approved the idea. At this point Pearson was intending a two-stage scheme. In the short first stage the troops available on the spot, largely British and French, but with an additional international component, perhaps American and Canadian, would separate the Israelis and the Egyptians. Thereafter, the force would be replaced as soon as possible by a proper UN police force recruited and controlled by a Committee of Five. In the meantime the British should be asked to undertake that there should be no unilateral landings.

The Americans were quite clear that the first stage of this scheme (which, of course, was the part which commended it to the British and French) would not do. The Canadians then decided that they must go for a full international 'intervention force' straightaway. President Eisenhower, anxious above all things to forestall any Anglo-French landing, personally suggested dropping the Committee of Five; action by the Secretary-General would be quicker. Finally Pearson, having accepted, with minor changes, a simplified draft from Lodge which had been cleared with the Egyptians and the Afro-Asian group, introduced on Saturday night, 3 November, a resolution which was extremely short, had no Committee of Five and gave Hammarskjöld sole responsibility. He was to submit a plan within forty-eight hours to set up an emergency force 'to secure and supervise the cessation of hostilities'. The sharp race was on to get his scheme adopted and in place before the British and French had landed.[22]

The idea gained warm approval all round. But for sheer unexpected midnight drama, the Oscar went to Abba Eban. The representative of Israel simply declared that, the General Assembly having called for an immediate cease-fire, 'My Government has given priority consideration to this recommendation and it now empowers me to announce that Israel agrees to an immediate cease-fire, provided a similar answer is forthcoming from Egypt.'

This was a sensational, deeply embarrassing and somewhat puzzling announcement. It was sensational because, combined with Egypt's acceptance of the Assembly's resolution the previous day, it seemed to mark the end of the war. It removed any excuse for the exercise of the international functions which Britain and France had arrogated to themselves. However much it could be argued that fighting troops were needed to hold apart two enemies who were actually fighting, the peacekeeping force being pressed by Pearson was clearly more suited to the new situation of a cease-fire.

The announcement was puzzling because, while it was easy to see why Ben-Gurion should not have felt that he owed much to Eden, he owed a great deal to the French; it was incongruous that he seemed to be depriving them of the excuse to strike their blow. But it is also puzzling from a more directly self-interested Israeli viewpoint. Sharm al-Sheikh, the point at the end of the peninsula, was not just Israel's proclaimed Number One target; it was peculiarly Ben-Gurion's own. Yet on the night of 3/4 November when Eban announced agreement to an immediate cease-fire, the Israelis, struggling down through the sharp-toothed mountain morass towards the Sharm, had not yet made it, were not in fact to make it until the early morning of 5 November. They had not even taken Ras Nasrani, from where the guns fired into the Enterprise Channel until 4 November. Presumably it was taken for granted that, as in 1948, and indeed, in Israel's later wars, it would always be possible, provided that one was on the winning side, to improve one's position in the twenty-four hours after a cease-fire before the international observers could be in place.

Following Eban's statement the Ceylonese delegate spoke for almost the entire Assembly when he said: 'Israel has made an open declaration that it is prepared to observe a cease-fire. What further reason is there for the UK and France to intervene?'

As the Assembly began to move towards a vote, Ronald Walker of Australia rose and read out a Reuters bulletin from Vienna: 'Premier Imre Nagy of Hungary declared over Budapest Radio today that the Russian Army was attacking the Hungarian capital and the Hungarians were fighting back.' Once more the affairs of Central Europe had become mixed with those of the Middle East. Walker immediately proposed that the President of the Security Council (for November, the Chilean) should meet with heads of delegations within half an hour in his office to plan the Council's next steps.

The General Assembly passed two resolutions in the early hours of Sunday, 4 November. The first was the Canadian resolution on UNEF, which was carried by fifty-seven votes to none, with nineteen abstentions (including the Soviet bloc, Britain, France and Israel). The second, proposed by India and eighteen other third world states, gave the parties twelve hours to implement the cease-fire and imposed a total ban on movement of military forces and arms into the area. It was carried by fifty-nine votes (including the USA and the USSR) to five (Britain, France, Israel, Australia and New Zealand) with twelve abstentions. Once again a delegate, this time Henry Cabot Lodge, rose immediately after the vote to speak of Hungary. 'We have just received word from our legation in Budapest that Budapest is under heavy bombardment, so much so that the staff of our own legation has had to take refuge in the cellar of the building.'

The General Assembly adjourned at five minutes past three on Sunday morning, 4 November. Five minutes before, at 3 a.m. the Security Council had gone into session to consider the situation in Hungary. Lodge began the debate by saying: 'A few minutes ago, we received word of the appeal of the Prime Minister of Hungary for help from the whole world while his capital city is burning.' On anyone who was present at these two debates or watched them live on American television, cutting from the one to the other, the juxtaposition left an unforgettable impression.

Cabling back his impressions of the Suez debate, Dixon said that, because of the time-limit in the Indian resolution, the Assembly would resume again in a very few hours. Britain would be in real trouble again if there were stepped-up military action. Above all, if there were heavy civilian casualties, 'the call for sanctions, which sounded hollow today, might gather momentum'. The Ambassador urged that, 'If we could swiftly announce that we were now in a position to suspend military action and were awaiting the arrival of an international force, the position would, of course, change at once.'[23]

The Agony of Decision

Sunday 4 November was a make-or-break day in the story of the Suez conflict. The British Cabinet had to decide between endorsing either the assault arranged for by Head in Cyprus or the advice to desist so urgently put by Dixon from New York.

One factor of which Eden had personal awareness that weekend was the intensity of the view taken on the infliction of civilian casualties in the current circumstances by the First Sea Lord. On Saturday (3 November), after the latest pessimism from Keightley about the likely scale of such casualties and the argument with General Templer, Admiral Mountbatten had hauled his Minister, Hailsham, back from the countryside to confront him 'in a fine state of excitement' with a draft letter proposing to resign because the honour of his Service was in danger of being compromised by what it was being required to do and the casualties that it would be called on to inflict.[24]

Hailsham had taken the robust line that, as a serving officer, Mountbatten could not just vacate his post 'at a time like this' and that the Navy's honour should be left in the hands of its political head. On 4 November Mountbatten redrafted his letter, acknowledging that his immediate resignation was not possible, for the first time disclosing to Hailsham that he had already written two days before to the Prime Minister and asking him after consulting Eden to 'give me an order to stay or go.' Hailsham replied on 5 November reaffirming his previous order to stay and his stand that, 'If anything happens to impair the honour of the Navy, I must resign.'[25]

On the Sunday there were two sessions of the Egypt Committee. At the first, which met at 12.30 p.m., Selwyn Lloyd discussed the two resolutions passed by the Assembly. The tactics were to back the implementation of the Canadian resolution as opposed to the Afro-Asian one. 'We should not defy the UN to the point at which they might feel compelled to sanction collective measures, including perhaps an economic boycott, against us.' But it was essential to occupy key points on the Canal 'if only as the advance guard of a UN force.' Lloyd believed that it was possible to get away with this rather surprising proposition provided that the Anglo-French landing took place without causing civilian casualties 'on a scale which would finally alienate opinion in the UN'.

In this connection Head brought back some good news. The Egyptians appeared to be withdrawing their forces towards Cairo, probably with the idea of safeguarding the seat of government until the UN force arrived. This might make it possible for Port Said to be occupied entirely by the paras, thus avoiding the necessity of a naval bombardment or a contested landing altogether. Should that not prove sufficient there would have to be air strikes along the length of the beach but without flying in towards the town and possibly a 'certain amount of naval bombardment on the fortified positions on the sea-front'; otherwise the landing would take longer and there would be greater risk of casualties among the troops. The commander should have discretion, but the Defence Minister was satisfied that it was understood that any bombardment would be the absolute minimum.[26]

At the second Egypt Committee meeting at 3.30 p.m. Lloyd reported on a despatch he had received from Sir Michael Wright in Baghdad. This was entirely in keeping with its predecessors. 'Today,' Wright announced dramatically, 'our contacts with Iraqis through the Administration who were previously our convinced friends have been closing down ... Almost all we have built up here over many years and with such pains has been shaken beyond repair.'[27]

There was also a letter from Hammarskjöld calling on Britain to end hostilities immediately and to reply in time for him to notify the other parties by 8 p.m. GMT. The Secretary-General had made it quite clear that, in his opinion, the inclusion of any British or French units would be quite unacceptable to the Assembly. This was a major blow to Eden's capacity for self-deception. During the course of the meeting, Pierson Dixon came through on the phone to Lloyd from New York. 'Unless I have your authority about a cease-fire', he told the Foreign Secretary, 'a sanctions resolution will be carried against Britain and France.' He made it clear that, in all probability, such a resolution would call for the withholding of oil supplies from them. On hearing this Harold Macmillan, who had been until now the foremost of the hawks, threw his hands up in the air, in one of those theatrical gestures to which he was partial, and said: 'Oil sanctions! That finishes it'. This was not a good augury for the battle to come.[28]

There then followed a debate in the committee on the fundamental question: were further military operations justified when both Israel and Egypt had agreed to a cease-fire? The discussion, as recorded in Cabinet Office Minutes, took what might be thought to be a rather peculiar course. A powerful case was made that, since the declared purpose of the Anglo-French intervention was to stop the fighting, it would look peculiar if it commenced after the fighting had stopped. The contrary arguments that prevailed seemed directed exclusively against the behaviour of Israel who appeared to have accepted a cease-fire but without agreeing to withdraw behind the armistice lines. Further, Israel had rejected the idea of an international force and, without some buffer inserted between Israel and Egypt, hostilities might well break out again. The moral seemed to be that Egyptians must be hit so that Israelis should be pushed back.

Hammarskjöld's bar on an Anglo-French component in the international force aroused the Egypt Committee's indignation. They thought it quite unauthorised in the Assembly's resolution. It could not be accepted. The Anglo-French forces should be landed in Egypt 'as advance elements of the international force or trustees on its behalf'. The backing of Menzies of Australia and Holland of New Zealand had both been mobilised behind the Canadian plan, on the ground that this was the way to reunite the Commonwealth. Eden and his colleagues were inclined to go for it but only in tandem with the Anglo-French landing.

However, if this was to be put forward as a proposition to the Secretary-General, some Ministers said, Britain and France should postpone the landing for twenty-four hours to give the UN an opportunity to reply. Someone suggested a compromise. Why not go ahead with the airborne landings due to take place at first light the next day and defer a decision about the sea-borne landings for the following day, until it was known whether the Egyptians would continue to resist? Against this, it was objected that there were military risks in leaving an airborne force without support for any length of time on Egyptian soil. Any delay, even of twenty-four hours, would make it politically more difficult to resume military operations. Eden decided that the full Cabinet should make the final decisions.[29]

The Sunday meeting of the Cabinet began at 6.30 p.m. Outside in Trafalgar Square a mass rally was taking place. A vast crowd demonstrating under the banner of 'Law, not War' was addressed by Aneurin Bevan. 'We are stronger than Egypt but there are other countries stronger than us. Are we prepared to accept for ourselves the logic we are applying to Egypt? If nations more powerful than ourselves accept this anarchistic attitude and launch bombs on London, what answer have we got?' He told the wildly applauding crowd, 'If Sir Anthony is sincere in what he says – and he may be – then he is too stupid to be Prime Minister . . .' Many people streamed down Whitehall and attempted to demonstrate in Downing Street. Mounted police charged the crowd in a manner which angered at least one of the journalists present.[30]

One man in the crowd (an off-duty soldier in mufti) has given this description of the scene: 'The star speaker was of course the great Welsh orator, Aneurin Bevan . . . Bevan's thin, squeaky voice echoed around the square (which was by then absolutely crammed with demonstrators) as he roundly condemned the assault on Egypt . . . (I clearly recall thinking at the time how strange it was that Bevan, whose speaking voice was so reedy and strained, had gained this reputation as one of the greatest orators of his generation) . . . As twilight fell and after Bevan had finished speaking a part of the enormous crowd began to mass together in the direction of Whitehall and to start chanting "Eden Must Go" in a determined effort to reach Downing Street . . . As we reached the entrance to Downing Street, we met a solid phalanx of police barring the way and, as the crowd jostled around in some confusion, a troop of mounted police came charging down Whitehall and rode directly into the demonstrators, scattering them far and wide up and down the pavements.'[31]

The noise penetrated the Cabinet room. Lloyd afterwards wrote: 'There was a steady hum of noise and then every few minutes a crescendo and an outburst of howling or booing.'[32] Against this background the final decisions were made. The Chiefs of Staff had given Keightley what was for him the highly disagreeable warning that 'although we hope otherwise, it may be essential to postpone tomorrow's operation for twenty-four hours'.[33] They asked him to say what was the latest time he must receive the decision. Keightley replied that it was physically possible to arrange a postponement up to 11 p.m. GMT, 'but consequences could be disastrous'. He listed five reasons: the weather was good now but likely to deteriorate; the morale and physical state of the troops; the enemy preparations were increasing daily and therefore every day's delay made a heavier bombardment by sea and air almost certainly necessary; the holding of the convoy in the open sea; and, finally, 'French command horrified'.[34] By the time that Keightley's reply was received the Cabinet had made its decision.

In the discussion, there was support for three different courses of action. One was that the British and French parachute landings should take place as already arranged but that the UN should be told that the allies would be willing to transfer responsibility at a later date to a UNEF which would have to include British and French detachments. The second was that the parachute landings should be suspended for twenty-four hours to give Egypt and Israel the chance to accept an Anglo-French force as the UN's advance guard. The third course would be to defer military action indefinitely on the ground that its object, the bringing of hostilities to an end, had been accomplished. At one point Eden went round the table, asking each Minister individually to make a choice. According to an additional record to which Rhodes James had access, the logic of the last course appealed to Salisbury, rather surprisingly perhaps, to Monckton, not surprisingly at all, and to Buchan-Hepburn, the Minister of Works; the twenty-four hours' postponement attracted Butler, the second ranking member of the Cabinet, Kilmuir the Lord Chancellor, and Heathcoat Amory (Agriculture) as well as a fourth unnamed Minister mentioned in the minutes, probably Macleod; the rest backed Eden in wanting the paratroops to go ahead and land at first light. All Ministers said that in the end they would support whichever view was in the majority except Monckton, whose name alone is therefore recorded in the official minutes.[35]

In *The Art of the Possible*, Butler says that he took the view that, were the news correct about the Israeli position, they could not possibly continue the expedition and that this argument was backed by Salisbury.[36] The apparent difference of recollection is probably accounted for by the fact that it was a long and exhaustive discussion, that some of the positions taken up, including Butler's, were conditional on confirmation of the Israeli position, and that there was an adjournment in the course of the meeting while guidance on that point was most urgently sought from Sir John Nicholls. The tension between personalities was caused not only by the appalling strain of the decision which had to be made, but also by the fact that, at the moment that the adjournment took place, Eden appeared to be opposed by at least two of his three most senior colleagues, Butler and Salisbury. He accordingly told these two and Macmillan that he would have to resign if it were decided not to go on. Butler commented that no one else could form a government; apparently Macmillan and Salisbury concurred.[37] The roars of the 'Law not War' crowd could be heard through the window. As Butler tells the story, Eden said at this point that he must go upstairs and consider his position. When Butler published this account, a number of those present including Eden agreed that they had no recollection of such an incident.[38] There is however independent confirmation that the Prime Minister did say that he was going upstairs; it is less clear for what purpose.[39]

The first message from Nicholls was little more than a holding statement and he cabled it *en clair*; it was received at 9.35 p.m. No reply, it said, had yet been sent to Hammarskjöld's communication. The Israelis found the communication obscure in several respects and their reply was still under consideration. The actual reason for the delay was the intense pressure that the Israelis were under from the French to withdraw or to qualify heavily Eban's pronouncement. But Nicholls went on: 'I think it likely that [the reply] will ask for clarifications, especially as regards the state of war and Egypt's readiness to negotiate a peace settlement. For your information some fighting is still going on and *fedayeen* are active'.[40] It was midnight before more precise information arrived from Nicholls. This was to the effect that before agreeing to a cease-fire Israel wanted to know whether Egypt still regarded herself as in a state of war with Israel; whether Egypt was prepared to start peace negotiations; whether the blockade and boycott would be terminated and the *fedayeen* gangs in neighbouring countries recalled.[41]

The Cabinet was able to conclude that a cease-fire had not been achieved and that the police action should go ahead. Both of the reasons given for undertaking military action against Egypt were violations committed by Israel: it was because Israel had neither accepted a UN force nor withdrawn from Egyptian territory that Ministers were recorded as agreeing that the 'initial phase' of the occupation of the Suez Canal should take place.[42] At the very last minute of the last hour the die had been cast. The police posse would set off to curb wrongdoing by Israel by effecting an opposed landing in Egypt.

24

The Empires Strike Back

Phase I: 5 November 1956

France and the world have their eyes on you . . . If necessary you will repeat the exploits of your forebears on Egyptian soil. Nor will you forget that Egypt was for a long while our friend. You will take pains, by your attitude and your conduct, to make known the grandeur and the humanity of our Fatherland.
General André Beaufre to his men on the eve of battle, 4 November 1956.

[W]ith the landings on Tuesday we had to go to it pretty hard and there was a hello bello of a shooting match all over the town all day.
General Sir Hugh Stockwell, letter, 17 November 1956.

At 7.15 a.m. (5.15 GMT, 0.15 in New York) on 5 November, 668 British paratroopers of 3 Parachute Battalion began dropping on Gamil airfield, on a narrow spit of land about 4 miles west of Port Said. After an anxious fly-in, because of obsolescent transport planes, the drop was executed with almost textbook precision, except for one man killed, another injured and two men dropped into the sea.[1] Fifteen minutes later 500 men of 2 Régiment Parachutistes Coloniaux, commanded by Colonel Pierre Château-Jobert (known universally as 'Conan') jumped from only 400 feet (well below regulation height) onto a very narrow dropping zone between Lake Manzala and the Canal to the south of Port Said at Raswa. Three months of preparation and of intense controversy and effort had, at last, produced a modest result, the presence of small Anglo-French forces on the soil of Egypt.

The British landing began fifteen minutes after the expiry of the extended deadline set by the Secretary-General of the UN for the complete cessation of all hostilities in accordance with the Assembly resolutions. And it came ten minutes before the UN General Assembly was to end another late-night session in which, by fifty-seven votes to none, with nineteen abstentions, it had created a United Nations Command with the mandate to recruit an international force with all conceivable speed to supervise the cessation of hostilities. The aim of the operation that was now being launched was no longer to bring down Nasser. It was to hold 'a gage' for the intense political bargaining that was to follow.

Abdul Hakim Amer and the Egyptian General Staff were still acting on the assumption that any Anglo-French landing must take place at Alexandria. Contrary to Nasser's wishes, high priority was not being given to the defence of the Canal Zone from which, as the allies had observed, military forces were pouring back towards Cairo. Separated at the Prime Minister's office from military headquarters, about half an hour's drive away towards the airport, President Nasser complained at being kept completely in the dark, despite his responsibilities and his military experience. It was agreed that two liaison officers would serve in his office. It was only from them that Nasser discovered on the evening of 3 November that Amer did not plan to organise a line of defence short of the west bank of the Rashid, the western of the two main branches of the Nile in the Delta. The water barrier should give the disorganised forces an opportunity to re-form.

Nasser objected that this meant that large parts of Cairo, including where they now were, were outside the defence perimeter. More fundamentally he was opposed to the apparent weakening of the Canal Zone. Amer's officers still maintained that, should the British and French attempt a landing, it would take place on the beaches to the west of Alexandria towards Mersa Matruh. Nasser disagreed: the wording of the ultimatum, with its mention of Port Said, Ismailia and Suez, was the clue. World public opinion would not permit the enemy to invade all Egypt to reach the Canal.[2]

As the news came in to him from the UN and from London, Nasser saw a battle for Port Said in psychological terms and acted accordingly. The normal garrison of two battalions of infantry reservists at Port Said was stiffened by a third; a couple of companies of regulars were sent in with orders to organise the population for partisan resistance. In addition there were 600 National Guards. The main fuel of the resistance arrived at the very last moment: on the evening of 4 November, four Russian SU-100 self-propelled guns arrived and the following morning, just before the allied paratroop drops, the small arms to be distributed among the people came in by train.[3]

Brigadier-General Salaheddin Moguy, the Chief of Staff, Eastern Command, who as the senior officer present was to be in nominal command of the defence of Port Said, arrived on an inspection trip on the evening of 4 November. Nasser himself, suffocated by the atmosphere at the Revolutionary Council Building in Cairo, oppressed by the thought that he had 'lost the State', and impatient to be again with troops, left Cairo just after midnight, accompanied by Boghdadi, to carry to Port Said his message of resistance. He did not inform Abdul Hakim Amer in advance of his intention to go, leaving him to be told in the morning. Boghdadi, drawing on a diary he kept at the time, portrays his leader in a melancholy mood as again and again they drove past the wreckage of vehicles and tanks on the road, where they had been strafed by the unopposed allied planes. Remarks like 'These are the remnants of a destroyed army', '£E 103 m down the drain', and, in English, 'I was defeated by my own army' escaped from him. Boghdadi watched Abdul Nasser, contrasting the way he looked with the times when he had been triumphant and had felt powerful. He felt, he writes, as if he were watching a broken man, though, when they arrived at Ismailia, Nasser's mood was improved by the high morale of its defenders. He was persuaded to go no further to avoid the dawn raids and the strafing of the Canal-side road into Port Said, and thus managed to escape being trapped by the French paras at Raswa. After a brief sleep he woke to news of the first landings, which seems oddly to have surprised him, and to Amer's urgent call for him to return at once to Cairo. To this he assented, though sounding troubled and confused about the apparent pointlessness of his trip.[4]

On the morning of 5 November the Israelis achieved their last and most coveted success, the capture of Sharm al-Sheikh. An attack the previous evening and another overnight assault on the town's defences by troops of 9 Brigade had both been repulsed. Dayan, getting desperate because of the need to be in possession of the Sharm at the moment of cease-fire, was urging Sharon's men on down the other coast. The Egyptians, superior in numbers, fought hard and only total Israeli air superiority, expressed in two days of strafing with rockets and napalm, enabled the daylight attack of 9 Brigade to succeed by 9.30 a.m., just in time for the paratroopers from 202 to arrive to find the battle already won.[5]

There was, thereafter, to be no more fighting in this war except that for which the self-constituted police force was responsible. On the outskirts of Port Said the paratroopers took their primary targets. At Gamil airfield many of them had come down within a few yards of the Egyptians defending the eastern edge. Sandy Cavenagh, one of the medical officers with the jump, wrote in his *Airborne to Suez*, 'Private Looker was involved straight away in hand-to-hand combat. As he neared the ground just off the airfield he watched an Egyptian shooting straight at him from below. The Egyptian had climbed out of his slit trench to get a better view. A late oscillation of Looker's parachute swung his container like a giant pendulum which knocked the Egyptian sprawling into the trench.'

The British paras cursed their equipment. Unlike their French allies they did not have sidearms that could be levelled instantly for action; theirs took thirty seconds longer to release from containers on landing. Cavenagh says that their Sten guns quickly jammed (as Sten guns frequently do, even without the aid of sand) and, as soon as they got access to the superior Egyptian weapons – Birettas, Schmeissers and Russian carbines – they thankfully replaced them. Their transport planes were so old-fashioned (in comparison to those used by the French and by the forces of five other countries) that the contents had to be made to match – old-model jeeps were specially conscripted and three clumsy wireless sets which so overloaded their 'chutes or their trailers that none of them landed in a usable condition. For the same reason more and more bundles had to be piled onto the backs of the fighting men. Loaded down with 320 lb of equipment – 40 lb above the maximum allowed – the men moved slowly about the airfield establishing their position and struggling for upwards of an hour to get the jeeps mobile.

Fifteen minutes after the drop the first air strikes went in from the 'cab rank' of British and French naval aircraft, whose pilots were poised ready to intervene against any source of defensive fire that was spotted.[6] They themselves were untroubled by opposition of any kind, an impression rather different from that supplied by the creative fiction writers of Cairo. 'The job of annihilating enemy forces at Gamil airport at Port Said has ended,' said Egyptian Communiqué No. 26 at 11.50. No. 27 at 2.30 p.m. said: 'The total number of aircraft show down this morning up to the issuing of this communiqué is fifteen'.[7] At the airfield the Egyptians, of about company strength, fought quite vigorously but were overcome within the hour. Twelve of the paras had been wounded by machine-gun or mortar fire, either in the air or on the ground.

The way of advance towards Port Said lay across 5,000 yards of ground to the beginning of Arab Town, the 'native quarter'. Flat sand and sand dunes gave way to very thick reeds, the marshes and ditches of a sewage farm, then a cemetery, coast guard barracks and, beyond that, the wooden shanty town. As with the southerly approach to Port Said this offered a narrow front – on average 500 yards in width – between sea and shallow lake. Like many others involved in the operation the paras complained afterwards of poor intelligence briefings about what opposition they might be likely to expect.

Without displaying great imagination or aggression, the Egyptians, with the aid of a couple of the Soviet self-propelled SU 100s, succeeded in making the invaders' progress sufficiently slow and uncomfortable for them to decide, by the time they had occupied the cemetery, that they had done enough for one day. Indeed they pulled back from the cemetery and settled down for the night in the sewage farm, in order to keep clear of the naval gunfire at dawn. The report on the operaton says: 'If there had been no seaborne attack to come the advance could undoubtedly have been continued, especially after the drop of the second lift at 1300 hours, which brought the mortars up to fifty rounds per gun. "C" Company could have carried out another attack and allowed "A" Company to pass through and seize the docks during the night.' But, the report says, since the sea-borne attack was coming anyway in the morning, they decided when darkness fell that there was no point in going on.[8] This is odd, since much of the point of Operation *Telescope* had been to make a contested sea-borne landing unnecessary. All the same, when later they heard of cease-fire talks, this must have reinforced their decision.

The airport would not take any plane above a Dakota but a Dakota containing Colonel Becq de Fouquières, the French Chief of Staff, landed there once the paras were in control and it is rather remarkable, considering the crucial importance of every hour of time, that this was not immediately followed up. The convoy from Malta was well ahead of timetable – the assault craft having managed an average of 8 knots, despite a head wind, instead of the 6.5 knots that had been estimated.[9] Consequently the Task Force Commanders were given the option of assaulting at dusk instead of waiting for the next morning. But this was considered too drastic an alteration, completely upsetting the fire support programme.

Admiral Power then intervened. He suggested that the helicopters that were mounted on the carriers *Ocean* and *Theseus* to demonstrate Mountbatten's controversial concept of 'vertical envelopment' be used to land the marine commandos at Gamil at once; with the paras they could take the entire harbour that afternoon.[10] That idea also failed to find favour. General Stockwell's main concern – and it was a genuine problem – was that, if the paratroops and commandos only partly completed the job, it would not in the morning be known precisely which of the naval gunfire areas they had already entered. The army's communications in 1956 were known to be unreliable. Still, this was a political operation in which speed was of the essence and the merits of avoiding an assault landing from the sea had been much stressed. The Egyptian resistance had forced the allied commanders to wait until the morning. That in itself was quite an achievement.

For a while, however, the French looked as if they would pull it off on 5 November.[11] The men of 2 Régiment Parachutistes Coloniaux who had dropped to the south of Port Said had as their task the capture of the two bridges at Raswa by which the causeway was linked to the town. The unit of the élite RAP (the French SAS) which dropped with them was to take over the waterworks which would enable them to shut off the complete water supply of Port Said. 'Even topographically the ground didn't seem very firm; water, humps and hollows everywhere,' wrote Pierre Leulliette, who took part in the drop. The French were instantly under fire. The water plant fell first, but the Canal Road bridge, which was only suitable for light traffic, was blown up as the paras approached it. But the really important bridge to the west – which carried the railway as well as the old 'Treaty Road' and was therefore strong enough when slightly reinforced to take Centurion tanks – was captured after a sharp battle. The paras found themselves outgunned, but they had air power on their side. 'Our fighters, hedge-hopping, machine-gunned every living thing ahead of us.'[12] A small contingent of British guardsmen and sappers who dropped with Colonel 'Conan' under Captain de Klee had another task: to reconnoitre the first stages of the road south towards Qantara and Ismailia. To their surprise they found it unmined for at least the first ten kilometres of its course.[13]

Two other French drops were made, a second at Raswa and then, in the afternoon, a drop into Port Fuad, the town on the opposite bank of the Canal to Port Said, where many of the French community of 1,600 lived, giving the place a recognisably Gallic appearance. The whole operation was co-ordinated from above by General Gilles, circling in an airborne command post. In an operation noteworthy for its weak communications, the only exception was when signals could be relayed through him.

It was obviously hoped that, when the Egyptians saw the invaders arriving from the sky, they would quickly surrender. In Port Fuad this was achieved overnight with the help of two local European residents, one British and one French. As a result the waterfront was in French hands at dawn and there was no need for an assault landing. But owing to the usual faulty signals, the ships were warned only just in time to stop that part of the support gunfire, while the ten-minute air strike against Port Fuad's coastal defence was only called off when the paras' tactical orders over radio/telephone happened to be overheard in the command ship.

But the story was not emulated in Port Said. The waterworks taken by Château-Jobert proved to have a functioning telephone; over it a meeting was arranged with the Egyptian commander. At 5 p.m. (3 p.m. GMT) Brigadier Butler, who had dropped with his men at Gamil and was the senior allied commander on the ground, helicoptered over to Raswa and, with Colonel Château-Jobert, received General Moguy and his staff. The encounter was cold and tense; no one sat down. The general asked that the water-supply be reconnected to the town and that the allies 'stop killing civilians'.

The French writer Henri Azeau is probably correct in saying that what Moguy was seeking was an informal truce of the kind that would make Port Said 'an open city', and that he preferred to deal only with the French. But it is difficult to see how any such concept could be reconciled with plans for making the port a bridgehead for large numbers of allied troops. Some of the French thought that, if it had been left to them, they could have finessed that problem, though General Jacques Massu, the Foreign Legion commander, afterwards held that Butler had been quite right to insist as he did on surrender in due and proper form. In that case, replied General Moguy, the terms for military and paramilitary forces – to lay down their arms and march out to Gamil airport – would have to be referred to Cairo. But he warned that insistence on an early answer would be likely to be treated as an ultimatum and as such would probably be rejected. A temporary cease-fire until 9.30 p.m. was agreed and later extended, at the British request, to 10.30. The British and French officers at first hoped and perhaps expected, despite unfavourable signs – Moguy's warning and some evidence that a 'political commissar' in the shape of an unprepossessing police officer was really calling the shots on the Egyptian side – that the 'temporary' would turn out to be permanent enough. The reference of the surrender terms to Cairo was thought to be a face-saving device on the part of the Egyptians, since the British flattered themselves that they had cut off all communications between Port Said and the outside world.[14]

Since Gilles was still aloft, Brigadier Butler got an initial message about the cease-fire through relatively quickly to Keightley and Barjot in Cyprus. But for a message to be quick does not guarantee that it is accurate and the message that reached the commanders gave them a greater impression of the chances of an unopposed landing than Butler could have intended. Worse, after that the flying command post was grounded, so that henceforth communications between *Tyne* and the shore were to be slow and doubtful.

Immediately it had been relayed to him in Cyprus, Keightley sent off the good news to London, realising that it would coincide with a parliamentary debate. Whitehall replied swiftly, the relief palpable: 'Your [signal] is splendid news. Our most sincere congratulations to you all. If surrender in Port Said is complete, your immediate and urgent aim should be to occupy Ismailia and Suez as quickly as possible and with minimum loss of life. If you consider this can best be done by direct approach to Governors of Ismailia and Suez, you have authority to go ahead. You should now cease all air bombing unless you receive special authority from us.'[15]

Stockwell and Beaufre began the planning work for an unopposed landing and a French parachute drop at Qantara, the exit from the causeway. The drive down the line of the Canal to Ismailia and beyond would begin in the dawn.[16]

Parliamentary Diversions

Regardless of wars, the British parliamentary calendar follows its predestined course. On 5 November the session was to be prorogued, thus cutting off the day's business at 5 p.m. The mood began building up even before Question Time as Tony Benn from the Labour benches presented a petition to the Commons, which he had read out by the Clerk. Since this petition was concerned with praising the principles of the United Nations in terms that implicitly condemned the policies of the Government, such remarks as '*Pravda!*' were soon being shouted across the House. The quick-talking Labour solicitor Lionel Hale objected to the Speaker: 'These people with their fingers drenched in blood have no right to come here and howl down the Clerk of the House and abuse the processes of the House.' The mood thus set was further heightened when Emrys Hughes asked Lloyd if he was aware of the widespread statements in the American press that he had misled the American Ambassador. 'Is he aware', he demanded, 'that we expect to be misled here, but does not he think that misleading the American Ambassador is going rather far?'

In a statement, Selwyn Lloyd read out the Anglo-French reply to the UN resolutions. It warmly welcomed the Canadian idea of an international force but noted that neither Egypt nor Israel had yet accepted it. Meanwhile some sort of international force was needed here and now 'to secure the speedy withdrawal of Israeli forces' – a form of reasoning that went down extremely badly in Israel – as well as to remove obstructions and to restore traffic through the Suez Canal. The two governments promised to stop all military action as soon as the Israelis and the Egyptians had accepted the UN Emergency Force (UNEF) and the UN had endorsed a plan for it. They thus relinquished control over their own military timetable though the assumption of the UN's tardiness was so ingrained that they may have thought that this would not do much harm. But, finally, they expressed 'their firm conviction that their action is justified'. They called for an early Security Council meeting at ministerial level to work out an international settlement in the Middle East which would endure, with the means to enforce it. Thus, at the very moment when the paras were first coming to grips with the Egyptians, Britain and France were putting forward a bid to elevate the issue to the highest ground.

Lloyd explained that this reply was already on its way to New York when it crossed news of the United Nations Command and the appointment of General Burns to head it. The Foreign Secretary had rather an awkward moment when, to cries of 'Shame', he had to explain why Dixon had abstained on this resolution. 'We have told the UN that we believe it is necessary to secure the speedy withdrawal of Israeli forces,' Lloyd said. 'But we cannot ensure that the Israelis withdraw from Egyptian territory until we are physically in the area to keep the peace, to give the necessary guarantees and to prevent a repetition of the events of the past few years.'

First, Tony Benn and, then, Aneurin Bevan rose and demanded whether the Foreign Secretary had authorised a broadcast on *Voice of Britain* from Cyprus at 5.45 a.m. on 4 November. They had got hold of the text of part of Brigadier Bernard Fergusson's output and they quoted from it, to great effect. 'We have the might and we shall use it to the limit if you do not give in ... It means that we are obliged to bomb you wherever you are ... You have committed a sin, that is you have placed confidence in Abdul Nasser and believed his lies. Now you are hearing the truth.' This was not, strictly speaking, neutral, peacekeeping stuff.

Lloyd was obviously thrown off his stride by this unanticipated line of questioning. 'In my respectful submission', said 'Nye' Bevan in his light Welsh lilt, 'we have here not a military action to separate Israeli and Egyptian troops; we have a declaration of war against the Egyptian Government in the most brutal terms ... Will the Government stop lying to the House of Commons?' Lloyd, hard pressed, answered only that the test was what had actually happened – which was that the Supreme Commander (*sic*) had been ordered to avoid civilian casualties. Pressed further, he was in the process of agreeing to consider publishing a White Paper setting out British pronouncements to the Egyptian people when the Prime Minister leapt up with some wonderful news. He had had a *FLASH* signal from General Keightley: 'Governor and Military Commander, Port Said, now discussing surrender terms with Brigadier Butler. Cease-fire ordered.'[17]

There was an immense release of emotion. Leaping up and down, waving their order papers, the triumphant Tories expressed in that moment immense pride in their leader, all the more so because many of them had at different stages of the crisis and for different reasons entertained doubts about him. The Opposition appeared at last to have been wrongfooted.[18] It seemed as though Anthony Eden, through keeping his nerve, had pulled it off after all. He summoned his Chiefs of Staff, led by Dickson, to Number Ten. Rushing forward and giving the diminutive Dickson a warm personal embrace he exclaimed: 'Oh my dear Chiefs, how grateful I am to you! You have been magnificent! It's all worked out perfectly!'[19]

Lieutenant Peter Mayo of the Royal Marines, a National Service officer who kept a diary, heard the same news over the BBC as he sat expectantly facing his first experience of war. 'Eight hours to go till H-hour and we have just heard that the Egyptian Commander-in-Chief [*sic*] has asked for an armistice to discuss surrender terms ... I can't help admitting I am very disappointed. It's a dreadful anti-climax for all concerned, though, I suppose, for the sake of humanity one should be pleased. It is certainly a tremendous triumph for Sir Anthony Eden.'[20]

A Ban on Bombing

In New York that morning (5 November) Pierson Dixon and de Guiringaud were being received by Hammarskjöld at 2.30 a.m. (7.30 GMT, 9.30 in Cairo). He seemed to be beside himself at what he termed the impudence of the Israeli reply to the Assembly's requirement of a cease-fire. It was a reply which, it will be recalled, incorporated a number of questions involving major controversies of long standing, the raising of which would be unlikely to contribute to an instant cease-fire. For that reason its content had been a great relief in London and Paris. Hammarskjöld described this document as 'an open insult to the UN'. He declared that it was impossible to do diplomatic business with such people and that he was sending an appropriately sarcastic reply.

On the other hand, the Anglo-French reply interested him, especially the proposal for a Security Council meeting at ministerial level to deal with the major issues. But, from now on, any international force would have to be a UN one; under a UN commander, subject to the Secretary-General. The pattern of the UN Command adopted in Korea would never work again. Hammarskjöld told Dixon and de Guirangaud that a dictated solution was now the only possible thing in the Middle East, 'particularly in the light of the Israelis' total defiance of the UN and disregard of diplomatic proprieties'.

The Secretary-General thought, mistakenly as it turned out, that it would be impossible for UNEF to take over directly from an Anglo-French force: the UN could never condone what it had virtually condemned. Therefore, everything would be far worse once the British and French were on Egyptian soil. Moreover, he could not see how they were going to force the Israelis, who were in no mood to negotiate or listen to reason, to withdraw.[21]

Dixon had not been gone long after this relatively cordial exchange when he got a phone call from Hammarskjöld to say that the UN's Colonel Ely had now reported that bombing of built-up areas in Cairo itself and Heliopolis was actually taking place. In fact, the targets were military – the main railway line 500 metres north-east of Cairo Central Station, Almaza military airport and the area of Abbassiah barracks. But the timing of these attacks was singularly unfortunate. They appeared to contradict declared British policy and so confirmed Hammarskjöld in the view that the UN could only intervene physically to restore peace once those who had first disturbed it and then refused the UN demand for the cessation of hostilities had been declared morally in the wrong. Dixon morosely predicted that, at the next Assembly session, delegates would be in a very ugly mood and 'out for our blood'. Specifically, the Afro-Asians and the Soviet bloc might rush through a resolution urging 'collective measures of some kind' against Britain and France. He recalled bitterly the telegrams in which he had urged that, 'unless we could announce that Anglo-French forces were suspending all further military activities, there would be no chance of our being able to move towards our objectives without alienating the whole world'. He went on: 'I must again repeat this warning with renewed emphasis. I do not see how we can carry much conviction in our protests against the Russian bombing of Budapest if we are ourselves bombing Cairo.'[22]

This last cable, whose tone of desperation was not unrelated to the fact that both Security Council and Emergency General Assembly were due to meet later that day, reached the Foreign Office at 9 p.m. (4 p.m. New York, 11 p.m. Middle East). Eden had already told Ivor Pink, Assistant Under-Secretary in charge of the UN Department, to contact Dixon by phone to obtain his assessment of the chances of the Anglo-French proposals being taken seriously. The answer came that those chances were nil and that the only measure that at this stage might possibly halt sanctions was an official statement that there would be no further bombing at all of targets in populated areas and within a short space of time no bombing whatsoever.

Eden then decided that, for the sake of getting troops ashore on the morrow, he must make this concession which, should there turn out to be serious Egyptian resistance, would in all probability prove to be a serious impediment to further operations. Knowing the cautious temperaments of Generals Keightley and Stockwell, Eden must have realised what yet another military limitation at this stage would do to the prospect of getting a lightning advance. As Bernard Fergusson wrote afterwards, the Services could cope with red lights and green but did not take well to perpetual flashings of amber. Thus the inevitability of an early cease-fire may already have been in the Prime Minister's mind.

During the afternoon in New York Dixon, who must have received authority from Eden by telephone, delivered a letter to Hammarskjöld. This contributed a culminating item to the cumulative optimism of the progress report which the Secretary-General inserted in advance of the published agenda at the Security Council's 8 p.m. session. Egypt had accepted a cease-fire without conditions, whereupon Israel had 'clarified' her earlier (unsatisfactory) reply and accepted likewise. The UN Command had been established by the Assembly; on the morrow (6 November) Hammarskjöld would be ready to present his plan for an international force. Then, to cap it all, there was the note from the British Representative which stated that 'orders have been given that all bombing should cease forthwith throughout Egypt'.

Arkady Sobolev, for the Soviet Union, did not hesitate to spoil the mood of euphoria by pointing out that the Secretary-General had omitted to read the next sentence in Dixon's note immediately after the one quoted. This said, 'Any other form of air action as opposed to bombing will be confined to the support of any necessary operation in the Canal area.' What 'other forms'?, he demanded. Parachute drops? Ground attack with rocket missiles? But the United States was prepared to co-operate with Britain and France to the extent of defeating 'inscription' (and hence immediate debate) of a Soviet item concerning the non-compliance with Assembly resolutions of three named aggressors, Britain, France and Israel. The Security Council, and shortly afterwards the General Assembly, adjourned for the night.

The Troops Prepare

Shortly after the decision about bombing was made in London, they knew at Port Said that there would be bloodshed on the morrow. Although the British thought they had cut all telephone lines out of Port Said, there was in fact still an underwater cable to which General Moguy had access. Boghdadi says that at the Revolutionary Council Building, to which Nasser had now returned, they heard that the British paratroop commander had asked for someone with whom to negotiate the surrender of Port Said. Nasser's reaction, he says, was that the British commander should be peremptorily told to give himself up with all his troops.[23] The President seems (perhaps unjustly) to have formed an indelibly unfavourable impression of Moguy from this report since he afterwards retired him prematurely from the army.

It is still uncertain what were the real motives of this old-fashioned Egyptian officer with his military bearing and correct English, who seemed to the allied officers who met him to be only imperfectly in charge. Sir Charles Keightley, in his published despatch, claimed that the surrender terms had been agreed and that the Egyptian troops had laid down their arms, which was not so. Then, he said, Cairo had ordered the fight to go on. Moguy himself, commenting in September 1957 on Keightley's despatch, claimed never to have relayed the allied terms to Cairo, regarding the talks and the cease-fire as a mere ruse on his own part to take the pressure off the population, to have the water reconnected (which was done), and to provide time for a universal distribution of firearms.[24]

At 10.30 p.m. (8.30 GMT, 3.30 in New York) fighting was resumed, the Egyptians having conveyed the rejection of the terms for cease-fire. In the hours beforehand masses of brand-new Czech rifles and machine-guns taken from their crates in the warehouses, often with the grease still on them, had been distributed freely throughout the town to civilians of whatever age from lorries and from piles dumped in the streets. Loudspeaker vans had toured Port Said, demonstrating again that in psychological war the allies were out-classed. It was claimed that World War Three had started, Russian help was on the way, London and Paris had been bombed. This was said by the allies to be all the work of the Russian consul, Anatoly Tchikov. But there was no evidence that the Egyptians had not thought it up for themselves. Afterwards Egyptian Communists in the Port Said area were to build on these myths of Soviet support during Egypt's hour of need and, to Nasser's displeasure, since he knew how slight was their substance, sought to use them to entrench their own position.[25] At the time however, Nasser's circle put the signals from Moscow to use to place salt under the tails of the Americans. According to a CIA cable (only partially declassified) Ali Sabri passed the word that he at least had been convinced by Moscow and the Russian Embassy that the Soviets were 'prepared to go all the way, risking a Third World War'. This was used as spice for the repeated and urgent request for the direct intervention of the Sixth Fleet. A still expurgated section of the cable refers to 'ominous information received from Egyptian Embassy, Moscow'.[26]

At midnight, 5/6 November (10 p.m. GMT) Keightley sent an emergency signal from Cyprus to his Land Force Commander, General Stockwell, on *Tyne*. '1. Hard Luck. 2. Grateful if you can give me the form so that I can handle political pressure. PM gave out in the House tonight that a cease-fire had taken place, so he will be reluctant to agree full-scale attack starting again. 3. I presume you have thought of all ways you can avoid the planned frontal assault such as landing behind the parachute battalion.'[27]

Stockwell was not about to change his entire plan yet once more. Under extreme pressure from London, Keightley issued precise instructions that supporting fire was to be confined strictly to 'known enemy defences and to those which engage our assault'. Orders like these, designed to capture Port Said without killing any of its inhabitants, made life difficult for junior officers at the end of the line, men like Douglas Clark, the author of *Suez Touchdown: A Soldier's Tale*. At the last minute they had received the order 'No gun of greater calibre than 4.5 inches will be fired.' This eliminated all cruisers from the bombardment programme and the whole task-table had to be worked out afresh. Then, overnight on 5/6 November, when they were studying the revised target list a further order – 'No bombardment' – came through. Various commanding officers sent off signals of protest against their men being expected to land unprotected on a defended beach. The nice distinction was remembered between a naval bombardment, which was not permitted, and naval gunfire support, which was not forbidden. While this was going on most other soldiers snatched what sleep they could get before the dawn.[28]

Moscow Finds Its Voice

Meanwhile a new element – or, rather, an old element up till now unusually muted – had in the early hours of 6 November returned with vigour to the scene. Moscow had been suspiciously silent through most of the past week, utterly absorbed no doubt in dealing a cruel and lethal blow at the neutral Hungary of the coalition under Imre Nagy. Now that Khrushchev and Bulganin had put their decision about Budapest into execution they felt free to address the parties to the Suez crisis with some highly moral advice. Purged of the fatal association with events in Central Europe, the series of letters sent by Marshal Bulganin on 5 November to Eden, Mollet, Ben-Gurion and Eisenhower might have amounted to an effective assertion of superpower authority.

Conceding to Eden that 'we understand your special interest in the Canal', the Soviet Premier denied the right of Britain and France to assume the role of judges in the matter of securing free navigation through it. 'There is no justification for the fact that the armed forces of Britain and France, two Great Powers that are permanent members of the Security Council, have attacked a country which only recently acquired national independence and which does not possess adequate means for self-defence. In what situation would Britain find herself if she were attacked by stronger states, possessing all types of modern destructive weapons? ... Were rocket weapons used against Britain and France you would, most probably, call this a barbarous action. But how does the inhuman attack launched by the armed forces of Britain and France against a practically defenceless Egypt differ from this?' Bulganin's message ended by summoning Parliament, the Labour Party and the trade unions to intervene and stop the bloodshed, and by informing Eden that he had invited the United States to use her naval and air forces jointly with other UN members to end the war in Egypt. 'We are fully determined to crush the aggressors by the use of force and to restore peace in the East.'

A similar self-righteousness informed the other letters. The letter to Mollet included the additional reproach that he headed a socialist government. 'During our meeting in Moscow last May you said that socialist ideals inspired you in all your work. But what has Socialism in common with the predatory armed attack on Egypt which is an open colonial war?'

In writing to Ben-Gurion Bulganin opened, for the first and only time in the history of the Soviet Union's relations (or, later, absence of relations) with Israel, the question of the state's existence. Its birth had been cherished by the Soviet Union: it had been identified as 'a peace-loving nation' and 'an instrument against imperialism'. The time was long past in the short history of the state when the Soviet Union could be labelled pro-Israel. But Ben-Gurion took extremely badly the reproach that, 'fulfilling the will of others, acting on instructions from abroad', the Government of Israel had betrayed the cause of anti-colonialism. 'It is', said Bulganin, 'sowing a hatred for the State of Israel among the peoples of the East such as cannot but make itself felt with regard to the future of Israel and which puts in jeopardy the very existence of Israel as a state.'[29]

Ben-Gurion was shaken by this tirade. 'The despatch with which Bulganin honoured me', he wrote in his diary, 'if his name had not been on it, I could have thought that it had been written by Hitler ... It worries me because Soviet arms are flowing into Syria and we must presume that the arms are accompanied by "volunteers".'[30]

After this epistolary effort, Bulganin came to the fellow-superpower to seek the recognition that all Russians thought they deserved from the United States as an equal arbiter of the world and more especially in a region that, in their perspective, was adjoining their own. On the one hand there was the spectacle of British, French and Israeli aggression, on the other the Soviet Union and the United States, both 'Great Powers possessing all types of weapon, including atomic and hydrogen weapons'. Consequently, 'we two bear a special responsibility for stopping the war and restoring peace and tranquillity in the area of the Near and Middle East'. The United States had a strong navy in the Mediterranean; the Soviet Union had both a strong navy and powerful air force. 'The joint and immediate use of these means by the United States and the Soviet Union, on a decision by the United Nations, would be a reliable guarantee for ending aggression.' Eisenhower was asked for immediate negotiations so that action could 'begin within the next few hours'.[31]

The President, on the very eve of his second-term election, made public his response, since Bulganin's letter had already been issued to the press in Moscow. 'Ike's' tone was harshly hostile: Bulganin's letter was 'an obvious attempt to divert world attention from the Hungarian tragedy'. Eisenhower dismissed the idea of the two of them joining forces to stop the fighting as an 'unthinkable suggestion'. It was to be regretted that the Soviet delegate had not voted in favour of UNEF (he had abstained along with Britain, France and Israel). The UN had decided that there should be no other forces in the area. Eisenhower personally strengthened the text prepared for him by the State Department by inserting at this point, 'The introduction of new forces under these circumstances would violate the UN Charter and it would be the duty of all UN members, including the US, to oppose any such effort.' Only when the Russians had conformed with the resolution on Hungary would it be seemly for them to suggest further steps towards world peace.[32] The Russians had left themselves wide open to this rebuke.

Thus Eisenhower had seized the chance of demonstrating that, despite everything, the United States would, where it counted, not let down her friends. He told Hoover and Allen Dulles on the morning of Election Day, 6 November, that 'if the Soviets attack the French and British directly, we would be in war and we would be justified in taking military action even if Congress were not in session'. Allen Dulles showed him the evidence from intelligence that the Russians had promised the Egyptians to 'do something'. He promptly ordered the U-2s into action over Syria and Israel (but not over the Soviet Union). If these flights disclosed Soviet air forces on Syrian bases, Eisenhower thought 'there would be reason for the British and French to destroy them'. But though he was not prepared to let his views on the weakness of the merits of his allies' action affect his determination not to allow the Soviet Union a strategic triumph, at the same time the apparent prospect of superpower confrontation did sharpen his will not to be manipulated by those allies.[33]

At one in the morning of 6 November, when the news from Moscow reached him, Eden was, to all appearances, not greatly affected by Bulganin's huffing and puffing.[34] Britain was herself a nuclear power and had access to American as well as her own intelligence estimates of Soviet nuclear capacity.[35] She would not at that date have considered that Bulganin's implied nuclear threat against Britain was a very real one, but some of Eden's advisers were not unaffected by the urgent tone of the cable from Sir William Hayter, the Ambassador to Moscow. 'Though there is an element of bullying bluff in this intolerable message', he said, 'I am afraid there is no doubt that the Soviet Government are working themselves up into a very ugly mood.' Hayter thought that the proposal for joint action with the US might have been intended to clear the ground for 'independent violent action against our forces'. To him it seemed to point to the fatal consequences of Britain being out of step with the US. Only clear and early proof that this was no longer so would 'stop these people from committing dangerous acts of folly'.[36]

There was no panic but members of the Cabinet were being shown ahead of their meeting that morning the consequences of being engaged in a public row with the Americans. At 5.30 in the morning of 6 November the Chiefs of Staff sent a *FLASH* signal to Keightley: 'You should know that Russia has just indicated readiness to intervene with force in the Middle East. United States has warned Russia that any attempt to use Russian forces in the Middle East would encounter American opposition.'[37]

At two o'clock in the morning Douglas Dillon, the American Ambassador in Paris, was woken and asked to go immediately to the Hotel Matignon. There, Guy Mollet, surrounded by most of his Cabinet, had tapes of the *Tass* summary of the Bulganin letter rather than the Note itself. The reference to rockets was even more unvarnished. Dillon's impression was that 'everybody was scared to death'. Mollet appeared to be under the misapprehension that French paratroopers had already advanced to the outskirts of Ismailia and might be at the Red Sea port of Suez in twelve hours.

What Mollet wanted to know from Dillon was what the Americans were going to do if France, which unlike Britain was not then a nuclear power, were attacked by Soviet rockets. The Ambassador replied at once: 'There's no doubt that it would be a violation of the Nato Treaty. I'm sure we'd be at your side.' When Mollet wanted to get instant confirmation of this from Washington, Dillon pointed out there would be no one there: it was, or would be in a few hours, Election Day in the United States. French Ministers said that they were prepared to discuss an early cease-fire provided that it should clearly be under American sponsorship so as to make plain that there had been no yielding to Soviet pressure. Less realism attached to Mollet's declared intention to call for free elections in Egypt.

Eden telephoned while Dillon was still in Mollet's office. He told the French Prime Minister that he would only be able to carry on until the next morning, 7 November. Mollet sent a telegram to change Eden's mind but he remarked to Dillon: 'If the British have decided, there's nothing we can do. They're in command and we shall have to stop.' But he added, misled by the fog of war about the position on the Canal, 'By ten o'clock tomorrow we might even have the whole thing.'[38]

The Service Attachés at the American Embassy in Moscow were working out an estimate of Soviet capacity to intervene in the Middle East fighting which was conveyed in a cable from Chip Bohlen, the Ambassador, who considered that the Bulganin messages had come as close to an ultimatum as possible without so stating', and that they made it very hard for the Russians to do nothing if the fighting continued. The attachés suggested the possibility of clandestine movement of volunteers by air or by submarine, open naval escort of transports containing volunteers or supplies, use of Adriatic-based submarine action disguised as Egyptian against Anglo-French forces, open Soviet naval visits to Egyptian ports, and the movement of bombers and fighters to or through Syrian bases.[39] Some of these had been foreseen as possibilities by the allies. Before the landings the Naval Task Force had been distinctly jumpy about submarines until told by the Ministry of Defence to disregard the threat. Reports of Soviet overflights of Turkey presumed to be *en route* for Syria were flashed around the Nato network. Although later they were held to have been a false alarm – and deliberate disinformation by the CIA – they contributed a particularly nerve-tingling feature to the other strains of Invasion Day.[40]

25

The Empires Strike Back

Phase II: 6 November 1956

The moment to which this entire story has been building up was approaching. More than the parachute drops, the sea-borne landing was the decisive gesture, the action which sceptics, a mounting breed during the leaden six-day approach march, had determined would not occur. Peter Mayo noted that, as he made his way down to the tank space, 'there was a wonderful dark red streaky dawn coming up'. At ten to six the guns opened up, firing at targets at the foot of the breakwater and along the beaches of Port Said. A series of loud bangs showed where the RAF were bombing the beaches, where there was a long row of huts. 'Soon many of the beach huts were blazing. At one moment there was a huge explosion and fire ball some way inland which was a large petroleum installation going up. It was to go on burning for three days.'[1]

Suddenly at 6.15 a.m., as Douglas Clark describes it, 'the shelling stopped as if cut off by a guillotine'. This enabled fighter planes to strafe the beach from left to right during the dangerous last two minutes of 40 and 42 Royal Marine Commandos' approach to shore in their amphibious 'Buffaloes' (Landing Vehicles Tracked) which had been launched into the sea from their landing ships. As each plane completed two runs, the Buffaloes made their last hundred yards to the beach. 'The wooden beach huts', says Clark, 'were burning fiercely in a broad curtain of fire across our path.'[2] They burned the more fiercely in that large quantities of ammunition from abandoned defensive positions were continually exploding.

The commandos got across the beach with only nominal opposition but then came under small arms fire from the buildings along the sea front. An SU 100 opened fire on one of the destroyers, which replied with a shell that set the whole shanty town area alight and burnt it to the ground.[3] Peter Mayo's commandos occupied three houses which were their first objective. 'Almost immediately several Wogs appeared running down the street immediately in front of us. They had rifles but no uniform and must have been Home Guard. Whatever they were, Soggers shot four of them with his bren gun ... [A] few minutes later another in a blue suit suddenly appeared from somewhere underneath our house and started running up the street. People said he had a pistol in his hand but I didn't see whether he had or not; but he hadn't taken more than a dozen crouching steps before five or six shots tore into him and, as he fell, he half twisted to look up where the fire came from, with a look of furious surprise on his face. He fell out of sight under a bush. I felt slightly sick. We weren't supposed to be shooting at civilians but it was very difficult to tell, as most of the people we met were civilians with rifles.'[4]

Supported by a squadron of tanks from 6 Royal Tank Regiment which had been deposited on the beaches to the west of Port Said by Landing Craft Tank (LCTs), 42 Commando were under orders to get through the town as fast as possible to seal off the southern exits. They set off in their lightly armoured landing vehicles down streets with tall houses on either side through 'a continual boil of fire'. 'We kept shooting all the time, half the time not at anyone in particular ... How we escaped more casualties I shall never know. I suppose the Wogs must have been very bad shots and, as we found throughout the day, practically without organisation.' Still, one of Mayo's companions was killed by his side and another hit. He himself got two superficial wounds. In the area of the Governorate an air strike was needed in order to keep up the pace. Some streets had to be cleared house by house and even room by room. General Keightley reported that, 'Failure to observe the normal street fighting drill and the wish of all ranks to get through Port Said as quickly as possible led in some cases to avoidable casualties to our own troops'.[5]

Some of the Egyptians with rifles had indeed had no military training whatsoever. 'My brother was out in the street holding a rifle in his hand for the first time in his life,' one young man subsequently told *Al Ahram*. 'He believed that the rifle was a big thing with which he could destroy any force facing him ... He stood in the middle of the street, rifle in hand ... The tank kept approaching nearer and nearer until the tank was as close as a single step. He then fired his rifle believing that he will hit the tank, but before hearing the sound of his shot my brother was a heap of flesh underneath the tank.'

By the original plans the area the British marines drove through was to have been softened by naval bombardment but that had been cancelled because of the tremendous emphasis on avoiding Egyptian casualties. By 9.30 a.m., 42 Commando had reached its objective and was taking up positions in the area of the gas works and the site of the old golf course to the south of the town. Egyptian infantry, apparently gathering for a counter-attack, were dispersed by another air strike.

The French paras, meanwhile, at Raswa were guarding their positions to the south of the town, 'waiting for the English' who arrived late through getting their tanks bogged down on the golf course. These Frenchmen were tough, ruthless professionals and they had had a tense night, 'completely alone, facing an entire town swarming with soldiers', Pierre Leulliette says.

In the dawn they noticed a dozen fishermen near some barges. 'Hands in the air, yelling something or other in their own language, they were trying to prove that they weren't soldiers ... "No unnecessary prisoners! They're a nuisance and a waste of food!" A voice in the hearts of my comrades was whispering: "Kill! Kill!" ... We emptied our magazines. The fishermen fell into the water, one by one!' These were not gentle policemen.[6]

40 Marine Commando was by no means having an easy time clearing the quay alongside the harbour in order to free the port facilities for use by the expedition. The Egyptians were difficult to dislodge from the Customs' Warehouse and held out at the Navy House and in the warehouses behind it until just before dusk when aircraft demolished that former symbol of British pre-eminence and power. 45 Commando was landed by helicopter not far from the de Lesseps statue, thus finally managing to bring off the 'first' that had been planned, and then worked methodically through streets that had been fought through but not cleared. This was not accomplished without one of those accidents that seem to be inevitable in military actions. Because the ship-based Joint Fire Support Committee worked off a large-scale map to give orders to planes using a twenty-times smaller scale one, the commanding officer of 45 Commando, his intelligence officer and fourteen other Marines were made casualties of a British attack.

Among the early prisoners to be brought in was General Moguy, which prompted the idea, based on the unsound assumption that he could command obedience on the Egyptian side, that it might now be possible to get his acceptance of the unconditional surrender of Port Said. Count Vicente Mareri, the energetic and resourceful Italian Consul, after turning his consulate into a refugee centre for the European population, was devoting himself to the negotiation of a cease-fire. With astonishing imprudence, all three Task Force Commanders, General Stockwell, Admiral Durnford-Slater and Air Marshal Barnett, together with General Beaufre and their planners travelled ashore from the command ships in their smartest uniforms on the same naval motor launch – in order, Keightley explained to the Chiefs of Staff, 'to insist on a firm surrender this time!'

The launch, with its high-ranking cargo, headed for the flamboyantly orientalist building which the Canal Company had erected for its offices and which, as it happened, was still in Egyptian hands. From the building they were greeted by a hail of bullets. A spent round landed at Stockwell's feet after glancing off his thigh. 'I don't think they are quite ready to receive us yet,' said Admiral Durnford-Slater.[7]

The commanders landed at a safer spot and, after some wandering around, were directed to the Italian consulate. The confusion was considerable. The place was overflowing with refugees and now with staff officers. The generals seem uncertain about whom they found there. In his despatch published in *The London Gazette*, General Keightley (who was not himself there) writes briskly, 'The Egyptian Commander, however, failed to come to the rendezvous,' and in his *Sunday Telegraph* article Sir Hugh Stockwell says that, 'After hanging about for some time for someone to turn up, we abandoned the idea.' But in his operational report Stockwell refers to 'the captured Egyptian Brigadier (often asleep)'. By this he seems to have meant a senior officer other than Moguy, although Beaufre describes in some detail how, after clambering over the bodies of the refugees, they eventually found a room where a man whom he certainly thought was General Moguy and whom he inaccurately describes as 'the Governor' was slumped in a chair. Whoever he was, he was exhausted, alone and out of touch.[8]

Macmillan's Reserves Depart

The British Cabinet met at 9.45 a.m. (11.45 a.m. in Port Said), on the second day of the land battle. Its outcome and duration lay in the hands of the British politicians. Harold Macmillan had been frantically telephoning the United States during the night. The sterling area's currency reserves were haemorrhaging as dealers hastened to get out of the currency of a country which was so manifestly isolated on the international scene. There had been heavy selling in New York; it seemed to Macmillan that the Federal Reserve Board was doing far more than was needed to protect the value of its other holdings although in fact there is little concrete evidence for this. Britain's reserves had fallen in September by £20.3 million ($57 million) and in October by £30 million ($84 million). According to his official biographer the Chancellor now told his Cabinet colleagues that another £100 million ($280 million or one-eighth of the total reserve) had run out in the first week of November. The awful prospect, which the Chancellor had spoken of ten days before, of devaluation and the death of the sterling area now loomed up before his eyes with a terrible immediacy. The curious thing is that there is no documentary evidence of his Treasury officials addressing him in such stark and inescapable terms over 5–6 November. The correct figure for sterling losses in the first week was £31.7 million ($85 million). But that night Macmillan felt sure that he was staring ruin in the face.

In the normal way, Britain would have expected immediate help from the United States, a temporary loan or American co-operation in raising funds swiftly from the International Monetary Fund by way of repayment of the British quota. Neither was available now. Macmillan saw Selwyn Lloyd before the Cabinet meeting opened and disclosed the extent of the flight from sterling. According to Lloyd, Macmillan told him that 'in view of the financial and economic pressures, we must stop'.[9] Considering the role he had played so far, his talk of 'all or nothing', of 'selling Britain's last securities', of 'dying in the last ditch', this was a sensational loss of nerve.

Tuesday, 6 November being the day for the Queen's Speech at the opening of the new session of Parliament, the Cabinet met beforehand in the Prime Minister's room in the Commons. Selwyn Lloyd explained the position. To the messages that had been received during the night from Hammarskjöld announcing that both Israel and Egypt had accepted an unconditional cease-fire and enquiring whether Britain and France accepted the Assembly resolution setting up a United Nations Command as meeting their condition for a cease-fire, it was now necessary to decide an answer. Lloyd said that Britain urgently required to regain the initiative and to enlist maximum sympathy and support from the American Government. At the same time, after Bulganin's letter, Britain must contrive a reply to Hammarskjöld that should not give the impression of yielding in the face of Soviet threats.

Some members of the Cabinet, particularly Head and James Stuart, the Secretary for Scotland, argued that if the allies accepted a cease-fire, having occupied only Port Said and not either Ismailia or Suez, they would be seen to have fallen short of their declared objective. Moreover, they would not then be in a position to undertake the huge job of unblocking the Canal. If they had to wait for this until UNEF had been established, free transit would not be restored for months. During the meeting Macmillan received definite confirmation that George Humphrey, the US Secretary of the Treasury, was obstructing Britain's efforts to draw from the IMF enough to protect sterling from speculation against it. In Lloyd's opinion this greatly enhanced the vigour with which the Chancellor now pressed for a cease-fire. This, in turn, wore away at the now desperately overtired Prime Minister who saw Butler and Salisbury, his other highest-ranking colleagues, presenting arguments to the same effect.[10]

The threat of Soviet intervention in the Middle East (as opposed to rocket attacks on Britain) counted with some Ministers. A possible Soviet invasion of Syria or even a direct attack on the Anglo-French forces in the Canal area were spoken of as real possibilities, should allied military action go any further. Other dangers mentioned were UN oil sanctions and the intervention of other Arab states. But, more fundamentally, the Cabinet was the victim of its own scenario; self-respect required that Britain at least try to act consistently with her story. Israel and Egypt had stopped fighting; the Secretary-General of the UN was raising an international force; the ostensible reason for the landing was no more.

As the clock approached 11 a.m., the hour at which all should process to the House of Lords to hear the Queen's Speech for the new Session of Parliament, Ministers decided that, subject to agreement with the French, the allies should cease fire that day. At the same time, Hammarskjöld should be told that the clearing of the Suez Canal of the numerous Egyptian blockages was in no sense to count as a military operation and that the technicians accompanying the Anglo-French force would begin this work without delay.

As soon as he was released from the ceremony in the House of Lords, Eden telephoned Mollet. As chance would have it, the climax of the Suez conflict coincided with one of the last stages in the negotiation of the European Economic Community. Konrad Adenauer, the Chancellor of West Germany, and Heinrich von Brentano, his Foreign Minister, had come to Paris to settle two of the major points still outstanding. The purpose of their visit was to overrule their own experts and to agree, for political reasons, that equal pay for men and women (which was the law in France) should be made the rule throughout the Community and to accept that there should be extra props for the French trading system to help it through the scary period of transition.

While the experts worked on the Common Market the leaders discussed what was to be made of the bevy of Russian notes. Adenauer had no doubt. Brushing aside the demurrers of his Foreign Minister, he expressed his profound mistrust of American policy, which he described as two-faced. He was convinced that Bulganin's call for joint superpower intervention could only be read against the background of two and a half years of direct exchanges between the White House and the Kremlin, by-passing the Department of State. With their new strategic concepts of mutual nuclear deterrence, the Americans were beginning to think that there was no one else in the world except themselves and the Russians. The old Chancellor insisted that the European states including Britain must be united against the United States and, once the presidential elections were over, require the Americans to say what they wanted.

The old man was getting increasingly animated. Mollet had put in that surely if Britain and France were attacked the Americans could not afford to do nothing or they would lose all that they had built up. To Brentano's obvious discomfiture, Adenauer was implacable. If Americans were not themselves attacked, would they have the nerve to start an atomic war? They had never known war themselves. For every one combatant in their army there were thirty if not fifty non-combatants. For the time being, American public opinion was all that was standing in the way of an American partition of the world with the Soviet Union. This was not comforting for Mollet to hear on that day of all others.

'Read Bulganin's letter [to Eisenhower] again,' said Adenauer. '. . . Bulganin would not have written it if he had not thought there was a chance of its acceptance.' At this moment the Suez war blew into the conference chamber. First Pineau, then Mollet had to leave to take the call from Anthony Eden. There is no written record available of the conversation between the two Prime Ministers. Pineau, who was listening on an extension, later gave an account, but one quotes it with a certain caution not only because in general Pineau's memory is sometimes demonstratively fallible but because in this particular case there are some features (not quoted here) that suggest a muddle with a later conversation. But the flavour sounds right. 'Anthony Eden said: "I don't think we can go on. The pressure on sterling is becoming unbearable. The English can take a lot of things, but I do not think they would be willing to accept the failure of sterling which would have considerable consequences for the Commonwealth. And the pressure is getting worse from day to day." '

Eden then declared that the British Cabinet wanted a cease-fire within a few hours. 'Guy Mollet said: "That's very quick. Could we not wait two or three days? In those two or three days we could gain some advantages. We could occupy more of the Canal which would put us in a better negotiating position when the final say of settlement comes." "No," said Anthony Eden, "I cannot hold out any longer."[11] "Try to", said Mollet. Then Eden indicated that Britain was letting the Americans know the nature of her reply.'

Mollet, who was keen to gain for his troops even a few hours of time, made the Adenauer visit an excuse to put off a meeting of the French Council of Ministers until the late afternoon. When the conversation with Eden ended, the old Chancellor said, 'France and England will never be powers comparable to the United States and the Soviet Union. Nor Germany, either. There remains to them only one way of playing a decisive role in the world; that is to unite to make Europe. England is not ripe for it but the affair of Suez will help to prepare her spirits for it. We have no time to waste: Europe will be your revenge.'[12]

The British Cabinet had made the decisive move because, at this late moment, after British troops had been committed and blood had been shed, the bulk of its members did not share their leader's nerve. Right from the beginning, when the Canal Company was seized, Eden had rejected the idea of basing policy on international law in the sense in which international lawyers were currently interpreting the impact of the UN Charter, because this did violence to his notion of equity. He recalled that this was not how Eisenhower and Dulles had behaved two years before in a matter concerning Guatemala, and he held passionately that Suez was every bit as important to Britain, both substantively and symbolically, as Central America was to the United States.

But Britain has Cabinet and not presidential government. These distinctions are tested in extreme cases. Throughout the three-month build-up of the crisis Eden had played an absolutely determining role. He dominated those around him, according to his Chairman of the Chiefs of Staff, to a greater extent even than Churchill in time of war, and he had taken on the detailed direction of every move in the game.[13] Yet when it came to the making of the final decisions he could not go or felt he could not go against the voices of his Cabinet. Seniority counts on occasions such as this:

when Butler, Macmillan and Salisbury were against going on in defiance of the United States, the Commonwealth and the United Nations, Eden felt he could do no more.

According to the Chief of the Imperial General Staff, General Sir Gerald Templer, who saw much of Eden during those last days, 'Once the operation was launched it became quickly apparent that his health would collapse unless the matter could be brought to an early solution ... But during such a time of intense stress and strain, a time when he was faced with what turned out to be an undefeatable alliance standing arm-to-arm against him (our American ally, Russia and India, all voting against us, Her Majesty's Opposition and a large part of the British press), he could hope to expect loyalty and support from his Cabinet colleagues. Did he get it at that moment? The answer of course is that he did not ...' Templer, a genuine admirer of Eden's, saw the scene in unrelieved black-and-white. 'I will never forget the last act of the Grecian tragedy,' he wrote. 'The Prime Minister in his bed at 10, Downing Street, his wife sitting on the bed holding his hand. Who else was there? The four Chiefs of Staff. Not a Minister. A broken man.'[14]

But despite this there is some reason to believe that, at the time, Eden was not thinking in so negative a way. He comforted himself with the reflection, as did Selwyn Lloyd, that he had perhaps done enough, that Britain and France had a 'gage' in Port Said. Eden would very much have preferred to have taken the whole Canal, and later told his party backbenchers that the main reason he could not do so was that Keightley, having tasted the strength of Egyptian resistance, had told him that it would take six days. Lloyd said that, for himself, he could not see much difference between a piece of it and all of it. But they both hoped and expected that, once they had been compelled to stop short of their objectives by the near-unanimity of world opinion, the United States would rapidly realign herself with her European allies in order to take full advantage of the leverage gained to promote those policies that they had in common.

It was the later American failure to meet this expectation more than the pressure over the cease-fire which so embittered Anthony Eden that, three years later, Selwyn Lloyd, commenting to Sir Norman Brook on the first draft of Eden's memoirs, could deplore 'the strong anti-American bias throughout'. Some criticisms made of American policy, Lloyd said, were legitimate but 'the legitimate ones lose force because there is such strong persistent prejudice running through the book'.[15]

Cease Fire

At 11.03 a.m. (1.03 p.m. in Port Said), immediately after the Cabinet meeting, the following signal was sent to Keightley: 'It may be essential politically to have an immediate cease-fire and to stand fast. Could you maintain the force at present ashore indefinitely from present positions assuming maintenance through Port Said?' Nearly two hours later, nothing having been heard, came the pressing request: 'Is answer "Yes" or "No"? Please reply plain soonest.' 'The answer', signalled Keightley, 'is Yes. Present forward positions midway between Port Said and Qantara.' At 1.30 p.m. (3.30 in Port Said), there was another *FLASH* signal from London. It told the Commander-in-Chief that, on receipt of the codeword STOP, he was to prepare for a cease-fire at 5 p.m. GMT (7 p.m. in Port Said) and not to reopen fire unless attacked. No forward movement from positions reached on land could afterwards be made.[16] Evidently Eden's intention was to bring all firing to a halt by the time (6 p.m.) that he expected to rise in the House of Commons in the first day's debate on the Address.

At that time in London there was no realisation of the tenacity of some parts of the Egyptian resistance, particularly to 40 Commando in the area round the Navy House, which in turn was helping to delay the landing of other forces. Eden had arranged for Winthrop Aldrich to come to his room at the Palace of Westminster at noon to show him the draft reply to Hammarskjöld accepting the UN cease-fire. He was 'extremely anxious' that the message should reach Eisenhower immediately (on Election Day, be it noted), and said that, if the President wished to telephone him about it he would be available at any time. In the last sentence of the Cabinet's draft a blank had been left where the timing of the cease-fire was to be stated. Eden was careful to say that this last sentence would be included and the blank filled in 'only if the military events of today justify its inclusion'. But he added that 'everything was going extremely well'.[17]

When, on account of French delays, Keightley was told that the cease-fire time was now likely to be later, the Commander-in-Chief, who with his villainous signals was not seriously in touch, was most relieved. He reported from Cyprus that he had no further news of the patrol moving south down the line of the Canal. He had given orders to hasten the speed of its advance. 'Any delay in cease-fire an advantage to enable us to clear up Port Said and push on further'.[18]

Having gained himself a few hours, Guy Mollet confronted his Ministers. He gave them an account of the reasons why Eden had called for an end to the operation, somewhat overstating, according to Pineau, the Soviet factor and playing down American pressure. He did not conceal the awkwardness of ending the operation leaving Nasser sitting in power and the Israelis held up ten miles short of the Canal. The eventual negotiations would unquestionably be easier if the allies had the whole Canal as a gage. Nevertheless, Mollet stood for Franco-British solidarity and this now demanded an immediate cease-fire. Bourgès-Maunoury, the Minister of Defence, was opposed. The landing had succeeded, the French troops had started advancing along the Canal and had no need of the British to continue the advance. In a few days they could get to Suez. Even though the Cairo part of the operation was abandoned, the French could then have something tangible to negotiate with.

The Ministers began discussing the operation to date, in particular what took the allies so long. Bourgès threw the blame onto General Keightley and asked whether he had not sabotaged the operation. At this point Mollet cut short this part of the discussion. Time pressed. They were not there to allot blame but to make a decision one way or the other. The Minister Resident in Algeria, Robert Lacoste, declared that a cease-fire would seem to millions of Arabs to spell victory for Nasser and hence a boost to the Algerian rebellion against France. A third Minister spoke with great fire of the need, regardless of risk, of exploiting their military advantage. Pineau favoured fudging the issue to gain more time but considered two days or just possibly three to be the utmost they could get. He says he failed to get a definite answer, Yes or No, out of Bourgès-Maunoury on whether this would be sufficient.

Despite such arguments to the contrary, the weight of the discussion supported Mollet's judgement. President Coty, who was in the chair, summed up in favour of a cease-fire but emphasised that the allies should stay in Port Said until the final settlement of the Canal problem was secured.[19] Mollet telephoned Eden in that sense.

Almost immediately after returning to the White House after voting at his private home in Pennsylvania, Eisenhower responded to Eden's invitation to call him at any time. Using the brand-new submarine cable, he caught the Prime Minister at 5.55 p.m. GMT just as he was about to go into the Commons. 'First of all,' said the President, 'I can't tell you how pleased we are that you found it possible to accept the cease-fire, having landed.' Eden replied calmly: 'We have taken a certain risk, but I think it is justified.' Eisenhower, clearly worried at the insistence on Franco-British conduct of salvage operations in the Canal in the British Note to the UN, quickly put in that he favoured accepting the resolution without any conditions and then afterwards talking about clearing the Canal. 'I don't want to give Egypt an opportunity to begin to quibble so that this thing can be drawn out for a week . . . I would like to see none of the great nations in [UNEF]. I am afraid the Red boy is going to demand the lion's share. I would rather make it "no troops from the Big Five". I would say: "Mr Hammarksjöld, we trust you. When we see you coming in with enough troops to take over, we go out . . .".'[20]

Eden said, before enquiring about the American election, 'If I survive here tonight, I will call you tomorrow.' The remark was evidently no casual one. He makes it clear in his memoirs that he was very doubtful as to what the parliamentary and the popular reaction to news of a cease-fire would be, particularly among the Conservative Party. 'The country had made up its mind that we were right to start, they would not be so easy to convince that we were right to stop.' On the other hand, the political danger threatening him in the immediate future was the opposite one: that if there were not an immediate cease-fire, Conservative members opposed to his Suez policy might contribute to an Opposition victory.

The announcement that Eden was to make would remove that immediate threat. In a curious passage in his memoirs he is anxious to defend his motives. 'If I had been playing politics, nothing would have suited me better than a defeat in the House of Commons at this juncture. I had no doubt that failure to assert international authority would result in a sharp deterioration in the Middle East within the next year or two until intervention became inevitable again. That would be the moment for me and those who shared my views. But I was not playing politics and I expected to stay in office until that moment came.'[21] Evidently he had become so addicted to the cyclical view of politics that he thought, however fleetingly, of his career repeating the same pattern as in the late thirties.

The Prime Minister entered the House immediately after speaking to the President. He was calm and self-possessed. He began at 6.04 p.m. (1.04 p.m., in New York, 8.04 p.m. in Port Said) by reading out the reply that was being sent to Hammarskjöld. If the Secretary-General were able to confirm that Egypt and Israel had accepted an unconditional cease-fire and that the international force would be competent to secure the aims of the General Assembly resolution (which included prompt withdrawal of all forces behind the armistice lines) Britain would agree to stop further military operations. There was a massive shout of approval from the Opposition benches. The clearing of the obstructions, he went on, was a matter of great urgency, for which the Franco-British force was specially equipped and ready to begin at once. Pending confirmation from the UN, Britain was ordering her forces to cease fire at midnight (Port Said time: 2 a.m.) that night. The House broke into cheering not only from Opposition members, who saw their own stand for the United Nations vindicated, but from many, though certainly not all, Government supporters. Such had been the tension in the House, building up for so long, that a great surge of relief was felt that such a divisive and emotionally charged war was over. Some MPs felt grimly and rather melodramatically that the scene resembled the acclaim given in the House to Neville Chamberlain when he came back from Munich.

Eden was artful enough to continue his account with the full text of his long answer to Bulganin, which resented the talk of Britain's 'barbaric actions' and rubbed the Russian's face in the Hungarian horrors. He then gave a sanitised version of the military operations at Port Said (partially justified by the misleading cables he had received from Cyprus), according to which the Egyptian 'Governor', having agreed completely to the allies' terms the previous day, suddenly informed them that he must resume hostilities. As the result of this, Eden said, the landing had taken place; it 'was virtually unopposed and no preliminary bombardment of any kind was ordered'. Anglo-French troops had then proceeded to clear Port Said of 'scattered opposition'. A very different impression was conveyed by a cable that was not sent by Keightley until a couple of hours later. It began: 'The main feature of the land operations is that the Egyptians have shown no sign of giving up the struggle easily.'

The last part of the Prime Minister's speech, although excited MPs were not in a mood to listen to it with much attention, was in some ways the most interesting. It formulated the essence of Eden's case, his version of why the apparent puzzles and contradictions of Middle East policy added up to a consistent and hopeful theme. He first answered the question: If the object was to get Israeli troops back, why was Britain attacking Egypt? The answer was that Israeli troops would not go back to the armistice line unless there was a force in between the belligerents, so that Israel would no longer fear attack by Egypt. It was because Israeli troops were within striking distance of the Canal that the Canal offered the only line on which a neutral force could be interposed. And the Israelis had indeed not got any nearer than the ten-mile limit. 'I do not think that anybody who has followed the military story of recent days can have the least doubt that had the Israeli forces so wished they could have gone very much further forward than they in effect did.' In other words, though it may not have felt like it to an Egyptian in Port Said, Britain had saved Egypt from the Israelis and had done it in a way that made it most unlikely that the Israelis would renew the attack.

Secondly, Eden was able to claim that British and French action had limited the scope of the conflict. He asked if any Member would have thought it possible when hostilities had broken out that the other Arab countries, all of them, would not have become immediately involved in the war.

Thirdly, he insisted that a return to the system which had continued to produce deadlock and chaos in the Middle East was 'now not only undesirable but impossible'. Eden had seen himself as the man who would bring order out of chaos in that region as he had done in Western Europe and, for the time being, in South-East Asia. He had confidence in his judgment and still thought that, despite the alarming extent to which he had been misunderstood and was now unsupported on major matters by his Cabinet, he could win through to what he termed 'a real settlement of the problems of the Middle East'. But that would only happen if the lesson were learnt that moral force alone in support of the UN was not enough. As the result of the Anglo-French action, it looked as though the UN might have been jolted into being 'more ready to employ force adequate to the duties it has to discharge'.[22]

This was the thesis and, thirty-five years of deadlock and chaos later, it does not sound an ignoble one.

Yet what kind of real settlement did Eden have in mind? A settlement like that visualised in the Guildhall speech of November 1955 could scarcely have been imposed on an Israel that had been incited to 'a real act of war' and had then won it so demonstratively. And the kind of UN force Eden had in mind would surely have required Security Council endorsement, that is Soviet approval as well as America's. But, above all, what was fatal to Eden's statesmanship was the absence of an essential link to reality – the failure of a man known for his 'anemone-like' sensitivity to atmospherics to understand that his credibility, something he had spent a lifetime creating, had been instantly destroyed throughout the world. Perhaps he had some insight of the truth. Eden's future biographer, Robert Rhodes James, who was then a junior clerk in the House of Commons, looked down on him when he made this speech from a seat in the Gallery immediately opposite him. 'Suddenly,' he recalls, 'he looked aged and ill, defeated and broken'. Rhodes James adds: 'I thought Eden looked strangely alone. I did not, of course, then know how alone he really was.'[23]

When Eden sat down in the House, the fighting still had five and a half hours to go. The first signal suggesting the possibility of a cease-fire reached Keightley and Barjot at luncheon in Cyprus. It caused dismay and, on the part of Barjot, frantic activity. His aim was to organise parachute drops immediately on Ismailia and perhaps also on Suez. Somehow the still uncertain deadline of a cease-fire must be beaten and control be asserted over the Canal. Jacques Baeyens remembers his British colleague Ralph Murray saying that it seemed to him now to be impossible to overthrow Nasser and, since that was so, what was the point of occupying Ismailia? Baeyens thought that nevertheless it would represent a serious threat to the Egyptian ruler provided he had domestic enemies. This was the view that was evidently held by Eden. 'Military dictators have more enemies at home than the foreigner ever dreams,' he wrote afterwards. 'It may be that even the Soviet entry into the lists would not have sufficed to save the regime in Cairo, humiliated by defeat and lacking the *Voice of Egypt* [*sic*] to call disaster victory.'[24] Would perhaps Colonel Siyyam have been able to move decisively if Stockwell had reached the town of Suez?

General Gilles had paratroops on Tymbou airfield poised to go. A French staff planner produced three emergency plans to match the desperation of the hour. Under the first scenario, Israelis, who were after all only ten miles from the Canal, would be asked to put on French uniforms and take the Canal. Under the second, the French would be landed by parachute behind the Israeli lines and from these points they would take the Canal. Under the third the Israelis would be asked to seize both banks of the Canal and, the next day, the allied policemen would take over from them. Despite the strong Israeli sense of gratitude to the French, which had caused Ben-Gurion to go back once on his acceptance of a cease-fire to the UN, it would have been unlikely that he would have done it again and at such short notice. In any case Keightley and Murray turned such ideas down.[25]

On *Tyne*, the sixteen transmitting and twenty-two receiving lines were proving much less than was needed for three commanders to control events.[26] Overnight there had been quite long periods of radio breakdown between Keightley in Cyprus and the ship; further delays occurred because of shortage of trained signals staff. *Tyne* and *Gustave Zédé*, the French command ship, were in turn not in close touch with their generals, Stockwell and Beaufre, for most of the day. Having gone ashore they were without adequate communication links. After the fiasco of the supposed cease-fire negotiation at the Italian consulate neither general had returned to his command-post afloat, Beaufre moving eventually to Port Fuad, while Stockwell saw to the overcoming of the last points of resistance in Port Said and issued orders for the morrow's break-out to the south. Neither was in effective command of the battle and neither was aware that a cease-fire was in prospect.

Later, when the matter of how far the allied advance party had got by 2 a.m. began to seem crucial, the question arose of whether, making better use of the resources at their command, the British and French could have pressed ahead with greater speed, leaving Port Said behind them. If everyone had been equally seized of the critical importance, for political reasons, of every hour, they could certainly have entered Qantara, and even by exceptional measures reached Ismailia. Stockwell, if only because of the failure of his rear link radio, gave the impression of being far from fully in control. The French, who had little to do in Port Fuad or were still waiting in Cyprus, felt that they could have been better used; and the British 2 Para, which had not been dropped but disembarked with difficulty on the wharf from a Hook-to-Harwich ferry could have been helicoptered across Port Said to exploit more swiftly Captain de Klee's surprising news that the route down the causeway was unimpeded.

It is a mistake to see this question only or even mainly in a Franco-British context. Beaufre states in his account that it was General Jacques Massu, due to take command of the column moving south along the Canal (with Brigadier Butler in charge of the advance guard), who preferred to wait until the following morning before setting out. Stung by what was to a French para the ultimate reproach of being responsible for being late, Massu, in his book *Vérité sur Suez 1956*, strikes back testily at Beaufre's performance during the day and at his inaccessibility at critical junctures.[27]

Towards the end of the afternoon, at a time when Cyprus already knew there would be no tomorrow, Stockwell was assembling his order group to plan the action for 7 November. There would be a morning para drop at

Qantara and an afternoon one at Ismailia. It was by now after dark in Egypt; Stockwell and Beaufre had to find their ways back to their respective ships. *Tyne* and *Gustave-Zédé* turned out not to be where they had last seen them, having been ordered to disperse in view of the threat of Soviet intervention. Helicopters did not then fly at night; so Stockwell was obliged to take to sea in a small landing craft. In a television interview twenty years later he vividly described the scene.

'It was pitch dark; and shooting, smoke, all the noises of battle were going on, and we set off. The coxswain said: "There's a break in the breakwater about here, Sir" . . . I said: "OK by me." And of course, when we got out there, there was a force-six sea running and the thing was going up and down and the sea coming in and one thing and another – and one of the engines went and I think some of the steering gear. Anyhow, we were adrift and couldn't possibly come back in again, didn't know the way in and all the sea was breaking over the breakwaters. No radio contact, nothing. We were just adrift. I said to the coxswain, "How long will it float?" He said: "About twenty minutes, Sir." "Oh," I said, "Christmas!" Luckily we saw a green standard light way up there and we edged up underneath that and a searchlight came down on us and a megaphone said: "Who's that? This is *Tyne*." It was our headquarters ship moving berth and we were picked up and hauled on board.' The Task Force Commander had been adrift about an hour and a half. In his book Beaufre tells of a rather similar experience. It was an extraordinarily haphazard way for both senior commanders to regain touch with their command posts in the middle of battle.

As Stockwell scrambled on board his Chief of Staff appeared holding an urgent signal. Incredulously he read the order to cease fire 'at midnight' (that is, 2 a.m. local time; the military were working to GMT). The news was very unexpected. 'I mean, after all we were in the full flush of battle. To stop short of victory was the last thing that entered my head. It never occurred to me, it's rather like blowing up a balloon and then putting a pin in it.' Sir Hugh comforted himself. 'I had learnt this lesson when I was dropped from the Marlborough XI on the morning of our match against Rugby at Lord's: there is always something else ahead.'

Putting aside his stiff whisky, Stockwell set himself to rush out fresh orders as fast as his defective communications would permit.[28] Brigadier Butler was told to rush paras and tanks as far down the Canal as they could get by the hour of the cease-fire. 6 RTR, whose tanks had gone farthest, had received orders to stop at Al Tina, ten miles to the south of Port Said, till the morning. The tanks were bedded down for the night, with their crews asleep on the engine decks, when fresh instructions at last got through to the commanding officer. There were just one and three quarter hours left. He decided to wait for the men of 2 Para who, unprovided with their own transport, had set out on foot from Port Said but were picked up on the way by a random collection of Coca Cola wagons, cattle truck and furniture vans that had been commandeered by the enterprising Major Anthony Farrar-Hockley. When Butler's men were ready to start moving together down the causeway from Al Tina, they had only forty-five minutes to go. Their best hope was to get to Qantara, where they could leave the causeway behind and take up proper tactical positions; at a minimum they must make the Canal station at Al Cap. They did not make either. They had a couple of breakdowns and at 2 a.m. (with their military watches showing midnight) they were still out in the open desert of the causeway. Butler ordered them to press on and, at twenty minutes past the deadline, they moved into Al Cap. (Those journalists who were with them were sworn to secrecy about the twenty minutes and did not let them down.) They dug in and waited, 'in disconsolate frustration'.[29] The lights of Qantara could be seen four miles away, mocking them. The military battle of Suez was over.

26

Picking up the Pieces

There are only two Great Powers in the world today, the United States and the Soviet Union ... The ultimatum put Britain and France in their right place, as Powers neither big nor strong ... It was the lesson of a lifetime for Britain and France.
Anwar Sadat, *Al Gumhouriya*, 19 November 1956.

Israel's attitude will inevitably lead to most serious measures such as the termination of all US governmental and private aid, UN sanctions and eventual expulsion from the UN. I speak with the utmost seriousness and gravity.
Herbert Hoover Jr, Acting US Secretary of State, to Abba Eban, Ambassador of Israel, 7 November 1956.

People found various ways of hailing Suez as a victory. First off the mark was the Israeli Prime Minister. In his speech before the Knesset on 7 November, David Ben-Gurion was in an exalted mood of antiquarian triumphalism. Israel's maritime commerce began in the Red Sea 3,000 years ago, in the reign of King Solomon, when Eilat was the first Hebrew port, he proclaimed; 1,400 years ago, an independent Hebrew state had existed on the island of Yotwat, which, the day before yesterday, had been 'liberated' by the Israeli Defence Forces. 'Because this matter is of such great importance', he said, 'I quote the words of Procopius in the original. Several modern historians who gathered their information from second- or third-hand sources distorted this important evidence.' Now Israelis held the island and the place opposite, which 'until two days ago was called Sharm al-Sheikh and whose name is now Mifratz Shlomo'.

Having settled his account with the centuries, Ben-Gurion came to the Sinai campaign, the thought of which sent him soaring to new heights of hyperbole and biblical reference. 'This was the greatest and most glorious military operation in the annals of our people and one of the most remarkable operations in world history ... The great booty which fell into our hands proves beyond any doubt that the Egyptian dictator had squeezed the last penny out of the starving masses of the Egyptian people for the purpose of providing the army, on which his rule and power depends, with abundant supplies and luxurious living. But all their modern arms and equipment were of no avail to the Egyptian soldiers because there was no spirit in them, and the words of the prophet Isaiah were fulfilled: "In that day shall Egypt tremble and be afraid and fear because of the shaking of the hands of the Lord of Hosts which he shaketh over it." '

What was the result of all this shaking? The speaker was in no doubt. 'The Armistice Agreement with Egypt is dead and buried and will never be resurrected.' It had been signed with the intention of its leading to permanent peace; Egypt had shown that that intention was not shared. Consequently, 'the armistice lines between us and Egypt have vanished and are dead', though Israel would respect the armistice agreements with other states so long as they reciprocated. Israel would negotiate peace with Egypt or any other Arab state, and would not go to war with them unless attacked. To the UN he gave his sternest warning: 'Israel does not agree in any circumstances that a foreign force – whatever its name may be – shall be stationed in its territory or in one of those territories which Israel now occupies.'[1]

This was defiance of the world. And the world took it badly. Overnight, on 6/7 November, it had become apparent that Dwight Eisenhower had won re-election to a second term by an overwhelming majority of ten million votes (almost double the margin of 1952) and that, as he had risen, so his party had fallen. The Opposition Democrats had won control of both Houses of Congress. But Eisenhower felt himself to be in supreme command. He sent off a message to Ben-Gurion about reports that Israel had no intention of withdrawing. 'I must say frankly, Mr Prime Minister, that the US views these reports, if true, with deep concern.' Any such decision could not but bring about the condemnation of Israel as a violator by the UN. It would be a matter of regret if Israeli policy should impair friendly American-Israeli relations.[2]

Abba Eban, the Israeli Ambassador both to Washington and the UN, dreaded the likely consequences of his Prime Minister's euphoria. Disinformation was circulating in Paris – originating, apparently, in the CIA – that the Soviet Union intended to 'flatten' Israel on 8 November. The French forwarded these reports straight away to the Israelis. Hoover mentioned in the White House a rumour that the Soviets had offered the Egyptians 250,000 'volunteers'. There were the supposed overflights of Turkey. Lester Pearson told Eban that whatever sympathy for Israel had existed in the UN and elsewhere had been unaccountably thrown away by Ben-Gurion.[3] On the night of 7 November, the vote in the Assembly for immediate withdrawal was sixty-five to one (Israel), with Britain and France only abstaining. The Israelis noted that, whereas Dillon had reassured Mollet that a Soviet missile attack on France or Britain would attract American retaliation, no such assurance was made to Israel. Instead, Hoover had sent for Eban's Washington deputy and told him: 'Israel's attitude will inevitably lead to most serious measures such as the termination of all US governmental and private aid, UN sanctions and eventual expulsion from the UN. I speak with the utmost seriousness and gravity'.[4]

'Eban, all terrified, called,' wrote Ben-Gurion in his diary. 'His cables also sow fear and horror.' The Americans were threatening to sever all ties and possibly have Israel expelled from the UN. 'Apparently, the fear of Russia has fallen on them.' Ben-Gurion asked Eban whether an immediate meeting with Eisenhower was possible, if necessary in secret. The Ambassador, who was aware of the American President's 'punitive' frame of mind, at once ruled out the possibility. The Israeli Cabinet met twice on 8 November, the second session going on from 5 p.m. till shortly before midnight, with some ministerial contributions referring to 'a second holocaust'. In the end the essential decision was left to Ben-Gurion. He was ready to face up to the necessity of changing course where staying in Sinai was concerned. The only choice that remained to him was between instant withdrawal or footdragging in the hope of being able to extract conditions on the way. He gave that choice back to Eban, on the grounds that the risk of losing American sympathies was the essential variable. After a series of taut phone calls to key Americans, Eban chose the second course.

Two texts for Ben-Gurion's radio address had been prepared to fit either answer. Although he was able to deliver the less humiliating one he sounded 'weary and dejected'. However many stages it took her, Israel was going to have to leave Sinai.[5]

This occasion is often cited as the one instance of the effective use of American pressure to change Israeli policy. (There had been a previous, less publicised occasion in 1954, also involving Eisenhower, when economic aid was cut off to prevent the Israelis diverting the waters of the Jordan at Gesher B'not Ya'acov.) Each American President since has been regularly called on in vain by Arabs and sometimes also by Europeans to emulate Eisenhower in this respect. It is worth remembering that in November 1956 two special circumstances prevailed: Eisenhower had just been handed a massive popular mandate, and Israel had been at the receiving end of peremptory pressure from not one but two Superpowers. 'Just as the US and Russian conjunction of policy led to the creation of the State, so on this occasion their conjunction led to our decision to withdraw.' Such was the view of one close adviser of Ben-Gurion. Another put it rather more apocalyptically: 'There was a genuine fear of world war that day. The conflict had escalated beyond the Middle East. The chasm of the unknown had opened for Israeli leaders. They shrank from the abyss.'[6]

UNEF

In London Sir Anthony Eden was also polishing his illusions. 'The President telephoned on his own account. There is no doubt at all that the friendship between us all is restored and even strengthened,' he rejoiced in a cable sent to Guy Mollet at 9.20 on the evening of 6 November. 'I feel that, as a result of all our efforts, we have laid bare the reality of Soviet plans in the Middle East and are physically holding a position which can be decisive for the future ... I am sure history will justify us.'[7] Yet Eisenhower had followed up his Election Day call by spelling out some of his requirements in a cable. Not for the first time the cordiality stood in the way of precise communication. The message, says Eden in *Full Circle*, 'contained some indications of the direction of American thinking which I was perhaps slow to recognise'.[8]

When Eisenhower told Eden that the Big Five should be ruled out from contributing to UNEF, the Prime Minister at first assumed that the sole motive was to avoid a Russian presence at the Canal. He did not personally attach so much importance to the Anglo-French expedition being integrated into the force because he expected the two to co-exist for quite some time before the allied 'police force' handed over. This was not at all what was in Eisenhower's mind. He, like Hammarskjöld, could not get the British and French out quickly enough.

On the morning of 7 November, Eden referred the question of the composition of the international force to the Cabinet. There the issue was vigorously debated since, as Eden had said, there were very deep feelings involved. The case put for a Small-Power force was that close relations must be re-established with the United States and that this could not be done without acceptance of the majority view of the General Assembly. Such a force in any case might not be too bad. As one Minister said, 'An international force which might be substantially composed of contingents from the older members of the Commonwealth and the Scandinavian countries could be expected to remain reasonably within the diplomatic control of the Western Powers.'

For some of the Cabinet this was not good enough. The single, tangible gain from the expedition would be lost unless, by participating in the international force, Britain was able to keep some of her own troops in place. These Ministers were prepared to accept the logical consequence that if any Permanent Member were to be part of the force Russia could not be kept out. The Soviet Union, they said, was evidently planning to push further into the Middle East in any case. She might rearm Egypt or occupy Syria. Her participation in the international force would at least bring this intervention into the open and keep it under some sort of control.[9]

Reading the record of this animated exchange leaves the uneasy sensation of a lack of contact with reality. Britain had yet to discover how little strength she had at Port Said even with so much local power. The United Nations was an instrument that was powerless against the Soviet Union or the United States. But it was effective enough when it came to calling Britain and France to order.

The Cabinet arrived at no decision, but in the afternoon in the Egypt Committee it became known that, contrary to what nearly everyone had expected, France was not now going to insist on being part of the force. This came about in a somewhat circular manner. Shortly after midnight, for the second night running, Douglas Dillon found himself in the presence of a French mini-Cabinet – consisting in this case of Mollet, Pineau and Gilbert Jules (the Minister of the Interior). It was, he wrote to Dulles, 'one of the strangest experiences of my whole career . . .' It did not take him long to convince Mollet of the validity of Eisenhower's view on the compilation of the force but he found Pineau quite intractable. For half an hour they were locked in fruitless argument while Mollet 'acted more or less as a referee'. Dillon finally suggested calling up Eden; when Mollet found Eden agreed with the President, Pineau's opposition collapsed. This made it possible for Eden to use the argument of France's new stand to get agreement in the Egypt Committee.[10]

The Committee finally decided that Britain should cast its vote for the Hammarskjöld model but to do so with an explanatory speech, stating that the Anglo-French force was not going away until it could be replaced by an international force 'which we accept as competent to fulfil the purposes which we have in view'. These purposes were the solution of the Palestine and Suez problems, no less. Dixon found a more conciliatory voice in which to convey these haughty reservations.[11]

By sixty-four votes to zero, with twelve abstentions (Israel, Egypt, South Africa and the Communist bloc) Hammarskjöld was empowered to establish UNEF as in effect his own armed force 'to secure and supervise the cessation of hostilities'. Originally a sceptic, Hammarskjöld had put his immense capacity for work and his ability to function without sleep wholeheartedly behind the fulfilment of Lester Pearson's idea. 'Thank God we have Dag Hammarskjöld as Secretary-General', Pearson wrote on 8 November. 'He has really done magnificent work under conditions of almost unbelievable pressure.' Dixon on the other hand viewed more wrily the emergence of the remarkable Swede as the hero of the hour. 'We may find it inconvenient', he said, 'to have to deal with a Secretary-General who will be elevated to the status of a Pope with temporal as well as spiritual powers.'[12]

The Secretary-General's report was now endorsed, which made it clear that this pioneer peacekeeping unit was not intended to be a fighting force. It was to enter Egyptian territory 'with the consent of the Egyptian Government' to help maintain order during 'and after' the withdrawal of all other outside troops and to secure compliance with the other terms of the Assembly's 2 November resolution, such as a return to the previous armistice lines. It was to be 'more than an observer corps, but in no way a military force'. Its functions were to 'cover an area extending roughly from the Suez Canal to the Armistice Demarcation Line'.[13]

On 8 November General Burns, the Chief of Command of this new force, flew in to Cairo to propose that it should be constituted without delay by raising contingents from Canada, Colombia, and the Scandinavian countries – Denmark, Finland, and Norway. As was so frequently the experience in dealing with the Egyptian Government, Burns's initial encounter with Mahmoud Fawzi seemed an entirely positive one. Difficulties then set in. Questions were asked. It was soon obvious that settling the ground rules was going to be a long business. Nasser was back at the task, of which he was a past master, of pushing out the boundaries of Egypt's sovereignty. He did not feel or act like a drowning man who was being thrown a rope by the UN. He insisted on himself having the last word on the composition of the force, rejecting the Canadians because they resembled the British – they had the same Queen, similar uniforms, regimental names like the Queen's Own Rifles – and querying the generally western character of the force as Pearson had originally conceived it. It was 11 November before Hammarskjöld had secured Egyptian agreement to a force composed of Colombian, Danish, Finnish, Norwegian, Swedish, Indian, Indonesian and Jugoslav contingents, but no Canadians (who were allowed to supply signals, air transport and the commanding officer). Brazilians joined the force in January 1957.[14]

Comes the Reckoning

Britain, meanwhile, had the task of saving what was to be saved from her botched endeavour. First of all, there was the Anglo-French army which was left by the cease-fire precariously poised on the northern tip of the Suez Canal in possession of what Admiral Barjot had first called a 'a gage'. It did not strike Brigadier Darling, General Stockwell's Chief of Staff, as that. 'Like everybody else I am foxed by the position in which we find ourselves,' he wrote to Stockwell on 8 November. 'About a week ago our aim was to secure a twenty-mile corridor astride the Canal; now we find ourselves halted in our tracks with a toehold in Egypt. Tactically our position could hardly be worse ... we are deployed on about a one-tank front. The main threat we have to meet is air attack against which we have little or no warning or defence ... A high proportion of the force is loaded in ships, many of which are now on the high seas ... Furthermore vehicles and equipment have been loaded for almost three months already ... The whole of this situation will produce ... a most ghastly administrative problem.'[15]

On 10 November the commander of the expedition's armoured brigade,

Brigadier Sleaman, at long last arrived in Port Said with his headquarters staff and part of 1 Royal Tank Regiment. Fretting and fuming, he was unable to land until three days later, such was the congestion in the port. If he had been landed on 6 November, as originally planned, he would have been in Ismailia and Abu Sueir by the time of the cease-fire, he declared as he was gently returned to the boat and shipped back to Malta.[16]

It was a paradox that, whereas total allied air superiority had contributed much to the military achievement so far, the allies, once in place, were feeling themselves naked to air attack should the Egyptian air force be revived by the Soviet bloc. Having never reached the Abu Sueir air base, the allies lacked land-based fighters nearby. Those from Cyprus could only spend about ten minutes over the Port Said area.

In a rather panicky signal on 8 November General Keightley declared that, unless the UN was strong enough to prevent Egypt attacking his troops (and he 'would require the most categorical assurances' on this point), he believed that 'the threat to the forces under my command, especially to the air forces in Cyprus and the merchant shipping now approaching and in Port Said, is ... a completely unacceptable risk'. Only Egypt's aircraft had been destroyed. Her pilots and all her maintenance backing still existed. Russia had said she would supply volunteers with fresh equipment. It would only require fifty MiGs using Syrian bases to deliver 'a most damaging or even disastrous blow'.[17]

As for the position on land, Keightley, having visited Port Said, was quite clear about one thing: after experiencing the tenacity of Egyptian resistance, there must be no question, if action was resumed, of fighting without killing. He foresaw in occupied Port Said itself an organised, fanatical resistance movement which might well be something far tougher to deal with than the British had encountered in Egypt before. There is no doubt, he said, that both in fighting spirit and in equipment the Egyptian army was much improved. 'I have been considering the situation if we are required to continue operation. I would say with all emphasis that we must not be required to do this unless we can have and use every weapon we require. Without bombing, for instance, we shall now clearly not break the Egyptian wish to resist and we can no longer fight with the warnings and care for property which we have exercised so far. If we try to do so, the war will be prolonged and our casualties high.'[18]

Now that the fighting was over, there remained the problem of the British and French nationals whom this great expedition was designed to protect. First, there were the civilian contractors on the Suez Canal base, a group of people for whom the British Government owed special consideration. They were still interned. But there was also the substantial permanent British community, including British nationals of Maltese, Cypriot and Lebanese origin. Many of them had lived in Egypt all their lives. By Military Law No. 5 of 1 November, Nasser sequestrated all goods and property belonging to the British and French Governments, companies, institutions and private individuals. These included nine banks, sixty-four insurance companies and shares in a large number of companies that belonged wholly or partly to British and French interests. Britain and France had thus lost within forty-eight hours of delivering their ultimatum all of what foreign policy might have been expected to preserve in Egypt.[19]

But the interest, above all others, for the sake of which the rest had been put at peril, was the Suez Canal itself. One of the security secrets that the Swinburn circle was accused of acquiring was the preparation of the Egyptian vessel *Akka* as a blockship in case of an attack on the Canal. She was off Ismailia when the 'police action' started. The British plan was to sink her in Lake Timsah before she could be manoeuvred into the Canal. Two strikes failed to do the job; according to the Egyptians, the second, which secured a hit, helped them sink her in exactly the right spot for the task of blockage.[20]

While most attention was paid at the time to the *Akka*, the Egyptians had not stinted themselves at the task of wrecking. Bridges, floating cranes, dredgers, pilot boats, tugs, a frigate and a floating dock were willingly sent to the bottom of the Canal and its approaches. There were a total of fifty-one wrecks in all, of which twenty-two, varying in weight from 100 tons to 4,000 tons were sunk in Port Said harbour. They made a dramatic spectacle since, while some were completely submerged, others had masts and superstructures above the water and six were sunk in shallow water. The Egyptians may not have been good at mining the causeway but there was nothing half-hearted about their sinking of ships.[21]

General Keightley had never made the slightest concealment of the fact that the operation he had planned, *Musketeer Revise*, would not be able to prevent the blocking of the Canal.[22] Lord Mountbatten had, therefore, made arrangements in advance for assembling a substantial salvage force at Cyprus and work was begun immediately after the initial landing at clearing Port Said harbour. But nothing had been occupied beyond Al Cap and that was the limit of what they were allowed to clear. The problem of opening the Canal to the precious oil and other traffic remained; it was not to be solved by Britain and France.

On the diplomatic front, Britain's most immediate problems were to restore relations with the United States and with the Arab states. Neither was going to be an easy task. Eden assumed that, with Washington, once he had agreed to a cease-fire all would immediately be forgiven. He was to have a nasty shock. Following the Cabinet meeting on 7 November, Eden spoke again with the President to congratulate him on his victory and to suggest that he and Mollet came over to Washington to decide what to do next in the Middle East and how to act on worrying intelligence reports about the Soviet Union. Two objects would thus be achieved: the breach in the western alliance would be visibly repaired and Eden's desire to be the instrument of securing a permanent settlement of the Palestine question would be dramatically endorsed. Eisenhower, in the mellow mood of electoral aftermath, readily agreed and asked what date Eden had in mind. Eden suggested they should come at once. Eisenhower did not demur, and although he said he would need to consult others, he authorised Eden to pass on the invitation to Mollet. Eden was overjoyed.[23]

In Washington the good-natured President was soon running into trouble. First, Sherman Adams, his powerful Chief of Staff, and Colonel Goodpaster, Adams's assistant and later successor, told him that Eden was trying to undermine Hammarskjöld's authority by fixing up his own deal with Washington. Eisenhower phoned Eden back to make certain that it was clearly understood that the United States was right behind Hammarskjöld and would stay that way. What Eden was coming to talk about must strictly be confined to policies for the future, to 'what the Bear will do and what we will do in the face of the Bear's acts'.[24] The President seemed satisfied by Eden's answers but, as they were speaking, Hoover arrived in the Oval Office. The United States, Hoover said, as soon as the President had put down the phone, must be very careful not to give the impression that she was teaming up with Britain and France. Moreover, there was Secretary Dulles. He might be in hospital after a cancer operation but Hoover had talked to him and he was very much opposed to the Eden–Mollet visit. Hammarskjöld's negotiations with the Egyptians, moreover, were at a very delicate point; there was a danger that he might not get their agreement.[25]

After his advisers, joined eventually by George Humphrey, the Secretary of the Treasury, had planted one objection after another, Eisenhower phoned Eden once again and rather unhappily retracted his original acceptance. He explained that he had been told that 'our timing is very, very bad': the Democrats had just won the congressional elections and he would have to spend the next few days conferring with their leaders. Also 'the boys at the UN are trying to put the pressure on Egypt and Israel; the general opinion is that any meeting until that gets done would exacerbate the situation, and they are going up in the air about that'. All of which meant that Eisenhower would have to postpone seeing Eden and Mollet. It was for Eden a deflating rebuff.[26]

Nevertheless the Americans were becoming concerned by intelligence reports of rapidly growing Soviet involvement in the Middle East. From the moment of the Anglo-French landing 'intimate Nasser advisers' had made it their business to see that Washington should be alerted to Moscow's moves. At the National Security Council meeting on 8 November the CIA produced a cable from their Cairo station containing information received from Mohamed Heikal about the latest Soviet line. This was that the Soviet Union should be seen as an armed camp surrounded by an inner ring of satellites and an outer ring of neutral states, both of which were now under assault from the West, the first in Hungary, the second in Egypt. In her own self-interest the Soviet Union could no more allow one to break than the other. Nasser, said Heikal, was 'fully aware of the Soviet game in the area, realizes that he must make a choice and has chosen the course of full co-operation with the United States'.

Allen Dulles told the National Security Council that the Soviet delegation at the UN had been urging the Arabs to hold out until the arrival of Soviet volunteers. However he stuck to his earlier view that the Russians would not risk anything that looked like leading to a general war. The worst immediate danger was of a Soviet-backed coup in Syria. Admiral Radford was more pessimistic. Basing himself on an erroneous report of the height at which a British reconnaissance plane had been shot down over Syria (too high for the Syrian air force) he thought the Russians were already in Syria in some strength.

Harold Stassen, fluent as ever with unfashionable ideas, wanted to provide real incentives to Nasser to align himself with the West. The United States, for example, could help to get the High Aswan Dam back on the tracks. Otherwise the Egyptians would simply refuse to admit UNEF to Egyptian territory. But, just because American policy had had the side-effect of rescuing Nasser, the other members of Council were not feeling disposed in his favour. Hoover replied coldly that in two years' experience of trying the carrot principle of dealing with the Egyptian President the failure had been pretty complete. That was the reason American plans called for the phasing out of Anglo-French forces only insofar as UN police forces were phased in.[27]

For President Eisenhower the real and puzzling sadness was the apparent failure of the Afro-Asian world to draw the obvious contrast between Soviet behaviour over Hungary and American behaviour over Suez. Nehru, the great moral standard bearer, condemned Britain and France outright but found it difficult to tell what was actually happening in Budapest. Eisenhower urged maximum distribution of film material about the Hungarian atrocities. But in the Middle East it was uphill work. President Quwwatly of Syria told the American Ambassador, 'Our first duty is to protect ourselves and we invoked [the] principle of non-aggression when it served that purpose ... [The s]ituation in Hungary is not our affair and I do not care if fifty Budapests are destroyed.'

To Save Pact and Commonwealth

President Iskander Mirza of Pakistan was, it will be remembered, at the time of Suez on a state visit to Iran. He regarded his Prime Minister's threat to leave the Commonwealth as bluff. Many constitutional processes would have to be gone through before anything like that could be done; the Prime Minister must be got to come to Teheran as soon as possible.[28] That message was conveyed to Hassan Suhrawardy through British channels complete with the news that the presidential jet had already left the Iranian capital to pick him up.

Meanwhile, in Karachi, Suhrawardy was telling Morrice James, the Acting High Commissioner, that if Britain did not obey the UN she would put herself in the same position as North Korea, branded as an aggressor with police action to follow. The Prime Minister said he well knew the difference between manufactured demonstrations and those that were based on genuine popular sentiment; those currently taking place were examples of the latter.[29]

On the night of 6/7 November in Baghdad, Sir Michael Wright went to the Palace at midnight to tell the King and Crown Prince that the landings at Port Said were going well and to reaffirm Britain's determination that Israel should withdraw. The royal family had some news, albeit false, for him. The Soviet Union, they said, was intervening in the Middle East with three warships coming in from Romania and eighty bombers arriving in Syria. As the night wore on, the Deputy Prime Minister, the Chief of the General Staff and three Cabinet Ministers joined them at the Palace. They were very worried men. The news that Soviet help was on the way was being broadcast by Damascus radio; the people were comparing the effectiveness of Russian friendship with the betrayal by the British.[30]

The Ambassador cabled twelve hours later on 7 November, after the cease-fire, that the only major card which Britain had left to play was to propose immediate Israeli withdrawal, to be backed up, in case of refusal, with enforcement measures, either military action or economic blockade. Failing this, the Government in Baghdad might fall in a few days and a breach of relations with Britain follow.[31] On 9 November the Foreign Office tried to dispel some of the gloom, at least about the stories of Soviet penetration. 'We are not alarmed,' it said. 'These reports of Soviet assistance are unconfirmed and we do not believe them. A few more Soviet aircraft may have reached Syria recently but, so far as we know, no fresh Soviet material or volunteers have yet arrived in either Syria or Egypt.'[32]

Nuri was at this time not in Baghdad but in Teheran for an emergency Baghdad Pact meeting held without the British. The draft of the proposed communiqué, drawn up before the meeting started, was communicated to the British Ambassador at 1 a.m. on the morning of 6 November. The final text was issued on 8 November. The British had succeeded in eliminating the word 'unwarranted' and replacing it by 'regrettable' as a characterisation of the Anglo-French attack. Otherwise the wording was little changed, nor did the British make more than a perfunctory attempt to do so.[33] The four countries laid stress on their intense loyalty to the UN and the demand for the withdrawal of the Anglo-French force. The 1947 Partition Resolution should be the basis of settling Palestine, and negotiations with Egypt through the UN that of settling Suez. The four Governments expressed themselves as pleased by the British statement that the joint action of the four had 'affected the decision for a cease-fire order at midnight on 6 November'. The British Government duly responded. They were 'most appreciative' of the initiative of Iraq, Iran, Pakistan and Turkey. 'The views offered both individually and collectively by these Governments have weighed heavily in the decision to bring an end to military action in Egypt.'[34]

The conference at Teheran served another purpose, that of keeping Pakistan in the Commonwealth. Hassan Suhrawardy caught the presidential plane, thereby removing himself from the overheated political atmosphere of Karachi, and joined Iskander Mirza at Teheran. By the time they both returned to Pakistan the agitation was dying down. The crisis was averted. The new Commonwealth remained intact.

The shock of British action had also to be absorbed in those parts of the Empire that still had the status of colonies. To them the Colonial Secretary, Lennox-Boyd, addressed the full-dress version of Britain's apologia. The message sent out to South-East Asia on 9 November can serve as an example. The British action 'has unlocked doors and opened up prospects for the future which until recently had been closed and sterile'. After ten years of uncertainty the 'situation has now been created in which the UN can play a truly effective part in the settlement of the area'. All this would never have happened 'except for the surgical operation undertaken by Britain and France', which, in addition, 'saved the Middle East from the holocaust of a new war'.[35]

'This is really too much,' exclaimed Jo Grimond reacting in his first speech as Liberal leader to similar lines of argument. 'This is like a burglar by his crime and violence claiming to have compelled the police to improve their methods.'

Dissenters and Loyalists

'More and more people in many countries are coming to see the wisdom of our course,' Selwyn Lloyd told the wireless audience on 7 November. He read out a long extract from an Oxford statement, conceived as a counterblast to the Alan Bullock *pronunciamento* that had been subscribed to by a pro-Suez group among university personalities, headed by the classicist and old League of Nations campaigner Dr Gilbert Murray. This concluded that 'Britain, in concert with France, has shown to the world that we still have the courage and the capacity to act when the need arises'. Scandalised, Lady Violet Bonham Carter wrote to Murray, 'I simply cannot believe it . . .' The nonogenarian idealist was unbowed: of the UN General Assembly he wrote that 'the original fifty members have been increased to seventy-nine, nearly all of them uncivilised, Asiatic, Arabic, or South American nations with a violent anti-West prejudice or anti-civilisation majority'.[36] The Foreign Secretary meanwhile had told Winthrop Aldrich that 'we believed that we had stopped a world war'.

With the cease-fire removing the self-imposed inhibition that had restrained some critics in Britain, the dam of controversy burst. It became apparent that the divisions did not, as might superficially have appeared until this point, run along strictly party lines. Many Conservatives or non-party people, who had felt the need to avoid speaking out so long as the troops were about to be or actually were in action, now openly expressed their astonishment and dismay that a government led by experienced statesmen should have got the country in such a mess, while showing such lack of regard for Commonwealth, Nato and United Nations opinion.

Nigel Nicolson was the first Tory MP of this camp to come out publicly with his criticism. At a United Nations Association meeting in Bournemouth on 7 November, he demonstrated that what the Government had done violated all the known axioms of Conservative foreign policy. There was a vote of confidence at the end of the House of Commons debate on 8 November, in which eight Conservatives abstained. They included Nicolson, the two resigning Ministers – Anthony Nutting and Sir Edward Boyle – Robert Boothby and J. J. Astor (one of three Astor brothers who all opposed Eden including Lord Astor who spoke out in the Lords and David Astor, the editor of the *Observer* and author of the phrase about the 'crookedness' of Eden). It was a smaller group than had been predicted: many thought before the vote that it might have been large enough to wipe out the Government's majority. This was a tribute not only to the immensely hard and sensitive efforts of Edward Heath's whips but to the unprecedented vehemence of constituency pressures.

The Government's real anxieties, once the vote of 8 November had taken place, were directed elsewhere towards those inflamed Conservatives who had identified passionately with the decision to intervene and were now aghast at the premature cease-fire. Their sentiments very rapidly turned into an intense anti-Americanism. The 'treachery' of Britain's great ally, who had 'always let us down' by coming in too late in both World Wars was a recurrent theme. The only purpose of American policy in the Middle East was seen to be to drive out British interests and influence. It was a view that came increasingly to be shared by the Prime Minister and the young wife who had weathered the crisis with him and who had coined the memorable phrase, 'I seem for months to have had the Suez Canal flowing through my drawing-room.'

The passions of the time, so uncharacteristic of British life, certainly in relation to an international issue, lashed with particular severity against those who were against Eden's use of force. The Conservative MPs who abstained on 8 November found themselves in immediate difficulties with their constituency associations. Some, like Sir Edward Boyle, member for the Handsworth division of Birmingham who had been Economic Secretary to the Treasury, escaped with relative impunity, but with a fresh insight into the nature of his party supporters that, in the long run, weakened the zest for political life of this most promising of the younger generation of Tories. At a 16 November meeting of Boyle's executive committee, two ex-Lord Mayors of Birmingham dominated the debate. One took the view that Sir Edward's behaviour in resigning from the Government was so unforgivable that he should immediately be repudiated and steps taken to adopt a new prospective candidate. The other, after favouring a strong endorsement of the Prime Minister, reminded the leaders of the Association that they had deliberately decided to adopt Boyle when he had been a young man of twenty-seven because they had wanted a Minister and felt sure that he would soon become one, an expectation that he had rapidly fulfilled. Surely just because a young man had made a single mistake, serious though it be, they ought not to repudiate him now. In the end, when the second view had prevailed, Boyle took the opportunity to thank personally the lone individual in the debate who had backed him on the substance of the issue, only to be disconcerted by the lady's reply: 'Oh yes, I have always thought that all the troubles of the world were caused by the Jews.'[37]

Sir Alexander Spearman, who was not even an abstainer but who had spoken out in criticism and had been reported as having taken the chair at gatherings of the 'liberal' rebels, was likewise summoned to a meeting of the Scarborough and Whitby executive. 'It would appear that every member of the executive disapproved of the line I was taking,' he afterwards said in a television interview. 'It was intimated to me that I would not be asked to stand again.' Spearman threatened in that case to resign straightaway, but they must realise that they would have him standing as an Independent in the subsequent by-election so as to 'let the constituency as a whole make the decision'. The party did not fancy a test under these circumstances and nothing more was heard of the threat to his career.[38]

But others did not get off so lightly. At Melton, Anthony Nutting's constituency, the members of the Finance and General Purposes Committee of the Conservative Association were so outraged that the Minister who had made such a stirring address at the party conference such a short time ago should let them down so disastrously when it counted that they unanimously sent a telegram to 10 Downing Street, dissociating themselves from their Member and endorsing the Prime Minister. Nutting, feeling unable to defend himself by disclosing state secrets even after the cease-fire, resigned his seat and did not publish his account until ten years later, after the failure of his one attempt at a political comeback.[39]

But the most prolonged and public sacrifice was that of Nigel Nicolson. A vote of no-confidence in him was carried at a public meeting of the Bournemouth East and Christchurch Conservatives in December and, since he declined to resign, a long and unpleasant struggle ensued between his supporters and those of the executive, who adopted a new, very right-wing candidate. The struggle was only finally resolved over two years later by a vote of the entire Association membership which Nicolson narrowly lost. The life of Bournemouth – normally tranquil to the point of somnolence – had been disrupted for two astonishing years.[40]

Nor was this an isolated experience, although its length was unusual. John Jacob Astor, who had already announced his impending retirement from his mother's old seat at Sutton (Plymouth) because he did not care for the life of politics, found that opinion heavily reinforced by the treatment to which he was now subjected. He was made to feel, he said, like an officer who had disgraced his regiment. He had described Eden's policy on 8 November as having been 'unnecessary and wrong'. Sir Frank Medlicott, who had had, as 'Conservative and Liberal' member for Central Norfolk, a cosy enough relationship with his supporters for seventeen years, found himself, after he abstained (without speaking) on 8 November, systematically 'frozen out' of the activities of his constituency association. Since this showed no sign of easing up and made it extremely difficult for him to do his job, it prompted his early retirement.[41]

The arguments and the uncharitableness sprang from primal emotions and basic convictions. Just as the attitudes of opponents of Suez seemed treasonable to its supporters, so the personal reputations and political credibility of leading members of the Government appeared to their critics so smirched that they should never be allowed to hold public office again. Because Iain Macleod and Derick Heathcoat Amory were widely rumoured to have been opposed in Cabinet to the use of force, there was some agitation to sweep the top leadership out of power and put them in charge. The *Observer* wanted to cut deeper still and put the thirty-three-year-old Sir Edward Boyle in command of the rescue operation, until he wrote a private note to the editor begging in high alarm that he forget the idea.[42] For the rest of the year there were doubts as to whether the Government and the parliamentary majority would be able to hold together.

In the gossip-shops of Westminster and in the country at large Eden's position was not unnaturally considered to be at risk. The Suez policy had been very personally connected with the Prime Minister and its execution had notoriously and to an unusual degree centred on him. Although true believers went on talking about its success, everybody else seemed convinced that it was a most total failure. Surely something ought to follow. On 6 November, when the military operation was still on, the *Daily Mail* wrote: 'If the operation against Egypt is short and successful and brings the desired result, Eden's fame is secure. If it drags on and this country is bogged down in the morass of a long, wasting guerrilla war, the Prime Minister will be cast out ... There is this too. If Nasser remains, Eden goes.' And, after the cease-fire, *The Economist* declared bluntly: 'As the dust swirls over the Middle East ... there is only one subject in domestic politics. It is the Prime Minister – should he go or stay? Sir Anthony Eden has always been, in a career of long public service, a man of principle and patriotism. There may rest upon him a painful but inescapable decision.'

But in Britain, nineteen years before the Tories adopted a system of annual leadership elections, thirty-four years before its effectiveness was demonstrated by the dispossession of Margaret Thatcher, it was far easier to speak of the fall of Premiers than to contrive it. And Eden was not ready to go. The feeling that something, though of course not all, had been achieved, that a bridgehead had been gained, which it would require all his unique skill to exploit, was still upon him. Those of little faith would yet be made to see. The Cabinet, though not all convinced or at any rate not to the same degree, felt that for the time being they must work on the assumption that he was right, lest all fall apart and the unspeakable Hugh Gaitskell prove the main beneficiary.

The Great American Freeze

The first problem which the Government had to face up to was the magnitude of the geological shift that had taken place in its relationship to the Americans. The Prime Minister had had some indication of this in the cancellation of the arrangement for him and Mollet to fly over to Washington. Worse was to follow. It is true that General Eisenhower's natural courtesy prevailed when on 9 November he received the new British Ambassador, Sir Harold Caccia, and asked him to convey to Eden the warmest message of personal friendship. Eisenhower had sharply differed from the Prime Minister on tactics regarding 'a single point', but his views on the vital need for the Anglo-American alliance were not changed in any way. This did not, however, stop him from quoting a letter from a member of the Nagy Government alleging that it was only the attack on Egypt by Israel, Britain and France that had allowed the Soviet Union to suppress freedom in Hungary. Nevertheless, he assured Caccia that he wanted to see Eden as soon as it could prudently be arranged. 'He could not personally have been more friendly or indeed more forgiving,' Caccia reported.[43]

But the Ambassador was soon to discover, to his dismay, that this initial impression could not have been more misleading. Word was out that Anglo-American relations were quite definitely in quarantine until British and French forces had disappeared from the Suez Canal. It was Sir Anthony Eden's assumption that in Port Said he had indeed an important 'gage', that he would offer it to Eisenhower and to Hammarskjöld to put more power to their elbows in bargaining with Nasser and even with Ben-Gurion. Eisenhower and Hammarskjöld were not interested in playing the game by those rules. They wanted UNEF on the ground and the Anglo-French force out as soon as they possibly could before the Russians found the way to play the Korea trick back against the West by appearing on the spot clothed in United Nations sanctity.

Caccia discovered that, once his credentials had been delivered, nobody of substance would talk to him. He could conduct formal business but little else. This applied not only to him: the hundreds of members of the British diplomatic and Service missions in Washington found themselves frozen out of their normal trusting and confidential relationships. Individual Americans found ways of notifying their British friends that nothing personal was intended when normal social contacts went into suspense, but nonetheless it was a traumatic experience for people long habituated to the genial social and diplomatic assumptions of the special relationship. The Ambassador appealed to British journalists, especially those who, representing papers critical of the Eden Government, were still receiving detailed briefings from American sources, to help keep him informed.[44] The experience was even more disconcerting in New York, where a tense Pierson Dixon found himself quite shut out from Henry Cabot Lodge's circle except for an occasional chat with Lodge himself, and at a loss to predict American tactics in the UN.[45]

Much the most important centre of action became the Secretary-General's offices on the thirty-eighth floor of the UN Secretariat building. This was partly because here the UNEF (United Nations Emergency Force) was being organised, whose members were to wear for the first time the famous *casques bleus* (American army helmet liners spray-painted blue for quick identification). The force's acceptability and effectiveness, on which much else depended, was seen to turn on the success of Hammarskjöld's personal diplomacy. But also the United States was, as a matter of conscious policy, delegating much of its policy-making in this area to the Secretary-General. This aggravated British officials, who, unable to withhold admiration for Hammarskjöld's exceptional qualities, found his department lacking in many of the facilities that would be normal in the government offices of a nation state.

The British, reinforced by a 'specialist group' in mufti, headed by the thinly disguised Admiral Dawnay, considered it their duty to supervise what appeared to their eyes the amateurish efforts of the Secretariat not only to establish an effective force but at the same time to clear the Canal. If UNEF was to replace the Anglo-French force it must resemble it as closely as possible. This approach made for difficulties in an atmosphere which a British UN official, (Sir) Brian Urquhart, recalls as one in which 'virtually everyone I knew was violently opposed to the Suez expedition, which we regarded as a doomed, dishonest and contemptible aberration by the British and French Governments'. Urquhart adds that, in his own indignation at the Anglo-French action, he was taught a lesson by Hammarskjöld. 'When the balance tipped and everyone was hounding the British and French, it was his tact and skill that helped them to withdraw and save face.'[46]

Selwyn Lloyd, considering the UN a familiar stamping ground, arrived in New York to take his place 'in the firing line' on 12 November. He remained there until 28 November. He and Urquhart had been brother-officers in the war; Urquhart says that it was with some embarrassment that he now greeted him. 'His bantering style ("I remember you as an exceedingly insubordinate young officer", etc) was more in evidence than ever.'[47]

Henry Cabot Lodge invited the Foreign Secretary and Dixon to dine on the evening of 13 November. 'He spoke of the shock which our action had been and the pain which it had caused him,' Lloyd reported. 'We had been guilty of aggression and what we had done was indefensible.' That opening was just the kind of remark that was making the British feel that they even missed Foster Dulles. 'I said that I did not agree with him at all.' It was legitimate self-defence and they had stopped a wider conflagration. Anyway, what about the CIA-mounted invasion of the Central American State of Guatemala two years before, which had overthrown the leftist but democratically elected Government? According to the American account Lloyd said it was monstrous to let small nations get away with aggression, while accusing Great Powers of aggression against them when they acted in self-defence. Dixon is recorded as adding in an aside that Britain could not be held to so-called Charter principles that she did not believe in.

If the United States had not 'led the hunt against us in the UN', the Foreign Secretary maintained, the British and French 'would have had a brilliant success and Nasser by now would have gone'. Britain had known that an Egyptian attack on Israel was planned to take place in five or six months' time (Lodge intervened here to remark that it was a pity Britain had not shared that knowledge with Washington), and that Soviet penetration, which had already gone farther than Americans believed, would then have reached its high point. 'You may think we acted rashly, immorally and behind your backs, but the UK had to do what it did. There was no alternative.' Dixon added that this was the historic moment to act and historians like Toynbee would say so in the future. (The Ambassador would have been well aware of the then current American craze for the British historian Arnold Toynbee's theories of the cyclical rise and fall of civilisations.)

The British force in Port Said, Selwyn Lloyd contended, was the only strong card the West or Hammarskjöld had to play against Nasser. If any force was going to replace it it would have to be a great deal stronger than the 3,000 Finns, Scandinavians and Colombians being assembled now. It would have to be at least as strong as the 15,000 British and the 3 or 4,000 French who were there now. As for the threat of Russian intervention, he reproached the United States with allowing herself to be bluffed by Moscow.

If there were to be 50,000 volunteers Britain would know how to take care of them.

All this made a lamentable impression upon Lodge, who felt that Lloyd's attitude was 'reckless and full of contradictions'; it had made him more pessimistic about the British than anything that had happened so far. 'He is in a dangerous state of mind which could touch off a war and which, I understand, reflects Eden's view.' Lloyd had had his say but had got nowhere.[48]

France Comes Clean

In France, where in the Palais Bourbon the Communist Party was the largest political group, the mood on 6 November was set by events in Hungary. The harsh divisions of the cold war once more dominated the chamber and in the prevailing anti-Communist mood Mollet and Pineau were able to get away with their extravagant claims of success: the humiliation of Nasser, the occupation of Ismailia as well as Port Said, the saving of Israel, the revelation of amazing stocks of Soviet arms near the Israeli border. Mollet himself made speech after speech, always laying great emphasis on the loyalty of Anthony Eden as an ally and the durability of the alliance. But, after a few days, doubts began creeping in. The press reported that the French and British were anything but united about whether Israel should withdraw from Sinai; Ismailia turned out not to have been taken after all; and there were worrying revelations about the atmosphere at the early morning Cabinet on the threatening Bulganin note. J. R. Tournoux wrote in the socialist daily *Le Populaire* of 9 November, 'The list of "agonising reappraisals" is open ... The French Government will without doubt take the decision shortly to manufacture nuclear weapons ... The Soviet threat to use rockets has dissipated all fictions and illusions.'[49]

The Soviet scare also prompted French politicians and civil servants to look for the repair of relations with the United States. The Political Department of the Quai d'Orsay, having bluntly recognised that France's British ally had proved herself to be 'hesitant in action, maladroit in execution and infirm of purpose when it counted', concluded that, 'either we must bring the United States to share our views ... on the policy to be followed [or] if we cannot arrange this we must adapt ourselves to theirs'. To ram the point home, the French officials went on, 'We have believed in a Franco-English magic formula. The setback has shown us that alone our two countries lack the weight sufficient to influence seriously the balance of power.' The need to 'make Europe' was never more urgent but it was not an instant solution and the danger was immediate.

The Minister, Christian Pineau, duly made his personal contribution on 16 November by seeing Allen Dulles and Admiral Radford during the course of a 'private' visit to Washington and confessing to each of them his version of the 'collusion', which ran on much the same lines as his talk to Dillon on 1 November and still omitted Sèvres. On 9 November the Foreign Affairs Commission of the Assembly called on Mollet to promote an immediate summit with Eisenhower and Eden to put an end to tripartite disunity over the Middle East. It was not for want of trying that Mollet was unable to comply. Dillon brought him the bad news on 12 November. The French Prime Minister rambled on gloomily about an immense Soviet plot which was now fully unmasked. If the Anglo-French had not pre-empted it, a joint Egyptian-Syrian-Jordanian attack, directed by Soviet officers and technicians, would have taken place against Israel in December or January. Since the Israelis would have been unable to withstand the impact of the Soviet volunteers, the choice for the West would have been between watching the annihilation of Israel or risking a war with the Soviet Union. Mollet admitted that Israeli propaganda was overdoing the amount of Soviet equipment that had been found in Sinai, but even so the extent and advanced design of the weapons that were found could only suggest that they were to be used in attack. Although the operation had spoiled Soviet plans, the method of ending it had resulted in a tremendous upsurge in Soviet prestige. The extent of Mollet's desperation can be judged by the fact that he now declared himself willing to do everything possible to strengthen the Baghdad Pact.[50]

Lloyd in Limbo

Anglo-American contacts through the intelligence networks, never totally severed, were the first to resume. Chester Crocker, the CIA's London station chief, was allowed to share information about the degree of reality of the Soviet rocket threat. But the vulnerability of British dispositions, especially in Cyprus, to assault from planes flown by 'volunteer' Soviet pilots was General Keightley's most constant anxiety. The possibility of jointly backed covert operations being undertaken in Syria, which was the country from which such planes were most likely to operate, was once more being discussed in the White House as early as 16 November. Eisenhower is recorded as having authorised Allen Dulles and Admiral Radford to accept direct invitations to separate sessions with someone (name deleted) who was coming to Washington 'incognito' to discuss such operations. 'The Iraqis and perhaps the Turks would be involved', it was noted, 'and the partition of Jordan seemed probable'. The circumstantial evidence points to the visitor being Selwyn Lloyd, based as he then was on the UN in New York.[51]

Lloyd was certainly in Washington that weekend. The experience left him very bewildered. Eisenhower declined to see him but he was by no means boycotted. He received from his visit two diametrically opposite impressions of the President's attitude to Britain and to Britain's leader. On the one hand, there was the pleasant manner to Caccia and the reports (which are borne out in the records) of the President's speaking up in the National Security Council in support of the alliance with Britain. On the other hand there were the impressions (from such friends as General Bedell Smith) that Eisenhower was deeply wounded by the deception that had been practised on him.[52]

It had always been known to those who had had experience of working with him that 'Ike' had a quick temper. William Clark had been telling stories of picking up a telephone during Suez week and being the innocent recipient of a stream of barrack-room language which the President thought he was addressing to the Prime Minister. The question which worried Lloyd and his colleagues from the moment that Eisenhower had 'disinvited' Eden to Washington was whether permanent damage had been done to the relationship for as long as Eden was at the British end of it. The evidence is not decisive either way. But Winthrop Aldrich, who for once was being used in a major role in Anglo-American relations, is a powerful witness for the theory of deep alienation. He was, he says, 'surprised at the vitrolic nature of Eisenhower's reaction to what happened. I think it was unstatesmanlike; indeed I think it was a dreadful thing the way the US Government permitted itself to act towards Eden because of pique or petulance ... the President just went off the deep end. He wouldn't have anything to do with Eden at all. He wouldn't even communicate with him.'[53]

Ben-Gurion was told by the head of Mossad on 1 December that 'the Americans will not make up with the English until Eden goes'.[54] On the other hand a message to Eden which Eisenhower drafted when he heard that the first troops had begun landing on 5 November and in the end did not send had been forgiving and affectionate ('... no matter what our differences, please remember that my personal regard and friendship for you, Harold, Winston and so many others is unaffected'), and when later he felt obliged to cancel his invitation to Eden he had expressed genuine regret to his advisers, saying that he had really looked forward to talking with the British Prime Minister.

Unable to assess Eisenhower's mood for himself, Lloyd, accompanied by Caccia, went to see Dulles in hospital on 17 November. They were both apparently dumbfounded when the sick man said: 'Selwyn, why did you stop? Why didn't you go through with it and get Nasser down?' It does not seem such a surprising remark. There is nothing inconsistent between being totally opposed to a course of action and observing afterwards that, if someone nonetheless insisted on doing it, he might as well do it properly. It was a view that many people in Britain also took. 'If you had so much as winked at us ...', gasped the discomforted visitor.[55]

'Good Faith' in Cairo

Lloyd returned to New York, more worried than ever about the future of Anglo-American relations, to await the return of Hammarskjöld, who had flown to Cairo via Abu Sueir accompanied by the advance guard of the Colombian contingent of UNEF. The Secretary-General, for whom the negotiations with Egypt since the cease-fire had been most difficult, had refused to come ahead of his troops as a suppliant to the Egyptian President.

Gamal Abdul Nasser had emerged from this ordeal much strengthened politically. He was unable to understand, he told the new American Ambassador Raymond Hare, why Britain and France had embarked on so senseless an adventure. As far as the UN was concerned his main anxiety, apart from a visceral dislike of yet another occupation force, arose from the link-up in his mind between the idea of an international force and that of the internationalisation of the management of the Suez Canal, which had been, after all, a Dulles proposal. He wanted to make sure not only that Egyptian sovereignty would not be compromised by UNEF but that the force was not going to be stationed for very long in the neighbourhood of the Canal which was precisely where Ben-Gurion wanted it to stay for ever. Nasser was also asking for what Hammarskjöld was determined that he should not have – a veto on every member state contributing forces.[56]

In London, the composition, character and functions of UNEF were already causing the Government trouble with its own supporters. Tory backbenchers, the Egypt Committee was told on 15 November, had expected that the international force would be 'fully equipped as a fighting force with armour and aircraft'. This was clearly far from the picture of the first blue-helmeted peacekeeping units which were now being put together at the Naples clearing base. Demands were heard for there being no complete withdrawal by Anglo-French forces until firm provisions were made 'for clearing the Canal, the settlement of the Suez Canal problem and the settlement of the Arab-Israel dispute'. The assertion was made that a majority of the people in the country shared that point of view.[57]

Hammarskjöld came back from Cairo on 19 November, 'clearly exhausted by his struggle with Nasser', according to Dixon. He had had three hard days of negotiation, seven hours of it going over the text alone with Nasser. To avoid a breakdown on the sticking points, which would have stood in the way of UNEF making its presence quickly felt, the Secretary-General produced the formula of a 'good faith' agreement, which was in fact 'a combination of one-sided but interlocking declarations'. From the agreed starting point that the international force would be on Egyptian territory only with the consent of the Egyptian Government, it followed that the Egyptian Government would be able at any time to withdraw that consent. But Egypt, unilaterally, declared that she would be 'guided in good faith' by her acceptance of the General Assembly resolution, which established the presumption that the force would stay in place until the objects, rather loosely defined, of that resolution had been achieved.[58]

Later, in 1967, this cat's cradle, depending as much of it did on the method, much favoured by both Hammarskjöld and Fawzi, of showing each other unilateral understandings of what was meant by deliberately imprecise wording, fell apart. According to an *aide-mémoire* drawn up by Hammarskjöld, but shown to no one else, his understanding was that the force should only withdraw on completion of its tasks and that, if there was a difference as to whether these 'tasks' had been completed, the issue should first go to the General Assembly. He says that Nasser made so many objections to the final text that 'I felt obliged, in the course of the discussion to threaten three times that, unless an agreement of this type was made, I would have to propose the immediate withdrawal of the troops'.[59]

The text completed, the international peacekeeping force would soon be ready to take up its positions. The question was becoming critical of when exactly the British and French were proposing to depart.

27

Forced to Quit

The United Kingdom is a burglar who has climbed through the window while Nasser is the householder in his nightshirt appealing to the world for protection.

George Humphrey, US Secretary of the Treasury, 27 November 1956.

We will not be sermonised. We do not propose to be sent to Coventry . . . I must warn the American people that if they continue to refuse to discuss practical problems in a practical way with their allies who have an interest in them . . . then those of us in public life who are half-American . . . are going to feel ashamed and humiliated before their fellow-countrymen and the Anglo-American friendship and alliance will stand in ruins.

Lord Hailsham, First Lord of the Admiralty, at Oxford, 30 November 1956.

Major pressure was now being felt in Britain from the economic effects of the crisis. It was this, after all, which had contributed mightily to bringing the operations to a halt. On 9 November Sir Roger Makins, who was the new Permanent Secretary to the Treasury, saw C. F. Cobbold, the Governor of the Bank of England. The Governor's verdict was that sterling was a major casualty of recent events and that radical treatment would be required to save it. He wanted to mobilise Treasury securities and raise money on them from New York banks, to get the Americans to agree to a waiver on the Anglo-American Loan, and, simultaneously, to borrow no less than three 'tranches' from the IMF. This would amount to the total British quota of $1,300 million (later expressed as a request for an actual drawing of $561m plus a stand-by arrangement of $739 million). But despite the urgency Cobbold did not think this grand slam, depending, as it would do, at almost every point on American goodwill, should be tried before relations with the Americans had improved.[1] This meant taking risks with the reserves even to the point of allowing them to fall below $2,000 million.

On the morning of 12 November Harold Macmillan announced to the Cabinet that British losses from the reserves in the three months up to the end of October amounted to $328 million. A meeting of top Treasury officials which was being held at the same time in Sir Leslie Rowan's room decided that it was impossible to go on losing reserves at the existing rate and avoid a second devaluation, which would risk the cohesion of the Commonwealth and threaten the structure of Nato. The stakes therefore were the highest. The approach to the United States should be that it was in her major interest that the sterling area should be firmly maintained. The remedies were the same as Cobbold's plus an Export/Import Bank loan for oil purchases; they would require, said the mandarins, 'a friendly and compliant attitude' on the American part; Macmillan was urged to approach the United States without further delay.[2]

The man who would have the chief burden of making such an approach was Lord Harcourt, the Economic Minister at the British Embassy, a merchant banker by profession rather than a diplomat. He was discovering that he met 'a brick wall at every turn with the Administration'. He found them to be 'hurt and piqued at our action which they look on as a blunder and they seem determined to treat us as naughty boys who have got to be taught that they cannot go off and act on their own without asking Nanny's permission first'.[3]

Moreover, a deadline was approaching: on 3 December the November reserve figures were due for release, when, it was feared, the discovery that they had fallen just below the (rather artificial) Plimsoll line of $2,000 million would, if no drastic measures were announced, cause a catastrophic flight from sterling.

There was also the parallel problem of oil. Macmillan was rebuffed at the OEEC meeting on 15 November when he approached the American observers for help with the re-direction of oil supplies. A plan had been discussed at the National Security Council meetings in Washington on 8 and 15 November but the decision was taken to make no move until UNEF was in place.[4]

On 19 November in a note prepared for the Chancellor's use in Cabinet, the Treasury predicted that the losses of reserves for November would prove very large; by the end of the month they would come to over $250 million (the actual figure, as published, was $279 million, but the 'real figure' was put by the Deputy Governor at $401 million). There were only two courses available: a floating rate, which would 'be a catastrophe, affecting not merely the cost of living and level of wages in this country but also having a disastrous effect on all our external relationships'; and what was described as 'seeing the present situation through', which required massive American help.[5]

Macmillan was at work on a major message to George Humphrey, cunningly tailored to appeal to the American's imagination. Laying it on with a trowel in the Macmillan manner, he painted the appalling consequences of 'the disintegration of the sterling system which, as you know, finances half the world's trade and payments'. That would represent 'the greatest triumph of the forces of Communism since the end of the war. They have always asserted that capitalism carried within itself the seeds of its own destruction. Here would be the proof.' As a counterpoint to this grim scene, Macmillan raised his eyes to the great prospects that he saw before him. 'We are, in Europe, on the threshold of developments which could transform the scene. The Government have definitely decided to take the lead in working for a free trade area connected with the Messina Custom Union [the EEC]. This could be the most important new factor in our own and Europe's history – both political and economic – during this century. I have never known any topic discussed more objectively and with a better sense of the major issues than this by all sectors of industrial and political parties here.'[6]

The letter in this form was never sent. But, to judge from the White House records, its substance – and probably much of its phraseology – entered into the long and frequent conferences that Macmillan was holding at this time with Winthrop Aldrich, the American Ambassador and former banker. Macmillan's sense of drama – of the 'war of the worlds' – was in every line of Aldrich's reports.

Anthony Eden was now fighting for a phased withdrawal from Suez to match the arrival of UNEF contingents, thus permitting an orderly take-over; and for the large allied salvage fleet, which had already partly cleared Port Said and the short stretch of the Canal that was occupied, to be allowed to help in clearing the rest. This Nasser was not going to permit, at least certainly not so long as these vessels used allied crews. But it was over this that the British had chosen to fight their last great battle of prestige. British salvage vesels, after all, had been declared (by Rab Butler in the House of Commons) to be 'the only ones in the world capable of clearing the Canal'.[7] But passions were still high; this was the unrepentant aggressor who was speaking. 'So long as there is a foreign force, one single foreign soldier in Egypt,' declared Abdul Nasser, 'we shall not begin repairing the Canal and we shall not begin running the Canal because this affects our plan for defence against aggression.' Hammarskjöld coolly obtained from the World Bank the services of an internationally famous engineer, the American General Raymond Wheeler, for the project and approached mainly Dutch and Danish salvage firms.

The Egyptians were still infuriatingly ahead in the psychological war. War crimes propaganda about Port Said received wide distribution. British initial estimates of Egyptian casualties – about 100 – were unfortunately many times too small. They were twice revised upwards by successive official investigators, Sir Walter Monckton and Sir Edwin Herbert, the President of the Law Society (foreign dignatories having declined British requests to undertake the enquiry), and, with the figures for Port Fuad added in, they could be assumed to be 750 killed, perhaps as many as 1,000. These were high figures compared both to the low allied losses –

twenty-three killed, one hundred and twenty-one wounded – and to the proclaimed peacekeeping purpose of the expedition.[8] Some British Ministers, aware of the lengths gone to organise an immaculate invasion, were shocked and surprised by them.[9] Port Said as a whole was not badly damaged, but certain areas, including one block of houses about a hundred yards square, for which the Egyptians had fought hard, had been destroyed by air strikes, the shanty town had been burnt down and the Navy House had been blown up. That was enough to provide the picture evidence to give an impression of devastation. The Egyptians were supplied by a Swedish journalist with the heightened prose to go with it.[10]

By December, as the inhabitants of Port Said became more conscious of its reputation as a 'martyred' town and of the impermanence of their conquerors the spirit of resistance flared and the military were seriously upset by a chain of incidents. But the impression Hammarskjöld and other visitors to Cairo were given in mid-November of a town seething with revolt, of ceaseless clashes between civilians and soldiers and a daily death toll was largely a work of the imagination. The Secretary-General was, however, seriously worried that such reports might set off anti-European riots in Cairo, which in turn could trigger off fresh British intervention and then an appeal by Nasser to the Russians. Lloyd, asked to admit the UN to Port Said without delay, agreed to the immediate token arrival of a mixed Danish/Norwegian company.[11]

To Jamaica

As the British Government prepared to abandon its policy over Suez and seek a new one, it was decided to prepare the way by spreading word of the country's true position. Rab Butler has given a pungent account of one such attempt. 'I dined with twenty influential Conservative members of the Progress Trust,' he wrote in *The Art of the Possible*, 'and was very open with them ... The small private room became like a hornets' nest. They all hurried off to the Carlton Club to prepare representations to the Government. Whenever I moved in the weeks that followed, I felt the party knives sticking into my innocent back.'[12]

Eden was now obviously suffering from advanced exhaustion – he had missed one Cabinet on 13 November because of the need for rest. His personal doctor was uncertain how seriously ill he was but was emphatic that he must not go on living, as he had been doing for some time, on stimulants. On the evening of 18 November, he recommended that Sir Anthony set aside the business of state and have several weeks' complete rest in the Caribbean sun. When told of this advice Harold Macmillan exploded with wrath at the doctor for its unsuitability. For the leader to disappear so totally when his troops were in such an exposed position seemed to him wrong. 'It did sound', Butler wrote later, 'the most extraordinarily remote suggestion in the middle of such unprecedented troubles.' The doctor was insistent; his patient must get right away, otherwise he would not relax.[13] Late at night on 19 November it was announced that Eden was cancelling his public engagements because of severe overstrain; on 21 November that he was flying to Jamaica.

The impact of this wholly unexpected announcement in the country was deeply damaging to the Prime Minister's position among his own supporters. The need for some rest after the exceptional strains of the past weeks was easily understandable. It was the fact that he was seeking it *in Jamaica* that had such unfortunate connotations. Here was the captain of the ship abandoning it in the middle of a storm to sun himself on a distant island that was in those days thought of as a haven for tax-evaders or a sybaritic holiday resort to which only the few could aspire. Actually, the remote bungalow without a telephone which was hastily made available for the Edens was the rather spartan retreat where Ian Fleming went to write the James Bond novels. But among the uncharitable, this did additional harm to his reputation. In explanation of the announcement, Anne Fleming, the novelist's wife and a considerable political hostess in her own right, was described as a close friend of Lady Eden. But she was also a close friend of Hugh Gaitskell. To the other ingredients of the shock was added for some Conservatives the special discomfort of seeing their leader accept this unsuitably placed hospitality from a female friend of the 'arch-traitor'.

The Edens actually left for Jamaica on 23 November. But already on the 20th in the White House they were discussing the succession. This is sometimes portrayed as if it were an American attempt to interfere in British politics, with the implication that an active American desire to remove Eden was egged on by Macmillan, but the facts do not necessarily require so loaded an interpretation. Macmillan, it is true, had been agitating to go to Washington but that was understandable in the light of Britain's economic perils and his special chance of gaining access to Eisenhower. At that stage Aldrich told him to wait until Eden was asked and then arrange to go with him. Macmillan agreed, remarking that he ought never to have been moved from the Foreign Office and that Selwyn Lloyd was 'too young and inexperienced for a position of such great responsibility'.

In the late afternoon of 18 November, the day before Eden announced his holiday, Macmillan was at the American Ambassador's Residence suggesting he might come over to Washington as 'Eden's deputy', because Eden was very tired and should have a rest. Aldrich could not help wondering 'whether this might not be a hint that some sort of movement is on foot in the Cabinet to replace Eden', but he added that he had no other evidence except Macmillan's conversation, in which he had portrayed the Cabinet as having to face within days 'a terrible dilemma': whether to withdraw from Egypt having accomplished nothing other than the entry of a completely inadequate token UN force, or, alternatively, to restart hostilities and take over the entire Canal to ensure its clearance and free operation and avoid the complete economic collapse of Europe. Macmillan claimed that some of the Cabinet favoured the second course and (like the old Macmillan) wanted to go down fighting. But both Salisbury and the latter-day Macmillan were quoted as being ready, once given an encouraging American word, to persuade their colleagues that the United States was willing to take over the burdens of clearing the Canal and establishing its operation.[14]

Decisions, too, would have to be taken soon in Washington about supporting the British economy, which must be co-ordinated tightly with the business of securing British compliance with the UN. The sudden withdrawal from the scene 'for weeks' just as the moment of decision approached of so central a figure as the British Prime Minister created a perfectly legitimate necessity for the Americans to locate a new centre of power. Eden's medical history would suggest the unlikelihood of his regaining his former position, quite aside from the likely political consequences of the collapse of his policy.

In these circumstances and with the absence of John Foster Dulles, Ike's friend George Humphrey, the Secretary of the Treasury, filled a central role, a man habitually sceptical of British pretensions. The record of a telephone conversation with the President on 19 November, however, shows Humphrey (no doubt under pressure from Aldrich) becoming more sensitive to the political consequences of American policy in Britain. 'I hate to have a man stick in there and get a vote of confidence and get licked,' he told the President. 'If they throw him out, then we have these Socialists to lick.' It is not absolutely clear from the context to whom Humphrey is referring – to Eden or to a Tory successor – but the American researcher Scott Lucas, who has written at length on this matter, is probably right in favouring the latter.[15] One did not have to be a political insider in Britain to be thinking that day of the succession.

Macmillan came round that night to the American Residence at his own request to tell Aldrich that Eden 'will have to go on vacation immediately, first for one week and then for another, and this will lead to his retirement'. Aldrich inferred that the successor government would be a triumvirate of Butler Prime Minister, Macmillan Foreign Secretary and Salisbury Lord President. Lloyd would be Chancellor. But, he added, 'Possibly Macmillan might be Prime Minister': he reported that his visitor was 'desperately anxious to see [the] President at [the] earliest possible opportunity'. The first action after Eden's departure would be on withdrawal of troops from Egypt. Macmillan said, 'If you can give us a figleaf to cover our nakedness, I believe we can get a majority of the Cabinet to vote for such withdrawal without requiring conditions ... although [the] younger members of the

Cabinet will be strongly opposed.' The situation was moving with great rapidity, he declared on leaving, as, with a touch of melodrama, he obtained Aldrich's pledge (which was most fulsomely granted) to be available to him 'at any minute of the day or night'.[16]

In the White House on 20 November, referring to Aldrich's cable about the British political scene, Humphrey said that, of the two candidates for the succession mentioned, he would think Butler the stronger choice. Eisenhower, who was given to reminiscing about the difficult days of his wartime command in North Africa, remarked that Macmillan was a straight, fine man, the outstanding Britisher he had served with during the war.

Macmillan had enquired of Aldrich if, in the event of an announcement of immediate withdrawal, the British could be brought back into the circle of consultation and helped economically. Eisenhower told his Ambassador that he should talk to Butler and Macmillan, preferably together; his main concern seems to have been not to show preference between them. Aldrich should tell them that, if the British acted sensibly, 'we can furnish a lot of fig-leaves'. But he remained quite clear about the sequence of events: first, withdrawal; secondly, talk to the Arab oil states about their willingness to resume supplying Western Europe; and thirdly, financial relief for Britain.[17]

Cross Words Across the Atlantic

The key to American Middle East policy at this point is Eisenhower's reversion to his earlier belief in building up King Saud of Saudi Arabia as a major figure in the region. Saudi Arabia, Iran and Iraq must be told that, once the withdrawal from Suez had begun, America was going to aid Western Europe financially. This was the moment for these oil states to be cooperative if they wanted to get back their European oil markets. Otherwise, once the United States had raised its own output (which was subject to major conservation restrictions), it would be very hard to cut it back. The President rejected a strong plea from Walter Robertson of the State Department for American adherence to the Baghdad Pact. That would forfeit all American influence with the Arabs. He repeatedly spoke of using Buraimi as 'an ace in the hole' with the Saudis; the British should be asked to express their willingness to leave the oasis.[18] Eisenhower, Humphrey and Hoover, presumably inspired by Macmillan's approach, were united in seeing 'some blessing in disguise coming to Britain out of this affair in the form of impelling them to accept the [European] Common Market'.

But things were still not going to be made too easy for Britain who, it emerged, was still interested in more substantial fig-leaves than the President had in mind. Sir Harold Caccia, after he had been some time enquiring at the State Department whether there was any intention of consulting with the British on Middle Eastern matters, was at length received by Hoover on 23 November as coldly as only Herbert Hoover knew how. Caccia's question about consultation had, he said, rather taken him aback. He had had the growing feeling that it was the British who wished to avoid frank discussion. First, there was Buraimi, then Jordan, now Suez. There had been a 'blackout' of British information over the last five weeks. Britain must recognise that much must be done if unqualified trust was again to be established. In reply Caccia blamed the whole present crisis on the way in which the United States had turned down the Aswan Dam project without any consultation and had failed to show that she understood that 'Nasser's action was calculated to bleed us to death'.

After this exchange of reproaches, Caccia said flatly that the British Government wanted to re-establish the close relationship which formerly existed and needed urgently to discuss many matters of vital importance. To this, Hoover responded that, before sitting down to frank discussion, there was a point of principle at stake: was Britain going to carry out UN resolutions or was she not?[19]

On the other side of the Atlantic, anti-Americanism was in danger of getting out of hand. An Early Day motion on the Commons Order Paper censuring the Eisenhower Administration for 'gravely endangering the Atlantic Alliance' picked up over a hundred signatures. Another attacked General Wheeler by name for his lack of appreciation of the obvious superiority of the British salvage team. This rather saddened an officer whose two honorary knighthoods spoke of an exceptional wartime ability to work with the British and who, when deputy to Lord Mountbatten as Supreme Allied Commander, SEATO, struck him as 'one of the nicest men I have ever met'.[20] The same attitude was reflected in the streets. Petrol rationing had just been announced and cases were reported of petrol stations refusing to fill up American cars and of taxis refusing to pick up Americans. The First Lord, Lord Hailsham, with his American mother and rumbustious style of oratory, found words for the feelings of many Suez supporters when he spoke at Oxford on 30 November. 'We will not be sermonised', he said. 'We do not propose to be sent to Coventry. We do not wish to hear any more lectures from those whose moral weakness and incapacity to see the facts was the precipitating factor in the present crisis.'

The first signal of a new policy of conformity with the UN was sent by Butler in a short statement to the House on 22 November, welcoming its progress in organising 'an effective intervention'. This intervention, he asserted rather desperately, 'has been made possible by Franco-British action. If this UN intervention succeeds, a precedent will have been set which will give mankind hope for the future.' The Conservative Party was not much deceived. It was touch and go for the survival of the Government. In the evening Butler put on a dual act with Macmillan before the 1922 Committee (of all Conservative backbenchers), which succeeded in holding the party together. But it was somewhat at the expense of Butler's reputation for leadership. James Ramsden, one of the Members present, remembers 'thinking, as both men entered the room, that the real proceedings were bound to be about which of them would succeed Eden'. It was penny plain or tuppence coloured and the audience knew which of those it needed at that moment. Butler, who spoke first, gave a flat, unadorned presentation of the hard facts and suggested that Macmillan might like to add a word or two on oil. At this the old actor-manager, with his hooded eyes and mastiff mouth, with the stagey pauses and the occasional baring of teeth in what looked very like a snarl, rose and delivered a thirty-five-minute, rounded oration which lifted all except a revolted few (like Enoch Powell) off the floor. There was a great deal of the 'long adventure of politics, full of hard knocks but still a game more worth playing than any other'. The Chancellor was rightly reported in the press the next day as having been 'particularly effective'.[21]

To Brendan Bracken, who had always considered that 'never since the days of Charles Townshend has the Treasury known a more unstable master',[22] Macmillan could be described as 'the leader of the bolters'. Having been, he put it to Beaverbrook on 7 December, 'an absentee from the Treasury, as he has been busily posturing as the scourge of Nasser', he had now 'returned to the bosom of his gloomy officials'. Now he was telling journalists that he intended to retire from politics and go to the morgue' – Macmillan's charming description of the chamber which, as the Earl of Stockton, he was to adorn in his tenth decade. 'He declares that he will never serve under Butler.' Bracken thought that his real intentions were to 'push his boss out of Number Ten'.[23] Macmillan was always one for large alternatives – double or quits over Suez, Chequers or the morgue for himself.

On 24 November at the United Nations the General Assembly staged a debate on a comparatively mild Afro-Asian motion 'noting with regret' British, French and Israeli failure to obey previous resolutions and calling on them to withdraw their troops 'forthwith'. Pineau, though of course opposed to the resolution, indicated privately to Lodge ahead of the debate a remarkable shift in his position; he was now prepared to leave it to General Burns to decide the timing of withdrawal. Lodge cabled, 'Today it was evident that he wanted to get out.' The British Foreign Secretary was not in the least amenable to any such suggestion. 'These bloody French', he blustered to Lodge, 'first they put planes all over Israel and now they flatten out completely.' He would rather go down fighting than have 'a UN General' decide such questions. Lloyd supposed that in England they would 'go right through the roof' at the very idea and he felt like doing the same.

The Americans were not going to let up. Lloyd discovered that Lodge had instructions to vote for the Afro-Asian resolution. He therefore persuaded the Belgian Foreign Minister, Paul-Henri Spaak, to propose an amendment which Britain could accept. When this Spaak amendment had been rejected by thirty-seven votes to twenty-three, with eighteen abstentions, one of them the United States, the Afro-Asian resolution was carried by sixty-three to five, with ten abstentions.[24]

The wave of anti-American feeling caused by this vote, Butler told Aldrich, could not possibly be exaggerated. If America did not act firmly about the immediate clearance of the Canal Britain might withdraw from the UN and might even ask the US to give up her bases in Britain. 'It is tragic', cabled the Ambassador on 26 November, 'to sit here in London and observe the rapidly changing attitude of the British public towards us. I believe it is not exaggerating in the slightest degree to say that we are rapidly reaching the point where we are thought of by the British public as enemies of Britain working against them with the Russians and the Arabs ...'[25]

In reporting from New York, Lloyd was obliged to confess that nothing was to be gained on clearance of the Canal or on arrangements for its future control by deferring withdrawal, since action on both was being postponed so long as the British and French were still there. Because of the rapidly encroaching dangers of financial crisis and communist penetration Britain and France simply could not outsit the rest. As Butler put it baldly to the Cabinet on 27 November, 'It is now necessary to consider how soon this withdrawal can be carried out without alienating that section of our [party] supporters who are opposed to an unconditional withdrawal.' The Foreign Secretary, his colleagues decided, had been away long enough. He was to be brought home. They also thought that it would be particularly difficult, politically, to convince their supporters that the withdrawal should take place without any reference to the work of clearance.[26]

The following day, the Cabinet ordered that steps should be taken to 'discourage Government supporters from stimulating further controversy about the situation in the Middle East'. When describing to Conservative Trade Unionists at Yarmouth how 'the Empire had stood alone and a third world war had been prevented', the Minister of Health, Robin Turton, was now not allowed to say that, 'The American eagle is like those seagulls we find stranded on the beach, their eyes smeared over and feathers begummed – with oil.'[27] There were to be no more hostages to fortune. But Sir Ivone Kirkpatrick told the American Ambassador that he knew what advice he would give Ministers if the UN let Britain down. It would be that Britain should quit the UN.[28]

Financially, the Americans were still turning the screws. 'Evidence is accumulating that Mr Humphrey is the most intransigent member of the Administration about our actions at Suez and he is the most vindictive,' Caccia reported on 23 November. 'In the light of this, I think we must abandon any approach on a "personal and informal basis" which also assumes that good relations still exist ... [T]he tone should I think be more that of a business statement. In this connection I should like to be able to face Mr Humphrey squarely with the effect of present trends on Nato forces in Germany'.[29] When he got to see the Treasury Secretary on 27 November, the Ambassador reported: 'It has been totally impossible (after a one-hour discussion) to persuade Mr Humphrey to discuss the problem in banking terms . . .' The terms he actually used more than once were that 'the United Kingdom was a burglar who had climbed in through the window, while Nasser was the householder in his nightshirt appealing to the world for protection'.[30]

Selwyn Lloyd, in his last message before returning to London, completed the picture of Britain's disaster. In America, he said, 'the hard core of policy-makers, some of whom have been strongly pro-British in the past, are now against us . . . Their feeling is that we have to purge our contempt of the President in some way.' He had felt obliged to tell Hammarskjöld that the force would be out of Port Said in fifteen days, that is by 14 December, provided that the clearance programme started in the meantime and British subjects in Egypt would cease being expelled.[31] When he got home and met the Cabinet he offered to resign. He had tried to do a deal with the Americans and he had failed.

The idea of the Foreign Secretary resigning, which clearly took his colleagues aback, did not appeal to them as a good one, and it was dropped.[32] Some eighteen months later Lloyd told Eden, 'We should all have been in a much stronger position if I had been allowed to resign.' Eden replied that this was when they all should have resigned. The trouble was that he was ill and away from London.[33]

The Decision to Withdraw

The Foreign Secretary did not have an easy time when he tried to sell to his colleagues the timetable of which he had spoken to Hammarskjöld. More than one took him to task for having mentioned a definite date (he had only done so, he said, *ad referendum*). He made no pretence of having obtained a package deal, saying there was no point in seeking guarantees from the Secretary-General which he was not in a position to give. His strongest support came from Macmillan. The goodwill of the United States was necessary and was not to be obtained without immediate and unconditional withdrawal. Ministers remained acutely uneasy about Conservative reactions to the unconditional nature of that formula. Some clutched at straws. 'The view was expressed', read the Minutes of this discussion, 'that the Government might still be able to extract some further advantage from the present situation.' Butler summed up against that assumption. The French should be consulted and, if they agreed, a rapid withdrawal should be announced.[34]

When Pineau came over to London on 30 November he confirmed his readiness to withdraw but on military grounds and not to a pre-announced timetable. He was willing for it to be announced that the Allied Commander-in-Chief and the UNEF commander, Generals Keightley and Burns, who had served together in Italy and once had a famous altercation on the battlefield, should decide between them the pace of the Anglo-French departure.[35] It emerged subsequently that Pineau wanted the troops to be still there when the French chamber debated foreign affairs on 18 December. When he got back from London he, like Lloyd, was given a difficult time by his colleagues. Outside the Cabinet, the Christian Democrats (MRP), on whose votes Mollet depended, were making a lot of trouble. The French Premier asked for another fig-leaf: a mention of the old, rejected, Eighteen-Power proposal as being still the 'best means' of settling the Suez question. The phrase was eventually put into a UN supplementary document which Hammarskjöld, on his own initiative, treated as an internal paper and refrained from circulating to the member states.[36]

By land, sea and air the UN troops had begun moving into Port Said. Despite all the fighting and bombing the railway line was found to be intact, so the first contingent, a Norwegian and Danish company, came in by train on 21 November. Others followed until by the end of the month there were 1,374 troops deployed in the Canal area.[37] The logistical arrangements were rightly called, in an article in *The Times* contributed by the Australian UN official George Ivan Smith, 'a triumph of improvisation'. Much of UNEF's food and other supplies, including trucks and petrol, were bought from the British. Some early rations of meat and fruit were acquired by a Canadian wing commander who hitched a lift along the Suez Canal until he came to the ships with cold storage which were still blocked there and, standing on the bank, shouted up to the masters for the bills of lading.[38]

On 25th UNEF's commander, General Burns, had flown in to be met on arrival by General Keightley. They had not seen each other since the fracas in Italy. Both were determined to be polite, though George Ivan Smith, who was present, felt that they were both aware of the ironies inherent in their position. One was that the British general and the UN general who was taking over from him wore almost identical uniforms. There was an initial silence. 'Keightley and Burns looked exactly the same, with the same hats and reds round the caps and they kept putting them on the desks and Keightley broke the silence: "Well, at least we wear the same cap, Burns." '[39]

A situation full of potential for embarrassment was handled with some tact and grace. Indian paras from UNEF moved into the causeway to create a buffer zone between the Egyptian army and the allies. The force also took over from the British and French the guarding of 'vulnerable points', thus markedly reducing Egyptian patriotic zeal for sabotage.

To underline the contrast with the British and French, the population treated the UN troops with the greatest enthusiasm. Hammarskjöld was laying the groundwork for what he regarded as one of the main functions of the UN – to help powers to remove themselves with some dignity from situations in which they should never have been. But the bridge for Britain and France should not be a golden one.[40]

An international police force, that long-held ideal, was becoming a reality, but it was very unlike the animal envisaged by Eden and Mollet two or three weeks before. Albert Gazier, the French Acting Foreign Minister, had reported that he had found Eden on 14 November full of confidence in Hammarskjöld and extremely satisfied at the creation of UNEF, of which the main element, he stressed, was going to be Canadian. The important thing was that it should have a strong base to the west of the Canal and that it should stay there until the whole Egyptian affair, including free circulation through the Canal, had been regulated.[41] By the beginning of December things looked rather different. It was apparent that, certainly at first, there would be nothing Canadian about the force except the force commander. Then, as Serge Bromberger of *Le Figaro* put it in a scathing message cabled to the French Ministry of Defence on 7 December, 'What one calls the force of the United Nations is not a force to be set in opposition to other forces, it is more like a float propelled by the waves according to the ebb and flow of the tide.'

Bromberger complained bitterly of the self-deception of those who had let themselves be persuaded that the Canal would be occupied for its entire length by an international force. It was not like that at all. As a journalist he had watched General Burns sending off his Jugoslav contingent, not south down the Canal but east into Sinai, following the footsteps of the retreating Israelis (who had, incidentally, left the desert equivalent of scorched earth behind them). 'Henceforth, things are very clear. UN troops in the Middle East are only there to push us into the sea, then to open up the Sinai route to the Egyptian army, and finally to line themselves up on the old border at Gaza.'[42]

On Saturday, 1 December, Dixon and his French colleague were summoned peremptorily to the Secretary-General's office, where Dixon reported, 'We found Hammarskjöld in a secure and pontifical mood.' The Secretary-General said he must make himself quite clear about the salvage fleet. Allied hardware was usable, allied crews were not. The Egyptian position was correct on this point since Britain and France were at present occupying part of Egypt. This was his considered opinion in view of the UN judgment about the armed intervention. Dixon ventured a political explanation: it was a characteristic difficulty of democratic systems that a question of this kind might assume disproportionate importance in the House and with British public opinion. Colonel Nasser, he could not refrain from adding, might not have such problems. Hammarskjöld retorted coldly, 'In the face of such difficulties, governments sometimes fall.'[43]

It was precisely this prospect of the fall of governments that particularly alarmed the 305th National Security Council at its meeting on Friday, 30

November, under Vice-President Nixon's chairmanship. When it came down to it American politicians lacked the *froideur* of the Secretary-General. Allen Dulles set the tone with his opening remarks. A series of dramatic cables had shown that Britain and France were in a highly psychopathic state, with a further acute rise in anti-Americanism in recent days. Hoover joined in with the remark that members of the Eden Cabinet, which was giving signs of extreme disorganisation, were telling Aldrich of their very great fear that the Government was about to fall. The extent to which even officials were 'rattled' was held to be illustrated by the way in which Sir Ivone Kirkpatrick had come up to Don Cook of the *New York Herald Tribune* and told him that the Government was going to fall on Monday if it had been found then to have accepted UN demands for withdrawal. (The journalist was said rather implausibly to have been so shaken by this that he did not write the story).

The thought of what might follow from these events did not leave those at the NSC meeting unmoved, and most especially George Humphrey, the most implacable foe of Eden's policies, and Richard Nixon. The Vice-President wanted to do something to help the Conservatives even before Monday, being, as he said, 'scared to death at the prospect of Nye Bevan in a position of power in a future British Government'. Humphrey, though insisting on waiting till Monday (since there would not be a vote in the Commons until Wednesday) said that 'the minute the British Cabinet acts next Monday, the [American] Government should be prepared to give Butler everything that he asks of us.' Nixon added that they were essentially engaged in trying to shore up Butler. Having settled that, the members, civilian and military, vied with one another in expression of extreme distrust of Abdul Nasser.[44]

One more Briton was to be heard from before the agonised statement of Monday, 3 December was made: the Prime Minister. Norman Brook, the Cabinet Secretary, had kept him a little informed. Anthony Eden gave his reactions in a telegram from Jamaica on 1 December. He considered the make-up of the international force to be unimpressive; he still wanted British troops not to leave before clearance had begun on the other sections of the Canal. 'There is also the question of the long-term future of the Canal. How do we stand about this?' For his colleagues the most worrying passage in his reply was that in which the absent leader said that he had set all this out 'because I can well understand and share Conservative and National feelings on these matters'. He was better, he said, and available for consultation.[45]

The statement to be read out by the Foreign Secretary was drafted by four other Ministers.[46] It was referred, in summary and with some background, to Jamaica. Eden replied, like Pineau before him, that he 'would have hoped for a reference to the Eighteen-Power proposals . . . I never thought the Six Principles amounted to anything much.' He also supposed that 'all available means of clearing the Canal will be used including our own'. To the last point Butler replied, misleadingly, 'The answer is "Yes".'[47] On the Sunday night before the statement Butler received a phone call from George Humphrey to reassure him that once the withdrawal had been announced the United States was 'ready, willing and anxious to help'.[48]

The statement which caused so much labour and tears was read out to the Commons by Selwyn Lloyd on Monday, 3 December. It was a proclamation of the success of the Suez expedition and of the achievement of its main objectives. 'We have stopped a small war and prevented a large one. The force which we temporarily interposed between the combatants is now to be relieved by an international force. We have by our action unmasked Soviet plots in the Middle East ... Responsibility for securing a settlement of the long-term problems of the area has now been placed squarely on the shoulders of the United Nations.' The UN force would be competent, in size and composition, to discharge its functions; the Secretary-General had accepted responsibility for clearing the Canal, negotiations on the future of the Canal would be resumed on the basis of the Six Principles. With these understandings Britain and France would withdraw without delay.[49]

Humphrey was as good as his word. A warm American statement expressed pleasure and support for the new British policy. Oil supplies began moving within three days from the Gulf of Mexico to Europe. At the International Monetary Fund, the British drawing for $561,470,000 and a further standby for $738,530,000 were approved by the Executive Board on 10 December, thanks to American support. The American Export-Import Bank announced on 21 December that a loan of $500 million would be made available. The Anglo-American Loan agreement was amended the following year, giving Britain the right to defer interest payments on up to seven occasions; the December 1956 payment, which had been placed in escrow, was returned. Thus the United States Government demonstrated in the most evident fashion the advantages of being a responsive rather than an unreliable ally.[50]

On 14 December, like a ghost from the past, bronzed, apparently healthy and ready for action, Sir Anthony Eden turned up in England to resume the battle. 'He seems very fit, *physically*,' said Rab Butler in his tantalisingly ambiguous way.

28

Last Stands and New Doctrine

As long as I live, I shall never apologise for what we did. . . . We have been patient with the US over a long time. We might have expected something in return.
Sir Anthony Eden to 1922 Committee, 18 December 1956.

It would have been disastrous for us in any plan in the Middle East if it seemed inspired by the British . . . [T]hey would be glad to ride back on our shoulders if they could.
John Foster Dulles to Senate Foreign Relations Committee, 2 January 1957.

The Britain to which Sir Anthony Eden returned in mid-December was very different from the one which he had left behind a month before. The processes of adjustment were quickly taking place and his colleagues were anxious that when he first spoke he should not sound as if he belonged to a perished world. A Prime Minister who travelled by aeroplane then was usually expected to make public statements at both ends of his journey. There was much to-ing and fro-ing about the text of what Eden should say, especially when he got out of the plane at London Airport. His wish was to come out fighting, but Butler, Salisbury and Lloyd combined to dilute his instinct to hit out at everyone at once, especially the UN and the United States. A sustained attack on Nasser would also be out of place, because it might 'support the contention that our real motive was to get rid of Nasser'.[1]

Thus restrained, he stepped from the plane, smoothing his hair in the breeze and looking marvellously tanned and fit next to the deathly pallor of Rab Butler. 'I thought I would make a statement,' he said. 'Some people have asked for one. As you know, I went away to get fit and I am now absolutely fit to resume my duties.' Understanding was growing that his actions had been right. Without them there would have been no UN force; drift would have allowed 'the Moscow–Cairo axis' to perfect its plans. Therefore he was convinced, 'more convinced than I have ever been about anything in all my public life, that we were right, my colleagues and I, in the judgements and decisions we took and that history will prove it so.' With a final toss that 'there are tasks a-plenty' and that he had 'come back reinvigorated to solve them', he walked briskly out to his waiting car.[2]

He had arrived to a courteous but not a rapturous welcome. Rhodes James quotes Clarissa Eden's expressive words about 'everyone looking at us with thoughtful eyes'. *The Times* said candidly: 'Either Sir Anthony Eden must now show that he can and will lead a vigorous, progressive, efficient government or the strains that have been set up will demand someone else. The times are too grave and Britain's position is too hazardous for a replica of the Balfour Administration from 1902 to 1905 to be supportable.' Eden presided over a Cabinet meeting on 17 December and entered the House of Commons during Question Time in the afternoon. There were some cheers from the Tory benches but they were not universal or prolonged and one Tory member, leaping to his feet to wave his order paper, found himself alone and silently resumed his seat.[3]

It was apparent that one of the first questions which Eden would be called on to address was the persistence of reports about collusion with Israel. Gaitskell, of course, had mentioned the word at the very outset, but, in the Cabinet meeting of 20 November, 'attention was drawn to the continuing speculation in certain sections of the press about the extent of the foreknowledge which the United Kingdom and French Governments had had of Israel's intention to attack Egypt'.[4] Foremost among these press sources was Jean-Jacques Servan-Schreiber's weekly *L'Express* which was supportive of Mendès-France, and the *K-H News Letter*, a private subscription weekly with a fairly influential circulation, written by an ex-MP and broadcaster, Commander Sir Stephen King-Hall. The history of the Suez crisis was beginning to catch up on the politics of the crisis.

There was never very much doubt about France's foreknowledge of and involvement in the Israeli attack. Shortly after the fighting was over James Morris sent back to the *Manchester Guardian* a series of circumstantial accounts of the activities of the French air force in Israel during the Sinai campaign which probably exaggerated their actual operational role but were broadly correct. But that in itself, though it muddied the waters, did not convict Anthony Eden of collusion. Stephen King-Hall, in his *News Letter* of 14 November asserted that, 'We can say with complete certainty, that French sources, who certainly do know the truth, have stated categorically that the British were made aware of the plan on 16 October and agreed to take part therein. The French sources may be telling lies in order to implicate us in retrospect.' But King-Hall rather discounted this possibility by saying that 'there is a great deal of circumstantial evidence to support the opinion that a very limited number of Ministers and senior military, air and naval officers knew what was expected to happen on 5 or 6 November but which did happen on 29 October, when Israel attacked prematurely because the secret had leaked and heavy warnings against action began to come from President Eisenhower.' Only such a miscue, it was suggested, could have caused such ill-conceived features as the twelve-hour ultimatum, the extraordinary delay between ultimatum and assault landings and the use of the British veto in the UN.[5] Indeed Eisenhower was saying on 12 November that he now thought the British had been telling the truth when they had denied collusion. He knew the British as meticulous military planners and they would have seen to it that they would have been ready to move into Egypt in a matter of hours if they had had any warning. They must have come in at the very last moment. For a decade until Nutting published his book *No End of a Lesson*, the one thing which conspiracy theorists found it impossible to contemplate was the truth, that 29 October had been deliberately picked beforehand as the trigger date.

Rumours of collusion plagued the British Embassy in Tel Aviv. At an early stage the Ambassador and his Third Secretary were themselves operating the cypher (as is done for messages of exceptional delicacy) to enquire of Ivone Kirkpatrick how they should handle such questions.[6] David Ben-Gurion, in his diary for Sunday, 25 November, has an account of a visit from Nicholls, their first meeting since the occasion just before the attack when the Israeli Premier had told him that he was not fully briefed by his Government. According to Ben-Gurion, the Ambassador 'took a piece of paper out of his pocket and, while looking at it from time to time, said that he had been requested by the Prime Minister to say that Eden had full confidence in him and that, whatever I wished to pass on to Eden, I could tell him'. Ben-Gurion replied that once he had had something to convey (his plan for the reorganisation of the Middle East) but that this had been on the assumption that Nasser would be destroyed. Since the British operation in Egypt did not succeed, Nasser remained. The Ambassador got round to talking about those who were enquiring about collusion, and Ben-Gurion formed the impression that this was the real purpose of the visit. 'Altogether', he noted in his diary, 'he was friendly, almost fawning. I suspect that this is due to the fear of collusion being discovered.'[7]

On 18 December, prominently displayed at the head of the letter columns of *The Times*, there was a message from the former Prime Minister, Earl Attlee, welcoming Eden back. It then requested from him a 'clear statement as to whether the British or French Government knew in advance of the Israeli attack on Egypt and whether the two governments prior to 29 October discussed the proposal for military intervention in that event' – wording which actually fell short of 'collusion'. In the evening Eden had a date with the 1922 Committee, the collectivity of Tory backbenchers, who received him politely. 'He has acquired the habit of asseveration,' Sir Edward Boyle observed.[8]

'We have been patient with the United States over a long time,' the Prime Minister said. 'We might have expected something in return.' By contrast there was a renaissance in France – he was much impressed by the young men of Mollet's Cabinet. He did not share the view that the next General Election at home had been lost. 'Our Suez action was supported by a great mass of ordinary men and women.' The reason that the army had not gone on was that 'according to the estimate we were given, it would have taken six days to get to Suez'. Eden was then questioned sharply by Nigel Nicolson, who described the operation as not just inexpedient but wrong in principle because it had forced honourable men, including the Prime Minister himself, to use methods and arguments which were in themselves dishonourable.

By way of reply Anthony Eden addressed himself to the question of 'half-truths'. He said: 'Some – and, if they existed at all, they were not serious or many in number – were necessary, and always are, in this sort of operation which demands extreme secrecy ...' Nicolson then asked why he had not invoked the Tripartite Declaration under which, if the Americans had refused to join in, the French and British were entitled to act alone. Some Members found it disconcerting when Eden responded uncertainly: 'I will have to look up your point about the Americans and the Tripartite Declaration. I haven't got it in my head.'[9] Sensing afterwards that his replies had not been wholly convincing, he concluded that the question of collusion must be directly and publicly met.

Two days later, on 20 December when Hugh Gaitskell was struggling to get his insistence on a straight answer on collusion past the Deputy Speaker's restrictive rulings on the Christmas adjournment debate, the Prime Minister broke in, eager to have his answer recorded. After distinguishing between foresight and incitement and dwelling at some length on the risk of a clash with Israel over Jordan, he came out flatly with the statement that, 'There were no plans got together to attack Egypt; there were military discussions of various kinds and finally the decision was made on that day.' Eden spoke again in winding up the short debate. 'I want to say this on the question of foreknowledge and to say it quite bluntly to the House that there was not foreknowledge that Israel would attack Egypt – there was not. But there was something else. There was – we knew it perfectly well – a risk of it and, in the event of the risk of it, certain discussions and conversations took place ... I would be compelled ... if I had the same very disagreeable decisions to take again, to repeat them.' These were the last words he was ever to speak in that chamber.[10]

Eden was holding a series of individual meetings with his Cabinet colleagues to ask whether they thought he should carry on. He told Kilmuir, for instance, that he was not sleeping well and felt it hard to get back to his normal vigour. Several Ministers, including the Lord Chancellor and Patrick Buchan-Hepburn, the Minister of Works who was a recent Chief Whip, urged him to stay. Buchan-Hepburn wrote to him that, 'it would be a grievous blow to us in every particular if it appeared that the United States could influence the tenure of the British Prime Minister'. Peter Thorneycroft, President of the Board of Trade, who remembers being asked the question over lunch with the Prime Minister when their wives were present, answered: 'No.' The first reason he gave was Eden's health, which he doubted would stand up to the tremendous effort required to rally the party in the country. His second was the paramount need to rebuild the Anglo-American alliance. Eden thanked him graciously for his opinion and gave no hint of what he planned.[11]

Eden's first move on taking back the helm was to make a renewed attempt to relate the fixing of a final date for the evacuation of British and French troops to the acceptance by the UN of all or some of the Anglo-French salvage fleet. This would provide some leverage, he thought, that could be used on the Egyptian government when it would become necessary once again for Britain and France, this time through intermediaries, to come to grips with Mahmoud Fawzi on how to implement the Six Principles.

He soon found that it was not going to be easy to get his way. General Wheeler was showing no sign of being in awe of the reputation of Anglo-French salvage. He appeared uncomfortably accommodating to President Nasser about alternatives. The UN would not take the Anglo-French fleet as one unit, though it was willing for the ships already working on Port Said harbour to finish the job there, and it was asking for two German heavy lifting ships to be released from their charter to the Admiralty. In addition six heavy-lift British ships were wanted but only provided they were crewed by Dutch, Swedish and Norwegian salvage men. Egypt was not prepared to permit British and French crews to operate beyond Al Cap and Lord Hailsham only heightened the atmosphere when he appeared, larger than life, at Port Said declaring that Wheeler's pledge to assemble in ten days a salvage fleet comparable to the Anglo-French one 'could only be greeted with total incredulity by my advisers'. In the hearing of the press General Wheeler, the honorary knight, was dismissed as 'an old mid-Western grocer'.[12]

Re-enter Mr Dulles

Anthony Eden was not the only ex-invalid to return to the scene. By mid-December John Foster Dulles was back attending a Nato Council meeting in Paris, with instructions from the presidential holiday home in Augusta, Georgia to the effect that Nasser was to be regarded as evil and that King Saud was to be built up as his Arab rival, with which competition Nasser would 'not last long'. To him Selwyn Lloyd bemoaned the fact that, 'as the result of what we had been told by the United States Administration', Britain had agreed to withdraw her forces 'virtually without conditions'. Now every bit of satisfaction was being denied to her – General Wheeler was not using her salvage ships; the Egyptians were either deporting British nationals outright or putting the rest under such heavy pressure that they would be obliged to leave with absolutely no security for their property; the 500 civilian contractors from the base were still interned with no assurance of when they would be released; British commercial assets had been sequestrated, the war material in the Canal base seized.

Dulles said the British and French action had caused revulsion throughout the United States; there could be no hope for world order if the Americans acquiesced in such behaviour. For instance – in a sly reference to Eden's diplomatic attitudes in the Far East – Presidents Synghman Rhee of South Korea and Chiang Kai-shek of Taiwan had, since Suez, been getting together to start a war of Asia by co-ordinated attacks north of the 38th parallel (in Korea) and against the Chinese mainland. The implication was that it was only because of the principled stand by the United States against the settlement of disputes by force that these disastrous moves had been averted.[13]

Reporting back to the President, Dulles said that the British were moving towards support of the European Common Market because Suez had shown that they could no longer act as an independent Great Power. He also observed that the Egyptians had been much cleverer than their opponents in dealing with Hammarskjöld, with the result that they often seemed in line with his objectives.[14] Hammarskjöld, who had not, according to Cabot Lodge, receded from his low opinion of President Nasser, his 'local and unsteady viewpoint' and his 'primitive character', showed no little resistance when put under pressure to go out to Cairo to negotiate with him again.[15]

Pierson Dixon confided his doubts about the 'amazing Swede' in a letter to the Permanent Under-Secretary on 22 December. He was finding, he said, that Hammarskjöld was increasingly difficult to deal with on Middle Eastern questions. 'In the first place he is a very obstinate creature with a unique gift for combining high moral principles with an obscurity of thought and expression, which makes it almost impossible sometimes to understand what he is saying, let alone what he is driving at.' The Secretary-General seemed, Dixon complained, to 'feel obliged to pay special deference to Egyptian susceptibilities and to seek Fawzi's approval on all points and at all stages'. The reasoning behind this the Ambassador knew perfectly well, although he found it difficult to swallow: 'He sees Egypt', he said, 'as the victim whose wishes must be consulted on all matters affecting her territory, whether this be Canal clearance or use of the U N force.'[16]

Evacuation

On 15 December – the date Lloyd had once mentioned to Hammarskjöld as a likely Evacuation Day – the British tried to bring the Canal clearance question to a head by saying that either the entire allied salvage fleet must be accepted for the work down the full length of the Canal and given adequate protection by the U N or it would all depart.

The unceasing strain on the Secretary-General was at last beginning to tell. 'Hammarskjöld, I think,' cabled Dixon in a personal message to Lloyd, 'is on the verge of collapse. He literally burst into tears this evening when I told him of the ... Monday ultimatum for withdrawing our salvage fleet.' For all Dixon's efforts to preserve a detached and critical attitude to the Swede he realised how much Britain now depended upon him. 'Surprisingly enough this strange intellectual whom we have elevated into a superman is made of flesh and blood. It may sound absurd but if this man collapses or turns against us our position will become immeasurably more complicated.'[17] In this extremity Selwyn Lloyd's personal regard for Hammarskjöld was an undoubted advantage. 'I am sorry he is upset,' he cabled back. 'You should tell him that he is the last person with whom we want to get at loggerheads.' As for the ultimatum, 'I am not quite clear (it being Sunday here) how the statement came to be made that the salvage fleet is to be used as a whole or not at all.'[18]

The ultimatum failed. General Wheeler declared that he could manage without the six heavy-lift ships, whose passage down the Canal was the most crucial part of the argument. This undermined the allied position. The only question now was how many British and French ships should be allowed to remain to finish up the work in Port Said.

Anthony Eden wished to retain as formidable a presence as possible. 'The British and French fought tooth and nail for every ship', recalls George Ivan Smith, the Australian UN official close to Hammarskjöld. The suspicions of covert action, always alive in the Middle East and now exceptionally well fuelled by the recent record, produced among the Egyptians the rumour that the Suez allies intended to 'blow the whole business up again and have a [fresh] dispute in the Canal'.

On 31 December Hammarskjöld told Dixon that his American Executive Assistant, Andrew Cordier, was just back from a four-hour session with Nasser with no others present; as a result at last the details of the salvage operation were sewn up. The UN fleet was to be a formidable force of thirty ships, of which fourteen would be provided by the Dutch and five each by the Danes, Germans and Italians. This did not include the eleven Anglo-French ships which would operate only in the Port Said section, and were to be phased out in between fourteen and thirty days. When Dixon showed himself less grateful for this news than Hammarskjöld thought he should have been, the latter did not hide his irritation and muttered that the British were getting more than they deserved.[19]

When the salvage agreement was reached, the British and French troops were no longer in Port Said. General Keightley, to whom the final decision on the date had been delegated, had decided to leave on 23 December, but this could not be announced in advance because of Pineau's requirement that troops still be there during the scheduled foreign affairs debate in the Palais Bourbon. There was a last minute flap, when Keightley, who had arranged that the civilian Base contractors should be released in return for

Egyptian prisoners-of-war, discovered that the French had just made off with their own prisoners, who were already at sea. Eden cabled Mollet that he was 'most deeply disturbed'. Mollet responded immediately: the ship carrying the prisoners was turned round and brought back to Port Said.[20]

For the French at Port Said, who had seen their prisoners as a 'gage' to use in securing the release of Frenchmen who had been arrested in Egypt, this seemed the last straw. Their temper was not improved when Sir Hugh Stockwell remarked that, unless they hurried up the exchange, which had been arranged without a word of consultation with them, the contractors would not be home for Christmas 'and that would be a tragedy'. This seemed to Beaufre and his political adviser Baeyens typical of the way everything was settled in private talks between the two Anglo-Saxon generals Stockwell and Burns without a word to the French, while Stockwell complained that his subordinate Beaufre seemed to prefer to get his instructions from Paris. Certainly they had different ideas about the occupation. Beaufre wanted to carry out aggressive patrols to show who was boss. Stockwell, for all his volatility, saw the advantages of circumspection and kept his head down.

In the circumstances, it is perhaps no surprise that Baeyens in his final report observed that it was not betraying any confidences to report that not one of the French officers at Port Said would ever again wish to be placed under the orders of this general.

On 23 December, the troops left Port Said, the British boarding by night because Stockwell wanted to avoid provoking incidents, the French by day because Beaufre wanted to preserve prestige and honour.[21] The UN mounted guard while the troopships pulled out past the proud statue of Ferdinand de Lesseps, prophet, promoter and digger of the Suez Canal, with a tricolour taped defiantly to his outstretched arm. They left behind one officer, 2nd Lieut. Moorhouse, who had been kidnapped and of whom no trace was found, until, subsequently, his asphyxiated body was discovered locked in a metal trunk. On Christmas Eve, a huge crowd assembled in Port Said harbour to watch Ferdinand de Lesseps blown off his pedestal at the third attempt. Today only his shoes, embedded in the concrete, are left behind.

The Texas Railroad Commission

Next to General Raymond Wheeler, the favourite butt of the anti-American critics in the British press had become the Texas Railroad Commission, the quaintly named body which regulated the production and conservation of Texas oil. The Commission had three members, of whom the best known was the colourful and opinionated General Ernest O. Thompson; the men met in the middle of each month at the state capital of Austin to fix the number of days' production that was 'allowable' for the following month. This was arrived at after receiving 'nominations' by the large companies of the amounts of oil they would expect to buy and also after listening to representations from other oilmen. It was of importance during the Suez crisis that the Commission had to take into account the contrasting interests of different parts of the Texas oil industry, and especially two parts, the 'majors' who owned the pipelines and refineries and were linked in with the multinationals, and the 'independents', who were not.[22]

Suez found the world supply of crude and refined products at an historic high; the Texas 'allowable' was only fifteen days. The multinationals acted immediately to assuage Europe's thirst for oil by running down their large East-coast stocks and by seeking to stimulate home production in Texas and Louisiana. On 15 November the man from Humble, the unsuitably named subsidiary of Standard Oil of New Jersey, rose before the Railroad Commissioners in Austin to make a proposition that scandalised the 'independents'. Citing Europe's desperate plight, he proposed that the Commission break its top sacred rule that the quota must be uniform for the 10,000 wells that it regulated. The object of the rule was not only to keep up the price but to prevent the majors from flooding the markets. Humble wanted, instantly in mid-month, to be allowed to move to nineteen days' production in eastern Texas, where the oil wells were mostly near the coast and hooked up with pipelines, while western Texas, where the majority of wells were not so hooked, should stay at fifteen.

'It seems to me like that today, inadvertently, the truth has slipped,' said Harry Jones, who described himself as 'a little independent from Kilgore'. The majors had been lecturing men like him for years about the perfect security of America's increasing dependence on foreign oil. 'Today they send one of their messenger boys and he tells us there is a little flurry somewhere – we couldn't even find it on the map if we wanted to. Now he's coming back to us and wanting more oil.'[23] Men like Harry Jones were not in favour of bailing the 'majors' out when they were in trouble without much more assurance than they had heard so far that they had learnt their lesson. Sob stories about Europe were not good enough. What they wanted was evidence that once the Canal was open again the majors would not revert straightaway to their preference for cheap, imported oil from the Middle East. As General Thompson himself had put it, 'The torrent of foreign oil ... robs Texas of her market.'[24] Furthermore the 'little men' were for having their (mainly) western wells linked up to pipelines and their existing (embarrassingly large) stocks taken off their hands.

A quavering voice from an old-timer ended the exceptionally long hearing at Austin. 'I was amazed this morning. In fact, as old as I am, my face turned red. I was very much worried that one of the companies here this morning was advocating selective buying.'[25] The Texas Railroad Commission, as yet under no pressure from the Federal Government who wanted to keep the squeeze on Britain and France, was sympathetic. Humble was humbled, the allowable was kept at fifteen days for another month, and General Thompson did not conceal his suspicion that the apocalyptic mood of crisis was being artificially worked up by the newspapers.

From the outset of the Suez crisis at the end of July the Federal Government, through Dr Arthur Flemming, the Director of the Office of War Mobilisation, working with the Department of the Interior, had activated an emergency procedure for use if supplies of oil were in danger. At the end of August, under its provisions, the Middle East Emergency Committee was set up with limited immunity from the anti-trust laws. On it were represented the fifteen leading oil companies with overseas operations, under a chairman drawn from Standard Oil of New Jersey. To this body, whose meetings were attended by government officials and by a strong contingent of British and French observers, the execution of a major item of US policy was to be delegated.[26] Its plans could not, however, be put into practice until a legal waiver had been issued by the Attorney-General. When the ultimatum was issued and the Canal blocked, the President, far from activating the plan, suspended all meetings of the Committee to make it painfully obvious that, until the UN was obeyed, not one finger would he raise to help the transatlantic flow of oil, which, for the time being only, nevertheless proceeded to run at a rather high level as the multinationals unloaded their East-coast stocks.

However, towards the end of November, when Rab Butler was known to be moving towards announcing evacuation and Vice-President Nixon was 'scared to death at the prospect of Nye Bevan in a position of power', Flemming was allowed to go ahead with the Middle East Emergency Committee, which was able to meet on 30 November and to proceed with the plan known as the 'voluntary agreement'. Flemming also undertook to 'work with the State Commissions' and to 'de-mothball' thirty-nine laid up tankers.[27]

There had thenceforward to be a massive exercise in switching of routes. Oil coming round the Cape was to be unloaded on the East coast of South America, thus releasing the same amount of Venezuelan oil for Europe. The 350,000 barrels of Saudi oil a day coming through the still functioning Tapline were to be unloaded in Europe (but not, on Saudi insistence, in Britain or France) instead of in the eastern United States, which was to get instead oil from the Caribbean and some from the Texas Gulf. 500,000 barrels a day from increased Gulf production was supposed to head direct to Europe. As Texas was the largest single source of oil in the United States and Flemming and the Emergency Committee were supposed to 'work with' the Texas Railroad Commission, the proceedings at Austin, Texas came under close, transatlantic scrutiny.

These were not, for the most critical period of the crisis, impressive. The Railroad Commissioners met on 19 December for the first time since the

President had given the go-ahead. They adjourned, without having made a decision, until the end of the month; then they decided not to put up the 'allowable'.[28] To Britain's press and politicians this seemed a preposterously frivolous response. Cartoons appeared showing the world being held up at pistol point by Texas and, since Texans were far from universally admired in the rest of the United States, that sentiment was echoed among many Americans. The total amounts of all petroleum products that were supplied kept Europe going at seventy-five to eighty per cent of normal consumption until the Canal was reopened, a level that was very considerably higher than disaster. On the other hand Britain wanted only crude, not petrol and refined products which America had in surplus, and this was to be got primarily from Texan wells. General Thompson felt his patience sorely tried. 'We have already shipped her many millions of barrels of crude', he said, 'but we only get criticism for not going all out at her bidding. England apparently still looks on us as a province or dominion.'[29]

In mid-February presidential and other pressure at last got through to the 'three bashaws' of Austin. The Texas 'allowable' was raised to eighteen days' production, which turned out, to many people's dismay, to be rather more than the system could readily manage. The crisis had been good for the oil companies. Humble raised the price of crude by 35 cents a barrel and twenty-eight competitors at once followed suit. Profits for the American based multinationals were up in the first quarter of 1957 by an average of eighteen per cent. When the Canal finally reopened, normal service was resumed; by August Texas was down to thirteen days' production.[30]

Petrol for Politicians

The Americans were not prepared to do a thing about oil for Britain until the British, by rationing, had shown willingness to do something for themselves. In any case there was a general feeling in Britain that it was time for industry and the general public to feel the impact of the Suez crisis. Aubrey Jones, the Minister of Fuel and Power, had ordered a first ten per cent cut in normal deliveries of fuels on 7 November. The full rationing scheme was announced on 20 November and came into effect on 17 December. The monthly allowance for the private motorist, adjusted to the make of his car, was supposed to enable him to drive 200 miles; 300 miles were allowed for business and the professions. There were cuts in public transport that ranged from a token five per cent on buses to a hefty fifty per cent on goods vehicles. Domestic heating was cut drastically to a third in the case of diesel and a quarter in that of fuel oil.

All this was taken calmly enough. Trouble arose over defining the special priority classes who were to get extra. One of these categories was political parties in the constituencies. Aubrey Jones has described that decision as a text-book case of what happens when a Minister is tired and distracted. The papers were laid before him at the end of a long hard day, he was told that there was all-party agreement about the political petrol and it went through on his nod.[31]

The Minister's advisers were right: there was no word of protest in the Commons. It was this which set off the row in the press. 'Tomorrow a time of hardship starts for everyone', wrote the acerbic John Junor on 16 December. (Having failed three times to get elected to the House for Scottish constituencies as a Liberal, he was to edit the *Sunday Express* for the next thirty years.) 'For everyone?' he went on. 'Include the politicians out of that. Petrol rationing will pass them by. They are to get prodigious supplementary allowances. Isn't it fantastic?' It had been no accident, he suggested, that there had been silence in the House. After all the strains of the past few weeks this was just too much, and Junor was found guilty by the Select Committee of Privilege of grave contempt. The committee had unanimously found that 'politicians' in his polemic would have been taken by the public to mean MPs.[32]

Summoned to the bar of the House he had so much wanted to enter, Junor availed himself of the opportunity to deliver an accomplished speech which, in appropriately respectful form, repeated the argument the committee had summarily rejected, namely that the politicians of whom he had written were the constituency workers who had received the extra petrol. Rab Butler, as Leader of the House, thereupon showed his quality as a parliamentarian by responding in a manner which in *Hansard* seems wholly incomprehensible but which had the effect on the House of inducing it to move on rather than make a bigger fool of itself than it had done already.[33]

The Eisenhower Doctrine

The obstacle of the British and French presence on Egyptian soil now having been removed, the American Administration felt that the time was ripe for propounding that independent American policy in the Middle East which had been much missed in recent weeks. It was clear that the post-war assumption, not ever adhered to completely, that Britain could be safely left to take the lead when the West was dealing with the region, had abruptly ended. In taking up for America the role (in which she has been cast ever since) of a major participant in Middle Eastern affairs, Eisenhower had a choice between building on his new credibility in the Afro-Asian world following his stand over Suez or seeking to force Middle Eastern issues into the thought patterns of the cold war.

There is evidence that the President was thinking along the former lines just immediately after the Suez invasion. On 15 November, in the context of deciding with Herbert Hoover, Allen Dulles, and the CIA official in charge of the U-2 high-altitude intelligence flights whether to send a mission over Soviet territory, Eisenhower suddenly said: 'Why need we go in? How much good will it do? Everyone in the world says in the last six weeks the United States has gained a place she hasn't held since World War II. To retain it, policies must be correct and moral.' In accordance with that mood, it was decided at the time not to schedule flights along the Soviet border.[34]

But this mood does not seem to have held for long. The message that Eisenhower sent to Congress, which launched what was to be labelled the 'Eisenhower Doctrine', was drawn out of the cold war locker. The President had decided that he needed more authority from Congress before he could pursue an active policy. Dulles told the Senate Foreign Relations Committee in a closed-door session that Eisenhower 'takes a more conservative view of the power of the Executive than some other Presidents have taken'. He was, therefore, asking Congress to agree in advance to military action in support of the territorial integrity and political independence of states in the Middle East, states who requested such aid 'against overt armed aggression from any nation controlled by International Communism'.

The issue was pressed with a great aura of haste. At the very beginning of January (1957) the new Democrat-led Congress was just meeting for the first time since the elections which had coincided with the Suez conflict. What Senator William Fulbright of the Senate Foreign Relations Committee later described as 'dramatic secret meetings of the Committee' were held 'after dark one evening before Congress was even organised, in an atmosphere of suspense and urgency'. Dulles felt it necessary to apologise for the fact that there had already been background briefings of key members of the press. For this he produced an ingenious reason. 'I was frankly much concerned lest, if we said nothing about it, our effort here would be portrayed as being responsive to the thinking of the United Kingdom ... and it would have been disastrous for us in any plan in the Middle East if it seemed to be inspired by the British ... On the other hand, they would very much have liked to have it appear that way. [T]hey would be glad to ride back on our shoulders if they could.'

Dulles argued that it had been Britain which for a century and more had been the bulwark against Czarist and now Soviet ambitions in the area; that bulwark had been swept away by the 'very improvident and unwise' British attack on Egypt. The British and French would very much like to know whether the formula Congress was being asked to endorse would mean that, if there was a communist government in Syria, the United States would overthrow it. The answer, Dulles said, was 'No', because 'we do not believe it is possible to invoke force for aggressive purposes – this is exactly the thing the British and French claimed they were doing in the case of Egypt, forestalling a Soviet-controlled government in there'.

Nevertheless, Dulles said he was convinced that 'with proper activity on our part', it would be possible, where Communists might take over, to help the non-communist people to overthrow the communist regime. This was in line with his thesis that it was only in countries adjacent to Soviet military power that communist revolutions were irreversible. 'I tell you, Albania is no exception because in Albania the Communist Government could be overthrown if we knew what in the world to do with Albania afterward ... Guatemala is, I think, a typical illustration.'

Hubert Humphrey, the loquacious liberal Senator from Minnesota, asked whether it would not be better for the United States to join the Baghdad Pact. Dulles replied: 'The British are in the Pact and if we go into the Pact the British are going to expect us to pull them back.' Also, King Saud was violently opposed to it and it remained American policy to build up the King as a counter-pole to Nasser. Finally, Iraq had the habit of offsetting its associations with the British by being more violently anti-Israel than anybody else, so it was as well for America not to get too close to Iraq.[35]

The Eisenhower Doctrine, which besides its military provisions – which Hubert Humphrey described as 'a predated declaration of war' – proposed economic aid for both civil and military purposes to the countries of the region, was launched on the public on 5 January with no little anti-Communist clatter. 'The reason for Russia's interest in the Middle East', declared the President bluntly, 'is solely that of power politics.' He explained that others had more estimable motives, such as economic self-interest. It was curious, in the light of America's palpable wish not to be confused with the British, how reminiscent the vocabulary of the new policy was of the more extravagant British expressions, with an extra dash of American morality. If 'alien forces' were to dominate the region, this would lead to the 'strangulation' of the free nations. 'Western Europe would be endangered just as though there had been no Marshall Plan.' Then again, it would be intolerable for the birthplace of three great religions to be 'subjected to a rule that glorifies atheistic materialism'. Free nations should 'look behind the mask ... Remember Estonia, Latvia and Lithuania.'[36]

Before it became public the tone and content of the message had been severely criticised within the Administration by the head of Policy Planning at the State Department, Robert Bowie. In his opinion it needed to be considerably revised. In its total effect it over-stressed the Soviet military threat, which most people would not consider the imminent danger, and relied too much on military cures. Furthermore it failed to 'recognise any legitimate Soviet interests in the area, even in terms of its security'. Bowie said that 'many will feel that this is hardly justified, especially in view of our position under the Monroe Doctrine'. The Soviet Union would interpret the initiative as aiming to create a strong American military position in the area and from this conclude that the only choice left to them was to stir up as much turmoil as possible. But the worst omission was that, in contrast to the Tripartite Declaration, the programme offered no means of controlling or limiting the risk of Arab-Israeli hostilities; Congress would be seen to authorise the use of force only against communist aggression, thus undermining other existing undertakings. If the Afro-Asian states interpreted the Eisenhower Doctrine as converting the Middle East into an area of the cold war, Bowie concluded, it was likely to impede America's ability to muster support.[37]

When the message was issued, the Syrian Government produced a prompt reply. It 'considers the vacuum theory to be an artificial one ... since there is no vacuum in the Middle East now that its countries have achieved their independence and freedom'.[38]

What Middle East Policy Now?

While America was going forward with the Eisenhower Doctrine to fill the vacuum that was assumed to be left by Britain's eclipse, the Eden Cabinet was still in the business of cutting losses. For example, Suleiman Nabulsi, the nationalist Prime Minister of Jordan, was firmly committed to bringing the Anglo-Jordanian Treaty to an end. On Lloyd's proposal, the British Cabinet decided that this Treaty now brought Britain no real advantages in return for the money it cost and the embarrassments it created. The Jordanians should be told that, in the light of their public statements, Britain had no wish to maintain an alliance that had evidently become onerous to them.[39] It only remained for Charles Johnston, Charles Duke's successor, to commence negotiating in amicable fashion the details of British disengagement. Three days later Egypt, Syria and Saudi Arabia agreed to pay between them £E 12.5 million a year to make up for the loss of the British subsidy.[40]

Yet it was not long before King Hussein was to show that he was not deaf to the anti-communist message that was coming out of Washington. It took him only a few months to disembarrass himself of both the civilian and the military leaders of Jordanian nationalism, Suleiman Nabulsi and Ali Abu Nuwar, and to anchor himself under the lee of the Eisenhower Doctrine.

This was the first outcome, in the end much better than could reasonably have been expected, of the Foreign Office's efforts from mid-December onward to pick itself up, brush itself down and come out with a Middle East policy that would make sense after Suez. The prime necessity was seen to be that of rebuilding the Western alliance. Philip Geyelin, the correspondent of the *Wall Street Journal*, described his conversations with (anonymous) Foreign Office officials at this time. 'After the Suez affair, galling as it may be, there should be no doubt that Britain cannot afford to go it alone,' said one. And another: 'Britain is going to be a very junior partner for a long while.'

Nevertheless the paper on 'Middle East Policy' drawn up in December by a committee chaired by Sir Paul Gore-Booth, while more modest than earlier documents would have been, evidently retained the instinct to meddle. The paper circulated in at least two drafts. Their content can only be inferred from letters of comment on them, since these have been released while the document itself has not. From these remarks it seems that policy post-Suez as outlined by Gore-Booth was to resemble Middle East policy pre-Suez, except that there was much more emphasis on the need for the Americans to play the major role in protecting Western interests and (no doubt, as the result of loss of enthusiasm for Jordan) there was to be even more reliance than before on Nuri's Iraq. There was evidently a shopping list of policies which Britain should advance, headed by Nuri's favourite, the Fertile Crescent. From this it could have been concluded that the Foreign Office had in mind years of continued close involvement in Arab domestic policies. In the Embassies the message of Suez had made a swifter impact. They foresaw a much more modest role.

The main difference between the two drafts concerned France. The first draft had Britain hastening to dissociate herself from the French, 'to escape the odium with which they were regarded by the Arabs'. The revision had the French being induced to bring their policies into line with Britain's. P. H. Laurence, who manned the Levant desk, clearly had a preference for the original version. If keeping in step with the United States was now so important, this was hardly compatible with keeping in step with the French, since the Americans could abide the French almost as little as could the Arabs.[41]

The idea of discriminating between the two compromised Western Powers appealed to the fertile mind of Nuri es-Said. He immediately broke off diplomatic relations with France and set about trying to get the French removed as minority shareholder in the Iraq Petroleum Company.[42] The degree of dependence of the proposed 'new' British policy on Nuri seemed to Gladwyn Jebb in Paris to be unhealthy. 'If Colonel Nasser fully recovers his power and Nuri is by chance bumped off or dies', he remarked in a letter to Kirkpatrick, 'the whole of the officials' report and the tentative policy based thereon will presumably have to be thrown into the waste-paper basket.'[43]

In the course of a long and thoughtful letter to Gore-Booth, Sir George Middleton, the Ambassador in Beirut, said bluntly: 'We can forget about the French in our Middle East policies. They have no position left . . .' As President Chamoun of the Lebanon had put it, 'It only remains to say a mass for their souls.' Even Gladwyn Jebb's letter to Kirkpatrick, who had sent him a copy (presumably of the first draft) of the paper on Middle East policy, acknowledges that 'our situation in the Arab world is at present so precarious that we must travel as light as possible'. Sir Ivone had made it clear in his covering letter that 'our recent close co-operation with the French in the Middle East cannot long survive'.

'My general criticism', wrote Middleton of the Foreign Office paper as a whole, 'is that the report assumes in places that we can control the evolution of the Middle East. We never could do that except in isolated instances and localities and we still less can attempt to do so now.' The same modesty was recommended from Ankara. 'It seems to me', Sir James Bowker wrote, 'that the moment has come, in view of our recent setbacks in the Middle East and our acute financial difficulties, to try and simplify and concentrate on essential objectives': these were oil and its effective delivery. Countering Soviet infiltration could be left to the Americans.[44] 'We have become very much junior partners in the Western Alliance', Middleton told Archibald Ross on 20 December, '... and in the Middle East this fact stands out a mile.'

Jebb questioned whether it was in Britain's interests to assume responsibility any more for the settlement of the Palestine problem. 'The general condemnation of our intervention in Egypt ... seems to give us an opportunity to put an end to the Tripartite Declaration and to leave the future handling of the Palestine question entirely to the UN.' As for the Fertile Crescent, was that really a possibility? 'We are more liable to burn our fingers ... than to achieve our aims.'

Finally, there was Egypt. Middleton thought that, 'In working for the downfall of Nasser [which, inferentially, must still have appeared as an objective in the report] ... we must bear in mind that Egypt, by virtue of its geographical position, size and culture, has many natural qualifications for leadership in the Arab world. It seems to me that in arriving at the *dénouement* of the Suez crisis ... we have had to accept the fact of Egypt as an independent sovereign state, supported by most of the world against our attempt to coerce her. We are relatively worse off from a bargaining point of view than we were in October and must adapt our policy accordingly.'[45]

29

The End of the Suez Conflict

It was evident that for us to remain in Gaza, ostracised by the world and facing terrorism . . . would not accord either with Israel's capabilities or with its vital requirements . . . What the British could not afford in Palestine or in India, we, too, cannot afford to do.

David Ben-Gurion to IDF commanders, 4 April 1957.

I do not pretend that the position is satisfactory. This is not a satisfactory settlement and the reason is that it is not a settlement at all . . .

Harold Macmillan to the House of Commons, 15 May 1957.

Sir Anthony Eden had now had a chance of seeing whether his health could take the strain of power at the top. Over the New Year the fevers and the sleepless nights returned. As he told his colleagues, since Nasser had 'seized the Canal' he had been 'obliged to increase the drugs considerably and also increase the stimulants necessary to counteract the drugs'. This had had 'an adverse effect on my rather precarious inside'.[1] There was a series of fraught medical consultations. Eden was most reluctant to go because, as he has expressed it in his memoirs, he was certain that events in the Middle East were about to vindicate him. 'I was more confident than in 1938 as to how, unhappily, the position would unfold. Further intervention would be inevitable in some part of the Middle East, certainly by ourselves and possibly by the Americans. I wanted to be there when that happened.'[2] From Washington were now coming noises attendant on the birth of the Eisenhower Doctrine. Eden was convinced that only American obtuseness had prevented him from carrying Suez off. With America on board, late as usual, there would soon be a new Suez.

It is sometimes suggested that factors other than his health affected Eden's final decision to resign. This is unlikely. He would not have got so far without very considerable tenacity; and, for all the rumours that make up a political correspondent's life, it used in fact to be extraordinarily difficult, and even in 1990 did not prove easy, to unseat an incumbent Prime Minister between elections, however unsuccessful the policies he has been pursuing may be shown to be. Eden had discussed the problem with his Cabinet Ministers; others besides Thorneycroft had doubtless advised against carrying on. But even in Thorneycroft's case the advice had been couched in a way that had stressed health rather than reputation or judgment. Some people were aware of Eisenhower's strong views about Eden's conduct but he himself was buoyed up by the courtesy of the messages that 'Ike' had exchanged with him on the occasion of his return. If the Prime Minister had been really determined to stay, it would have been hard to see what (in the short run, at least) would have stopped him.

But Eden had had recent experience of an unfit Prime Minister hanging on. He asked the doctors whether he could 'last out till the summer or Easter at the earliest', but they told him they would not give him more than six weeks before the likelihood of another collapse. On that basis he decided to go without delay. There were two Cabinet meetings on 8 January but Eden did not attend the second. He had gone to Sandringham. From there he wrote to Churchill: 'I have heavy news about health. The benefit of Jamaica is not significant.' Salisbury and Norman Brook had agreed that it would be of no use for him 'to drag on for such a short period of time' as the doctors allowed.[3]

The following day, after a final Cabinet, he resigned. The Queen made no formal request for advice about a successor, but gave him a chance 'to signify that my own debt to Mr Butler while I have been Prime Minister was very real' and that Butler had done very well while he had been away.[4]

The contingency which many people had anticipated, either because they hated the Suez policy or because they despised its failure or because they simply thought Eden's health insufficiently robust, had occurred. The change had to a considerable extent been discounted; when it was announced the country expected as a formality that Rab Butler, who had for two extended periods presided over the Cabinet under Churchill and under Eden, would be sent for by the Palace. Among political correspondents, only Randolph Churchill trumpeted in the *Evening Standard* that it would, without question, be Harold Macmillan. At this time the Conservative Party retained a curiously tribal method of 'evolving' a leader rather than electing him. People remembered the Baldwin succession in 1923, when the sovereign exercised choice but in a somewhat hieratic manner. On this occasion, a less mystical method of taking the views of the Cabinet was devised. Lord Salisbury, having been asked to advise the Palace (as was Churchill), combined with the Lord Chancellor to ask the Ministers one by one for their opinion. The result was overwhelmingly for Macmillan.

One cannot help but reflect on the irony of the choice. Butler had admittedly not had a good year in 1956. He had been very much at the periphery of the Suez story until Eden had been clever enough to win his backing for the final adventure. Then he had shown considerable skill in guiding the Cabinet, party and country along the tricky path out of the swamp. He might well have thought that the succession was his by right. Macmillan's emergence as the victor was amazingly reminiscent of Churchill's in 1940, with triumph rapidly crowning failure. Churchill had been deeply implicated in the disasters of the Norwegian campaign, to the extent that Lord Hankey, then a member of the War Cabinet, described its course as threatening to be a re-enactment of Gallipoli, the campaign which had nearly wrecked Churchill's career for good. If there had been one person more set on destroying Nasser than Eden it had been Macmillan; one person more responsible for the most serious misjudgement of all, that of Eisenhower's likely reaction to an Anglo-French ultimatum; one man whose abrupt change of front contributed most of all to the aborted nature of the campaign. Yet, two months after his talk of being ready for the morgue, Harold Macmillan's was the older blood to which Eden gave way.

Talking to survivors from the Eden Cabinet, the impression they give is that the main reason for Macmillan's victory was that Rab Butler was the alternative. 'I could not imagine Rab taking a coherent decision about anything,' was one Minister's recollection. After describing Macmillan as a charlatan, Aubrey Jones (who as a Minister outside the Cabinet was not asked his opinion) says that he would nevertheless have voted for him because Butler was 'indecisive'. Butler was intellectually very gifted. His personality, enlivened by a whimsical sense of humour that was the stuff of affectionate anecdote, was much to the taste of political journalists. But his fellow-Ministers disliked his unfortunate habit of asking a large number of people for advice in a manner that did not convey democratic scruple so much as chronic uncertainty. He was a great back-room boy, everyone seems to have felt, but he was a pedestrian speaker, not a man, for all his qualities, to lift the Tory Party out of the ditch.[5]

End of the Freeze

The Suez Canal crisis could not be counted as over until the Canal had been reopened to traffic and the world could see on what terms that was done and with what result. In a telegram that went out from the Foreign Office on the day that Eden resigned, Pierson Dixon was told optimistically that 'we continue to aim at a Canal regime in which there would be an equilibrium of power between an Egyptian Canal administration on the one hand and an organisation of users on the other'.[6] But the British had reconciled themselves to there being no final Canal settlement by the time a channel was cleared for shipping; thus provisional arrangements must be made before Nasser got a chance of laying his hands on all the Canal dues.

Almost precisely similar sentiments were being expressed in Washington. George Humphrey, of all people, was now so thoroughly aroused by the thought of the dangers involved in Nasser's having complete control over the Canal that, when Allen Dulles reported to the National Security Council on 7 February that clearance was proceeding at a very rapid pace, he insisted that every single minute was important to them in securing a binding agreement. The trouble was, as Secretary Dulles explained, Hammarskjöld rather than the State Department was in charge of this negotiation and he had a number of other things on his hands. In any case, under the still operating Omega Memorandum, the United States was already applying about every sanction she possessed against Egypt except the ultimate one of military force. Admiral Radford was obviously longing to do more. He wanted the Israelis to 'prove themselves smart ... bring their own ships to the Canal' in time for the opening, and then, if they were stopped, 'we and the UN would be in a position to impose sanctions on Nasser'.[7]

London and Washington were agreed in preferring the World Bank as an interim collecting agent. The Bank should pay half the dues over to Egypt and retain the balance against final settlement. Co-operation between the Western allies was beginning to resume. Duncan Sandys, Macmillan's Minister of Defence, a hard man determined to cut the costs of defence and reshape the armed services in a drastic way, was in Washington at 27 January, and was invited to the White House to see the President, the first such contact there had been since the 'great freeze'.[8] When Harold Caccia joyfully disclosed the fact of this ice-breaking meeting to British press correspondents at the Embassy that evening, Sandys, who seemed much put out by his exposure to the privileged treatment reporters receive in America ('you even find them walking about the corridors of the Pentagon, including the *Tass* correspondent'), remained sourly unforthcoming.

In February, Guy Mollet and Christian Pineau at the head of a full delegation from France were received in Washington by Eisenhower and Dulles. Mollet, invited to start, turned the proceedings over to his Foreign Minister, who gave a complete exposition of the main features of the Treaty of Rome, which was now ready for signature. When he had finished, Eisenhower said that the day this became a reality would be one of the finest in the history of the free world, perhaps even more so than the winning of the war.[9] The French had found a stylish way back to grace.

Peacekeeping in Gaza

Relations between the United States and France's ally Israel were by now at a low ebb. Continuous application of American and UN pressure, with the prospect of another severe Afro-Asian resolution with full American backing laying the foundation for sanctions, prompted the Israelis to announce on 13 January their withdrawal from all occupied territory except for Gaza and Sharm al-Sheikh. They were determined not to abandon these two prizes unless they had worthwhile guarantees that neither *fedayeen* raids from the first nor naval blockade from the second would be possible. The Egyptian response to this was to encourage the Palestinians to resume the *fedayeen* campaign. On 2 December Cairo Radio had announced that '*Fedayeen* HQ has decided to carry out large-scale action during the coming winter season'. On 24 December it said that 'the Arab Governments are training *fedayeen* and instructing them in warfare which is neither forbidden nor shameful. The Government of Egypt is organising the *fedayeen* and instilling in them readiness to fight.' On 11 December the railway line was blown up three miles inside Israel by two landmines; on 15 December a house was completely demolished killing a man inside; on 23 December an Israeli Health Service clinic was destroyed in one place, a reservoir and water pipeline in another. The message being sent was that the Arabs were not intimidated and would not stop, at least so long as Israel was on Egyptian soil.[10]

Eban, in a skilful propaganda campaign in the United States, concentrated on the Staits of Tiran, where Israel had a good case. The General Assembly, he contended in an *aide-mémoire* given to Hammarskjöld on 23 January, could not have intended its resolutions to lead to the restoration of an illegal situation with a consequent eruption of conflict. The Israelis wanted UNEF to take over Sharm al-Sheikh to ensure freedom of navigation and stay there until there was a peace settlement. They did not seek to annex Gaza or maintain a military force there, but Egypt should never go back and UNEF was not needed to go in. The Strip should continue to be administered and policed by the Israelis who would supply services and develop local government. 'Israel will make its full contribution towards any UN plan for the permanent settlement of the refugees, including those of Gaza.' The commitment that the Israelis carefully avoided making was that this 'full contribution' would take the form of the settlement of all the Gaza refugees inside Israel, though they would have taken some. The fact was that Israel wanted Gaza out of Egypt's hands for security reasons but was no more willing than before to absorb into Israel the enormous number of Palestinians that it contained.

The *aide-mémoire* was a shock both to the Secretary-General and the Americans. Henry Cabot Lodge thought it 'a very unfortunate turn of events on a par with the invasion of Sinai on 29 October of which it is a continuation', and Hammarskjöld, who thought (correctly) that some of the proposals were personal to Ben-Gurion, labelled them as 'impossible'. The same day Hammarskjöld made what turned out to be an equally impossible suggestion of his own, though it commanded American and Canadian support, which was that UNEF should be stationed on both sides of the demarcation line, the Israeli side as well as the Arab. In no way would Ben-Gurion, who was having his own difficulties with four especially hawkish members of the Cabinet who threatened to resign, countenance such a proposition.[11]

Although now classed by Ben-Gurion as 'our Number One enemy after Russia', Hammarskjöld was by no means insensitive to the fact that while Israel had been responsible for aggression, it had not been unprovoked aggression. The aggression had to be vacated, but should not the provocations also be made to disappear? 'You will note my insistence on the withdrawal of Israeli troops behind the Armistice Demarcation Lines as a prerequisite for everything else', the Secretary-General wrote to Nasser on 24 January, 'but you will also note that I feel that there can be no return to conditions as they were before the crisis, although the change, of course, should be in spite of and not because of Israel's military action'.[12]

On 11 February Dulles read Eban an *aide-mémoire* which commanded a withdrawal from Gaza that should be prompt and unconditional but said that, when Israel had obeyed, the UN should move in and 'be on the boundary' between her and the Strip (a phrase which presumably meant, though it did not say so, on both sides of that boundary). Also, if Israel left Sharm al-Sheikh without conditions (thereby in effect vacating her offence) UNEF would come in and the United States would be pledged to exercise the right of free passage into the Gulf of Aqaba for herself and would encourage others to do the same. 'We have a strong sense of moral responsibility', said the Presbyterian Secretary, 'to take further steps if Israel withdraws and the blockade is resumed.' Israel and the United States with their high moral standards should work together and proceed hand in hand down the path towards peace and progress.[13]

This did not make a very brilliant impression in Israel. David Ben-Gurion, still showing the effects of his recent bout of pneumonia, laboured through a whole day's Cabinet on the subject on 14 February. He emerged at the halfway point, after a morning in which he had been the sole speaker, subjecting the American document to extended exegesis, to give an interim report to the American Ambassador. He seemed to Lawson 'completely spent' by the effort, his voice nearly gone. The Armistice Agreements did not any longer exist, he croaked, and nothing would make Israel return to them. There must be an Israeli civil administration in Gaza, the nature of which he would like two, three or four weeks to explore with the United States.[14]

The situation at the United Nations was becoming acute. Israel had still not complied with the Assembly resolution. Cabot Lodge said that a two-thirds vote for sanctions against Israel would be obtained at any time if the United States voted for it or merely abstained. With mounting reluctance he was holding off the heavy pressures from week to week.

It was indicative of the intensity of the controversy as to whether or not the American vote should eventually be cast for sanctions that both sides thought they were losing the propaganda war. To the beleaguered Israeli

Ambassador it seemed that even sections of the American press that were normally favourable to Israel were becoming impatient at her delays. 'It is now Israel's turn to be reasonable,' said the *Washington Post* of 13 February. Moreover, untiring advocate though he was, Eban could no longer believe in the briefs he was getting from Ben-Gurion. Although it had been the Ambassador who in the first place had determined that Israel should give ground only slowly, he was now thoroughly shaken by the Prime Minister's stand that Israel's positions should not alter even under the immediate prospect of sanctions.[15]

To Dulles, on the other hand, the most worrying factor was, he told Lodge, 'the terrific control the Jews have over the news media and the barrage [to] which the Jews have [subjected] Congressmen'. The opposition to sanctions in Congress was overwhelming and, if it went to a vote, it would probably be unanimous against them in both Houses. Dulles wanted Lodge to stall still further; 'We don't want the Israelis to know we are weak on this thing at all'. Lyndon Johnson, the leader of the Democratic majority in the Senate, had written saying it was impossible to organise economic weight against little states when the UN had made no pretence of doing so against large states (like the Soviet Union in the case of Hungary). The Republican Senate leader, William Knowland, had wanted to have notice of any American vote in favour of sanctions so that he could resign in advance from the American delegation to the General Assembly.[16]

At this stage, on 20 February, Eisenhower addressed the nation, confronting with his immense prestige and recent electoral success the high-powered bipartisan opposition to sanctions against Israel. 'We are approaching a fateful moment', he said, 'when either we must recognise that the United Nations is unable to restore peace in the area or the United Nations must renew with increased vigour its effort to bring about Israeli withdrawal.' The President discussed the nature of Israel's replies and said that he would be 'untrue to the standards of the high office to which you have chosen me if I were to lend the influence of the United States to the proposition that a nation which invades another should be permitted to exact conditions for withdrawal'. He had no choice, he said, but to exert pressure upon Israel to comply. To the Israelis this meant not just the cut-off of official aid – that had already started – but interception of private aid as well. Dulles told Lodge that this, if it could be enforced, would be 'fatal for Israel'.[17]

On the days following the speech the White House anxiously examined its mail. It was a relief, in a way, that ninety per cent of it was from Jews (other Americans did not seem all that worried) but, of that percentage, ten per cent was for the President, ninety per cent against. Secretary Dulles phoned an ex-colleague on the National Council of Churches and, in a mood bordering on despair, begged for some strong Sunday sermons in Protestant churches on the morality of getting Israel out of Egypt. 'It is impossible to hold the line because we get no support from the Protestant elements of the country,' he complained. 'All we get is a battering from the Jews.'[18]

Eban meanwhile was back in Israel. He had decided that it was vital to reason with Ben-Gurion, to persuade him that, with America's willingness to uphold Israel's rights established, the declared objectives of the *Kadesh* campaign had been achieved. He was sent on his way by what he described as a 'downright unpleasant interview' with Dulles and his officials, an interview in which, according to the American record, his arguments were dismissed by Dulles as 'only of secondary importance' and one of the officials sharply remarked that in Gaza it made no sense to say that an Israeli civil administration could remain after the departure of Israeli troops. When he went in to see Ben-Gurion, Eban demanded to know what exactly he did have in mind for the future of Gaza.

The 'old man' burst out in a torrent of words: 'Gaza as a part of Israel would be like a cancer. In return for a small sliver of territory we would take responsibility for some 250–300,000 Arabs ... Our interest in Gaza is security. To take a small territory with a vast Arab population would be the worst possible exchange.' When Eban returned he had the authority to accept an understanding with America about the Straits of Tiran, provided that each detail of the arrangement was satisfactorily clarified; in return the Americans should, if possible, be persuaded to put off consideration of what to do about Gaza.

Dulles warmed somewhat to the change in Israeli tone. But there was to be no relaxation over Gaza. His legal logic was remorseless. The American commitment over the Straits, which the Israelis so much wanted, depended on the assumption of the absence of belligerency; this would hardly be compatible with the Israelis exercising the right of belligerency to administer Gaza. But, he observed not unkindly, the French were in Washington and had put forward a plan which, if acceptable to the Israelis, would gain American support.[19]

Christian Pineau, to whom Eban then turned, proposed a solution which, surprisingly perhaps from a man who appeared sometimes to hold the United Nations in such low regard, was founded on Hammarskjöld's favourite device of advancing by a series of unilateral statements and assumptions. Pineau felt that Hammarskjöld should first have to be able to 'state with confidence' that Egypt had agreed that the orderly take-over of Gaza from Israel should, 'in the first instance', be undertaken exclusively by UNEF; he should also state that Egypt had 'the willingness and readiness to make special and helpful arrangements' to allow the UN to take over the administration of refugee affairs. Then the Israelis should go, on the clear understanding that UN forces would put 'a definite end to all incursions and raids across the border from either side'.

Eban tried to get Hammarskjöld to go several stages further: to say, for instance, that UNEF would not be withdrawn from Sharm al-Sheikh, even at Egypt's request, until the General Assembly had first had a chance of debate. Dulles was prepared to agree this, but the furthest the Secretary-General judged it practicable to go in writing was that, if asked by Egypt to leave, he would seek the advice of the Advisory Committee of nations contributing to the UN force before acting. This apparently trivial distinction was to be of absolutely crucial importance during the build-up for war in 1967. Hammarskjöld was also asked to say that *de facto* UN administration of Gaza precluded the direct or indirect return of Egypt to the territory. He replied simply that he was bound by the Armistice Agreement which entrusted control of the Strip to Egypt; his statements must be interpreted within that framework.[20]

Golda Meir accompanied her announcement of Israel's withdrawal on both fronts to the UN Assembly on 1 March with a couple of clear warnings. Israel would treat any interference with Israeli shipping in the Gulf of Aqaba or the Straits as entitling her to exercise self-defence under Article 51; Israel would likewise reserve the freedom to act if pre-war conditions returned to the Gaza Strip. The text of Mrs Meir's address was gone through in advance in the State Department with a fine toothcomb and Dulles reported triumphantly to the President over the phone, 'Mrs Meir made her speech precisely as agreed.' No comparable tribute was paid to Henry Cabot Lodge by the French and the Israelis. Christian Pineau and Golda Meir had been shown a less-than-final draft of his reply to her, they checked its delivery in detail and both got worked up about last-minute changes in wording which in their view weakened American assurances. Another letter from Eisenhower to Ben-Gurion was needed before the arrangements stuck.[21]

All dangers were not over yet. The status of Gaza remained uncomfortably ambiguous. General Burns cabled Hammarskjöld anxiously for instructions as to what to do if Egypt tried to send back elements of her civilian administration and her military presence as soon as the Israelis had gone. Hammarskjöld replied that the 'initial' take over was to be done 'exclusively' by UNEF. Burns was not to commit himself to anybody about the future and not to give an impression of tacit acceptance of Israeli 'assumptions'. UNEF would run 'a full administration' for 'a couple of weeks necessary in order to negotiate more definite arrangements with the Egyptians'.[22] This was not quite what Ben-Gurion and Abba Eban had in mind. In a private note, Hammarskjöld recorded that, in order to 'get over the hump', Israel, France and the United States had 'had to hide the underlying conflict of views so as not to provoke open discussion in the General Assembly'. On Mrs Meir's statement of 18 March that everyone who had not criticised what she had said on 1 March had assumed responsibility for all its 'assumptions', Hammarskjöld wrote that, had he acted on this basis, he would have wrecked the opportunity 'in a certain atmosphere of vagueness, pragmatically to get around a difficult corner'.[23]

On 6 March the Israelis began evacuation of both places and were out in forty-eight hours. UNEF in both cases replaced them. The Egyptians promptly opened up the Suez Canal to vessels of 500 tons and gave permission to General Wheeler's men to start raising the two remaining blockships. The links between the two events were never explicit but were quite apparent.

Back in February Hammarskjöld had been thinking in terms of establishing in Gaza a full-dress international administration. He told Dixon that it would be an immense operation, far bigger than what the League of Nations had tried to do in Danzig. He had been thinking of appointing an Indian general as governor and bringing in the American General Lucius Clay as adviser.[24] But this was to reckon without the Palestinian people who, rather to the surprise of some of the UN staff, now demonstrated in favour of renewed Egyptian rule. 'It was perfectly clear from the attitude of the crowds', General Burns wrote, 'that, whatever they wanted, they did not want rule by outsiders'. On 10 March UN troops had to disperse a mob by firing over their heads and one man was killed by a ricochet. The following day the appointment was announced in Cairo of General Mohamed Abdul Latif as Administrative Governor of Gaza and three days later he arrived to take up his duties.

The Israelis were appalled. Bourgès-Maunoury informed the American Chargé that, in concert with the British, he was making preparations to provide air cover for the Israelis in case they found it necessary to reoccupy Gaza. But this was no replay of Suez: the Foreign Office dismissed the idea as 'absolute nonsense'; the Quai d'Orsay had the satisfaction of accusing the Defence Minister of taking 'mere military planning exercises and perhaps his own desires for fact'. It was now once more the hour of the Quai; together with the Americans it calmed the Israelis down. What did it matter having an Egyptian Governor in Gaza if the Egyptian army was not there and UNEF provided a safeguard against the *fedayeen*? As Fawzi said to Burns on 19 March, the UNEF was 'now all over Gaza, but it would create trouble to announce it'. The question of co-operation with the UN should be left to Egypt without anyone 'pressing too much'.[25] This formula was found to work. The presence of General Abdul Latif seemed to satisfy the feelings of the residents, at least to the extent of avoiding riots.

When Hammarskjöld arrived in Cairo on 21 March, it was possible for him to reach a twelve-point oral agreement on Gaza with President Nasser which lasted. Deliberately avoiding issues of principle, this was based on a list of practical requirements which Burns had drawn up for the UN in order to put a stop to infiltration and maintain order. For a few weeks there were still some incidents of infiltration but, since the Egyptians had orders to co-operate with UNEF in stamping them out, they rapidly dwindled. Bitter initial criticism in Israel of UN ineffectiveness died away. Gaza became an advertisement for successful peacekeeping. Palestinian activists now encountered a hostile climate, while in Cairo Yasser Arafat found that it was time for him to move on to Kuwait.[26]

A month after Israel's withdrawal from Gaza, on 4 April 1957, Ben-Gurion produced an explanation to his military commanders for his decision. 'During the few months we governed in Gaza', he said, 'we saw that we could, apparently, make order there, but it was evident that for us to remain in Gaza, ostracised by the world and facing terrorism ... would not accord either with Israel's capabilities or with its vital requirements ... In this we're no better or worse than the British. What the British could not afford in Palestine or in India, we, too, cannot afford to do.'[27] It was a remarkable concession.

Two Old Comrades in Bermuda

After the French had been in Washington, it was Harold Macmillan's turn. Eisenhower and Dulles were Britain's guests in Bermuda from 20 to 23 March. The Middle East, unsurprisingly, played a large part in the agenda, but the restoration of the 'special relationship' was the main theme. Fletcher Knebel, the American humourist, caught the mood best when he visualised this dialogue:

'Eisenhower: What are we gonna do, Mac, about the Middle East?
Macmillan: I dunno, Ike, but it's nice to be asked for a change.'

Both men recorded in personal accounts the instant re-establishment of the rapport which had existed between them in North Africa during the war. They established a pattern for future contacts, in which a happy glow almost succeeded in obliterating the considerable divergences that continued between them without obscuring the realities of power. The President wrote at the end of the first day: 'The meeting was by far the most successful international meeting that I have attended since the close of World War II'.[28] 'There is no doubt,' Macmillan triumphantly reported to Menzies in Australia, 'that, as far as the President is concerned, things are back on the old footing. Dulles, who by temperament and conviction is a sort of Gladstonian Liberal who dislikes the nakedness of facts, has also come a long way, but still, I think, lags a little behind his Head of State.'[29]

Selwyn Lloyd, whom Macmillan, despite his former doubts as to his adequacy, had kept on at the Foreign Office as a symbol of continuity, weighed in on 20 March with 'a tirade against Nasser, saying he was not only an evil, unpredictable and untrustworthy man but was ambitious to become a second Mussolini'. Macmillan took over the next morning. 'If Nasser is absolutely obdurate, if we all have in the short run to eat dirt and accept a bad and unjust settlement, I hope you won't say in public or in private that it's a good settlement,' he told 'Ike'. '... If we have to accept a humiliating defeat don't let's call it a victory or even a draw. Let's make it clear that we'll get him down – sooner or later.' Anything else would cause a rift in the British public's feelings towards America that would take a long time to repair.[30]

The American response to this struck the British as being very mild. Dulles, in particular, gave the impression of trying to make things up. Macmillan's account, however, does not dwell on the substance of the President's reply. According to Eisenhower, this centred on the inconsistency between this polemical approach and the urgent political and economic need, also stressed by the British, for a rapid outcome to the negotiations, which the Americans had now partly taken over from Hammarskjöld. 'If we were at this moment to begin an attack on Nasser (and we admit that he is far from an admirable character) and do everything in our power overtly and covertly to get rid of him, then the hope of getting an early and satisfactory settlement on the Canal would be completely futile.'

On the Palestine question, there was little difficulty in the two sides agreeing to give a formal burial to Alpha and all thought of a comprehensive solution. What was needed was a period of tranquillity and a tackling of individual issues as opportunity arose, though Selwyn Lloyd emphasised that the present frontiers of Israel could not be 'justified and would have to be adjusted'. On the Middle Eastern situation as a whole, the Foreign Secretary produced his list of Suez accomplishments: the Israelis no longer felt hemmed in and were more relaxed, the bubble of Egyptian military power had been pricked ('no chance of Nasser's becoming a new Saladin'), UNEF was on the ground, Soviet penetration had been revealed.

The President told Macmillan that he never read the newspapers or listened to the radio, but that his Press Secretary told him about foolish speeches by members of Congress and foolish articles that made bad blood across the Atlantic. He recognised that British attacks on him and Dulles were natural, though they pained him all the same. But the conference had 're-established complete confidence between himself and the Head of the British Government'. Macmillan took the precaution of intruding on his friend's euphoria the thought that 'he must realise that my difficulty was that it was the most patriotic and traditionalist elements in my country which were the most disturbed'.[31]

Suez Canal Reopened

Harold Watkinson, the Minister of Transport, was quite blunt when he reported to the Prime Minister the results of his consultation with British shipowners on 12 March. From their meetings with their foreign colleagues the position seemed plain: if the Suez Canal was cleared before any agreement had been made, 'there is no likelihood that there would be sufficient support internationally to give a boycott any chance of success'. If that was correct it would remove such leverage as Britain and France still hoped to exercise. Watkinson had warned the shipowners that tactically it was important to keep the Egyptians guessing for the present. They agreed to do what they could but they made it clear that 'once some shipowners start using the Canal, others will be very tempted to do the same and it would then be impossible to hold the position'.[32]

The jointly sponsored scheme of the United States, Britain, France and Norway for the World Bank to collect Canal dues and hold back half of them, which, to Washington's fury, the British leaked, was in any case dead before birth. The Egyptians announced on 18 March that they were going to collect all the dues themselves. On the other hand, according to the rather sketchy six-point draft which was circulated to the diplomatic missions in Cairo, Egypt would stick to certain rules. She would abide by the Constantinople Convention, 'having proved herself thoroughly able to manage the navigation', would levy dues according to the last agreement negotiated with the Canal Company and would create a special fund for improvements which should be fed by a certain proportion of the revenue. Canal dues should be paid in advance to the Suez Canal Authority 'or its nominees'.[33]

This document did not make a good impression in London, Washington or Paris, but only the French talked immediately about organising a boycott. When they realised that the British would not go along, they begged them not to mention a word about this to the Americans. The Foreign Office's objection to the Egyptian draft was to its unilateral form, its failure to mention the Six Principles, and the absence of provision for any organised co-operation between the Egyptian Authority and the users. Among officials, Archibald Ross declared downright that 'as it stands, this document would represent a hands-down victory for Nasser at a very undesirable moment'.[34]

Hammarskjöld also attempted to get the Egyptians to accept 'organised co-operation', not necessarily through SCUA but perhaps through a body with more universal membership. His financial adviser, John McCloy, chairman of Chase Manhattan, spent five hours with President Nasser on 1 April and spoke 'with the utmost bluntness'. According to his own account, McCloy drummed it into Nasser that the Canal was a diminishing asset unless the Egyptians did something to recognise its international character. Otherwise alternatives would be, indeed already were being, devised. Nasser said he was afraid of 'tying himself up for eternity'; he did not want to limit Egypt's sovereignty for another hundred years.[35]

The British Cabinet considered on 3 April what to do when the Canal was completely cleared, which would take place on 8 April, one month ahead of General Wheeler's initial schedule. It was not a very satisfactory discussion and arrived at no conclusion.[36]

Britain and France were visibly beginning to diverge, after nine months of holding themselves in line. Gladwyn Jebb was told by Louis Joxe, the Secretary-General at the Quai d'Orsay, that Britain seemed to think that, since she was not going to be able to stop her ships from using the Canal much longer, she must bow to the inevitable. France felt that was wrong; she favoured a meeting of the Security Council as soon as possible to reaffirm the Six Principles and to insist on a multilateral negotiation about the Canal.[37]

The Foreign Secretary, meanwhile, was reporting to the Cabinet that a revised Egyptian memorandum, fleshing out in a helpful way several of the original points, had now been circulated and might be said to cover five of the Six Principles (the sixth being insulation from the politics of one country). The main objection was still to a unilateral document, which the Egyptians would be at liberty to withdraw at will. There lacked any sanction to compel the Egyptian Government either to observe its terms or to accept the award of any of the arbitration proceedings for which there was now some provision. But by the Cabinet of 17 April, Ministers had come round to the notion that the best they could get was a unilateral declaration, registered at the UN as an international commitment.[38]

On 24 April Fawzi transmitted to Hammarskjöld a letter stating that 'the Government of Egypt are pleased to announce that the Suez Canal is now open for normal traffic'. He accompanied it with a very much fuller and more sophisticated version of his Government's declaration. Any increase in the tolls of more than one per cent per year would have to be negotiated and, failing agreement, be referred to international arbitration. The Canal was to be developed 'in accordance with the progressive requirements of modern navigation', including the eighth and ninth Programmes already laid down by the old Company. The Egyptian Government declared that it would welcome and encourage regular co-operation between the Canal Authority and representatives of shipping and trade. Tolls would be payable in advance to any bank authorised by the Canal Authority, and the Bank of International Settlements (rather than the World Bank) should be one of these. Twenty-five per cent of all gross receipts should be paid into a separate Suez Canal Capital and Development Fund. Disputes about discrimination, violation of the Canal Code, or proposed changes in that Code should go before an arbitration tribunal. Also questions of compensation and claims in connection with the nationalisation of the 'ex-company' should likewise be referred to arbitration. Differences arising out of the Convention of 1888 would go to the International Court of Justice, Egypt having now for the first time accepted its compulsory jurisdiction.[39]

On 6 May Selwyn Lloyd, in a lengthy cable to Hammarskjöld, accepted reality, recognising that time had run out, that the Egyptians had offered rather more than many people had expected, and that they were not going to offer any more.[40] Next day Whitehall sent out a circular to SCUA members declaring that information from British shipowners 'shows that the common front among the members of the shipping conferences in the dry cargo trades has virtually collapsed'. The only alternatives were to let the present position crumble rapidly or to act in accordance with the realities. Advice to British shipping not to use the Canal would be withdrawn.[41]

Gladwyn Jebb waited on Guy Mollet on 11 May to give him two days' notice of what Macmillan was going to say in the House of Commons and to consider how the damage of their divergence of opinion could be limited. Mollet, as always, played the part of a gentleman. He showed every understanding of the economic realism of the British move, of which he displayed not the slightest resentment. Macmillan's new policy was, however, not possible for him. He and Sir Anthony Eden had made declarations that they would never accept complete individual control by Nasser of the Canal. Eden no longer had any responsibility for the conduct of affairs; but Mollet did. He declared to Jebb that, unless he were prepared to resign, he personally could not adopt the same attitude as Britain now proposed to do. For him it would be like Munich all over again; it was better, therefore, to go down fighting. No doubt, he added, his successor, whoever he was, would wish to associate himself with Britain's views.[42]

France's tone and Mollet's political fate no longer in May exercised the Svengali-like hold on British policy that they had done the previous October. Macmillan was pre-eminently a man who knew *force majeure* when he saw it. On 13 May he announced in the House of Commons what eight Tory MPs promptly labelled 'HMG's capitulation to Nasser'. The news – that the Government could no longer advise British shipowners to refrain from using the Canal – was received in blank silence. The eight rebels met under Lord Hinchingbroke's lead and announced that they had dropped the Conservative whip. Another member, Lord Lambton, resigned as Parliamentary Private Secretary to Selwyn Lloyd. The Hinchingbroke Eight issued a statement declaring Macmillan's decision to be 'one episode in a long series of retreats that started off with the Labour Government's weakness at the time of Abadan ... [E]ven though all the alternatives are unpleasant, the final surrender to Nasser will be interpreted by the people of Britain and by friends of Britain overseas as a sign both of national weakness and, far worse, of decaying will.'

Mollet offered his resignation to President Coty because of 'the British capitulation'. The President refused it, but Mollet made no secret that his only reason for staying on was that he did not want to be accused of 'funking' the parliamentary battle ahead. Macmillan prepared his dispositions carefully for his own ordeal, the two-day debate to which he had agreed. First, he made plans to launch a programme for the building of as many supertankers as possible and to prepare the special harbour and repair facilities that they would need. Next, on the morning of Monday, 15 May, as *hors d'œuvre* to the parliamentary debate, the Government announced the end of petrol rationing.

It was in a mood of 'extreme ... nervous strain', that the Prime Minister prepared himself for the last act, as far as Britain was concerned, in the drama of the Suez conflict. For all the appearance of poise, sense of occasion and perfect timing that Harold Macmillan increasingly supplied as he settled into his Premiership and which continued to extreme old age when, although too blind to read any notes, he would thrill younger generations with his evocative and witty addresses, he was in fact a very nervous speaker. For his Suez Canal speech, he wrote afterwards, he worked until 2 a.m. on its preparation and was 'wholly unprepared for the ordeal that awaited me'.

The Opposition were out to shake his nerve. 'They kept up', Macmillan said in a diary entry for that day, 'a sort of wave of laughter, jeers, catcalls, etc., just not enough for the Speaker to interfere but very disconcerting. This quite spoiled the serious parts of the speech – especially the long passage on the future transit of oil – and made me rather fumble other parts.'

Macmillan started by asserting that the decisions Eden took had been 'with the full, complete and unanimous support of his colleagues', and that 'his actions and those of his colleagues will be fully justified by history'. Nevertheless, the Government had to face facts as they were. 'I do not pretend that the position is satisfactory. This is not a satisfactory settlement and the reason is that it is not a settlement at all. It is a unilaterally drawn prospectus of the terms on which the Egyptian Government are prepared to offer the use of the Canal to potential customers.'

But, nevertheless, he conceded that 'on the face of it, if – and, of course, this is the big "if" – these conditions are kept, then the Egyptian proposals in these respects are not so very far from what the Six Principles envisaged'. It would not be tolerable if the rest of international traffic were to use the Canal and Britain alone were excluded by her own will. 'We have, therefore, thought it right to advise our British shipowners accordingly.' Macmillan struggled through the speech 'as manfully as I could; still, I got to the end'. His press notices were not too severe – except for the 'Suez Betrayal: Eden Was Deserted By His Colleagues', of the *Daily Express* – but he noted unsparingly of his performance on this testing occasion, 'It was not a success.'

A two-day debate gives a Prime Minister a second chance. Also there was a special factor: news had come that morning from Christmas Island that Britain had exploded her first H-bomb. Worrying about the effect of Tory abstentions on his majority, Macmillan wound up the debate. 'We hope that it will be better than yesterday,' shouted a Glaswegian Socialist, as Macmillan formally asked leave to speak again. 'By some miracle' this speech was 'as great a success as that of the day before had been a failure,' the Prime Minister recorded afterwards, much relieved. His own party had responded most warmly, members rising to wave their order papers at the end as he headed triumphantly towards the voting lobby. Despite fourteen Tory abstentions – the Hinchingbroke Eight and six more, including Lambton – the Labour motion expressing 'concern' at the Government's Suez policy was thrown out with a majority of forty-nine. Harold Macmillan was well content – his Government had passed its first big test. For Britain the Suez conflict was over.[43]

How much it was over was illustrated on 1 July when Independent Television News brought President Nasser into British drawing rooms to be interviewed in Cairo by Robin Day. There was no great outcry at the appearance of this erstwhile hate-figure. Day questioned him firmly and persistently but with courtesy. Abdul Nasser's answers displayed an absence of rancour and a desire to resume normal relations. He seemed evasive only about the status of Israel, which he linked to the fate of the Palestinian refugees. The day of 'telediplomacy' had arrived.[44]

For France the conflict was to carry on for one month longer. The Government was defeated at the end of May, and it took France a fortnight to get another. The man to emerge as Prime Minister was Maurice Bourgès-Maunoury, the dynamo behind the Israeli alliance. His initial vote of confidence was the lowest given to any new government since the Liberation. Jebb said that he already had a reputation as a poor orator but he had never seen him put up such an indifferent performance. His investiture speech was 'long, disconnected, insufficiently prepared and delivered in a series of nervous and sometimes almost hysterical shouts'.[45]

Both allies had now decided to abandon the conflict by promoting their premier hawks. Bourgès's first act as Prime Minister was to lift the French boycott of the Canal. He told Macmillan that he was not in the least opposed to the Baghdad Pact.[46] When he came to London, in the capacity of 'Polygone', for celebrations of the Resistance and de Gaulle's leadership of it, Bourgès-Maunoury asked his Ambassador, Jean Chauvel: 'Am I right in thinking that the British Government is anxious to put the memories of Suez firmly behind them?' When Chauvel answered in the affirmative, the French Prime Minister said that this was his object also. For him Suez was a completely closed chapter and he was most anxious to achieve complete co-ordination of British and French policy in the Middle East. But for the British, putting the memories of Suez behind them did not mean exactly that. A minute to Macmillan about Chauvel's account of this conversation sounded the authentic post-Suez note: 'For us, of course, it is far more important to achieve a meeting of minds with the Americans ... For some time to come, close relations with the French in the Middle East will be far more of a handicap than an advantage.'[47]

30

Epilogue

Of the two leading protagonists at Suez, the loser, Anthony Eden, for all his fragile health, lived on in retirement for twenty years, sustained by the devotion of his second wife, supported financially by the commercial success of his memoirs and, from 1961 onwards, known as the Earl of Avon. The winner, Gamal Abdul Nasser, received the adulation of the Arab crowds in most streets in the Middle East for having successfully withstood the 'triple aggression' of Israel and the two imperialist powers and for having broken the spirit of colonialism. Now, for everyone in Egypt and for many far beyond, he was the *Rais*, the Leader. He was to go on to other moments when he seemed to be riding high, most especially in 1958 when Syrian revolutionaries under Abdul Hameed Sarraj decided to pre-empt their communist rivals and, against Nasser's instinct of caution, proclaim straight political union with Egypt under his leadership. The same year the Iraqi army took over Baghdad, killed King, Crown Prince and Nuri es-Said, and destroyed for ever the pro-British regime. In 1962 the young new Emir of Yemen was believed to have been blown up in his castle by the Yemeni Chief of Staff who was a known admirer of President Nasser. The force seemed to be with Nasser. It looked as if the Arab world might well be united in the twentieth century as Germany and Italy had been in the nineteenth.

But Nasser's star was also crossed. Each of the bright successes was followed before long by a reversal of fortune. General Qassim, the austere soldier with the staring eyes who was the new military leader of Iraq, took Baghdad out of the Baghdad Pact, but, in alliance with the Iraqi Communist Party, was able to resist the efforts of those who wanted Iraq to join the United Arab Republic of Egypt and Syria. That union, which was intended to be the kernel of the Arab nation, broke up in 1961 after only three years of existence, as Syrians wearied of the clumsy efforts of Nasser's Damascus Viceroy, Field-Marshal (as he now was) Abdul Hakim Amer, to force them into an Egyptian political mould. And in Yemen, instead of collecting quick benefits from one dramatic coup in that remote and feudal land, Egypt was to find that the Emir, against all the odds, had escaped from the ruins of his castle and that large parts of the Egyptian army were committed to an endless and unrewarding civil war.

The Suez crisis enabled Egypt to sweep away at a stroke the non-Egyptian elements who had hitherto played such a prominent part in the commercial, academic and social life of the country. British, French and Australian management was removed. Laws were enacted requiring all banks, insurance companies and commercial enterprises to be Egyptian registered, with majority Egyptian shareholding and Egyptian management. Some 15,000 stateless persons, mainly Jews, were turned out over the next four years. The Suez Canal under Egyptian management was a success story. But the same cannot be said for much of the rest of now Egyptian-owned enterprise. With some exceptions in banking, the Egyptian private sector was not allowed the chance of taking over the sequestrated businesses. All the emphasis was put on developing heavy industry under state direction, which resulted in a top-heavy and over-centralised structure being super-added to an already cumbersome bureaucratic tradition.

Nasser's great and lasting achievement in the economic sphere lay in the construction of the High Aswan Dam. It was not until October 1958 that Khrushchev agreed to finance it, an action for which he was criticised in the Soviet Union, not least because the recipient of this largesse had such a short way with Egyptian Communists. The dam was essentially completed in Nasser's lifetime, though it was formally opened after his death. Two years after that all Soviet advisers were expelled from Egypt.

Nasser's relations with Moscow were, as someone once remarked of Mussolini's relations with King Victor Emmanuel, 'cordial but not friendly'; they could not conceal the fact that throughout the region it could be said that the Nasserites were the most effective counter to the Communists as, in the blocking of Egyptian hegemony, the Communists were the most effective counter to the Nasserites. Though Nasser's alliance with Khrushchev was to hold during Nasser's lifetime, neither side had many illusions about the other and Dulles's dictum – that no country not immediately adjacent to the Soviet bloc could be irretrievably lost to the other side – was surprisingly rapidly upheld.

In 1959 there was a famous quarrel relating to the story of Suez. It started in March with a Nasser speech, to which Khrushchev took exception, claiming that after the 'triple aggression', the Egyptians had only had Allah and themselves on whom to rely. In April, in the course of a long letter to the Egyptian leader, Khrushchev angrily took high credit for the effect of the Soviet threats of 5–6 November 1956. Unabashed, Nasser in his reply pointed to Moscow's earlier comprehensive rebuff to the Syrian President. As for the Soviet ultimatum, Nasser observed drily that it was issued without his knowledge after nine days had passed during which Egypt had been alone on the battlefield. 'Of what use would the ultimatum have been that day, Mr Chairman, if we had come to an end and fallen?'

The great Egyptian writer Tawfiq al-Hakim has written of Nasser's 'emotional and agitational nature' which he claims distinguished him from 'true politicians' like Nehru and Tito. He had, he says, 'more of the nature of a dreamy, emotional, artistic writer'.[1] And in the correspondence between them in 1959 Khrushchev wrote to Nasser, 'Knowing your impulsiveness we feared that our unlimited support of your belligerent sentiments might have prompted you to take military action which we have always regarded as undesirable.'[2] But while Nasser was one to take abrupt actions like the nationalisation of the Suez Canal Company he also knew how to sit back and wait. It was this ability that drove the British and French to the folly that ruined them.

Nasser had the most extraordinary luck in finding the Americans coming to his rescue in a way he would not have predicted. Unfortunately this led to his being convinced by his own propaganda that his forces had suffered no defeat in Sinai and to his retaining in command of his forces that ineffable pair, Field-Marshal Hakim Amer and the unready air force commander, General Mohamed Mahmoud Sidqi. They were still in charge when the next test came, in 1967. Then, unlike 1956, Israel had no allies in the field and Egypt had two, Syria and Jordan.

For Israel the settlement of 1957 brought ten valuable years of peace with Egypt at a critical period of her development, without incidents on her borders and with free passage of the Straits of Tiran, albeit the development of Eilat was disappointingly slow and Israeli shipping in the Red Sea not numerous. The war had not brought territorial expansion but Israel had obtained quiet frontiers, thanks to the services of the UN (whose emergency force grew to a maximum strength of 6,073 in March 1957 and was at rather more than half that number ten years later), which Israel enjoyed without ever admitting the peacekeepers to her side of the demarcation line. In the case of Jordan also, there was no serious incident between Suez and the autumn of 1966.

On Israel's northern border with Syria, from 1960 onwards there were incidents and reprisals of the familiar kind. By May 1967 the Syrians, perhaps led to it by the Russians, were of the belief that they were to be the victims of a major Israeli attack and called on Egypt for support. An erroneous Soviet intelligence report, passed to Cairo, appeared to confirm the danger. Nasser, stung by hostile Arab radios reproaching him for sheltering behind the UN, moved his troops up to the international frontier in Sinai, the local Egyptian general telling the UN to remove their posts. Hammarskjöld was dead. U Thant, his Burmese successor, took the position that Egypt could not pick and choose; all UN posts should be withdrawn or none. The Egyptian Government then officially requested the former.

Here the material insubstantiality of the pieces of sealing wax and string, which was all that Hammarskjöld had had at his disposal for performing his diplomatic wonderwork, became apparent. The principle was that Israel must not be seen to benefit from her aggression. Yet, if peace were to last, common prudence suggested that she must be shielded from repetition of past provocations. The square could only be circled if Egypt unilaterally bound herself to be policed at the borders by UNEF 'until UNEF's task was completed'. What Egypt unilaterally granted she could unilaterally take away. Hammarskjöld had written in a private memo to himself that, if he were ever confronted with such a request, he would summon the General Assembly so they could decide whether 'the task' had been completed – and gain time in the process. Thant did not do that, or go immediately himself to Cairo, or use his special authority under Article 99 of the Charter to refer the situation on his own responsibility to the Security Council. He did speak to his Advisory Committee, whose opinions were divided, and he complied with Nasser's request.[3] Having militarily reoccupied Sharm al-Sheikh Nasser announced the reimposition of the blockade of the Straits. Israel had made it abundantly plain in 1957 that in such circumstances she would regard herself, in the absence of swift American or international intervention on her behalf, as entitled to act in self-defence under Article 51.

'I have read every word written about the 1956 events', said President Nasser in publicly announcing the renewed blockade, 'and I know exactly what happened in 1956. Thus in 1956 we did not have an opportunity to fight Israel. We decided to withdraw before the actual fighting with Israel began.' He went on to explain that now all the secrets of Suez were exposed. 'The most important secret concerns Ben-Gurion when the imperialists brought him to France to employ him as a dog for imperialism to begin the operation. Ben-Gurion refused to undertake anything unless he was given a written guarantee that they would protect him from the Egyptian bombers and the Egyptian air force. All this is no longer secret. The entire world knows.'

Eleven years back, Nasser proclaimed, Egypt had only a few bombers; now she had many. Israel was no longer backed by Britain and France. 'The Jews threaten war. We tell them: You are welcome, we are ready for war ... War might be an opportunity for the Jews ... to test their forces against ours and to see that what they wrote about the 1956 battle and the occupation of Sinai was all a lot of nonsense.'[4] War began on 5 June with a pre-emptive low-flying air strike by Israel which eliminated at one blow the entire Egyptian air force, a task which, the Israeli fliers pointed out, had taken the British and French air forces all of two and a half days. The war lasted six days, at the end of which the Israelis had occupied Syria's Golan Heights, the West Bank and Gaza and the whole of Sinai. Nasser was shattered and resigned. But what he had stood for – the restoration of dignity to the Egyptian people – and what he still meant to the man in the street did not stand for nothing; there was a genuine surge of public opinion in his support and he resumed office.

Eden and Nasser, then, were both defeated, the one by world opinion orchestrated by both superpowers, the other by the force of Israeli arms.

In the case of both (Nasser being much the younger man) their health was gone. Nasser did not enjoy twenty years of retirement but struggled on for three more years in office. They were an anti-climax. He was chronically unwell, suffering great pain from severe circulatory complications in both legs. His diabetic condition, which first appeared in 1958, worsened. He died of heart-failure at the close of an exhausting inter-Arab conference in 1970 at the age of 52. He was succeeded by the man who, if Nasser had indeed been Hitler, would have had some claim to be accounted his Goebbels, Colonel Anwar Sadat. A brilliant propagandist, he had had little executive experience and had been only for a few months Nasser's Vice-President. His record from the time of Suez seemed to be polemically anti-Western. What he did as President was to throw out the Soviet experts, redeem the honour of the Egyptian army in the third war against Israel in 1973 (though without actually winning it), gain the confidence of the American Government and public opinion and sign a peace treaty with Israel on 26 March 1979.

Suez in Retrospect

Looking back on the story of Suez one asks: granted that Nasser had decided to nationalise the Canal Company, could the crisis have been handled differently? It is perfectly possible to see now, as it was sometimes possible to see then, what an agreed outcome of the dispute would have looked like. It would not have looked vastly different from what finally emerged in 1957 and has worked satisfactorily since, with Egypt accepting some voluntary limitations on her ability to dispose of revenues and to alter their amount. Probably but not certainly, sufficient diverse pressures could have been brought to bear on Nasser to secure his agreement to some form of 'organised co-operation' between the Egyptian Canal Authority and an association of users somewhat differently constituted from the body dreamed up by the three Western Powers, with provision for independent arbitration in case of conflict.

It was this type of solution that appealed to Eisenhower from the beginning and which was the basis of the various schemes proposed by the Indians. What Nehru and Menon said during the crisis made a great deal of common sense; it was unfortunate that Menon, the putative conciliator, antagonised in turn everybody in sight and that Nehru, who was after all himself the Indian Foreign Minister, did not play a more personal role. Though the idea of an Eisenhower–Nehru mediation was dreamed up by the American President's press secretary with an eye to the coming election, it was not, given the two men's instinctive approach to the problem, all that misplaced.

The major obstacle to such an approach and the reason why Dulles talked the President out of it was the strength of opinion in Britain and France at the beginning of August with the political leaderships talking mainly in terms of military force. Thanks to Dulles's leadership at the London Conference eighteen nations were lined up behind the innovative concept of an international regime for an international waterway. But Egypt was not present, let alone consenting; there was no way that, through the United Nations machinery, Egypt could be forced to accept a new treaty on penalty of legalised military action. The proposition was delivered to Egypt by Menzies, who was more than a postman, less than a negotiator – an orator, perhaps. If Dulles had himself led or even replaced the five-nation group, as Eisenhower wished, he might have engaged with the Egyptians in real negotiation. American mediation did not fail, as Alexander Haig's did between Britain and Argentina over the Falklands; it was not tried. Neither was co-belligerency, as recommended in America's own strategic interest, by the Joint Chiefs of Staff.

It was Mollet, not Eden, who described Nasser as a Hitler. Eden subscribed to the Mussolini analogy. Mollet thought he needed to destroy Nasser in order to set the stage for a negotiated settlement in Algeria. Eden saw Nasser acting as Russia's stooge to destroy the political and commercial basis of Britain's cheap fuel supply in the Middle East. Having got control of the Suez Canal, he would succeed in all his conspiratorial plans and thus acquire hegemony over oil states like Kuwait, Iraq and even Saudi Arabia as well as non-oil states such as Jordan and (at that time) Libya. The oil companies would be nationalised, the prices soar upwards and the European economies, just rescued at high cost by the Marshall Plan, would be put into immense jeopardy. Control over the Canal would enable the Egyptian President to set off oil consumers against each other by discriminating between those deemed friendly and those (namely Britain and France) deemed hostile. The dimensions of these fears might not seem so archaic in 1990 when measured against the alarm created in that year, above all in the United States, by Saddam Hussein, the dictator of Iraq, in acquiring nineteen per cent of the world's reserves of oil and threatening to seize twenty-five per cent more.

When Suez struck, Anthony Eden had dangerously little room for political manoeuvre: to the image of his unconvincing domestic leadership was added party discontent caused by his reputation as an appeaser in the Middle East. For some time his anger at Nasser had in private been rising while in the Commons his judgement had since the turn of the year been challenged from a pro-Israeli direction by the fresh voice of Hugh Gaitskell. For Eden's desire to strike back at once, he had at first the human rights excuse supplied by the official threats of imprisonment made by the Egyptians against non-compliant foreign staff, and in this respect he would have been backed by Gaitskell and (probably) by Eisenhower. But Britain no longer had the right hardware in the right place, and Nasser was quick to correct this one major error. If there had to be delays the Americans wanted to fill them with proper diplomatic moves, not with Selwyn Lloyd's first idea of a hole-in-the-corner get-together of a few friends to launch a hasty ultimatum. The result was that the task of matching the push-button military timetable with the more ragged and contingent political and diplomatic timetables was allowed to get out of hand, especially as one of the three powers with a hand on the levers, the United States, was not working to the same assumptions as the other two.

Washington and Whitehall were each manoeuvring to co-opt the other to its policies; Whitehall wanted to use SCUA to entrap the United States into co-belligerency, Washington hoped that the same device would entangle Britain in long-term pressures towards long-term solutions. Likewise, inside the British Cabinet, the one phrase – the use of force 'as a last resort' – was used as a means of carrying a consensus forward in the face of a wide variety of views until something else could determine the course to be followed. As time went by, it became indeed obvious that a 'new fact' or *casus belli* would be needed. Just as Nasser amazed Ahmed Hussein by suddenly switching the subject from the Aswan Dam to the nationalisation of the Canal Company, so General Challe at Chequers opened before Eden the way in which he could resolve his dilemma by changing the context. To deal with an adventurer, he was advised to use an adventurer's panache.

It is wrong to assume that all those involved took an identical attitude in each stage of the crisis. Selwyn Lloyd, one of the most bellicose at the beginning, had by early October to the dismay of the French come round to favouring international supervision rather than management. Pierson Dixon told his son at the end of August that, 'The Americans and Russians will hold the ring while we deal with Nasser.' A month later he was telling Macmillan in New York that 'the UK could not have a violent solution'.[5] Even Eden gave the impression during the days before the fateful interview at Chequers that he would have been resigned to Lloyd's negotiations reaching some compromise in New York. But if he was a waverer he was a reluctant one and, after all the weeks of tension aggravated by lack of sleep, which was partly due to the time differences with Washington and New York, and partly to the strains of his exhausting illness, he fell an easy prey to an over-ingenious idea.

The Suez operation was crippled by the inability of British political leadership, having embarked on the cynicism business, to be sufficiently cynical about the follow-up, and by Harold Macmillan's obsession (shared with his department) about the overriding importance of the integrity of the sterling area. If Eden was determined to win he should have seen to it that the Anglo-French armada was 'just over the horizon' when the ultimatum expired and the risk should have been taken of allowing those like General Gilles and Brigadier Kenneth Darling, who wanted to start operations by airborne landings at key positions along the Canal, to carry them out.

Those who professed so much faith in psychological warfare should have made immediate and utmost use of the confusion caused in the Egyptian command at the moment when they discovered that they had three enemies rather than one. They should have learnt from the Israeli example that, when planning an operation that is likely to be disapproved of by the UN, especially with American sympathy not secured in advance, there is the heaviest premium on speedy, sharp and even risky action.

Eden's worst mistake was in simply not realising – as a man with his sensitive international antennae might have been expected to do – the utter implausibility of the cover story. He was not himself a cynic by nature and he does not seem to have approached the question in a cynical mood. After all, if Israel was going to attack (and, for all he knew, the French and the Israelis might have persuaded each other to dispense with British help) there would indeed have been a danger of fighting across the Suez Canal (as was to occur during the War of Attrition between Egypt and Israel from 1967 to 1970). This would have constituted a threat to British shipping interests. Eden tried conscientiously to arrange events so as to conform to that picture and in doing so wrecked his chance of success.

If tripping over the logic of the Anglo-French scenario was one reason why the British stopped, the other was the critical state of the British currency and hence the threat to Britain's position as banker of the sterling area (which largely overlapped but was not co-terminous with the Commonwealth). The supreme irony of this crisis was that while Britain paid next to no attention to what was being said in the Commonwealth during its course (with the personal exception of the Prime Minister of Australia, who, after an initial wobble, was throughout supportive of Eden), thus making a farce of the special consultation features of Commonwealth membership and putting aside the sensible (if tiresomely projected) ideas of India, the preservation of what was substantially a Commonwealth institution was, when it came down to it, afforded absolute priority. If Commonwealth solidarity was that important, it would have made more sense to pay greater heed to Nehru's and Menon's views in the first place. The sterling area gave some lingering substance to the notion that Britain was still a World Power. It was to uphold that notion that Britain was at Suez. One aspect of fading greatness was sacrificed to save another.

Eden entered the Suez war with the dream of emerging from it as what he had volunteered to be in the Guildhall speech of a year before: the arbitrator of the Arab–Israel dispute. He would either stay on the Suez Canal or facilitate the UN's staying there if it proved itself capable of creating a genuine international police force until there was a final peace settlement, as well as a permanent regime installed for the Canal itself. But it is difficult indeed to imagine how he expected this to be done, how he thought he could impose his type of settlement, with some loss of Israeli territory and some return of refugees, on an Israel to whom he had placed himself under such an obligation or how he imagined his good faith would be accepted by any Arabs, at least until he had inflicted as much punishment on Israel as he had already done on Egypt. If genuine international settlements were being called for, would the UN be prepared to play a walk-on part in a script written by Eden? And how long would Britain have been willing or able, in her state of financial health, to maintain an occupation army of, say, three divisions until all these other matters had been sorted out?

Conceding that the task of a British Prime Minister placed as was Eden on 26 July 1956 was an exceedingly tricky one, it is clear nevertheless that he made a series of misjudgements fatal for a man in his exposed situation and disconcerting to the many people who believed in his star. It may have been on account of his health, though he was not the only invalid in high places (Ben-Gurion and Dulles were both taken ill during Suez and Eisenhower approached it as a recent heart patient) and afterwards he always rejected suggestions that his condition had been disabling. However, when he entered a Boston clinic in April 1957 his American specialist said that his condition then was such that his judgement could well have been impaired during the preceding six months. It could have been, as some eminent men including at least one member of his Cabinet have said, that, for all his brilliant accomplishments, he always, regardless of his health, lacked prime ministerial qualities. Signs of this, it is said, had been detected before Suez and by Suez this lack was pitilessly exposed.

But there is something to be said for a different or perhaps an additional proposition: that men often, in the end, fail at what they are best at doing; that having time after time emerged with reputation enhanced from some mission impossible until they are thought to have or think themselves to have some singular quality, they attempt or are trapped by cruel circumstance into attempting to pull off a last, unachievable trick. Eden's failure has, in this perspective of time, something of that tragic quality. Not many years were to pass before the man who emerged with most credit from Suez, Dag Hammarskjöld, was to suffer a fate not utterly different in the Congo.

Eden's partner in this affair, the French Government of Guy Mollet, was preoccupied with two things: the rebellion in Algeria, of which Colonel Nasser was regarded as the external head, and the negotiation of the European Common Market. Mollet and some (though not all) of his Ministers were convinced that until the external factor had been removed the political compromise over Algeria which they as socialists sought was beyond their reach. A number of the key Ministers were also influenced by a strong pro-Israeli bias, on the part of a Council for Ministers that was full of youngish *résistants* who also thought of the Israelis as fellow-Socialists. In addition French Socialists had some of the same reactions to Colonel Nasser as Aneurin Bevan in Britain – that he was a right-wing military despot, articulating an old-fashioned nationalism whose fallacies had been exposed in Europe, and that, by his abrupt nationalisation of the Canal Company, he was jeopardising the chances of an enlightened foreign policy that would place the main emphasis on rapid economic investment in developing countries. The main political difficulty with which Mollet had to contend was the feeling in right-wing circles that as a Socialist and pre-war pacifist he would not be sufficiently tough.

Fearing erroneously that Eden's objectives if he acted alone would be limited to the Canal and stop short of dumping Nasser, and being persuaded also of the critical importance for an operation against Egypt of Cyprus and the Canberra bomber, Mollet from the outset decisively offered to place French forces under British military leadership. He accepted the logical consequences of that decision; while others dreamed of acting alone, Mollet invariably opted for joint action and thus for acceptance of Eden's judgement of the time when it was necessary to halt that action. General de Gaulle, informed throughout of France's plans, disapproved only of the integrated command; the outcome seemed to vindicate him down to the last syllable.

The organisation which emerged with enhanced credit from the whole crisis was the United Nations; the individual was Dag Hammarskjöld. That sense of accomplishment was real enough to survive Hammarskjöld's subsequent controversial handling of the crisis in the former Belgian Congo and the sense after his death that his dispositions in the Middle East had been seen to fall to pieces in 1967. The lesson that was hammered home was that the Charter had singled out going to war for the sake of the national interest as forbidden ground; it outlawed not only unprovoked but provoked aggression. Lord McNair, who held the legally not highly subscribed view that the Suez Canal Company was sufficiently 'impressed' with an international character that Nasser's nationalisation of it was contrary to international law, nevertheless argued firmly that Britain and France were not entitled to resent that seizure by force. This might indeed reveal a lacuna in international relations, a class of grievance with no effective redress, but the alternative would be to fail to make that crucial break in the circuit of cause and effect in the use of violence which was the Charter's aim.

No serious attempt was ever made on this occasion to invoke the one Article, 51, which does permit the use of force – singly and collectively – in response to direct attack. What was done to the company could not effectively be portrayed as a direct attack on another state. Later, when it came to attempts to settle matters by negotiation, first the British and French in October 1956 over the future regulation of the Canal and then the Israelis in March/April 1957 over freedom of passage of the Straits of Tiran made it their aim to arrange things so that, should they ever again be aggrieved, they would not find themselves at such a disadvantage.

The *dénouement* of Suez was the most striking and immediate triumph ever achieved by economic sanctions, and it was achieved against that Power, Britain, which has, ever since, appeared as the chief sceptic of the effectiveness of sanctions whenever their use has been proposed. The impact was almost entirely psychological. There was no formal application of such measures either by the UN or by the United States alone; but the mere talk of them in the former and the refusal of the latter to respond instantly to Britain's urgent currency requirements were enough, in the circumstances of 4–6 November 1956, to put paid to the attempt to do a superpower's job on a British-style economy.

For the UN to achieve anything inevitably invites the reproach of 'double standards' because the UN does not achieve everything. This was especially the case over Suez because of its exact coincidence with the Hungarian Revolution, in relation to which the UN was almost wholly ineffective. The Soviet Union was able to withstand international pressures where Britain and France were not because 'their' superpower not only failed, in their estimation, to protect them, but was 'the leader of the pack' against them. It was not entirely a fair reproach. In the first place, the United States was not formally an ally in the Middle East. (In 1956, as opposed to thirty-five years later, it was the Americans who were most inclined to stress the limited area to which Nato commitments applied.) Secondly, Britain and France had, in any case, not behaved very much like allies of the United States in the immediate run-up to the expedition.

The United States did not in fact entirely neglect the duty of protection; she used her considerable skills in the management of the United Nations, for example, to ensure that Britain and France were never formally found to be aggressors, and of course she was firm enough when there was a question of Soviet military intervention. But, first and foremost, she was worried lest the Soviet Union be presented with a way of turning the almost universal reaction against the Anglo-French invasion of Egypt into a means of manipulating the machinery of the United Nations to suit her own purposes. That, at the time of Hungary, would have been a paradox indeed.

Thirty-five Years On

Experience with the Suez partnership determined Britain and France – that 'odd couple' in international relations – to try going their separate ways. With the failure to overthrow Nasser the heart went out of French resistance to the Algerian rebellion and also out of the Fourth Republic's ability to resist the constitutional notions of de Gaulle. Mollet's Government was the last Fourth Republic government of any length and stature, though, before it became the turn of the General, two short-lived Ministries took decisive steps which have conditioned France's role ever since. Under Bourgès-

Maunoury's premiership France ratified the Treaty of Rome, thus ensuring the birth of the European Community, that 'revenge' of which Chancellor Adenauer had spoken on the morning of 6 November. Under Bourgès-Maunoury's successor it was decided that France should be a nuclear power, so that she should never feel again as naked and exposed as she had done in the early hours of 6 November. When de Gaulle formed the Fifth Republic and served as its first President, Algerian independence was recognised, Israel's privileged access to the Ministry of Defence was ended, France withdrew from the integrated command system of Nato and, when Macmillan finally decided that Britain should apply to join the European Community, France cast her veto, reasoning that Britain was too entangled both with the United States and the Commonwealth to pursue a 'European vocation'.

After Suez Britain's overwhelming desire, to an extent which, to judge from his wife's letters to Lord Beaverbrook,[6] repelled Sir Anthony Eden, was to get back into good standing with Washington. This she succeeded in doing so that the 'special relationship' was interrupted, not severed, by Suez. But the relationship between the two countries in the Middle East was permanently altered. The pretence that Britain could take the lead was abandoned. What Churchill had said over Palestine in 1945 was effectively said for the whole region; it was someone else's turn now. Eisenhower and Dulles, turning down the contrary advice of the State Department's chief planner Robert Bowie, brought the United States fully into the Middle East on a strictly 'cold war' basis, the basis which since the beginning of 1956 Eden had been urging on her.

The open acknowledgement after Suez of what the British had begun in their hearts to suspect – that Britain was no longer a World Power – was dramatically made in the 1957 White Paper on Defence which ended the call-up in three years and abolished conscription in five and sharply circumscribed Britain's capacity for independent action. The final stages of decolonisation went rapidly ahead under a Conservative government, not without moments of great political tension but with the outcome conditioned by the demonstration effect at Suez of the harsh limits of British power. Although it was true in any case that the writing was on the wall for the British Empire by the mid-fifties, it was perhaps too much to hope that it could have all silently evaporated without one 'last stand'. In the circumstances it was a great mercy that this lasted just one week.

Because history's edges are seldom sharp, Britain's role in the Middle East enjoyed a brief Indian summer, when British troops returned to Amman at the urgent request of King Hussein to protect his throne at the time of the Baghdad coup of 1958. But they flew in by arrangement with the United States, which at the same time landed marines on the beaches of Beirut. Both forces left, but the American presence had signified much for the future, the British little. In the Gulf British influence lasted for a further decade. When Britain recognised the complete independence of Kuwait in 1961 and General Abdul Karim Qassim of Iraq promptly announced that his own men would walk in, the British were still able to produce troops who, sweltering in insufferable heat, held the line until they could hand over to an Arab League force organised by Nasser. A Labour Prime Minister, Harold Wilson, cherished the idea of a defence role 'east of Suez' and it was dropped not through any demand of the sheikhdoms (rather to the contrary) nor any influence of the United States (which was emphatically in favour of Britain staying) but through the factor that was basic, the decline of the British economy.

Since the day of the supertanker had by then come, the closing down of the Suez Canal after the 1967 war did not present the type of oil crisis which was feared in 1956. However, when the Canal was re-opened in 1975 it was found that competitive forms of transit had not replaced it. Few of those who in 1956 so dreaded the power of cheap radios to spread the word of Nasserite nationalism would have credited that so many of the traditional regimes would withstand the impact, that King Hussein would still be sitting on the Hashemite throne of Jordan in 1991, and that governments that were extensions of one family would still be the rulers of Saudi Arabia, Abu Dhabi, Kuwait, Bahrein, Qatar and Oman. The oil revolution did not, after all, come through the instrumentality of one revolutionary personality or his imitators. But it came, nevertheless, bringing the scale of price increases that Eden feared in 1973 and again in 1979–80. The industrialised West shuddered but survived; the non-oil producing Third World suffered far more harshly.

In Britain after Suez it became a general assumption that, regardless of the provocation, there would be no more solo flights. Britain would not use force in Rhodesia after UDI, though she had the sovereign right and would have been supported by the vast majority of the United Nations. There were, in any case, serious geographical obstacles to swift, effective military action. But there were also fears that a Labour government acting against white settlers with friends and sympathisers in the Tory party and in the army itself would be exposed to Tory reprisals for what was done to Eden at the time of Suez. Again, Britain would not use force in Cyprus in 1974 either, in the first instance against Greece or, later on, against the Turkish invasion, despite Britain's treaty rights and her having troops on the spot. The Foreign Secretary of the time, James Callaghan – the man who had regularly berated Eden, Head and Lloyd from a recumbent position on the Labour front bench in the Suez debates – cites directly the lesson taught him by Suez when in his memoirs he describes his reaction to the renewed Turkish attack which overran the northern third of Cyprus. Britain, he says, would have been ready to threaten and, if necessary, use force to hold the Turks back but, remembering Suez, not without specific

American support. This the American Secretary of State, Henry Kissinger, withheld.[7]

Since then, two events, the Falklands conflict of 1982 and the Gulf crisis beginning in August 1990 with the Iraqi conquest of Kuwait and culminating in the Gulf War of January and February 1991, have in their very different ways opened fresh historical perspectives on Suez. The Falklands War showed that Britain, contrary to what was generally thought after Suez, could after all act alone at a great distance from home base without abortion or catastrophe. The Gulf crisis of 1990–1 showed that in a post-cold war climate the United States, obtaining from the UN Security Council a succession of enabling resolutions, was prepared to intervene in strength, with allies that included Egypt, Syria and Saudi Arabia as well as Britain and France, against the threat of a single Arab dictator, exploiting the clichés of Arab nationalism in a bid to control the 'jugular' of the world's oil supply. It seemed at times as if the ghost of Anthony Eden were writing the speeches of George Bush. Both these instances, however, differed decisively from Suez in certain critical respects.

The Falkland Islands were a British territory to which Argentina had a longstanding claim. The peace was breached on 2 April 1982 by the Argentines. The UN Security Council thereupon passed a resolution, demanding the immediate withdrawal of all Argentine forces. In these circumstances British use of force was clearly covered by Article 51. Margaret Thatcher had the same problem as Anthony Eden of fitting the diplomatic moves into the necessary interval before the Task Force reached the area of conflict and thereafter of winding up the diplomacy and the political preparation promptly so that the Task Force was not left tossing about at sea. Secretary of State Alexander Haig's mediatory flights may at times have looked like John Foster Dulles's moves before Suez. But the differences were crucial. In the first place, because of his refusal to go to Cairo after the London Conference, Dulles did *not* engage in any negotiations with Nasser. Haig on the other hand *did* bargain with President Galtieri and his colleagues and, having found them intractable, came down decisively in favour of supporting Britain. Thanks to this, Mrs Thatcher was enabled to wind up the politicking (a little brusquely, perhaps) on cue for the landings. The Americans gave the British the type of assistance that the Joint Chiefs of Staff had unsuccessfully recommended should be given to them at the time of Suez.

The invasion of Kuwait was a clear case under the terms of the UN Charter of aggression by one state, Iraq, in order to annex the complete territory of another. The claim that this was merely a case of parts of one Arab nation coming together carried weight with some Arab crowds but not with Egypt, Syria or Saudi Arabia. Saddam Hussein was a much more coarse-grained, violent and cynical man than Abdul Nasser. There were echoes of Suez because some of President Bush's rhetoric sounded very much like Anthony Eden's and his words were certainly what Eden would have liked to have heard from the lips of an American President. 'Half a century ago the world had the chance to stop a ruthless aggressor and missed it. I pledge to you we will not make that mistake again.' Eden, had he been alive to hear that from Bush, would have felt himself truly vindicated.

But the American President in 1956 did not consider that either legally or politically was the Suez Canal issue suited to that kind of response. The legal side was clearly deficient by comparison with the Falklands case, let alone Kuwait. Politically in 1956 the United States carried the main responsibility for conducting the cold war. Eden and Mollet decided, from whatever motives, to act on their own, to deceive the United States about an enterprise that could have ended up with triggering World War III, and to violate what in 1956, just as in 1990, was considered the first rule of making a stand against a Middle East state: never allow the issue to be confused with the Arab–Israel dispute.

In the event Suez failed because a political scenario that was too clever by half was fitted clumsily onto a military plan that had been drawn up under other assumptions. A. J. P. Taylor supplied the right verdict when he wrote nine years later, 'The moral for British Governments is clear. Like most respectable people, they will make poor criminals and had better stick to respectability. They will not be much good at anything else.'[8]

Appendix A

THE PROTOCOL OF SÈVRES, 24 OCTOBER 1956

The document was drafted in French at the end of the tripartite discussions. It showed signs of hasty preparation and had not been proof-read for spelling, syntax and typographic consistency. The British representatives did not participate in its drafting and no English version was prepared. Three copies were signed by the three chief representatives who each retained one. Sir Anthony Eden wished it to be destroyed and it is not to be found in the British Archives. Christian Pineau in his book *1956 – Suez* gives the substance of the document in French, interspersed with his own comments. Moshe Dayan in his *Story of My Life* gives a version in English.

The following is a complete English translation of the original French. Its authenticity has been confirmed by Sir Donald Logan.

PROTOCOL

The results of the conversations which took place at Sèvres from 22–24 October 1956 between the representatives of the Governments of the United Kingdom, the State of Israel and of France are the following:

1 The Israeli forces launch in the evening of 29 October 1956 a large scale attack on the Egyptian forces with the aim of reaching the Canal zone the following day.
2 On being apprised of these events, the British and French Governments during the day of 30 October 1956 respectively and simultaneously make two appeals to the Egyptian Government and the Israeli Government on the following lines:

A *To the Egyptian Government*
- (a) halt all acts of war.
- (b) withdraw all its troops ten miles from the Canal.
- (c) accept temporary occupation of key positions on the Canal by the Anglo-French forces to guarantee freedom of passage through the Canal by vessels of all nations until a final settlement.

B *To the Israeli Government*
   (a) halt all acts of war.
   (b) withdraw all its troops ten miles to the east of the Canal.

In addition, the Israeli Government will be notified that the French and British Governments have demanded of the Egyptian Government to accept temporary occupation of key positions along the Canal by Anglo-French forces.
It is agreed that if one of the Governments refused, or did not give its consent, within twelve hours the Anglo-French forces would intervene with the means necessary to ensure that their demands are accepted.

C The representatives of the three Governments agree that the Israeli Government will not be required to meet the conditions in the appeal addressed to it, in the event that the Egyptian Government does not accept those in the appeal addressed to it for their part.

3 In the event that the Egyptian Government should fail to agree within the stipulated time to the conditions of the appeal addressed to it, the Anglo-French forces will launch military operations against the Egyptian forces in the early hours of the morning of 31 October.

4 The Israeli Government will send forces to occupy the western shore of the Gulf of Akaba and the group of islands Tirane and Sanafir to ensure freedom of navigation in the Gulf of Akaba.

5 Israel undertakes not to attack Jordan during the period of operations against Egypt.

But in the event that during the same period Jordan should attack Israel, the British Government undertakes not to come to the aid of Jordan.

6 The arrangements of the present protocol must remain strictly secret.

7 They will enter into force after the agreement of the three Governments.

(signed)

DAVID BEN-GURION   PATRICK DEAN   CHRISTIAN PINEAU

French-Israeli Protocol

On the same day the French and Israeli representatives signed another protocol but did not mention it to the British representatives. It is reproduced in Christian Pineau's book. In English it would read:

The French Government undertakes to station on the territory of Israel to ensure the air defence of Israeli territory during the period from 29–31 October 1956 a reinforced squadron of Mystères IV A, a squadron of fighter bombers. In addition two ships of the Marine Nationale will during the same period put into Israeli ports.

(signed) M. Bourgès-Maunoury

NOTE ON BRITISH RATIFICATION

According to Ben-Gurion's *Diary* for 26 October Artur Ben-Natan (an Israeli Ministry of Defence representative in Europe) arrived in Israel in a French plane at lunchtime that day with three documents:

1 A letter from Guy Mollet which confirmed the French Government's agreement to 'the results of the Sèvres talks and the terms of the final protocol' and reported that he had received a letter from Eden in which he had confirmed the agreement of the British Government;
2 A photocopy of the letter from Eden to Mollet which read: 'HMG have been informed of the course of the conversations held at Sèvres on 22–24 October. They confirm that in the situation there envisaged they will take the action described. This is in accordance with the declaration enclosed with my communication of 21 October.'
3 A letter from Bourgès-Maunoury confirming the terms of the French-Israeli Protocol.

Ben-Gurion sourly comments that Eden's note was 'typical of the British Foreign Office' because, in contrast to the openness of the French, there were various ways in which it could be interpreted. As applied to the Foreign Office the stricture seems unfounded since the note must have originated in 10 Downing Street and was probably drafted by Eden himself.

Appendix B

LETTER OF RESIGNATION FROM THE DIPLOMATIC SERVICE FROM EVAN LUARD, SUBSEQUENTLY MP AND FOREIGN UNDER-SECRETARY

FOREIGN OFFICE, SW1.

November 5, 1969.

Dear Henniker-Major,

I promised this morning that I would let you know in writing about my decision to resign and to explain to you the reasons for it.

I belong to a generation which was brought up in the belief that for one nation to undertake the use of armed force against another in order to promote its own interest is morally wrong. I grew up during a war which, I understood, was fought for the establishment of that principle.

When I joined the Foreign Service I was conscious that this country was a member of the United Nations and had entered into a solemn undertaking to act in accordance with the Charter of that Organisation. I knew that successive Governments, formed by different political parties, had pledged their support for the purpose and principles embodied in the Charter and had repeatedly declared their readiness to comply with its terms. And I therefore assumed that any Government under which I was likely to serve would act in accordance with these undertakings.

It now appears that this assumption was mistaken. The Government of which I am a servant have decided to initiate an armed attack against a nation which was at the time itself already the victim of aggression; at the same time they have publicly formulated certain demands relating to a political question in dispute between our two countries; and they have persisted in their decision to launch this assault two days after fighting between the other two parties concerned had ceased and twenty-four hours after both had indicated their readiness to agree to a cease-fire.

I am not at present concerned with the wisdom or otherwise of an action which seems likely not only to blacken the reputation of this country throughout the world for many years to come but gravely to endanger those very material interests which it was supposedly designed to protect. When I became a member of the Service I recognised that it was in the nature of this career that I might from time to time during the course of my service be called upon to carry out policies of whose wisdom I personally was in doubt; and, where such occasions arose, I have, as a matter of course, conscientiously done everything in my power to promote and, when necessary, to defend such policies. The present case is different. Here it is a question of an action of the Government that I serve which in my eyes seems to have betrayed everything for which I had believed that this country stood, and to have violated the most fundamental principles of international morality, in accordance with which I had assumed the foreign policy of any Government I was likely to serve under would be formulated. Since it appears that I can no longer have any assurance that the decisions which principally condition the nature of the work I do will be cast within the framework of these principles, I am afraid that I can no longer feel this career to be one which I wish any further to pursue.

For these reasons I should like to offer my resignation from the Foreign Service.

Yours sincerely,

D. E. T. Luard

Notes

Glossary

The files kept in the Public Record Office, Kew, which have been used for this book are designated PREM (Prime Minister's Office), CAB (Cabinet Office), FO (Foreign Office), FO 800 (the Personal Files of the Foreign Secretary), DO (Commonwealth Relations Office), DEFE (Ministry of Defence), ADM (Admiralty), WO (War Office), AIR (Air Ministry) and LCO (Lord Chancellor's Office).

The Avon Papers (AP) of Anthony Eden are in the library of the University of Birmingham; those of Earl Mountbatten of Burma, consulted for this book at his residence at Broadlands, are now at the University of Southampton. Other collections of private papers referred to below are at Churchill College, Cambridge.

The papers of Dwight D. Eisenhower (DDE) are in the Eisenhower Library at Abilene, Kansas. Those of John Foster Dulles (JFD) are also mainly at Abilene but there are some at the Seeley G. Mudd Library, Princeton, which also holds the transcripts from the extensive JFD Oral History Project. The papers of Allen Dulles (AWD) and C.D. Jackson (CDJ) are to be found in the Eisenhower Library.

Printed documentary collections used include:–

FRUS *Foreign Relations of the United States 1955–57* (Government Printing Office, Washington, DC). Vol. XIII Near East: Jordan–Yemen (1988); Vol. XIV Arab–Israeli Dispute, 1955 (1989); Vol. XV Arab–Israeli Dispute, January 1–July 26, 1956 (1989). Vol. XVI Suez Crisis, July 26–December 31, 1956 (1990); Vol. XVII Arab–Israeli Dispute, 1957 (1990).

DDF *Documents Diplomatiques Français* (Paris, Imprimerie Nationale) *1955*, Vol. I 1 Jan–30 June (1987), Vol. II 1 July–31 December (1988); *1956* Vol. I 1 Jan–30 June (1988), Vol. II 1 July–23 Oct (1990), Vol. III 24 October–31 December (1990).

DFPI *Documents on the Foreign Policy of Israel* (Israel State Archives, Vols 1–5 and *Companion Volumes* (English)).

Chapter One
Swing-Door of the British Empire

1. DEFE 4/43 COS(51) 86 Confidential Annex, 23.5.51. Cited by Wm Roger Louis, *The British Empire in the Middle East, 1945–1951* (OUP, 1984), pp. 673–4. Iran was still known to the Foreign Office, though not to the Service Ministries, as Persia. HMG finally conformed to local practice, at the Shah's special request, in 1955.
2. James Bill and Wm Roger Louis (eds), *Musaddiq, Iranian Nationalism and Oil* (I.B. Tauris, 1988), p. 4. Louis (1984), op. cit., p. 9.
3. In 1951 traffic through the Canal was 80,356,338 tons, of which 26,900,063 (33.48%) were British. By 1955 it had gone up to 115,756,398 tons in total, British ships

accounting for 32,789,874 tons (28.33%). In 1955 66.9 m metric tons of oil and oil products passed northwards through the Canal. This was no less than 76% of total traffic northward and 62% of all traffic in both directions. 20.5% of the oil came to Britain.

4. Fakhreddin Azimi, 'The Political Career of Dr Muhammad Musaddiq', pp. 47–68, and Wm Roger Louis, 'Musaddiq and the Dilemmas of British Imperialism', pp. 232–56 in Bill and Louis (eds), *Musaddiq*, op. cit.
5. FO 371/02806 Winston Churchill to Bedell Smith, 15.4.53.
6. CAB 128/10 CM 60 (51) 27.9.51. Cited Louis (1984), op. cit., p. 687.
7. Robert Rhodes James, *Anthony Eden* (Weidenfeld and Nicolson, 1986), p. 265.
8. David Butler, *The British General Election of 1951* (Macmillan, 1952), pp. 86–7 and 112–28.
9. Rhodes James, op. cit., p. 87.
10. Anthony Eden, *Another World, 1897–1917* (Allen Lane, 1976), p. 150.
11. John Vincent (ed.), *The Crawford Papers: The Journals of David Lindsay, 27th Earl of Crawford and 10th Earl of Balcarres* (Manchester University Press, 1984), pp. 590, 578.
12. Martin Gilbert, '*Never Despair*'. *Winston S. Churchill, 1945–1965* (Heinemann, 1988), p. 227.
13. Viscount Stuart of Findhorn, *Within the Fringe* (Bodley Head, 1967), p. 178.
14. David Carlton, *Anthony Eden. A Biography* (Allen Lane, 1981), pp. 278–86.
15. C. W. Hallberg, *The Suez Canal, Its History and Diplomatic Importance* (Columbia University Press, 1931); Douglas Farnie, *East and West of Suez* (Clarendon Press, 1969); Ferdinand de Lesseps, *The History of the Suez Canal. A Personal Narrative* (Blackwood, 1876).
16. John Pudney, *Suez: de Lesseps' Canal* (J. M. Dent, 1969), pp. 75–80.
17. Pudney, op. cit., pp. 81–124. Egyptian Embassy, Washington, 'The Suez Canal. Facts and Figures', 4.8.56. Central Office of Information, London, 'The Suez Canal', July 1957.
18. J. T. Bunce in *Birmingham Weekly Post*, 4.12.1875, p. 4. *Cheltenham Free Press*, 4.12.1875, p. 2. *Daily Bristol Times and Mirror*, 29.11.1875, p. 3. Farnie, *East and West of Suez*, pp. 238–41.
19. Farnie, op. cit. Chapter 17.
20. Michael Haag, 'The City of Words' in E. M. Forster, *Alexandria, A History and A Guide* (Michael Haag, 1982), pp. 236–7. For an impression of the extent to which the minorities, especially the Copts, began to be treated as 'foreigners' see Lawrence Durrell, *Mountolive* (Faber and Faber, 1963 edn), *passim* but especially pp. 37–42 and 97–106.
21. Peter Mansfield, *The British in Egypt* (Weidenfeld and Nicolson, 1971) pp. 17–55.
22. A. J. P. Taylor, *The Struggle for Mastery of Europe, 1848–1918* (OUP, 1954), p. 289.
23. Ronald Robinson and John Gallagher, *Africa and the Victorians. The Official Mind of Imperialism* (Macmillan, 1961), pp. 76–159.
24. Full text in D. Cameron Watt, *Britain and the Suez Canal* (RIIA, 1956), Annex II, pp. 27–34.
25. Taylor, op. cit., pp. 289–90.
26. Farnie, op. cit., p. 549.
27. Lloyd to Admiral Sir Roger Keyes, 19.6.27. Quoted in John Charmley, *Lord Lloyd and the Decline of the British Empire* (Weidenfeld and Nicolson, 1987), p. 140.
28. *Cmd 5360* (1936). Extracts in Watt, op. cit., pp. 35–6.
29. *Tribune*, 14.8.56. Letter from H. B. Bennett (Kidderminster). For an inspired impression of relationships in wartime Egypt see Artemis Cooper, *Cairo in the War, 1939–1945* (Hamish Hamilton, 1989).
30. Anwar Sadat, *Revolt on the Nile* (Allan Wingate, 1957), pp. 39–51.
31. Gamal Abdul Nasser, *Egypt's Liberation. The Philosophy of the Revolution* (Public Affairs Press, Washington, 1955), pp. 24–5.

32. Ahmed Gomaa, *The Foundation of the League of Arab States* (Longman, 1977), Chapter 6 *passim*.
33. Aweed Dawisha, *Egypt in the Arab World. The Elements of Policy* (Macmillan, 1976), pp. 79–83.
34. Gomaa, op. cit., Chapter 7 *passim*.
35. Elizabeth Monroe, *Britain's Moment in the Middle East* (Chatto & Windus, 1963), p. 156.
36. For a good description of the size and complexity of the Suez Base see Wm Roger Louis (1984), op. cit., pp. 8–11.

Chapter Two
A Jewish State

1. Keith Kyle, 'Death of a Plan' in *The Listener*, 13.1.72, pp. 57–8. Sir Llewellyn Woodward, *British Foreign Policy in the Second World War*, Vol. IV (HMSO, 1975), pp. 366–83. CAB 95/14 War Cabinet. Committee on Palestine. P(M)(44)11. 'The Case Against Partition'. Memo by the S. of S. for Foreign Affairs, 15.9.44.
2. Nicholas (Lord) Bethell, *The Palestine Triangle* (André Deutsch, 1979), p. 201.
3. See, for example, Ilan Pappé, *Britain and the Arab-Israeli Conflict, 1948–51* (St Antony's/Macmillan, 1988).
4. PREM 11/398 PM's Minute M512/52,19.10.52. Churchill to Eden. Lord Bullock, *Ernest Bevin, Foreign Secretary* (Heinemann, 1983), pp. 164–83 discusses Bevin's attitude to Jews and to Zionism.
5. FO 371/68649 Bevin to Lord Inverchapel (Washington) 19.4.48 'Conversation with the US Ambassador'.
6. David McDowell, *The Palestinians* (Minority Rights Group, 1987), discusses the demographical problems involved, p. 32 (n. 47).
7. *Political and Diplomatic Documents, 1947–48* (Israel State Archives), Doc. 483, Moshe Shertock [Sharett], (Washington) to Ben-Gurion, 8.5.48.
8. *Foreign Relations of the United States, 1948*, Vol. V, pp. 632–3. Diary entry in Forrestal Papers for 18.2.48. See also Warren Austin to George Marshall, 10.2.48. *FRUS 1948 V*, op. cit., pp. 614–16.
9. Wm Roger Louis, *The British Empire in the Middle East*, pp. 528–9.
10. Michael Bar-Zohar, *Ben Gurion. A Political Biography* (Weidenfeld and Nicolson, 1978), p. 272.
11. Avraham Avi-hai, *Ben-Gurion. State-Builder* (Israel Universities Press, Jerusalem, 1974), p. 283.
12. Benny Morris, *The Birth of the Palestinian Refugee Problem, 1947–1949* (Cambridge UP, 1987). Morris, 'The Causes and Character of the Arab Exodus from Palestine' in *Middle Eastern Studies*, January 1986, pp. 5–19.
13. Walid Khalidi, 'Plan Dalet: Master Plan for the Conquest of Palestine' in *Journal of Palestine Studies*, Autumn 1988, pp. 3–70.
14. Morris, op. cit. Shabtai Teveth, 'The Palestine Arab Refugee Problem and its Origins', in *Middle Eastern Studies*, April 1990, pp. 214–49.
15. *Documents on the Foreign Policy of Israel*, May–Sept. 1948, Moshe Shertok [Sharett] to Nahum Goldmann (London), 15.6.48, pp. 162–4.
16. David Shipler, *New York Times*, 22.10.79 reprinting censored passage from Yitzhak Rabin, *The Rabin Memoirs*. Ben-Gurion to Aharon Zisling, Minister of Agriculture, quoted by Teveth, op. cit., p. 243. Arieh Itzchaki, 'Latrun, the Battle for the Road to Jerusalem' (Hebrew) Vol. II, p. 394.
17. *FRUS 1948 V*, Pinkerton (Beirut) to George Marshall, 16.5.48, pp. 1002–4.
18. Thomas Mayer, 'Egypt's Invasion of Palestine', in *Middle Eastern Studies*, Winter 1987, pp. 21–34. Simha Flapan, *Zionism and the Palestinians* (Croom Helm, 1979), pp. 338–41.

19. Walid Khalidi, 'Nasser's Memoirs of the First Palestinian War', in *Journal of Palestine Studies*, February 1973.
20. Chaim Herzog, *The Arab–Israeli Wars*, p. 74.
21. Ben-Gurion, *War Diaries*, 16.6.48. Speech to Provisional Government. Cited Flapan, *The Birth of Israel*, p. 105. B. G. also noted the success of the Greek-Turkish exchange of populations in the 1920s.
22. Count Folke Bernadotte of Wisborg, *To Jerusalem* (Hodder and Stoughton, 1951), pp. 236–44. Mordechai Gazit, 'American and British Diplomacy and the Bernadotte Mission' in *The Historical Journal*, Sept. 1986, pp. 676–96.
23. Cary, David Stenger, 'A Haunting Legacy. The Assassination of Count Bernadotte' in *Middle East Journal*, Spring 1988. Amitzur Ilan, *Bernadotte in Palestine, 1948* (Macmillan, 1990).
24. Herzog, *The Arab-Israeli Wars*, pp. 97–104. 'Political pressure was mounting in the UN Security Council to force Israel to withdraw to the lines of 14 October. This political pressure, in which Britain played a major role, convinced the Israeli Command that it was essential to drive the Egyptians out of the country.'
25. Louis, *The British Empire in the Middle East*, pp. 564–6. Segev, 1949, op. cit., pp. 3–5.
26. Avi Shlaim, *Collusion Across the Jordan*, pp. 386–433. There is a map showing what King Abdullah had to surrender at p. 413.
27. Shlaim, op. cit., pp. 530–1. In Appdx 4, pp. 634–9 Shlaim prints the text of an (unsigned) draft Treaty of Amity and Non-Aggression between Israel and Jordan of March 1950.
28. *D.F.P.I. V (Companion Volume)*, Doc. 125. Meeting of Eban and Rafael with Abd al-Mun'im Mustafa (Geneva), 27.2.50, pp. 88–9.
29. Beryl Cheal, 'Refugees in the Gaza Strip, December 1948–May 1950' in *Journal of Palestine Studies*, Autumn 1988, pp. 138–57.
30. Tom Segev, *1949*, pp. 6–8, 32–4. Morris, *The Birth of the Palestinian Refugee Problem*, pp. 266–75.
31. *D.F.P.I. V* (*Companion Volume*), Doc. 129. Sharett to Eban and Rafael (Geneva), 6.3.50, p. 91.
32. Quoted by Segev, *1949*, p. 34.
33. *D.F.P.I. V* (*Main Volume*), Doc. 202.
34. Shlomo Slonim, 'Origins of the 1950 Tripartite Declaration on the Middle East' in *Middle Eastern Studies*, April 1978, pp. 135–49, quotes (p. 144) the official UK interpretation of the crucial last sentence of the Declaration. 'None of the three Governments is by this statement giving any undertaking of any character towards any Government except the other two parties to the statement. In particular, no undertaking of any character is thereby given to Israel or any of the Arab states.'
35. For NEACC system see Paul Jabber, *Not By War Alone* (University of California Press, 1981). The difficulties and ambiguities of the idea of a Middle Eastern balance were analysed on 3.1.55 in a memorandum by Sir John Sterndale Bennett, Head of the British Middle East Office (FO 371/115552).
36. Louis, *British Empire in the Middle East*, p. 355. The terms of the alliance were cosmetically revised in February 1948, the main difference being the establishment of a Joint Defence Board, giving Jordan somewhat more of the appearance of equality (ibid., p. 368).
37. L. M. Bloomfield, *Egypt, Israel and the Gulf of Aqaba in International Law* (Carswell, Toronto, 1957), pp. 8–9. Farnie, *East and West of Suez*, pp. 664–8.
38. *Parliamentary Debates (Hansard), House of Commons*, Vol. 485, 15.3.51. cols 1766–71; 16.3.57. cols 1967–70; 20.3.51 cols 2301–3 and 2333–90.
39. Martin Gilbert, '*Never Despair*'. *Winston S. Churchill, 1945–65*, pp. 657–8.

Chapter Three
Eden and Nasser

1. William Rees-Mogg, *Sir Anthony Eden* (Rockcliff, 1956), p. 105.
2. CAB 128/29 CM 34 (55) 8, 4.10.55.
3. Julian Amery to author, April 1988. Also, Amery, 'The Suez Group' in Troën and Shemesh (eds), *The Suez-Sinai Crisis 1956: Retrospective and Reappraisal* (Frank Cass), pp. 110–26.
4. Peter Mansfield, *The British in Egypt* (Weidenfeld and Nicolson, 1971), pp. 296–8.
5. Mansfield, op. cit., p. 298.
6. Anwar Sadat, *Revolt on the Nile* (Allan Wingate, 1957), p. 119, gives the text of the broadcast. Sadat says that it was written by Abdul Hakim Amer, the future War Minister and Commander-in-Chief.
7. PREM 11/392 PM's Personal Minutes, M441/52 19.9.52, M458/52 26.8.52.
8. Lord Hankey was Secretary of the Cabinet (1916–38) and of the Committee of Imperial Defence (1912–38).
9. These included words of praise conveyed by the staff at Number Ten for a speech by Julian Amery which was highly critical of Eden's policy. Amery, 'The Suez Group' in Troën and Shemesh, op. cit., p. 115.
10. Sir Evelyn Shuckburgh, *Descent to Suez* (Weidenfeld and Nicolson, 1986), pp. 75–6.
11. Julian Amery to author, April 1988. Troën and Shemesh, op. cit., p. 112.
12. PREM 11/636 Lord Hankey, 'The Suez Canal Company. Military Evacuation of the Zone', 7.2.53.
13. CAB 129/52. Printed as Doc. 11 in A. N. Porter and A. J. Stockwell, *British Imperial Policy and Decolonization, 1938–64* (Macmillan, 1989), pp. 164–75.
14. Wm Roger Louis, *The British Empire in the Middle East, 1945–1951* (Clarendon Press, 1984), pp. 595–600. Irvine H. Anderson, 'The American Oil Industry and the Fifty-Fifty Agreement of 1950', in James A. Bill and Wm Roger Louis, *Mussadiq. Iranian Nationalism and Oil* (I. B. Tauris, 1988), pp. 143–63.
15. Samuel Flagg Bemis, Preface to *The American Secretaries of State and their Diplomacy, Vol. XVII, John Foster Dulles*, by Louis L. Gerson (Cooper Square, New York, 1967), p. xi.
16. Shuckburgh, *Descent to Suez*, op. cit., p. 329.
17. Sir John Colville, *The Fringes of Power. Downing Street Diaries 1939–1955* (Hodder and Stoughton, 1985), p. 662.
18. Lord Moran, *Struggle for Survival* (Constable, 1966), p. 441.
19. Lord Sherfield to author, January 1988.
20. Shuckburgh, *Descent to Suez*, op. cit., p. 23. Lord Sherfield described this passage to the author as 'exactly right'.
21. Memorandum of Discussion, 133rd Meeting of the National Security Council, 24.2.53. Eisenhower Library, Abilene. PREM 11/701 Churchill to Eisenhower, 18.2.53. Churchill told the Chiefs of Staff that their paper 'seems to assume that the Egyptian forces are really effective fighting men'. No prisoners were to be released. 'As soon as violence is used upon us, good cages should be made' (PREM 11/392).
22. Amin Hewedy, 'Nasser and the Crisis of 1956', in Wm Roger Louis and Roger Owen, *Suez 1956. The Crisis and its Consequences* (OUP, 1989). pp. 163–4.
23. Miles Copeland, *The Game of Nations* (Weidenfeld and Nicolson, 1969), pp. 85–90.
24. FO 371/102764 John de Courcy Hamilton to Michael Creswell, Cairo Embassy, 9.3.53.
25. FO 371/102807 Sir James Bowker to Michael Creswell, 25.4.53. JE 1192/246.
26. Jefferson Caffery to Dulles 8.5.53. National Archives (Diplomatic), Washington.
27. *Parliamentary Debates (Hansard). House of Commons*, Vol. 515, 11.5.53, cols 883–

98. Memconv. between Parker T. Holt (Director Near East, State Department) and Ronald Bailey (First Secretary, British Embassy). National Archives (Diplomatic), Washington.
28. Memorandum of Discussion, 147th Meeting of the National Security Council, 1.6.53. Eisenhower Library, Abilene. FO 371/103515 from Makins (Washington) 2.6.53. Sir Roger Makins commented: 'It is the innuendo which is the most objectionable part.'
29. FO 371/102765 Handwritten memorandum by Robin Hankey 22.5.53. JE 1052/121.
30. FO 371/102810 Minute, 11.5.53. PREM 11/629 Hankey to Bowker, 17.5.53: 'They really have not the first idea of how to govern a modern country, though Gamal Abdul Nasser is more willing to learn than some of them.' FO 371/102860 from Hankey, 1.9.53: 'No better government is in sight; whatever happens ... Nasser and his friends have the character and brain-power to maintain the lead.'
31. FO 371/102860 from Hankey, 1.9.53. JE 11915/62.
32. FO 371/102860 from General Sir Brian Robertson, 20.9.53. JE 11915/72.
33. Caffery to Dulles, 22.11.53, National Archives (Diplomatic), Washington.
34. PREM 11/699. PM's personal tel. T310/53, 19.12.53.
35. Livingston Merchant, 'Memorandum for the Files', Paris 16.12.53. National Archives (Diplomatic), Washington.
36. General Neguib remained with the title of President until 17.11.54 when he was deposed. The Presidency was kept vacant from then until 23.6.56.
37. Under Caffery there was a reasonable liaison between formal and informal diplomacy, since William Lakeland, a young member of the Embassy staff, was involved with the Free Officers. Later the Ambassador might not know that Roosevelt was in Cairo and seeing Nasser. The best accounts of this are in Miles Copeland's books, *Game of Nations* (Weidenfeld and Nicolson, 1969) and *The Game Player* (Aurum, 1989), pp. 158–205.
38. FO 371/108415, from Makins (Washington) 9.3.54. JE 1192/67.
39. PREM 11/702 Churchill to Eisenhower. PM's personal tel. T197/54, 21.6.54.
40. FO 371/108464 Ralph Murray (Cairo) to Thomas Bromley (African Dept), 3.6.54. Roosevelt found Nasser's conversation 'notably devoid of the usual references to a Samsonic policy of conflict with the British'. Nasser also expressed worry at accusations that he was becoming a tool of American imperialism.
41. PREM 11/701 CCz (54), 12.1.54.
42. Sir Norman Kipling, *The Suez Contractors* (Kenneth Mason, 1969).
43. FO 371/118984 from Humphrey Trevelyan (Cairo) 29.6.56, Minute by R. C. Blackham, 13.7.56.
44. FO 371/118984 Minute by Evelyn Shuckburgh, 12.6.56, JE 11912/21. DEFE 4/87, 'UK Requirements in the Middle East', Annex to JP (56) 71 (Revised) (Final) 28.5.56.
45. FO 371/111076 Nutting, 'Record of Nile Barrage Conversation with Nasser', 25.10.54, VR 1072/242.
46. Richard P. Mitchell, *The Society of the Muslim Brothers* (OUP, 1969), pp. 125–62.
47. Professor Ali Mahafzah to author, Amman, November 1987.
48. 'Abd al-Nasir [Abdul Nasser], *Falsafat al-Thawrah*, translated as *The Philosophy of the Revolution Book I* (Cairo, Dar al Ma'arif, 1954) and in the United States as *Egypt's Liberation* (Public Affairs Press, 1955) with a laudatory introduction by Dorothy Thompson whose whole celebrity as a journalist had been based on her early recognition and denunciation of *Mein Kampf*.
49. FO 371/108317 Sir Ralph Stevenson (Cairo) to Eden, 14.9.54.
50. Eden had been made Knight of the Garter in recognition of his exceptional achievement at the Geneva Conference on Indo-China, 20.10.54.
51. FO 371/111045 Eden to Makins (Washington), 4.11.54.
52. FO 371/111045 Makins (Washington) to Eden, 5.11.54.
53. Shuckburgh, unpublished diary of Middle East tour, Nov.–Dec. 1954.

54. See Footnote 45.
55. FO 371/111002 Paul Falla, 'Revision of Anglo-Iraqi Treaty', 6.1.54. VQ 1054/1. Minute by Eden, 9.1.54. The Turkish base in question was Mardin.
56. Ahmed Gomaa, *The Foundation of the League of Arab States* (Longman, 1977), p. 66.
57. Robert Belgrave to author, Chatham House, 1986.
58. FO 371/115488 Minute by J. G. Ward (Deputy Under-Secretary of State), 1.2.55. V 1073/175. Shuckburgh, unpublished diary, op. cit.
59. FO 371/115488 from Sir James Bowker (Ankara), 8.2.55.
60. Mohamed Heikal, *Cutting the Lion's Tail*, p. 56.
61. FO 371/115488 J. G. Ward to Sir Ivone Kirkpatrick, 2.2.55. VR 1973/154 'A'.
62. FO 371/115490 from Bowker (Ankara), 8.2.55, V 1073/219. FO 371/115487 from Sir Michael Wright (Baghdad), 9.3.55, V 1073/463.
63. The British did not favour much in the way of structure for the Baghdad Pact. Again, it was the Turks who slipped in at the last moment a permanent Council of Ministers as soon as membership went up to four.
64. FO 371/115493 'Discussion between the Secretary of State and Egyptian Leaders'. 21.2.55.
65. *Foreign Relations of the United States, Vol. XIV, Arab-Israel Dispute, 1955*, pp. 30–1, 35, 46. FO 371/115838 Shuckburgh to Kirkpatrick, 2.2.56, VR 1076/106. FO 371/115865 Shuckburgh 'Brief for the Secretary of State's Visit to Cairo'.
66. Mohamed Heikal, *Nasser: The Cairo Documents*, op. cit., pp. 78–81.
67. Heikal, *Cutting the Lion's Tail*, p. 65.
68. Robert Rhodes James, *Anthony Eden* (Weidenfeld and Nicolson, 1986), p. 398. In the following paragraph Rhodes James himself cites evidence that as late as April 1956, Nasser's opinion of Eden was 'not as hostile as he later alleged'.

Chapter Four
Arms and the Dam

1. Chaim Herzog, *The Arab-Israeli Wars*, p. 120.
2. Ariel Sharon (with David Chanoff), *Warrior* (Macdonald, 1989), pp. 76–85. FO 371/111069. General Glubb, 'After Qibya', 26.1.54, VR 1072/10.
3. Sharon, op. cit., pp. 86–91.
4. FO 371/111070 Antony Moore (Tel Aviv) to Paul Falla (Levant Dept), 6.4.54. VR 1072/46.
5. FO 371/115905, General Moshe Dayan, 'Military Operations in Peacetime', Lecture to commanders in *Bamahane* No. 51, 5.9.55.
6. FO 371/111074, Eden to Sir Francis Evans (Tel Aviv), 'Conversation between the Secretary of State and the Israeli Ambassador', 22.9.54. JE 11916/86.
7. Sharon, op. cit., pp. 102–9.
8. Ehud Ya'ari, *Mitzrayim ve-Hafedayeen, 1953–1956* ('Egypt and the *Fedayeen*') (Givat Havivar Centre, 1975). Avi Shlaim, 'The Gaza Raid: Was it a Turning Point?', *Middle East International*, April 1978.
9. Alan Hart, *Arafat, Terrorist or Peacemaker?* (Sidgwick and Jackson, 1984), pp. 107–10. Sharon, op. cit., p. 102.
10. Patrick Seale, *The Struggle For Syria* (RIIA/OUP, 1965). Hakim Amêr made a similar statement to the Egyptian Parliament 2.9.57.
11. Heikal, *Cutting the Lion's Tail*, op. cit., p. 66.
12. Avi Shlaim, 'Egypt and the *Fedayeen*' in *Middle East International*. Hart, *Arafat*, op. cit. Yunes al-Katari, *Lost Link in the Struggle of the Palestine People: 141 Fedayeen Battalion* (Arabic) (PLO Mustaqbal al-Arabi, Cairo, 1987). I am grateful to Dr Yazid Sayigh for his assistance with material about the *fedayeen*.
13. FO 371/111071 from Evans (Tel Aviv), 10.5.54. Sharett made out the case for Israel

being *sui generis* 'because there is no parallel to Jewish history in the annals of Mankind'. The Knesset resolution repudiated Byroade by name.

14. Stephen Ambrose, *Eisenhower. The President* (George Allen and Unwin, 1984), p. 387. The Soviet Union's first pro-Arab veto came in January 1954, on a Western resolution concerning the division of the Jordan waters. The second was used against a New Zealand resolution reaffirming the 1951 condemnation of Egypt's blockade of Israeli trade through the Suez Canal.
15. Avi Shlaim, 'Conflicting Approaches to Israel's Relations with the Arabs: Ben-Gurion and Sharett, 1953–1956', in *The Middle East Journal*, Spring 1983, pp. 189–91. *FRUS 1955–57, XIV*, Doc. 66, 5.4.55, pp. 139–40.
16. FO 371/115825 Sir John Nicholls (Tel Aviv) to Shuckburgh, 8.3.55, VR 1051/8.
17. See e.g. Shuckburgh, *Descent to Suez*, p. 284. 'I think that A. E. really models himself on W. S. C. in a sort of perverted way. For instance, all that bedroom-work is an imitation. H. M. [Harold Macmillan] would never dream of being so indelicate as to have the FO staff in his bedroom.'
18. Michael Cockerell, *Live from Number 10. The Inside Story of Prime Ministers and Television* (Faber and Faber, 1988), pp. 27–37.
19. William Clark, unpublished diary for Sept.–Dec. 1955. Clark, *From Three Worlds*, p. 148.
20. Clark, unpublished diary, op. cit.
21. Lord Butler, *The Art of the Possible* (Hamish Hamilton, 1971), p. 184.
22. Lord Home to author, House of Lords, April 1988.
23. Robert Rhodes James, *Anthony Eden*, op. cit., p. 597.
24. Shuckburgh, *Descent to Suez*, p. 14. 'He was constantly having troubles with his insides. We used to carry around a black tin box containing various forms of analgesic supplied by his doctor, ranging from simple aspirins to morphia injections. It was understood that if an injection was required the detective was sent for to perform it . . .'
25. FO 371/113608 T. E. Bromley, 'Instructions to Sir Humphrey Trevelyan', 5.8.55. JE 1057/9.
26. FO 371/113608 Minute by Bromley, 24.6.55. Macmillan to Eden, 29.6.55, JE 1057/7.
27. FO 371/113608. Minutes by Bromley, Leslie Fry (Eastern Dept), Shuckburgh, Kirkpatrick, Nutting and Macmillan on PM's Minutes, 13–15.7.55, JE 1057–8.
28. *FRUS XIV*, Docs 58, 27.3.55, pp. 120–5; 62, 3.4.55, pp. 229–33; and 67, 5.4.55, p. 141. FO 371/115867 Stevenson to Shuckburgh, 1.4.55, VR 1076/51; from Stevenson, 6.4.55, 1076/57.
29. Shimon Shamir, 'The Collapse of Project Alpha' in Louis and Owen (eds), *Suez 1956. The Crisis and its Consequences*, pp. 73–100.
30. FO 371/115813 Nicholls (Tel Aviv) to Macmillan, 26.7.55, VR 1015/25. Thomas R. Bransen (ed.), *Recollections. David Ben-Gurion* (MacDonald, 1970), pp. 146–7.
31. The full text of the Alpha proposals is in FO 371/115866 VR 1076/34 and a summary version for use by President Eisenhower in *FRUS XIV*, pp. 200–4. Memo on economic inducements to Egypt from Francis Russell to Dulles, 18.5.55, *FRUS XIV*, pp. 204–5. Russell to Hoover, 'Present Status of Efforts to Secure Israel-Arab Settlement', *FRUS XIV*, pp. 175–6.
32. Shamir, op. cit. Jon Kimche, 'Suez: The Inside Story', in *The Jewish Chronicle*, 31.10.86.
33. William J. Burns, *Economic Aid and American Policy Toward Egypt, 1955–1981* (SUNY, Albany, 1985), pp. 13–19. Paul Jabber, *Not By War Alone* (University of California Press, 1981), pp. 133–6, 144–50, 156–61.
34. FO 371/113674 from Terence Garvey (Counsellor, Cairo), JE 1194/159.
35. *FRUS XIV*, pp. 237–40 (from Byroade, 9.6.55). Jabber, *Not By War Alone*, p. 163.
36. Joel Beinin, 'The Communist Movement and Nationalist Political Discourse in Nasirist Egypt' in *Middle East Studies*, Autumn 1987, pp. 568–84.
37. *FRUS XIV*, pp. 255–6, 266, 270–6, 304–5, 307–8, 332–3, 337–9, 387. Egypt was

ineligible to receive straightforward grants of military aid under the American Mutual Aid legislation because Nasser would not allow a Mutual Aid Advisory Group (MAAG) mission to administer them on the grounds that, having at long last got rid of the British, he would not have Americans replacing them.

38. *FRUS XIV*, pp. 355–8.
39. *FRUS XIV*, pp. 481, 483–4, 492–3. FO 371/113673 from Trevelyan (Cairo), 21.9.55. JE 1194/140.
40. FO 371/113674 Macmillan to Makins, 23.9.55. JE 1194/151.
41. FO 371/113674 Shuckburgh to Macmillan, 23.9.55. JE 1194/151. Minute by Caccia.
42. FO 371/113574 from Trevelyan (Cairo), 26.9.55. JE 1194/158.
43. *FRUS XIV*, pp. 520–3. Allen Dulles was worried that Roosevelt might leave Nasser with the impression that a nice statement could mitigate the effects of the deal. Lord Trevelyan, *The Middle East in Revolution* (Macmillan, 1970), pp. 29–30. FO 371/113675 from Trevelyan (Cairo), 1.10.55. JE 1194/202. Miles Copeland, *The Game of Nations*, pp. 134–5.
44. Frankland (ed.), *Documents on International Affairs, 1955* (RIIA), pp. 370–2. The intelligence report, reproduced in facsimile in *Al Gumhouriya* (3.10.55) came from *Military Intelligence Review*, May 1955. The French document was *Bulletin Hebdominaire, No. 19*, 20.5.55, published by the Centre d'Information du Proche-Orient and edited by Edouard Sablier. This exaggerated British delivery of arms supplied to Israel. The correct figures were that in the previous 12 months Egypt had got 2 destroyers, 45 jet planes, and 32 modern Centurion tanks while Israel had received 2 destroyers, 9 jets, and 20 disarmed and older Sherman tanks.
45. *FRUS XIV*, pp. 516–19 Memconv. New York: Dulles, Macmillan and officials.
46. FO 371/113675 ff 35–6 Harold Caccia to Harold Macmillan (New York) (draft using Ali Maher's name at f 34), 30.9.55. JE 1194/221.
47. *FRUS XIV*, pp. 537–40, Allen to Dulles, 1.10.55.
48. FO 371/113675 Macmillan to Eden, 3.10.55. JE 1194/221.
49. FO 371/113736 Macmillan to Makins (Washington), 20.10.55.
50. *FRUS XIV*, pp. 542–9, 'Call of the British Foreign Secretary re: Soviet-Egyptian Arms Agreement', 3.10.55.
51. Memconv. Dulles and Abba Eban, 30.9.55 (copy in FO 371/113670).
52. Moshe Dayan, *Story of My Life*, p. 147.
53. Professor Y. Harkabi to author, Jerusalem, Oct. 1986.
54. Jacob Tsur, *Prélude à Suez. Journal d'une Ambassade, 1953–1956*, pp. 259–60. FO 371/115537 Meetings of Sharett with Macmillan at Paris (26.10.55, V 1076/4) and at Geneva (1.11.55, V 1076/5). Sharett complained that Britain had sold the Israelis 17 Meteor planes which were not enough for a unit and refused the additional 7. Above all, Israel needed Centurion tanks.
55. Colonel (Res) Mordechai Bar-On, 'Ben-Gurion and the War of 1956', Leonard Davies Institute lecture, June 1987.
56. *Parliamentary Debates (Hansard), House of Commons*, Vol. 56, 30.11.55, cols 287–8.
57. General (Res) Rahavam ('Gandhi') Ze'evi, then Chief of Staff Southern Command, to author, Tel Aviv, Oct. 1986.
58. Bar-On, 'Ben-Gurion and the War of 1956', op. cit. Bar-On, 'David Ben-Gurion and the Sèvres Collusion' in Louis and Owen, *Suez 1956. The Crisis and its Consequences*, p. 147. The British Chiefs of Staff had shown interest in 1948 in the relocation of British troops and planes from the Suez Canal Zone in bases in the Negev, should this be awarded to 'Greater Transjordania'. But in the 1950s the Foreign Office was scratching its head about the origin of Ben-Gurion's obsession about this subject.
59. Abba Eban, *An Autobiography*, p. 198, comments severely on the complete absence of proportion about this reprisal. Dayan and Sharon were told by a glowering Ben-Gurion that the raid had been 'too successful'. (Sharon, *Warrior*, pp. 125–6.)

60. PREM 11/859, from Trevelyan (Cairo), 13.10.55.
61. PREM 11/859, 27.10–1.11.55.
62. FO 371/113608 Sir Ivone Kirkpatrick to Macmillan, 28.10.55.
63. Frankland (ed.), *Documents on International Affairs 1955* (RIIA), pp. 382–5.
64. FO 371/115880 from Trevelyan (Cairo), 10.11.55. *FRUS XIV*, pp. 781–3 from Byroade, 17.11.55.
65. *FRUS XIV*, pp. 784–6 (from Lawson, Tel Aviv, 17.11.55).
66. *FRUS XIV*, pp. 643–4. John Waterbury, *Hydropolitics of the Nile Valley* (Syracuse University Press, 1979), pp. 98–105. FO 371/113735 'High Aswan Dam', 30.8.55. FO 371/113740 Outward Tel. from Commonwealth Relations Office, 10.12.55, JE 1423/318(a).
67. Winthrop Aldrich, J. F. Dulles Oral History Project, Seeley G. Mudd Manuscript Library, Princeton University. *FRUS XIV*, pp. 632–6, from Aldrich, 20.10.55.
68. George Humphrey and Herbert Hoover Jr, J. F. Dulles Oral History Project, Princeton.
69. *FRUS XIV*, pp. 645–7. FO 371/113739 Makins (Washington) to Eden, 29.11.55.
70. Wilbur C. Eveland to Allen Dulles, 1.5.56. Eveland, *Ropes of Sand* (W. W. Norton, New York, 1980), pp. 169–72. Major Eveland was a consultant to the CIA.
71. William Clark, unpublished diary, entry for 29.11.55.
72. Shuckburgh, *Descent to Suez*, p. 305.
73. FO 371/113739 Eden to Eisenhower, 26.11.55, JE 1423/269. *FRUS XIV*, pp. 808–10.
74. FO 371/113738 from Makins (Washington), 27.11.55, JE 1423/252.
75. FO 371/113738 Memorandum by Shuckburgh, 28.11.55.
76. FO 371/113738 to Makins, 28.11.55, JE 1423/252.
77. *FRUS XIV*, pp. 868–70. FO 371/113741 from Makins, 16.12.55, JE 1423/340.

Chapter Five
Turning against Nasser

1. Alistair Horne, *Macmillan*, I (Macmillan, 1988), pp. 371–2.
2. D. R. Thorpe, *Selwyn Lloyd* (Jonathan Cape, 1988), p. 439.
3. Sir Evelyn Shuckburgh, *Descent to Suez*, p. 337, entry for 25.2.56. Selwyn Lloyd, *Suez 1956. A Personal Account* (Jonathan Cape, 1978), p. 4.
4. Avon Papers, A P 20/49/1–17. Shuckburgh, op. cit., p. 314, entry for 19.12.55.
5. Sir Con O'Neill, 'Ivone Kirkpatrick', in E. T. Williams and C. S. Nicholls (eds), *Dictionary of National Biography 1961–1970* (OUP, 1981), pp. 616–17. Shuckburgh to author, 1987. Shuckburgh, op. cit., p. 335, entry for 20.2.56.
6. Marshal of the RAF Sir William Dickson to author, 1986.
7. FO 371/115526 from Charles Duke (Amman), 4.11.55, V 1073/1228.
8. FO 371/115526 from Sir James Bowker (Ankara), 2.11.55, V 1075/1206. *Foreign Relations of the United States, 1955–57, Vol. XIV*, Doc. 391, 9.11.55, pp. 720–2. Shuckburgh, op. cit., p. 299, entry for 10.11.55.
9. FO 371/115653 from Bowker (Ankara), 10.11.55, VJ 1051/22.8.FO.
10. FO 371/115532 from General Glubb (Amman), 28.11.55, V 1073/1348.
11. FO 371/115532 'Record of the Restricted Session of the Baghdad Pact Ministers', 22.11.55. Macmillan conveyed his impressions of the meetings to Dulles in a telegram on 25.11.55. In his reply, which he did not send until 5.12.55, Dulles said, 'An immediate move to expand the Baghdad Pact would probably deny us Nasser's co-operation. Therefore I think we should wait a little...' *FRUS XIV*, Doc. 434, 5.12.55, pp. 820–1.
12. Macmillan, *Tides of Fortune*, p. 573.
13. Ali Abu Nuwar to author, Amman, December 1987.
14. FO 371/115650 'Report of General Sir Gerald Templer on Mission to Jordan'.
15. Anwar Sadat, *Al Gumhouriya*, 24–27.12.55. Hazza al Majali, *The Story of the*

Templer Talks (Arabic, Amman, 1956). Templer, 'Report . . .', op. cit.

16. FO 371/121241 C.E. Fouracres (First Secretary, Information, Amman) to Alan Goodison (Information Policy Dept, FO), 29.12.55. V 1071/8.
17. See footnote 13.
18. DDE Diaries, entry for 10.1.56. Eisenhower Library, Abilene.
19. *Daily Telegraph*, 16.1.56.
20. FO 371/121233 Heads of Mission Conference, Middle East, 4–5.1.56. Shuckburgh, *Descent to Suez*, pp. 316–17.
21. FO 371/121722 from Duke (Amman), 21.1.56. Minute by P.H. Laurence, VR 1073/20. FO 371/121723 Glubb to Duke, 18.1.56. E.M. Rose (Head, Levant Dept), 'Military Planning with Jordan', 6.2.56, VR 1073/37A. FO to Duke, 7.2.56, VR 1073/37.
22. DEFE 4/82 COS(56) 12th Meeting, 26.1.56. Annex to JP (55) 137 (Final), 19.1.56.
23. FO 371/121724 Trevelyan (Cairo) to Adam Watson (Head, African Dept), 13.2.56. Watson to Trevelyan, 1.3.56, VR 1073/79, Annexes I and II.
24. FO 371/121724 Glubb to Generals Templer (CIGS) and Keightley (C-in-C, Middle East Land Forces), 17.2.56, VR 1073/56.
25. FO 371/121543 King Hussein, 'The Reasons that Led Me to Relieve General Glubb of his Post . . .' Glubb, *Soldier with the Arabs*. Ali Abu Nuwar to author, December 1987. Peter Snow, *Hussein. A Biography* (Barrie and Jenkins, 1972), pp. 80–90. In the event Glubb was allowed twenty-two hours to leave. He never came back.
26. CAB 128/30 Pt 1. CM(56) Conclusions, 22.2.56.
27. *FRUS XV*, Doc. 157, 4.3.56, pp. 287–9 and Doc. 162, 5.3.56, pp. 295–300.
28. FO 371/121243 Lloyd (Cairo) to Eden, 2.3.56, FO 371/121709 Lloyd (Bahrein) to Eden, 3.3.56, VR 1071/34. Lloyd, *Suez 1956*, pp. 45–8. Heikal, *Cutting the Lion's Tail*, pp. 95–8. Lord Caccia to author, 1986.
29. FO 800/734 Lloyd (New Delhi) to Eden, 4.3.56. Sir Michael Weir to author, 1986. Sir Charles Belgrave should not be confused with his relative, Robert Belgrave, who was in the Diplomatic Service at the time. (Shuckburgh, *Descent to Suez*, p. 348).
30. Shuckburgh, op. cit., p. 345, entries for 7 and 8.3.56.
31. Shuckburgh, op. cit., p. 342, entry for 4.3.56.
32. William Clark, unpublished diary entry for 7.3.56. Clark, *From Three Worlds*, p. 162.
33. *Parliamentary Debates (Hansard) House of Commons, Vol.* 549, 7.3.56, cols 2223–33.
34. See footnote 31.
35. FO 800/734 Nutting to Lloyd (Karachi), 5.3.56.
36. Shuckburgh, op. cit., p. 346, entry for 12.3.56.
37. William J. Burns, *Economic Aid and American Policy toward Egypt*, pp. 58–61. *FRUS XV*, Doc. 10, 6.1.56, p. 15.
38. *FRUS XV*, Doc. 15. 'Diary Entry by the President', 11.1.56, p. 23.
39. *The Independent*, 17.6.87, 'Anderson's Tardy Fall from Grace'. *The Times*, 26.6.87.
40. *FRUS XV*, Doc. 54, 30.1.56, pp. 101–7. FO 371/121759 Eden and Lloyd to Rab Butler, 31.1.56.
41. David Ben-Gurion, *My Talks with Arab Leaders* (Keter, Jerusalem, 1972), pp. 298 and 313. Anderson is referred to anonymously as 'The Emissary'.
42. *FRUS XV*, Doc. 9, 6.1.56, pp. 13–14. Doc. 48, 29.1.56, pp. 92–4.
43. *FRUS XV*, Doc. 32, 24.1.56, pp. 60–3. Doc. 64, 1.2.56, pp. 122–4. Doc. 78, 5.2.56, pp. 143–5. Doc. 84, Memorandum, 'The Problem of Tension Between the Arab States and Israel: Obstacles to Settlement', handed to Ali Sabri, 8.2.56, pp. 152–6. Doc. 107, 20.2.56, pp. 195–6. Doc. 109, 21.2.56, pp. 198–202.
44. *FRUS XV*, Doc. 108, 21.2.56, pp. 196–8.
45. This extreme detestation of Jews Dulles attributed, by factual blunder, to Saudi belief that Jews had been involved in the assassination of the Prophet Mahomed. Although erased from the official record of the hearing, this bizarre quotation received worldwide circulation.

46. *84th Congress, Second Session. Senate Foreign Relations Committee Hearings*, 24.2.56.
47. *FRUS XV*, Doc. 150, 2.3.56, pp. 275–6.
48. *FRUS XV*, Doc. 140, 29.2.56, pp. 257–60. Doc. 151, 2.3.56, pp. 276–81.
49. *FRUS XV*, Doc. 75, pp. 138–40. The letter, dated 6.2.56, was in two parts. The first, signed by Nasser, pledged that Egypt would 'never be party to an aggressive war' and recognised the need 'to eliminate the tensions between the Arab States and Israel'. The second, an unsigned attachment, lists 'principles' for a settlement, which included, 'The establishment of Arab sovereignty over a satisfactorily substantial territory connecting Egypt and Jordan.'
50. *FRUS XV*, Doc. 164, 6.3.56, pp. 302–7.
51. *FRUS XV*, Doc. 187, 'Diary Entry by the President', 13.3.56, pp. 342–3.
52. Sir Anthony Nutting, *No End of a Lesson ... The Story of Suez* (Constable, 1967), pp. 33–4.
53. Nutting to author, 1986. Nutting, idem, pp. 34–5.
54. *FRUS XV*, Docs 223–7, 28.3.56, pp. 419–26. A special office for the Omega programme was set up under Douglas MacArthur III.
55. *FRUS Vol. XIII*, Doc. 213, 30.1.56, pp. 329–34. *FRUS XV*, Doc. 225. Memconf. with the President, 28.3.56, pp. 423–4.
56. FO 371/114618 'Note on Buraimi Arbitration', 16.9.55.
57. FO 371/114618 Sir Harold Caccia (Deputy Under-Secretary, FO) to Makins (Washington), 21.10.55. For a description of the operation and the local background see Edward Henderson, *The Strange, Eventful History. Memoirs of Earlier Days in the UAE and Oman* (Quartet, 1988).
58. FO 371/115532 Harold Macmillan, 'Memorandum to the Prime Minister, PM 55/172', 25.11.55, V 1073/1336.
59. Dulles was still fulminating about British 'aggression' in Saudi Arabia to the Dutch Foreign Minister as late as 27.12.56. Avon Papers AP 14/4/157. Mason (The Hague) to Lloyd.
60. Memconv. Eisenhower, Louis St Laurent, Dulles, Pearson at White Sulphur Springs, West Va., 27.3.56. Eisenhower Library, Abilene.
61. FO 371/118861 Trevelyan (Cairo) to Shuckburgh, 5.4.56.
62. *FRUS XV*, Doc. 265 Dulles, Meeting with Congressional Leaders, 10.4.56, pp. 504–11.
63. Wilbur Crane Eveland, *Ropes of Sand, America's Failure in the Middle East* (Norton, 1980, pp. 169–71).
64. *FRUS XV*, Doc. 197 Eden to Eisenhower, 15.5.56, with enclosure, 'Egyptian Plans for a United Arab States' (January 1956). In PREM 11/1177 the enclosure is withheld.
65. Eveland to Allen Dulles, 1.5.56.
66. Winthrop Aldrich to Dulles, 9.10.56, Eisenhower Library, Abilene.
67. Eveland, *Ropes of Sand*, op. cit., p. 229.
68. *FRUS XV*, Doc. 65, 1.2.56, pp. 125–6. Doc. 143, 1.3.56, pp. 263–5.
69. *FRUS XV*, Doc. 54, 30.1.56, pp. 101–7. Doc. 56, 31.1.56, pp. 109–12.
70. FO 371/121761 Marshal for the RAF Sir William Dickson to General Sir John Whiteley, 15.3.56, VR 1076/64.
71. FO 371/121761 Dickson to Whiteley, 16.3.56, VR 1076/64 'A'.
72. FO 371/121761 Sir Roger Makins (Washington) to Eden, 18.3.56, VR 1076/58.
73. Admiral Arleigh Burke, Dulles Oral History Project, Princeton.
74. PREM 11/1626 'Visit of the Soviet Leaders to the UK', p. 46. *FRUS XV*, Editorial Note, pp. 585–6.
75. FO 371/121759 Barbara Salt, 'Meeting between US and UK to examine the Possibility of Taking Advance Action in the UN', 8.2.56.
76. Sir Brian Urquhart, *A Life in Peace and War* (Weidenfeld and Nicolson, 1987), pp. 125–7.

77. FO 371/121724 from Paul Gore-Booth (Rangoon), 9.2.56, VR 1073/55.
78. FO 800/735 'Conversation in London between S. of S. and the S-G. of the UN', 7.4.56. Hammarskjöld also told the American, French and British Permanent Representatives at a luncheon on 7.5.56 that his 'eyes had been opened' on Nasser, but he liked Fawzi and got along splendidly with Ben-Gurion. *FRUS XV*, Doc. 338, pp. 621–2.
79. Dag Hammarskjöld Priv. 20. Meeting with Henry Cabot Lodge and Sir Pierson Dixon, 13.3.56. Hammarskjöld Archives, Royal Library, Stockholm.
80. FO 371/115905 from Amman, 10.10.55, enclosing special report to General Glubb from Radi Abdullah, Jordanian Military Attaché in Cairo, 'Incidents on the Egyptian-Israeli Boundaries'. VR 1092/326.
81. Sir Brian Urquhart, *Hammarskjold* (The Bodley Head, 1972), pp. 140–5.
82. Hammarskjöld to Lloyd, 11.6.56. Hammarskjöld Archive, Royal Library, Stockholm. Glubb's immediate successor was Major-General Radi Anab, but he was replaced by Abu Nuwar before the end of May.
83. Lieutenant-General E. L. M. Burns, *Between Arab and Israeli*, pp. 151–9. FO 371/121729 from Duke (Amman), 7.7.56, VR 1073/213. 'We hope Burns knew what he was doing', commented the American Embassy in Jordan. *FRUS XV*, Doc. 424, 5.7.56, pp. 774–6.
84. *FRUS XV*, Doc. 259, 9.4.56. pp. 469–70. Doc. 282, 14.4.56, pp. 532–7. Doc. 342, 10.5.56, pp. 628–32. Doc. 345, 14.5.56, pp. 634–5. Doc. 349, 16.5.56, pp. 639–41. Doc. 358, 23.5.56, pp. 655–6. Doc. 364, 24.5.56, pp. 670–1. Doc. 423, 5.7.56, pp. 773–4. Doc. 445, 12.7.56, pp. 818–19. Doc. 456, 13.7.56, p. 835. Doc. 462, 16.7.56, pp. 840–1. Doc. 480, 19.7.56, pp. 874–5.
85. *FRUS XV*, Doc. 510, 26.7.56 and Footnote 4. Memo by George Allen, 30.7.56, p. 906.
86. Urquhart, *Hammarskjold*, op. cit., pp. 153–8. *FRUS XVI*, Doc. 637, 5.12.56, p. 1251. *FRUS XVII*, Doc. 3, 31.12.56, pp. 6–7.

Chapter Six
Code-Word 'De Lesseps'

1. Even now (1990), when President Mitterrand calls a conference of Francophone states, Egypt is among those who attend.
2. FO 371/115494 Sir Gladwyn Jebb to Shuckburgh, 23.2.55. 'The French have always held us responsible in a large measure for their eviction from the Levant.'
3. FO 371/115500 Sir John Gardener (Damascus) to Michael Rose (Head of Levant Dept), 9.3.55. V 1073/53.
4. FO 371/115860 Nicholls (Tel Aviv) to Eden, 22.2.55 with minutes. VR 10317/1. FO 371/115502 from Jebb (Paris), 24.3.55. Minuted by Eden, V 1073/569.
5. FO 371/115818 Nicholls (Tel Aviv) to Eden, 22.2.55. Minute by Rose, 16.3.55, VR 10317/1.
6. Colonel Abdul Monheim al-Nagar to author, Cairo, November 1986. *FRUS XIV*, Doc. 364, 28.10.55, p. 673. *FRUS XV*, Doc. 463, 16.7.56, pp. 843–4. 'Various elements in the French Government wish to send huge quantities of arms to Israel. It is difficult for the Quai d'Orsay to resist the pressure.'
7. Ze'ev Schiff, *A History of the Israeli Army* (Macmillan, 1985), pp. 87–8. Matti Golan, *The Road to Peace* (Warner, New York, 1989), pp. 28–38. CAB 30/104/477 Cabinet Committee on Supply of Arms to the Middle East, 24.11.54. FO 371/115552 from Jebb (Paris), 12.1.55. Minuted by Eden and Macmillan, V 1192/30. The sharp French reply to British representations was described by Macmillan as 'an insolent and blackmailing one'.
8. FO 371/115818 Nicholls to Eden, 22.2.55, VR 10317/1. *FRUS XIV*, Doc. 364, 28.10.55, p. 673.

9. A useful summary and analysis of the French election of 1956 is given by Jean-Louis Thiébault, 'Le Gouvernement de Guy Mollet' in B. Ménager *et al.*, *Guy Mollet, Un Camarade en République*, pp. 299–306. There is a detailed narrative by Sir Anthony Meyer, subsequently a Conservative MP but then at the Paris Embassy, in FO 371/124421, WF 1015/27.
10. Roger Bullen and M. E. Pelly, *Documents of British Policy Overseas, Series II, Vol. 1* (HMSO, 1986), p. 764 n.20.
11. For Mollet's career see Bernard Ménager *et al.*, *Guy Mollet*, op. cit. especially Denis Lefebvre, 'Du Pacifisme à la Résistance', and Jérôme Jaffre, 'Guy Mollet et la Conquête de la SFIO en 1946'.
12. Christian Pineau, *1956 Suez* (Editions Robert Laffont, Paris, 1976), pp. 15–16.
13. FO 371/124430 from Gladwyn Jebb, 4.2.56. WF 1022/1.
14. FO 371/124421 Memo by Sir Ivone Kirkpatrick of conversation with French Ambassador, 4.1.56.
15. FO 371/124422 from Jebb (Paris), 2.3.5. Two telegrams, WF 1015/61 and/65.
16. FO 371/124422 from Jebb (Paris), 2.3.56. WF 1022/6.
17. FO 80–0/734 'Record of a Meeting Held at Chequers, Sunday, 11 March, 1956'.
18. FO 371/124430 Eden to Jebb, 12.3.56. WF 1022/24. The bargaining over the wording of the speech of reparation was conducted by Jebb and Emile Noël, Mollet's *chef de cabinet*, rather in the fashion of the drafting of the settlement of a libel action (Jebb to Eden, 19.3.56).
19. FO 371/124430 Eden to Jebb, 25.3.56. FO 370/121244 Jebb to Kirkpatrick, 26.3.56. V 1072/35. Jebb to Eden, 27.3.56. WF 1022/35.
20. Pineau, *1956 Suez*, op. cit., pp. 34–44.
21. FO 371/124431 from Jebb (Paris), 27.3.56. WF 1022/35.
22. Abel Thomas, *Comment Israel Fut Sauvé. Les Secrets de l'Expédition de Suez* (Albin Michel, Paris, 1978), pp. 86–90.
23. Roger Faligot and Pascal Krop, *La Piscine. Les Services Secrets Français 1944–1984* (Seuil, Paris, 1985), p. 149. Ilan Troën (ed.) 'Ben-Gurion's Diary' in Troën and Shemesh, *The Suez-Sinai Crisis 1956* (Frank Cass, 1989). Diary entry for 29.12.56, pp. 328–9. *FRUS XIV*, Doc. 364, 28.10.55, p. 673.
24. Maurice Vaïsse, 'La France et la Crise de Suez d'après les Documents Diplomatiques Français', in Louis and Owen, *Suez 1956: The Crisis and its Consequences* (OUP, 1989), p. 133. *FRUS XV*, Doc.336, 6.5.56. pp. 615–19.
25. 'Ben-Gurion's Diary' entry for 14.12.56, in Troën and Shemesh, op. cit., pp. 326–7.
26. Professor Yehosafat Harkabi to author, Jerusalem, October 1986. Matti Golan, *Shimon Peres* (Weidenfeld and Nicolson, 1982), pp. 45–6.
27. FO 371/124431 Jebb (Paris) to Eden, 13.6.56.
28. FO 371/124443 Memorandum by Julian Amery, MP, 4.6.56.
29. FO 371/124431 from Jebb (Paris), 13.7.56.
30. FO 371/124431 Jebb to Kirkpatrick, 10.7.56. WF 1051/66, Memconv. Lloyd/Chauvel, 26.7.56.
31. From the President, François Charles-Roux (75), downwards the Suez directors were nearly all old men. The British list was headed by Lord Hankey (78), and included the notoriously quirkish Sir Harrison Hughes (74) who had been a director for 35 years. The company prided itself on never having refused re-election to a director who offered himself for it.
32. According to Sir Francis Wylie, one of the three British Government directors who was responsible for a delightfully pithy and sardonic weekly letter received by the Foreign Office on the company's affairs, Georges-Picot was known in Cairo for his rudeness and insensitivity (FO 371/113743, 21.3.55. JE 1424/31). He struck Wylie, an old India hand, as being 'extremely quick and clever but, I should say, dubiously well-bred'.
33. FO 371/113746 Conversation Armstrong/Georges-Picot, 26.7.55. JE 1424/94.

34. Engineer Ezzat Adel to Afro-Asian Solidarity Committee Seminar on the Suez War, Ismailia, October 1986.
35. FO 371/113743. William Armstrong thought that Nasser's speech 'seems to make it less likely that the Egyptians will attempt to take over the Canal before the end of the concession.' 23.1.55. Tel from Stevenson (Cairo) 24.2.55, JE 1424/25.
36. Frankland (ed.), *Documents on International Affairs, 1956* (RIIA), p. 513.
37. FO 115/4522 from Trevelyan (Cairo), 18.2.56. FO 371/119067 Robert Isaacson (Minister, Paris) to Adam Watson (Head, African Dept), 6.2.56. FO 115/4522 Wylie to Bromley, 'Suez Canal Company: Policy of HMG', 29.12.55.
38. Dr Hefnaoui's thesis was published as *Le Canal de Suez et Ses Problémes Contemporains*. The author gave up diplomacy and devoted himself to propaganda against the Company. After 26.7.56 he was a member of the Canal Authority Board.
39. Jacques Georges-Picot, *The Real Suez Crisis* (Harcourt Brace Jovanovich, 1978), pp. 45–6.
40. CAB 129/78. CP(55)152, 14.10.55 'Middle East Oil: Report by the Middle East (Official) Committee'. The secretary of the committee was Robert Belgrave. Also see FO 371/114963, UE 51171/33.
41. Martin Gilbert, '*Never Despair*', pp. 689, 701–2, 718–20.
42. PREM 11/1626 'Visit of the Soviet Leaders to the UK', pp. 13–14.
43. *Parliamentary Debates (Hansard), House of Commons*, Vol. 552, 7.5.56, cols 820–2; 15.5.56, cols 1961–70.
44. See Footnote (40).
45. *FRUS XV*, pp. 96–100, 115–17, 128–30. Eugene Black, Dulles Oral History Project, Princeton. Richard Lamb, *The Failure of the Eden Government*, p. 186. I do not share Mr Lamb's view that Black's negotiations were abortive and that 'a great opportunity of bringing peace to the Middle East was lost'. Despite the moments of tension, agreement with the World Bank was finally reached.
46. FO 371/119050 from Trevelyan (Cairo), 8.2.56. JE 1422/86. FO 371/119053 from Trevelyan, 5.3.56. JE 1422/135.
47. FO 371/119052 from Makins (Washington), 14.2.56. JE 1422/108. FO 371/119053 from Trevelyan (Cairo), 3.3.56. JE 1422/137. The Egyptians, becoming aware of the hazards of running over the fiscal year, began to press for the money for the Dam to be hypothecated and deposited with the World Bank or elsewhere. Eden minuted crossly, 'They certainly won't get the money at present.'
48. FO 371/121885 from Trevelyan (Cairo), 17.5.56. FC 10316/1. Eisenhower had told Eden that, if the UN voted to admit the People's Republic of China, the US would have to leave the UN. *FRUS XV*, pp. 435–7, 450–1, 646. The Russians had told Nasser, following the Eden–Khrushchev talks, that the West might promote a UN Security Council ban on arms exports to the Middle East. Thinking it 'not impossible' that Russia would agree, Nasser wanted to establish alternative lines of supply with China. (Heikal, *Cutting the Lion's Tail*, pp. 102–3.)
49. Burns, *Economic Aid and American Policy Towards Egypt*, pp. 85–9.
50. FO 371/119055 Adam Watson, 'Aswan Dam', 6.6.56. JE 1422/194. Draft letter from Frederick Bishop (10 Downing Street) to Patrick Hancock (Private Secretary to Selwyn Lloyd).
51. FO 371/118985 Trevelyan (Cairo) to Shuckburgh, 'Secretary of State for War's Visit to Egypt', 19.3.56. JE 11913/13. Minutes by John Wilton and Antony Moore. The other British journalist whose articles met with Nasser's approval was Alastair Forbes of the *Sunday Despatch*. He was said in the FO to be 'a purely polemical writer with whom we have no contact'.
52. FO 371/118861 Tom Little's Interview with Colonel Nasser in *The Observer*, 25.3.56, in which Nasser attacked the Baghdad Pact, British 'spheres of interest' and Britain's 'springing of surprises', but declared himself not opposed to British interests. JE 1053/12.
53. FO 371/119055 Michael Johnston (Treasury) to J. F. S. Phillips (FO), 6.6.56.

54. FO 371/119055 Trevelyan (Cairo) to Watson, 23.6.56. JE 1422/211. FO 371/119057 Archibald Ross, 'High Aswan Dam', 22.6.56. JE 1422/269.
55. *FRUS XIV*, Doc 371, 26.5.56, pp. 682–3. Doc. 399, 16.6.56, pp. 731–4.
56. *Senate Foreign Relations Committee, 84th Congress, Second Session, 1956, Executive Sessions (Historical Series)*, pp. 514–16.
57. Some Free Officers were dropped from the Cabinet, including Colonel Anwar Sadat whose highly polemical nationalism caused him to be regarded (mistakenly) by Nuri as pro-communist. But he retained his true power base: the editorship of *Al Gumhouriya* and access to the airwaves of Cairo Radio. He proved a powerful propagandist during the Suez crisis.
58. FO 371/119056 from Terence Garvey (Counsellor, Cairo). The Foreign Office's informant was Tom Little of the Middle East News Agency and *The Economist*, who named several (Egyptian) sources to the British Embassy. See also *FRUS XV*, pp. 751–4 (Allen Dulles to Foster Dulles, 'Shepilov's Visit to Egypt', 27.6.56, partially censored) and 754–6. The CIA's source was probably Ahmed Hussein (see *FRUS XV*, Doc. 476, 19.7.56, p. 865).
59. PREM 11/1098 f 240 from Trevelyan (Cairo) 30.7.56, includes Ahmed Hussein's account to Byroade. *FRUS XV*, Doc. 439, 10.7.56. pp. 806–7.
60. FO 371/119056 from Makins (Washington), 11.7.56. JE 1422/226. CAB 128/30 CM(56)2, 17.7.56.
61. Avon Papers, AP 20/34/40, January 1957. FO 371/119056 from Makins (Washington), 14.7.56. JE 1422/230. *FRUS XV*, p. 855.
62. FO 371/119056 to Makins, 17.7.56. JE 1422/230 'G'.
63. FO 371/119056 from Makins, 18.7.56. JE 1422/230 'A'.
64. FO 371/119056 to Makins, 19.7.56. JE 1422/230. Lord Sherfield to author, London, 1988.
65. FO 371/119056 from Makins, 19.7.56. JE 1422/241. *FRUS XV*, Doc. 474, 19.7.56, pp. 863–4. According to the American account, Makins promised to telephone London before the interview to say that Dulles would have preferred to have received Britain's 'advice' if there had been time. Dulles remarked, amid general amusement, that that depended what construction was placed on the word 'advice'.
66. *FRUS XV*, Doc. 478, 19.7.56, pp. 867–73. Mohamed Heikal, *Cutting the Lion's Tail*, pp. 119–22.
67. FO 371/119056 'Aswan Dam'. Handwritten, unsigned note, JE 1422/243.
68. PREM 11/1106 f 140–2 Sir Harold Caccia (Washington) to Lloyd, 23.11.56.
69. C. D. Jackson Papers. Log, Friday July 20, 1956, Eisenhower Library, Abilene.
70. Maurice Couve de Murville, J. F. Dulles Oral History Project, Seeley G. Mudd Manuscript Library, Princeton University.
71. 'Suez. The Nine-Day War.' Transcript BBC documentary (producer: David Wheeler), 20.9.66.
72. Lord Thorneycroft to author, House of Lords, March 1988.
73. Heikal, op. cit., pp. 119–22. Nasser was accustomed to this manner of calculating risks. He told Robert Anderson (19.2.56) that, if there was an Egyptian-Israeli settlement he would lose 60% of his popular support at once; with a good programme of public works he would recover 30% within 30 to 60 days and within 6 months all except 10%. (*FRUS XV*, p. 32.)
74. Heikal, ibid. pp. 123–4. Sayyid Mar'i, *Awraq Siyasiyya* [Political Papers] (Cairo, 1978), Vol. II, Chapter XVI, ed. and tr. Moshe Shemesh, in Troën and Shemesh, *The Suez-Sinai Crisis 1956*, pp. 359–61.
75. This was a reference back to the nadir of Ismail's regime in 1878 when an Englishman (Sir Rivers Wilson) and a Frenchman (de Blignières) were appointed respectively Minister of Finance and Minister of Public Works under an Armenian Prime Minister (Nubar Pasha).
76. According to Herodotus, the Pharaoh Necho built a canal from the Nile to the Red Sea. 'In the prosecution of this work under Necho no less than 100,000 Egyptians

perished.' The Suez Canal Company never published statistics of mortality among its labour force during the construction of the Canal. It was high but not that high.

77. A full text of Nasser's Alexandria speech is in Frankland (ed.), *Documents on International Affairs, 1956* (RIIA), pp. 77–113.

Chapter Seven
Plotting Nasser's Downfall

1. Philip Williams (ed.), *The Diary of Hugh Gaitskell, 1945–56*. pp. 552–3.
2. Clark, *From Three Worlds*, p. 166. *FRUS XV*, Doc. 2, 27.7.56, pp. 3–5.
3. Earl Mountbatten of Burma, 'The First Sea Lord's Part in the Suez Canal Crisis up to 7 Sept. 1956'. N.106, Broadlands Archive. Philip Ziegler, *Mountbatten, the Official Biography*, pp. 537–8.
4. Admiral Sir Guy Grantham to Anthony Seldon, Seldon Oral History Archive.
5. Mountbatten, 'The First Sea Lord's Part . . .', op. cit.
6. Sir Frank Cooper in *RAF Historical Society Proceedings 3*, p. 19.
7. Julian Amery in Troën and Shemesh (ed.), *Suez–Sinai Crisis 1956: Retrospective and Reappraisal*, p. 117. Amery to author, March, 1988.
8. PREM 11/1098 ff 410–15 CM(56) 54th Conclusions. Confidential Annex, 27.7.56.
9. According to Macmillan's diary, cited by Horne, *Macmillan*, Vol. 1, p. 397, Eden had first intended to run the crisis with a 'Suez Committee' consisting only of himself, Salisbury, Macmillan and Home.
10. PREM 11/1098 ff 410–15, op. cit. The Egypt Committee, which was usually attended by all or some of the Chiefs of Staff, also practised variable geometry with additional civilian members. Several other Ministers, including Butler, Lennox-Boyd (Colonies) and Watkinson (Transport) attended quite frequently.
11. Eden, *Full Circle*, op. cit., pp. 427–8.
12. Robert Murphy, *Diplomat Among Warriors* (Collins, 1964), p. 461. 'The President was not greatly concerned and there was no talk of recalling Dulles from Peru.' Lloyd cites this, contrasts it with Eisenhower's later comment 'The fat was really in the fire' (Dwight D. Eisenhower, *Waging Peace*, 1966, p. 34) and remarks bitterly, 'I think that Murphy's recollection is probably more accurate . . .' Lloyd, *Suez 1956*, p. 87.
13. *FRUS XV*, Doc. 3, 27.7.56, pp. 5–7. Doc. 6, 27.7.56, pp. 11–12. Doc. 15, 28.7.56, pp. 26–7.
14. *FRUS XVI*, Doc. 15, 28.7.56, pp. 26–7.
15. *FRUS XVI*, Doc. 16, 28.7.56, Supplementary Note, pp. 27–8.
16. FO 371/119080 Sir Francis Wylie to Adam Watson, 30.7.56. Jacques Georges-Picot, *The Real Suez Crisis* (Harcourt Brace Jovanovich, 1978), pp. 78–9.
17. PREM 11/1098 f 284, Egypt Committee, 4th Meeting. 30.7.56, Minute 9, 'Military Operations'.
18. FO 371/119080 Wylie to Watson, 30.7.56.
19. PREM 11/1098 f 244, 30.7.56, Donald Logan (FO) to Guy Millard (Number Ten). f 153–4 A. D. M. Ross, 'Suez Canal Company's Instructions to Employees', 2.8.56; Wylie to Watson, 3.8.56, Cadogan Papers, Churchill College, Cambridge. PREM 11/1098 ff 81–2, Record of 7th Meeting held in Council Chamber, FO 2.8.56, FO 37/119092, Record of Conv. between S. of S. and French Ambassador, 3.8.56.
20. PREM 11/1098 ff 350–2 from Trevelyan (Cairo), 28.7.56.
21. PREM 11/1098 f 282 Egypt Committee, 4th Meeting, 30.7.56.
22. Georges-Picot, *The Real Suez Crisis*, pp. 74–6.
23. Christian Pineau, *1956 Suez* (Robert Laffont, Paris, 1976), p. 41. Henri Azeau, *Le Piége de Suez*, p. 120 and n.1.
24. Azeau, ibid., p. 125.

25. Kennett Love, *Suez. The Twice Fought War*, p. 368.
26. Maurice Vaïsse, 'France and the Suez Crisis', pp. 131–43, in Louis and Owen, *Suez 1956: The Crisis and Its Consequences*, discusses some of the contradictions between Pineau's description of his motives in *1956, Suez* and his contemporary remarks. Briefly the former put him into Azeau's 'smash-Nasser-because-of-Israel' category; the latter into the 'smash-Nasser-because-of-Algeria' one.
27. Pineau, *1956 Suez*, p. 58. Incredibly enough, Georges-Picot in his book, *The Real Suez Crisis*, pp. 82–3, adds himself to the lengthening list of those who claimed to have realised in advance that the pilots' phenomenal expertise was largely bluff.
28. C. D. Jackson Papers 1931–67, Box 58, Luce, H. R. and Clare, 1956 (2). Eisenhower Library, Abilene.
29. Jean Chauvel, *Commentaire, Vol. III 1952–1962 De Berne A Paris* (Fayard, Paris, 1973), pp. 182–5. Mountbatten, 'The First Lord's Part in the Suez Canal Crisis, 1956'. Broadlands Archives N.106.
30. Couve de Murville (Washington) to Pineau, 28 July, cited by Maurice Vaïsse in Louis and Owen, *Suez 1956: The Crisis and its Consequences*, p. 139.
31. PREM 11/1098 ff 346–7 from Makins (Washington), 29.7.56.
32. PREM 11/1098 ff 269–70. 'Record of Conversation between the Secretary of State and M. Pineau, at 1, Carlton Gardens, at 5.45 pm on 29 July, 1956.'
33. PREM 11/1098 ff 269–70. 'Record of Meeting Held at 1, Carlton Gardens at 6 pm on Sunday, 29 July, 1956.'
34. PREM 11/1098 ff 318–21. 'Record of Meeting Held at 1, Carlton Gardens at 9.30 pm on 29 July, 1956.' Selwyn Lloyd, *Suez 1956*, op. cit., pp. 87–9.
35. PREM 11/1098 f 237. 'Record of Conversation with Mr. Murphy and Mr. Barbour at 10, Downing Street on 30 July 1956.'
36. PREM 11/1098 f 311 Egypt Committee, 30.7.56 (EC (56) 3rd Meeting.
37. FO 371/121662 Abdul Ilah to Colonel de Gaury, forwarded by Julian Amery to Lloyd, 1.8.56. VQ 1051/44.
38. *BBC Summary of World Broadcasts, Part IV*, No. 435, 24.12.57. Middle East News Agency account of 'Restoration Plot'. For dynastic links, see *Burke's Royal Families of the World, Vol. II, Africa and the Middle East*, p. 36.
39. Yaacov Caroz, *The Arab Secret Services*, p. 22. *Al Ahram*, 25.12.57.
40. Caroz, ibid.
41. *BBC SWB IV*, 24.12.57. *SWB IV*, No. 471, 8.2.58. Caroz, op. cit., p. 24. FO 371/125423, 26.12.57. JE 1019/7 (b) and (d). Enclosed: Claude G. Ross, Foreign Service Despatch to State Department, Washington.
42. FO 371/125423, 25.8.57, JE 1091/1 (e).
43. Sir Anthony Eden, 'Suez', January 1957 in Avon Papers, AP 20/34/40. Miles Copeland, *The Game Player*, pp. 165–6, 200–5.
44. BBC Radio 4, 'The Profession of Intelligence, Part IV', presented by Christopher Andrew, 24.8.81.
45. Peter Wright (with Paul Greengrass), *Spycatcher. The Candid Autobiography of a Senior Intelligence Officer*, Viking Penguin, New York, 1987, pp. 84–5, 160–1.
46. *BBC Summary of World Broadcasts*, IV, Daily Series No.7, 31.7.56, 'Unidentified Broadcasts Attacking Gamal Abdul Nasser in Arabic, 28.7.56.' No.8, 1.8.56. No.11, 4.8.56. The exiled Egyptian journalist Mustafa Abul-Fath was later reported in *Al-Ahram* as confessing that he had undertaken anti-Nasser broadcasts at a station in the south of France. The MI6-owned station on Cyprus, Sharq al-Adna, was also implying, a little more gently, that 'a coup d'état against Nasser was a serious possibility'. (Peter Partner, *Arab Voices* (BBC, 1988), p. 100.) *FRUS XVI*, Doc. 637, 5.12.56, p. 1258. *FRUS XVII*, Doc. 13, 10.1.57, p. 20.
47. *BBC SWB IV*, Unidentified station in Arabic, 1.8.56, 15.8.56.

Chapter Eight
A Matter of Timetables

1. PREM 11/1098 ff 310–15, EC(56) 3rd Meeting, 30.7.56.
2. *Parliamentary Debates (Hansard), House of Commons, Vol. 557*, cols 918–20.
3. PREM 11/1098 ff 275–84, EC(56) 4th Meeting, 30.7.56.
4. PREM 11/1098 ff 257–60 from Makins (Washington), 30.7.56.
5. *FRUS XVI*, Doc. 33, 31.7.56, pp. 60–2.
6. *FRUS XVI*, Doc. 34, 31.7.56, pp. 74–7.
7. *FRUS XVI*, Doc. 38, 31.7.56, pp. 74–7.
8. DO 35/6314 General Sir Archibald Nye to Sir Gilbert Laithwaite, 1.8.56.
9. FO 800/739 from Makins (Washington), 31.7.56.
10. Sarvepalli Gopal, *Jawaharlal Nehru. A Biography, Vol. II, 1947–1956*, p. 278. Nehru to Vijayalakshi [Mrs Pandit], 27.7.56.
11. Gopal, 'India, the Crisis and the Non-Aligned Nations' in Louis and Owen, *Suez 1956: The Crisis and Its Consequences*, pp. 174–7.
12. Text in Mohamed Heikal, *Cutting the Lion's Tail*, pp. 135–7.
13. FO 371/119182 'Record of a Conversation with the Jugoslav Minister at Luncheon on Thursday, 4 October 1956 in New York'.
14. Sir Anthony Eden to author, Washington, 1954.
15. DO 35/6317 Malcolm MacDonald to Home, 2.8.56.
16. James Eayrs, *The Commonwealth and Suez* (OUP, 1964), p. 70. The speaker was Tamizuddin Khan, President of the East Pakistan Muslim League.
17. DO 35/6317 Morrice James to Home, 1.8.56.
18. Eayrs, op. cit., pp. 15–16, 60.
19. ADM 116/6097 Admiralty to C-in-C, Mediterranean, 14.8.56.
20. *DDF 1956, II*, Doc. 105, pp. 209–10.
21. PREM 11/1098 f 184 6th Meeting, Council Chamber, FO, 1.8.56.
22. Rhodes James, *Anthony Eden*, pp. 471–3. Selwyn Lloyd, *Suez 1956*, p. 98. Rhodes James prints the complete text of Eisenhower's letter. *FRUS XVI*, Doc. 35, 31.7.56, pp. 69–71.
23. PREM 11/1098 ff 187–8 CM(56) 56th Conclusions, 1.8.56.
24. PREM 11/1098 ff 77–84 7th Meeting, Council Chamber, FO. 2.8.56.
25. Frankland (ed.), *Documents on International Affairs, 1956* (RIIA), pp. 151–5.
26. Anthony Eden, *Full Circle*, pp. 437–8.
27. Clark, *From Three Worlds*, p. 168.
28. *Parliamentary Debates (Hansard), House of Commons, Vol. 557*, cols 1602–1721, 2.8.56.
29. Martin Gilbert, *'Never Despair'*, p. 1202. To his doctor (Lord Moran, *The Struggle for Survival*, p. 702), Churchill said on 1.8.56, 'Whoever he [Nasser] is, he's finished after this. We can't have that malicious swine sitting across our communications.'
30. Salisbury to Eden, 2.8.56. Text in Rhodes James, *Anthony Eden*, pp. 483–4.
31. PREM 11/1099 Lloyd to Makins (Washington). Minute by Eden, who even turned down a French proposal to notify Hammarskjöld officially about the Maritime Conference and the list of invitees.
32. Clark, *From Three Worlds*, p. 170.

Chapter Nine
Musketeer

1. DEFE 4/89 ff 48–51 Confidential Annex to COS (56) 74th Meeting, 30.7.56. JP (56) 134 (Final).
2. Air Marshal Sir Michael Armitage and Air Commodore R. A. Mason, *Air Power in the Nuclear Age. 1945–84. Theory and Practice* (1985), p. 220.

3. DEFE 4/89 ff 54/60. Annex to JP (56) 134 (Final). 'Availability of Forces for Action Against Egypt'. 31.7.56. ff 86–8. 'Action Against Egypt. Outline Plan', Report by the Joint Planning Staff', JP (56) 135 (Final), 31.7.56.
4. AIR 20/10746 Air Marshal Denis Barnett, 'Report by the Air Task Force Commander on Operation *Musketeer*': 'In general the equipment supplied to the French Air Force ... was so superior ... that at times the RAF looked almost Victorian'.
5. Air Chief Marshal Sir David Lee, *Wings in the Sun* (HMSO, 1989). Sir David Lee was in 1956 the Secretary to the Chiefs of Staff Committee. 'Even before reinforcements arrived,' he writes of Nicosia, 'about 1,000 men were living in tents and all of the new arrivals had to be similarly accommodated. A vigorous programme of tent erection ran into difficulty as compressors had to be used to drill holes through solid rock to take tent pegs. Understandably there were not enough compressors readily available' (p. 64). For French experiences in Cyprus, see Paul Gaujac, *Suez 1956* (Lavauzelle, Paris, 1987), 'Installation à Chypre', p. 80.
6. WO 106/5986 contains an excellent short summary of the principal military plans and arguments.
7. PREM 11/1099 ff 270–2. 'Record of a Meeting at 11, Downing Street on Friday, 3 August, 1956.' 'All history shows that Statesmen of any character will seize a chance like this and the Jews have character' (Macmillan to Eden, 3.8.56). Eden was said to be 'very shocked' (Alistair Horne, *Macmillan*, I, p. 401).
8. FO 371/121662 Lloyd to R. W. J. Hooper (Baghdad), 8.8.56.
9. WO 288/77. Report on Operation *Musketeer* by the Land Task Force Commander, 'Phase I – The Preliminary Period, 31 July to 9 Aug. 1956'. PREM 11/1098 ff 61–8 EC (56)5, Memo by COS: 'Action Against Egypt – Outline Plan, 1.8.56.'
10. Kenneth Macksey, *The Tanks. The History of the Royal Tank Regiment, 1945–1975* (Arms and Armour Press, 1979), pp. 124–9.
11. Air Marshal Barnett, 'Report ...' op. cit.
12. The codename *Musketeer* was recommended by the Chiefs of Staff Committee as early as 1.8.56 (DEFE 4/89 ff 82–4 Confidential Annex to COs (56) 76th Meeting). However, the operation was at first called *Hamilcar*, but this was changed when it was discovered that the French spelled the classical name *Amilcar*. The French assault force, commanded by General Beaufre, remained, however, known as 'Force A'; and, internally, the French referred to the Suez expedition as *Opération 700* (Gaujac, *Suez 1956*, pp. 28–9).
13. Sir Frank Cooper, *RAF Historical Society Proceedings* 3, p. 20. Sir Ewen Broadbent, op. cit., p. 33.
14. Stockwell, 'Suez from the Inside', *Sunday Telegraph*, 30.10.66. p. 6.
15. WO 288/77 Stockwell, 'Report', p. 12.
16. Martin Gilbert, '*Never Despair*', p. 1203–4.
17. PREM 11/1098 f 278–9 EC (56)8 'Action Against Egypt'. Note by the Chancellor of the Exchequer, 7.8.56. It carries the notation: 'This memo was not circulated but discussed at the beginning of the Egypt Committee meeting on 7 Aug 1956.'
18. Quoted by Horne, *Macmillan*, I, pp. 404–5.
19. 'Ben Gurion's Diary' in Troën and Shemesh, *Suez-Sinai Crisis 1956*, p. 292, entry for 3.8.56.
20. WO 32/16709 Secretary of State's file, War Office. COS to Keightley and Grantham, 31.7.56; BDCC (ME) to COS, 2.8.56; COS to BDCC (ME), 2.8.56; Halford (Tripoli) to FO, 2.8.56; Graham (Tripoli) to FO, 9.8.56. Stockwell, 'Report', p. 11.
21. WO 106/5986 Plans for *Musketeer*. Horne, *Macmillan*, I, pp. 405–6.
22. PREM 11/1099 f 225–6, Lloyd to Eden. PM 56/166, 8.8.56.
23. PREM 11/1099 f 230–1. FO to Jebb (Paris), 8.8.56. Clark, *From Three Worlds*, op. cit., p. 169.
24. *DDF 1956 III*, Doc. 321, Baeyens Report, 22.12.56, pp. 592–3.
25. General Sir Kenneth Darling, 'The Suez Canal Crisis, July–Dec 1956: The Problem of Intervention', Imperial War Museum. General Beaufre's description of this

encounter is in Beaufre, *The Suez Expedition* (tr. Richard Barry, Faber & Faber, 1969), p. 28, and General Stockwell's in WO 288/77, Stockwell, 'Report' . . ., p. 14.

26. PREM 11/1099 f133 'Minutes of a Staff Conference held at Chequers on Saturday, 11 August, 1956.'
27. PREM 11/1099 ff 197A–200 'Military Operations: Force Commanders' Outline Plan. Memo by COS'. EC (56) 15, 10.8.56. WO 288/77 Stockwell, *Report*, p. 15.
28. Stockwell, *Sunday Telegraph*, 30.10.66. See CAB 134/1225 and CAB 21/3094 for successive drafts of a 'Political Directive to the Allied Commander-in-Chief'. Dickson to author, 1986.
29. Paul Gaujac, *Suez 1956*, op. cit. Barjot was backed by an engineer, General Gazin, who favoured his own quick landing system of mobile pontoons and ramps. Beaufre, *The Suez Expedition 1956*, pp. 41–3.
30. PREM 11/1099 f 264 Selwyn Lloyd: 'France and the Middle East', 7.8.56. EC(56)10.
31. PREM 11/1098 Eden to Eisenhower, Prime Minister's Personal Tel. T352/56, 5.8.56.

Chapter Ten
The First London Conference

1. DDE Papers as President, Diary Series, Box 8, 6.8.56. JFD Papers, White House Memoranda Series, 8.8.56. Eisenhower Library, Abilene. *FRUS XVI*, Doc. 71, 8.8.56, p. 164.
2. Record Group 218: Records of the Joint Chiefs of Staff, 'Joint Chiefs of Staff, History', Vol. VI, Chapter X, pp. 322–3. *FRUS XVI*, Doc. 68, 7.8.56, pp. 153–6 and Doc. 72, 9.8.56, pp. 170–6.
3. Admiral Arleigh Burke, J. F. Dulles Oral History Project, Princeton.
4. *FRUS XVI*, Doc. 73, 9.8.56, pp. 176–7 and Doc. 74, Editorial Note, pp. 177–8. Bourgès-Maunoury, TV interview, Sde Boqer, Oct. 1986.
5. *FRUS XVI*, Doc. 76, 10.8.56. pp. 182–3.
6. PREM 11/1098 ff 66–7 Final Protocol of the Meeting of the Three Ministers of Foreign Affairs. Annex C: 'Proposed Basis for the International Conference'.
7. *FRUS XVI*, Doc. 40, 31.7.56, pp. 78–93. Doc. 58, Editorial Note, pp. 132–3. Doc. 66, 6.8.56, pp. 149–50. Doc. 69, 7.8.56, pp. 156–60.
8. Nehru to Nasser, quoted in Heikal, *Cutting the Lion's Tail*, pp. 138–40. Heikal says that Nehru was 'doing what he enjoyed almost more than anything – that is, thinking and speaking on behalf of someone else'.
9. Mahmoud Fawzi, *Suez 1956. An Egyptian Perspective*, p. 50.
10. PREM 11/1099 f 22 from Trevelyan (Cairo), 8.8.56.
11. PREM 11/1098 f 18–19 from Trevelyan (Cairo), 4.4.56.
12. See footnote 10.
13. Clark, *From Three Worlds*, op. cit., p. 171.
14. Frankland (ed.), *Documents on International Affairs, 1956* (RIIA), pp. 158–61.
15. Rhodes James, *Anthony Eden*, op. cit., p. 492. Douglas (later Lord) Jay had used the adjective 'hysterical'.
16. FO 371/118809. 'Letters from the Public on the Suez Crisis'. Doris M. Clayton to Selwyn Lloyd, 12.8.56.
17. Heikal, *Cutting the Lion's Tail*, op. cit., pp. 140–2.
18. FO 800/739 Lloyd to Sir William Hayter (Moscow), 16.8.56, JE 14211/826.
19. Information from Professor Ali Hillal Dessouki, Wilson Center, Washington, September 1987. Also see Veljko Mićunović (tr. David Floyd), *Moscow Diary* (Chatto and Windus, 1980), pp. 102–4, entry for 23.8.56.
20. FO 371/119108 Reading to Lloyd, 13.8.56.
21. CAB 134/1302 Cabinet Official Committee on the Middle East, Suez Sub-

Committee, ME(O) (SC) (56) 3rd Meeting, 13.8.56 'International Conference on the Future of the Suez Canal', briefs A and B.
22. CAB 134/1302 'Record of Meeting on the Suez Canal', 10.8.56.
23. Frankland (ed.), *Documents ... 1956*, op. cit., pp. 155–7.
24. PREM 11/1099 ff 112–16. CM(56)59th Conclusions, Minute 3, 14.8.56.
25. The two timetables are set out by J. A. Sellers in Troën and Shemesh, *The Suez-Sinai Crisis 1956*, pp. 29–32.
26. Clark, *From Three Worlds*, op. cit., p. 170.
27. PREM 11/1099 f 109. EC (56) 15 Meeting, 14.8.56.
28. Gaitskell to Eden, 3.8.56. Philip Williams (ed.), *The Diary of Hugh Gaitskell, 1945–1956*, pp. 570–1.
29. Rhodes James, *Anthony Eden*, p. 493.
30. FO 371/118809. 'Letters from the Public on the Suez Crisis'.
31. Williams (ed.), *The Diary of Hugh Gaitskell*, p. 581.
32. Clark, op. cit., pp. 172 (Brook) and 174 (Eden).
33. BBC Written Archives, Board of Management Minutes. BMM 391 WAC/R34/1580/1. Cited by John King, 'The BBC and Suez', *The Round Table*, October 1987. FO 953/1642.
34. FO 371/118999 Trevelyan (Cairo) to Kirkpatrick, 15.8.56. Minute by Eden, 17.8.56.
35. *FRUS XVI*, Doc. 78, 10.8.56, pp. 185–7.
36. *FRUS XVI*, Doc. 86, 16.8.56, pp. 210–11.
37. FO 800/739 'Record of Conversation between the S. of S. and Mr Dulles', 15.8.56, JE 14211/796. Dulles to Eisenhower (DULTE 1) see 36 footnote.
38. CAB 134/1217 f 84. Menon told *The Hindu* (23.5.56), 'We will have a great deal of difficulty even on these with the Egyptians but all negotiations are difficult.' The British Government's opinion of Menon's performance was that 'it almost looked as if Mr Krishna Menon was anxious to make the dispute more serious in order to leave greater openings for himself as a mediator'. DO 35/6316 CRO Outward Telegram, 29.8.56.
39. Frankland (ed.), *Documents ... 1956*, pp. 174–5.
40. Menon (London) to Ali Yavar Jung (Cairo), 20.8.56. Menon to Nehru, 2.6.56. Files of Ministry of External Affairs, Delhi, cited by Sarvepalli Gopal, 'India, the Crisis and the Non-Aligned States', in Louis and Owen, *Suez 1956: The Crisis and its Consequences*, p. 180.
41. Menon to Nehru, 22.8.56. Nehru to Menon, 23.8.56. MEA, cited in Gopal. op. cit.
42. Frankland (ed.), *Documents ... 1956*, pp. 175–7. The Western plan became known as 'the Five-Nation Proposal' when amendments were accepted from Ethiopia, Iran, Pakistan and Turkey. *FRUS XVI*, Doc. 110, Editorial Note, pp. 250–2.
43. T. Michael Ruddy, *The Cautious Diplomat. Charles E. Bohlen and the Soviet Union, 1929–1969* (Kent State University Press, 1986), p. 139.
44. Frankland (ed.), *Documents ... 1956*, pp. 177–86.
45. *FRUS XVI*, Doc. 94, 18.8.56, p. 227.
46. *DDF 1956, II*, Doc. 137, pp. 279–82.
47. *FRUS XVI*. Doc. 98, 19.8.56, pp. 232–3.
48. *FRUS XVI*, Doc. 99, 19.8.56, pp. 233–5.
49. FO 800/739 'Record of a Meeting with Representatives of the Baghdad Pact Powers', 20.8.56. Lloyd told Halvard Lange, the Norwegian Foreign Minister, that the Asians were keen on having a committee talk to the Egyptians so that the plan did not look like an ultimatum.
50. *FRUS XVI*, Doc. 99, pp. 233–5.
51. *FRUS XVI*, Doc. 97, 19.8.56, pp. 231–2.
52. *FRUS XVI*, Doc. 101, 20.8.56, pp. 237.
53. *FRUS XVI*, Doc. 103, 20.8.56, pp. 241–2.
54. *FRUS XVI*, Doc. 111, 21.8.56, pp. 253–4.
55. *FRUS XVI*, Doc. 120, 23.8.56, pp. 269–73 and Doc. 125, 23.8.56, pp. 280–1.

56. *FRUS XVI*, Doc. 107, 20.8.56, p. 248.
57. *FRUS XVI*, Doc. 109, 21.8.56, pp. 249–50.
58. *FRUS XVI*, Doc. 126, 23.8.56, p. 281.
59. *FRUS XVI*, Doc. 129, 24.8.56, pp. 285–6.
60. *FRUS XVI*, Doc. 119, 23.8.56, pp. 267–9.

Chapter Eleven
Keightley in Command

1. PREM 11/1152 f 43 Eden to Sandys. PM's Personal Minute M188/56, 22.8.56.
2. PREM 11/1152 f 42 Sandys to Eden, 23.8.56.
3. Lord Birkenhead, *Monckton*, op. cit., p. 307. Marshal of the RAF Sir William Dickson to author, 1986. Clark, *From Three Worlds*, op. cit., p. 173. Also entry for 14 August: 'I saw Walter Monckton who is also depressed by the prospects of military op. and feels that the senior civil servants are against it. But he realises that to row back now would be fatal for the Government.'
4. Lord Mountbatten, 'The First Sea Lord's Part in the Suez Canal Crisis, up to 7 September, 1956'. Broadlands Archives N.106. Ziegler, *Mountbatten*, p. 542.
5. DEFE 4/89 f 191 COS (56) 80th Meeting, Confidential Annex, 14.8.56.
6. DEFE 4/89 f 123 COS (56) 83rd Meeting, Confidential Annex, 23.8.56.
7. Salisbury to Eden, 24.8.56, Avon Papers, AP 20/33/4.
8. PREM 11/1100 ff 337–9. Pierson Dixon, 'Possible Security Council Action in Connection with the Suez Situation', 23.8.56.
9. CAB 134/1216 ff 160–2. EC(56) 21st Meeting, 24.8.56.
10. PREM 11/1152 ff 26–41. Alan Lennox-Boyd to Eden (24.8.56); Earl of Home to Eden (24.8.56); Sir Norman Brook to Eden (25.8.56); Marquess of Salisbury to Eden (24.8.56). Macmillan noted in his diary: 'Walter Monckton was calm but obviously distressed' (Horne, *Macmillan*, I, p. 410).
11. Clark, *From Three Worlds*, p. 180, diary entry for 27.8.56. 'In conversation with Walter Monckton it became clear that PM is pressing Cabinet to decide for the immediate use of force.'
12. *FRUS XVI*, Doc. 108, 21.8.56, pp. 248–9.
13. Macmillan, *Riding the Storm, 1956–59*, p. 112. FO 371/121257, 24.8.56.
14. PREM 11/1100 ff 283–4 'The United Nations and Suez'. Note by the Foreign Secretary, 27.8.56.
15. PREM 11/1100 ff 253–5 Lloyd to Makins (Washington), 28.8.56.
16. *FRUS XVI*, Doc. 151, 30.8.6, pp. 334–5.
17. 'Joint Chiefs of Staff, History Vol. 6', Chapter 10, pp. 324–5. National Archives, Washington (Record Group 218 – Records of the Joint Chiefs of Staff). *FRUS XVI*. Doc. 149, 30.8.56, pp. 324–32.
18. DEFE 4/89 COS (56) 78th Meeting, Confidential Annex, 9.8.56. General Sir Charles Keightley: Supplement to *The London Gazette*, 12.9.57, p. 5327. Merry and Serge Bromberger, *Secrets of Suez* (Sidgwick and Jackson, 1957), pp. 54 and 65.
19. ADM 116/6209 Vice-Admiral Richmond, 'Report on Operation *Musketeer*', p. 27.
20. CAB 134/1225 ff 4–7. Minutes of Egypt (Official) Committee, EOC (56) 1st Meeting. 24.8.56. PREM 11/1100, ff 304–6, E C (56) 28, 20.8.56, 'Egypt: Military Planning'. Memo by the Foreign Secretary.
21. Julian Amery to author, March 1988.
22. CAB 134/1225 EOC (56) 1st Meeting, ff 4–7, op. cit. EOC (56) 3rd Meeting ff 15–16, 30.8.56. Annex, 'Nature of Hostilities Contemplated in Egypt'. 'Whatever they were called, the hostilities would in fact (and in most respects also in law) be war ... and Egypt would be entitled to treat them as such. There would however be political advantages in not ourselves claiming for the operations the status of war

and *a fortiori* in not making any declaration of war.' CAB 21/3049 EOC 'Political Directive for the Allied Commander-in-Chief'.

23. CAB 21/3049 'Political Directive. Note by the Foreign Office' by Patrick Dean, 20.9.56. EOC (56) 3rd Meeting, f 16.
24. *FRUS XVI*, Doc. 139, 28.8.56, pp. 306–8. PREM 11/1100 f 277 Conversation between Lloyd and Henderson, 27.8.56.
25. *FRUS XVI*, Doc. 142, 28.8.56, p. 312. FO 371/119124 Note on Eden–Henderson meeting, 28.8.56. Eden expressed horror to Cabinet at 24 hours' delay (CM(56)62nd Conclusions).
26. PREM 11/1104 ff 145–50, 28.8.56.
27. They all seem to have forgotten or preferred not to remember Admiral Lord Fisher, who resigned as First Sea Lord in May 1915, though Hailsham and Mountbatten were to recall this inhibiting precedent on 3.11.56.
28. Mountbatten, 'The First Sea Lord's Part in the Suez Canal Crisis'. Cilcennin to Mountbatten, 21.8.56. Broadlands Archives, N.106.

Chapter Twelve
The Birth of SCUA

1. William Clark, *From Three Worlds*, pp. 182–3. FO 800/739. Lloyd (Personal) to Trevelyan, 30.8.56.
2. Dillon to Dulles, 2.9.56, JFD Papers, Box 82 Suez Canal Crisis, Eisenhower Library, Abilene. FO 800/740 f 10 'Conversation between the S. of S. and Mr Barbour, the US Chargé d'Affaires, 3.9.56'. The French troops' arrival in Cyprus could not be treated with total discretion because, thanks to the island's status as a British colony, a Royal Proclamation had to be published before it could accommodate foreign forces.
3. 'Ben Gurion's Diary' in Troën and Shemesh, *The Suez–Sinai Crisis 1956*, pp. 291–2, 296, entries for 30.7.56, 3.8.56 and 1.9.56. Moshe Dayan, *Story of My Life*, p. 151.
4. Heikal, *Cutting the Lion's Tail*, p. 154n.
5. PREM 11/1100 f 209 from Trevelyan (Cairo), 31.8.56.
6. Heikal, ibid., p. 149.
7. Loy Henderson to Dulles, 3.9.56. JFD Papers, Box 82 Suez Canal Crisis, Eisenhower Library, Abilene. Henderson thought Nasser looked ill at ease. 'I had the impression that he was not quite sure whether it would be appropriate for him to relax like those around him or to assume the pose of a strongman. He apparently compromised. At times he smiled in friendly, cordial fashion. At other times his face took on a Mussolini-like mask. So far as I could ascertain, his facial expression had no relation to the Menzies presentation.' *FRUS XVI*, Doc. 169, Summary No. 1, Developments in Suez Situation, Executive Secretariat, DOS, 4.9.56, pp. 366–9.
8. Mahmoud Fawzi, *Suez 1956*, p. 57.
9. Henderson to Dulles, op. cit. Fawzi, op. cit., p. 58.
10. Sir Robert Menzies, 'My Suez Story', in *Afternoon Light* (Cassell, 1967), pp. 164–5, 167–8. PREM 11/1101 f 75 Makins (Washington) to Lloyd, 15.9.56.
11. Eden, *Full Circle*, p. 471.
12. *FRUS XVI*, Doc. 173, Summary No. 2, Exec. Sec., 5.9.56, pp. 375–8. PREM 11/1100 f 152–3 from Trevelyan (Cairo), 5.9.56.
13. PREM 11/1100 ff 123–4 Menzies to Eden, PM's Personal Tel. T 388/56. *FRUS XVI*, Doc. 178, Summary No. 3, Exec. Sec., 6.9.56, pp. 393–4.
14. *FRUS XVI*, Doc. 194, Editorial Note, pp. 441–3. Anwar Sadat, *Al Gumhouriya*, 8.9.56.
15. Frankland (ed.), *Documents on International Affairs, 1956* (RIIA), pp. 199–201. 'Egyptian Memorandum to the United States, 10.9.56'. Identical memoranda were

sent to other Governments and to the S-G of the UN. FO 371/119130 A. D. M. Ross, 'The Egyptian Proposal of 10 September', 11.9.56.

16. Ambassador Henry Byroade to author, Maryland, August 1986.
17. FO 800/740 f 19 Lloyd to Menzies (Cairo), 6.9.56.
18. Duck Island is in the eastern extremity of Lake Ontario. Dulles's holiday home was not on the telephone but radio messages could be relayed by the lighthouse.
19. *FRUS XVI*, Doc. 161, 2.9.56, pp. 351–2, and Doc. 172, 5.9.56, pp. 374–5. PREM 11/1100 ff 158–9 from Coulson (Washington), 5.9.56.
20. *FRUS XVI*, Doc. 170, 4.9.56, pp. 369–72 and Doc. 180, 6.9.56, pp. 398–400.
21. PREM 11/1100 ff 93–7 Lloyd to Makins (Washington), 6.9.56.
22. Complete text in Dwight D. Eisenhower, *Waging Peace*, pp. 666–7 and in *FRUS XVI*, Doc. 163, 2.9.56, pp. 355–8.
23. Clark, *From Three Worlds*, pp. 183–4.
24. Eden, *Full Circle*, pp. 464–7 and *FRUS XVI*, Doc. 181, 6.9.56, pp. 400–3.
25. DDE Diary, Presidential Tel. Calls, 7.9.56. Eisenhower Library, Abilene. A different version of this conversation is printed in *FRUS XVI*, Doc. 182, 7.9.56, pp. 403–4 and n.1.
26. Dulles Memconv. with the President, 8.9.56. Eisenhower Library, Abilene. *FRUS XVI*, Doc. 192, 8.9.56, pp. 435–8. An earlier draft by Eisenhower is at Doc. 190, pp. 431–3.
27. FO 800/740 Kirkpatrick to Makins (Washington), 10.9.56.
28. PREM 11/1123 Oliver Poole to Eden, 29.8.56.
29. PREM 11/1123 William Clark to Eden, 10.9.56.
30. PREM 11/1100 CM (56) 63rd Conclusions, Confidential Annex, 6.9.56.
31. *DDF 1956 II*, Note du Secrétariat des Conférences, 10.9.56, pp. 360–3. PREM 11/1100 ff 74–6 and 64–5 from Makins, 7 and 8.9.56. *FRUS XVI*, Doc. 188, 7.9.56, pp. 420–30 and Doc. 193, 8.9.56, pp. 438–41.
32. PREM 11/1100 ff 44–5 Lloyd to Makins (Washington), 8.9.56.
33. *FRUS XVI*, Doc. 201, 10.9.56, pp. 461–2 and Doc. 202, Editorial Note, pp. 462–3.
34. PREM 11/1100 f 22 from Jebb (Paris), 9.9.56. See also *DDF 1956 II*, Doc. 169, 8.9.56, pp. 348–9 and 349 n.2.
35. T 236/4188 Edward Bridges to Macmillan, 7.9.56. Horne, *Macmillan*, I, pp. 414–16 and 402. Richard Lamb, *The Failure of the Eden Government*, pp. 282–3.
36. FO 800/740 f 33 Makins to Selwyn Lloyd, 9.9.56.
37. FO 371/119136 Record of Meeting in Foreign Office, 8.9.56. At a subsequent meeting with British officials on 14.9.56, Georges-Picot described the possibility of Nasser accepting CASU as 'a catastrophe'. The colonel would simply accept the use of the Company's pilots until he had recruited enough of his own and then break off collaboration. CASU would amount to 'playing Colonel Nasser's cards for him'. CAB 134/1302 'Notes of a Meeting on CASU in Mr. Beeley's Room', 14.9.56 [CASU later became SCUA. *DDF 1956 II*, Doc. 164, 4.9.56, pp. 340–1 and 340 n.1.
38. FO 800/740 f 38 Lloyd to Makins, 10.9.56. *FRUS XVI*, Doc. 205, 10.9.56, pp. 469–72 and Doc. 206, 10.9.56, pp. 472–3.
39. *DDF 1956 II*, Docs. 172 and 173, 10.9.56, pp. 356–60.
40. *DDF 1956 II*, Doc. 176, 11.9.56, p. 369. *FRUS XVI*, Doc. 200, 10.9.56.
41. *DDF 1956 II*, Doc. 177, 11.9.56, p. 367–73.
42. FO 800/740 f 38 Lloyd to Makins ('drafted by I.K. [Kirkpatrick]', 10.9.56.

Chapter Thirteen
Musketeer Revise

1. PREM 11/1104 ff 105, 121–30, WM(56)118, 7.9.56 (Keightley's Note begins at f

128). A revised version of the new plan was circulated to the Egypt Committee on 17.9.56, with a further Note by Keightley (WM 120/56 ff 74–85).
2. Lord Hailsham to author, House of Lords, December 1987. Hailsham, *A Sparrow's Flight* (Collins, 1990), pp. 288–9.
3. WO 106/5986 Musketeer.
4. Earl Mountbatten, 'Naval Responsibility for Inflicting Civilian Casualties', and 'First Sea Lord's Part in the Suez Canal Crisis 1956'. Broadlands Archives (N. 106).
5. PREM 11/1104 ff 101–2 EC(56) 25th Meeting, Minute 1.
6. Eden Diary for 7.9.56, Avon Papers, AP 20/1/32. Eden was a most episodic diarist. Using a standard-issue office diary he would put down quite full narrative entries for a day or two and then leave a gap of several weeks before the next entry. He kept no continuous record during the Suez Crisis.
7. Clark, *From Three Worlds*, p. 185. Although usually described as Churchill's idea, the 1940 scheme for Franco-British Union was proposed by Jean Monnet and René Pleven, with some drafting help from Lord Vansittart. Churchill adopted it reluctantly.
8. Emile Noël to author, London, April 1988.
9. Ely, *Mémoires. Suez ... Le 13 mai*, pp. 105–6.
10. PREM 11/1104 ff 77–8 COS (56)350 (Revise) 'Alternative to *Musketeer*'. Memorandum by the Chiefs of Staff, 12.9.56.
11. PREM 11/1104 ff 81–5 Note by General Sir Charles Keightley.
12. AIR 8/1940 Annex to JP (57) 142 (Final). Sir Charles Keightley 'Lessons of Suez', 11.12.57. Brigadier Fergusson was later Lord Ballantrae and Governor-General of New Zealand.
13. *Jewish Observer and Middle Eastern Review*, 21.9.56. The British weekly, edited by Jon Kimche, kept up a campaign against these broadcasts, despite the efforts of Sir Keith Joseph, one of the only two Jewish MPs then on the Conservative benches, to persuade them to drop it.
14. PREM 11/1149 ff 183/190 Langardge (FO) to Bishop (Number Ten), 3.10.56, enclosing text of SCANT No. 44, 25.9.56.
15. AIR 20/9570 Papers by Brigadier Bernard Fergusson. Comment by Air Marshal Barnett. This is one of the few files on Psychological Warfare at the PRO that have not been withheld.
16. WO 288/77 Sir Hugh Stockwell, 'Operational Report', p. 25.
17. AIR 20/10746 Air Marshal Denis Barnett, 'Summary of Operations during Operation *Musketeer*'.
18. WO 288/77 Stockwell, op. cit., p. 22.
19. AIR 8/2081 Brief for Sir Dermot Boyle for COS Committee, 25.9.56. Air Vice-Marshal R. B. Lees, Assistant Chief of Staff (Operations) to Boyle, 24.9.56.
20. Beaufre, *The Suez Expedition, 1956*, pp. 54–60; Paul Gaujac, *Suez 1956*, pp. 94–7; Colonel John Sellers, 'Military Lessons: the British Perspective', in Troën and Shemesh (ed), *The Suez–Sinai Crisis 1956*, pp. 36–7.
21. WO 32/16079 Parliamentary Under-Secretary of State for War, 28.9.56.
22. PREM 11/1104 ff 86–8 Antony Head to Eden, 14.9.56.
23. CAB 128/36 ff 537–40 CM (56) 64.
24. Frankland (ed.), *Documents on International Affairs, 1956* (RIIA), pp. 210–19.
25. Lloyd, *Suez 1956*, p.140.
26. Eden, *Full Circle*, pp. 481–2.
27. Tel. call, J. F. Dulles – Arthur Fleming. Dulles Telephone Series, Box 5, Eisenhower Library, Abilene.
28. *Parliamentary Debates (Hansard), House of Commons, Vol. 558*, 12.9.56, cols 2–15 (Eden).
29. *FRUS XVI*, Doc. 216, 13.9.56, pp. 491–2.
30. Frankland (ed.), *Documents*, op. cit., pp. 210–19.
31. Eden, *Full Circle*, p. 483. There is a note in the Dulles Papers in the Eisenhower

Library of a phone call from Sir Roger Makins praising Dulles lavishly for his 'tremendous' performance, saying 'he does not know how admirable he thinks it is', and adding that it would enable Eden to make an effective reply to the debate. Alphand also sent an enthusiastic report to his Government. (*DDF 1956 II*, Doc. 181, pp. 378–9.) The Russians treated the press conference as evidence of the Americans inciting Britain and France to use force.

32. Alistair Horne, *Macmillan*, I, p. 417. *Parliamentary Debates*, op. cit., cols 219 and 287–308.
33. Eden Diary, entry for 12.9.56. Avon Papers, AP 20/1/32.
34. PREM 11/1125 Eden to Sir Robert Boothby, 16.9.56. Horne, *Macmillan*, I, p. 418.
35. Kenneth Harris, *David Owen, Personally Speaking* (Weidenfeld and Nicolson, 1987), pp. 16–17.
36. *Parliamentary Debates (Hansard), House of Lords, Vol. 199*, 12.9.56, col. 724.
37. Of the 90 foreign pilots who left, 40 were British, 24 French, 10 Dutch, 5 Norwegian, 3 Danish, 2 Italian, 2 American, and one each Spanish, Polish, Belgian and Swedish FO 115/4579 from Cairo, 17.9.56.
38. FO 115/4580 from Cairo. Text from Gamal Abdul Nasser's speech at Bilbeis Air Academy, 15.9.56.
39. PREM 11/1101 f 89. EC(56) 28th Meeting, Minute 2, 14.9.56.
40. CAB 128/30 Pt 2. Memorandum by Harold Watkinson, 10.9.56. JE 14211/1784.
41. PREM 11/1102 f 490. EC(56) 29th Meeting, Minute 3, 17.9.56.
42. FO 115/4578, from Cairo, 16.9.56. FO 371/118999 Trevelyan (Cairo) to Ross, 16.9.56.
43. FO 371/119138 Marshal Bulganin to Eden, 11.9.56, JE 14211/1667. The text of the Soviet statement of 15.9.56 is in Frankland (ed.), *Documents*, op. cit., p. 226.
44. PREM 11/1102 ff 479–83 Letter from Permanent Representative of Egypt to the President of the UN Security Council, 17.9.56.
45. See Footnote (38).
46. FO 371/119134, Minute by Sir Ivone Kirkpatrick, 12.9.56.
47. PREM 11/1101 ff 309/11 from Hankey (Stockholm), 12.9.56.
48. FO 115/4576 from Oslo, 1424/709/56. On the other hand the Danes were offended by Egypt's diplomatic style. They did not take kindly to being told that Danish membership of CASU would, since Egypt did not intend to co-operate with it, be tantamount to being in favour of war. The folly of this communication, the British Embassy was told, struck the Danish Government even more than its impudence. FO 115/4579, 18.9.56, 1424/797/56.
49. FO 371/119140 Martino to Lloyd, 10.9.56. Minutes by Ross (12.9.56) and Ward (13.9.56).
50. DO 35/6314 Outward Telegram from Commonwealth Relations Office.
51. FO 115/4579 from Pierson Dixon (New York), 15.9.56, 1424/799/56.
52. CAB 21/3093 'Proceedings of SCUA Conference'.
53. Clark, *From Three Worlds*, p. 191.
54. Lloyd, *Suez 1956*, pp. 146–8. PREM 11/1102 ff 423–8. 'Record of Conversation between S. of S. and Mr. Dulles at Lancaster House', 21.9.56. *FRUS XVI*, Doc. 247, 21.9.56, pp. 548–50.
55. *DDF 1956 II*, Doc. 212, 24.9.56, pp. 445–8.

Chapter Fourteen
The Israeli Factor

1. PREM 11/1102 ff 422–3 to Makins (Washington), 22.9.56.
2. PREM 11/1102 ff 394–5, Eden to Macmillan, 23.9.56, T406/56.
3. PREM 11/1103 ff 356–60 from Makins, 26.9.56. *FRUS XVI*, Doc. 263, 25.8.56, pp. 577–9.

4. PREM 11/1102 f 355 Macmillan to Eden, 25.9.56.
5. Lord Bracken to Lord Beaverbrook, 22.11.56. Beaverbrook Papers, House of Lords Library. Macmillan was, Bracken went on, 'like the character in O'Casey's play who cried:
   Let me like a hero fall,
   My breast expanding to the ball.'
6. PREM 11/1102 ff 302–4 Macmillan, 'Note of a Private Talk with Mr Dulles, 25 September 1956', *FRUS XVI*, Doc. 265, 25.9.56, pp. 580–1.
7. PREM 11/1102 ff 297–300 Macmillan to Eden, 26.9.56. *FRUS XVI*, Doc. 264, Editorial Note, p. 580.
8. William Clark to author, December 1956.
9. J. F. Dulles, 'Memorandum of Conversation with Mr Ellsworth Bunker', 30.9.56. Dulles–Herter Papers, Eisenhower Library, Abilene. *FRUS XVI*, Doc. 291, 2.10.56, p. 626, n.2.
10. Michael Brecher, *Decisions in Israel's Foreign Policy* (OUP 1974), pp. 265–6. Brecher cites Shimon Peres's diary (in Y. Evron, *B'Yom Sagrir: Su'ets Me'ahorei Ha-Klayim* (Tel Aviv, 1968)), recording Bourgès-Maunoury on Pineau's talks in London.
11. Matti Golan, *Shimon Peres. A Biography* (Weidenfeld and Nicolson, 1982), pp. 48–9.
12. Golan, op. cit., p. 50.
13. CAB 128/36 CM 65(56)2, 14.9.56.
14. CAB 130/120 Franco-British Union. GEN 551/1 Memo by Treasury. GEN 551/2 Memo by Foreign Office. GEN 551/3 Draft Report to Cabinet.
15. FO 800/740 Eden (Paris) to R. A. Butler, 26.9.56.
16. PREM 11/1102 ff 321–2, EC(56) 31st Meeting, 25.9.56. FO 800/741 John Graham to Donald Logan, 3.10.56.
17. See footnote 15.
18. *Le Monde*, 26.9.56.
19. PREM 11/1125 Eden to Sir Robert Boothby, 'I found your French friends vigorous and firm. They are young by our standards – I felt a doyen.'
20. Terence Robertson, *Crisis. The Inside Story of the Suez Conspiracy* (Hutchinson, 1965), p. 136.
21. CAB 130/120 Meetings of Ministers, 1–2.10.56, both presided over by Eden and the second attended by Macmillan on his return from Washington. Nutting in *No End of a Lesson*, p. 68, states that the French had disclosed nothing at this time about their talks with the Israelis and that Eden 'returned to London only a very little less depressed than when he left'.
22. CAB 130/120, GEN 551/2, 21.9.56. 'Other possibilities of less substance but with sentimental appeal' that were mentioned included the Channel Tunnel.
23. Dulles news conference, 26.9.56, *Department of State Bulletin*, p. 543.
24. FO 371/121778 E. M. Rose, 'Incidents on Jordan Border'. VR 1091/236.
25. FO 371/121778 from Sir Charles Duke (Amman), 18.9.56, VR 1091/237. FO 371/121779 from Wikeley (Jerusalem), 25.9.56, VR 1091/257.
26. Golan, *Shimon Peres*, op. cit., p. 50.
27. Mordechai Bar-On, 'With Golda Meir and Moshe Dayan to the Conference of St. Germain' (Hebrew), *Ma'ariv*, 29.10.76. 'Ben-Gurion's Diary', entries for 25 and 27.9.56, in Troën and Shemesh, *The Suez–Sinai Crisis 1956*, pp. 299–300.
28. General E.L. M. Burns, *Between Arab and Israeli*, pp. 167–8. FO 371/121779 from Westlake (Tel Aviv), 26.9.56, VR 1091/261; 28.9.56, VR 1091/273.
29. Ben-Gurion to Hammarskjöld, 27.9.56. Dag Hammarskjöld Archive, Royal Library, Stockholm.
30. Mordechai Bar-On to author, Jerusalem, October 1986.
31. The Jordanian election of November 1989 represented a near-return of democratic politics, despite parties not being expressly allowed.
32. FO 371/121780 Fitzmaurice to Kirkpatrick, 27.9.56, VR 1091/289.

33. Speech by Shimon Peres, Ben-Gurion Centennial Symposium, Sde Boqer, 29 October 1986.
34. Golan, *Shimon Peres*, op. cit., p. 51.
35. Abel Thomas, *Comment Israel Fut Sauvé* (Albin Michel, Paris, 1978), p. 153–4. Dayan, *Story of My Life*, pp. 158–65. Maurice Bourgès-Maunoury at Ben-Gurion Centennial, Sde Boqer, October 1986.
36. Dayan, op. cit., pp. 166–7. Bar-On to author, Jerusalem, October 1986.
37. Major General Shlomo Gazit to author, Tel Aviv, October 1986.
38. Dayan, op. cit., p. 170.
39. 'Kadesh' was the last site in Sinai occupied by the Children of Israel before moving into the Promised Land.
40. Mordechai Bar-On, 'The Influence of Political Considerations on Operational Planning in the Sinai Campaign' in Troën and Shemesh, *The Suez–Sinai Crisis*, pp. 200–1.
41. Beaufre, *The Suez Expedition 1956*, p. 70.
42. General Paul Ely, *Mémoires: Suez . . . Le 13 Mai*, pp. 126–32.

Chapter Fifteen
Taking it to the UN

1. PREM 11/1102 ff 202–3 Eden to Eisenhower, T 423/56, 1.10.56.
2. For text of Menon's proposal see Donald Cameron Watt, *Documents of the Suez Crisis* (RIIA, 1957), pp. 77–80. PREM 11/1102 ff 256–8, Egypt Committee, Confidential Annex, EC(56) 32nd Meeting, 1.10.56.
3. *Department of State Bulletin*, 15.10.56.
4. Iverach McDonald, *The History of The Times. Vol. V. Struggles in War and Peace*, 1939–66, pp. 267–8.
5. PREM 11/1174 f 2 Makins to Eden, 4.10.56.
6. *FRUS XVI*, Doc. 298, 4.10.56, pp. 634–7.
7. Memconf with the President, 6.10.56, Hoover/Goodpaster, Eisenhower Library, Abilene. The relevant paragraph has been deleted in the printed version in *FRUS XVI*, Doc. 303, 6.10.56, pp. 650–2. Doc. 637, 5.12.56, CIA Annex, pp. 1270–1.
8. PREM 11/1102 ff 190–4, 5.10.56. *FRUS XVI*, Doc. 300, 5.10.56, pp. 639–45.
9. PREM 11/1102 f 185 Eden to Lloyd, T 437/56, 6.10.56.
10. Rhodes James, *Anthony Eden*, op. cit., pp. 523–4, 556.
11. Summary No. 24 of 'Developments in Suez Situation', Executive Secretariat of Department of State, 5.10.56, *FRUS XVI*, Doc. 301, pp. 645–6. PREM 11/1102 ff 170–1 and 158 Lloyd to Eden, Eden to Lloyd, T 444/56 and T 445/56, 8.10.56.
12. *FRUS XVI*, Docs. 310 and 311, 8.10.56, pp. 661–3.
13. PREM 11/1102 Eden to Lloyd, T 440/56, 7.10.56.
14. Heikal, *Cutting the Lion's Tail*, p. 164.
15. Heikal, idem, pp. 163 and 168.
16. Fawzi to Nasser, 'I notice that everyone is fed up with Krishna Menon. Hammarskjöld, Lloyd, Pineau and Shepilov have all separately told me so' (Heikal, p. 166–8).
17. Urquhart, *Hammarskjold*, pp. 151–2 and note.
18. FO 800/728 Lloyd, 'M. Pineau and Mr Dulles in New York'.
19. Y. Harkabi to author, Jerusalem, October 1986.
20. PREM 11/1102 ff 116–18 Lloyd to Eden, T 449/56, 10.10.56. Heikal, *Cutting the Lion's Tail*, p. 167.
21. PREM 11/1102 f 110 EC(56) 34th Meeting, 10.10.56. *FRUS XVI*, Doc. 319, 10.10.56, pp. 676–7.
22. PREM 11/1102 ff 107–8 Eden to Lloyd, 10.10.56.
23. *FRUS XVI*, Doc. 326, 10.10.56, pp. 689–92.
24. *DDF 1956 II*, Doc. 263, 10.10.56, pp. 556–7.

25. Heikal, idem, p. 168. Hammarskjöld was irritated by Menon's interventions and tantrums. 'How can we explain politely to him that we are quite prepared to survive his threat to go back to India?' he asked Fawzi. Lloyd noted that 'Shepilov is very angry that he is not playing a larger part'. Fawzi was not telling him what was happening. (PREM 11/1102 f 92 Lloyd to Eden, 10.10.56.)
26. PREM 11/1102 ff 90 Lloyd to Eden, T 454/56, 11.10.56.
27. Lord Lambton, the PPS to Selwyn Lloyd, later wrote that Nutting was given a choice by the Chief Whip, Edward Heath, as to whether the speech was to be publicly attributed to Salisbury or to him. (Lambton, *Sunday Telegraph*, 2.7.67.) Avon Papers, AP 20/49/42A.
28. The National Union of Conservative and Unionist Associations, *The 76th Annual Conservative Conference, Verbatim Report*.
29. Nutting, *No End of a Lesson*, p. 82. Avon Papers, AP 20/49/42A.
30. PREM 11/1102 ff 78–80 Meeting of Ministers, 11.10.56.
31. Heikal, idem, p. 171.
32. PREM 11/1102 ff 73–4 Lloyd to Eden, T 459/56, 12.10.56. Lloyd to FO, ff 69–72, 67–72, 67–8, 12.10.56.
33. PREM 11/1102 f 42 Lloyd to Eden, T 466/56, 13.10.56. 'I gather that we shall be criticised on the ground that we have abandoned the purpose for which we came to New York.' Eden replied (ibid. f 34,T 468/56, 13.10.56), proposing to strengthen the reference to the 18-Power plan and declaring 'We are not at all worried about a Russian veto.' *FRUS XVI*, Doc. 329, 11.10.56, pp. 659–7.
34. Duncan Sandys to Piers Dixon, 21.10.62. Information by courtesy of Piers Dixon. Eden, *Full Circle*, p. 508.
35. *The 76th Annual Conservative Conference*, op. cit.
36. Pineau, *1956, Suez*, pp. 118–19.
37. *UN Security Council Records (11th Year, Jan.–Dec. 1956)*, 742nd Meeting, pp. 1–19. The second negative vote was Jugoslavia's, so that Lloyd could plume himself on having gained a clean sweep of the non-communist members of the Council.
38. *FRUS XVI*, Doc. 343, 14.10.56, p. 721.
39. PREM 11/1102 ff 10–12 Lloyd to Eden, T 476/56, 14.10.56.
40. PREM 11/1102 ff 13–14 Eden to Lloyd, T 475/56, 14.10.56.
41. Pineau, *1956 Suez*, pp. 119, 123.
42. PREM 11/1102 f 17 Lloyd to Eden, T 472/56, 13.10.56.
43. PREM 11/1175 ff 3–5 'Note on American Undertakings on a Canal Users' Association', n.d.
44. *FRUS XVI*, Doc. 347, n.2, p. 734. PREM 11/1103 ff 76–7 Lloyd to Dulles, 15.10.56. Also FO 800/728 Lloyd, 'M. Pineau and Mr Dulles in New York'.
45. PREM 11/1103 ff 76–7 Lloyd to Dulles, 15.10.56. *FRUS XVI*, Doc. 347 and 348, 15.10.56, pp. 734–40.

Chapter Sixteen
Two Frenchmen at Chequers

1. Alastair Horne, *Macmillan*, I, pp. 427–8.
2. FO 371/121487 Gladwyn Jebb to Anthony Nutting, 3.10.56. Jebb to Kirkpatrick, 3.10.56, VJ 10393/91.
3. FO 371/121781 from Ronald Higgins (Tel Aviv). Incidents Report for w.e. 11 October. FO 371/121487 Westlake (Tel Aviv) to Rose (FO), 27.9.56, VJ 10393/77.
4. *DDF 1956 II* Doc. 222, 27.9.56, p. 471.
5. FO 371/121467 from Makins (Washington), 3.10.56. FO 371/121487 Archibald Ross, 'Iraq–Jordan', 4.10.56, VJ 10393/87. *FRUS XVI*, Doc. 277, Editorial Note, pp. 599–600. Doc. 289, Editorial Note, pp. 662–3. Doc. 295, 3.10.56, pp. 630–1. Doc. 296, Editorial Note, pp. 631–2.

6. FO 371/121780 from Jebb (Paris), 10.10.56, VR 1091/290. Also, VR 1091/297 from Makins (Washington), 10.10.56. Minute by P.H. Laurence, 'One cannot help suspecting that the French and Israelis are in collusion over all this.' *FRUS XVI*, Doc. 318, 9.10.56, pp. 675–6.
7. CIA, 'Impression of Israel–Jordan Affair', 11.10.56, Eisenhower Library, Abilene. FO 371/121781 Higgins, Incidents Report, 11.10.56. Ariel Sharon, *Warrior*, pp. 135–40 provides the Israeli commander's account of the operation. He blames Dayan's interference for the mishaps.
8. FO 371/121780 from Thomas Wikeley (Jerusalem), 11.10.56, VR 1091/298.
9. FO 371/121780 from Duke (Amman), 11.10.56. FO to Duke, 12.10.56, VR 1091/303.
10. FO 371/121488 from Peter Westlake (Tel Aviv), 12.10.56, VJ 10393/126.
11. FO 371/121781 Memorandum by Kirkpatrick of conversation with Eliahu Elath, 11.10.56. 'Our refusal to supply Centurions had been a great disappointment. Another irritating factor was the hostile attitude of our radio station in Cyprus.'
12. FO 371/121781 from Duke (Amman), 13.10.56, VR 1091/316. 'The Husan incident could be a reconnaissance in force for a right hook to cut off Jerusalem, and Qalqilya an exercise in co-ordination of all arms in attack.'
13. FO 371/121781 to Duke (Amman), 14.10.56.
14. DEFE 4/90 ff 180–2. COS (56) 96th Meeting, Confidential Annex, 2.10.56. FO 371/121535 COS JP (56) n.9, 17.10.56. Political Office, Middle East Forces, to FO, 20.10.56, VJ 1192/114.
15. DEFE 4/91 ff 10–11. COS(56) 98th Meeting, Confidential Annex, 10.10.56. According to Sir William Dickson, if the United States came in it would be possible to take on Israel and Egypt at the same time.
16. FO 371/121488 from Jebb (Paris), 12.10.56 (VJ 10393/127) and 13.10.56 (VJ 10393/134).
17. Nutting, *No End of a Lesson*, p. 89.
18. Jean Chauvel, *Commentaire. Vol. III*, pp. 194–5.
19. FO 371/121488 Eden to Wright (Baghdad), 14.10.56. Only the Israel–Jordan–Iraq item features in the telegrams about Gazier's visit.
20. General Maurice Challe, *Notre Révolte*, pp. 27–8. Ely, *Suez ... Le 13 Mai*, pp. 137–8.
21. FO 800/741 to Wright (Baghdad), 15.10.56. Nutting, op. cit., p. 95.
22. FO 371/121782 Full text in English of Ben-Gurion's speech to the Knesset, including translation of the Alterman poem, 15.10.56, VR 1091/356.
23. 'Ben-Gurion's Diary', entry for 17.10.56, in Troën and Shemesh (eds), *The Suez–Sinai Crisis 1956*, pp. 302–3.
24. Mordechai Bar-On, 'David Ben-Gurion and the Sèvres Collusion' in Wm Roger Louis and Roger Owen (eds), *Suez 1956. The Crisis and Its Consequences* (Clarendon Press, 1989), p. 148. Shimon Peres, 'Mivtza Suffa' (unpublished, Hebrew), cited by Bar-On.
25. See footnote 23.
26. FO 371/121781 from Wikeley (Jerusalem), 16.10.56 and from Nicholls (Tel Aviv), 18.10.56, VR 1091/332 and /350. Before the era of *Private Eye*, 'tired and emotional' was not yet a term of art.
27. FO 371/121781 from Sir Charles Duke (Amman), 15.10.56, VR 1091/337.
28. FO 371/121781 from Wikeley (Jerusalem), 16.10.56, VR 1091/337.
29. *FRUS XVI*, Doc. 387 301st Meeting of the National Security Council, 26.10.56, p. 784.
30. Michael R. Beschloss, *Mayday. Eisenhower, Khrushchev and the U-2 Affair* (Faber and Faber, 1986), pp. 136–7. *FRUS XVI*, Doc. 345, Appendix, 15.10.56, p. 726.
31. Ferrell (ed.), *The Eisenhower Diaries*, pp. 330–2.
32. J.F. Dulles, Memconv. with the President, 'Israeli Reaction to Iraqi Troops in Jordan', 15.10.56, Eisenhower Library, Abilene.
33. FO 371/121781 Higgins, Incidents Report for w.e. 18.10.56. 'Mr Ben-Gurion is

personally fearless, but he does not underestimate his own value for Israel.'

34. Selwyn Lloyd, *Suez 1956*, pp. 164–5.
35. Sir Archibald Ross to author. No record was kept in the files. An informal record was kept for a while by Ross but now no longer exists. Also see Nutting, *No End of a Lesson*, pp. 96–7. No minute was kept of the subsequent ministerial meeting at which Ross was not present.
36. Lloyd, *Suez 1956*, p. 166.
37. PREM 11/1126 Gladwyn Jebb to Selwyn Lloyd, 17.10.56. Eden to Lloyd, PM's Personal Minute No. M 220/56, 19.10.56.
38. Sir Anthony Nutting to author, December 1987.
39. Nutting, *No End of a Lesson*, p. 99.
40. Memorandum by Lloyd, FO 800/725.
41. The Editor of *The Times* and the retiring Editor of *The Economist* (Geoffrey Crowther) had driven into Salt Lake City, Utah, in the air-conditioned Cadillac in which they were touring America when Haley was urgently summoned home on 21.10.56 following the briefing of McDonald. McDonald's handwritten note was never put in the paper's archives and Haley later told him that he had taken steps to ensure that it should never be seen. McDonald to author, May 1989. Iverach McDonald, *The History of The Times, Vol. V* (Times Books, 1984), pp. 268–9.
42. See footnote 40. The text of the British declarations is given by Bar-On in Louis and Owen, *Suez 1956. The Crisis and its Consequences*, p. 150. It derives from the Official Diaries of the Bureau of the Chief of Staff (Hebrew), IDF Archives.
43. 'Ben-Gurion's Suez Diary', entry for 18.10.56, Troën and Shemesh (eds), *The Suez–Sinai Crisis*, pp. 303–5.
44. Not Chancellor of the Duchy of Lancaster as in Roy Jenkins, *Baldwin* (Collins, 1987). The Chancellor of Oxford University stumbles over his sinecures.
45. Lord Monckton, 'Note on Suez', n.d., quoted by Birkenhead, *Monckton*, p. 307.
46. Nutting, *No End of A Lesson*, p. 107. William Clark, *From Three Worlds*, p. 203. The issues of conduct involved are discussed in Keith Kyle, 'Morality and Conscience in Politics', *The Listener*, 18.5.67. It is remarkable that no minuted session of the Egypt Committee took place between the 35th Meeting of 17 October and the 36th Meeting of 1 November.
47. PREM 11/1104 f 11 COS(56)380 'Operation *Musketeer* – Winter Plan'.
48. WO 32/16713, 'The Reservists', 19.10.56. There was a total call-up from civilian life of 1,000 officers and 26,000 other ranks, while 6,000 regulars were retained with the Colours after they became due for discharge. In mid-October 3,000 reservists were in Germany and 17,000 still in the UK. It took three to four weeks for families to get a National Assistance Grant and the forms were complicated.
49. Robin Esser, interviewed for BBC *Tonight* Programme, Suez series (prod. Peter Hill), November 1976.
50. Major Kenneth Macksey, *The Tanks: The History of the Royal Tank Regiment, 1945–1975* (Arms and Armour, 1979), p. 126.
51. *The Times*, 4.10.56 and 9.10.56.
52. PREM 11/1104 ff 13–24. 'Operation *Musketeer*. Appreciation by General Sir Charles Keightley', 12.10.56.
53. DEFE 6/37 JP(56)158 (Final), 5.10.56. 'Suggested Alternative to the Winter Plan for Operation *Musketeer*'. Marked 'WITHDRAWN'.
54. The Ministers present at the vital but thinly attended Cabinet of 18.10.56 were: Eden, Butler, Lloyd, Macmillan, Kilmuir, Home, Monckton, Sandys, Heathcoat Amory, Eccles, Buchan-Hepburn and Head, with Heath in attendance.
55. Lloyd, *Suez 1956*, p. 179.
56. FO 800/728 Cabinet Meeting, 18.10.56.
57. Butler, *The Art of the Possible*, p. 192.
58. ADM 205/137 Vice-Admiral Davis to Mountbatten. Mountbatten to Admiral Grantham (181514Z October), 18.10.56.

59. ADM 205/137 Mountbatten to Grantham ('by secure means'), 19.10.56.
60. ADM 205/137 Grantham to COS and Keightley (201814), 20.10.56.
61. AIR 20/9965 Air Vice-Marshal R. B. Lees, Assistant Chief of the Air Staff (Operations) to Air Marshal H. C. Patch, Commander-in-Chief, Middle East Air Forces.
62. AIR 20/9965 Patch to Air Chief Marshal Boyle, CINC 190, 25.10.56.
63. WO 106/5986 '*Musketeer*'. Report prepared for CIGS, 19.11.56.
64. Beaufre, *The Suez Expedition 1956*, pp. 79–81.
65. Douglas Dillon, J. F. Dulles Oral History Project, Princeton.
66. Townsend Hoopes, *The Devil and John Foster Dulles* (André Deutsch, 1974), pp. 131–2.
67. Dag Hammarskjöld to Mahmoud Fawzi, 24.10.56. Dag Hammarskjöld Archive. Royal Library, Stockholm. Hugh Thomas, *The Suez Affair* (Weidenfeld and Nicolson, 1986 edition), Appdx 5, pp. 211–15.

Chapter Seventeen
Sèvres, Conference of Collusion

1. Shimon Peres, diary for 16.10.56. Yosef Evron, *B'Yom Saqrir: Su'ets Me'ahorei Haklayim* (Tel Aviv, 1968).
2. Dayan, *The Story of My Life*, p. 175.
3. Troën (ed.), 'Ben-Gurion's Diary: The Suez–Sinai Campaign' in Troën and Shemesh, *The Suez–Sinai Crisis: 1956*, entry for 18.10.56, pp. 303–5.
4. Ben-Gurion, ibid., 19.10.56, p. 305.
5. Ben-Gurion, ibid., 19.10.56, also see 22.10.56 ('on the plane'), pp. 305–6.
6. Dayan, op. cit., p. 176.
7. Dayan, ibid., pp. 176–7. As Dayan tells the anecdote, Ben-Gurion would seem to have made the discovery about the Kingdom of Yotwat afresh during the flight. But Ben-Gurion's *My Talks with Arab Leaders* (Keter Books, Jerusalem, 1972), contains the transcript of his talks with Eisenhower's emissary, Robert Anderson, during the second of which (23.1.56) Ben-Gurion tells the identical story about Procopius and Yotwat (p. 284).
8. The clearest reference is in one version of the British Cabinet Minutes for 23 Oct. (CAB 128/30 ff 610–11. CM (56) 72 Confidential, Annex). A reference by Donald Logan to his and Lloyd's narrow escape from a bad driving accident on 22 Oct. (which in fact occurred in France) is to be found in Lloyd's Personal Papers (FO 800/716).
9. This account is based on: Ilan Troën (ed.), 'Ben-Gurion's Diary' in Troën and Shemesh, *The Suez–Sinai Crisis*, op. cit; Selwyn Lloyd, *Suez 1956*, pp. 180–90; Christian Pineau, *1956 Suez*, pp. 149–55; Moshe Dayan, *Story of My Life*, pp. 176–94; Abel Thomas, *Comment Israel fut Sauvé*, pp. 166–99; and Mordechai Bar-On, *Etqar va Tiqra* (written 1958, to be published shortly) and 'David Ben-Gurion and the Sèvres Collusion', op. cit. I am especially indebted to the scholarly generosity and personal kindness of Mordechai Bar-On in connection with these as well as several other passages of this book.
10. Lloyd, *Suez 1956*, pp. 181–3.
11. Bar-On, 'David Ben-Gurion and the Sèvres Collusion', op. cit. Bar-On formed a much more favourable impression of Lloyd's personality after reading his 'most honest, humble and humane memoirs'. Interview with Moshe Dayan, BBC-TV, a *Tonight* programme – Suez series, November 1976.
12. Bar-On, BBC 2 interview, *Secrets of Suez* programme, November 1986.
13. In his diary entries both for the 22nd and for the 24th Ben-Gurion refers to the operation beginning at 7 p.m., whereas Dayan's plan called for a 5 p.m. attack, which was approximately when it took place. Bar-On says that Ben-Gurion often

made mistakes on military detail and was probably thinking of 1700 hours when he wrote it down.

14. Lloyd, *Suez 1956*, pp. 260–1.
15. CAB 128/30 ff 610–11. CM (56)72 Confidential Annex. There are two versions of this Confidential Annex in this bound volume: one, reinserted in the body of the minute, does not contain the reference to the secret conference with the Israelis; the other, reproduced as an appendix does. Versions in the PREM files and in Selwyn Lloyd's Papers also omit the reference.
16. Mountbatten to Sir Guy Grantham, 23.10.56, Broadlands Archives (N.106).
17. WO 288/77 General Sir Hugh Stockwell, 'Reports on Operation *Musketeer*', p. 38.
18. *Parliamentary Debates (Hansard). House of Commons, Vol. 558*, 23.10.56, cols 491–6.
19. FO 371/121470 Sir Charles Duke (Amman), 26.10.56, VJ 1015/292.
20. Christian Pineau, *1956 Suez*, pp. 139–46.
21. Pineau, ibid., p. 137. See also Lloyd, *Suez 1956*, pp. 186–7. When using Pineau it should be borne in mind that he has got the time sequence wrong in this phase (as is explained in Lloyd).
22. CAB 128/30 CM (56) 73.
23. The most recent assertion of Patrick Dean's presence at Sèvres on 22 October is contained in the 1986 edition of Hugh Thomas, *The Suez Affair*, p. 122.
24. See Appendix 'A', p. 565 for an English text of the Protocol (which was drafted in French only).
25. Mordechai Bar-On, 'David Ben-Gurion and the Sèvres Collusion', in Louis and Owen, *Suez 1956. The Crisis and its Consequences*, pp. 154–8.
26. Dayan, *Story of My Life*, p. 193.
27. Rhodes James (*Anthony Eden*, p. 532) says that, besides Eden, Butler, Macmillan, Lloyd, Head and Mountbatten were present. He adds that on that occasion, 'Mountbatten willingly assented' to what was agreed at Sèvres.
28. Sir Donald Logan, interviewed by Keith Kyle for BBC 2's *Secrets of Suez* (prod. Peter Hill), 14.11.86. Also Logan, 'Collusion at Suez', *Financial Times*, 8.1.86.

Chapter Eighteen
A Parachute Drop at the Mitla

1. Mohamed Heikal, *Cutting the Lion's Tail*, p. 176.
2. Heikal, op. cit., pp. 157–9. Crown Prince Faisal told Nasser: 'Brother Gamal, the mob is a fickle and unprincipled force ... If you let them out of their cage, you will never be able to get them back again.'
3. FO 800/741 from Sir Charles Duke (Amman), 27.10.56.
4. Cardinal John Morton, Henry VII's Chancellor, used the notorious argument when assessing for benevolences (forced loans) that he who spent ostentatiously could obviously afford to pay and he who lived modestly clearly had enough savings.
5. PREM 11/1103 ff 31–2 CM 74(56) of 25.10.56.
6. PREM 11/1100 ff 21–7 Egypt Committee. 'Military Implications of Mounting Operation *Musketeer*.' Memorandum by Chiefs of Staff. EC(56)63, 25.10.56.
7. Keightley to Mountbatten, 26.5.58. Broadlands Archives, N.106.
8. Nutting, *No End of a Lesson*, pp. 107–8.
9. FO 953/1645 Lord Privy Seal's Committee on Overseas Broadcasting. Peter Partner, *Arab Voices. The BBC Arabic Service, 1938–1988*, pp. 104–5.
10. Harman Grisewood, *One Thing at a Time. An Autobiography* (Hutchinson, 1968), p. 200.
11. Grisewood, ibid., p. 199. F.R. MacKenzie, 'Eden, Suez and the BBC – a Reassessment' in *The Listener*, 18.12.69. Leonard Miall (BBC History of Broadcasting Unit), Record of Conversation with William Clark, 10.4.76. 'Clark admitted that

he might have exaggerated in talking to Grisewood about the specific plans afoot.' To Robert Allan (Eden's PPS) Clark denied in 1969 that he had ever known of or mentioned any documents prepared by Kilmuir (Allan to Avon, 16.9.69. Avon Papers, AP 20/51/1).

12. FO 953/1643 Minute by Kirkpatrick, 28.8.56, PB 1011/43. For some leading Conservatives the problem went beyond false notions of impartiality. According to the Foreign Under-Secretary, Douglas Dodds-Parker, 'Many people far beyond the confines of the Tory Party believe that there are sinister extreme left-wing influences in the BBC who since the war have slanted news against HMG's long-term interests' (Quoted by Partner, op. cit., p. 97.)
13. Partner, op. cit., p. 109.
14. *FRUS XVI*, Doc. 383, 26.10.56, pp. 789–90.
15. The French also helped, the Quai d'Orsay confirming reports of the King's death. The King promptly appeared on the *Voice of the Arabs* (26.10.56), 'his voice full of vitality, Arabism and sincerity', to refute the report and to say that he had been working all day 'to implement our agreement with Egypt and Syria for the notification of our three fronts'. (*BBC Summary of World Broadcasts, Pt IV*, No. 83, 29.10.56.)
16. Chester L. Cooper, *The Lion's Last Roar* (New York, 1978). On 26 October a meeting of the CIA's Watch Committee saw pictures of French arms being loaded at Toulon and Marseilles and of a British convoy gathering at Malta and Cyprus. (Michael R. Beschloss, *Mayday*, p. 137.)
17. *FRUS XVI*, Doc. 382, Editorial Note, p. 788.
18. *FRUS XVI*, Doc. 387, 27.10.56, pp. 793–4. Doc. 378, 301st Meeting of the National Security Council, 26.10.56, p. 784. Wilbur C. Eveland, *Ropes of Sand*, pp. 217–23, 225.
19. *FRUS XVII*, Doc. 314, 3.5.57, p. 593.
20. *FRUS XVI*, Doc. 371, 24.10.56, p. 775 and Doc. 376, 25.10.56, pp. 781–2.
21. James Jesus Angleton (CIA) to author, Washington, 1976.
22. Admiral Sir William Davis, 'My Life. Vol. VI. Feb. 1954–July 1960', unpublished. Churchill College Archive, Cambridge. The two shipowners were Sir William Currie (Chairman and Managing Director, P&O) and Kenneth Pelly (Chairman and Managing Director, Wm France Fenwick).
23. WO 288/77 Sir Hugh Stockwell, 'Report of Allied Land Task Force Commander on Operation *Musketeer*'.
24. André Beaufre, *The Suez Expedition, 1956*, pp. 57, 79.
25. AIR 8/2081 'Suez Canal Crisis: Planning for Military Operations'. 'Points for PM', 26.10.56.
26. General Sir John Cowley, unpublished memoir, Churchill College Archive, Cambridge.
27. General Stockwell gave more than one version of the exchange with Beaufre. In the *Sunday Telegraph* of 30.10.66 he said, 'Although I didn't discover all that was afoot, it became clear to me as the result of our talks that the Israelis were about to launch an attack on Egypt. General Beaufre never in fact said as much.' Ten years later, in a television interview for BBC 2, he said bluntly that Beaufre 'told me that the Israelis were going to launch an attack against Egypt on 29 October'. According to his Operational Report (WO 288/77, p. 38) Stockwell had been given by French staff officers at his corps headquarters some information 'concerning a probable D-Day and L-Day in the near future'.
28. Admiral Sir Manley Power, unpublished autobiography, p. 100, Churchill College Archives, Cambridge.
29. AIR 20/9965 Boyle to Patch, 270930z, 27.10.56.
30. Paul Gaujac, *Suez 1956*, p. 140.
31. Douglas Clark, *Suez Touchdown. A Soldier's Tale*.
32. Sir Denis Barnett to author, 1986.

33. Mordechai Bar-On, 'The Influence of Political Considerations on Operative Planning in the Sinai Campaign' in Troën and Shemesh, *The Suez–Sinai Crisis, 1956*, pp. 204–7.
34. (Sir) Denis Smallwood (then Group Captain (Plans), Air Task Force) in *RAF Historical Society, Proceedings 3*, p. 26. General Lucien Robineau in 'Les Porte-à-Faux de l'Affaire de Suez', in *Revue Historique des Armées*, December 1986, pp. 44–5.
35. Moshe Dayan, *Diary of the Sinai Campaign*, pp. 68–70.
36. *FRUS XVI*, Doc. 388, 27.10.56 (transmitted 12.25 p.m. Washington time, 7.25 p.m. Middle East time) and Doc. 393, Editorial Note, pp. 800–1.
37. *FRUS XVI*, Doc. 401, 28/29.10.56, pp. 811–13. Dayan, op. cit., pp. 71–4.
38. *FRUS XVI*, Docs. 391 and 392, 28.10.56, pp. 798–800.
39. *FRUS XVI*, Doc. 384, 26.10.56, p. 790. Doc. 395 Statement by the President, 28.10.56, p. 802. Docs. 396, 397 and 398, 28.10.56, pp. 803–7. Allen Dulles to Herman Phleger, 11.5.64 ('We predicted the attack ... by matter of hours rather than days'), Allen Dulles Papers, Eisenhower Library, Abilene. FO 800/741 from Coulson (Washington), 28.10.56.
40. Sir Harold Beeley and Nigel Bruce to author, 1987.
41. Sir Frank Cooper in *RAF Historical Society, Proceedings 3*, p. 21. William Clark, *From Three Worlds*, p. 197.
42. Winthrop Aldrich in J. F. Dulles Oral History Project, Princeton. Sir Harold Beeley to author, 1987. *FRUS XVI*, Doc. 405, 29.10.56, pp. 817–20.
43. FO 800/741 from Sir John Nicholls (Tel Aviv), 29.10.56. No. 568. Despatched *en clair* at 8.16 a.m. (local time).
44. FO 800/741 from Nicholls, 29.10.56. No. 569. Despatched *en clair* at 8.53 a.m. (local time).
45. *FRUS XVI*, Doc. 441, Editorial Note, pp. 883–4.
46. FO 371/121782 from Nicholls, 29.10.56. No. 567. Despatched 9.23 a.m. (local time), VR 1091/378.
47. FO 371/121782 from Nicholls, 29.10.56. No. 580. Despatched 7.40 p.m. (local time), VR 1091/378.
48. FO 371/121782 from Nicholls, 29.10.56. No. 572. Despatched *en clair* 12 noon (local time), VR 1091/375. The author is indebted for information on the put-up nature of the incident to Colonel (Res) Bar-On, then Chief of Bureau to General Dayan.
49. See footnote 46.
50. FO 371/121782 from Nicholls, 29.10.56. No. 583. Despatched *en clair* 10.22 p.m. (local time), VR 1091/380.
51. FO 371/171283 from Nicholls, 30.10.56. No. 584. Despatched *en clair* 12.54 a.m., VR 1091/397.
52. Akiva Orr, 'The '56 War – Another Sordid Chapter', in *Middle East International*, 27.6.87.
53. Dayan, *Diary*, op. cit., p. 83. Ariel Sharon, *Warrior*, gives a vivid account of the operation from his point of view, pp. 142–5.
54. R. J. Penney in *RAF Historical Society, Proceedings 3*, pp. 32–3.
55. Lloyd, *Suez 1956*, p. 195.
56. Amin Hewedy, 'Nasser and the Crisis of 1956' in Louis and Owen (eds), *Suez 1956: The Crisis and its Consequences*, pp. 168–9. Hewedy to author, Cairo, October 1986.
57. Yonah Bandman, 'The Egyptian Armed Forces during Operation *Kadesh*' in Troën and Shemesh, *The Suez–Sinai Crisis 1956*. pp. 337–8.
58. General S. L. A. Marshall, *Sinai Victory* (William Murrow, New York, 1968), pp. 94–7, 141–6.
59. Ian Black and Benny Morris, *Israel's Secret Wars* (Hamish Hamilton, 1991), pp. 132–3, citing *Ma'ariv*, 20.1.89. Maj-Gen Ali Abu Nuwar to author, Amman, December 1987.

60. Heikal, *Cutting the Lion's Tail*, p. 177.
61. 'Abd al-Latif al-Bughdadi, *Muddakarat II* (Cairo, 1977), 'From the Memoirs of Abd al-Latif Bughdadi', in Troën and Shemesh, op. cit., pp. 337–8.
62. Amin Hewedy, 'The Suez Crisis and the Use of Force'. Paper delivered at the seminar of the Egyptian Committee for Afro-Asian People's Solidarity, 'Thirty Years After the Suez Canal Nationalisation', held in Cairo, 30.10–3.11.86.
63. Kennett Love, *Suez, The Twice-Fought War*, pp. 501–2, 515–16. Raphael Ryan, 'Sinai Campaign 1956' in *War Monthly*, July 1982.

Chapter Nineteen
Ultimatum

1. *FRUS XVI*, Doc. 409, 29.10.56, pp. 829–31.
2. *FRUS XVI*, Doc. 413, Editorial Note, pp. 840–1.
3. *FRUS XVI*, Doc. 411, 29.10.56, pp. 833–9.
4. *FRUS XVI*, Doc. 412, 29.10.56, pp. 839–40.
5. Dulles Papers, General Telconvs., 10 p.m., 29.10.56. President's tel. calls, 8.40 a.m., 30.10.56. Eisenhower Library, Abilene. *FRUS XVI*, Doc. 413, Editorial Note, pp. 841–2.
6. Winthrop W. Aldrich, JFD Oral History Project, Princeton. Aldrich, 'The Suez Crisis: A Footnote to History', *Foreign Affairs*, April 1967, pp. 541–52. *FRUS XVI*, Doc. 416, 30.10.56, pp. 846–7.
7. PREM 11/1105 ff 530–2. Eisenhower to Eden, 30.10.56. *FRUS XVI*, Doc. 418, 30.10.56, pp. 848–50.
8. Lord Hankey, 'Catastrophic Disaster' (unpublished, Churchill College Archive, Cambridge).
9. CAB 128/30 ff 632–3 C(56)75th Conclusions, Min. 1, 30.10.56.
10. Earl of Selkirk to author, 1990.
11. Eden, *Full Circle*, p. 525. *FRUS XVI*, Doc. 421, pp. 856–7.
12. Whitman File, Staff Memos, DDE Diaries, Abilene. *FRUS XVI*, Doc. 419, n.5, 30.10.56, p. 853.
13. PREM 11/1105 ff 501–3 to Tel Aviv and Cairo, 30.10.56. The cruiser *Jamaica* was ordered to take up station 3 miles off Port Said at 4 a.m. (local time) on the 31st in case the ultimatum should be accepted. Eden's message to Menzies is in DO 35/6336.
14. PREM 11/1105 ff 576–7 Eden to Eisenhower, PM's Personal Tel. T 485/6, 30.10.56. *FRUS XVI*, Doc. 434, 30.10.56, pp. 871–2.
15. *Parliamentary Debates (Hansard), House of Commons, Vol. 558*, 30.10.56, cols 1274–98.
16. *UN Security Council. Proceedings, 748th Session*, 30.10.56.
17. Aldrich, JFD Oral History, op. cit. President's Tel. calls with Dulles, 2.17 p.m., 30.10.56. *FRUS XVI*, Doc. 420, Editorial Note, pp. 855–6 and Doc. 430, 30.10.56, p. 866.
18. George Ivan Smith to author, 1987.
19. *Parliamentary Debates (Hansard), House of Commons, Vol. 558*, 30.10.56, cols 1341–82.
20. Clark, *From Three Worlds*, p. 200.
21. *UN Security Council. Proceedings, 749th Session and 750th Session*, passim. Sydney Bailey, *Four Arab-Israeli Wars and the Peace Process* (Macmillan, 1990), pp. 144–5.
22. Winston Churchill, *The Second World War. Triumph and Tragedy*, pp. 310–11.
23. Bernard Cornut-Gentille went on to become a Cabinet Minister, and was for 18 years the Mayor of Cannes. *DDF 1956 III*, Doc. 65, 30.10.56, p. 105. Doc. 68, 31.10.56, pp. 109–13. Bailey, *Four Arab-Israeli Wars*, op. cit., pp. 145–6.
24. PREM 11/1105 ff 509–11 from Dixon (New York), 30.10.56.

25. PREM 11/1105 f 476 from Coulson (Washington), 30.10.56. *FRUS XVI*, Doc. 437, 30.10.56, pp. 875–6. *DDF. 1956 III*, Doc. 51, 29.10.56, pp. 72–4. Doc. 68, 31.10.56, p. 111.
26. PREM 11/1105 f 327 from Coulson, 31.10.56.
27. *FRUS XVI*, Doc. 455, 1.11.56, pp. 902–16.
28. Telcom. John Foster and Allen Dulles, 5.31 p.m., 30.10.56. Dulles Papers, Abilene.
29. FO371/121783 from Nicholls (Tel Aviv), 31.10.56, VR 1091/403. PREM 11/1105 ff 483–4. Ronald Higgins, *The Seventh Enemy* (Hodder and Stoughton, 1978), pp. 36–9. Higgins to author, 1986.
30. PREM 11/1105 from Trevelyan (Cairo), 30.10.56.
31. PREM 11/1105 from Trevelyan. Sent 11 p.m. (local time), 30.10.56.
32. BBC-TV, *Suez, the Nine-Day War* (producer: David Wheeler), 20.9.66.
33. 'Abd al-Latif al-Bughdadi's Memoirs' in Troën and Shemesh, *The Suez–Sinai Crisis 1956*, p. 338. Abdel Majid Farid to author, London, April 1988.
34. Dayan, *Diary of the Sinai Campaign*, pp. 91–3. Bar-On, 'The Influence of Political Considerations on Operational Planning in the Sinai Campaign' in Troën and Shemesh, op. cit., pp. 196–217.
35. Dayan, *Diary*, p. 96.
36. Gamal Abdul Nasser in BBC-TV interview for *Suez, The Nine-Day War*, repeated in *Secrets of Suez*, BBC 2, 14.11.86. The Israelis also had problems of absorption. Of their Mystères only 14 were serviceable in time for this campaign (Fullick and Powell, *Suez, The Double War*, p. 88).
37. Sir William Dickson to author, 1986.
38. Shimon Peres to author, Sde Boqer, 26.10.86, in BBC 2 interview for *Secrets of Suez* (producer: Peter Hill), 14.11.86.
39. General Paul Ely, *Mémoires. Suez . . . Le 13 Mai*, p. 158.
40. Mordechai Bar-On in BBC 2, *Secrets of Suez*.

Chapter Twenty
The Die is Cast

1. ADM 205/161 Vice-Admiral L. F. (Robin) Dunford-Slater, 'Report of the Allied Naval Task Force Commander on Operation *Musketeer*' (draft). The naval report was finally written by Vice-Admiral Richmond.
2. Air Chief Marshal Sir Thomas Prickett (in 1956, Chief of Staff, Air Task Force) in *RAF Historical Society Proceedings* 3, p. 45.
3. AIR 20/9967 Group Captain G. C. O. Key, 'Report of Bomber Wing, Cyprus, on Operation *Musketeer*'. AIR 20/9557 Air Task Force Reports. The author would like to thank Group Captain Gordon Key for his assistance. The 31 Valiants taking part in the operation were all based on Malta. Of the 81 Canberras, 22 flew from Malta and 59 from Nicosia (Cyprus) (AIR 20/9557 Bomber Participation Annex 'A').
4. AIR 8/1490 COSKEY 2 Chiefs of Staff to Keightley, 301440z, 30.10.56. COSKEY 4, 301700z, 30.10.56. AIR 8/2111 Keightley to Chiefs, 301735z, 30.10.56. COSKEY 5, 310145z, 31.10.56. *FLASH* signals were supposed to have absolute priority, but still at times took longer than would have seemed possible. It is important to bear in mind that the Services were on GMT (Z = Zulu) throughout the operation. Except where indicated, however, this book uses local time, known to the Services as B = Bravo, which in the case of the Middle East was two hours ahead of Zulu.
5. AIR 20/9557 'Bomber Participation Report'. The Air Task Force had decided to stick to its attack sequence commencing at dusk, 'even if clearance was given for attacks to start earlier'.
6. AIR 20/9964 A.V.-M. Crisham, 'Report on Air Aspects of Operation *Musketeer*', 14.3.57. AIR 20/9967 'Report of Bomber Wing, Cyprus', op. cit.

7. ADM 116/1104 Amplified Report of Flag Officer, Aircraft Carriers. At 1.30p.m. (local time) on 30.10.56 Vice-Admiral Power received the order from Admiral Grantham, 'Do NOT start briefing yet'. With some satisfaction Power replied, 'This was received too late ...'
8. Eric Grove, *Vanguard to Trident*, pp. 189–92. In addition the British and French contingents each carried four rescue helicopters. Power's flagship was *Eagle*, which carried fifty planes but was operationally somewhat handicapped because its starboard catapult had broken. Before the end of the battle on 6.1.56 the port catapult also gave out, making the carrier unserviceable for eight to ten days (ADM 116/6104 Power, 'Report', f 29 103).
9. The sceptics, included most notably Admiral Sir William Davis, the Vice-Chief of the Naval Staff. After this British 'first', the use of helicopters on the battlefield became a feature of American operations, e.g. in Vietnam.
10. Admiral Sir Guy Grantham to Anthony Seldon, 11.6.81, Seldon Oral History Archive.
11. William Rees-Mogg, 'The day that Anthony Decided to Invade Egypt', in *The Independent*, 4.11.86.
12. See e.g. Brian McCauley, 'Hungary and Suez, 1956: The Limits of Soviet and American Power' in Bela K. Kiraly *et al., The First War Between Socialist States: The Hungarian Revolution of 1956 and its Impact* (Brooklyn College Press, 1984), pp. 291–315.
13. Keith Kyle, 'Background to the Eisenhower Doctrine', in *National and English Review*, February 1957. Access to shorthand notes of the dinner discussion.
14. *Parliamentary Debates (Hansard), House of Commons, Vol. 558*, 31.10.56, cols 1441–572.
15. Sir Brian Urquhart, *Hammarskjöld*, pp. 174–5.
16. *UN Security Council. Proceedings. 751st Session.* Bailey, *Four Arab-Israeli Wars and the Peace Process*, pp. 147–8. Dixon challenged the legality of this proceeding, but failed by 6 votes to 4 (Piers Dixon, *Double Diploma*, p. 267).
17. Lord Trevelyan, *The Middle East in Revolution*, p. 115.
18. *The Egyptian Gazette*, 1.11.56. Anwar Sadat is quoted in that day's Arabic Press Review as writing that Eden had 'not bothered to make a declaration of war, thus ignoring a formality which even the nineteenth-century gunboat diplomatists generally observed'.
19. Sir Norman Kipping, *The Suez Contractors* (Kenneth Mason, 1969).
20. Trevelyan, op. cit., p. 122.
21. Dayan, *Story of My Life*, pp. 204–5.
22. Abel Thomas, *Comment Israel Fut Sauvé*, pp. 207, 284.
23. Air Chief Marshal Sir Lewis Hodges and Air Chief Marshal Sir Kenneth Cross in *RAF Historical Society, Proceedings 3*, pp. 35–6. AIR 8/21111 *FLASH*, Air Marshal Patch to Chiefs of Staff, 310006z. 'Have taken all possible steps to turn aircraft around ... You will appreciate the implications of cutting out the most vital of all their airfields ...'
24. AIR 20/10746 Air Marshal Barnett, 'Summary of Operations During Operation *Musketeer*. Appdx D. Bomber Participation'. Air Force Staff College, 'Operation *Musketeer*' (unpublished). 'It was unfortunate that the RAF's first raid was to be on the wrong target but the last minute change of plan ... made an error highly probable.' MoD Air Historical Branch, Lacon House.
25. AIR 20/9967 Group Captain G. G. O. Key, 'Report of Bomber Wing, Cyprus'.
26. Air Force Staff College, 'Operation *Musketeer*', op. cit.
27. AIR 20/10746 Barnett, 'Summary of Operations', op. cit.
28. PREM 11/1169. Nigel Birch to Eden, 14.12.56. Minute by Eden. *The Times*, 18, 29, 30.1.57.
29. Heikel, *Cutting the Lion's Tail*, pp. 177–81.
30. 'Abd al-Latif al-Bughdadi, *Mudhakkirat* II (Cairo, 1977). Extracts printed in trans-

lation in Troën and Shemesh (eds), *Suez-Sinai Crisis 1956*, pp. 333–4.

31. Frankland (ed.), *Documents on International Affairs, 1956* (RIIA), pp. 265–9.
32. *FRUS XVI*, Doc. 435, 30.10.56, pp. 873–4.
33. Telcons. Dulles/Humphrey, 9.15 and 9.46 am, 30.10.56, General Telephone Conversations, Dulles Papers, Abilene. *FRUS XVI*, Doc. 419, 30.10.56, p. 852 and Doc. 446, 31.10.56, pp. 890–1 and n.1.
34. *FRUS XVI*, Doc. 447, 31.10.56, pp. 891–3 and Doc. 455, 1.11.56, pp. 905–6.
35. *FRUS XVI*, Doc. 451, 31.10.56, pp. 898–900.
36. Clark, *From Three Worlds*, p. 202.
37. Aldrich to Dulles, 1.11.56. Eisenhower Library, Abilene.
38. *Parliamentary Debates (Hansard), House of Commons, Vol. 558*, 1.11.56, cols 1619–25.
39. Interview with Iverach McDonald for BBC *Tonight* programme, Suez series, November 1976.
40. *Parliamentary Debates*, op. cit., cols 1625–1744 (Yates, 1716–17).
41. *Parliamentary Debates (Hansard), House of Lords, Vol. 199*, 1.11.56, cols 1243–1316. Following this debate Archbishop Fisher wrote to the Prime Minister, 'I am sure that Christians in general and a vast number of citizens would say not only that we were on slippery ground, but that we have slipt' (*sic*). LCO 2/5760.
42. FO 800/747 Fitzmaurice to Kirkpatrick, 31.10.56. Manningham-Buller to Kirkpatrick, minuted by Fitzmaurice, 5.11.56. Fitzmaurice to Legal Staff, FO, 1.11.56. 'I should like all my colleagues to know that, throughout the Suez affair ... we have from the beginning and at all times strongly opposed the use of force as having no legal justification in any of the circumstances that had or have arisen hitherto ... The Prime Minister has, however, taken his advice on the matter from the Lord Chancellor and virtually all the legal arguments which the Government have put forward on the question of the use of force and which I have constantly queried have emanated from that quarter.'

Chapter Twenty-One
World Opinion Speaks

1. Lord Casey, *Australian Foreign Minister. The Diaries of R. G. Casey, 1951–60*, p. 251. For the wide differences between Menzies and Casey about Suez see Lord Carrington, who had just gone to Canberra as High Commissioner, in *Reflect on Things Past* (Collins, 1988), pp. 127–31.
2. FO 371/121788 Pearson to Robertson, 1.11.56.
3. Robert Belgrave to author, Chatham House, 1986.
4. FO 371/121791 St Laurent to Eden. PM's Personal Tel. T 505/56, 1.11.56.
5. James Eayrs (ed.), *The Commonwealth and Suez. A Documentary Survey*. Extract from St Laurent's speech, 26.11.56, p. 417.
6. FO 371/121790 Press interview by Eric Louw, Capetown, VR 1091/643E.
7. ADM 116/6097 *Royalist* to NZ Navy Board, 15.9.56. Holland to Eden, 21.9.56.
8. ADM 205/139 Speaking note for Mountbatten's discussions with Chiefs of Staff and Prime Minister, n.d.
9. FO 371/121790 f 61 General Sir Geoffrey Scoones (Wellington) to Home, 1.11.56, VR 1091/643Y. ADM 116/6118 Chief, Naval Staff, RNZN to Vice-Chief, Naval Staff. ADM 116/6097 Holland to Eden, 1.11.56.
10. ADM 116/6097 Scoones (Wellington) to Sir Gilbert Laithwaite (CRO), 4.11.56.
11. FO 371/121783 from Malcolm MacDonald (New Delhi), 31.10.56, VR 1041/573g.
12. FO 371/121788 from Morrice James (Karachi), 31.10.56, VR 1091/573E.
13. FO 371/121789 from James (Karachi), 1.1.56, VR 1091/642A.
14. Eayrs, *Commonwealth and Suez*, op. cit., pp. 197–8.
15. ADM 116/6119 from James (Karachi), 3.11.56. It was characteristic of Mount-

batten's outlook that Commonwealth telegrams are to be found bound in with operational signals in the Naval Records of Suez.

16. Sir William Hayter, *A Double Life* (Hamish Hamilton, 1974), pp. 1412–13. FO 371/121291 from Con O'Neill (Peking), 2.11.56. Malcolm MacDonald, *Titans and Others* (Collins, 1972), pp. 225–6.
17. Lord Gore-Booth, *With Great Truth and Respect* (Constable, 1974), pp. 229–30. For Evan Luard's letter of resignation see below, Appendix 'B', p.568–9. Luard was Foreign Under-Secretary from 1969–70 and from 1976–9. John Wilson was another junior Foreign Office official who resigned, (Anthony Adamthwaite, 'Suez Revisited' in *International Affairs*, Summer 1988, p. 458).
18. FO 371/121783 from Wright (Baghdad), 31.10.56, VR 1091/407. Also VR 1091/416.
19. FO 371/121783 Selwyn Lloyd to Wright (Baghdad), 31.10.56, No. 2343.
20. FO 371/121783 from Wright, 1.11.56. VR 1091/432 Lloyd to Wright, 1.11.56.
21. FO 371/121785 Crown Prince to Eden, 1.11.56. VR 1091/423.
22. FO 371/121785 Eden to Crown Prince, 2.11.56. No. 2400.
23. FO 371/121786 from Wright, 3.11.56. VR 1091/515.
24. FO 371/121786 from Wright, 3.11.56. VR 1091/511.
25. FO 371/121785 from Stevens (Teheran), 1.11.56. VR 1091/465.
26. FO 371/121785 to Stevens, 1.11.56. No. 1062.
27. FO 371/121785 from Stevens, 2.11.56. VR 1091/488.
28. Kennett Love, *Suez, The Twice-Fought War*, pp. 514–15. Ali Abu Nuwar and Suleiman Musa to author, Amman, Nov.–Dec. 1987.
29. Ali Abu Nuwar to author.
30. Love, op. cit., pp. 532–3 prints a signal from the Supreme Command in Cairo addressed to the commanders of the Syrian and Jordanian armies, despatched at 6 a.m., 1.11.56. It read in part, 'Halt all offensive preparations. Postpone *Beisan* until further orders. Secure borders and prepare defences ...'.
31. Information from Suleiman Musa.
32. FO 371/121783 from Sir Charles Duke (Amman), 30.12.56, VR 1091/396.
33. Heikal, *Cutting the Lion's Tail*, pp. 189–91.
34. Heikal, op. cit., pp. 192–3.
35. FO 371/121784 from Walter Graham (Tripoli), 31.10.56, VR 1090/422.
36. ADM 116/6118 from Graham, 1.11.56. No. 396.
37. FO 371/121783 from Sir Christopher Steel (NATO), 31.10.56, VR 1091/425.
38. FO 371/131684 Sir Frederick Hoyer Millar (Bonn), 'Annual Report on the FRG for 1956', 19.1.57. WG 1011/1. *DDF 1956.III*, Doc. 102, 3.11.56, pp. 162–3.
39. Frankland (ed), *Documents on International Affairs, 1956* (RIIA), pp. 269–70.
40. *UN General Assembly. Official Records, 1st and 2nd Emergency Special Sessions, 1956*, 561st and 562nd Plenary Meetings, 1–2.11.56. Resolution 997 (ES–1).
41. The full text of Pearson's speech is reproduced in Rosalyn Higgins, *UN Peace-keeping Vol I The Middle East* (RIIA/OUP), pp. 228–9. Pearson first put the idea forward when he saw Eden on 14.11.55.
42. *Parliamentary Debates (Hansard), House of Commons*, Vol. 558, 2.11.56, cols 1753–71.
43. Interview with David Astor, BBC *Tonight* programme, Suez series, Nov. 1976. The Trustees of the *Observer* who resigned were Marshal of the RAF Lord Portal of Hungerford, who had been the wartime Chief of the Air Staff, and Arthur Mann, former editor of the *Yorkshire Post*. After the 4 November leader, the *Observer* received during the first week 866 hostile readers' letters (474 of them announcing that the writers were giving up the paper) and 302 favourable ones. The week after, those who supported the paper were in a 3-to-1 majority. (Ralph Negrino, 'The Press and the Suez Crisis: A Myth Re-examined' in *The Historical Journal*, Vol. 25 No. 4, 1982.) There was no net loss of circulation because of compensating new readers, but the latter were not considered as being so interesting by advertisers as the readers who had been lost. The paper's upward surge had not been halted, but

it had been lamed. David Astor and Roy Harris at Institute of Contemporary British History summer school, London School of Economics, July 1989.

Chapter Twenty-Two
France's War

1. Jacques Baeyens, *Un Coup d'épée dans l'eau du canal. La seconde campagne d'Egypte* (Paris 1976), pp. 59–64. To Mangin's uncomplimentary language about the Quai d'Orsay, Baeyens says he replied, 'The Quai has not been informed nor enlisted nor called on to express any opinion whatsoever in this affair. Besides which, how can you ask the Ministry of Foreign Affairs to promote violence, aggression and adventure?'
2. Patrick Facon, 'L'Armée de l'Air et l'Affaire de Suez', and General Lucien Robineau, 'Les Porte-à-Faux de l'Affaire de Suez', in *Revue Historique des Armées*, 4–1986, pp. 36, 45–6. The single reference to this force in the French military archives is a note of 4.10.56, calling for the creation of two squadrons to furnish 'maximum aid to Israeli forces crossing their frontier to secure the east bank of the Suez Canal', *Service Historique de l'Armée de l'Air*, C-2218, Note du ler CATAC No. 317.
3. General Lucien Robineau in *RAF Historical Society, Proceedings* 3, p. 53. FO 371/141941, VG 1091/6.
4. Paul Gaujac, *Suez 1956*, op. cit., pp. 174–5.
5. AIR 8/1940 Keightley to Chiefs, KEYCOS 2, 31.10.56.
6. FO 800/727 Ralph Murray to Kirkpatrick, 1.11.56. ADM 116/6117 Marine Paris to Admiral Grantham 301932z, 31.10.56. Grantham to *Newfoundland* 310610z, 31.10.56. Admiralty to Grantham 3110905z, 31.10.56. The impression that the Israelis had taken the Ras Nasrani batteries and Sharm al-Sheikh at the beginning of the campaign must have arisen through some hangover from Dayan's pre-Sèvres planning.
7. FO 800/727 Eden to Mollet, 1.11.56.
8. AIR 8/1940 Keightley to Chiefs *FLASH* 021026z, 2.11.56. KEYCOS 16.
9. FO 800/727 Murray to Kirkpatrick, 3.11.56.
10. *FRUS XVI*, Doc. 459, 1.11.56, pp. 919; Doc. 579, 16.11.56, pp. 1135–7 and Doc. 637, 5.12.56, pp. 1263–71. Pineau's statement that the question of entry of Iraqi troops into Jordan was 'primarily a smokescreen' is belied by the entries in Ben-Gurion's diary except for the days after Sèvres.
11. ADM 116/6117 Admiralty Signals, *Musketeer*. Durnford-Slater to Admiralty 311705Z, 31.10.56. ADM 116/6118 Grantham to Power 021702Z, 2.11.56.
12. AIR 8/194 General Sir Charles Keightley, 'Lessons of Suez'.
13. AIR 20/10746 'The Suez Campaign (Air)'. Appdx A. 'Report of Flag Officer, Aircraft Carriers'.
14. Admiral Arleigh Burke, JFD Oral History Project, Princeton.
15. AIR 8/1940. Extracts from Minutes, COS(56) 11th Meeting, 5.11.56.
16. Love, *Suez – The Twice-Fought War*, pp. 549–50. Dayan, *Diary of the Sinai Campaign*, pp. 132–3. Chaim Herzog, *The Arab-Israeli Wars*, pp. 126–32.
17. Love, op. cit., p. 550.
18. Dayan, *Story of My Life*, p. 204. Yonah Bandman, 'The Egyptian Armed Forces during the Kadesh Campaign' in Troën and Shemesh, *The Suez-Sinai Crisis 1956*, p. 86.
19. See, for example, Erskine Childers, *The Road to Suez* (MacGibbon and Kee, 1962), pp. 281–304. Bernard Fall, 'The Two Sides of the Sinai Campaign' in *Military Review – USA*, July 1957, was an early effort by an experienced commentator to give a balanced view.
20. Mordechai Bar-On to author, Jerusalem, Oct. 1986.

21. AIR 8/1940 Chiefs to Keightley, COSKEY 20, Keightley to Chiefs, KEYCOS 15, *FLASH*, 22.11.56.
22. RAF Staff College, 'Operation *Musketeer*'. MoD Air Historical Branch, Lacon House.
23. AIR 20/10369 'This is the Voice of the Allied Command'.
24. Peter Partner, *Arab Voices*, pp. 108–9. AIR 20/10369 Keightley to Sir Reginald Powell (Perm. Sec., Ministry of Defence), 16.11.56.
25. AIR 20/10369.
26. AIR 20/10746 Air Marshal Barnett Report.
27. FO 371/125423 'Trial of Conspirators against Nasser', 25.8.57 JE 1019/1(E). *Mideast Mirror*, 18.8.57.
28. 'Abd al-Latif al-Bughdadi's Memoirs' in Troën and Shemesh, *The Suez–Sinai Crisis 1956*, pp. 338–68.
29. *Egyptian Gazette*, 3.11.56.
30. 'al-Bughdadi's Memoirs', op. cit.
31. *DDF 1956 III* No. 127, 6.11.56, pp. 213–14.
32. PREM 11/1090 ff 10–11 Mountbatten to Eden, 2.11.56. Eden spoke to Mountbatten by phone saying he fully understood his feelings but was not prepared to turn back the convoy; operations were directed only against military targets.
33. Philip Ziegler, *Mountbatten. The Official Biography* (Collins, 1985).
34. PREM 11/1090 Mountbatten to Priv. Sec. to the Prime Minister, 2.11.56.
35. General Ely, *Mémoires Suez ... le 13 Mai*, pp. 162–3.
36. Wright, *Spycatcher*, pp. 82–6.
37. AIR 8/1940 Confidential Annex to COS (56) 109th Meeting, 'Meeting with General Ely', 2.11.56.
38. Ely, op. cit., pp. 165–6.
39. Dickson to Keightley, *FLASH*, 022125z, 2.11.56, COSKEY 23. Keightley to Dickson, *FLASH*, 030455z, 3.11.56, KEYCOS 19.
40. Colonel de Fouquières, 'Guerre des Six Jours', in *Forces Aériennes Françaises*, 1957, p. 817.
41. WO 288/138.
42. AIR 8/1940, Keightley to Chiefs, 022135z, 2.11.56, KEYCOS 17.
43. Mountbatten, 'Naval Responsibility for Inflicting Civilian Casualties', Broadlands Archives (N.106). AIR 8/1940 'Operation *Musketeer*. Reconsideration of Phase III', 3.11.56.
44. PREM 11/1105 f 250 EC(56) 38th Meeting, 3.11.56.
45. PREM 11/1169 Sir John Nicholls, 'An Account of the Israeli Campaign in Sinai and Connected Events, 29 Oct.–7 Nov.', p. 3.

Chapter Twenty-Three
Slow March to Suez

1. Three decades later, Nixon revised his contemporary view of the Suez crisis ('My Debt to Macmillan', *The Times*, 28.1.87), describing the American handling of it as 'not admirable' and quoting Eisenhower as having said after he had left office that it was his 'major foreign policy mistake'.
2. Allen Dulles to author, November 1956.
3. Eisenhower to General Al Gruenther, 2.11.56. Eisenhower Library, Abilene.
4. *FRUS XVI*, Doc. 469, 2.11.56, p. 935 and Doc. 470, 2.11.56, pp. 936–7.
5. PREM 11/1105 ff 264–5 Frederick Bishop (PM's Private Secretary) to Eden.
6. PREM 11/1105 ff 311–14 CM (56) 78th Conclusions, 2.11.56.
7. *Parliamentary Debates (Hansard), House of Commons, Vol. 558*, 3.11.56, cols 1857–81. *Manchester Guardian*, 5.11.56.
8. Sir Robin Day, *Grand Inquisitor* (Weidenfeld and Nicolson, 1989), pp. 89–93. Sir

Geoffrey Cox, *See It Happen. The Making of ITN* (The Bodley Head, 1983), pp. 74–87.

9. PREM 11/1105 ff 214 and 212–13 from Dixon (New York), 3.11.56.
10. *FRUS XVI*, Doc. 477, 3.11.56, pp. 947–9.
11. Full text of Sir Anthony Eden's broadcast in *The Listener*, 8.11.56, pp. 735–6.
12. John Grigg, 'Sir Christopher Chancellor – obituary', *Independent*, 11.9.89. Papers of Lieutenant-General Sir John Cowley in Churchill College, Cambridge.
13. Harman Grisewood, *One Thing at a Time*, pp. 201–4.
14. Hugh Gaitskell's text in *The Listener*, 8.11.56, pp. 737–8.
15. Quoted in Philip Williams, *Hugh Gaitskell*, p. 437.
16. Interview with Anthony Howard for BBC-TV *Tonight* programme, Suez series, November 1976.
17. Admiral Pierre Barjot, 'Réflexions sur les Opérations de Suez 1956' in *Revue de Défense Nationale*. André Beaufre, *The Suez Expedition 1956*, p. 97.
18. AIR 8/1490 COSKEY 24 Chiefs of Staff to Keightley, 3.11.56.
19. AIR 8/1940 KEYCOS 20, 3.11.56.
20. Beaufre, *The Suez Expedition, 1956*, p. 91. Beaufre, who strongly disapproved of Barjot's attempt to go it alone, says that he subsequently discovered that the Admiral's supposed abandonment of *Telescope* was a ruse while he mobilised political support.
21. Jacques Baeyens, *Un Coup d'Epée dans l'Eau du Canal*, pp. 82–7.
22. Lester Pearson, *Memoirs. Vol. II. 1948–1957. The International Years*, pp. 247–51. Michael Fry, 'Canada, the North Atlantic Triangle and the UN', in Louis and Owen (eds), *Suez 1956: the Crisis and Its Consequences*, pp. 306–16. *FRUS XVI*, Doc. 481, 3.11.56 and Doc. 485, Editorial Note, p. 964 for text of Resolution 998 (ES-1).
23. UN General Assembly, *First Emergency Session, 1956, 563rd Plenary Meeting*. PREM 11/1105 ff 185–6 from Dixon (New York), 4.11.56. Bailey, *Four Arab-Israeli Wars*, pp. 149–51.
24. Lord Hailsham, *A Sparrow's Flight. Memoirs*, pp. 291–2.
25. PREM 11/1090 ff 6–8 Mountbatten to Hailsham, 4.11.56. Hailsham to Mountbatten, 5.11.56. Hailsham wrote to Eden, 'I think it would be disastrous to relieve him now, which is the only other possible course.'
26. PREM 11/1105 EC (56) 39th Meeting, 4.11.56.
27. FO 371/121786 from Sir Michael Wright (Baghdad), 4.11.56, VR 1091/523.
28. Sir William Dickson to author, 1986. Rhodes James, *Anthony Eden*, p. 565.
29. PREM 11/1105 EC (56) 40th Meeting, 4.11.56.
30. 'Law Not War', in *The Economist*, 10.11.56, p. 493. The paper's correspondent found the mounted police to be 'thoroughly undisciplined and far too rough'. He described how, when the crowd was already in retreat towards Trafalgar Square, 'they made an entirely needless charge at speed on their horses, knocking down and injuring at least one middle-aged man ...'
31. David Painting to author, February 1987.
32. Lloyd, *Suez 1956*, pp. 206–7.
33. PREM 11/1105 f 176 COS to Keightley, 4.11.56.
34. PREM 11/1105 f 178 Keightley to COS, 4.11.56.
35. PREM 11/1105 ff 180–4. CM (56) 79th Conclusions, 4.11.56. Rhodes James, op. cit., pp. 566–7.
36. R. A. Butler, *The Art of the Possible*, p. 193.
37. Rhodes James, op. cit., p. 567.
38. Butler, op. cit., p. 193.
39. Evidence of a civil servant.
40. PREM 11/1105 f 174 from Nicholls (Tel Aviv). Received 9.35 p.m. GMT, 4.11.56.
41. PREM 11/1105 f 171 from Nicholls. Received 11.39 p.m. GMT, 4.11.56.
42. PREM 11/1105 ff 180–4. CM (56) 79th Conclusions, 4.11.56. Rhodes James, op. cit., p. 567, quoting Lady Eden's diary describes the scene when the tension was

broken by definite information from Tel Aviv. 'Everyone laughed and banged the table with relief – except Birch and Monckton, who looked glum.' Birch, the Air Minister, who was not a member of the Cabinet, was in attendance as was Hailsham.

Chapter Twenty-Four
The Empires Strike Back
Phase I: 5 November 1956

1. AIR 20/9577 'Report on Gamil Operation'.
2. 'Abd al-Latif al-Bughdadi, *Muddakarat, ii* (Memoirs). I am very grateful for Abdel Majid Farid's assistance with the Arabic text. Translated extracts can be found in Troën and Shemesh, *The Suez-Sinai Crisis 1956: Retrospective and Reappraisal*, pp. 333–56.
3. Kennett Love, *Suez – The Twice-Fought War*, pp. 598–9.
4. al-Bughdadi, *Memoirs*, op. cit.
5. Chaim Herzog, *The Arab-Israeli Wars*, pp. 134–8. Love, op. cit., pp. 589–95.
6. Sandy Cavenagh, *Airborne to Suez* (William Kimber, 1965), p. 128. Julian Thompson, *Ready for Anything. The Parachute Regiment At War* (Weidenfeld and Nicolson, 1989), pp. 253–63. WO 288/74.
7. *BBC Summary of World Broadcasts, IV*, No. 93, 9.11.56.
8. See Footnote 1. Also see A. J. Barker, *Suez, The Seven Day War*, Azeau, *Le Piège de Suez* (Robert Laffont, 1964); Fullick and Powell, *Suez: The Double War* (Leo Cooper, 1979 and 1990).
9. ADM 116/6136 General Keightley's Sitreps, 4.11.56.
10. Admiral Sir Manley Power, 'Autobiography' (unpublished), Churchill College, Cambridge.
11. André Beaufre, *Suez Expedition*; Jacques Massu and Henri Le Mire, *Vérité sur Suez* (Plon, 1978), Pierre Leulliette, *St Michael and the Dragon; Memoirs of a Paratrooper* (Houghton Mifflin, 1964); Azeau, op. cit.
12. Leulliette, op. cit. 'Le RAP 700' in Paul Gaujac, *Suez 1956*, pp. 238–9, contains a long list of imaginative missions dreamed up for the RAP (le Service Renseignements – Action – Protection) scarcely any one of which turned out to be practicable except for the capture of the waterworks. The report on that operation observes drily that if the unit had been properly briefed it could have taken care of the Canal Road bridge as well in sufficient time.
13. Captain M. P. de Klee, 'A Jump with the French', *The Household Brigade Magazine*, 1957.
14. Azeau, op. cit. Massu and Le Mire, op. cit. DEFE 11/111 'Strategic Policy in the Middle East: *Musketeer* Cease-Fire'. WO 288/152 HQ 2 (British) Corps War Diary, 5.11.56. ADM 116/6104 Amplified Report of FOAC. .
15. AIR 8/1940 Chiefs of Staff to General Keightley, COSKEY 37, *FLASH*, 0518002, 5.11.56. An allied press communiqué read: 'Terms for the surrender of the Egyptian garrison of Port Said have been agreed. Egyptian troops have laid down their arms and Egyptian police are functioning under allied control.' DEFE 11/111.
16. WO 288/152 Stockwell to Keightley 051818Z, 5.11.56.
17. AIR 8/1940 *FLASH* from Keightley, KEYCOS 33, 051555z. *Parliamentary Debates (Hansard), House of Commons*, Vol. 558, 5.10.56, cols 1956–78 (Eden's announcement, col. 1966).
18. *The Times* (6.11.56) wrote, 'The Prime Minister achieved a powerful dramatic effect and swept the Conservative ranks to almost delirious heights of joy ... immediately a thunder of cheering burst from the Government side – shouting and gestures directed at the passive ranks opposite.'
19. Sir William Dickson to author, 1986.
20. Peter Mayo's Diary (unpublished), Imperial War Museum.

21. PREM 11/1105 ff 123–5 from Dixon (New York), received 7.20 p.m. GMT, 5.11.56.
22. PREM 11/1105 ff 118–19 from Dixon (New York), received 9 p.m. GMT, 5.11.56. Lamb, *The Failure of the Eden Government*, pp. 265–7.
23. al-Bughdadi, *Memoirs*, op. cit.
24. General Sir Charles Keightley, 'Despatch. Operations in Egypt – November to December 1956', in *Supplement to The London Gazette*, 10.9.57. Love, *Suez – The Twice-Fought War*, p. 605.
25. Joel Beilin, 'The Communist Movement and Nationalist Political Discourse in Nasirist Egypt' in *The Middle East Journal*, Autumn 1987, pp. 577–8.
26. *FRUS XVI*, Doc. 526, 6.11.56, pp. 1027–8.
27. WO 288/152 Keightley to Stockwell, 052201Z, 5.11.56.
28. D.M.J. Clark, *Suez Touchdown. A Soldier's Tale*, pp. 63–5.
29. Frankland (ed.), *Documents on International Affairs, 1956* (RIIA), pp. 288–92.
30. Ben-Gurion 'Diary' in Troën and Shemesh, *The Suez-Sinai Crisis 1956*, entry for 7.11.56.
31. Frankland (ed.), *Documents*, op. cit., pp. 292–4.
32. Ibid., pp. 294–5.
33. *FRUS XVI*, Doc. 518, 6.11.56, p. 1014.
34. In the early afternoon of 6 November Sir Patrick Reilly, the Ambassador-designate to Moscow, went to Number Ten in connection with the reply to Bulganin. Lloyd was sitting at a table, Eden walking about the room. Neither seemed to be paying much attention to the Russian Note. (Sir William Hayter at St Antony's College, Oxford, June 1986.)
35. But the CIA was stopped from passing on to the British the assessment it made at 1.30 a.m. (6.30 British time, 8.30 in Port Said) on the 6th. This said that Soviet Russia had the capability of launching low-yield atomic weapons by ballistic missile at a range of 800 miles from satellite states. On the whole the assessment tended to play down the dangers. (*FRUS XVI*, Doc. 521, Special National Intelligence Estimate, 6.11.56, pp. 1018–20 and see n.2.)
36. PREM 11/1105 from Hayter (Moscow), 5.11.56.
37. AIR 8/1940 Chiefs of Staff to Keightley, COSKEY 41, *FLASH* 060536Z.
38. C. Douglas Dillon in J.F. Dulles Oral History Project, Princeton. Love, op. cit., p. 613.
39. Charles (Chip) Bohlen (Moscow) to Dulles, despatched 7.00 p.m. (Moscow time), received 3.31 p.m. (Washington time), 6.11.56. Dulles Papers, Eisenhower Library, Abilene. *FRUS XVI*, Doc. 520, 6.11.56, pp. 1016–17, especially n.3.
40. AIR 20/9890 Keightley to Chiefs of Staff, 062240Z, 6.11.56. The *New York Times* correspondent, Kennett Love established that, 'The US Embassy in Syria connived at false reports issued in Washington and London through diplomatic and press channels to the effect that Russian arms were pouring into the Syrian port of Latakia and that 'not more than 123 MiGs' had arrived in Syria. I travelled all over Syria without hindrance in November and December and found that there were indeed "not more than 123 MiGs". There were none' (Love, *Suez – The Twice-Fought War*, p. 655).

Chapter Twenty-Five
The Empires Strike Back
Phase II: 6 November 1956

1. Mayo, unpublished diary, op. cit.
2. D.M.J. Clark, op. cit., pp. 71–2.
3. There were other claimants to responsibility for the fire in the shanty town. The British paras who had captured Gamil the previous day resumed their advance and thought that they had started the blaze (AIR 20/9577).

4. Mayo, unpublished diary, op. cit.
5. Keightley, 'Despatch', *London Gazette*, p. 5334.
6. Leulliette, *St Michael and the Dragon*.
7. General Sir Hugh Stockwell, BBC–2 television interview, November 1976.
8. Keightley, 'Despatch'. Stockwell, *Sunday Telegraph*, 6.11.66. Stockwell. 'Report', WO 288/77, p. 52, para, 17.
9. Lloyd, *Suez 1956*, p. 209. Diane Kunz, *The Economic Diplomacy of the Suez Crisis* (Croom Helm, 1990), and 'Did Macmillan Lie over Suez?' in the *Spectator*, 3.11.90. Alastair Horne, *Macmillan*, I, pp. 440–7.
10. Rhodes James, *Anthony Eden*, p. 574.
11. *DDF 1956 III*, Doc. 138, Procès-Verbal Mollett/Adenauer, 6.11.56, pp. 231–8. BBC television interview with Christian Pineau, Paris, 1976, transmitted BBC *Tonight* programme, Suez series, 19.11.76 (producer: Peter Hill).
12. Pineau, *1956 Suez*, p. 191.
13. Sir William Dickson to author, 1986.
14. John Cloake, *Templer, Tiger of Malaya* (Harrap, 1985), p. 355.
15. FO 800/728 Selwyn Lloyd to Sir Norman Brook, 8.8.59.
16. AIR 20/9890 Chiefs to Keightley, COSKEY 42, 061103z, Chiefs to Keightley 061255z. Keightley to Chiefs 061308z. Chiefs to Keightley, COSKEY 43, 061330z *FLASH*.
17. *FRUS XVI*, Doc. 519, 6.11.56, sent 2 p.m., received 10.16 a.m., pp. 1015–16.
18. AIR 20/9890 Chiefs to Keightley, COSKEY 44. Keightley to Chiefs, KEYCOS 49.
19. Pineau, *1956 Suez*, pp. 178–80.
20. *FRUS XVI*, Doc. 525, 6.11.56, telcon., 12.55 p.m. (Washington), 5.55 p.m. (GMT), pp. 1025–7. Contrary to Lloyd, op. cit., p. 209, this was the first Eden–Eisenhower conversation, of 6.11.56. The conversation at 1.43 p.m. GMT, to which Lloyd refers, took place on 7.11.56.
21. Eden, *Full Circle*, p. 557.
22. *Parliamentary Debates* (*Hansard*) *House of Commons*, *Vol. 560*, 6.11.56, cols, 25–84 (Eden 75–81).
23. Rhodes James, *Anthony Eden*, p. 576.
24. Baeyens, *Un Coup d'Epée dans l'Eau du Canal*, p. 109. Eden, *Full Circle*, p. 559.
25. Gaujac, *Suez 1956*, pp. 270–2.
26. DEFE 5/72 ff 86–9. 'Amphibious Warfare Problems Arising During Operation *Musketeer*'. '*Tyne* could not be fully efficient without major alterations.'
27. Thompson, *Ready for Anything*, pp. 268–9. Massu and Le Mire, *Vérité sur Suez, 1956*, pp. 199–210.
28. General Sir Hugh Stockwell, interview on BBC–2, November 1976 (producer: Peter Hill). Stockwell, *Sunday Telegraph*, 6.11.66.
29. Kenneth Macksey, *The Tanks*, pp. 134–5. A. J. Barker, *Suez. The Seven-Day War*, pp. 162–4. General Sir Anthony Farrar-Hockley to author, October 1989.

Chapter Twenty-Six
Picking Up The Pieces

1. *BBC Summary of World Broadcasts, IV*, 7.11.56. Many scholars still think that Ben-Gurion was wrong about the identification of ancient Yotwat. Shlomo Avineri (Troën and Shemesh, *The Suez-Sinai Crisis, 1956*, p. 247) finds it more likely that it was at Gezirat al-Faraoun, a few miles south of Eilat.
2. *FRUS XVI*, Doc. 550, 7.11.56.
3. Abba Eban, *An Autobiography*, p. 229.
4. Ibid., pp. 230–1. *FRUS XVI*, Doc. 551, 7.11.56, pp. 1065–7.
5. Brecher, op. cit., pp. 283, 288–9. Eban, op. cit., pp. 231–4. 'Ben-Gurion's Diary' in Troën and Shemesh, *The Suez-Sinai Crisis 1956*, entry for 8.11.56, pp. 318–19.

Troën and Shemesh, *The Suez-Sinai Crisis 1956*, entry for 8.11.56, pp. 318–19.
6. Brecher, op. cit., pp. 290–1. The opinions were those of Yitzhak Navon (later President of Israel) and Yaacov Herzog respectively.
7. PREM 11/1105 f 1 Eden to Mollet, sent 9.21 p.m., 6.11.56.
8. Eden, *Full Circle*, p. 561. *FRUS XVI*, Doc. 527, 6.11.56, pp. 1028–9.
9. PREM 11/1105 ff 58–62. CM (56) 81st Conclusions, 7.11.56, pp. 1028–9.
10. *FRUS XVI*, Doc. 527 n.2, 6.11.56. p. 1029.
11. PREM 11/1105 ff 25–8. EC(56) 41st Meeting, 7.11.56.
12. Lester Pearson, *Memoirs II*, p. 260. PREM 11/1105 ff 40–2 from Dixon (New York), 7.11.56. Sir Pierson fancied the papal analogy and several times reverted to it.
13. United Nations A/3302, *Second and Final Report of the Secretary-General on the Plan for an Emergency International UN Force*, 6.11.56.
14. Burns, *Between Arab and Israeli*, pp. 196–202.
15. WO 288/1 Brigadier Darling to General Stockwell, 8.11.56.
16. Macksey, *The Tanks, 1945–75*, pp. 136–7.
17. AIR 20/9890 KEYCOS 57, Keightley to Chiefs, 8.11.56.
18. AIR 20/9890 KEYCOS 54, Keightley to Chiefs, 7.11.56. Allied casualties up to the cease-fire were: British 16 killed and 96 wounded; French 10 killed and 33 wounded.
19. Roger Owen, 'The Economic Consequences of the Suez Crisis for Egypt' in Louis and Owen (eds), *Suez 1956: The Crisis and its Consequences*, pp. 363–75. In January–February 1959, Egypt agreed to pay Britain a lump sum of £27.5 million in final settlement of all claims. (CAB 128/33 ff 22–3, CC1(59)3, 16.1.59; ff 28–9, CC 2(59)3, 22.1.59; ff 80–1, CC11(59)1, 19.2.59; ff 92–5, CC 12(59)5, 26.2.59.)
20. ADM 116/6209 Vice-Admiral Richmond, 'Report on Operation *Musketeer*', p. 73, para. 293.
21. ADM 116/6209 Richmond, idem, p. 204 Appdx VI Salvage. List of Wrecks in Annex. ADM 116/6131 Admiralty Sitrep No. 11, 26.11.56.
22. PREM 11/1104 f 38, 18.9.56. Note by Keightley to Egypt Committee, para. 17, Blockage of Canal.
23. *FRUS XVI*, Doc. 536, 7.11.56, 8.43 a.m. (Washington time), 1.43 p.m. GMT, p. 1040. This is the 1.43 p.m. GMT phone call which Lloyd (*Suez 1956*, p. 209) erroneously assigns to 6.11.56.
24. *FRUS XVI*, Doc. 538, 7.11.56, telcon. 9.55 a.m., pp. 1042–3.
25. *FRUS XVI*, Doc. 539, 7.11.56, pp. 1043–5.
26. *FRUS XVI*, Doc. 540, 7.11.56, telcon. 10.27 a.m., pp. 1045–7.
27. *FRUS XVI*, Doc. 554, 303rd National Security Council Meeting, 8.11.56, pp. 1070–86.
28. FO 371/121788 from Sir Roger Stevens (Teheran), 4.11.56, VR 1091/589.
29. ADM 116/6119 Morrice James (Karachi) to CRO, 4.11.56.
30. FO 371/121791 from Wright (Baghdad) sent 3.30 a.m. (local time), 7.11.56, VR 1091/688.
31. FO 371/121791 from Wright sent 3.05 p.m. (local time), 7.11.56, VR 1091/691.
32. FO 371/121791 to Wright (Baghdad), 9.11.56.
33. FO 371/121789 from Stevens (Teheran), 6.11.56. FO to Stevens, 6.11.56.
34. Frankland (ed.), *Documents on International Affairs, 1956* (RIIA), pp. 313–14.
35. FO 371/121789 Alan Lennox-Boyd to Sir Donald MacGillivray (Singapore), 9.11.56, VR 1091/886.
36. Selwyn Lloyd text in *The Listener*, 15.11.56. Gilbert Murray and others, *The Times*, 7.11.56. Letter from Murray, *Time and Tide*, 10.11.56. Sir Duncan Wilson, *Gilbert Murray* (Clarendon Press, 1988), pp. 392–4.
37. Sir Edward (later Lord) Boyle to author, December 1956.
38. Keith Kyle, 'Footnotes to Suez', in *The Listener*, 16.12.76.
39. Nutting, *No End of a Lesson*, pp. 159–62.
40. Nigel Nicolson, *People and Parliament* (Weidenfeld and Nicolson, 1958). The right-

wing candidate, Major Friend, had meanwhile exceeded the limits of the possible and was himself replaced.

41. Leon D. Epstein, *British Politics in the Suez Crisis* (Pall Mall Press, 1964), pp. 98–102 (Nicolson), 112–14 (Astor). The only Labour MP who openly supported Eden, Stanley Evans, was likewise penalised by the Wednesbury Divisional Labour Party, whose general management committee unanimously called for his resignation. This was promptly tendered. Epstein, pp. 130–2.
42. David Astor to author, 1987.
43. PREM 11/1106 ff 514–16 from Sir Harold Caccia (Washington), 9.11.56. Memconv. with the President, 9.11.56. The new Ambassador was recorded at the White House by his middle name as Sir Anthony Caccia, Eisenhower Library, Abilene.
44. Among journalists so recruited were Max Freedman (*Manchester Guardian*), Patrick O'Donovan (*The Observer*) and Keith Kyle (*The Economist*). There may have been others. Not all senior members of the Embassy staff appreciated the press having access to official sources that were denied to them.
45. e.g. PREM 11/1106 ff 523–4, 9.11.56. Dixon complained of learning what was happening by chance 'since the US delegation continues to ignore us'. Sir Pierson went on, 'It is appalling to be stampeded in this way ... If however we get up and say that the Assembly must not be rushed, we shall be reminded about our statement about the urgency of a solution ...'
46. Sir Brian Urquhart, *A Life in Peace and War*, p. 135, has a hilarious description of this generally neglected team of British 'civilian' specialists whose leader, while objecting to being addressed as 'Admiral', stood in the window 'swaying gently to and fro with a roll of secret Admiralty charts under his arm'. Rear-Admiral Peter Dawnay was the Deputy Controller of the Royal Navy, 1956–8.
47. Ibid., p. 135.
48. PREM 11/1106 ff 343–5 Lloyd to Eden. PM's Personal Tel. T 557/56, 14.11.56. *FRUS XVI*, Doc. 575, 16.11.56, pp. 1123–5.
49. J.-R. Tournoux, 'Relance de la Guerre Froide', in *Le Populaire*, 9.11.56.
50. *DDF 1956 III*, Doc. 158, 10.11.56, pp. 271–7; Doc. 196, 18.11.56, pp. 340–2. *FRUS XVI*, Doc. 572, 12.11.56, pp. 1117–20; Doc. 579, 16.11.56, pp. 1135–7.
51. White House Memorandum, 16.11.56. DDE Diaries, Box 19, Staff Memoranda, Eisenhower Library, Abilene.
52. Lloyd, *Suez 1956*, pp. 220–1.
53. Winthrop Aldrich, Eisenhower Oral History Project, Columbia University, and Dulles Oral History, Princeton.
54. 'Ben-Gurion's Diary' in Troën and Shemesh, *The Suez-Sinai Crisis 1956*, entry for 1.12.56, pp. 324–5.
55. PREM 11/1106 ff 266–7 Lloyd to Eden, 17.11.56. PM's Personal Tel. T 574/56. According to *FRUS XVI*, Doc. 582, n.2, p. 1142, no American record was kept of the Dulles–Lloyd conversation but an almost identical remark about the British and Suez was made by Dulles to Eisenhower during a hospital visit on 12.11.56 (Doc. 570, p. 1114).
56. Raymond Hare (Cairo) to Hoover, 10.11.56, Dulles–Herter Series, Box 6, Eisenhower Library, Abilene. Hammarskjöld Priv. 21(a); Doc. VIII, 10.11.56. Monthly digest for November 1956, Hammarksjöld Archive, Royal Library, Stockholm.
57. PREM 11/1106 ff 320–2. EC(56) 44th Meeting, 15.11.56.
58. Hammarskjöld Priv. 21 (a) Doc. XII Hammarskjöld to Fawzi, 12.11.56; Doc. XX Fawzi to Hammarskjöld, 13.11.56; Doc. XXII Hammarskjöld to Fawzi, 13.11.56; Doc. XXIII Hammarskjöld, 'Functions of UNEF', internal memo, November 1956. Hammarskjöld Archive, Stockholm.
59. Major-General Indar Jit Rikhye, *The Sinai Blunder* (Frank Cass, 1980), Appdx J, pp. 221–6. 'Aide-mémoire by Dag Hammarskjöld' on 'Conditions Governing Withdrawal of UNEF'.

Chapter Twenty-Seven
Forced to Quit

1. T 236/4189 Sir Roger Makins to Macmillan, RM/56/3.
2. T 236/4189 'Note of a Meeting held in Sir Leslie Rowan's Room', 12.11.56.
3. Lord Harcourt to Sir Leslie Rowan, Bank of England G1/124 19.11.56. Cited by Diane Kunz, 'The Importance of Having Money: The Economic Diplomacy of the Suez Crisis' in Louis and Owen (eds), *Suez 1956: The Crisis and Its Consequences*, p. 228.
4. *FRUS XVI*, Doc. 554, 303rd Meeting of National Security Council, 8.11.56, pp. 1070–89, Doc. 577, 304th Meeting, NSC, 15.11.56, pp. 1129–32 and Doc. 583, 17.11.56, pp. 1142–3. Macmillan, *Riding the Storm*, p. 169.
5. T 236/4189 'Sterling. Notes for Chancellor's Statement in Cabinet', 19.11.56. Humphrey Mynors, Deputy Governor was responsible for the statement that 'the real figure is £401m', Treasury Memo T 236/4190, 30.11.56.
6. T 236/4189 Draft of Message from Chancellor of the Exchequer to Mr Humphrey.
7. *Parliamentary Debates (Hansard), House of Commons, Vol. 560*, 13.11.56.
8. PREM 11/1149 Sir Edwin Herbert concluded that 'a reasonable estimate' was 650 killed in Port Said and another 100 in Port Fuad. Another 900 were sufficiently wounded to be detained in hospital. The US Naval Attaché estimated 1,000 deaths. The most damaging allegations were made by a Swedish journalist, Olof Perelew Anderssen, who wrote that between 7,000 and 12,000 had died. 'Is it police action', he demanded, 'to fly planes through streets, machine-gunning the inhabitants of a city?' (PREM 11/1149 ff 146 and 35).
9. Lord Hailsham to author, Dec. 1987.
10. The illustrated magazine *Scribe* (Cairo) was used as a major vehicle for atrocity stories. The records show the Government as very seriously worried by the campaign. *FRUS XVI*, Doc. 561, 8.11.56, pp. 1096–7.
11. PREM 11/1106 f 216 from Selwyn Lloyd (New York), 20.11.56. 'Nasser has clearly frightened Hammarskjöld into believing that the situation in Port Said may get out of hand.'
12. Butler, *The Art of the Possible*, p. 194.
13. Ibid.
14. *FRUS XVI*, Doc. 571, 12.11.56, pp. 1115–7 and Doc. 588, 19.11.56, pp. 1150–2.
15. Telcon. Eisenhower/Humphrey, 19.11.56, DDE Diaries, Box 19, Eisenhower Library, Abilene. *FRUS XVI*, Doc. 592, Editorial Note, p. 1162. W. Scott Lucas, 'Suez, the Americans and the Overthrow of Anthony Eden' in *LSE Quarterly* (Autumn 1987).
16. *FRUS XVI*, Doc. 593, 19.11.56, p. 1163.
17. Telcon. Eisenhower/Aldrich, 20.11.56, DDE Diaries, Box 19. Memconv. with the President, Humphrey and Hoover, 20.11.56, Eisenhower Library, Abilene. *FRUS XVI*, Doc. 597, 20.11.56, pp. 1169–70.
18. *FRUS XVI*, Doc. 595, 20.11.56, p. 1165. Memconf. with the President, Humphrey, Hoover, Allen Dulles, Radford *et al.*, 21.11.56, DDE Diaries, Box 19, Eisenhower Library, Abilene.
19. *FRUS XVI*, Doc. 605, 23.11.56, p. 1181. PREM 11/1106 ff 140–2 Caccia to Lloyd, 23.11.56.
20. Philip Ziegler, *Mountbatten*, p. 248. Quotation from Mountbatten's personal diary, 18.9.45.
21. Anthony Howard, *RAB: The Life of R. A. Butler* (Jonathan Cape, 1987), pp. 240–1. James Ramsden, 'Rab did sometimes miss tricks which Macmillan managed to take', in *The Listener*, 19.3.87.
22. Charles Townshend was the eighteenth-century Chancellor of the Exchequer who in 1767 introduced the duties that lost Britain her American colonies and made a brilliant but scandalous 'champagne speech' in which he ridiculed his own Cabinet

colleagues. (Sir Lewis Namier and John Brooke, *Charles Townshend*, pp. 169–79.)

23. Brendan (Lord) Bracken to Lord Beaverbrook, 22.11.56 and 7.12.56. Beaverbrook Collection, House of Lords.
24. PREM 11/1106 f 97 Lloyd to Butler, 24.11.56. *FRUS XVI*, Doc. 606, 23.11.56. pp. 1182–5 and Doc. 611, Editorial Note, pp. 1192–3.
25. *FRUS XVI*, Doc. 614, 26.11.56, pp. 1196–7.
26. CAB 128/30 ff 689–90, CM 88(56), 27.11.56.
27. CAB 128/30 f 692, CM 89(56), 28.11.56. FO 371/121238 Denis Laskey to Robin Turton, 27.11.56. V 1054/140.
28. PREM 11/1106 f 55, to Dixon (New York), 27.11.56.
29. T 236/4190 from Sir Harold Caccia (Washington), 23.11.56.
30. T 236/4190 from Caccia, 27.11.56.
31. PREM 11/1106 ff 41–4 and 39–40 from Selwyn Lloyd (New York).
32. Lloyd, *Suez 1956*, p. 232. 'The expression on the faces of the colleagues needed some interpretation. One or two were clearly doubtful of my motives. All were against it.'
33. FO 800/728 Selwyn Lloyd's record of conversation with Eden, 30.5.58. Lloyd, *Suez 1956*, p. 232.
34. CAB 128/30 ff 695–7, CM 90(56), 28.11.56.
35. PREM 11/1107 ff 480–3. Record of Anglo-French Meeting at 10 Downing Street, 30.11.56.
36. PREM 11/1107 f 450 from Sir Gladwyn Jebb (Paris), 1.12.56.
37. PREM 11/1106 ff 34–5 from Dixon (New York), 28.11.56. 4,500 troops had been accepted from eight states for service in UNEF.
38. 'The UN Force Assembles: A Triumph of Improvisation. By a UN official recently returned from Egypt' [George Ivan Smith] in *The Times*, 12.12.56.
39. George Ivan Smith to author, 1986.
40. Dag Hammarskjöld, in 'Internal Memorandum, 17.11.56' rejected as 'untenable' the British and French assumption that because they had stopped military action, the UNEF were obliged to achieve their goals for them. Hammarskjöld Archive, Royal Library, Stockholm.
41. *DDF 1956 III*, Doc. 186, Gazier to Pineau, 15.11.56, pp. 325–7. The British account of the same conversation in PREM 11/1106 is withheld until 2007.
42. *DDF 1956 III*, Doc. 269, 7.12.56, pp. 484–6.
43. PREM 11/1107 ff 440–1 from Dixon (New York), 1.12.56.
44. *FRUS XVI*, Doc. 626, 30.11.56, pp. 1218–29.
45. PREM 11/1107 f 464 Eden (Jamaica) to Sir Norman Brook, 1.12.56. PM's Personal Tel. T 597/56.
46. The Cabinet entrusted the task to Lord Salisbury, with the assistance of Lord Kilmuir, Alan Lennox-Boyd and Antony Head (CAB 128/30 f 708 CM 93(56), 29.11.56).
47. PREM 11/1107 ff 410–11 Butler to Eden (Jamaica), 2.12.56, PM's Personal Tel T 600/56; f 407 Eden to Butler, T 608/56; f 403 Butler to Eden, T 609/56.
48. PREM 11/1107 ff 376–8. 'Note of a [telephone] conversation' between George Humphrey and R. A. Butler, 2.12.56.
49. *Parliamentary Debates (Hansard), House of Commons, Vol. 561*, 3.12.56, cols 877–96.
50. Diane Kunz, 'The Importance of Having Money', Postscript and Appendix, in Louis and Owen, *Suez 1956*, pp. 231–2.

Chapter Twenty-Eight
Last Stands and New Doctrine

1. Rhodes James, *Anthony Eden*, pp. 590–1.
2. *The Times*, 15.12.56.
3. Rhodes James, op. cit., pp. 591 (Clarissa Eden) and 592 (Commons entry).
4. CAB 128/30 CM 85(56), f 64, 20.11.56.
5. Sir Stephen (later Lord) King-Hall, *National Newsletter*, issues 1060, 14.11.56, and 1062, 28.11.56. In response to 'the astonishing volume of correspondence' which the first of these issues produced, he wrote in the second, 'World public opinion and, we are glad to say, all but the most irresponsible types of person in Britain would be deeply shocked if it were to be proved that HMG – or even a limited number of senior Ministers – were aware of what was likely to happen and decided to take advantage of the event to press forward with policies which, it seemed, had been abandoned at the end of August.' *FRUS XVI*, Doc. 570, 12.11.56, p. 1114.
6. Ronald Higgins to author, Chatham House, March 1988.
7. 'Ben-Gurion's Diary' in Troën and Shemesh (eds), *The Suez–Sinai Crisis, 1956*, entry for 25.11.56, p. 324.
8. Sir Edward (later Lord) Boyle to author, December 1956.
9. Hugh Thomas (Lord Thomas of Swynnerton), *The Suez Affair* (Weidenfeld and Nicolson, 1986 edition) Appdx 8 'Meeting of the 1922 Committee, 18.12.56'.
10. *Parliamentary Debates (Hansard), House of Commons, Vol. 562*, 20.12.56, cols 1456–1518.
11. Lord Kilmuir, *Political Adventure*, pp. 283–4. Lord Thorneycroft to author, House of Lords, March 1988.
12. Urquhart, *Hammarskjöld*, p. 200.
13. PREM 11/1107 ff 199–201 'Record of a Conversation between the S. and S. and Mr Dulles on Monday, 10 December 1956 in Paris'. *FRUS XVI*, Doc. 650, 12.12.56, pp. 1296–8 and Doc. 654. 14.12.56.
14. Memconv. with the President, 15.12.56, JFD Papers, White House Memoranda Series, Eisenhower Library, Abilene. *FRUS XVI*, Doc. 657, 15.12.56, pp. 1309–10.
15. Tel. call, Lodge to Dulles, 27.12.56. JFD Papers, tel. calls series, Eisenhower Library, Abilene. *FRUS XVI*, Doc. 654, 14.12.56, pp. 1302–4 and Doc. 666, 27.12.56, pp. 1334–6.
16. FO 371/119217 from Dixon (New York), 21.12.56, JE 14217/201. FO 371/119189 Dixon to Kirkpatrick, 22.12.56, JE 14214/405.
17. FO 800/743 Dixon, 'Personal' for Lloyd, 16.12.56.
18. FO 800/743 Lloyd, 'Personal' for Dixon, 16.12.56.
19. FO 371/125348 from Dixon, 31.12.56.
20. PREM 11/1107 f 84 Mid-East Main to MoD, 20.12.56, KEYCOS 151. Eden to Mollet, PM's Personal Tel. T 671/56.
21. *DDF 1956 III*, Doc. 321, Baeyens to Pineau, 22.11.56, pp. 587–94.
22. Robert Engler, *The Politics of Oil. A Study of Private Power and Democratic Directions* (Macmillan, New York, 1961), pp. 134–6, 141–2. *The Economist*, 26.1.57, p. 290, 'Two Tangles in Texas:(1) Over Oil for Europe'.
23. The Railroad Commission of Texas, Statewide Hearing, 15.11.56, reprinted in US Senate Joint Subcommittee Hearings, *Emergency Oil Lift Program and Related Oil Problems*, Part 3, Appdx A, pp. 1711–20, 1724.
24. Engler, op. cit., p. 231.
25. The Railroad Commission of Texas, p. 1727.
26. Middle East Emergency Committee, Membership and Minutes, *Emergency Oil Lift Program*, op. cit., Part 3, Appdx A, pp. 1835–1980.
27. *FRUS XVI*, Doc. 626, 30.11.56, pp. 1218–19. Engler, op. cit., pp. 261–2.
28. *Wall Street Journal*, 21.12.56 and 31.12.56.
29. Engler, op. cit., p. 144. *Wall Street Journal*, 18.2.57.

30. *The Economist*, 23.2.57, pp. 643–4. 'Texas Catches the Oil Bus'. Engler, op. cit., p. 244. Humble and the twenty-eight other companies were subsequently indicted by a federal grand jury for price fixing under the Sherman Anti-Trust Act (an offence not covered by the immunity granted). After an immensely complicated trial they were acquitted on the ground that evidence against them 'did not rise above the level of suspicion'.
31. Aubrey Jones to author, April 1988.
32. *Sunday Express*, 16.12.56.
33. *Parliamentary Debates (Hansard), House of Commons*, Vol. 563, 24.1.57, cols 403–5.
34. Memconf. President with Herbert Hoover, Allen Dulles, Richard Bissell, 15.11.56. US Declassified documents.
35. *Senate Foreign Relations Committee, 1957, 96th Congress, 1st Session, Vol. 7. Nominations and Historical Series, Resolutions Regarding the Middle East.*
36. Frankland (ed.), *Documents on International Affairs, 1957* (RIIA/OUP, 1960), 'Message to Congress by President Eisenhower, 5.1.57', pp. 233–40.
37. Robert R. Bowie, 'Comments on Middle East Message', 27.12.56. Eisenhower Library, Abilene.
38. Frankland (ed.), *Documents 1957*, op. cit., pp. 241–7.
39. CAB 128/30 Pt 2 CM(57) 1st Conclusions, 3.1.57. CAB 123/31 Pt 1 ff 24–5 CC(57)1st Conclusions, 15.1.57.
40. Sir Charles Johnston, *The Brink of Jordan* (Hamish Hamilton, 1972).
41. FO 371/121238 ME (O) (56)80, 'Middle East Policy'. Minute by P. H. Laurence, 14.12.56, V 1054/150(b).
42. CAB 134/1299 ME (O) (56)76, 'Nuri es-Said's Proposals Concerning IPC'.
43. FO 371/127747 Gladwyn Jebb (Paris) to Ivone Kirkpatrick, 'British Policy in the Middle East', 4.1.57.
44. FO 371/127747 James Bowker (Istanbul) to Paul Gore-Booth, 'Future Middle East Policy', 4.1.57.
45. FO 371/127747 George Middleton (Beirut) to Gore-Booth, 'Future Middle East Policy', 20.12.56.

Chapter Twenty-Nine
The End of the Suez Conflict

1. Rhodes James, *Anthony Eden*, p. 597. Notes prepared by the Prime Minister for Cabinet of 9.1.57.
2. Eden, *Full Circle*, p. 582.
3. Eden to Churchill, 8.1.57. Text in Rhodes James, op. cit., p. 596.
4. Dictated by Eden, 11.1.57. Avon Paper, University of Birmingham.
5. Lord Thorneycroft, Lord Home of the Hirsel and Aubrey Jones to author, March 1988.
6. FO 371/125548 to Dixon (New York), 9.1.57.
7. *FRUS XVII*, Doc. 63, 312th Meeting National Security Council, 7.2.57, pp. 99–101. *FRUS XVI*, Doc. 665, 26.12.56, pp. 1333–4.
8. Memconv. with the President, Duncan Sandys and Harold Caccia, Eisenhower Library, Abilene. *FRUS XVII*, Doc. 41, 27.1.57, pp. 63–4.
9. *FRUS XVII*, Doc. 160, 26.2.57, p. 296.
10. AIR 20/10370 Cairo Radio, 23.11.56. FO 371/121804 from Nicholls (Tel Aviv), 27.12.56, VR 1091/1055A. *FRUS XVI*, Doc. 671, 28.12.56, p. 1341.
11. Frankland (ed.), *Documents on International Affairs, 1957* (RIIA), pp. 185–9. UN Doc. A/3512, 'Report of the Secretary-General in pursuance of G.A. Res. 1123 (XI)', 24.1.57. *FRUS XVII*, Doc. 32.
12. Hammarskjöld to Nasser, 26.1.57, Priv. 26, Hammarskjöld Archive, Royal Library, Stockholm. 'Ben-Gurion Diary', entry for 14.11.56 in Troën and Shemesh, *The Suez–Sinai Crisis 1956*, p. 321.

13. Abba Eban, *An Autobiography*, pp. 238–40. *FRUS XVII*, Docs. 77–9, 11.2.57, pp. 125–36.
14. *FRUS XVII*, Doc. 100, 14.2.57.
15. Eban, op. cit., pp. 241–4.
16. *FRUS XVI*, Doc. 86, 12.2.57, pp. 142–4. Doc. 104, 16.2.57, pp. 187–8. Docs. 106–7, 17.2.57, pp. 195–6. Doc. 127, 21.2.57, pp. 231–2.
17. Frankland (ed.), *Documents ... 1957*, op. cit., pp. 193–9. *FRUS XVII*, Doc. 86, op. cit.
18. *FRUS XVII*, Doc. 133, 22.2.57, pp. 239–40.
19. Eban, op. cit., pp. 245–8. *FRUS XVII*, Doc. 143, 24.2.57, pp. 254–67.
20. *FRUS XVII*, Docs. 155–60, 26.2.57, pp. 283–98. Schmidt Priv. 27, 26.2.57, Hammarskjöld Archive, Stockholm.
21. *FRUS XVII*, Docs. 161–2, 26–27.2.57, pp. 298–303. Doc. 167, 28.2.57, pp. 311–17. Doc. 170, 28.2.57, pp. 320–1. Doc. 173, 28.2.57, pp. 325–9. Doc. 174, 1.3.57, p. 330. Docs. 178–81, 1–2.3.57, pp. 337–47.
22. Burns to Hammarskjöld, Hammarskjöld to Burns, 2.3.57. Summarised in Priv. 28, Hammarskjöld Archive, Stockholm.
23. S-G's private note, 18.3.57, Priv. 28, Hammarskjöld Archive, Stockholm. *FRUS XVII*, Doc. 233, 18.3.57, pp. 433–41.
24. FO 371/128143 from Dixon (New York), 13 and 14.2.57, VR 1082/8. *FRUS XVII*, Doc. 86, 12.2.57, pp. 142–4 and Doc. 90, 12.2.57, pp. 149–50.
25. General E.L.M. Burns, *Between Arab and Israeli*, pp. 264–70. *FRUS XVII*, Docs. 210–11, 11.3.57, pp. 396–9. Doc. 21, Editorial Note, p. 399. Docs 217–18, 13.3.57, pp. 404–11. Doc. 230, 17.3.57, pp. 429–30. Burns to Hammarskjöld, 19.3.57. Summarised in Priv. 27, Hammarskjöld Archive, Stockholm. *FRUS XVII*, Doc. 220, n.2 and end note, 13.3.57, pp. 414–15.
26. Burns, op. cit., pp. 273–6. Urquhart, *Hammarskjöld*, pp. 220–2. Alan Hart, *Arafat*, pp. 119–20.
27. Yoav Lavi, 'Ben-Gurion on Gaza' in *Davar*, 3.2.88.
28. Dwight D. Eisenhower, 'Bermuda Conference'. Eisenhower Library, Abilene.
29. PREM 11/1789 Macmillan to Menzies, 25.3.57.
30. Macmillan, *Riding the Storm*, pp. 253–4. *FRUS XVII*, Doc. 239, 20.3.57, pp. 450–1. Doc. 241, 21.3.57, pp. 452–8.
31. PREM 11/1838 'Bermuda Conference. Proceedings'. *FRUS XVII*, Docs. 242–7, 21–23.3.57, pp. 452–8.
32. PREM 11/1789 Harold Watkinson to Macmillan, 12.3.57.
33. Frankland (ed.), *Documents ... 1957*, p. 215. *FRUS XVII*, Doc. 231, 13.3.57, p. 430–1.
34. PREM 11/1789 Adam Watson, 'Proposed Egyptian Declaration on Suez Canal'. Minute by Archibald Ross.
35. *FRUS XVII*, Doc. 262, 2.4.57, pp. 500–2 and Doc. 267, 4.4.57, pp. 512–14. PREM 11/1789 from Dixon (New York), 6.4.57.
36. CAB 128/31 Pt 1 CC(57) 29th Conclusions, 3.4.57.
37. PREM 11/1787 from Jebb (Paris), 16.4.57.
38. CAB 128/31 Pt 1 CC(57) 35th Conclusions f 243, 17.4.57.
39. Frankland (ed.), *Documents ... 1957*, pp. 222–6.
40. PREM 11/1787 Lloyd to Hammarskjöld (Geneva), 6.5.57.
41. PREM 11/1787 Lloyd to all SCUA members, 10.5.57.
42. PREM 11/1787 from Jebb (Paris), 11.5.57.
43. Macmillan, *Riding the Storm*, pp. 236–7.
44. Sir Robin Day, *Grand Inquisitor*, pp. 94–7. Transcript, ITN.
45. PREM 11/1850 from Jebb (Paris), 13.6.57. Bourgès-Maunoury was confirmed by 240 votes to 194, with 74 abstentions. The opponents included the leader of his (Radical) party, Pierre Mendès-France.
46. PREM 11/1850 Bourgès-Maunoury to Macmillan, 15.6.57, WF 1051/34.
47. PREM 11/1946 Minute to Macmillan on conversation with French Ambassador (Chauvel), 11.7.57.

Chapter Thirty
Epilogue

1. Tawfiq al-Hakim, *The Return of Consciousness* (Macmillan, 1985), pp. 21–2.
2. Mohamed Heikal, *Nasser. The Cairo Documents*, p. 138.
3. Sydney D. Bailey, *Four Arab–Israeli Wars and the Peace Process*, pp. 191–221 and 406–10. U Thant did go to Cairo later 'but,' writes Bailey, 'it was not in his style to rush.' Maj.-Gen. Indar Jit Rikhye, *The Sinai Blunder*, *passim*.
4. 'Speech by President Nasser on Closing the Gulf of Aqaba, 22 May, 1967'. Text printed as Appdx. 'E' of Rikhye, op. cit., pp. 198–203.
5. Information from Piers Dixon.
6. Beaverbrook Papers, House of Lords Library.
7. James Callaghan, *Time and Chance* (Collins, 1987), pp. 331–57.
8. A.J.P. Taylor, review of Terence Robertson, *Crisis*, in the *Observer*, 13.2.65.

Bibliography

In addition to the unpublished sources on which this book is primarily based and which are listed in the Acknowledgements, I have consulted the following published books and articles:

AGRES, Eliyahu, 'Ben-Gurion, the Arabs and Zionism', in *New Outlook*, March/April 1988.

AHMED, J. M., *The Intellectual Origins of Egyptian Nationalism* (OUP, 1960).

ANDREWS, Burton, 'Suez Canal Controversy', in *Albany Law Review*, January 1957.

ARMITAGE, Air Marshal Sir Michael, and MASON, Air Commodore R. A., *Air Power in the Nuclear Age, 1945–84. Theory and Practice* (Macmillan, 1983).

ARONSON, Geoffrey, *From Side Show to Center Stage: US Policy Towards Egypt, 1946–1956* (Boulder, 1986).

AVI-HAI, Avraham, *Ben-Gurion. State Builder* (Israel Universities Press, Jerusalem, 1974).

AVRAM, Benno, *The Evolution of the Suez Canal Status from 1869 up to 1956. A Historico-Juridical Study* (Librairie E. Droz, Geneva, 1958).

AZEAU, Henri, *Le Piège de Suez* (Robert Laffont, 1964).

BAILEY, Sydney D., *Four Arab–Israeli Wars and The Peace Process* (Macmillan, 1990).

BARJOT, Admiral Pierre, 'Réflexions sur les operations de Suez, 1956', in *Revue du défense nationale*, 22 (1966).

BARKER, A. J., *Suez: The Seven-Day War* (Faber and Faber, 1964).

BAR-ON, Mordechai, 'The St Germain Conference' (Hebrew), *Ma'ariv*, 29.10.76.

BAR-ON, Mordechai, 'Ma'arekhet Sinai 1956: Matarot ve Tsipiot' (The Sinai Campaign: Aims and Expectations), in *Zemanim* 24. Winter 1987.

BAR-ON, 'Ben-Gurion and the War of 1956' in Papers Presented to the Leonard Davis Institute Seminar on Innovative Leadership (Jerusalem, 1987).

BAR-ZOHAR, Michael, *Ben Gurion, A Political Biography* (Weidenfeld and Nicolson, 1978).

BAR-ZOHAR, Michael, *Suez, Ultra Secret* (Fayard, Paris, 1964).

BEAUFRE, General André, *The Suez Expedition 1956* (Faber and Faber, 1969).

BEININ, Joel, 'The Communist Movement and Nationalist Political Discourse in Nasirist Egypt', in *The Middle East Journal*, Autumn 1987.

BELL, J. Bowyer, *Terror Out of Zion. Irqun Zvai Leumi, LEHI, and the Palestine Underground* (The Academy Press, Dublin, 1979).

BEN-GURION, David, *Israel's Security and her International Position Before and After the Sinai Campaign* (Jerusalem, 1960).

BEN-GURION, David, *My Talks with Arab Leaders* (Jerusalem, 1973).

BEN-GURION, David, *Israel: Years of Challenge* (Holt, Reinhart Winston, 1963).

BERNADOTTE of WISBORG, Count Folke, *To Jerusalem* (Hodder and Stoughton, 1951).

BESCHLOSS, Michael R., *Mayday. Eisenhower, Khrushchev and the U-2 Affair* (Faber and Faber, 1986).

BETHELL, Nicholas (Lord), *The Palestine Triangle* (André Deutsch, 1979).

BILL, James A., and LOUIS, Wm Roger, *Musaddiq, Iranian Nationalism and Oil* (I. B. Tauris, 1988).

BIRKENHEAD, Earl of, *Monckton* (Weidenfeld and Nicolson, 1969).

BLACK, Ian, and MORRIS, Benny, *Israel's Secret Wars* (Hamish Hamilton, 1991).

BLOCH, Jonathan, and FITZGERALD, Patrick, *British Intelligence and Covert Action* (Brandon, Ireland, 1983).

BOGHDADI, Abdul Latif ['Abd al-Latif al-Bughdadi], *Mudhakkirat II* (Cairo, 1977).

BOWIE, Robert, *Suez 1956: International Crisis and the Rule of Law* (OUP, 1974).

BRADDON, Russell, *Suez, Splitting of a Nation* (Collins, 1973).

BRANSTEN, Thomas (ed), *Recollections. David Ben-Gurion* (Macdonald, 1970).

BRECHER, Michael, *Decisions in Israel's Foreign Policy* (OUP, 1974).

BRECHER, Michael, *The Foreign Policy System of Israel: Setting, Images, Process* (OUP, 1972).

BRIGGS, Lord (Asa), *Governing the BBC* (BBC, 1979).

BROMBERGER, Merry and Serge, *Secrets of Suez* (Sidgwick and Jackson, 1957).

BULGANIN, N.A., and SHEPILOV, D.T., *Suez. The Soviet View. Statements by the Soviet Government on the Suez Canal Issue* (Soviet News, 1956).

BULLOCK, Lord, *Ernest Bevin, Foreign Secretary* (Heinemann, 1983).

BURNS, General E. L. M., *Between Arab and Israeli* (Harrap, 1962).

BURNS, William J., *Economic Aid and American Policy Toward Egypt, 1955–1981* (SUNY, Albany, 1985).

BUTLER, Lord, *The Art of the Possible* (Hamish Hamilton, 1971).

CABLE, Sir James, *The Geneva Conference of 1954 on Indo-China* (Macmillan, 1986).

CALLAGHAN, Lord, *Time and Chance* (Collins, 1987).

CAMERON WATT, Donald, *Britain and the Suez Canal* (RIIA, 1956).

CAMERON WATT, Donald, *Documents on the Suez Crisis* (RIIA, 1957).

CANDOLE, E. A. V. de, *The Life and Times of King Idris of Libya* (privately printed, London, 1988).

CARLTON, David, *Anthony Eden. A Biography* (Allen Lane, 1981).

CARLTON, David, *Britain and the Suez Crisis* (ICBH/Blackwell, 1988).

CAROZ, Yaacov, *The Arab Secret Service* (Corgi Books, 1978).

CARRINGTON, Lord, *Reflect on Things Past* (Collins, 1988).

CARY, David Stenger, 'A Haunting Legacy. The Assassination of Count Bernadotte', in *Middle East Journal*, Spring 1988.

CASEY, Lord (R. G.), *Australian Foreign Minister. The Diaries of R. G. Casey, 1951–60* (Collins, 1972).

CAVENAGH, Sandy, *Airborne to Suez* (William Kimber, 1965).

CHARMLEY, John, *Lord Lloyd and the Decline of the British Empire* (Weidenfeld and Nicolson, 1987).

CHAUVEL, Jean, *Commentaire Vol III 1952–1962* (Fayard, Paris, 1973).

CHEAL, Beryl, 'Refugees in the Gaza Strip, Dec. 1948 to May 1950', in *Journal of Palestine Studies*, Autumn 1988.

CHILDERS, Erskine B., *The Road to Suez* (MacGibbon and Kee, 1962).

CHURCHILL, Randolph S., *The Rise and Fall of Sir Anthony Eden* (MacGibbon and Kee, 1959).

CLARK, Douglas, *Suez Touchdown. A Soldier's Tale* (P. Davies, 1964).

CLOAKE, John, *Templer, Tiger of Malaya. The Life of Field Marshal Sir Gerald Templer* (Harrap, 1985).

COCKERELL, Michael, *Live from Number 10. The Inside Story of Prime Ministers and Television* (Faber and Faber, 1988).

COCKETT, Richard (ed), *My Dear Max. The Letters of Brendan Bracken to Lord Beaverbrook, 1925–58* (The Historians' Press, 1990).

COLVILLE, Sir John, *The Fringes of Power. Downing Street Diaries 1939–1955* (Hodder and Stoughton, 1985).

COOPER, Artemis, *Cairo in the War, 1939–45* (Hamish Hamilton, 1989).

COOPER, Chester L., *The Lion's Last Roar* (New York, 1978).

COPELAND, Miles, *The Game of Nations. The Amorality of Power Politics* (Weidenfeld and Nicolson, 1969).

COPELAND, Miles, *The Game Player. Confessions of the CIA's Original Political Operative* (Aurum, 1989).

COX, Sir Geoffrey, *See It Happen. The Making of ITN* (The Bodley Head, 1983).

CRANKSHAW, Edward (ed), *Khrushchev Remembers* (André Deutsch, 1971).

CROSBIE, Sylvia K., *A Tacit Alliance: France and Israel from Suez to the Six-Day War* (Princeton University Press, 1974).

CRUISE O'BRIEN, Conor, *The Siege. The Saga of Israel and Zionism* (Weidenfeld and Nicolson, 1986).

DARBY, Phillip, *British Defence Policy East of Suez 1947–1968* (RIIA/OUP, 1973).

DAY, Sir Robin, *Grand Inquisitor* (Weidenfeld and Nicolson, 1989).

DAYAN, General Moshe, *Diary of the Sinai Campaign* (Weidenfeld and Nicolson, 1966).

DAYAN, General Moshe, *Story of My Life* (Weidenfeld and Nicolson, 1976).

DE KLEE, Captain M.P., 'A Jump with the French', in *The Household Brigade Magazine*, 1957.

DIXON, Piers, *Double Diploma. The Life of Sir Pierson Dixon, Don and Diplomat* (Hutchinson, 1968).

DODDS-PARKER, Sir Douglas, *Political Eunuch* (Springwood Books, 1986).

'Dossier: La Crise de Suez', in *L'histoire*, 38 (Oct. 1981).

'Dossier: L'Affaire de Suez trente ans après', in *Revue Historique des Armées*, 165 (Dec. 1986).

EAYRS, James, *The Commonwealth and Suez* (OUP, 1964).

EBAN, Abba, *An Autobiography* (Weidenfeld and Nicolson, 1978).

EDEN, Sir Anthony [Earl of Avon], *Full Circle* (Cassell, 1960).

EISENHOWER, Dwight D., *The White House Years*, Vols I and II (Doubleday, 1963 and 1965).

ELY, General Paul, *Mémoires, Suez ... Le 13 Mai* (Plon, Paris, 1969).

ENGLER, Robert, *The Politics of Oil. A Study of Private Power and Democratic Directions* (Macmillan, New York, 1961).

EPSTEIN, Leon D., *British Politics in the Suez Crisis* (Pall Mall Press, 1964).

EVELAND, Wilbur C., *Ropes of Sand. America's Failure in the Middle East* (Norton, 1980).

EVRON, Yosef, *B'Yom Sagrir: Su'ets Me'ahorei Ha-klayim* (Tel Aviv, 1968) [In Stormy Days: Suez Behind the Scenes].

FALIGOT, Roger, and KROP, Pascal, *La Piscine. Les Services Secrets Français 1944–1984* (Editions du Seuil, 1985).

FALL, Bernard, 'The Two Sides of the Sinai Campaign' in *Military Review – USA*, July 1957.

FARNIE, Douglas, *East and West of Suez. The Suez Canal in History 1854–1956* (Clarendon Press, Oxford, 1969).

FAWZI, Mahmoud, *Suez 1956. An Egyptian Perspective* (Shorouk International, 1987).

FERRELL, Robert (ed), *The Eisenhower Diaries* (W. W. Norton, New York, 1981).

FINER, Herman, *Dulles Over Suez* (Heinemann, 1964).

FLAPAN, Simha, *Zionism and the Palestinians* (Croom Helm, 1979).

FLAPAN, Simha, *The Birth of Israel. Myths and Realities* (Croom Helm, 1987).

FORSTER, E. M., *Alexandria: a History and Guide* (Michael Haag, 1982).

FOUQUIÈRES, Colonel Becq de, 'Guerre des Six Jours', in *Forces Aeriennes Françaises*, 1957.

FRANKLAND, Noble (ed), *Documents on International Relations*, 1955/1956/1957 (RIIA/OUP, 1958/1959/1960).

FULLICK, Roy, and POWELL, Geoffrey, *Suez: the Double War* (Hamish Hamilton, 1979).

GALLMAN, Waldemar J., *Iraq Under General Nuri* (Johns Hopkins Press, 1964).

GAUJAC, Paul, *Suez 1956* (Lavauzelle, Paris, 1987).

GAZIT, Mordechai, 'American and British Diplomacy and the Bernadotte Mission', in *The Historical Journal*, Sept. 1986.

GEORGES-PICOT, Jacques, *The Real Suez Crisis* (Harcourt Brace Jovanovich, 1978).

GERSON, Louis L., *The American Secretaries of State and their Diplomacy, Vol. XVII, John Foster Dulles* (Cooper Square, New York, 1967).

GILBERT, Martin, *'Never Despair'. Winston S. Churchill, 1945–1965* (Heinemann, 1988).

GLUBB, General Sir John Bagot, *A Soldier with the Arabs* (Hodder and Stoughton, 1957).

GOLAN, Matti, *Shimon Peres* (Weidenfeld and Nicolson, 1982).

GOLAN, Matti, *The Road to Peace* (Warner, N.Y., 1989).

GOMAA, Ahmed, *The Foundation of the League of Arab States* (Longman, 1977).

GOODHART, Arthur L., *Israel, the United Nations and Aggression* (Anglo-Israel Association, 1968).

GOPAL, Sarvepalli, *Jawaharlal Nehru Vol II 1947–1956* (Jonathan Cape, 1979).

GORE-BROWN, Lord, *With Great Truth and Respect* (Constable, 1974).

GORST, Anthony, JOHNMAN, Louis, and LUCAS, W. Scott (eds) *Post-War Britain, 1945–64. Themes and Perspectives* (Pinter, 1989).

GORST, Anthony, and LUCAS, W. Scott, 'Suez 1956: Strategy and the Diplomatic Process', in *The Journal of Strategic Studies*, Dec. 1988.

GREEN, Stephen, *Taking Sides. America's Secret Relations with a Militant Israel, 1948–1976* (Faber and Faber, 1984).

GRISEWOOD, Harmam, *One Thing At A Time. An Autobiography* (Hutchinson, 1968).

GROVE, Eric, *Vanguard to Trident. British Naval Policy Since World War II* (Bodley Head, 1987).

GUHIN, Michael A., *John Foster Dulles. A Statesman and His Times* (Columbia University Press, 1972).

HAILSHAM, Lord, *A Sparrow's Flight* (Collins, 1990).

HAKIM, Tawfiq al-,' *'Awdat al-Wa'i. The Return of Consciousness* (Beirut, 1974, English edn, Macmillan, 1985).

HALLBERG, C. W., *The Suez Canal. Its History and Diplomatic Importance* (Columbia University Press, 1931).

HANDEL, Michael I., *Israel's Political-Military Doctrine* (CFIA, Occasional Papers No. 30, Harvard, 1973).

HARRIS, Kenneth, *Attlee* (Weidenfeld and Nicolson, 1982).

HARRIS, Kenneth, *David Owen, Personally Speaking* (Weidenfeld and Nicolson, 1987).
HARRIS, Lillian Craig (ed), *Egypt: Internal Challenges and Regional Stability* (Chatham House Papers 39) (RIIA, 1988).
HART, Alan, *Arafat. Terrorist or Peacemaker* (Sidgwick and Jackson, 1984).
HAYTER, Sir William, *A Double Life* (Hamish Hamilton, 1974).
HEIKAL, Mohamed, *Nasser: The Cairo Documents* (New English Library, 1972).
HEIKAL, Mohamed, *Cutting the Lion's Tail* (André Deutsch, 1986).
HERZOG, Chaim, *The Arab–Israeli Wars* (Arms and Armour Press, 1982).
HEWEDY [Huwaidi], Amin, *Hurub 'Abd al-Nasir* [Nasser's Wars] (Beirut, 1977).
HIGGINS, Ronald, *The Seventh Enemy. The Human Factor in the Global Crisis* (Hodder and Stoughton, 1978).
HIGGINS, Rosalyn, *United Nations Peacekeeping. 1946–67 Documents and Commentary I The Middle East* (OUP, 1969).
HOOPES, Townsend, *The Devil and John Foster Dulles* (Andre Deutsch, 1974).
HORNE, Alistair, *Macmillan, Vols I and II* (Macmillan, 1988 and 1989).
HOURANI, Albert, *The Emergence of the Modern Middle East* (St Antony's, Macmillan, 1981).
HOWARD, Anthony, *RAB. The Life of R. A. Butler* (Jonathan Cape, 1987).
HUSSEINI, Mohrez Mahmoud al-, *Soviet–Egyptian Relations, 1945–85* (Macmillan, 1987).

ILAN, Amitzur, *Bernadotte in Palestine, 1948* (Macmillan, 1990).

JABBER, Paul, *Not By War Alone. Security and Arms Control in the Middle East* (University of California Press, 1981).
JOHNSON, Paul, *The Suez War* (MacGibbon and Kee, 1957).
JOHNSON, Sir Charles, *The Brink of Jordan* (Hamish Hamilton, 1972).

KAPELIOUK, Amnon, 'New Light on the Israeli–Arab Conflict and the Refugee Problem and its Origins', in *Journal of Palestine Studies*, Spring 1987.
KATARI, Yunes al-, *Lost Link in the Struggle of the Palestine People: 141 Fedayeen Battalion* (Arabic) (PLO/Mustaqbai al-Arabi, Cairo, 1987).
KEIGHTLEY, General Sir Charles, 'Operations in Egypt, Nov to Dec 1956', in *Supplement to London Gazette*, 10.9.57.
KHADDURI, Majid, *Arab Contemporaries. The Role of Personalities in Politics* (John Hopkins University Press, 1973).
KHALIDI, Walid, 'Nasser's Memoirs of the First Palestinian War', in *Journal of Palestine Studies*, Feb. 1973.
KHALIDI, Walid, 'Plan Dalet: Master Plan for the Conquest of Palestine', in *Journal of Palestine Studies*, Autumn 1988.
KILMUIR, Earl of, *Political Adventure* (Weidenfeld and Nicolson, 1964).
KIMCHE, Jon, 'Suez. The Inside Story', in *Jewish Chronicle*, 31.10.86.
KING, John, 'The BBC and Suez', in *The Round Table*, Oct. 1987.
KIPPING, Sir Norman, *The Suez Contractors* (Kenneth Mason, 1969).
KUNZ, Diane, *The Economic Diplomacy of the Suez Crisis* (Chapel Hill, 1991).
KYLE, Keith, 'Background to the Eisenhower Doctrine', in *The National and English Review*, Feb. 1957.
KYLE, Keith, 'Morality and Conscience in Politics', in *The Listener*, 18.5.67.
KYLE, Keith, 'Death of a Plan', in *The Listener*, 13.1.72.
KYLE, Keith, 'Footnotes to Suez', in *The Listener*, 16.12.76.

LA GORCE, Paul Marie de, *Naissance de la France moderne. II. Apogée et mort de la 4e République 1952–58* (Grasset, 1979).

LAMB, Richard, *The Failure of the Eden Government*, (Sidgwick and Jackson, 1987).

LAUTERPACHT, Elihu (ed), *The Suez Canal Settlement* (Stevens, 1960).

LEE, Air Marshal Sir David, *The RAF and the Mediterranean* (HMSO, 1989).

LESSEPS, Ferdinand de, *The History of the Suez Canal. A Personal Narrative* (Blackwood, 1876).

LEULLIETTE, Pierre, *St Michael and the Dragon. Memoirs of a Paratrooper* (Houghton Mifflin, 1964).

LOUIS, Wm Roger, *The British Empire in the Middle East, 1945–1951* (Clarendon Press, Oxford, 1984).

LOUIS, Wm Roger, and OWEN, Roger (ed), *Suez, 1956: The Crisis and Its Consequences* (Clarendon Press, 1989).

LOVE, Kennett, *Suez: The Twice-Fought War* (Longman, 1970).

LUARD, Evan, *A History of the United Nations, Vol II. The Age of Decolonisation, 1955–1965* (Macmillan, 1989).

LUCAS, W. Scott, 'The Path to Suez: Britain and the Struggle for the Middle East, 1953–56', in Anne Deighton (ed.), *Britain and the First Cold War* (Macmillan, 1990).

LUETHY, Herbert, and RODMICH, David, *French Motivations in the Suez Crisis* (Princeton, 1956).

LUTTWAK, Edward, and HOROWITZ, Dan, *The Israeli Army* (Allen Lane, 1975).

McDONALD, Iverach, *The History of 'The Times'. Vol V. 1939–1966* (Times Books, 1984).

MACDONALD, Malcolm, *Titans and Others* (Collins, 1972).

McDOWELL, David, *The Palestinians* (Minority Rights Group, 1987).

McKENZIE, F. R., 'Eden, Suez and the BBC – A Reassessment', in *The Listener*, 18.12.69.

MACKSEY, Kenneth, *The Tanks. The History of the Royal Tank Regiment, 1974–1975* (Arms and Armour, 1979).

MACMILLAN, Harold [Earl of Stockton], *Tides of Fortune, 1945–1955* (Macmillan, 1969).

MACMILLAN, Harold [Earl of Stockton], *Riding the Storm, 1956–1959* (Macmillan, 1971).

MANSFIELD, Peter, *Nasser's Egypt* (Penguin, 1969).

MANSFIELD, Peter, *Nasser* (Methuen, 1969).

MANSFIELD, Peter, *The British in Egypt* (Weidenfeld and Nicolson, 1974).

MARSHALL, General S. L. A., *Sinai Victory* (William Morrow, New York, 1968).

MASSU, General Jacques, and LE MIRE, Henri, *Vérité sur Suez 1956* (Plon, 1978).

MAYER, Thomas, 'Egypt's Invasion of Palestine', in *Middle Eastern Studies*, Witner, 1987.

MÉNAGER, Bernard, *et al.* (eds), *Guy Mollet, un camarade en république* (Presses Universitaires de Lille, 1987).

MENZIES, Sir Robert, *Afternoon Light* (Cassell, 1967).

MEZERIK, A. G., *The Suez Canal. Nationalization, Invasion, International Action* (International Review Series, 1957).

MIĆUNOVIĆ, Veljko, *Moscow Diary* (Chatto & Windus, 1980).

MITCHELL, Richard P., *The Society of Muslim Brothers* (OUP, 1969).

MONCRIEFF, Anthony (ed.), *Suez Ten Years After* (BBC, 1967).

MONROE, Elizabeth, *Britain's Moment in the Middle East* (Chatto and Windus, 1963 and 1981).

MORRIS, Benny, *The Birth of the Palestinian Refugee Problem, 1947–1949* (Cambridge University Press, 1987).

MORRIS, Benny, 'Yosef Weitz and the Transfer Committee, 1948–49', in *Middle Eastern Studies*, Oct. 1986.

MORRIS, Benny, 'The Causes and Character of the Arab Exodus from Palestine: the Israeli Defence Forces Intelligence Branch analysis of June 1948', in *Middle Eastern Studies*, Jan. 1986.

MORRIS, Benny, 'Operation Dani and the Palestinian Exodus from Lydda and Ramle in 1948', in *The Middle East Journal*, Winter 1986.

MOSLEY, Leonard, *Dulles: A Biography of Eleanor, Allen and John Foster Dulles and Their Family Network* (Hodder and Stoughton, 1978).

MURPHY, Robert, *Diplomat Among Warriors* (Collins, 1964).

NASSER, Gamal Abdul ['Abd al-Nasir], *Egypt's Liberation. The Philosophy of the Revolution* (Public Affairs Press, Washington, 1955).

NEFF, Donald, *Warriors of Suez. Eisenhower Takes America into the Middle East* (Linden Press, New York, 1981).

NEGRINO, Ralph, 'The Press and the Suez Crisis: A Myth Re-examined', in *The Historical Journal*, No. 4, 1982.

NEUSTADT, Richard E., *Alliance Politics* (Columbia University Press, 1970).

NICOLSON, Nigel, *People and Parliament* (Weidenfeld and Nicolson, 1958).

NUTTING, Sir Anthony, *No End of a Lesson. The Story of Suez* (Constable, 1967).

NUTTING, Sir Anthony, *Nasser* (Constable, 1972).

OBIETA, Father Joseph A., *The International Status of the Suez Canal* (Martinus Nijhoff, The Hague, 1960).

ORBACH, Maurice, 'The Orbach File', in *New Outlook*, Oct. and Nov./Dec. 1974.

ORR, Akiva, 'The '56 War – Another Sordid Chapter', in *Middle East International*, 27.6.87.

PAPPÉ, Ilan, *Britain and the Arab–Israeli Conflict, 1948–1951* (St Antony's Macmillan, 1988).

PARTNER, Peter, *Arab Voices. The BBC Arabic Services 1938–1988* (BBC, 1988).

PEARSON, Lester, *Memoirs, Vol II 1948–1957. The International Years* (Victor Gollancz, 1974).

PERES, Shimon, *David's Sling: the Arming of Israel.*

PERRAULT, Gilles, *A Man Apart. The Life of Henri Curiel* (Zed Books, 1987).

PINEAU, Christian, *1956 Suez* (Robert Laffont, Paris, 1976).

PUDNEY, John, *Suez: de Lesseps' Canal* (Dent, 1969).

QAWUQJI, Fawzi al-, 'Memoirs 1948', in *Journal of Palestine Studies*, Autumn 1972.

RA'ANAN, Uri, *The USSR Arms the Third World: Case Studies in Soviet Foreign Policy* (MIT Press, Boston, 1969).

RABIN, General Yitzhak, *The Rabin Memoirs* (Weidenfeld and Nicolson, 1979).

RAF HISTORICAL SOCIETY, *Proceedings 3*, Jan. 1988, 'A Seminar on the Air Aspects of the Suez Campaign, 1956'.

RAFAEL, Gideon, *Destination Peace. Three Decades of Israeli Foreign Policy* (Weidenfeld and Nicolson, 1981).

RAMM, Agatha, *Political Correspondence of Mr Gladstone and Lord Granville, 1876–1886, Vol 1* (Clarendon Press, Oxford, 1962).

RAMSDEN, James, 'Rab Did Miss Tricks which Macmillan Managed to Take', in *The Listener*, 19.3.87.

REES-MOGG, William (Lord), *Sir Anthony Eden* (Rockcliff, 1956).

RHODES JAMES, Robert, *Anthony Eden* (Weidenfeld and Nicolson, 1986).

RIAD, Mahmoud, *The Struggle for Peace in the Middle East* (Quartet Books, 1981).

RIKHYE, General Indar Jit, *The Sinai Blunder* (Frank Cass, 1980).

ROBERTS, Adam, and KINGSBURY, Benedict (eds), *United Nations in a Divided World* (Clarendon Press, Oxford, 1988).

ROBERTSON, Terence, *Crisis. The Inside Story of the Suez Conspiracy* (Hutchinson, 1965).

ROBINSON, Ronald, and GALLAGHER, John, *Africa and the Victorians. The Official Mind of Imperialism* (Macmillan, 1961).

RO'I, Yaacov (ed), *From Encroachment to Involvement: A Documentary Study of Soviet Policy in the Middle East* (Israeli Universities Press, Jerusalem, 1974).

ROOSEVELT, Kermit, *Countercoup. The Struggle for the Control of Iran* (McGraw-Hill, 1979).

ROSKILL, Stephen, *Hankey, Man of Secrets. Vol III 1931–1963* (Collins, 1974).

RUBIN, E., *The Suez Canal. The Great Internationale* (De Vero, 1956).

RUDDY, T. Michael, *The Cautious Diplomat. Charles E. Bohlen and the Soviet Union, 1929–1969* (Kent State University Press, 1986).

RYAN, Raphael, 'Sinai Campaign 1956', in *War Monthly*, July 1982.

SADAT, Anwar, *Revolt on the Nile* (Allan Wingate, 1957).

SADAT, Anwar, *In Search of Identity. An Autobiography* (Collins, 1978).

SALTER, Lord, *Memoirs of a Public Servant* (Faber and Faber, 1961).

SAYIGH, Rosemary, *Palestinians: From Peasants to Revolutionaries* (Zed Press, 1979).

SCHIFF, Ze'ev, *A History of the Israeli Army* (Macmillan, N.Y., 1985).

SEALE, Patrick, *The Struggle for Syria: A Study in Post-War Arab Politics, 1945–1958* (RIIA/OUP, 1965).

SEGEV, Tom, *1949, The First Israelis* (Collier Macmillan, 1986).

SELWYN-LLOYD, Lord, *Suez 1956. A Personal Account* (Jonathan Cape, 1978).

SHARON, Ariel (with David Chanoff), *Warrior. An Autobiography* (Macdonald, 1989).

SHLAIM, Avi, *Collusion Across the Jordan. King Abdullah, the Zionist Movement and the Partition of Palestine* (Clarendon Press, 1988).

SHLAIM, Avi, 'Britain and the Arab–Israel War of 1948', in *The Journal of Palestine Studies*, Summer 1987.

SHLAIM, Avi, 'Conflicting Approaches to Israel's Relations with the Arabs: Ben-Gurion and Sharett, 1953–1956', in *The Middle East Journal*, 37, 1983.

SHONFIELD, Sir Andrew, *British Economic Policy Since the War* (Penguin, 1958).

SHUCKBURGH, Sir Evelyn, *Descent to Suez* (Weidenfeld and Nicolson, 1986).

SLONIN, Shlomo, 'Origins of the 1950 Tripartite Declaration on the Middle East', in *Middle Eastern Studies*, Apr. 1978.

SMITH, Captain R. J., 'Suez and the Commando Carrier Concept', in *The Royal United Services Institution Journal*, Feb. 1963.

SMOLANSKY, Oles, *The Soviet Union and the Arab East under Khrushchev* (Bucknell University Press, 1974).

SNOW, Peter, *Hussein. A Biography* (Barrie and Jenkins, 1972).

STOCKWELL, General Sir Hugh, 'Suez from the Inside', in *Sunday Telegraph*, 30.10.66, 6.11.66.

STUART of FINDHORN, Viscount, *Within the Fringe* (Bodley Head, 1967).

TAYLOR, A. J. P., *The Struggle for Mastery in Europe, 1848–1918* (Clarendon Press, Oxford, 1954).

THOMAS, Abel, *Comment Israel Fut Sauvé. Les Secrets de l'Expédition de Suez* (Albin Michel, Paris, 1978).

THOMAS, Hugh (Lord Thomas of Swynnerton), *The Suez Affair* (Weidenfeld and Nicolson, 1966 and 1986).

THOMPSON, Julian, *Ready for Anything. The Parachute Regiment at War, 1940–1982* (Weidenfeld and Nicolson, 1989).

THORPE, D. R., *Selwyn Lloyd* (Jonathan Cape, 1989).

TIVNAN, Edward, *The Lobby. Jewish Political Power and American Foreign Policy* (Simon and Schuster, 1987).

TOUVAL, Saadia, *The Peace Brokers. Mediators in the Arab–Israeli Conflict, 1948–1979* (Princeton University Press, 1982).

TREVELYAN, Lord (Humphrey), *The Middle East in Revolution* (Macmillan, 1970).

TROËN, Selwyn Ilan, and SHEMESH, Moshe (eds), *The Suez–Sinai Crisis 1956. Retrospective and Reappraisal* (Frank Cass, 1989).

TSUR, Jacob, *Prélude à Suez: journal d'une ambassade, 1953–1956* (Presses de la Cité, 1968).

URQUHART, Sir Brian, *Hammarskjold* (The Bodley Head, 1972).

URQUHART, Sir Brian, *A Life in Peace and War* (Weidenfeld and Nicolson, 1987).

WATERBURY, John, *Hydropolitics of the Nile Valley* (Syracuse University Press, 1979).

WEIZMAN, Ezer, *On Eagles' Wings* (Steimatzky's, Tel Aviv, 1979).

WIGHT, Martin, *Power Politics* (RIIA/Penguin, 1979).

WIGHT, Martin, 'Brutus in Foreign Policy', in *International Affairs*, July 1960.

WILLIAMS, Philip, *Hugh Gaitskell* (Jonathan Cape, 1979).

WILLIAMS, Philip (ed.), *The Diary of Hugh Gaitskell, 1945–56* (Jonathan Cape, 1983).

WILSON, Mary C., *King Abdullah, Britain and the Making of Jordan* (Cambridge University Press, 1987).

WOODWARD, Sir Llewellyn, *British Foreign Policy in the Second World War Vol IV* (HMSO, 1975).

WRIGHT, Peter, *Spycatcher. The Candid Autobiography of a Senior Intelligence Officer* (Viking, 1987).

YOUNES, Mahmoud, 'La Nationalisation du Canal de Suez', in *Le Scribe* (May 1963).

ZIEGLER, Philip, *Mountbatten. The Official Biography* (Collins, 1985).

Index